The

Oral History

Reader

SECOND EDITION

Edited by

Robert Perks and Alistair Thomson

Routledge
Taylor & Francis Group

LONDON AND NEW YORK

First published 1998
by Routledge
2 & 4 Park Square, Milton Park, Abingdon, Oxon OX14 4RN

Simultaneously published in the USA and Canada
by Routledge
270 Madison Avenue, New York NY 10016

Reprinted 2000, 2002, 2003
2nd edition published 2006

Routledge is an imprint of the Taylor & Francis Group

Typeset in Bell Gothic and Perpetua by
Florence Production Ltd, Stoodleigh, Devon
Printed and bound in Great Britain by
TJ International Ltd, Padstow, Cornwall

British Library Cataloguing in Publication Data
A catalogue record for this book is available from the British Library

Library of Congress Cataloging in Publication Data

ISBN10: 0–415–34302–X (hb)
ISBN10: 0–415–34303–8 (pb)

ISBN13: 9–78–0–415–34302–2 (hb)
ISBN13: 9–78–0–415–34303–9 (pb)

The Oral History Reader

Praise for the first edition:

'This is the book I've been waiting for: a fat, stimulating and carefully selected and edited collection of significant contributions on oral history theory and practice ... I recommend it to anyone embarking on or already immersed in the challenges, delights and stimulation of oral history work.' *Janis Wilton, Oral History*

'It provides a rich resource for oral history students, practitioners and researchers in diverse settings. And it offers more traditional historians another powerful perspective on history.' *Dorothy Atkinson, Social History of Medicine*

Fully updated to include the most recent discussions on key issues, this second edition of *The Oral History Reader* is a comprehensive, international anthology of major, 'classic' articles and cutting-edge pieces on the theory, method and use of oral history. Arranged in five thematic sections, the collection details issues in the theory and practice of oral history and covers influential debates in its development over the past sixty years. New chapters and issues include:

*   interview methods and the oral history relationship
*   the use of testimony in truth and reconciliation politics
*   memory and interpretation
*   the digital revolution and new technologies for the creation, use and dissemination of oral history
*   community oral history projects
*   memory and history.

Including new introductions to each of the chapters, each section contains an overall introduction which contextualizes the selection by reviewing key debates and relevant literature. Extensive cross-referencing and indexing provide an aid to research and a crucial comparative dimension.

This comprehensive volume illustrates similarities and differences in oral history from around the world, including examples from North and South America, Britain and Europe, Australasia, Asia and Africa. It also details the subjects – such as women's history, family history, gay and lesbian history, ethnic history and disability history – to which oral history has made a significant contribution.

With an updated bibliography and useful contacts list, this second edition of *The Oral History Reader* is an essential tool for all students of modern history, memory studies, sociology, anthropology, media studies, cultural and h   LIVERPOOL JMU LIBRARY   library and information studies.

Robert Perks is Curator of O   ive and Director of the National Life Story Collection. His p   story (1998) and *Oral History, Health and Welfare* (Routlec.

Alistair Thomson is a Reader in Continuing Education and History at the Centre for Continuing Education, University of Sussex. His publications include *Anzac Memories* (1994) and *Ten Pound Poms: Australia's Invisible Migrants* (2005). They are both editors of *Oral History: The Journal of the Oral History Society.*

Contents

Introduction to second edition   ix

PART I
Critical developments   **1**

Introduction   1

1 Alex Haley
   BLACK HISTORY, ORAL HISTORY AND GENEALOGY   14

2 Paul Thompson
   THE VOICE OF THE PAST: ORAL HISTORY   25

3 Alessandro Portelli
   WHAT MAKES ORAL HISTORY DIFFERENT   32

4 Popular Memory Group
   POPULAR MEMORY: THEORY, POLITICS, METHOD   43

5 Valerie Yow
   'DO I LIKE THEM TOO MUCH?': EFFECTS OF THE ORAL
   HISTORY INTERVIEW ON THE INTERVIEWER AND
   VICE-VERSA   54

6 Susan H. Armitage and Sherna Berger Gluck
   REFLECTIONS ON WOMEN'S ORAL HISTORY: AN EXCHANGE   73

7 Daniel James
   LISTENING IN THE COLD: THE PRACTICE OF ORAL
   HISTORY IN AN ARGENTINE MEATPACKING COMMUNITY   83

8 Michael Frisch
   ORAL HISTORY AND THE DIGITAL REVOLUTION: TOWARD
   A POST-DOCUMENTARY SENSIBILITY   102

PART II

Interviewing   **115**

    Introduction   115

  9   Studs Terkel, with Tony Parker
      INTERVIEWING AN INTERVIEWER   123

10   Kathryn Anderson and Dana C. Jack
      LEARNING TO LISTEN: INTERVIEW TECHNIQUES AND
      ANALYSES   129

11   Hugo Slim and Paul Thompson, with Olivia Bennett and
      Nigel Cross
      WAYS OF LISTENING   143

12   Belinda Bozzoli
      INTERVIEWING THE WOMEN OF PHOKENG   155

13   Susan K. Burton
      ISSUES IN CROSS-CULTURAL INTERVIEWING: JAPANESE
      WOMEN IN ENGLAND   166

14   Ruth Finnegan
      FAMILY MYTHS, MEMORIES AND INTERVIEWING   177

15   Jan Walmsley
      LIFE HISTORY INTERVIEWS WITH PEOPLE WITH LEARNING
      DISABILITIES   184

16   Mark Klempner
      NAVIGATING LIFE REVIEW INTERVIEWS WITH SURVIVORS
      OF TRAUMA   198

PART III

Interpreting memories   **211**

    Introduction   211

17   Fred H. Allison
      REMEMBERING A VIETNAM WAR FIREFIGHT: CHANGING
      PERSPECTIVES OVER TIME   221

18   Mark Roseman
      SURVIVING MEMORY: TRUTH AND INACCURACY IN
      HOLOCAUST TESTIMONY   230

19   Alistair Thomson
      ANZAC MEMORIES: PUTTING POPULAR MEMORY THEORY
      INTO PRACTICE IN AUSTRALIA   244

20   Trevor Lummis
     STRUCTURE AND VALIDITY IN ORAL EVIDENCE   255

21   Linda Shopes
     ORAL HISTORY AND THE STUDY OF COMMUNITIES:
     PROBLEMS, PARADOXES, AND POSSIBILITIES   261

22   Elizabeth Lapovsky Kennedy
     TELLING TALES: ORAL HISTORY AND THE CONSTRUCTION
     OF PRE-STONEWALL LESBIAN HISTORY   271

23   Ann Laura Stoler, with Karen Strassler
     MEMORY-WORK IN JAVA: A CAUTIONARY TALE   283

24   Katherine Borland
     'THAT'S NOT WHAT I SAID': INTERPRETATIVE CONFLICT
     IN ORAL NARRATIVE RESEARCH   310

25   Kathleen Blee
     EVIDENCE, EMPATHY AND ETHICS: LESSONS FROM ORAL
     HISTORIES OF THE KLAN   322

PART IV
Making histories   **333**

     Introduction   333

26   Ellen D. Swain
     ORAL HISTORY IN THE ARCHIVES: ITS DOCUMENTARY
     ROLE IN THE TWENTY-FIRST CENTURY   343

27   Francis Good
     VOICE, EAR AND TEXT: WORDS, MEANING, AND
     TRANSCRIPTION   362

28   Jane Mace
     REMINISCENCE AS LITERACY: INTERSECTIONS AND
     CREATIVE MOMENTS   374

29   Marjorie Shostak
     'WHAT THE WIND WON'T TAKE AWAY': THE GENESIS OF
     NISA – THE LIFE AND WORDS OF A !KUNG WOMAN   382

30   Charles Hardy III
     AUTHORING IN SOUND: AURAL HISTORY, RADIO AND THE
     DIGITAL REVOLUTION   393

31   Dan Sipe
     THE FUTURE OF ORAL HISTORY AND MOVING IMAGES   406

32   Anna Green
     THE EXHIBITION THAT SPEAKS FOR ITSELF: ORAL
     HISTORY AND MUSEUMS   416

33 Toby Butler and Graeme Miller
LINKED: A LANDMARK IN SOUND, A PUBLIC WALK OF ART 425

34 Rina Benmayor
CYBER-TEACHING IN THE ORAL HISTORY CLASSROOM 434

PART V
Advocacy and empowerment **447**

Introduction 447

35 Joanna Bornat
REMINISCENCE AND ORAL HISTORY: PARALLEL UNIVERSES
OR SHARED ENDEAVOUR? 456

36 Cliff Kuhn and Marjorie L. McLellan
VOICES OF EXPERIENCE: ORAL HISTORY IN THE CLASSROOM 474

37 Daniel Kerr
'WE KNOW WHAT THE PROBLEM IS': USING VIDEO AND
RADIO ORAL HISTORY TO DEVELOP COLLABORATIVE
ANALYSIS OF HOMELESSNESS 485

38 William Westerman
CENTRAL AMERICAN REFUGEE TESTIMONIES AND
PERFORMED LIFE HISTORIES IN THE SANCTUARY
MOVEMENT 495

39 Rosanne Kennedy
STOLEN GENERATIONS TESTIMONY: TRAUMA,
HISTORIOGRAPHY, AND THE QUESTION OF 'TRUTH' 506

40 Irina Sherbakova
THE GULAG IN MEMORY 521

41 Patricia Lundy and Mark McGovern
'YOU UNDERSTAND AGAIN': TESTIMONY AND POST-CONFLICT
TRANSITION IN THE NORTH OF IRELAND 531

42 Nigel Cross and Rhiannon Barker
THE SAHEL ORAL HISTORY PROJECT 538

43 Sanjiv Kakar
LEPROSY IN INDIA: THE INTERVENTION OF ORAL HISTORY 549

Select bibliography 560
Useful contacts 564
Index 570

Introduction to second edition

MEMORIES ARE LIVING HISTORIES. According to the African proverb, 'Every old man that dies is a library that burns.'[1] Over the past sixty years oral history – 'the interviewing of eye-witness participants in the events of the past for the purposes of historical reconstruction'[2] – has transformed the practice of contemporary history in many countries. While interviews with members of social and political elites have complemented existing documentary sources, the most distinctive contribution of oral history has been to include within the historical record the experiences and perspectives of groups of people who might otherwise have been 'hidden from history', perhaps written about by social observers or in official documents, but only rarely preserved in personal papers or scraps of auto-biographical writing.[3] Through oral history interviews working-class men and women, indigenous peoples or members of cultural minorities, among others, have inscribed their experiences on the historical record and offered their own inter-pretations of history. Interviews have also documented aspects of historical experience which tend to be missing from other sources, such as domestic work or family life, and they have resonated with the subjective or personal meanings of lived experience.

Oral history has challenged the historical enterprise in other ways. Oral history research is not the privileged preserve of academic or professional historians, and groups as diverse as school students, day centre residents or development project workers have all proved to be adept interviewers. Oral historians of all kinds have had to learn skills required for the creation and documentation of recorded inter-views. We have drawn upon different intellectual disciplines – including sociology, anthropology, psychology and linguistics – to better understand the narratives of memory, and we have worked alongside museum curators, artists or media professionals to create public histories that combine sound, image and text.

Most significantly, and uniquely, oral historians speak to their sources, and this active human relationship transforms the practice of history in several ways. The narrator not only recalls the past but also asserts his or her interpretation of that past, and in participatory oral history projects the interviewee can be a historian as well as the source. Moreover, for some practitioners oral history has not just been about making histories. In certain projects a primary aim has been the empowerment of individuals or social groups through the process of remembering and reinterpreting the past, with an emphasis on the value of process as much as historical product. In this regard oral history has influenced and overlapped with some of the most important contemporary uses of historical memory: in the 'truth and reconciliation' projects of post-conflict societies, or in legal responses to human rights abuses, such as war crime tribunals or the land claims of indigenous peoples.

Yet historians have been notoriously wary of memory as a historical source. In challenging orthodoxies about historical sources, methods and aims, and by using memory for contemporary political purposes, oral history has generated fierce debates – for example, about the reliability of memory, the psychology of the interview relationship or the interpretation and re-presentation of people's lives; or more generally about the relationships between memory and history, past and present, scholarship and politics. By bringing together some of the best writings by practitioners in the field, this *Oral History Reader* explores the issues at stake in these debates and the distinctive nature and contribution of oral history.

Since the first edition of the *Oral History Reader* was published in 1998 it has become a core anthology for undergraduate and postgraduate students in oral history and an important reference book for academic oral historians, and for researchers and practitioners moving into oral history from other fields. When we were invited to compile a second edition we were keen to update the contents and respond to comments and suggestions we have received from users around the world. The positive feedback we received about the first edition – particularly from the main readership in higher education – convinced us that the aims and structure of the *Reader* worked well.

The *Reader* is not, primarily, a handbook which details the practical nuts and bolts of doing oral history, though there are practically-oriented articles within each section (for beginners, this book might best be used alongside one of the oral history handbooks available in most countries and listed in our Select Bibliography at the end of the volume). Nor does the *Reader* argue for a particular, 'right' way to do oral history. One review of the first edition argued that our efforts 'reflect the variety of oral history rather than give shape to it'.[4] We believe this is a strength rather than a weakness. The contributors draw upon diverse oral history experiences to explore issues in the theory and practice of oral history, from the creation of oral evidence through to data analysis and historical production – and they do not always agree about best practice. They highlight the complexity of the oral history relationship, the richness of oral testimony, and the extraordinary variety of ways of interpreting the past and making histories using oral sources.

Yet there are subtle ways in which an anthology like this can indeed 'shape the field'. As editors of the British journal *Oral History*, and in our research for the second edition of the *Reader*, we have noticed that since 1999 many new writings about oral history cite chapters from the *Reader*. We know from conversations with teachers of oral history that students use the *Reader* as a short cut into the extensive, though not always accessible, oral history literature. In editing the second edition we were acutely aware of a responsibility not to shape the field in a particular narrow direction but to introduce contrasting and cross-disciplinary approaches that offer instructive lessons for the novice or experienced oral historian whilst also stimulating debate and challenging convention. Of course, advances in information technology are widening electronic access to an international literature and diligent readers can now follow up leads and discover other, full-text articles on the internet. We hope that the *Reader* will continue to serve as a starting point for discovery and learning.

In this second edition of the *Oral History Reader* we have retained the structure of five thematic sections, each of which focuses on a related set of issues, and which take the reader through the different stages of oral history. An introduction to each part contextualizes the selection, reviews the relevant literature, and notes significant issues and recent developments. Part I, 'Critical developments', includes a selection of articles which represent key debates in the post-war development of oral history – up to 2005 – from arguments about the value and validity of oral evidence through to more sophisticated explorations of memory, narrative and subjectivity, and of the oral history relationship, and reflections about the current and future impact of digital technology. In Part II, 'Interviewing', the contributions introduce a variety of different interview experiences and approaches, and consider issues posed by the interview relationship. Part III, 'Interpreting memories', includes articles that consider the nature of memory, approaches to the interpretation of oral testimony, and the interpretative relationship between oral historian and narrator. Part IV, 'Making histories', considers the practical, ethical and interpretative issues that arise as we transcribe, document and archive oral testimony and then use it to make histories in a wide variety of forms: in books, exhibitions or artworks, on stage and in college projects, in radio, film or multimedia. The articles in Part V, 'Advocacy and empowerment', explore some of the ways in which oral history projects can be used to empower individual narrators and particular social groups, and highlight the personal and political significance of oral history.

Rather than structuring the *Oral History Reader* around particular historical subjects – such as labour history or women's history – we have tried to ensure that most of the subjects to which oral history has made a significant contribution are represented in one or several of the articles. The index allows readers to trace subjects which cut across our arrangement of the book, and to follow up their own areas of interest.[5] Inevitably, many of the articles in the *Reader* relate to the concerns of more than one section, and the index thus enables users to find references to a particular issue – such as Holocaust memory – which occur in different sections. The index also provides a guide to the different countries and regions represented in oral history projects discussed by contributors. One of the aims of the *Oral History Reader* is to provide an international collection of writings which introduces the range of ways in which oral history is used in different countries, suggesting common and distinctive features and showing how the shared concerns of oral history are faced in rather different ways in diverse cultural and national contexts.

In 1975, North American oral historian Ron Grele lamented the rather limited critical discussion among oral historians about the theoretical and methodological issues underpinning their work.[6] That charge could not be levelled at oral historians

in the early twenty-first century; our research for the first edition of this *Reader*
turned up a wealth of insightful writing in which oral historians reflect on their
practice in different parts of the world, and while updating the second edition we
were astonished by the extent and variety of recent oral history literature. Perhaps
most notably, oral historians are researching and writing from a wide range of
scholarly disciplines (including, but not only, history, sociology and anthropology),
and the literature of oral history is increasingly cross-disciplinary, borrowing and
blending from the many intellectual and professional contexts that consider memory,
orality and the interview.

Our problem has been to narrow the selection down. We decided to retain the
principle of the first edition that we would only include previously published material
(about a third from books, two conference papers and the balance from journals,
including – but not only – the established national oral history journals), but were
keen to include pieces which are out of print or not readily available. Apart from
the opening section on 'Critical developments' we have favoured recent pieces –
including twenty-one published since we completed research for the first edition in
1997 – though each section includes a number of older pieces with continuing relevance for oral historians. In order to open up the *Reader* to as wide a range of
different experiences and perspectives as possible, we opted for a larger number
of shorter pieces (or extracts from longer articles), and we have stuck with our first
edition limit of one contribution per author. For a number of notable oral historians who have published extensively in the field, our selection is not necessarily the
'best' piece they had written, but the publication which best fitted the needs of the
Reader. For example, Alessandro Portelli's 'The death of Luigi Trastulli: memory
and the event',[7] is a classic exploration of individual and social remembering, but
it is not included here because a short extract from the long article would not have
worked, because we had several other excellent pieces exploring similar issues,
and because Portelli's shorter article, 'What makes oral history different', which is
included in 'Critical developments', is a fine introductory analysis of oral history's
distinctive features.

Experience of teaching with the first edition of the *Reader*, and electronic
conversations with teachers and other users, have also guided our selection – and
deletions – in the second edition. Some articles in the first edition 'worked' for
students but others didn't. We wanted a reasonable number of contributions that
would be accessible and stimulating for students encountering oral history for the
first time, alongside a selection of more sophisticated and challenging pieces. We
have favoured pieces, written in lively and engaging prose, that are relatively free
of unexplained jargon and accessible to students and practitioners with different
levels of oral history experience and theoretical understanding. Wherever possible
we have opted for writings which are grounded in the author's own oral history
practice, and which use examples from interviews. We have also favoured writings
which situate critical reflection on practice within the relevant historiographical
literature, and which therefore introduce readers to the concerns and approaches of
oral historians and others using the interview methodology. In many cases there
were several equally apt and effective pieces about a particular oral history concern
(for example the interview relationship), and our final selection was influenced by

an attempt to achieve a balance – across the *Reader* as a whole – in terms of geographical spread and historical subject matter.

One innovation in this second edition is the inclusion of a number of pieces which use a dialogue format instead of formal written prose: Tony Parker's interview with Studs Terkel; a roundtable discussion amongst school teachers who use oral history; an email exchange between feminist oral historians Susan Armitage and Sherna Gluck. Each of these pieces evokes the spontaneity of oral narrative and the animated interchange of dialogue that are key features of an oral history interview, and together they show how speaking about your life to another person might generate distinctive ways of articulating and comprehending experience.

There are still some gaps in our selection. We did not have a budget for translation for either edition and so were limited to pieces published in English. This is an English-language publication primarily aimed at an English-speaking readership, and it includes a strong selection of writings from North America, Britain and Ireland, Australasia and Africa, with a smaller number of articles from continental Europe, Asia and Latin America. For continental Europe the works by Alessandro Portelli and Irina Sherbakova represent only the tip of the significant contribution which oral historians from the Continent have made to the field over the last forty years.[8] Similarly, the two English-language pieces from Latin America do not adequately represent the vibrant development of oral history in that region in recent decades.[9] We repeat our first edition challenge for a publisher to commission an English-language anthology of translated writings from Latin American oral history experience.

Once again, certain aspects of oral history practice remain under-represented in the literature and in this *Reader*. Oral historians in museums, libraries, archives and the arts have improved the literature about their practice over the past decade. There is a proliferation of excellent new writing about oral history interviewing and about the uses of oral testimony as a historical source. But there is still a very limited range of reflective writing about radio, video and television oral history, and the burgeoning growth of oral history on the world wide web is not reflected in substantial critical reflection about oral history and the internet. Not surprisingly, most media practitioners prefer to make multimedia oral histories rather than write critically about the method and theory of their work. This is a gap to fill.

In editing the selection we have standardized reference styles, and we have reduced the length of some of the longer pieces by choosing self-contained extracts or by deleting discursive footnotes. Wherever possible we have left the contributions in their original form. Deletions from original texts are represented thus, [. . .], and explanatory editorial notes are also contained within square brackets. We thank the authors and original publishers for their cooperation. We also thank our oral history colleagues from around the world – at conferences, on the H-OralHist internet discussion group, and as anonymous referees for the publisher – who have provided invaluable advice about the structure and selection for this collection – in particular: Federico Lorenz and Dora Schwarzstein (Argentina – Dora was a pioneering Argentinian oral historian who died in 2002); Rosie Block, Heather Goodall, Paula Hamilton and Janis Wilton (Australia); Verena Alberti, Sonia Maria de Freitas and Daisy Perelmutter (Brazil); Joanna Bornat, Rena Feld,

Graham Dawson, Siân Edwards, Donny Hyslop, Dorothy Sheridan, Lorraine Sitzia, Dan Weinbren and Krista Woodley (Britain); Richard Lochead (Canada); Tuula Juvonen (Finland); Anna Green and Megan Hutching (New Zealand); Belinda Bozzoli, Jonathon Grossman and Sean Field (South Africa); Rina Benmayor, David Dunaway, Jim Fogarty, Michael Frisch, Sherna Gluck, Ron Grele, Charles Hardy, Cliff Kuhn, Anne Ritchie, Don Ritchie, Rebecca Sharpless, Linda Shopes, Andor Skotnes and Valerie Yow (USA).

Notes

1   Amadou Hampâté Bâ is credited with coining this phrase: http://people.africadatabase/org/en/profile/1929.html.

2   R.K. Grele, 'Directions for oral history in the United States', in D.K. Dunaway and W.K. Baum (eds), *Oral History: An Interdisciplinary Anthology*, Walnut Creek, Calif.: AltaMira Press, second edition, 1996, p. 63.

3   S. Rowbotham, *Hidden from History*, London: Pluto, 1973.

4   R.C. Whiting, 'Short notices', *English Historical Review*, April 1999, p. 530.

5   For surveys of the oral history literature on particular historical subjects, see the bibliographies listed in our Select Bibliography, and P. Thompson, *The Voice of the Past: Oral History*, Oxford, Oxford University Press, 2000, pp. 331–334; D. Ritchie, *Doing Oral History: A Practical Guide*, New York: Oxford University Press, 2003, pp. 293–303.

6   R.J. Grele, 'Movement without aim: methodological and theoretical problems in oral history', in R.J. Grele (ed.), *Envelopes of Sound: The Art of Oral History*, New York: Praeger, 1991 (original edition, 1975), pp. 126–155.

7   A. Portelli's 'The death of Luigi Trastulli: memory and the event', in *The Death of Luigi Trastulli and Other Stories: Form and Meaning in Oral History*, Albany: State University of New York Press, 1991, pp. 1–26.

8   See, for example, Portelli, *The Death of Luigi Trastulli and Other Stories*; A. Portelli, *The Battle of Valle Giulia: Oral History and the Art of Dialogue*, Madison: University of Wisconsin Press, 1997; L. Passerini, *Fascism in Popular Memory: The Cultural Experience of the Turin Working Class*, Cambridge: Cambridge University Press, 1987; P. Thompson and N. Burchardt (eds), *Our Common History: The Transformation of Europe*, London: Pluto, 1982; R. Samuel and P. Thompson (eds), *The Myths We Live By*, London: Routledge, 1990; the chapters by Karen Hartewig (Germany), Danièl Voldman (France) and Alessandro Portelli (Italy) in Dunaway and Baum, *Oral History*; and the journals *BIOS* (Germany) and *Historia y Fuente Oral* (Spain).

9   See, for example, V. Alberti, *Ouvir contar: textos em história oral*, Rio de Janeiro: Editora Fundação Getulio Vargas, 2004; J.C.S.B. Meihy (ed.), *(Re)introduzindo a história oral no Brasil*, São Paulo: Xamã, 1996; M. de Moraes Ferreira and J. Amado (eds), *Usos & Abusos da História Oral*, Rio de Janeiro: Fundação Getulio Vargas, 1996; A. T. Montenegro, *História oral e memória: a cultura popular revisitada*, São Paulo: Contexto, 1992; D. Schwarzstein (ed.), *La História Oral*, Buenos Aires: Centro Editorial de América Latina, 1991; and the chapters by Eugenia Meyer (Mexico and the Caribbean) and Dora Schwarzstein (Argentina) in Dunaway and Baum, *Oral History*.

PART I

Critical developments: introduction

THIS FIRST SECTION OF THE *READER* outlines critical developments
in the history of oral history. It does not attempt to survey the national or
regional histories of oral history, which are readily available in other publications.[1]
Although the points of genesis and patterns of development for oral history have
varied from one country to another, particular social and intellectual forces shaped
contemporary approaches to oral history and have influenced oral historians
around the world. The readings selected for this section illustrate and explore these
critical developments. This introduction contextualizes those readings within a
survey of four paradigm shifts in oral history theory and practice: the post-war
renaissance of memory as a source for 'people's history'; the development, from the
late 1970s, of 'post-positivist' approaches to memory and subjectivity; a transformation in perceptions about the role of the oral historian as interviewer and
analyst from the late 1980s; and the digital revolution of the late 1990s and early
2000s.[2] Threaded through discussion of these paradigm shifts are reflections upon
four factors that have impacted upon oral history and, in turn, been significantly
influenced by oral historians: the growing significance of political and legal practices
in which personal testimony is a central resource; the increasing interdisciplinarity
of approaches to interviewing and the interpretation of memory; the proliferation
from the 1980s of studies concerned with the relationship between history and
memory; and the evolving internationalism of oral history.

The first paradigm transformation – and the genesis of contemporary oral
history – was the post-Second World War renaissance in the use of memory as a
source for historical research. Paul Thompson, among others, charts the prehistory
of the modern oral history movement, explaining that historians from ancient times
relied upon eyewitness accounts of significant events, until the nineteenth-century
development of an academic history discipline led to the primacy of archival research
and documentary sources, and a marginalization of oral evidence. Gradual acceptance of the usefulness and validity of oral evidence, and the increasing availability

of portable tape recorders, underpinned a revival of oral history after the Second World War. The timing and pattern of this emergence differed markedly around the world. For example, the first organized oral history project was initiated by Allan Nevins at Columbia University in New York in 1948, and his interest in archival recordings with white male elites was representative of early oral history activity in the United States. In Britain in the 1950s and 1960s oral history pioneers were more interested in recording the experiences of so-called 'ordinary' working people and had initial links with folklore studies;[3] George Ewart Evans, for example, determined to 'ask the fellows who cut the hay'.[4] The lived experience of working-class, women's or black history was undocumented or ill-recorded and oral history was an essential source for the 'history from below' fostered by politically committed social historians in Britain and around the world from the 1960s onwards. Our first two readings evoke the excitement and political commitment of the first, pioneer generation of oral historians.

Alex Haley's best-selling books, *Autobiography of Malcolm X* (first published in 1965) and *Roots*: *The Saga of an American Family* (1976), encouraged black Americans to explore their past and helped to popularize oral history and family history in the United States.[5] Our first extract is from a talk which Haley gave to an early meeting of the United States Oral History Association, published in the very first issue of the Association's journal *Oral History Review* in 1973. Haley describes the transmission of memories within his African-American family, and the oral traditions which are preserved in precise detail and retold by the *griot* or historical storyteller of a West African tribal community. Critics have expressed grave concerns about the accuracy of the evidence which Haley used to link his African and American ancestors.[6] The *griot* may well have presented the family connections that Haley wanted to hear; and in tracing his American family history Haley probably embellished the oral tradition and overstepped the boundary 'where fictional line diverged from factual basis'.[7] Haley's work offered ample ammunition for critics of memory as a historical source, and the debates it generated exemplify the blurred boundaries between fact and fiction, personal memory and oral tradition, and oral history and journalism. Despite these concerns, we have retained Haley's talk in this second edition of the *Reader* because it evokes for oral history newcomers the passion and commitment of early oral historians as they set out to uncover and record forgotten histories, and because Haley's writing reminds us that oral history recording taps into a vast, rich reservoir of oral traditions sustained through family, community and national memories.[8]

Paul Thompson, a social historian at the University of Essex, played a leading role in the creation of the British Oral History Society in the early 1970s and the subsequent development of an international oral history movement from the end of that decade. His book, *The Voice of the Past*: *Oral History*, became a standard textbook for oral historians around the world when it was first published in 1978.[9] As a socialist, Thompson was committed to a history which drew upon the words and experiences of working-class people. Yet he also sought to defend oral history against critics who claimed that memory was an unreliable historical source, and determined to prove the legitimacy and value of the approach. In the extract from *The Voice of the Past* which we use here, Thompson explains how oral history has transformed both the content of history – 'by shifting the focus and opening new areas of inquiry, by challenging some of the assumptions and accepted judgements of historians, by bringing recognition to substantial groups of people who had been ignored' – and the processes of writing history, breaking 'through the barriers between the chroniclers and their audience; between the educational institution and the outside world'. For many oral historians, recording experiences which have been ignored in history and involving people in exploring and making their own histories, continue to be primary justifications for the use of oral history.[10] And in most countries oral history has developed powerful roots outside higher education, in schools, community projects and reminscence work.[11]

The second paradigm shift in oral history was, in part, a response to positivist critics – for the most part traditional documentary historians of a conservative political persuasion – who feared the politics of people's history and who targeted the 'unreliability' of memory as its weakness.[12] At the core of criticisms of oral history in the early 1970s was the assertion that memory was distorted by physical deterioration and nostalgia in old age, by the personal bias of both interviewer and interviewee, and by the influence of collective and retrospective versions of the past. For example, the Australian historian Patrick O'Farrell wrote in 1979 that oral history was moving into 'the world of image, selective memory, later overlays and utter subjectivity . . . And where will it lead us? Not into history, but into myth.'[13] Goaded by the taunts of historian critics, early oral historians developed their own handbook guidelines to assess the reliability of oral memory (while shrewdly reminding the traditionalists that documentary sources – many of which were created as records of spoken events – were no less selective and biased). From social psychology and anthropology they showed how to determine the bias and fabulation of memory, the significance of retrospection and the effects of the interviewer upon remembering. From sociology they adopted methods of representative sampling, and from documentary history they brought rules for checking the reliability and internal consistency of their sources. These guidelines provided useful signposts for reading memories and for combining them with other historical sources to find out what happened in the past.[14]

By the late 1970s imaginative oral historians turned these criticisms on their head and argued that the so-called unreliability of memory was also its strength, and that the subjectivity of memory provided clues not only about the meanings of historical experience but also about the relationships between past and present, between memory and personal identity, and between individual and collective memory. For example, Luisa Passerini's study of Italian memories of interwar fascism highlighted the role of subjectivity in history – the conscious and unconscious meanings of experience as lived and remembered – and showed how the influences of public culture and ideology upon individual memory might be revealed in the silences, discrepancies and idiosyncrasies of personal testimony.[15] Also writing in the 1970s, North American oral historian Michael Frisch argued against the attitude that oral memory was 'history as it really was', and asserted that memory – 'personal and historical, individual and generational' – should be moved to centre stage 'as the object, not merely the method, of oral history'. Used in this way, oral history could be 'a powerful tool for discovering, exploring, and evaluating the nature of the process of historical memory – how people make sense of their past, how they connect individual experience and its social context, how the past becomes part of the present, and how people use it to interpret their lives and the world around them'.[16] Memory thus became the subject as well as the source of oral history, and oral historians began to use an exhilarating array of approaches – linguistic, narrative, cultural, psychoanalytic and ethnographic – in their analysis and use of oral history interviews.

Our third reading, first published by Alessandro Portelli in 1979, exemplifies the second paradigm shift in approaches to memory and oral history. Portelli challenged the critics of 'unreliable memory' head-on by arguing that 'what makes oral history different' – orality, narrative form, subjectivity, the 'different credibility' of memory, and the relationship between interviewer and interviewee – should be considered as strengths rather than as weaknesses, a resource rather than a problem. Portelli's article, reproduced here in full, is a subtle exploration of 'the peculiarities of oral history' and an ideal introduction for newcomers to the field.[17] The interpretative opportunities that Portelli outlined are explored in more depth through the detailed case studies about interpreting memories in Part III.

Though conservative historians were the most vocal critics of oral history in the 1970s, oral history was also challenged from the Left. In the late 1970s and early 1980s some socialist historians were particularly critical of the notion that the method of oral history was necessarily radical and democratic. Luisa Passerini cautioned against the 'facile democratisation' and 'complacent populism' of oral history projects which encouraged members of oppressed groups to 'speak for themselves' but which did not see how memories might be influenced by dominant histories and thus require critical interpretation.[18] At the Centre for Contemporary Cultural Studies in Birmingham, the Popular Memory Group developed a similar critique of British oral history in an article about 'popular memory' which is extracted here. The Group situated professional and other historical practices within the much wider process of 'the social production of memory', and argued that public struggles over the construction of the past are profoundly significant both in contemporary politics and for individual remembering. For example, oral history as used within the community and women's history movements could be a significant resource for making more democratic and transformative histories.[19] Yet the Popular Memory Group concluded that this radical potential was often undermined by superficial understandings of the connections in oral testimony between individual and social memory and between past and present, and by the unequal relationships between professional historians and other participants in oral history projects.

These arguments highlight two related concerns, that the increasing theoretical sophistication of academic oral history is incomprehensible to, or ignored by, oral historians outside the academy – for example those working in schools, community projects and the media – and that our interviewees may be bewildered by the deconstruction of their memories. Several articles in the *Reader*, such as the email exchange about women's oral history by Susan Armitage and Sherna Gluck, and Linda Shopes's piece about community oral history, highlight these tensions. A reflective, critical approach to memory and history undoubtedly makes for better oral history, yet at the same time oral historians who are committed to a dialogue with their interviewees and a wider public audience need to write and speak in terms that make accessible sense.

The Popular Memory Group's writing highlights the political possibilities and contradictions for oral history projects which have a radical agenda.[20] Yet in the early 1980s the political scope and impact of oral history and memory work was still comparatively limited. The increasingly diverse range of contexts within which memory has come to be used for advocacy and empowerment are explored through case studies in Part V that range from intergenerational oral history projects with elders and young people; health, social care and development work; community-based projects with marginalized groups such as the homeless and refugees; and the use of testimony in legal and political processes related to indigenous people's rights and restitution, post-conflict resolution and national truth and reconciliation. Indeed, though oral history has often played a significant role within such projects, commentators such as Fuyuki Kurasawa argue that memory and testimony have become critical constituents of a more general 'witnessing fever' in the late twentieth century and the early twenty-first, in which 'bearing witness' is 'a mode of ethico-political practice'.[21]

A third transformation in oral history involved a paradigmatic shift in our approach to the 'objectivity' of the oral historian as interviewer and analyst. Throughout the 1980s positivist notions of researcher objectivity were increasingly questioned by feminist theorists, post-modern anthropologists and qualitative soci-ologists – and by some interviewers who were deeply reflective about the relationships they formed with their narrators. Oral historians were also influenced by the developments in reminiscence work that highlighted the benefits of remem-bering for older people and reminded interviewers to consider the value of the exchange for both parties.[22] In an article published in the *Oral History Review* in 1997, and reproduced here, Valerie Yow argues that from the late 1980s a new oral history 'paradigm [. . .] permits awareness and use of the interactive process of interviewer and narrator, of interviewer and content'.[23] Oral historians were increasingly alert to the ways that they were affected by their interviews and how the interviewer, in turn, affected the interview relationship, the data it generated and the interpretative process and product. Quoting Victor Turner, Yow argues for 'an objective relation to our own subjectivity', and explains how oral historians can use this reflexive alertness to enhance interviews and their interpretation.

Valerie Yow's article also exemplifies the interdisciplinarity that has been one of the most significant features of oral history from the 1980s onwards. Though memory is now a respected historical source, history is just one of many academic disciplines and emergent intellectual fields that work with memories. Yow writes about the 'trickle over effect' from other disciplines such as qualitative sociology,[24] anthropology,[25] biographical and literary studies,[26] feminist theory and life review psychology.[27] To this list we could add cultural studies,[28] linguistics, communication and narrative studies,[29] folklore studies[30] and interdisciplinary work exploring the relationship between memory, narrative and personal identity.[31] While theoretical and methodological developments in each of these fields have enriched the practice of oral history, oral historians themselves, as represented by the authors in this and other sections, have made substantial contributions to the theory, method and politics of qualitative research and memory work through their interdisciplinary reflections on interview relationships and the interpretation and use of recorded memories.

Oral history and feminist history have enjoyed an especially significant symbiotic connection since the late 1960s. Interviews with women have provided an invaluable source for uncovering and exploring experiences which have been, in Sheila Rowbotham's resonant phrase, 'hidden from history', and for challenging historical interpretations based upon the lives and documents of men.[32] Feminist oral historians have also made significant contributions to theoretical and method-ological developments in oral history, illuminating issues about oral history relationships and the interconnections between language, power and meaning.[33] In 1977, *Frontiers: A Journal of Women's Studies* introduced a special issue on women's oral history with an article by Sherna Berger Gluck about the interview process, 'What's so special about women? Women's oral history'. In the second *Frontiers* women's oral history issue in 1983, Susan Armitage wrote 'The next step' about women's oral history projects. In 1998 the journal devoted two more issues to women's oral history and published an email exchange, which we include here, in which Armitage and Gluck discussed the development of women's oral history.[34] As Gluck comments, the email dialogue format 'reproduce[s] some of the spon-taneity of the oral history interview and pose[s] some of the questions about presentation' which are considered in the exchange. Armitage and Gluck note the importance within feminist history of the turn to subjectivity from the late 1970s, and the tensions between necessary but 'wearying' analytical sophistication and the naïve enthusiasm of pioneering 'recovery' history. They argue that oral history retains an urgent political importance in many parts of the world where women's oppression is reinforced by the silencing of women's voices and histories. Like Valerie Yow, they consider the significant challenges faced by women interpreting other women's lives and the opportunities and difficulties of collaborative inter-pretation. The email exchange evokes the efforts of many contemporary oral historians to link theoretical sophistication about subjectivity, narrative and memory with the political commitment to the history of oppressed and marginal groups which motivated the first generation of feminist and socialist oral historians.[35]

Daniel James's book, *Dona María's Story: Life History, Memory and Political Identity*, published in 2000, is an exemplary work of women's oral history from South America. The first half of the book comprises Dona María's own testimony, as recorded and edited by James, and vividly recalls the life and times of a working-class woman activist in a twentieth-century Argentinian industrial community. The interpretative essays that follow consider Dona María's experience and testimony, and the history and memory of her community, from cutting-edge interdisciplinary perspectives. 'Listening in the cold', which is extracted here, explores the challenges of recording, hearing and comprehending testimony that is influenced by prevalent narrative forms, by the political and psychological identity of the narrator, and by an interview relationship that can enable or disable recollection.

James also considers the importance of remembering – as 'embodied in cultural practices such as storytelling' – for individuals and for their communities, and poses the problem of modern memory for working-class communities faced with deindustrialization and the destruction of sites for social and collective memory. In this regard his work exemplifies the 'ascent of "memory" as an object of investigation by historians' in the last two decades of the twentieth century. Omer Bartov offers a compelling explanation for this trend, in which memories recorded by oral historians have played a significant role:

> The stream of 'memory studies' was clearly related to the pervasive cultural sense of an end of an era, both as a chronological fact and as a reflection of rapid socioeconomic transformation. The 'rediscovery' of Maurice Halbwach's theories on collective memory; the publication of Pierre Nora's massive tomes on *lieux de mémoire*; the growing scholarly interest in the links between history and memory, documentation and testimony; the popularity of works of fiction and films on memory; debates among psychologists over 'deep' and repressed memory; and, not least, the public controversies on forms and implications of official commemoration. All seemed to indicate that 'memory' had firmly established itself as a central historical category.[36]

James's work also highlights the increasing internationalism of oral history. In 1979 a number of North American oral historians met up with their European counterparts at an International Conference on Oral History held in Essex, England. This meeting was to be the first of many international exchanges, and was a catalyst for the publication of an *International Journal of Oral History* (from 1980 until 1990) and a series of collaborative, international oral history anthologies.[37] In 1996 the international oral history conferences were formalized within a newly constituted International Oral History Association (IOHA), for which representatives from each continent were elected to a council responsible for the biennial conference and a bilingual (Spanish and English) newsletter and journal, *Words and Silences/ Palabras y Silencios*. The conferences and publications have sustained and propelled a cross-fertilization of ideas and practices across the different national contexts of oral history, and have shifted the centre of gravity in oral history away from Europe and North America. The recent sequence of conferences in Turkey, Brazil, South Africa and Australia have showcased the rich histories and extraordinary growth of oral history in the 'South'. Indeed, Latin American oral historians are challenging the European and North American oral history hegemony. In an editorial introducing a 2003 issue of *Words and Silences* about 'Oral history and the experience of politics', the Mexican IOHA vice-president Gerardo Necoechea suggests that whereas in the 'North' oral history is often 'directed to problems of identity and cultural recognition within democratic regimes . . . Latin America continues to be a space for utopia, for thinking about the far-away relatively just society and fearing the fracture of the ever fragile present. Politics there jumps at you', and oral history is intertwined with politics.[38] In the same issue the Brazilian, José Carlos Sebe Bom Meihy, argues that the international conference in Rio de Janeiro in 1998 was a turning point, with Latin American oral history in particular offering a more radical political context and purpose.[39] In fact, articles in Part V of this *Reader* by Daniel Kerr (about homeless people in Cleveland, Ohio) and Patricia Lundy and

Mark McGovern (about a commemorative project in Northern Ireland) point to significant political aims and outcomes for oral history projects in the 'North'. Yet it is undoubtedly true that different national and regional contexts make for different types of oral history, and that all oral historians gain from international dialogue and comparative insights.

We are in the middle of a fourth, dizzying digital revolution in oral history, and its outcomes are impossible to predict. Email and the internet are certainly fostering oral history's international dialogue. But, more than that, new digital technologies are transforming the ways in which we record, preserve, catalogue, interpret, share and present oral histories. Very soon we will all be recording interviews on computers, and we can already use satellite links and conference call facilities to conduct virtual interviews with people on the other side of the world. Audio-visual digital recordings will be readily accessible in their entirety via the internet, and sophisticated digital indexing and cataloguing tools – perhaps assisted in large projects by artificial intelligence – will enable anyone, anywhere, to make extraordinary and unexpected creative connections within and across oral history collections, using sound and image as well as text. Our interviewees may well think rather differently about telling a story that will be instantly accessible and easily manipulated. The future of oral history, and the role of the oral historian, has never been so exciting, or so uncertain.

In the past decade oral historians have been grappling with the technical, ethical and epistemological implications of the digital revolution.[40] In the concluding contribution to this review of Critical Developments, Michael Frisch writes from the cusp of the digital frontier. He argues that the digitization of sound and image will challenge the current dominance of transcription and return aurality to oral history. Furthermore, non-text-reliant digital index and search mechanisms will enable users to find and hear the extracts they are looking for in their own interviews – and across countless interviews from other projects – and will enable imaginative, unforeseen interpretations. Frisch concludes that we are witnessing the emergence of a 'post-documentary sensibility' which breaks down the distinction between the oral history document source and the oral history documentary product, and suggests that 'new digital tools and the rich landscape of practice they define may become powerful resources in restoring one of the original appeals of oral history – to open new dimensions of understanding and engagement through the broadly inclusive sharing and interrogation of memory'.

Notes

1   See P. Thompson, 'Historians and oral history', in *The Voice of the Past: Oral History*, Oxford, Oxford University Press, 3rd edition, 2000, pp. 25–82; D.A. Ritchie, *Doing Oral History: A Practical Guide*, New York: Oxford University Press, 2nd edition, 2003, pp. 19–46; C.T. Morrissey, 'Why call it oral history? Searching for early uses of a generic term', *Oral History Review*, 1980, vol. 8, pp. 20–48; the chapters by Allan Nevins, Louis Starr and Ronald J. Grele (United States), Eugenia Meyer (Mexico and the Caribbean), Paul Thompson (Britain), Karen Hartewig (Germany), Danièle Voldman (France), Alessandro Portelli (Italy) and Dora Schwarzstein (Latin America)

in D.K. Dunaway and W.K. Baum (eds), *Oral History: An Interdisciplinary Anthology*, Walnut Creek, Calif.: AltaMira Press, 1996 (many of these articles were initially published in *BIOS*, Special Issue, 1990); L. Douglas and P. Spearitt, 'Talking history: the use of oral sources', in W. Mandle and G. Osborne (eds), *New History: Studying Australia Today*, Sydney, Allen & Unwin, 1988, pp. 59–68; R. Lochead, 'Preface', in N. Fortier, 'Guide to oral history collections in Canada', published in *Canadian Oral History Association Journal*, vol. 13, 1993; P. la Hause, 'Oral history and South African studies', *Radical History Review*, 1990, nos. 46–47, pp. 346–356; R. Jamieson, 'Aspects of oral history projects and archives in New Zealand, the United States and the United Kingdom', *Oral History*, 1990, vol. 20, no. 2, pp. 53–60; I. Jaksic, 'Oral history in the Americas', *Journal of American History*, vol. 79, September 1992, p. 590; P. Huen, J.H. Morrison and K.C. Guan, *Oral History in Southeast Asia: Theory and Method*, Singapore, National Archives of Singapore and Institute of Southeast Asian Studies, 1998; J.C. Sebe Bom Meihy, 'Oral history in Brazil: developments and challenges', *Oral History Review*, 1999, vol. 26, no. 2, pp. 127–130. The various national and international oral history journals which are cited in the Select Bibliography reference other national and regional surveys, and see also references in R. Perks, *Oral History: An Annotated Bibliography*, London: British Library National Sound Archive, 1990.

2   The physicist Thomas Kuhn popularized the idea of 'paradigm' shifts in his book *The Structure of Scientific Revolutions*, Chicago, University of Chicago Press, 1962. Kuhn was also a pioneering oral historian of American science: see R.E. Doel, 'Oral history of American science: a forty-year review', *History of Science*, 2003, vol. xli, p. 349.

3   The relationship between folklore studies and oral history has varied in different parts of the world. In England, despite initial links, oral history and folklore studies tended to travel different paths; Paul Thompson argues that English folklore studies 'never escaped from the stigma of amateurism' (Thompson, *The Voice of the Past*, pp. 71–72). A shared interest in aurality – fuelled by digital technologies, may be bringing the two fields closer again (see R. Perks and J. Robinson, '"The way we speak": web-based representations of changing communities in England', *Oral History*, 2005, vol. 33, no. 2, pp. 79–90). The nationalist politics of Britain's Celtic nations – Wales, Scotland and Northern Ireland – have forged closer relationships between folklore studies and oral history, and in Scandinavia folklore studies have had a profound impact upon the development of oral history.

4   G.E. Evans, *Ask the Fellows Who Cut the Hay*, London: Faber, 1956. See also Evans's anthology, *Spoken History*, London: Faber, 1987. For later but comparable developments in Australia see M. Loh and W. Lowenstein, *The Immigrants*, Melbourne: Hyland House, 1977; and W. Lowenstein, *Weevils in the Flour: An Oral Record of the 1930s Depression in Australia*, Melbourne: Hyland House, 1978. Notable work by the North American Studs Terkel, perhaps the best-known oral history pioneer, includes: *Hard Times: An Oral History of the Great Depression*, New York: Pantheon Books, 1970; *Division Street, America*, Harmondsworth, Penguin, 1970; and '*The Good War*': *An Oral History of World War Two*, Harmondsworth: Penguin, 1986.

5   A. Haley, *Autobiography of Malcolm X*, Harmondsworth: Penguin, 1968; and *Roots: The Saga of an American Family*, London: Hutchinson, 1977.

6   See Thompson, *The Voice of the Past*, pp. 24–26; C.T. Morrissey, 'Oral history and the boundaries of fiction', *The Public Historian*, 1985, vol. 7, no. 2, pp. 41–46; L. Woodward and A. Collings, 'The limits of "faction"', *Newsweek*, 25 April 1977.

7   J. Berry, *The Nation*, 2 October 1976, p. 313, quoted in Morrissey, 'Oral history and the boundaries of fiction', p. 42.

8   On family memory and history see Chapter 14 by Finnegan and Chapter 24 by Borland in this *Reader*. Also V.R. Yow, *Recording Oral History: A Guide for the Humanities and Social Sciences*, Walnut Creek: AltaMira Press, 2nd edition, 2005, pp. 253–281; Ritchie, *Doing Oral History*, pp. 293–294; A. Kikemura, 'Family life histories:

a collaborative venture', *Oral History Review*, vol. 14, 1986, pp. 1–7. On oral tradition and oral history, see J. Vansina, *Oral Tradition as History*, Madison: University of Wisconsin Press, 1985; J.C. Miller (ed.), *The African Past Speaks*: *Essays on Oral Tradition and History*, Folkestone: Dawson, 1980; D. Henige, *Oral Historiography*, London: Longman, 1982; J. Binney, 'Maori oral narratives, Pakeha written texts: two forms of telling history', *New Zealand Journal of History*, 1987, vol. 21, no. 1, pp. 16–28; R. Finnegan, *Oral Tradition and the Verbal Arts*, London: Routledge, 1991; I. Hofmeyer, '*We spend our years as a tale that is told*': *Oral Historical Narrative in a South African Chiefdom*, London: James Currey, 1993; J. Cruikshank, 'Oral tradition and oral history: reviewing some issues', *Canadian Historical Review*, 1994, vol. 75, no. 3, pp. 403–418; E. Tonkin, *Narrating Our Pasts*: *The Social Construction of Oral History*, Cambridge: Cambridge University Press, 1995; J. Cruikshank, 'Discovery of Gold in the Klondike: perspectives from oral tradition', in J.S.H. Brown and E. Vibert (eds), *Reading Beyond Words*: *Contexts for Native History*, Orchard Park, N.J.: Broadview, 1996, pp. 433–457; J. Cruikshank, *The Social Life of Stories*: *Narrative and Knowledge in the Yukon Territory*, Lincoln: University of Nebraska Press, 1998; B. Attwood and F. Magowan (eds), *Telling Stories*: *Indigenous History and Memory in Australia and New Zealand*, Crows Nest, NSW: Allen & Unwin, 2001; L. White, S.F. Miescher and D.W. Cohen (eds), *African Words, African Voices*: *Critical Practices in Oral History*, Bloomington: Indiana University Press, 2001; T. Falola and C. Jennings (eds), *Sources and Methods in African History*: *Spoken, Written, Unearthed*, Rochester, N.Y.: University of Rochester Press, 2003.

9   Subsequent editions published in 1988 and 2000 expanded the initial chapters about the history and achievements of oral history, and explored new thinking about memory, subjectivity and psychoanalysis.

10   A recent example of how oral history continues to be used to recover hidden histories – as noted in a series of reviews in the June 2001 issue of the *American Historical Review* – is the use of oral history to recover African experiences of and perspectives on the First World War: J. Lunn, *Memoirs of the Maelstrom*: *A Senegalese Oral History of the First World War*, Portsmouth, N.H.: Heinemann, 1999; A. Jackson, *Botswana 1939–1945*: *An African Country at War*, New York: Clarendon Press, 1999; M.E. Page, *The Chiwaya War*: *Malawians and the First World War*, Boulder, Colo.: Westview Press, 2000.

11   J. Bornat, 'Oral history as a social movement: reminiscence and older people', *Oral History*, 1989, vol. 17, no. 2, p. 17.

12   Among early critics were: William Cutler III, 'Accuracy in oral history interviewing', *Historical Methods Newsletter*, 1970, no. 3, pp. 1–7; B. Tuchman, 'Distinguishing the significant from the insignificant', *Radcliffe Quarterly*, 1972, no. 56, pp. 9–10 (these two articles are reproduced in Dunaway and Baum (eds), *Oral History*); E. Powell, 'Old men forget', *The Times*, 5 November 1981. For a critique from the Left of oral historians' naïve use of memory, see E. Hobsbawm, 'On history from below', in E. Hobsbawm, *On History*, London: Weidenfeld & Nicolson, 1997, pp. 266–286 (written in 1985 and first published in 1988).

13   P. O'Farrell, 'Oral history: facts and fiction', *Oral History Association of Australia Journal*, 1982–83, no. 5, pp. 3–9.

14   See, for example, the first edition (1978) of Thompson's *The Voice of the Past* for a defence of oral history in these terms.

15   L. Passerini, *Fascism in Popular Memory*: *The Cultural Experience of the Turin Working Class*, Cambridge: Cambridge University Press, 1987. Passerini's pioneering article on subjectivity and silence, 'Work ideology and consensus under Italian fascism' (*History Workshop*, 1979, no. 8, pp. 82–108) is one of the most widely referenced contributions to the literature of oral history, and is used by several contributors to this *Reader*. Readers are urged to refer to the article in its original form.

16   M. Frisch, *A Shared Authority*: *Essays on the Craft and Meaning of Oral and Public History*, Albany: State University of New York Press, 1990, p. 188 (from his article 'Oral history and *Hard Times*: a review essay', first published in 1972). See also, A. Thomson, M. Frisch and P. Hamilton, 'The memory and history debates: some international perspectives', *Oral History*, 1994, vol. 22, no. 2, pp. 33–43. Ron Grele was another notable North America critic of oral history's theoretical naïvety in the 1970s who suggested new ways of working with memory. See R. Grele (ed.), *Envelopes of Sound*: *The Art of Oral History*, New York: Praeger, 1991.

17   For outstandingly imaginative oral history see Portelli's other seminal work, including *The Death of Luigi Trastulli and Other Stories*: *Form and Meaning in Oral History*, Albany: State University of New York Press, 1991; *The Battle of Valle Giulia*: *Oral History and the Art of Dialogue*, Madison: University of Wisconsin Press, 1997; *The Order Has been Carried Out*: *History, Memory, and Meaning of a Nazi Massacre in Rome*, Palgrave Macmillan, 2003. See also, *Oral History Review*, 2005, vol. 32, no. 1, pp. 1–34, special section on 'History, memory and the work of Alessandro Portelli'.

18   Passerini, 'Work ideology and consensus under Italian fascism', p. 84. Michael Frisch also criticized the populist 'no history' approach to oral history in 'Oral history and *Hard Times*: a review essay'. Louise Tilly criticized oral historians' atheoretical and individualist tendencies, though from a more conventional academic standpoint, in her article, 'People's history and social science history', *Social Science History*, 1983, vol. 7, no. 4, pp. 457–474, reprinted with responses from leading oral historians in the *International Journal of Oral History*, 1985, vol. 6, no. 2, pp. 5–46. For a comparable and contemporary Australian critique see J. Murphy, 'The voice of memory: history, autobiography and oral memory', *Historical Studies*, 1986, vol. 22, no. 87, pp. 157–175.

19   A contemporary overview of oral history's radical potential is provided in the introduction to J. Green, 'Engaging in people's history: the Massachusetts History Workshop', in S.P. Benson *et al.*, (eds), *Presenting the Past*: *Essays on History and the Public*, Philadelphia: Temple University Press, 1986, pp. 337–359. For a critique of the assumption that the disempowered have rich memory resources to draw upon for empowerment through oral history, see J. Daklia, 'New approaches in the history of memory?', in Angelika Neuwirth and Andreas Pflitsch (eds), *Crisis and Memory in Islamic Societies*, Beirut: Orient Institute, 2001.

20   For a critique of the Popular Memory Group, see T. Lummis, *Listening to History*: *The Authenticity of Oral Evidence*, London: Hutchinson, 1987.

21   F. Kurasawa, 'A message in a bottle: bearing witness as a mode of ethico-political practice', (http://research.yale.edu/ccs/papers/kurasawa_witnessing.pdf). See also the introduction and articles in Part V, 'Advocacy and empowerment'.

22   J. Bornat, 'Oral history as a social movement: reminiscence and older people', *Oral History*, 1989, vol. 17, no. 2, pp. 16–20.

23   V. Yow, '"Do I Like Them Too Much?" Effects of the oral history interview on the interviewer and vice-versa', *Oral History Review*, 1997, vol. 24, no. 1, pp. 55–79. See also the introduction and articles in Part II and Part III of this *Reader*.

24   See D. Bertaux (ed.), *Biography and Society*: *The Life History Approach in the Social Sciences*, Beverly Hills: Sage, 1981; K. Plummer, *Documents of Life 2*: *An Invitation to a Critical Humanism*, London: Sage, 2001; 'Autobiography and Society' issue of *Sociology*, 1993, vol. 27, no. 1; *Auto/Biography* journal (from 1992); P. Chamberlayne, J. Bornat and T. Wengraf (eds), *The Turn to Biographical Methods in Social Sciences*, London: Routledge, 2000; B. Roberts, *Biographical Research*, Buckingham: Open University Press, 2001; M. Andrews, S.D. Sclater, C. Squire and A. Treacher (eds), *The Uses of Narrative*: *Explorations in Sociology, Psychology and Cultural Studies*, New Brunswick: Transaction Publishers, 2004 (previously published by Routledge, 2000, as *Lines of Narrative*: *Psychosocial Perspectives*).

25   See L.L. Langness and G. Frank, *Lives: An Anthropological Approach to Biography*, Novato, Calif., Chandler & Sharp, 1981; L. Watson, and M. Watson-Franke, *Interpreting Life Histories: An Anthropological Inquiry*, New Brunswick, N.J.: Rutgers University Press, 1985; J. Okely and H. Callaway (eds), *Anthropology and Autobiography*, London and New York: Routledge, 1992; S. Mintz, 'The anthropological interview and the life history', in Dunaway and Baum (eds), *Oral History*, pp. 298–305; J.C. Climo and M.G. Cattell (eds), *Social Memory and History: Anthropological Perspectives*, Walnut Creek, Calif.: AltaMira Press, 2002. See also note 8 in this introduction.

26   See J. Olney (ed.), *Studies in Autobiography*, New York: Oxford University Press, 1988; J. Swindells (ed.), *The Uses of Autobiography*, London: Taylor & Francis, 1995; A. Portelli, *The Text and the Voice*, New York: Columbia University Press, 1994; S. Smith and J. Watson, *Reading Autobiography: A Guide for Interpreting Life Narratives*, Minneapolis: University of Minnesota Press, 2001; and the North American journals *Biography* and *Journal of Narrative and Life History*.

27   See W.M. Runyan, *Life Histories and Psychobiography: Explorations in Theory and Method*, New York and Oxford: Oxford University Press, 1982; T.R. Sarbin (ed.), *Narrative Psychology: The Storied Nature of Human Conduct*, New York: Praeger, 1986; R. Josselson and A. Leiblich (eds), *Narrative Study of Lives*, Newbury Park, Calif.: Sage, from 1993; Andrews, *et al.*, *The Uses of Narrative*.

28   R. Johnson *et al.* (eds), *Making Histories: Studies in History-writing and Politics*, London: Hutchinson, 1982; C. Steedman, *Past Tenses: Essays on Writing, Autobiography, History*, London: Rivers Oram Press, 1992; R. Samuel, *Theatres of Memory: Past and Present in Contemporary Culture*, London: Verso, 1994; Andrews, *et al.*, *The Uses of Narrative*.

29   See E. McMahan, *Elite Oral History Discourse: A Study of Cooperation and Coherence*, Tuscaloosa: University of Alabama Press, 1989; R.J. Grele, 'A surmisable variety: interdisciplinarity and oral testimony', in Grele, *Envelopes of Sound*, pp. 156–195; C. Joyner, 'Oral history as communicative event', in Dunaway and Baum (eds), *Oral History*, pp. 292–297; R. Jossleson and A. Leiblich (eds), *Making Meaning of Narrative*, Thousand Oaks, Calif.: Sage, 1999; M. Chamberlain and P. Thompson (eds), *Narrative and Genre: Contexts and Types of Communication*, New Brunswick, N.J.: Transaction Publishers, 2004 (previously published by Routledge, 1998); A. Leiblich, R. Tuval-Mashiach and T. Zilber (eds), *Narrative Research: Reading, Analysis and Interpretation*, Thousand Oaks, Calif.: Sage, 1998.

30   W. Schneider, *So They Understand: Cultural Issues in Oral History*, Logan: Utah State University Press, 2002.

31   G.C. Rosenwald and R.L. Ochberg (eds), *Storied Lives: The Cultural Politics of Self-Understanding*, New York and London: Yale University Press, 1992; B. Ross, *Remembering the Autobiographical Past: Descriptions of Autobiographical Memory*, Oxford: Oxford University Press, 1992; M. Freeman, *Rewriting the Self: History, Memory, Narrative*, London and New York: Routledge, 1993, C. Linde, *The Creation of Coherence*, Oxford: Oxford University Press, 2003; R. Fivush and C.A. Haden (eds), *Autobiographical Memory and the Construction of a Narrative Self: Developmental and Cultural Perspectives*, Mahwah, N.J.: Lawrence Erlbaum, 2003.

32   Sheila Rowbotham, *Hidden from History*, London: Pluto, 1973.

33   The core texts for feminist oral history are S. Berger Gluck and D. Patai (eds), *Women's Words: The Feminist Practice of Oral History*, New York and London: Routledge, 1991; and S.H. Armitage (ed.), *Women's Oral History: The Frontiers Reader*, University of Nebraska Press, 2002. See also Personal Narratives Group, *Interpreting Women's Lives: Feminist Theory and Personal Narratives*, Bloomington and Indianapolis: Indiana University Press, 1989; M. Stuart, 'You're a big girl now: subjectivities, oral history and feminism', *Oral History*, 1994, vol. 22, no. 2, pp. 55–63;

the four women's history issues of *Oral History* (1977, vol. 5, no. 2; 1982, vol. 10, no. 2; 1993, vol. 21, no. 2; 2002, vol. 30, no. 1); *Canadian Oral History Association Journal*, 1991, no. 11, special issue on 'Women and oral history'; T. Cosslett, C. Lurie and P. Summerfield (eds), *Feminism and Autobiography: Texts, Theories, Methods*, London: Routledge, 2000; and the articles by Anderson and Jack, Borland, Bozzoli, James, Kennedy, Shostak and Stoler in this *Reader*.

34   S.H. Armitage and S.B. Gluck, 'Reflections on Women's Oral History: An Exchange', originally published in *Frontiers: Journal of Women's Studies*, 1998, vol. 19, no. 3, pp. 1–11. The women's oral history issues of *Frontiers: A Journal of Women's Studies* comprise vol. 2, no. 2, 1977; vol. 7, no. 2, 1983; vol. 19, no. 2, 1998; vol. 19, no. 3, 1998. A selection of *Frontiers'* articles about women's oral history is available in Armitage, *Women's Oral History*.

35   See, for example, Joan Sangster's, 'Telling our stories: feminist debates and the use of oral history', *Women's History Review*, 1994, vol. 3, no. 1, pp. 5–28.

36   O. Bartov, in a review of three books about the European memory of the Holocaust and the Second World War, in *American Historical Review*, 2001, vol. 106, no. 2, p. 660. Bartov also notes signs that in the new millennium 'this preoccupation with memory will gradually diminish', particularly in relation to the scholarly focus on 'the Nazi occupation of Europe and the material reconstruction and identity reformation of the postwar period'. Books about history and modern memory include: D. Thelen, *Memory and American History*, Bloomington: Indiana University Press, 1990; J. Le Goff, *History and Memory*, New York: Columbia University Press, 1992; R. Terdimann, *Present Past: Modernity and the Memory Crisis*, Ithaca, N.Y.: Cornell University Press, 1993; K. Darian-Smith and P. Hamilton (eds), *Memory and History in Twentieth Century Australia*, Melbourne: Oxford University Press, 1994; A. Huyssen, *Twilight Memories: Marking Time in a Culture of Amnesia*, London: Routledge, 1995; D. Gross, *Lost Time: On Remembering and Forgetting in Late Modern Culture*, Amherst, University of Massachusetts Press, 2000; S. Radstone and K. Hodgkin (eds), *Regimes of Memory*, London: Routledge, 2003.

37   Early examples included P. Thompson and N. Burchardt (eds), *Our Common History: The Transformation of Europe*, London: Pluto, 1982; R. Samuel and P. Thompson (eds), *The Myths We Live By*, London: Routledge, 1990. There have been several successors or alternatives to the *International Journal of Oral History*, which lapsed in the late 1980s: *Life Stories/Recits de Vie*, Colchester, Biography and Society Research Committee, International Sociological Association, 1985–89; R. Grele (ed.), *Subjectivity and Multi-Culturalism in Oral History, The International Annual of Oral History*, New York, 1992; *International Yearbook of Oral History and Life Stories*, Oxford: Oxford University Press, 1992–96; *Memory and Narrative*, book series, London: Routledge, 1997–2004 (from 2004 published by Transaction); *Words and Silences* (journal of the IOHA from 1997).

38   G. Necoechea, 'Editorial', *Words and Silences*, 2003, new series vol. 2, no. 1, p. 2.

39   J.C.S.B. Meihy, 'The radicalization of oral history', *Words and Silences*, 2003, new series vol. 2, no. 1, pp. 31–41. See the bibliography for key oral history texts from Latin America.

40   S.B. Gluck, D.A. Ritchie and B. Eynon, 'Reflections on oral history in the new millennium: roundtable comments', *Oral History Review*, 1999, vol. 26, no. 2, pp. 1–27; M.A. Larson, 'Potential, potential, potential: the marriage of oral history and the world wide web', *Journal of American History*, vol. 88, no. 2, 2001, pp. 596–603; Brewster, 'Internet access to oral recordings: finding the issues', (www.uaf.edu/library/oralhistory/brewster1/research.html). See also articles by Benmayor and Swain in Part IV of this *Reader*, and Perks and Robinson, 'The way we speak'.

Chapter 1

Alex Haley

BLACK HISTORY, ORAL
HISTORY AND GENEALOGY

Alex Haley's best-selling and controversial books, *Autobiography of Malcolm X* (first published in 1965) and *Roots*: *The Saga of an American Family* (1976), encouraged black Americans to explore their past and helped to popularize oral history and family history in the United States. In this extract from a talk to an early meeting of the United States Oral History Association, Haley describes the transmission of memories within his African-American family, and the oral traditions which are preserved in precise detail and retold by the *griot* or historical storyteller of a West African tribal community. Reprinted from *Oral History Review*, 1973, vol. 1, pp. 1–17. © 1973, Oral History Association. All rights reserved. Used by permission.

WHEN I WAS A LITTLE BOY I lived in a little town which you probably never heard of called Henning, Tennessee, about fifty miles north of Memphis. And I lived there with my parents in the home of my mother's mother. And my grandmother and I were very, very close. Every summer that I can remember growing up there in Henning, my grandmother would have, as visitors, members of the family who were always women, always of her general age range, the late forties, early fifties. They came from places that sounded pretty exotic to me – Dyersburg, Tennessee, Inkster, Michigan – places like that, St Louis, Kansas City. They were like Cousin Georgia, Aunt Plus, Aunt Liz, so forth. And every evening, after the supper dishes were washed, they would go out on the front porch and sit in cane-bottomed rocking chairs, and I would always sit behind grandma's chair. And every single evening of those summers, unless there was some particularly hot gossip that would overrule it, they would talk about otherwise the self same thing. It was bits and pieces and patches of what I later would learn was a long narrative history of the family which had been passed down literally across generations.

As a little boy I didn't have the orientation to understand most of what they talked about. Sometimes they would talk about individuals, and I didn't know what these individuals were often; I didn't know what an old massa was, I didn't know what an old missus was. They would talk about locales; I didn't know what a plantation was. And then at other times, interspersed with these, they'd talk about anecdotes, incidents which had happened to these people or these places. The furthest-back person that they ever talked about was someone whom they would call 'The African'. And I know that the first time I ever heard the word Africa or African was from their mouths, there on the front porch in Henning.

I think that my first impression that these things they spoke of went a long way back, came from the fact that they were wrinkled, greying, or completely grey in some cases, and I was a little boy, three, four, five, and now and then when some of them would get animatedly talking about something, they would fling their finger or hand down towards me and say something like 'I wasn't any bigger than this young 'un here'. And the very idea that someone as old and wrinkled as she had at one time been no older than I was just blew my mind. I knew it must be way, way back that they were talking about.

When they were speaking of this African, the furthest-back person of all, they would tell how he was brought on a ship to this country to a place they pronounced as 'Naplis'. And he was bought off this ship by a man whose name was John Wailer, who had a plantation in a place called Spotsylvania County, Virginia. And then they would tell how he was on this plantation and he kept trying to escape. The first three times he escaped he was caught and given a worse beating than previously as his punishment. And then the fourth time he escaped he had the misfortune to be caught by a professional slave catcher. And I grew up hearing how this slave catcher decided to make an example of him. And I grew up hearing how he gave the African the choice either to be castrated or to have a foot cut off. And the African chose the foot. And I grew up hearing how his foot was put against a stump, and with an ax was cut off across the arch. It was a very hideous act. But as it turned out that act was to play a very major role in the keeping of a narrative down across a family for a long time.

The reasons were two. One of them was that in the middle 1700s in Virginia, almost all slaves were sold at auction. A male slave in good condition would bring on the average about $750. At the end of every slave auction they would have what they called the scrap sale, and those who were incapacitated, ill, or otherwise not so valuable for market, would be sold generally for amounts of $100 or less in cash. And this particular African managed to survive and then to convalesce, and he posed then to his master an economic question. And his master decided that he was crippled and he hobbled about, but he still could do limited work. And the master decided that he would be worth more kept on that plantation than he would be worth sold away for cash of less than $100. And that was how it happened that this particular African was kept on one plantation for quite a long period of time.

Now that came at a time when, if there was any single thing that probably characterizes slaves, it was that they had almost no sense of what we today know and value and revere as family continuity. And the reason simply was that slaves were sold back and forth so much. Characteristically slave children would grow up without an awareness of who their parents were, and particularly male parents. This African, now kept on the plantation by his master's decision, hobbling about and doing the limited work he could, finally met and mated with another slave on that plantation, and her name (in the stories told by my grandmother and the others on the front porch in Henning) was Bell, the big house cook. And of that union was born a little girl who was given the name Kizzy. As Kizzy got to be four or five or so, this African would take that little girl by the hand, and he would take her around and point out to her various natural objects, and he would tell her the name for that thing – tree, rock, cow, sky, so forth. The names that he told her were instinctively in his native tongue, and to the girl they were strange phonetic sounds which in time, with repetitive hearing, the girl could repeat. He would point at a guitar and he would make a single sound as if it were spelled *ko*. And she came in time to know that *ko* was guitar in his terms. There were other strange phonetic sounds for other objects. Perhaps the most involved of them was that contiguous to the plantation there was a river, and whenever this African would point out this river to his daughter Kizzy he would say to her '*Kamby Bolongo*'. And she came to know that *Kamby Bolongo* in his terms meant river.

There was another thing about this African which is in the background of all the Black people in this country, and that was that whoever bought them off the slave ship, when they got them to a plantation, about their first act was giving them an Anglicized name. For all practical purposes that was the first step in the psychic dehumanization of an individual or collectively of a people. And in the case of this particular African his master gave him the name Toby. But whenever any of the other adult slaves would address him as Toby, this African would strenuously rebuff and reject it and he would tell them his name was '*Kin-tay*', a sharp, angular two-syllabic sound that the little girl Kizzy came to know her father said was his name.

And there was yet another thing about this African characteristic of all those original Africans in our background, and that was that they had been brought from a place where they spoke whatever was their native tongue, and brought to this place where it became necessary to learn English for sheer survival's sake. And gradually, haltingly, all those original Africans learned a word here, a phrase there, of the new tongue – English. As this process began to happen with this African, and he began to be able to express himself in more detailed ways, he began to tell his little daughter Kizzy little vignettes about himself. He told her, for instance, how he had been captured. He said that he had not been far away from his village chopping wood to make himself a drum when he had been set upon by four men, overwhelmed, and taken thusly into slavery. And she came to know along with many other stories the story of how he was chopping wood when he was captured.

To compress what would happen over the next decade, the girl Kizzy stayed on the plantation in Spotsylvania County directly exposed to her father who had come directly from Africa, and to his stories, until she had a considerable repertoire of knowledge about him from his own mouth. When the girl Kizzy was sixteen years of age, she was sold away to a new master whose name was Tom Lea and he had a much smaller plantation in North Carolina. And it was on this plantation that after a while the girl Kizzy gave birth to her first child, a boy who was given the name George. The father was the new master Tom Lea. And as George got to be four or five or so, now it was his mother Kizzy who began to tell him the stories that she heard from her father. And the boy began to discover the rather common phenomenon that slave children rarely knew who their fathers were, let alone a grandfather. He had something which made him rather singular. And so it was with considerable pride the boy began to tell his peers the story of his grandfather; this African who said his name was *Kin-tay*, who called a river *Kamby Bolongo*, and called a guitar *ko* and other sounds for other things, and who said that he had been chopping wood when he was set upon and captured and brought into slavery.

When the boy George got to be about twelve, he was apprenticed to an old slave to learn handling the master's fighting gamecocks. And this boy had innate, green thumb ability for fighting gamecocks. By the time he was in his mid-teens he had been given (for his local and regional renown as an expert slave handler and pitter of fighting gamecocks) the nickname he would take to his grave decades later – Chicken George.

When Chicken George was about eighteen he met and mated with a slave girl. And her name was Matilda, and in time Matilda gave birth to seven children. Now for the first time that story which had come down from this African began to fan out within the breadth of a family. The stories as they would be told on the front porch in Henning by grandma and the others were those of the winter evenings after the harvest when families would entertain themselves by sitting together and the elders would talk and the young would listen. Now Chicken George would sit with his seven children around the hearth. The story was that they would roast sweet potatoes in the hot ashes, and night after night after night across the winters, Chicken George would tell his seven children a story unusual among slaves, and that was direct knowledge of a great-grandfather; this same African who said his name was *Kin-tay*, who called the river *Kamby Bolongo*, and a guitar *ko*, and who said that he was chopping wood when he was captured.

Those children grew up, took mates and had children. One of them was named Tom. And Tom became an apprenticed blacksmith. He was sold in his mid-teens to a man named Murray who had a tobacco plantation in Alamance County, North Carolina. And it was on this plantation that Tom, who became that plantation's blacksmith, met and mated with a slave girl whose name was Irene and who was the plantation weaver. And Irene also in time bore seven children. Now it was yet another generation, another section of the state of North Carolina and another set of seven children who would sit in yet another cabin, around the hearth in the winter evenings with the sweet potatoes in the hot ashes. And now the father was Tom telling his children about something virtually unique in the knowledge of slaves, direct knowledge of a great-great-grandfather, this same African, who said his name was *Kin-tay*, who called the river *Kamby Bolongo*, who said he was chopping wood when he was captured, and the other parts of the story that had come down in that way.

Of that second set of seven children, in Alamance County, North Carolina, the youngest was a little girl whose name was Cynthia, and Cynthia was my maternal grandmother. And I grew up in her home in Henning, Tennessee, and grandma pumped that story into me as if it were plasma. It was by all odds the most precious thing in her life – the story which had come down across the generations about the family going back to that original African.

I stayed at grandma's home until I was in my mid-teens. By that time I had two younger brothers, George and Julius. Our father was a teacher at small black land grant colleges about the South and we began now to move around wherever he was teaching. And thus I went to school through two years of college. When World War II came along I was one of the many people who thought that if I could hurry and get into an organization of which I had recently heard called the US Coast Guard, that maybe I could spend the war walking the coast. And I got into the service and to my great shock rather suddenly found myself on an ammunition ship in the Southwest Pacific, which was not at all what I had in mind. But when I look back upon it now, it was the first of a series of what seemed to be accidental things, but now seem to be part of a pattern of many things that were just meant to be, to make a certain book possible, in time. On the ships in the Coast Guard, totally by accident, I stumbled into the long road to becoming a writer. It was something I had never have dreamed of. [. . .]

[Many years later]

One morning, I was in the British Museum and I came upon something, I had vaguely heard of it, the Rosetta Stone. It just really entranced me. I read about it, and I found how, when this stone was discovered in 1799, it seemed to have three sets of texts chiseled into the stone: one of them in Greek characters, which Greek scholars could read, the second in a then-unknown set of characters, the third in the ancient hieroglyphics which it was assumed no one would ever translate. Then I read how a French scholar, Jean Champollion, had come along and had taken that second unknown set of script, character for character, matched it with the Greek and finally had come up with a thesis he could prove – that the text was the same as the Greek. And then in a superhuman feat of scholarship he had taken the terribly intricate characters of the hieroglyphics and cross matched them with the preceding two in almost geometric progression, and had proved that too was the same text. That was what opened up to the whole world of scholarship, all that hitherto had been hidden behind the mystery of the allegedly undecipherable hieroglyphics.

And that thing just fascinated me. I would find myself going around London doing all sorts of other things and at odd times I would see in my mind's eye, almost as if it were projected in my head, the Rosetta Stone. And to me, it just had some kind of special significance, but I couldn't make head or tail of what it might be. Finally I was on a plane coming back to this country, when an idea hit me. It was rough, raw, crude, but it got me to thinking. Now what this scholar worked with was language chiseled into the stone. And what he did was to take that which had been unknown and match it with that which was known, and thus found out the meaning of what hitherto had been unknown. And then I got to thinking of an analogy: that story always told in our family that I had heard on the front porch in Henning. The unknown quotient was those strange phonetic sounds. And I got to thinking, now maybe I could find out where these sounds came from. Obviously these strange sounds are threads of some African tongue. And my whole thing was to see if maybe I could find out, just in curiosity, what tongue did they represent. It seemed obvious to me what I had to do was try to get in touch with as wide a range of Africans as I could, simply because there were many, many tongues spoken in Africa. I lived in New York, so I began doing what seemed to me logical. I began going up to the United Nations lobby about quitting time. It wasn't hard to spot Africans, and every time I could I'd stop one. And I would say to him my little sounds. In a couple of weeks I stopped a couple of dozen Africans, each and every one of which took a quick look, quick listen to me, and took off. Which I well understand; me with a Tennessee accent trying to tell them some African sounds, I wasn't going to get it.

I have a friend, a master researcher, George Sims, who knew what I was trying to do and he came to me with a listing of about a dozen people renowned for their knowledge of African linguistics. And one who intrigued me right off the bat was not an African at all, but a Belgian. Educated at England, much of it at the School of Oriental and African Studies, he had done his early work living in African villages, studying the language or the tongue as spoken in those villages. He had finally written a book called in French, *La Tradition Orale*.[1] His name: Dr Jan Vansina, University of Wisconsin. I phoned Dr Vansina. He very graciously said I could see him. I got on a plane and flew to Madison, Wisconsin, with no dream of what was about to happen. In the living room of the Vansina's that evening I told Dr Vansina every little bit I could remember of what I'd heard as a little boy on the front porch in Henning. And Dr Vansina listened most intently. And then he began to question me. Being himself an oral historian, he was particularly interested in the physical transmission of the story down across the generations. And I would answer everything I could. I couldn't answer most of what he asked. Around midnight, Dr Vansina said, 'I wonder if you'd spend the night at our home,' and I did stay there. The following morning, before breakfast, Dr Vansina came down with a very serious expression on his face; I was later to learn that he had already been on the phone with colleagues, and he said to me: 'The ramifications of what you have brought here could be enormous.' He and his colleagues felt almost certain that the collective sounds that I had been able to bring there, which had been passed down across the family in the manner I had described to him, represented the Mandinka tongue. I'd never heard the word. He told me that that was the tongue spoken by the Mandingo people. He began then to guess translate certain of the sounds. There was a sound that probably meant cow or cattle; another probably meant the bow-bow tree, generic in West Africa. I had told him that from the time I was knee-high I'd heard about how this African would point to a guitar and say *ko*. Now he told me that almost surely this would refer to one of the oldest of the stringed instruments among the Mandingo people, an instrument made of a gourd covered with goat skin, a long neck, 21 strings, called the *kora*. He came finally to the most involved of the sounds that I had heard and had brought to him – *Kamby Bolongo*. He said without question in Mandinka, *bolongo* meant river; preceded by *Kamby* it probably would mean Gambia River. I'd never heard of that river.

It was Thursday morning when I heard those words; Monday morning I was in Africa. I just had to go. There was no sense in messing around. On Friday I found that of the numerous African students in this country, there were a few from that very, very small country called Gambia. And the one who physically was closest to me was a fellow in Hamilton College, Clinton, New York. And I hit that campus about 3:30 Friday afternoon and practically snatched Ebou Manga out of an economics class and got us on Pan American that night. We flew through the night to Dakar, Senegal, and there we got a light plane that flew over to a little airstrip called Yundum – they literally had to run monkeys off the runway to get in there. And then we got a van and we went into the small city of Bathurst, the capital of Gambia. Ebou Manga, his father Alhaji Manga (it's a predominantly Moslem culture there), assembled a group of about eight men, members of the government, who came into the patio of the Atlantic Hotel, and they sat in kind of a semi-circle as I told them the history that had come down across the family to my grandmother and thence to me; told them everything I could remember.

And when I finished, the Africans irritated me considerably because *Kamby Bolongo*, the sounds which had gotten me specifically to them, they tended almost to poo-poo. They said, 'Well, of course *Kamby Bolongo* would mean Gambia River; anyone would know that.' What these Africans reacted to was another sound: a mere two syllables that I had brought them without the slightest comprehension that it had any particular significance. They said, 'There may be some significance in that your forefather stated his name was *Kin-tay*.' I said, 'Well, there was nothing more explicit in the story than the pronunciation of his name, *Kin-tay*.' They said, 'Our oldest villages tend to be named for those families which founded those villages centuries ago.' And then they sent for a little map and they said, 'Look, here is the village of Kinte-Kundah. And not too far from it is the village of Kinte-Kundah-Janneh-Ya.' And then they told me about something I never had any concept existed in this world. They told me that in the back country, and particularly in the older villages of the back country, there were old men called *griots*, who are in effect walking, living archives of oral history. They are the old men who, from the time they had been in their teen-ages, have been part of a line of men who tell the stories as they have been told since the time of their forefathers, literally down across centuries. The incumbent *griot* will be a man usually in his late sixties, early seventies, and underneath him will be men separated by about decade intervals, sixty, fifty, forty, thirty, twenty, and a teen-age boy, and each line of *griots* will be the experts in the story of a major family clan; another line of *griots* another clan; and so on for dozens of major clans. Another line of *griots* would be the experts in the history of a group of villages. Another would go into the history of the empires which had preceded it, and so forth. And the stories were told in a narrative, oral history way, not verbatim, but the essential same way they had been told down across the time since the forefathers. And the way they were trained was that the teen-age boy was exposed to that story for forty or fifty years before he would become the oral historian incumbent.

It astounds us now to realize that men like these, in not only Africa but also other cultures, can literally talk for days, telling a story and not repeating them-selves, and telling the details in the most explicit detail. The reason it astounds us is because in our culture we have become so conditioned to the crush of print that most people in our culture have almost forgotten what the human memory is capable of if it is trained to keep things in it. These men, I was told, existed in the back country. And the men there told me that since my forefather had said his name was *Kin-tay* they would see what they could to do help me.

I came back to this country enormously bewildered. I didn't know what to do. It embarrasses me to say that up to that time I really hadn't thought all that much about Africa. I knew where it was and I had the standard cliché images of it, the Tarzan Africa and stuff like that. Well, now it was almost as if some religious zealotry came into me. I just began to devour everything I could lay eyes on about Africa, particularly slavery. I can remember after reading all day I'd sit on the edge of a bed at night with a map of Africa, studying the positions of the countries, one with relation with the other.

It was about six weeks later when an innocuous-looking letter came to me which suggested that when it was possible I should come back. I was back over there as quickly as I possibly could make it. The same men, with whom I had previously talked rather matter-of-factly, told me that the word had been put out in the back country and that there had indeed been found a *griot* of the Kinte clan. His name, they said, was Kebba Kanga Fofana. When I heard there was such a man I was ready to have a fit. Where is he? I figured from my experience as an American magazine writer, the government should have had him there with a public relations man for me to talk to. And they looked at me oddly and they said, he's in his village.

I discovered at that point that if I was to see this man, I was going to have to do something I'd never dreamed before: I would have to organize a safari. It took me three days to rent a launch to get up the river, lorry, Land-Rover to take supplies by the back route, to hire finally a total of fourteen people, including three interpreters, four musicians (they told me in the back country these old oral historians would not talk without music in the background), bearers and so forth. And on the fourth day we went vibrating in this launch up the Gambia River. I was very uncomfortable. I had the feeling of being alien. I had the queasy feeling of what do they see me as, another pith-helmet? We got on up the river to a little village called Albreda on the left bank. And then we went ashore. And now our destination by foot was a village called Juffure where this man was said to live.

There's an expression called 'the peak experience'. It is that which emotionally nothing in your life ever can transcend. And I know I have had mine that first day in the back country in black West Africa. When we got up within sight of the village of Juffure, the children who had inevitably been playing outside African villages gave the word and the people came flocking out of their huts. It's a rather small village, only about seventy people. And villages in the back country are very much today as they were two hundred years ago, circular mud huts with conical thatched roofs. And from a distance I could see this small man with a pillbox hat and an off-white robe, and even from a distance there was an aura of 'somebodiness' about him. I just knew that was the man we had come to see. And when we got closer the interpreters left our party and went straight to him. And I had stepped unwittingly into a sequence of emotional events that always I feel awkward trying to describe, simply because I never ever verbally could convey the power, the physical power, of emotional occurrences.

These people quickly filtered closely around me in kind of a horseshoe design with me at the base. If I had put up my hands I would have touched the nearest ones on either side. There were about three, four deep all around. And the first thing that hit me was the intensity of the way they were staring at me. The eyes just raped. The foreheads were forward in the intensity of the staring. And it was an uncomfortable feeling. And while this was happening there began to occur inside me a kind of feeling as if something was turgid, rolling, surging around. And I had this eerie feeling that I knew inside me why it was happening and what it was about, but consciously I could not identify what had me so upset inside. And after a while it began to roll in: it was rather like a galeforce wind that you couldn't see but it just rolled in and hit you – bam! It was enough to knock you down. I suddenly realized what so upset me was that I was looking at a crowd of people and for the first time in my life every one of them was jet black. And I was standing there rather rocked by that, and in the way that we tend to do if we are discomforted we drop our glance. And I remember dropping my glance, and my glance falling on my own hand, my own complexion, in context with their complexion. And now there came rolling in another surging galeforce thing that hit me perhaps harder than the first one. A feeling of guilt, a feeling rather of being hybrid, a feeling of being the impure among the pure.

And the old man suddenly left the interpreters, walked away, and the people as quickly filtered away from me and to the old man. And they began a very animated talking, high metallic Mandinka tongue. One of the interpreters, his name was A.B.C. Salla, whispered in my ear and the significance of what he whispered probably got me as much as all the rest of it collectively. He said, 'They stare at you so because they have never seen a black American.' And what hit me was they were not looking at Alex Haley, writer, they didn't know who he was, they couldn't care less. But what they saw me as was a symbol of twenty-five million of us over here whom they had never seen. And it was just an awesome thing to realize that someone had thrust that kind of symbolism upon me. And there's a language that's universal. It's a language of gestures, noises, inflections, expressions. Somehow looking at them, hearing them, though I couldn't understand a syllable, I knew what they were talking about. I somehow knew they were trying to arrive at a consensus of how did they collectively feel about me as a symbol for them of all the millions of us over here whom they never had seen. And there came a time when the old man quickly turned. He walked right through the people, he walked right past three interpreters, he walked right up to me, looking piercingly into my eyes and spoke in Mandinka, as if instinctively he felt I should be able to understand it. And the translation came from the side. And the way they collectively saw me, the symbol of all the millions of us black people here whom they never had seen was, 'Yes, we have been told by the forefathers that there are many of us from this place who are in exile in that place called America and in other places.' And that was the way they saw it.

The old man, the *griot*, the oral historian, Kebba Kanga Fofana, seventy-three rains of age (their way of saying seventy-three years, one rainy season a year), began now to tell me the ancestral history of the Kinte clan as it had been told down across the centuries, from the times of the forefathers. It was as if a scroll was being read. It wasn't just talk as we talk. It was a very formal occasion. The people became mouse quiet, rigid. The old man sat in a chair and when he would speak he would come up forward, his body would grow rigid, the cords in his neck stood out and he spoke words as though they were physical objects coming out of his mouth. He'd speak a sentence or so, he would go limp, relax, and the translation would come. Out of this man's head came spilling lineage details incredible to behold. Two, three centuries back. Who married whom, who had what children, what children married whom and their children, and so forth, just unbelievable. I was struck not only by the profusion of details, but also by the biblical pattern of the way they expressed it. It would be something like: 'and so and so took as a wife so and so and begat and begat and begat', and he'd name their mates and their children, and so forth. When they would date things it was not with calendar dates, but they would date things with physical events, such as, 'in the year of the big water he slew a water buffalo', the year of the big water referring to a flood. And if you wanted to know the date calendar-wise you had to find when that flood occurred.

I can strip out of the hours that I heard of the history of the Kinte clan (my forefather had said his name was *Kin-tay*), the immediate vertical essence of it, leaving out all the details of the brothers and the cousins and the other marriages and so forth. The *griot* Kebba Kanga Fofana said that the Kinte clan had been begun in a country called Old Mali. Traditionally the Kinte men were blacksmiths who had conquered fire. The women were potters and weavers. A branch of the clan had moved into the country called Mauretania. It was from the country of Mauretania that a son of the clan, whose name was Kairaba Kunta Kinte (he was a *Marabout*, which is to say a holy man of the Moslem faith), came down into the country called the Gambia. He went first to a village called Pakali n'Ding. He stayed there for a while. He went next to a village called Jiffarong; thence he went to a village called Juffure. In the village of Juffure the young *Marabout* Kairaba Kunta Kinte took his first wife, a Mandinka maiden whose name was Sireng. And by her he begat two sons whose names were Janneh and Saloum. Then he took a second wife; her name, Yaisa. And by Yaisa he begat a son whose name was Omoro. Those three sons grew up in the village of Juffure until they came of age. The elder two, Janneh and Saloum, went away and started a new village called Kinte-Kundah Janneh-Ya. It is there today. Literally translated it means 'The Home of Janneh Kinte'. The youngest son, Omoro, stayed in the village until he had thirty rains, and then he took a wife, a Mandinka maiden, her name Binta Kebba. And by Binta Kebba, roughly between 1750 and 1760, Omoro Kinte begat four sons, whose names were Kunta, Lamin, Suwadu and Madi.

By the time he got down to that level of the family, the *griot* had talked for probably five hours. He had stopped maybe fifty times in the course of that narrative and a translation came into me. And then a translation came as all the others had come, calmly, and it began, 'About the time the king's soldiers came.' That was one of those time-fixing references. Later in England, in British Parliamentary records, I went feverishly searching to find out what he was talking about, because I had to have the calendar date. But now in back country Africa, the *griot* Kebba Kanga Fofana, the oral historian, was telling the story as it had come down for centuries from the time of the forefathers of the Kinte clan. 'About the time the king's soldiers came, the eldest of these four sons, Kunta, went away from this village to chop wood and was seen never again.' And he went on with his story.

I sat there as if I was carved out of rock. Goose-pimples came out on me I guess the size of marbles. He just had no way in the world to know that he had told me that which meshed with what I'd heard on the front porch in Henning, Tennessee, from grandma, from Cousin Georgia, from Aunt Liz, from Cousin Plus, all the other old ladies who sat there on that porch. I managed to get myself together enough to pull out my notebook, which had in it what grandma had always said. And I got the interpreter Salla and showed it to him and he got rather agitated, and he went to the old man, and he got agitated, and the old man went to the people and they got agitated.

I don't remember it actually happening. I don't remember anyone giving an order, but those seventy people formed a ring around me, moving counterclockwise, chanting, loudly, softly, loudly, softly, their bodies were close together, the physical action was like drum majorettes with their high knee action. You got the feeling they were an undulating mass of people moving around. I'm standing in the middle like an Adam in the desert. I don't know how I felt; how could you feel a thing like that? And I remember looking at the first lady who broke from that circle (there were about a dozen ladies who had little infant children slung across their backs), and she with a scowl on this jet black face, broke from that circle, her bare feet slapping against the hard earth, came charging in towards me. And she took her baby and roughly thrust it out. The gesture said, 'Take it!' and I took the baby and I clasped it, at which point she snatched it away and another lady, another baby, and I guess I had clasped about a dozen babies in about two minutes. It would be almost two years later at Harvard when Dr Jerome Bruner told me, you were participating in one of the oldest ceremonies of humankind called 'the laying on of hands'; that in their way they were saying to you, 'through this flesh which is us, we are you, and you are us'. There were many, many other things that happened in that village that day, but I was particularly struck with the enormity of the fact that they were dealing with me and seeing me in the perspective of, for them, the symbol of twenty-five millions of us black people in this country whom they never had seen. They took me into their mosque. They prayed in Arabic which I couldn't understand. Later the crux of the prayer was translated, 'Praise be to Allah for one long lost from us whom Allah has returned.' And that was the way they saw that.

When it was possible to leave, since we'd come by water, I wanted to go out over the land. My five senses had become muted, truncated. They didn't work right. If I wanted to feel something, I would have to squeeze to register the sense of feeling. Things were misty. I didn't hear well. I would become aware the driver sitting right by me was almost shouting something and I just hadn't heard him up to that point. I began now, as we drove out over the back country road, with drums distantly heard around, to see in my mind's eye, as if it were being projected somehow on a film, a screen almost, rough, ragged, out of focus, almost a portrayal of what I had studied so, so much about: the background of us as a people, the way that ancestrally we who are in this country were brought out of Africa. [. . .]

Note

1   J. Vansina, *De la Tradition Orale*: *Essai de Methode Historique*, Belgique, Tervuren, 1961. Translated as *Oral Tradition*: *A Study in Historical Methodology*, Chicago: Routledge & Kegan Paul, 1965.

Chapter 2

Paul Thompson

THE VOICE OF THE PAST
Oral history

Paul Thompson, a Research Professor at the University of Essex, played a leading role in the creation of the British Oral History Society and the international oral history movement. In this extract from his classic textbook, *The Voice of the Past*, Thompson explains how oral history has transformed both the content of history – by shifting the focus and opening new areas of enquiry, by challenging some of the assumptions and accepted judgements of historians, by bringing recognition to substantial groups of people who had been ignored – and the processes of writing history, breaking 'through the barriers between the chroniclers and their audience; between the educational institution and the outside world'. Extracted from P. Thompson, *The Voice of the Past: Oral History*, Oxford: Oxford University Press, 1988 (2nd edition), with permission.

A LL HISTORY DEPENDS ultimately upon its social purpose. This is why in the past it has been handed down by oral tradition and written chronicle, and why today professional historians are supported from public funds, children are taught history in schools, amateur history societies blossom, and popular history books rank among the strongest bestsellers. Sometimes the social purpose of history is obscure. There are academics who pursue fact-finding research on remote problems, avoiding any entanglement with wider interpretations or contemporary issues, insisting only on the pursuit of knowledge for its own sake. They have one thing in common with the bland contemporary tourism which exploits the past as if it were another foreign country to escape to: a heritage of buildings and landscape so lovingly cared for that it is almost inhumanly comfortable, purged of social suffering, cruelty, and conflict to the point that a slavery plantation becomes a positive pleasure. Both look to their incomes free from interference, and in return stir no challenge to the social system. At the other extreme the social purpose of history can be quite blatant: used to provide justification for war and conquest, territorial seizure, revolution and counter-revolution, the rule of one class or race over another. Where no history is readily at hand, it will be created. South Africa's white rulers divide their urban blacks between tribes and 'homelands'; Welsh nationalists gather at bardic eisteddfods; the Chinese of the cultural revolution were urged to construct the new 'four histories' of grass-roots struggle; radical feminists looked to the history of wet-nursing in their search for mothers without maternal instinct. Between these two extremes are many other purposes, more or less obvious. For politicians the past is a quarry for supportive symbols: imperial victories, martyrs, Victorian values, hunger marches. And almost equally telling are the gaps in the public presentation of history: the silences in Russia on Trotsky, in West Germany on the Nazi era, in France on the Algerian war.

Through history ordinary people seek to understand the upheavals and changes which they experience in their own lives: wars, social transformations like the changing position of youth, technological changes like the end of steam power, or personal migration to a new community. Family history especially can give an individual a strong sense of a much longer personal lifespan, which will even survive their own death. Through local history a village or town seeks meaning for its own changing character and newcomers can gain a sense of roots in personal historical knowledge. Through political and social history taught in schools, children are helped to understand, and accept, how the political and social system under which they live came about, and how force and conflict have played, and continue to play, their part in that evolution.

The challenge of oral history lies partly in relation to this essential social purpose of history. This is a major reason why it has so excited some historians, and so frightened others. In fact, fear of oral history as such is groundless. We shall see later that the use of interviews as a source by professional historians is long-standing and perfectly compatible with scholarly standards. American experience shows clearly enough that the oral history method can be regularly used in a socially and politically conservative manner; or indeed pushed as far as sympathy with Fascism in John Toland's portrait of *Adolf Hitler* (New York, 1976).

Oral history is not necessarily an instrument for change; it depends upon the spirit in which it is used. Nevertheless, oral history certainly can be a means for transforming both the content and the purpose of history. It can be used to change the focus of history itself, and open up new areas of inquiry; it can break down barriers between teachers and students, between generations, between educational institutions and the world outside; and in the writing of history – whether in books, or museums, or radio and film – it can give back to the people who made and experienced history, through their own words, a central place.

Until the present century, the focus of history was essentially political: a documentation of the struggle for power, in which the lives of ordinary people, or the workings of the economy or religion, were given little attention except in times of crisis such as the Reformation, the English Civil War, or the French Revolution. Historical time was divided up by reigns and dynasties. Even local history was concerned with the administration of the hundred and parish rather than the day-to-day life of the community and the street. This was partly because historians, who themselves then belonged to the administering and governing classes, thought that this was what mattered most. They had developed no interest in the point of view of the labourer, unless he was specifically troublesome; nor – being men – would they have wished to inquire into the changing life experiences of women. But even if they had wished to write a different kind of history, it would have been far from easy, for the raw material from which history was written, the documents, had been kept or destroyed by people with the same priorities. The more personal, local, and unofficial a document, the less likely it was to survive. The very power structure worked as a great recording machine shaping the past in its own image.

This has remained true even after the establishment of local record offices. Registers of births and marriages, minutes of councils and the administration of poor relief and welfare, national and local newspapers, schoolteachers' log books – legal records of all kinds are kept in quantity; very often there are also church archives and accounts and other books from large private firms and landed estates, and even private correspondence from the ruling landowner class. But of the innumerable postcards, letters, diaries, and ephemera of working-class men and women, or the papers of small businesses like corner shops or hill farmers, for example, very little has been preserved anywhere.

Consequently, even as the scope of history has widened, the original political and administrative focus has remained. Where ordinary people have been brought in, it has been generally as statistical aggregates derived from some earlier admin-istrative investigation. Thus economic history is constructed around three types of source: aggregate rates of wages, prices, and unemployment; national and inter-national political interventions into the economy and the information which arises from these; and studies of particular trades and industries, depending on the bigger and more successful firms for records of individual enterprises. Similarly, labour history for long consisted of studies on the one hand of the relationship between the working classes and the state in general, and on the other of particular but essen-tially institutional accounts of trade unions and working-class political organizations; and, inevitably, it is the larger and more successful organizations which normally leave records or commission their own histories. Social history has remained espe-cially concerned with legislative and administrative developments like the rise of the welfare state; or with aggregate data such as population size, birth rates, age at marriage, household and family structure. And among more recent historical specialisms, demography has been almost exclusively concerned with aggregates; the history of the family, despite some ambitious but ill-judged attempts to break through to a history of emotion and feeling, has tended to follow the lines of conven-tional social history; while at least until quite recently women's history has to a remarkable extent focused on the political struggle for civil equality, and above all for the vote.

There are, of course, important exceptions in each of these fields, which show that different approaches are possible even with the existing sources. And there is a remarkable amount of unexploited personal and ordinary information even in official records – such as court documents – which can be used in new ways. The continuing pattern of historical writing probably reflects the priorities of the majority of the profession even if no longer of the ruling class itself – in an age of bureaucracy, state power, science, and statistics. Nevertheless, it remains true that to write any other kind of history from documentary sources remains a very difficult task, requiring special ingenuity. It is indicative of the situation that E.P. Thompson's *The Making of the English Working Class* (1963) and James Hinton's *The First Shop Steward's Movement* (1973) each depended to a large extent on reports by paid government informers, in the early nineteenth century and First World War respectively. When socialist historians are reduced to writing history from the records of government spies, the constraints imposed are clearly extreme. We cannot, alas, interview tombstones, but at least for the First World War period and back into the late nineteenth century, the use of oral history immediately provides a rich and varied source for the creative historian.

In the most general sense, once the life experience of people of all kinds can be used as its raw material, a new dimension is given to history. Oral history provides a source quite similar in character to published autobiography, but much wider in scope. The overwhelming majority of published autobiographies are from a restricted group of political, social, and intellectual leaders, and even when the historian is lucky enough to find an autobiography from the particular place, time, and social group which he happens to need, it may well give little or no attention to the point at issue. Oral historians, by contrast, may choose precisely whom to interview and what to ask about. The interview will provide, too, a means of discovering written documents and photographs which would not have otherwise been traced. The confines of the scholar's world are no longer the well-thumbed volumes of the old catalogue. Oral historians can think now as if they themselves were publishers: imagine what evidence is needed, seek it out and capture it.

For most existing kinds of history, probably the critical effect of this new approach is to allow evidence from a new direction. The historian of working-class politics can juxtapose the statements of the government or the trade union head-quarters with the voice of the rank and file – both apathetic and militant. There can be no doubt that this should make for a more realistic reconstruction of the past. Reality is complex and many-sided; and it is a primary merit of oral history that to a much greater extent than most sources it allows the original multiplicity of stand-points to be recreated. But this advantage is important not just for the writing of history. Most historians make implicit or explicit judgements – quite properly, since the social purpose of history demands an understanding of the past which relates directly or indirectly to the present. Modern professional historians are less open with their social message than Macaulay or Marx, since scholarly standards are seen to conflict with declared bias. But the social message is usually present, however obscured. It is quite easy for a historian to give most of his attention and quotations to those social leaders whom he admires, without giving any direct opinion of his own. Since the nature of most existing records is to reflect the standpoint of authority, it is not surprising that the judgement of history has more often than not vindicated the wisdom of the powers that be. Oral history by contrast makes a much fairer trial possible: witnesses can now also be called from the under-classes, the unprivileged, and the defeated. It provides a more realistic and fair reconstruction of the past, a challenge to the established account. In so doing, oral history has radical implications for the social message of history as a whole.

At the same time oral history implies for most kinds of history some shift of focus. Thus the educational historian becomes concerned with the experiences of children and students as well as the problems of teachers and administrators. The military and naval historian can look beyond command-level strategy and equipment to the conditions, recreations, and morale of other ranks and the lower deck. The social historian can turn from bureaucrats and politicians to poverty itself, and learn how the poor saw the relieving officer and how they survived his refusals.

The political historian can approach the voter at home and at work; and can hope to understand even the working-class conservative, who produced no newspapers or organizations for investigation. The economist can watch both employer and worker as social beings and at their ordinary work, and so come closer to understanding the typical economic process, and its successes and contradictions.

In some fields, oral history can result not merely in a shift in focus, but also in the opening up of important new areas of inquiry. Labour historians, for example, are enabled for the first time to undertake effective studies of the ill-unionized majority of male workers, of women workers, and of the normal experience of work and its impact on the family and the community. They are no longer confined to those trades which were unionized, or those which gained contemporary publicity and investigation because of strikes or extreme poverty. Urban historians similarly can turn from well-explored problem areas like the slums to look at other typical forms of urban social life; the small industrial or market town, for example, or the middle-class suburb, constructing the local patterns of social distinctions, mutual help between neighbours and kin, leisure and work. They can even approach from the inside the history of immigrant groups – a kind of history which is certain to become more important in Britain, and is mainly documented only from outside as a social problem. These opportunities – and many others – are shared by social historians: the study of working-class leisure and culture, for example; or of crime from the point of view of the ordinary, often undetected and socially semi-tolerated poacher, shoplifter, or work-pilferer.

Perhaps the most striking feature of all, however, is the transforming impact of oral history upon the history of the family. Without its evidence, the historian can discover very little indeed about either the ordinary family's contacts with neighbours and kin, or its internal relationships. The roles of husband and wife, the upbringing of girls and boys, emotional and material conflicts and dependence, the struggle of youth for independence, courtship, sexual behaviour within and outside marriage, contraception and abortion – all these were effectively secret areas. The only clues were to be gleaned from aggregate statistics, and from a few – usually partial – observers. The historical paucity which results is well summed up in Michael Anderson's brilliant, speculative, but abstract study of *Family Structure in Nineteenth-Century Lancashire* (1971): a lop-sided, empty frame. With the use of interviewing, it is now possible to develop a much fuller history of the family over the last ninety years, and to establish its main patterns and changes over time, and from place to place, during the life cycle and between the sexes. The history of childhood as a whole becomes practicable for the first time. And given the dominance of the family through housework, domestic service, and motherhood in the lives of most women, an almost equivalent broadening of scope is brought to the history of women.

In all these fields of history, by introducing new evidence from the underside, by shifting the focus and opening new areas of inquiry, by challenging some of the assumptions and accepted judgements of historians, by bringing recognition to substantial groups of people who had been ignored, a cumulative process of transformation is set in motion. The scope of historical writing itself is enlarged and enriched; and at the same time its social message changes. History becomes, to put it simply, more democratic. The chronicle of kings has taken into its concern the life experience of ordinary people. But there is another dimension to this change, of equal importance. The process of writing history changes along with the content. The use of oral evidence breaks through the barriers between the chroniclers and their audience; between the educational institution and the outside world.

This change springs from the essentially creative and co-operative nature of the oral history method. Of course oral evidence once recorded can be used by lone scholars in libraries just like any other type of documentary source. But to be content with this is to lose a key advantage of the method: its flexibility, the ability to pin down evidence just where it is needed. Once historians start to interview they find themselves inevitably working with others – at the least, with their informants. And to be a successful interviewer a new set of skills is needed, including an understanding of human relationships. Some people can find these skills almost immediately, others need to learn them; but in contrast to the cumulative process of learning and amassing information which gives such advantage in documentary analysis and interpretation to the professional historian well on in life, it is possible to learn quite quickly to become an effective interviewer. Hence historians as field-workers, while in important respects retaining the advantages of professional knowledge, also find themselves off their desk, sharing experience on a human level. [. . .]

The co-operative nature of the oral history approach has led to a radical questioning of the fundamental relationship between history and the community. Historical information need not be taken away from the community for inter-pretation and presentation by the professional historian. Through oral history the community can, and should, be given the confidence to write its own history.

[. . .] oral historians have travelled a long way from their original aim – and there is, undoubtedly, some danger of conflict between the two. On the level of the interview itself, for example, there have been telling criticisms of a relationship with informants in which a middle-class professional determines who is to be inter-viewed and what is to be discussed and then disappears with a tape of somebody's life which they never hear about again – and if they did, might be indignant at the unintended meanings imposed on their words. There are clear social advantages in the contrasting ideal of a self-selected group, or an open public meeting, which focuses on equal discussion and encourages local publication of its results; and of individual recording sessions which are conversations rather than directed interviews. But there are also drawbacks in the alternative.

The self-selected group will rarely be fully representative of a community. It is much more likely to be composed from its central groups – people from a skilled working-class or lower middle-class background. The local upper class will rarely be there, nor will the very poor, the less confident especially among women, or the immigrant from its racial minority. A truer and socially more valuable form of local oral history will be created when these other groups are drawn in. Its publi-cations will be much more telling if they can juxtapose, for example, the mistress with the domestic servant, or a millowner with the millworkers. It will then reveal the variety of social experience in the community, the groups which had the better or the worse of it – and perhaps lead to a consideration of what might be done about it. Local history drawn from a more restricted social stratum tends to be more complacent, a re-enactment of community myth. This certainly needs to be recorded and a self-sufficient local group which can do this is undoubtedly helping many others besides itself. But for the radical historian it is hardly sufficient. History should not merely comfort; it should provide a challenge, and understanding which helps towards change. For this the myth needs to become dynamic. It has to encompass the complexities of conflict. And for the historian who wishes to work and write as a socialist, the task must be not simply to celebrate the working class as it is, but to raise its consciousness. There is no point in replacing a conservative myth of upper-class wisdom with a lower-class one. A history is required which leads to action: not to confirm, but to change the world.

In principle there is no reason why local projects should not have such an object, while at the same time continuing to encourage self-confidence and the writing of history from within the community. Most groups will normally contain some members with more historical experience. They certainly need to use tact; to undervalue rather than emphasize their advantage. But it is everybody's loss in the long run if they disown it: their contribution should be to help the group towards a wider perspective. Similar observations apply in the recording session where the essential need is mutual respect. A superior, dominating attitude does not make for a good interview anyway. The oral historian has to be a good listener, the informant an active helper. As George Ewart Evans puts it – 'although the old survivors were walking books, I could not just leaf them over. They were persons.'[1] And so are historians. They have come for a purpose, to get information, and if ultimately ashamed of this they should not have come at all. A historian who just engages in haphazard reminiscence will collect interesting pieces of information, but will throw away the chance of winning the critical evidence for the structure of historical argument and interpretation.

The relationship between history and the community should not be one sided in either direction: but rather a series of exchanges, a dialectic, between information and interpretation, between educationists and their localities, between classes and generations. There will be room for many kinds of oral history and it will have many different social consequences. But at bottom they are all related.

Oral history is a history built around people. It thrusts life into history itself and it widens its scope. It allows heroes not just from the leaders, but also from the unknown majority of the people. It encourages teachers and students to become fellow-workers. It brings history into, and out of, the community. It helps the less privileged, and especially the old, towards dignity and self-confidence. It makes for contact – and thence understanding – between social classes, and between generations. And to individual historians and others, with shared meanings, it can give a sense of belonging to a place or in time. In short it makes for fuller human beings. Equally, oral history offers a challenge to the accepted myths of history, to the authoritarian judgement inherent in its tradition. It provides a means for radical transformation of the social meaning of history.

Note

1   *Oral History*, 1973, vol. 1, no. 4, p. 57.

Chapter 3

Alessandro Portelli

WHAT MAKES ORAL HISTORY
DIFFERENT

This article, first published in 1979, challenged oral history's critics head-on by arguing that 'what makes oral history different' – orality, narrative form, subjectivity, the 'different credibility' of memory, and the relationship between interviewer and interviewee – should be considered as strengths rather than as weaknesses, a resource rather than a problem. Alessandro Portelli holds a Chair in American Literature at the University of Rome. Reprinted by permission from *The Death of Luigi Trastulli and Other Stories: Form and Meaning in Oral History* by Alessandro Portelli, the State University of New York Press © 1991 State University of New York. All rights reserved. A first version, 'Sulla specificita della storia orale', appeared in *Primo Maggio* (Milano, Italy), 1979, vol. 13, pp. 54–60, reprinted as 'On the peculiarities of oral history' in *History Workshop Journal*, 1981, no. 12, pp. 96–107.

'Yes,' said Mrs. Oliver, 'and then when they come to talk about it a long time afterwards, they've got the solution for it which they've made up themselves. That isn't awfully helpful, is it?' 'It is helpful,' said Poirot . . . 'It's important to know certain facts which have lingered in people's memories although they may not know exactly what the fact was, why it happened or what led to it. But they might easily know something that we do not know and that we have no means of learning. So there have been memories leading to theories.'

Agatha Christie, *Elephants Can Remember*

His historical researches, however, did not lie so much among books as among men; for the former are lamentably scanty on his favorite topics; whereas he found the old burghers, and still more their wives, rich in that legendary lore, so invaluable to true history. Whenever, therefore, he happened upon a genuine Dutch family, snugly shut up in its low-roofed farmhouse, under a spreading sycamore, he looked upon it as a little clasped volume of black-letter and studied it with the zeal of a book-worm.

Washington Irving, 'Rip Van Winkle'

Memories leading to theories

A SPECTER IS HAUNTING THE HALLS of the academy: the specter of oral history. The Italian intellectual community, always suspicious of news from outside and yet so subservient to 'foreign discoveries' – hastened to cut oral history down to size before even trying to understand what it is and how to use it. The method used has been that of charging oral history with pretensions it does not have, in order to set everybody's mind at ease by refuting them. For instance, *La Repubblica*, the most intellectually and internationally oriented of Italian dailies rushed to dismiss 'descriptions "from below" and the artificial packages of "oral history" where things are supposed to move and talk by themselves', without even stopping to notice that it is not *things*, but *people* (albeit people often considered no more than 'things') that oral history expects to 'move and talk by themselves'.[1]

There seems to be a fear that once the floodgates of orality are opened, writing (and rationality along with it) will be swept out as if by a spontaneous uncontrollable mass of fluid, amorphous material. But this attitude blinds us to the fact that our awe of writing has distorted our perception of language and communication to the point where we no longer understand either orality or the nature of writing itself. As a matter of fact, written and oral sources are not mutually exclusive. They have common as well as autonomous characteristics, and specific functions which only either one can fill (or which one set of sources fills better than the other). Therefore, they require different specific interpretative instruments. But the undervaluing and the overvaluing of oral sources end up by cancelling out specific qualities, turning these sources either into mere supports for traditional written sources, or into an illusory cure for all ills. This chapter will attempt to suggest some of the ways in which oral history is intrinsically different, and therefore specifically useful.

The orality of oral sources

Oral sources are *oral* sources. Scholars are willing to admit that the actual document is the recorded tape; but almost all go on to work on the transcripts, and it is only transcripts that are published.[2] Occasionally, tapes are actually destroyed: a symbolic case of the destruction of the spoken word.

The transcript turns aural objects into visual ones, which inevitably implies changes and interpretation. The different efficacy of recordings, as compared to transcripts – for classroom purposes, for instance – can only be appreciated by direct experience. This is one reason why I believe it is unnecessary to give excessive attention to the quest for new and closer methods of transcription. Expecting the transcript to replace the tape for scientific purposes is equivalent to doing art criticism on reproductions, or literary criticism on translations. The most literal translation is hardly ever the best, and a truly faithful translation always implies a certain amount of invention. The same may be true for transcription of oral sources.

The disregard of the orality of oral sources has a direct bearing on interpretative theory. The first aspect which is usually stressed is origin: oral sources give us information about illiterate people or social groups whose written history is either missing or distorted. Another aspect concerns content: the daily life and material culture of these people and groups. However, these are not specific to oral sources. Emigrants' letters, for instance, have the same origin and content, but are written. On the other hand, many oral history projects have collected interviews with members of social groups who use writing, and have been concerned with topics usually covered by the standard written archival material. Therefore, origin and content are not sufficient to distinguish oral sources from the range of sources used by social history in general; thus, many theories of oral history are, in fact, theories of social history as a whole.[3]

In the search for a distinguishing factor, we must therefore turn in the first place to form. We hardly need repeat here that writing represents language almost exclusively by means of segmentary traits (graphemes, syllables, words, and sentences). But language is also composed of another set of traits, which cannot be contained within a single segment but which are also bearers of meaning. The tone and volume range and the rhythm of popular speech carry implicit meaning and social connotations which are not reproducible in writing – unless, and then in inadequate and hardly accessible form, as musical notation.[4] The same statement may have quite contradictory meanings, according to the speaker's intonation, which cannot be represented objectively in the transcript, but only approximately described in the transcriber's own words.

In order to make the transcript readable, it is usually necessary to insert punctuation marks, which are always the more-or-less arbitrary addition of the transcriber. Punctuation indicates pauses distributed according to grammatical rules: each mark has a conventional place, meaning, and length. These hardly ever coincide with the rhythms and pauses of the speaking subject, and therefore end up by confining speech within grammatical and logical rules which it does not necessarily follow. The exact length and position of the pause has an important function in the understanding of the meaning of speech. Regular grammatical pauses tend to organize what is said around a basically expository and referential pattern, whereas pauses of irregular length and position accentuate the emotional content, and very heavy rhythmic pauses recall the style of epic narratives. Many narrators switch from one type of rhythm to another within the same interview, as their attitude toward the subjects under discussion changes. Of course, this can only be perceived by listening, not by reading.

A similar point can be made concerning the velocity of speech and its changes during the interview. There are no fixed interpretative rules: slowing down may mean greater emphasis as well as greater difficulty, and acceleration may show a wish to glide over certain points, as well as a greater familiarity or ease. In all cases, the analysis of changes in velocity must be combined with rhythm analysis. Changes are, however, the norm in speech, while regularity is the norm in writing (printing most of all) and the presumed norm of reading: variations are introduced by the reader, not by the text itself.

This is not a question of philological purity. Traits which cannot be contained within segments are the site (not exclusive, but very important) of essential narrative functions: they reveal the narrators' emotions, their participation in the story, and the way the story affected them. This often involves attitudes which speakers may not be able (or willing) to express otherwise, or elements which are not fully within their control. By abolishing these traits, we flatten the emotional content of speech down to the supposed equanimity and objectivity of the written document. This is even more true when folk informants are involved: they may be poor in vocabulary but are often richer in range of tone, volume and intonation than middle-class speakers who have learned to imitate in speech the monotone of writing.[5]

Oral history as narrative

Oral historical sources are *narrative* sources. Therefore the analysis of oral history materials must avail itself of some of the general categories developed by narrative theory in literature and folklore. This is as true of testimony given in free interviews as of the more formally organized materials of folklore.

For example, some narratives contain substantial shifts in the 'velocity' of narration, that is, in the ratio between the duration of the events described and the duration of the narration. An informant may recount in a few words experiences which lasted a long time, or dwell at length on brief episodes. These oscillations are significant, although we cannot establish a general norm of interpretation: dwelling on an episode may be a way of stressing its importance, but also a strategy to distract attentions from other more delicate points. In all cases, there is a relationship between the velocity of the narrative and the meaning of the narrator. The same can be said of other categories among those elaborated by Gérard Genette, such as 'distance' or 'perspective', which define the position of the narrator toward the story.[6]

Oral sources from nonhegemonic classes are linked to the tradition of the folk narrative. In this tradition distinctions between narrative genres are perceived differently than in the written tradition of the educated classes. This is true of the generic distinction between 'factual' and 'artistic' narratives, between 'events' and feeling or imagination. While the perception of an account as 'true' is relevant as much to legend as to personal experience and historical memory, there are no formal oral genres specifically destined to transmit historical information; historical, poetical, and legendary narratives often become inextricably mixed up.[7] The result is narratives in which the boundary between what takes place outside the narrator and what happens inside, between what concerns the individual and what concerns the group, may become more elusive than in established written genres, so that personal 'truth' may coincide with shared 'imagination'.

Each of these factors can be revealed by formal and stylistic factors. The greater or lesser presence of formalized materials (proverbs, songs, formulas, and stereotypes) may measure the degree in which a collective viewpoint exists within an individual's narrative. These shifts between standard language and dialect are often a sign of the kind of the control which speakers have over the narrative.

A typical recurring structure is that in which standard language is used overall, while dialect crops up in digressions or single anecdotes, coinciding with a more personal involvement of the narrator or (as when the occurrences of dialect coincide with formalized language) the intrusion of collective memory. On the other hand, standard language may emerge in a dialect narrative when it deals with themes more closely connected with the public sphere, such as politics. Again, this may mean both a more or less conscious degree of estrangement, or a process of 'conquest' of a more 'educated' form of expression beginning with participation in politics.[8] Conversely, the dialectization of technical terms may be a sign of the vitality of traditional speech and of the way in which speakers endeavor to broaden the expressive range of their culture.

Events and meaning

The first thing that makes oral history different, therefore, is that it tells us less about *events* than about their *meaning*. This does not imply that oral history has no factual validity. Interviews often reveal unknown events or unknown aspects of known events; they always cast new light on unexplored areas of the daily life of the nonhegemonic classes. From this point of view, the only problem posed by oral sources is that of verification (to which I will return in the next section).

But the unique and precious element which oral sources force upon the historian and which no other sources possess in equal measure is the speaker's subjectivity. If the approach to research is broad and articulated enough, a cross section of the subjectivity of a group or class may emerge. Oral sources tell us not just what people did, but what they wanted to do, what they believed they were doing, and what they now think they did. Oral sources may not add much to what we know, for instance, of the material cost of a strike to the workers involved, but they tell us a good deal about its psychological costs. Borrowing a literary category from the Russian formalists, we might say that oral sources, especially from nonhegemonic groups, are a very useful integration of other sources as far as the *fabula* – the logical, causal sequence of the story – goes; but they become unique and necessary because of their *plot* – the way in which the story materials are arranged by narrators in order to tell the story.[9] The organization of the narrative reveals a great deal of the speakers' relationships to their history.

Subjectivity is as much the business of history as are the more visible 'facts'. What informants believe is indeed a historical *fact* (that is, the fact that they believe it), as much as what really happened. When workers in Terni misplace a crucial event of their history (the killing of Luigi Trastulli) from one date and context to another, this does not cast doubts on the actual chronology, but it does force us to arrange our interpretation of an entire phase of the town's history. When an old rank-and-file leader, also in Terni, dreams up a story about how he almost got the Communist Party to reverse its strategy after World War II, we do not revise our reconstructions of political debates within the Left, but learn the extent of the actual cost of certain decisions to those rank-and-file activists who had to bury into their subconscious their needs and desires for revolution. When we discover that similar stories are told in other parts of the country, we recognize the half-formed legendary complex in which the 'senile ramblings' of a disappointed old man reveal much about his party's history that is untold in the lengthy and lucid memoirs of its official leaders.[10]

Should we believe oral sources?

Oral sources are credible but with a *different* credibility. The importance of oral testimony may lie not in its adherence to fact, but rather in its departure from it, as imagination, symbolism, and desire emerge. Therefore, there are no 'false' oral sources. Once we have checked their factual credibility with all the established criteria of philological criticism and factual verification which are required by all types of sources anyway, the diversity of oral history consists in the fact that 'wrong' statements are still psychologically 'true' and that this truth may be equally as important as factually reliable accounts.

Of course, this does not mean that we accept the dominant prejudice which sees factual credibility as a monopoly of written documents. Very often, written documents are only the uncontrolled transmission of unidentified oral sources (as in the case of the report on Trastulli's death, which begins: 'According to verbal information taken . . .'). The passage from these oral 'ur-sources' to the written document is often the result of processes which have no scientific credibility and are frequently heavy with class bias. In trial records (at least in Italy, where no legal value is accorded to the tape recorder or shorthand transcripts), what goes on record is not the words actually spoken by the witnesses, but a summary dictated by the judge to the clerk. The distortion inherent in such procedure is beyond assessment, especially when the speakers originally expressed themselves in dialect. Yet, many historians who turn up their noses at oral sources accept these legal transcripts with no questions asked. In a lesser measure (thanks to the frequent use of shorthand) this applies to parliamentary records, minutes of meetings and conventions, and interviews reported in newspapers: all sources which are legitimately and widely used in standard historical research.

A by-product of this prejudice is the insistence that oral sources are distant from events, and therefore undergo the distortion of faulty memory. Indeed, this problem exists for many written documents, which are usually written some time after the event to which they refer, and often by nonparticipants. Oral sources might compensate chronological distance with a much closer personal involvement. While written memoirs of politicians or labor leaders are usually credited until proven to be in error, they are as distant from some aspects of the event which they relate as are many oral history interviews, and only hide their dependence on time by assuming the immutable form of a 'text'. On the other hand, oral narrators have within their culture certain aids to memory. Many stories are told over and over, or discussed with members of the community; formalized narrative, even meter, may help preserve a textual version of an event.

In fact, one should not forget that oral informants may also be literate. Tiberio Ducci, a former leader of the farm workers' league in Genzano, in the Roman hills, may be atypical: in addition to remembering his own experience, he had also researched the local archives. But many informants read books and newspapers, listen to the radio and TV, hear sermons and political speeches, and keep diaries, letters, clippings, and photograph albums. Orality and writing, for many centuries now, have not existed separately: if many written sources are based on orality, modern orality itself is saturated with writing.

But what is really important is that memory is not a passive depository of facts, but an active process of creation of meanings. Thus, the specific utility of oral sources for the historian lies, not so much in their ability to preserve the past, as in the very changes wrought by memory. These changes reveal the narrators' effort to make sense of the past and to give a form to their lives, and set the interview and the narrative in their historical context.

Changes which may have subsequently taken place in the narrators' personal subjective consciousness or in their socio-economic standing, may affect, if not the actual recounting of prior events, at least the valuation and the 'coloring' of the story. Several people are reticent, for instance, when it comes to describing illegal forms of struggle, such as sabotage. This does not mean that they do not remember them clearly, but that there has been a change in their political opinions, personal circumstances, or in their party's line. Acts considered legitimate and even normal or necessary in the past may be therefore now viewed as unacceptable and literally cast out of the tradition. In these cases, the most precious information may lie in what the informants *hide*, and in the fact that they *do* hide it, rather than in what they *tell*.

Often, however, narrators are capable of reconstructing their past attitudes even when they no longer coincide with present ones. This is the case with the Terni factory workers who admit that violent reprisals against the executives responsible for mass layoffs in 1953 may have been counterproductive, but yet reconstruct with great lucidity why they seemed useful and sensible at the time. In one of the most important oral testimonies of our time, *Autobiography of Malcolm X*, the narrator describes very vividly how his mind worked before he reached his present awareness, and then judges his own past self by the standards of his present political and religious consciousness. If the interview is conducted skillfully and its purposes are clear to the narrators, it is not impossible for them to make a distinction between present and past self, and to objectify the past self as other than the present one. In these cases – Malcolm X again is typical – *irony* is the major narrative mode: two different ethical (or political, or religious) and narrative standards interfere and overlap, and their tension shapes the telling of the story.

On the other hand, we may also come across narrators whose consciousness seems to have been arrested at climactic moments of their personal experience: certain Resistance fighters, or war veterans; and perhaps certain student militants of the 1960s. Often, these individuals are wholly absorbed by the totality of the historical event of which they were part, and their account assumes the cadences and wording of *epic*. The distinction between an ironic or an epic style implies a distinction between historical perspectives, which ought to be taken into consideration in our interpretation of the testimony.

Objectivity

Oral sources are not *objective*. This of course applies to every source, though the holiness of writing often leads us to forget it. But the inherent nonobjectivity of oral sources lies in specific intrinsic characteristics, the most important being that they are *artificial, variable, and partial*.

Alex Haley's introduction to *Autobiography of Malcolm X* describes how Malcolm shifted his narrative approach not spontaneously, but because the interviewer's questioning led him away from the exclusively public and official image of himself and of the Nation of Islam which he was trying to project. This illustrates the fact that the documents of oral history are always the result of a relationship, of a shared project in which both the interviewer and the interviewee are involved together, if not necessarily in harmony. Written documents are fixed; they exist whether we are aware of them or not, and do not change once we have found them. Oral testimony is only a potential resource until the researcher calls it into existence. The condition for the existence of the written source is emission; for oral sources, transmission: a difference similar to that described by Roman Jakobson and Piotr Bogatyrev between the creative processes of folklore and those of literature.[11]

The content of the written source is independent of the researcher's need and hypotheses; it is a stable text, which we can only interpret. The content of oral sources, on the other hand, depends largely on what the interviewer puts into it in terms of questions, dialogue, and personal relationship.

It is the researcher who decides that there will be an interview in the first place. Researchers often introduce specific distortions: informants tell them what they believe they want to be told and thus reveal who they think the researcher is. On the other hand, rigidly structured interviews may exclude elements whose existence or relevance were previously unknown to the interviewer and not contemplated in the question schedule. Such interviews tend to confirm the historian's previous frame of reference.

The first requirement, therefore, is that the researcher 'accept' the informant, and give priority to what she or he wishes to tell, rather than what the researcher wants to hear, saving any unanswered questions for later or for another interview. Communications always work both ways. The interviewees are always, though perhaps unobtrusively, studying the interviewers who 'study' them. Historians might as well recognize this fact and make the best of its advantages, rather than try to eliminate it for the sake of an impossible (and perhaps undesirable) neutrality.

The final result of the interview is the product of both the narrator and the researcher. When interviews, as is often the case, are arranged for publication omitting entirely the interviewer's voice, a subtle distortion takes place: the text gives the answers without the questions, giving the impression that a given narrator will always say the same things, no matter what the circumstances – in other words, the impression that a speaking person is as stable and repetitive as a written document. When the researcher's voice is cut out, the narrator's voice is distorted.

Oral testimony, in fact, is never the same twice. This is a characteristic of all oral communication, but is especially true of relatively unstructured forms, such as autobiographical or historical statements given in an interview. Even the same interviewer gets different versions from the same narrator at different times. As the two subjects come to know each other better, the narrator's 'vigilance' may be attenuated. Class subordination – trying to identify with what the narrator thinks is the interviewer's interest – may be replaced by more independence or by a better understanding of the purposes of the interview. Or a previous interview may have simply awakened memories which are then told in later meetings.

The fact that interviews with the same person may be continued indefinitely leads us to the question of the inherent incompleteness of oral sources. It is impossible to exhaust the entire memory of a single informant; the data extracted with each interview are always the result of a selection produced by the mutual relationship. Historical research with oral sources therefore always has the unfinished nature of a work in progress. In order to go through all the possible oral sources for the Terni strikes of 1949 to 1953, one ought to interview in depth several thousand people: any sample would only be as reliable as the sampling methods used, and could never guarantee against leaving out 'quality' narrators whose testimony alone might be worth ten statistically selected ones.

The unfinishedness of oral sources affects all other sources. Given that no research (concerning a historical time for which living memories are available) is complete unless it has exhausted oral as well as written sources, and that oral sources are inexhaustible, the ideal goal of going through 'all' possible sources becomes impossible. Historical work using oral sources is unfinished because of the nature of the sources; historical work excluding oral sources (where available) is incomplete by definition.

Who speaks in oral history?

Oral history is not where the working classes speak for themselves. The contrary statement, of course, would not be entirely unfounded: the recounting of a strike through the words and memories of workers rather than those of the police and the (often unfriendly) press obviously helps (though not automatically) to balance a distortion implicit in those sources. Oral sources are a necessary (not a sufficient) condition for a history of the nonhegemonic classes; they are less necessary (though by no means useless) for the history of the ruling classes, who have had control over writing and leave behind a much more abundant written record.

Nevertheless, the control of historical discourse remains firmly in the hands of the historian. It is the historian who selects the people who will be interviewed; who contributes to the shaping of the testimony by asking the questions and reacting to the answers; and who gives the testimony its final published shape and context (if only in terms of montage and transcription). Even accepting that the working class speaks through oral history, it is clear that the class does not speak in the abstract, but speaks *to* the historian, *with* the historian and, inasmuch as the material is published, *through* the historian.

Indeed, things may also be the other way around. The historian may validate his or her discourse by 'ventriloquizing' it through the narrator's testimony. So far from disappearing in the objectivity of the sources, the historian remains important at least as a partner in dialogue, often as a 'stage director' of the interview, or as an 'organizer' of the testimony. Instead of discovering sources, oral historians partly create them. Far from becoming mere mouthpieces for the working class, oral historians may be using other people's words, but are still responsible for the overall discourse.

Much more than written documents, which frequently carry the impersonal aura of the institutions by which they are issued – even though, of course, they are composed by individuals, of whom we often know little or nothing – oral sources involve the entire account in their own subjectivity. Alongside the first person narrative of the interviewee stands the first person of the historian, without whom there would be no interview. Both the informant's and the historian's discourse are in narrative form, which is much less frequently the case with archival documents. Informants are historians, after a fashion; and the historian is, in certain ways, a part of the source.

Traditional writers of history present themselves usually in the role of what literary theory would describe as an 'omniscient narrator'. They give a third-person account of events of which they were not a part, and which they dominate entirely and from above (above the consciousness of the participants themselves). They appear to be impartial and detached, never entering the narrative except to give comments aside, after the manner of some nineteenth-century novelists. Oral history changes the writing of history much as the modern novel transformed the writing of literary fiction: the most important change is that the narrator is now pulled into the narrative and becomes a party of the story.

This is not just a grammatical shift from the third to the first person, but a whole new narrative attitude. The narrator is now one of the characters, and the *telling* of the story is part of the story being told. This implicitly indicates a much deeper political and personal involvement than that of the external narrator. Writing radical oral history, then, is not a matter of ideology, of subjective sides-taking, or of choosing one set of sources instead of another. It is, rather, inherent in the historian's presence in the story, in the assumption of responsibility which inscribes her or him in the account and reveals historiography as an autonomous act of narration. Political choices become less visible and vocal, but more basic.

The myth that the historian as a subject might disappear in the objective truth of working-class sources was part of a view of political militancy as the annihilation of all subjective roles into that of the full-time activist, and as absorption into an abstract working class. This resulted in an ironical similarity to the traditional attitude which saw historians as not subjectively involved in the history which they were writing. Oral historians appear to yield to other subjects of discourse, but, in fact, the historian becomes less and less of a 'go-between' from the working class to the reader, and more and more of a protagonist.

In the writing of history, as in literature, the act of focusing on the function of the narrator causes this function to be fragmented. In a novel such as Joseph Conrad's *Lord Jim*, the character/narrator Marlow can recount only what he himself has seen and heard; in order to tell the 'whole story', he is forced to take several other 'informants' into his tale. The same thing happens to historians working with oral sources. On explicitly entering the story, historians must allow the sources to enter the tale with their autonomous discourse.

Oral history has no unified subject; it is told from a multitude of points of view, and the impartiality traditionally claimed by historians is replaced by the partiality of the narrator. 'Partiality' here stands for both 'unfinishedness' and for 'taking sides': oral history can never be told without taking sides, since the 'sides' exist inside the telling. And, no matter what their personal histories and beliefs may be, historians and 'sources' are hardly ever on the same 'side'. The confrontation of their different partialities – confrontation as 'conflict', and confrontation as 'search for unity' – is one of the things which make oral history interesting.

Notes

1   B. Placido in *La Repubblica*, 3 October 1978.
2   One Italian exception is the Instituto Ernesto De Martino, an independent radical research organization based in Milan, which has published 'sound archives' on

long-playing records since the mid-1960s – without anyone in the cultural
establishment noticing: see F. Coggiola, 'L'attivitá dell'Istituo Ernesto de Martino',
in D. Carpitella (ed.), *L'etnomusicologia in Italia*, Palermo: Flaccovio, 1975, pp.
265–270.

3   L. Passerini, 'Sull'utilità e il danno delle fonti orali per la storia'. Introduction to
Passerini (ed.), *Storia Orale. Vita quotidiana e cultura materiale delie classi subalterne*,
Torino: Rosenberg & Sellier, 1978, discusses the relationship of oral history and social
history.

4   On musical notation as reproduction of speech sounds, see G. Marini, 'Musica
popolare e parlato popolare urbano', in Circolo Gianni Bosio (ed.), *I giorni
cantati*, Milano: Mazzotta, 1978, pp. 33–34. A. Lomax, *Folk Song Styles and Culture*,
Washington DC: American Association for the Advancement of Sciences, 1968,
Publication no. 88, discusses electronic representation of vocal styles.

5   See W Labov, 'The logic of non-standard English', in L. Kampf and P. Lauter (eds),
The Politics of Literature, New York: Random House, 1970, pp. 194–244, on the
expressive qualities of non-standard speech.

6   In this article, I use these terms as defined and used by G. Gennete, *Figures III*, Paris:
Seuil, 1972.

7   On genre distinctions in folk and oral narrative, see D. Ben-Amos, 'Categories analy-
tiques et genres populaires', *Poétique*, 1974, no. 19, pp. 268–293; and J. Vansina,
Oral Tradition, Harmondsworth: Penguin Books, [1961], 1973.

8   For instance, G. Bordoni, Communist activist from Rome, talked about family and
community mainly in dialect, but shifted briefly to a more standardized form of Italian
whenever he wanted to reaffirm his allegiance to the party. The shift showed that,
although he accepted the party's decisions, they remained other than his direct experience. His recurring idiom was 'There's nothing you can do about it.' See Circolo
Gianni Bosio, *I giorni cantati*, pp. 58–66.

9   On fabula and plot see B. Tomaševskij, 'Sjužetnoe postroenie', in *Teorija literatury
Poetika*, Moscow-Leningrad, 1928; Italian trans., 'La costruzione dell'intreccio', in
T. Todorov (ed.), *I formalisti russi*, Torino: Einaudi, 1968, published as *Théorie de la
littérature*, Paris: Seuil, 1965.

10   These stories are discussed in chapters 1 and 6 of A. Portelli, *The Death of Luigi
Trastulli*, Albany: State University of New York Press, 1991.

11   R. Jakobson and P. Bogatyrev, 'Le folklore forme spécifique de creation', in
R. Jakobson, *Questions de poétique*, Paris: Seuil, 1973, pp. 59–72.

Chapter 4

Popular Memory Group

POPULAR MEMORY
Theory, politics, method

In the early 1980s the Popular Memory Group at the Centre for Contemporary Cultural Studies in Birmingham (England) highlighted the political possibilities and contradictions for radical oral history projects. In this extract the Group argues that this radical potential is often undermined by superficial understandings of the connections in oral testimony between individual and social memory and between past and present, and by the unequal relationships between professional historians and other participants in oral history projects. Extracted with permission from R. Johnson *et al.* (eds), *Making Histories*: *Studies in History-writing and Politics,* London: Hutchinson, 1982, pp. 206–220.

> Must become historians of the present too.
> (Communist Party Historians' Group Minutes,
> 8 April 1956)

IN THIS ARTICLE we explore an approach to history-writing which involves becoming 'historians of the present too'. It is important to stress 'explore'. We do not have a completed project in 'popular memory' to report. We summarize and develop discussions which were intended as an initial clarification. These discussions had three main starting-points. First, we were interested in the limits and contradictions of academic history where links were attempted with a popular socialist or feminist politics. Our main example here was 'oral history', a practice that seemed nearest to our own preoccupations. Second, we were attracted to projects which moved in the direction indicated by these initial criticisms. These included experiments in popular autobiography and in community-based history, but also some critical developments with a base in cultural studies or academic historiography. Third, we tried [. . .] to relate problems of history-writing to more abstract debates which suggested possible clarifications.

What do we mean, then, by 'popular memory'? We give our own provisional answers in the first part of this essay. We define popular memory first as an *object of study* but, second, as a *dimension of political practice*. We then look, in the second part, at some of the resources for such a project, but also sketch its limits and difficulties. [. . .]

Popular memory as an object of study

The first move in defining popular memory is to extend what we mean by history-writing (and therefore what is involved in historiographical comment) [. . .] to expand the idea of historical production well beyond the limits of academic history-writing. We must include *all* the ways in which a sense of the past is constructed in our society. These do not necessarily take a written or literary form. Still less do they conform to academic standards of scholarship or canons of truthfulness. Academic history has a particular place in a much larger process. We will call this 'the social production of memory'. In this collective production everyone participates, though unequally. Everyone, in this sense, is a historian. As Jean Chesneaux argues, professionalized history has attempted to appropriate a much more general set of relationships and needs: 'the collective and contradictory relationship of our society to its past' and the 'collective need' for guidance in the struggle to make the future.[1] We have already noted a similar stress in Christopher Hill's work: the recognition of a larger social process in which 'we ourselves are shaped by the past' but are also continually reworking the past which shapes us.[2] The first problem in the pursuit of 'popular memory' is to specify the 'we' in Hill's formulation or 'our society' in Chesneaux's. What *are* the means by which social memory is produced? And what practices are relevant especially outside those of professional history-writing?

It is useful to distinguish the main ways in which a sense of the past is produced: through public representations and through private memory (which, however, may also be collective and shared). The first way involves a public 'theatre' of history, a public stage and a public audience for the enacting of dramas concerning 'our' history, or heritage, the story, traditions and legacy of 'the British People'. This public stage is occupied by many actors who often speak from contradictory scripts, but collectively we shall term the agencies which construct this public historical sphere and control access to the means of publication 'the historical apparatus'. We shall call the products of these agencies, in their aggregate relations and combinations at any point of time, 'the field of public representations of history'. In thinking about the ways in which these representations affect individual or group conceptions of the past, we might speak of 'dominant memory'. This term points to the power and pervasiveness of historical representations, their connections with dominant institutions and the part they play in winning consent and building alliances in the processes of formal politics. But we do not mean to imply that conceptions of the past that acquire a dominance in the field of public representations are either monolithically installed or everywhere believed in. Not all the historical representations that win access to the public field are 'dominant'. The field is crossed by competing constructions of the past, often at war with each other. Dominant memory is produced in the course of these struggles and is always open to contestation. We do want to insist, however, that there are real processes of domination in the historical field. Certain representations achieve centrality and luxuriate grandly; others are marginalized or excluded or reworked. Nor are the criteria of success here those of truth: dominant representations may be those that are most ideological, most obviously conforming to the flattened stereotypes of myth.

[. . .] the various sites and institutions do not act in concert. To make them sing, if not in harmony at least with only minor dissonances, involves hard labour and active intervention. Sometimes this has been achieved by direct control (censorship for example) and by a violent recasting or obliteration of whole fields of public history. More commonly today, in the capitalist West, the intersections of formal political debates and the public media are probably the crucial site. Certainly political ideologies involve a view of past and present and future. Ranged against powers such as these, what price the lonely scholar, producing (also through commercial channels) the one or two thousand copies of the latest monograph?!

There is a second way of looking at the social production of memory which draws attention to quite other processes. A knowledge of past and present is also produced in the course of everyday life. There is a common sense of the past which, though it may lack consistency and explanatory force, none the less contains elements of good sense. Such knowledge may circulate, usually without amplification, in everyday talk and in personal comparisons and narratives. It may even be recorded in certain intimate cultural forms: letters, diaries, photograph albums and collections of things with past associations. It may be encapsulated in anecdotes that acquire the force and generality of myth. If this is history, it is history under extreme pressures and privations. Usually this history is held to the level of private remembrance. It is not only unrecorded, but actually silenced. It is not offered the occasion to speak. In one domain, the modern Women's Movement well understands the process of silencing and is raising the 'hidden' history of women's feelings, thoughts and actions more clearly to view. Feminist history challenges the very distinction 'public'/'private' that silences or marginalizes women's lived sense of the past. But similar processes of domination operate in relation to specifically working-class experiences, for most working-class people are also robbed of access to the means of publicity and are equally unused to the male, middle-class habit of giving universal or 'historic' significance to an extremely partial experience. But we are only beginning to understand the class dimensions of cultural domination, partly by transferring the feminist insights. Nor is this only a question of class or gender positions. Even the articulate middle-class historian, facing the dominant memory of events through which he has actually lived, can also be silenced (almost) in this way. One telling example is the difficulty of writers of the New Left in speaking coherently about the Second World War:

> One is not permitted to speak of one's wartime reminiscences today, nor is one under any impulse to do so. It is an area of general reticence: an unmentionable subject among younger friends, and perhaps of mild ridicule among those of radical opinions. All this is understood. And one understands also why it is so.
>
> It is so, in part, because Chapman Pincher and his like have made an uncontested take-over of all the moral assets of that period; have coined the war into Hollywood blockbusters and spooky paper-backs and television tedia; have attributed all the value of that moment to the

mythic virtues of an authoritarian Right which is now, supposedly, the proper inheritor and guardian of the present nation's interests.

I walk in my garden, or stand cooking at the stove, and muse on how this came about. My memories of that war are very different.[3]

This is followed by a reassuringly confident passage which is a classic text for studying the popular memory of the 1940s, but the struggle is intense, the victory narrow, and the near-silencing of so strong and masculine a voice in the shape of its domestication is very revealing.

It is this kind of recovery that has become the mission of the radical and democratic currents in oral history, popular autobiography and community-based publishing. We will look at these attempts to create a socialist or democratic popular memory later in the argument. But we wish to stress first that the study of popular memory cannot be limited to this level alone. It is a necessarily *relational* study. It has to take in the dominant historical representation in the public field as well as attempts to amplify or generalize subordinated or private experiences. Like all struggles it must needs have two sides. Private memories cannot, in concrete studies, be readily unscrambled from the effects of dominant historical discourses. It is often these that supply the very terms by which a private history is thought through. Memories of the past are, like all common-sense forms, strangely composite constructions, resembling a kind of geology, the selective sedimentation of past traces. As Gramsci put it, writing about the necessity of historical conscious-ness for a Communist politics, the problem is '"knowing thyself" as a product of the historical process to date which has deposited in you an infinity of traces, without leaving an inventory'. Similarly the public discourses live off the primary recording of events in the course of everyday transactions and take over the practical knowledge of historical agents. It is for these reasons that the study of 'popular memory' is concerned with *two* sets of relations. It is concerned with the relation between dominant memory and oppositional forms across the whole public (including academic) field. It is also concerned with the relation between these public discourses in their contemporary state of play and the more privatized sense of the past which is generated within a lived culture.

Popular memory as a political practice

[. . .] The political uses of history do seem to us more problematic even from a Marxist perspective. This is especially the case when history is defined as 'the study of the past'. We have come to see this as one of the key features of professional history, and indeed, of historical ideologies. Certainly it is deeply problematic from the viewpoint of 'popular memory'. For memory is, by definition, a term which directs our attention not to the past but to *the past–present relation*. It is because 'the past' has this living active existence in the present that it matters so much politically. As 'the past' – dead, gone or only *subsumed* in the present – it matters much less. This argument may be clarified if we compare a number of approaches to the political significance of history. [. . .]

The construction of traditions is certainly *one* way in which historical argument operates as a political force, though it risks a certain conservatism; similarly any adequate analysis of the contemporary relations of political force has to be historical in form as well as reaching back to more or less distant historical times. It must also attempt to grasp the broader epochal limits and possibilities in terms of a longer history of capitalist and patriarchal structures. What we may insist on in addition is that all political activity is intrinsically a process of historical argument and definition, that all political programmes involve some construction of the past as well as the future, and that these processes go on every day, often outrunning, especially in terms of period, the preoccupations of historians. Political domination involves historical definition. History – in particular popular memory – is a stake in the constant struggle for hegemony. The relation between history and politics, like the relation between past and present, is, therefore, an *internal* one: it is about the politics of history and the historical dimensions of politics. [. . .]

The formation of a popular memory that is socialist, feminist and antiracist is of peculiar importance today, both for general and for particular reasons. Generally, as Gramsci argued, a sense of history must be one element in a strong popular socialist culture. It is one means by which an organic social group acquires a knowledge of the larger context of its collective struggles, and becomes capable of a wider transformative role in the society. Most important of all, perhaps, it is the means by which we may become self-conscious about the formation of our own common-sense beliefs, those that we appropriate from our immediate social and cultural milieu. These beliefs have a history and are also produced in determinate processes. The point is to recover their 'inventory', not in the manner of the folklorist who wants to preserve quaint ways for modernity, but in order that, their origin and tendency known, they may be *consciously* adopted, rejected or modified.[4] In this way a popular historiography, especially a history of the commonest forms of consciousness, is a necessary aspect of the struggle for a better world.

More particularly, the formation of a popular socialist memory is an urgent requirement for the 1980s in Britain. Part of the problem is that traces of a politicized memory of this kind chart, on the whole, a post-war history of disillusionment and decline. In particular, there is a sense of loss and alienation so far as the Labour Party is concerned. But the problem is deeper than this difficulty (which, even now, the socialist revival within and outside the Labour Party may be lessening). For what are to be the forms of a new socialist popular memory? A recovery of Labour's past will hardly do; nor is it helpful to chart the struggles only of the male, skilled, white sectors of the working class who have formed the main subjects of 'labour history' to this day. We need forms of socialist popular memory that tell us about the situation and struggles of women and about the convergent and often antagonistic history of black people, including the black Britons of today. Socialist popular memory today has to be a *newly constructed enterprise*; no mere recovery or re-creation is going to do. Otherwise we shall find that nostalgia merely reproduces conservatism.

Resources and difficulties

Resources

The resources for such a project are great but they are also, in important ways, very disorganized, systematically disorganized that is, not merely 'lacking organization'.

This has much to do with the diverse social origins of different kinds of resources and the immense difficulties of their combination. For many resources have, in the last two decades, been created through the critical work of academic practitioners – especially, in our field, historians, sociologists, philosophers and so on, dissatisfied with the limits and ideologies of their professional discipline. 'Cultural studies' has developed along these lines, but belongs to a very much wider field of radical and feminist intellectual work where much of the stress has been, till lately, upon theoretical clarification and development. But there have been important breaks outside the academic circles too, or in a tense relation to them. They have been most commonly connected to adult education (especially the WEA) or to school-teaching or to post-1968 forms of community action. The principal aim of these tendencies has been to democratize the practices of authorship; in the case of 'history' to lessen or remove entirely the distance between 'historian' and what Ken Worpole has called 'the originating constituency'. The characteristic products of this movement have been popular autobiographies, orally based histories, histories of communities and other forms of popular writing. But it has also developed a characteristic critique of academic practice that stresses the inaccessibility even of left social history in terms of both language and price, and the absorption of authors and readers in the product (book or journal) rather than the process by which it is produced and distributed. Partly because of the stress on 'language' and the commitment to 'plain speech', oral-historical or popular-autobiographical activists are often deeply critical of the dominant forms of theory. It is this division that is, in our opinion, a major source of disorganization. The tensions between the 'activist' and 'academic' ends of radical historical tendencies are explosive to a degree that is often quite destructive. They are often qualitatively less productive than directly cross-class encounters in which working-class people directly interrogate academic radicals. Even so there is a beginning of useful connections between academic 'critics' and community activists (who are not always different persons); where patience holds long enough on either side there are the beginnings of a useful dialogue. Some of this can be traced in the pages of *History Workshop Journal*, the conference volume to History Workshop 13 and in the writings, especially, of some authors whose experience spans an 'amateur' and 'professional' experience.[5] In general History Workshop (as journal and as 'movement') has been distinguished by its attempt to hold together these two unamiable constituencies along with other groups under the banner of 'socialist' or 'people's' history. In this sense History Workshop is the nearest thing we have to an *alternative* 'historical apparatus', especially if its own recently-formed federation is placed alongside the older Federation of Worker Writers and Community Publishers.[6] In what follows we want simply to note some developments, within and outside the History Workshop movement that seem to us already to point towards the study of popular memory.

It is oral history – the evocation and recording of individual memories of the past – which seems, at first sight, nearest to the popular memory perspective, or one aspect of it. In fact the term oral history embraces a very large range of practices only tenuously connected by a 'common' methodology. What interests us most about oral history is that it is often the place where the tension between competing historical and political aims is most apparent: between professional procedures and amateur enthusiasm, between oral history as recreation (in both senses) and as politics, between canons of objectivity and an interest, precisely, in subjectivity and in cultural forms. Later, we want to illustrate these tensions by looking at the early work of the oral and social historian Paul Thompson.[7] [. . .]

In focusing part of our argument around Thompson's work, we do not mean to imply that there are not alternative models. Other adaptations of oral history are, indeed, much nearer to our own concerns. We would cite for example the critique of oral history, in its more empiricist forms, to be found in Luisa Passerini's work.[8] Her pursuit of the structuring principles of memory and of forgetfulness, her concern with representation, ideology and subconscious desires, her focus on 'subjectivity' as 'that area of symbolic activity which includes cognitive, cultural and psychological aspect',[9] and her understanding of subjectivity as a ground of political struggle, all bring her work very close to British traditions of cultural studies, especially where they have been influenced by feminism. Her critique of oral history seems to us much more radical than its sometimes guarded expression might suggest. And we agree absolutely with her criticisms of English debates for the failure to connect oral history as a *method* with more general theoretical issues.[10] The beginnings of her analysis of popular memories of Italian fascism in Turin mark a large advance on most thinking about the cultural and political (as opposed to merely 'factual') significance of oral history texts.

Although there is a beginning of a more self-reflexive mood in Britain, the strengths here lie more in a developed practice of popular history, often building on the social and labour history traditions. This is the case, for example, with the most stunning single work drawing on evoked memories of participants – Ronald Fraser's *Blood of Spain*.[11] The lessons of this book for future practice lie more in the way it is written than in any self-conscious prescriptions by the author, a long-time practitioner of oral history or 'qualitative sociology'. What we found interesting in *Blood of Spain* was the use of oral remembered material in something like the form in which it is first evoked: not as abstracted 'facts' about the past, but as story, as remembered feeling and thought, as personal account. The whole book is woven from such stories and retrospective analyses, sometimes quoted, sometimes paraphrased, clustered around the chronology of the Spanish Civil War or the make-or-break issues that were debated and literally fought out in its course. There is a sense in which Fraser's interviewees actually 'write' *Blood of Spain* by providing the author with the cellular form of the larger work: innumerable tiny personal narratives from which is woven a larger story of heroic proportions and almost infinite complication. *Blood of Spain* is history through composite autobiography, the re-creation of experience in the form of a thousand partial and warring viewpoints.[12]

But it is arguable that the most significant development has been the growth of community history, popular autobiography and working-class writing more generally, where the terms of authorship have been more completely changed. In one sense, *all* these texts and projects are evidence for the forms of popular memory; they are all about the relation of past to present, whether self-consciously 'historical' or not. Some projects, however, have specifically focused on these themes: the chronologically-ordered sequence of accounts of work in Centreprise's *Working Lives*, part of the *People's Autobiography of Hackney*, is one example,[13] the work of the Durham Strong Words Collective, especially *Hello Are You Working?* (about unemployment) and *But the World Goes on the Same* (about past and present in the pit villages) is another.[14] The Durham work is especially organized around contrasts of 'then' and 'now', often viewed through inter-generational comparisons. As the editors put it:

> The past exerts a powerful presence upon the lives of people in County Durham. The pit heaps have gone but they are still remembered, as is the severity of life under the old coal owners and the political battles that were fought with them. As they sit, people try to sort things out in their minds how *were* things then? How different are they now? And why?[15]

Different from either of these projects are the politically located, culturally sensitive projects around history and memory that have developed within the contemporary Women's Movement. There is already a strong past–present dialogue at work within contemporary feminism. [. . .] Much feminist history also draws on oral materials, sometimes using them in innovative ways.[16] The autobiographies evoked by Jean McCrindle and Sheila Rowbotharn, and published as *Dutiful Daughters*, are framed by the editors' feminism and by a distinctive politics of publication. The aim is to render private feminism oppression more public and more shared, thereby challenging dominant male definitions and the silencing of women.[17] Works like this continue a long feminist tradition of writing about past and present through autobiographical form. We might also note in this collection, in the Durham work, in Jeremy Seabrook's *What Went Wrong?* and elsewhere the beginnings of an interest in a specifically socialist popular memory. It was interesting that both *Dutiful Daughters* and *What Went Wrong?* were the subjects of 'collective reviews' at History Workshop 14.[18]

Not all relevant practices and debates belong to what would usually be thought of as 'historical' work. Indeed, there is a real danger that 'History', who is often a very tyrannous Muse, will draw the circumference of concerns much too narrowly. That is one reason why the broader categories – black, or women's or working-class 'writing' for example – are sometimes preferable. Even here, though, there are unhelpful limitations: the commitment, for example, to the *printed* word and the tendency to neglect other practices including the critique of dominant memory in the media. It is here that debates on 'popular memory' which come out of a completely different national and theoretical tradition are so important, especially debates in France around Michel Foucault's coinage of 'popular memory' as a term.[19] French debates focus on such issues as the representation of history in film and around the 'historical' policies of the French state – for example the Ministry of Culture's promotion of popular history and archival retrieval during the official Heritage Year of 1979.[20] Another important French voice for us has been Jean Chesneaux's *Pasts and Futures: What is History For?*, a militant and sometimes wildly iconoclastic attack on French academic history, including academic social history written by Marxists.

One importance of the French debates is that they have directed attention to the possibility of radical cultural practice of a 'historical' kind outside the writing of history books.[21] It is important to note developments of this kind in film, community theatre, television drama and radical museum work. The film *Song of the Shirt*, the television series *Days of Hope*, the television adaptation of Vera Brittain's *Testament of Youth* and the strong historical work of radical theatre groups like 7:84, Red Ladder and The Monstrous Regiment are examples of 'history-making' often with a real popular purchase, yet usually neglected by historians. Innovations in this area are intrinsic to popular memory both as a study and as a political practice. They should certainly receive as much interest and support from socialist and feminist historians as the latest historical volume, or the newest issue of 'the journal'.

Difficulties and contradictions

What, then, are some of the difficulties in realizing the potential of these resources? Oral history and popular autobiography have, after all, now been around for some time, initially generating a real excitement. Why have the political effects been fairly meagre? What are the remaining blocks and inhibitions here?

There are, perhaps, four main areas of difficulty. Very often these have to do with the tensions that exist between the academic or professional provenance of new practices and their adaptation to a popular politics. We will summarize the four areas of difficulty briefly here. [. . .]

The first set of difficulties is epistemological in character. They arise from the ways in which 'historical' objects of study are defined. They revolve around the empiricism of orthodox historical practice. They are not purely technical matters for philosophers to adjudicate. The historian's empiricism is a real difficulty. It blocks political progress. That is why it is so important to return to these questions once more, showing the political effects of this persistently empiricist stance.

The second set of difficulties derive initially from the form in which the 'raw material' of oral history or popular autobiography first arises: the individual testimony, narrative or autobiography. This poses, in a very acute form, the problem of the individual subject and his or her broader social context. In what sense is individual witness evidence for larger social changes? How can these changes themselves be understood, not as something that evades human action, but also as the product of human labour, including this individual personality? This difficulty runs through the oral history method and through the autobiographical form. It is also reflected in larger divisions of genres: history, autobiography, fiction (with its particular experiential truth). Such diversions in turn encapsulate hierarchies of significance. The oral-historical witness or the autobiographer, unless held to be a personage of exceptional public power, speaks only for herself; it is the historian who, like the Professor in Lucky Jim, speaks literally for 'History'. Some resolution of this persistent problem, some way of thinking the society of individuals, would be an important additional resource.

We have already touched on a third set of difficulties: the tendency to identify the object of history as 'the past'. This largely unquestioned feature of historical common sense has extremely paradoxical results when applied to oral history or popular autobiography. Indeed it shows us that this definition cannot be held without a radical depoliticization of the practice of research. What is interesting about the forms of oral-historical witness or autobiography are not just the nuggets of 'fact' about the past, but the whole way in which popular memories are constructed and reconstructed as part of a contemporary consciousness. In this section we will look at some of the characteristic ways in which a sense of the past has been constructed in private memories.

The fourth set of difficulties is more fundamental. It concerns not just the manifest intellectual and theoretical blockages, but the social relations which these inhibitions express. In oral history and in similar practices the epistemological problem – how historians are going to use their 'sources' – is also a problem of human relationships. The practice of research actually conforms to (and may in practice deepen) social divisions which are also relations of power and of inequality. It is cultural power that is at stake here, of course, rather than economic power or political coercion. Even so research may certainly construct a kind of economic relation (a balance of economic and cultural benefits) that is 'exploitative' in that the returns are grossly unequal ones. On the one hand there is 'the historian', who specializes in the production of explanations and interpretations and who constitutes himself as the most active, thinking part of the process. On the other hand, there is his 'source' who happens in this case to be a living human being who is positioned in the process in order to yield up information. The interviewee is certainly subject to the professional power of the interviewer who may take the initiative in seeking her out and questioning her. Of course, the problem may be solved rhetorically or at the level of personal relations: the historian may assert that he has 'sat at the feet of working-class witnesses' and has learnt all he knows in that improbable and uncomfortable posture. It is, however, *he* that produces the final account, *he* that provides the dominant interpretation, *he* that judges what is true and not true, reliable or inauthentic. It is his name that appears on the jacket of his monograph and his academic career that is furthered by its publication. It is he who receives a portion of the royalties and almost all the 'cultural capital' involved in authorship. It is his *amour propre* as 'creator' that is served here. It is his professional standing among his peers that is enhanced in the case of 'success'. In all this, at best, the first constructors of historical accounts – the 'sources' themselves – are left untouched, unchanged by the whole process except in what they have given up – the telling. They do not participate, or only indirectly, in the educational work which produces the final account. They may never get to read the book of which they were part authors, nor fully comprehend it if they do.

We have deliberately overdrawn this case, to make the point polemically. But we do not describe an untypical situation for the more professionalized types of oral-historical practice. The question is what are the wider effects of such social divisions? Are they transformable? To what extent, locally, fragilely, have they already been transformed? And what are the difficulties and opportunities involved in further transformations? Much is at stake here. We are discussing a particular form of class relation (that between working-class people and sections of the professional middle class) and how it can be transformed into a more equal alliance. It is an alliance that happens to have a crucial one in the history of left politics and one which is certainly central to the future of socialism and feminism today. [. . .]

Notes

1   J. Chesneaux, *Pasts and Futures or What is History For?*, London: Thames & Hudson, 1978, especially pp. 1 and 11.

2   C. Hill, *Change and Continuity in Seventeenth Century England*, London: Weidenfeld & Nicolson, 1974, p. 284.

3   E.P. Thompson, *Writing by Candlelight*, London: Merlin, 1980, pp. 130–131.

4   Q. Hoare and G. Nowell-Smith (eds and trans.), *Selections from the Prison Notebooks of Antonio Gramsci*, London: Lawrence & Wishart, 1971, *passim* but especially pp. 324–325.

5   See especially the debate between K. Worpole, J. White and S. Yeo in R. Samuel (ed.), *People's History and Socialist Theory*, London: Routledge & Kegan Paul, 1981, pp. 22–48.

6   The FWWCP was founded in 1976 and 'links some twenty or more working class writers' workshops and local publishing initiatives around the country'. For a useful account of the history of History Workshop see R. Samuel, 'History Workshop, 1966–80', in Samuel, *People's History*, pp. 410–417.

7   [See pp. 221–227 and 231–234 of the original article – eds.]

8   L. Passerini, 'Work ideology and consensus under Italian fascism', *History Workshop Journal*, 1979, no. 8, pp. 82–108; L. Passerini, 'On the use and abuse of oral history' (mimeo translated from L. Passerini (ed.), *Storia Orale: Vita Quotidiana e Cultura Materiale delii Classe Subalterne*, Torino, Rosenberg & Sellier, 1978). We are grateful to the author for sending us a copy of this paper. See also her position paper given at History Workshop, 13: 'Oral history and people's culture' (mimeo, Nov.–Dec. 1979).

9   Passerini, 'Italian fascism', p. 83.

10 Passerini, 'Use and abuse', pp. 7–8.

11 R. Fraser, *Blood of Spain: The Experience of Civil War 1936–39*, London: Allen Lane, 1979. See also R. Fraser, *Work: Twenty Personal Accounts*, 2 vols, Harmondsworth: Penguin, 1967.

12 We are grateful to Bill Schwarz for sharing his responses to this book.

13 'A people's autobiography of Hackney', *Working Lives*, 2 vols, Hackney WEA and Centreprise, n.d. For Centreprise more generally see K. Worpole, *Local Publishing and Local Culture: An Account of the Centreprise Publishing Project 1972–77*, London: Centreprise, 1977, and *Centreprise Report*, December 1978.

14 K. Armstrong and H. Beynon (eds), *Hello, Are you Working? Memories of the Thirties in the North East of England*, Durham: Strong Words, 1977; Strong Words Collective, *But the World Goes on the Same: Changing Times in Durham Pit Villages*, Durham, Strong Words, 1979. We are grateful to Rebecca O'Rourke for introducing us to the work of this collective.

15 Strong Words, *But the World Goes on the Same*, p. 7.

16 For example, the use of autobiographical material in J. Liddington and J. Norris, *One Hand Tied Behind Us*, London: Virago, 1978.

17 J. McCrindle and S. Rowbotham (eds), *Dutiful Daughters*, Harmondsworth: Penguin, 1979.

18 J. Seabrook, *What Went Wrong? Working People and the Ideals of the Labour Movement*, London: Gollancz, 1978.

19 M. Foucault, 'Interview', in *Edinburgh '77 Magazine* (originally published in French in (*Cahiers du Cinéma*, 1974). See also *Radical Philosophy*, 1975, no. 16.

20 P. Hoyau, 'Heritage year or the society of conservation', *Les Révoltes Logiques* (Paris), 1980, no. 12, pp. 70–77. See also the report on *Cahiers du Forum – Histoire in Les Révoltes Logiques*, 1979–80, no. 11, p. 104, a group with similar interests and aims to our own.

21 Hence the debate in Britain on radical filmic practices and historical drama. See, for example, C. MacCabe, 'Memory, phantasy, identity: *Days of Hope* and the politics of the past', *Edinburgh '77 Magazine*; K. Tribe, 'History and the production of memories', *Screen*, 1977–8, vol. xvii, no. 4; C. McArthur, *Television and History*, London: British Film Institute, 1978.

Chapter 5

Valerie Yow

'DO I LIKE THEM TOO MUCH?'
Effects of the oral history interview on the interviewer and vice-versa

In this article Valerie Yow argues that from the late 1980s a new oral history paradigm encouraged 'awareness and use of the interactive process of interviewer and narrator, of interviewer and content', and that oral historians were increasingly alert to the ways that they were affected by their interviews and how the interviewer, in turn, affected the interview relationship, the data it generated and the interpretative process and product. Valerie Yow is book review editor for *Oral History Review* and an independent scholar based in North Carolina. Reprinted from *Oral History Review*, 1997, vol. 24, no. 1, pp. 55–79. © Oral History Association. All rights reserved. Used by permission.

TWENTY YEARS AGO this might have been an unspeakable topic. Oral history textbooks and articles in the *Oral History Review* scarcely mentioned this in the 1970s and early 1980s. My students would talk about their reactions to an interviewing experience, sometimes mention their realization about how an interviewing project had changed them. I remember vividly a student who told me that in interviewing Jewish immigrants in Providence she had touched on their experiences in the Holocaust and that this had forced her to change drastically her views about justice and human society. I also remember remarking to a student after I had listened to a tape, 'I wonder why you didn't pursue the topic the narrator mentioned?' And she said, 'I didn't hear him say that.' And a colleague asked me, 'You didn't want to write about your narrators' race prejudice?' And I said, 'Never even thought about it.' And then I added, 'Do I like them too much?'

I was aware of some effects on myself but not nearly as cognizant of the influences of interviewing women mill workers as I should have been. Now I sometimes catch my breath when I read critically a play I've written or an essay on oral history I'm working on and see appear something told to me twenty years ago.

But usually we treated such concerns as if they were not an integral and important part of the interview – they didn't occupy the main stage, they were the side show. They were, as anthropologist Paul Rabinow, has described them, 'corridor talk' – the remarks you made about your reactions to your research while you were standing with a colleague in the corridor. You were about to go into the room where you would discuss the really important research matters.[1]

In this essay, I'll outline the conceptual shift which makes acknowledgment of the interviewer's reactions to, and intrusions into, research speakable. I'll briefly survey disciplines that use the in-depth interview as a research method because all contributed to the change in the paradigm. Last, I'll suggest questions the interviewer can ask to become more aware of the impact of the process on himself or herself and of the interviewer's influence on the research and analysis.

When I refer to interview effects on the interviewer and to the ways the interviewer interacts with narrator and with content, I include motives for doing the project, feelings about the narrator, interviewer's reaction to the narrator's testimony, and intrusion of the interviewer's assumptions and of the interviewer's self-schema into the interviewing and interpretive processes.

At times subjectivity has been discussed in the literature as cognitive process as opposed to observable behavior; this is not the definition I use here. Rather, I use the traditional definition of objectivity as value-free research which requires the elimination of researcher intrusion

Most often, in the early years of the Oral History Association, there was not any acknowledgment that the interviewer was affected by the interviewing. There was not even a lot of discussion about the effects on the narrator – sometimes, two or three sentences, and at the most, a paragraph here and there. James Hoopes' oral history manual (1979), for example, advised students to ask themselves this question, 'As far as you can tell, what was the interviewee's idea of you, and how might it have affected what he said?'[2] He suggested students spend a few minutes examining their own preconceptions, especially about the narrator.[3]

Elliot Wigginton started publishing his writings about the Foxfire projects in the 1970s. Wigginton described the way students interviewing members of their own community began to respect their own culture and themselves.[4] Possibly, Wigginton's statements about students being changed by the interviewing they were doing was acceptable because these were adolescents learning to like history. They could be seen as impressionable.

But it is *Envelopes of Sound*, first published in 1975, that articulated an awareness both of the effects of the interview process on the interviewer and of the effects of the interviewer on the process. Alice Kessler Harris wrote in the introduction to the book that oral history researchers began to realize that the interjection 'of the historian, first as interviewer and transcriber and later as analyst, posed serious theoretical problems.'[5] One of the things that worried oral historians, she said, was that they knew the 'intrusion of differences between the interviewer and his subjects, distinctions in dress, speech and manners imposed on the subject a set of classbound attitudes that inevitably distorted the information.'[6]

In Ronald Grele's interview with Studs Terkel which the book presented, the issue of interviewer's intrusion into the interview came up again when Terkel said, 'You try to be objective but sometimes you become involved with the narrator.'[7] And later, in a roundtable discussion entitled 'It's Not the Song: It's the Singing,'

Saul Benison talked about how he had been changed by oral history interviewing. Grele commented,

> There is some kind of dialectical process that occurs in which you are working jointly on something and you come to share the creation itself. In my own mind, there's always the problem of detachment because, as a historian, I have to stand back.[8]

Alice Kessler Harris answered him,

> I'm not so sure that that's not an asset, in some sense. I think that to become emotionally involved, while it's true that it violates the first canon of the historian, which is objectivity, nevertheless, puts you intimately into a situation and thus enables you to understand it in a way, I think, you can't understand it if you remain outside the situation.[9]

Benison added that there is no such thing as objective history – such a thing would be like reading the telephone book.[10] In the last essay in *Envelopes of Sound*, Grele reminded readers that 'the relationship created by the interaction of the interviewer and interviewee' requires analysis of the social and psychological kind.[11]

Another notable exception in the 1970s is Luisa Passerini's article, published in *History Workshop*, entitled 'Work Ideology and Consensus Under Italian Fascism.' She frankly acknowledged that oral history research is subjective and argued that we have to be able to use subjectivity – both for narrator and for interviewer – in understanding social history because both invest events with meaning.[12]

Acknowledgment that the historian is not an objective observer was admitted on other occasions, as well. Oscar Handlin's *The Uprooted*, published in 1952, was a study in which the author frankly declared he had a passionate interest.[13] Martin Duberman candidly reflected on his reactions to the historical movement he observed and described in *Black Mountain: An Exploration in Community* (published in 1974):

> Yet the issue is not, I believe, whether the individual historian should appear in his books, but *how* he should appear – covertly or overtly. Every historian knows that he manipulates the evidence to some extent simply because of who he is (or is not), of what he selects (or omits), of how well (or badly) he empathizes and communicates. Those 'fallibilities' have been frequently confessed in the abstract. Yet the process by which a particular personality intersects with a particular subject matter has rarely been shown, and the intersection itself almost never regarded as containing materials of potential worth. Because 'objectivity' has been the ideal, the personal components that go into historical reconstruction have not been candidly revealed, made accessible to scrutiny.[14]

In the preface to *All God's Dangers*, historian Theodore Rosengarten stated frankly that to him Ned Cobb is a hero.[15] In 1979, in an article for the anthology, *Telling Lives: The Biographer's Art*, Rosengarten wrote that he would raise the question of love in social science inquiry. He commented that this was an embarrassing thing to do, but we need an accurate description of the relationship of the interviewer and narrator so we can figure out what is going on. He dared to write,

> Perhaps we divest our motivations of love because we fear an attack on our objectivity. Yet, no claim of objectivity survives the generation in which it is made.[16]

Undoubtedly, Rosengarten was influenced by participation in political debate in the 1960s when a new ethos among students was evolving – a conviction that a scholar must do the work that is meaningful to her or him, that detachment edges one towards perfunctory research and dull interpretation.

And like many historians, he may reveal the influence of Benedetto Croce's and R.G. Collingwood's writings on the philosophy of history. Both were read routinely in graduate courses, and both stressed the centrality of the observer. Following Croce's lead on this, Collingwood argued that the historian cannot be objective, even in beginning the research. He said that it is only when we have a problem in mind that we can begin to look for evidence.[17] Collingwood reminded historians that history cannot exist outside of human consciousness – a statement that puts the interpreter at the center of the process of understanding the past.

Both Croce and Collingwood were usually shunted aside, however, as historians clung to the idea of objectivity in historical research. The 1970s and early 1980s were the years, after all, when quantification of historical data was uppermost in many historians' minds and nobody admitted having an emotional connection to numbers. Oral historians, on the defensive anyway because we were using the testimony of *living* witnesses, wanted to show that our method was a rigorous, disinterested pursuit of truth and therefore respectable. As interviewers, we were simply observers of verbal behavior.

By the early 1980s, however, there was a discernible chink in that armor, that soon became a gaping hole. In *That Noble Dream: The 'Objectivity Question' and the American Historical Profession*, Peter Novick traced the notion of objectivity among historians and concluded that although in the eighties many continued to adhere to an 'antitheoretical and antiphilosophical objectivist empiricism' and praised historical writings for approaching objectivity, among others a strong current of skepticism was developing.[18] Now historians were more and more prone to pay attention to their 'hidden ideological agendas.'[19]

Much questioning of the ideal of scientific objectivity was going on in other disciplines, as well. Concurrent developments that led to acknowledgment of effects on the researcher and of the researcher on the process of research were taking place in anthropology and sociology (both influenced by hermeneutics and phenomenology), biography (influenced by psychoanalytic writings), and feminist theory. So, while I don't see much 'trickle down effect' in the economic sphere, I do see a 'trickle over effect' in the cultural sphere as ideas developed in one discipline are taken up and considered by people working in another discipline. Oral historians could hardly escape being vitally interested in, and influenced by, scholars in these disciplines who were using the recorded life review in research. Kristin M. Langellier observed that 'the personal narrative as a communication phenomenon crosses disciplinary boundaries everywhere and every which way.'[20]

Novick summed up the influence on historians of the paths other disciplines were taking toward candid acknowledgment of the subjective nature of research:

> The influence of antiobjectivist currents of thought coming from other disciplines is difficult to evaluate exactly and all but impossible to trace in the case of any given individual. But in the aggregate they clearly made many historians aware of how problematic received views of objectivity had become in contemporary thought.[21]

The impact of hermeneutics and phenomenology on social science disciplines shows up occasionally even in the late 1950s and early 1960s.[22] For example, Abraham Kaplan in *The Conduct of Inquiry: Methodology for Behavioral Science* published in 1964 argued that no human observation can be 'immaculate':

> We always know something already, and this knowledge is intimately involved in what we come to know next, whether by observation or in any other way. We see what we expect to see, what we believe we have every reason for seeing. . . . In sum, in making an observation we are not passive but active; and we are doing something, not only with our eyes and our minds, but also with our lips, hands, feet – and guts.[23]

It was the seventies, however, when the examples of the influence of the new paradigm first became numerous in sociology, although the stance that objectivity is the proper goal for social observers was dominant (and still is).[24] The decade opened with Rosalie Wax's book *Doing Fieldwork* in which she admitted the effects on her of fieldwork among Japanese Americans, saying that it had made her a different person.[25] (It is not clear just how.) At the end of the decade Shulamit Reinharz in her book *On Becoming a Social Scientist* summed up the struggle between the two paradigms: 'Social camps are split between those who wish to depersonalize the process of knowing in the hopes of obtaining universal, "pure" knowledge and those who acknowledge that since the self of the observer is always implicated, it should be converted into an invaluable tool.'[26]

And in the seventies, a few manuals on the in-depth interview for sociologists took up the discussion. There was the excellent book by Raymond Gorden, *Interviewing: Strategy, Techniques, and Tactics* published in 1969, which does present a discussion of effects of the interviewing process on the interviewer. Gorden defined a 'triadic relationship,' that is, 'The interrelationships between the nature of the *information* sought, the nature of the *respondent*, and the nature of the *interviewer*.'[27] Jack Douglas' text, *Investigative Social Research*, also discussed the interactive process of interviewer and narrator extensively.[28] At the end of the decade, two textbooks were published, *Qualitative Sociology: A Method to the Madness* and *New Rules of Sociological Method: A Positive Critique of Interpretative Sociologies*, which dealt with the effects of the interviewer on the interview.[29] Also, at the end of the decade sociologists founded the journal *Qualitative Sociology* and began to publish articles by interviewers like Arlene Daniels who admitted how much she had invested two of her narrators with glittering personality because *she* needed for them to have a glittering personality.[30]

Anthropologist Victor Turner argued in the foreword to an ethnographic study by a sociologist that one can have 'an objective relation to one's own subjectivity,' and can therefore use self-scrutiny to gain greater understanding of the research one is engaged in.'[31] In anthropology in the sixties, a few researchers were developing ethnographic theory based on this awareness of the intrusion of one's self into the research and interpretation of data. 'Reflexivity' was a term used more and more often. In *Reinventing Anthropology* (1969), a collection of essays scrutinizing the discipline, Bob Scholte described the question anthropologists confronted in his essay, 'Toward a Reflexive and Critical Anthropology:'

> If our perceptions, descriptions, and analyses are influenced by language, and if our language is in turn related to a given cultural setting, then our efforts are potentially subject to various 'ethnocentricities of weaning.' Nor can a scientific language be assumed to be neutral. . . . It follows that all ethnographic descriptions and any ethnological analyses derived from such accounts are, and must he, part hermeneutics, that is, interpretive activities based on contextual information and mediated texts.[32]

Many anthropologists who were writing in the 1970s used reflexivity as a means of critiquing and understanding their own research process. Anthropologist Barbara Myerhoff described her work, the recording of life histories of Jewish elders: 'How a tale is heard and how profoundly it affects the one who hears it as well as the one who tells it is an important theme in my work.'[33]

Peter Novick commented on the anxiety caused by the debate among anthropologists concerning subjectivity in research: 'Of all the social science disciplines, it was in anthropology that the "objectivity question" assumed the greatest centrality in recent decades, and where it was most divisive.'[34]

Outstanding anthropologists, such as James Clifford[35] and Clifford Geertz[36] argued persuasively that subjectivity must be acknowledged, indeed that it can be used to enhance understanding of the research process. Dennis Tedlock used as his model intersubjectivity: it is the researcher's questions as well as the informant's answers that must be scrutinized, he argued. It is the *dialogue* that is important.[37]

A remarkable book, *People Studying People*: *The Human Element in Fieldwork*, published in 1980, presented essays dealing with the role that the researcher's emotions play. Authors Robert A. Georges and Michael Jones declared frankly: 'In this book we have attempted to counter the view, widely held and generally reinforced by conventional fieldwork guides and manuals, that individuals can conduct fieldwork involving people studying people without being human.'[38] Just three years later, George Stocking edited a collection of essays on ethnographic fieldwork, *Observers Observed*, which revealed the ways the ethnographer's desires, fears, and eccentricities impinged on the work of such well-known anthropologists as Bronislaw Malinowski and Franz Boas.[39]

In the 1980s, Renato Rosaldo became a spokesman for the argument that the ethnographer 'occupies a position or structural location and observes with a particular angle of vision.' He reminded readers that age, gender, outsider's position, identification with a particular political regime, and certain life experiences all influence what an ethnographer learns in fieldwork. 'The truth of objectivity has lost its monopoly status,' he stated.[40]

At the same time (the 1970s) that the philosophical writings in hermeneutics and phenomenology were becoming more widely known in the social sciences, a few biographers were bravely admitting that they were anything but detached, objective observers. Often they described explicitly the influence on their work of psychoanalytic theory, especially Erik Erikson's model of stages of development and the Freudian concept of transference. Therapists are used to asking themselves, 'Why am I reacting to this client the way I am? Am I attributing to this client personality characteristics of someone in my past or feelings I have had in my past?' But biographers also began to use the concept of transference to analyze their writing. And Erikson's model of stages of development led them to ask, 'What are the issues I'm confronting in my own life now? How does this research relate to these questions I have now about how to live a life?'

A collection of articles on writing biography, *Introspection in Biography: The Biographer's Quest for Self-Awareness*, edited by Samuel Baron and Carl Pletsch and published in 1985, offered reflections by biographers who were writing in the seventies. In one of the articles, Richard Lebeaux said he chose his subject Henry David Thoreau during the period of the anti-war movement because he saw Thoreau as one of the founding fathers of the counterculture. He wrote, 'Thoreau, with his stress on individual action, nonviolence, and the preeminence of the natural, was highly compatible with my ideological and emotional needs.'[41] Later Lebeaux used this awareness of affinity to examine the process of his research and interpretation, to take a step back and look at what he had done. Trained in English and sociology, he said that he had used Eriksonian and other psychoanalytical concepts to critique his writing.[42]

Carl Pletsch ended the book *Introspection in Biography* by stating, 'Biographers have felt obliged to subscribe to the ideal of objectivity. But biography is the perfect enterprise in which to transcend that ideal and show the value of assimilating subjectivity in a larger conception of knowledge.'[43]

Among psychologists who were using the life review method in their research, there was a growing awareness of the ways the researcher interacts with the informant and the process. Psychologist Thomas Cottle, carrying out life studies, noted in 1973 that we interviewers watch ourselves as much as we watch our narrators. He wrote,

> As best we can, therefore, we play out political roles, the politics, that is, of our own experiences together, hoping to combat the asymmetries produced by the culture, the society, our age, sex, and race and social standing, and by the rights and privileges that put me at an advantage. . . . There is little, then, about this form of research that allows for so-called objective inquiry.[44]

By 1983, Ken Plummer in his chapters 'The Doing of Life Histories' and 'Theorizing Lives' in *Documents of Life* offered specific questions the researcher/writer must ask about how he or she has influenced the research and interpretation, such as, how have my attitudes, demeanor, personality, and expectancies shaped the outcome?[45]

In the 1970s, almost at the same time as the developments in the writing of biography and the conceptual changes among some sociologists and anthropologists (and even a few psychologists who were using the life review as a research method), feminist theorists were raising questions about relationships of power in society. Working separately in the fields of English, education, anthropology, psychology, sociology, and history, but also talking together, they discussed the ways class position and sexual asymmetry operated in interpersonal relations. Their ideas were inevitably applied to the interview situation.

Sociologist Dorothy Smith made an early commentary on research methodology from the feminist point of view by arguing that 'objective' sociology has depended upon class and sex biases. Now it is impossible, she wrote, for 'sociology to evade the problem that our kind of society is known and experienced rather differently from different positions within it.'[46] In 1975, *Another Voice: Feminist Perspectives on Social Life and Social Science*, a collection of original articles by sociologists, edited by Marcia Millman and Rosabeth Kanter, presented work on the influence of gender on every aspect of society, even interpersonal relationships in research.[47] The 1977 edition of *Frontiers* was devoted entirely to oral history as a way of recovering the history of women. Sherna Gluck and other contributors speculated on how the difference in culture between interviewer and narrator – 'including gender, race, class, ethnicity and regional identification' – affects the interview.[48] In an article 'Feminist Criticism of the Social Sciences' for the *Harvard Educational Review* in 1979, Marcia Weskott declared that the ideal of objectivity, by trying to eliminate subjectivity, prevented the searcher from realizing that meanings are arrived at through the intersubjectivity of subject and object.[49]

And feminist researchers using the in-depth interview were concerned with how the dominant position of the researcher – who knows all the questions to ask and by implication all the answers – can subdue the narrator. By the late 1970s, they began to publish assertions that the cult of scientific objectivity was a means of maintaining the researcher in a 'one-up' position.[50] Liz Stanley and Sue Wise in '"Back Into the Personal" or: Our Attempt to Construct Feminist Research' argued,

> We reject the idea that scientists, or feminists, can become experts in other people's lives. And we reject the belief that there is one true reality to become experts about. We feel that feminism's present renaissance has come about precisely because many women have rejected other people's (men's) interpretations of our lives.[51]

Feminists pointed out that the notion of scientific objectivity is androcentric.[52] They talked about how the questions men asked and what they chose to define as important, using their objective scientific methods, had led them to leave out a lot of information about women.[53] They decided they would have to use subjectivity. In the spring issue of the *Oral History Review* in 1987, historian Kathryn Anderson summed up a realization many shared: 'Reviewing my interviews, I have found that my training in the history of facts and action triumphed over my awareness of a decade of historical research pointing to the importance of relationships and consciousness in women's lives.'[54]

That same spring, Daphne Patai's article in the *International Journal of Oral History*, 'Ethical Problems of Personal Narratives, or Who Should Eat the Last Piece of Cake?' emphasized that the possibility of the interviewer's exploitation of the narrator is built into every research project.[55] The implication of her work is that we cannot go about research without questioning ourselves, our biases, our purposes, our reactions to the narrator and the process, and the effects our research have on the narrator.

In the eighties, a flood of articles by women in specific social science disciplines critiqued positivism. In *Analyzing Gender: A Handbook of Social Science Research*, published in 1987, editors Myra Marx Ferree and Beth Hess summed up feminists' critiques of positivism developed over nearly 20 years:

> Feminist methodology rejects the positivist division between theory and practice, between the researcher and the 'object' of research. The image of science as establishing mastery over subjects, as demanding the absence of feeling, and as enforcing separateness of the knower from the known, all under the guise of 'objectivity,' has been carefully critiqued even in reference to the physical sciences. Elements that are present in scientific knowing but devalued because they are associated with femaleness – intuition, empathy, and passion – are ignored in the positivist account and eventually distort the actual process of doing science.[56]

Critiques like these notwithstanding, mainstream sociology, psychology, economics, and political science continue to champion the ideal of scientific objectivity in research. Historians, according to Novick, have not arrived at a consensus.[57] However, qualitative sociology, ethnography, biography, and feminist theory have embraced this conceptual shift to insist on awareness of the interactive process involving interviewer and narrator, interviewer and content.[58]

Has the paradigm shifted for oral history? Reading articles in the *Oral History Review*, I notice that a rejection of old notions of objectivity was very much influencing how some oral historians thought about what they were doing in the late seventies and early eighties. Beginning in 1987, however, in nearly every article in the first volume in that year, writers discussed their motivation and feelings about the interviewing project they were engaged in. From that time, contributors have often explored the ways their class, gender, age, or ethnicity affected their interaction with the narrator. And they have briefly mentioned the ways their reactions to the narrator affected the research and interpretive processes.[59] They have talked about the interview as a collaborative effort, not between authority and subject but between two searchers of the past and present. In the recently published collection of essays, *Interactive Oral History Interviewing*, Allan Futrell and Charles Willard declared, 'We want to emphasize the emerging relationship between the interviewer and the interviewee as the key component in understanding the meaning created during the interview.'[60] Certainly, the paradigm has shifted in oral history.

As practitioners and instructors we have to be more than just aware of this shift in the paradigm for oral historians, we have to begin incorporating the concept of reflexivity into our writing and teaching. In the past, it was always easier to talk about effects on the narrator than to take a hard look at ourselves, at how we affect the process of research and analysis, how we are affected. And we historians have concentrated on providing full citations for the location of the document rather than on the search itself or on our process during the search and analysis; it has not been our custom to put our reflections on the ways we reacted to the documents into print. But we need to not only question our own work, we need to place the published writing in a total context which includes revelation of our own agendas when the reader needs this information to evaluate the research. The fear is sometimes expressed that every research article or book will deal with the researcher's personal experiences and the research topic itself will take second place in the presentation. I am not advocating that the researcher's personal reactions become the emphasis of the research. What I am suggesting is that when we pretend there is nothing going on inside of us that is influencing the research and interpretation, we prevent ourselves from using an essential research tool. And in some cases, the reader needs to know what influenced the research and interpretation.

Anthropologist Victor Turner's goal of having 'an objective relation' to our own subjectivity is something to aim for.[61] Devereux expressed this stance well, 'The scientific study of man . . . must use the subjectivity inherent in all observation as the royal road to an authentic, rather than fictitious, objectivity.'[62]

Do I try to have my cake and eat it, too? Yes. I am talking about two aims which I see as indissoluble, not antithetical – (1) understanding the subjective aspects of the research and interpretation so that (2) we can carry out the project with as much objectivity as possible and use subjectivity to advantage. A value-free research process, the definition of objectivity I use here,[63] is not possible. But the intent of that definition is that we should not ignore evidence because it does not fit our prior assumptions – we have to be conscious therefore of what our prior assumptions are. To my mind, objectivity in research has two aspects: (1) the collection of all information, including the subjective, bearing directly on the research question and (2) the critical examination of the evidence with the methods of examination themselves under scrutiny. These aspects of research can only be goals, not actual attainments: we can never gather all the evidence, we can never be completely aware of all researcher intrusion. And the 'complex web' in the interpersonal relations in an interview prevents us from sorting things out in discrete boxes.[64]

Although this matter of researcher influence on the research is often mentioned now in oral history literature, it is not often dealt with in any detail. Even works on intersubjectivity have little to say that is specific about effects on the interviewer.[65] This kind of analysis is not simple or easy, but we can glean some information from research in psychology and communication studies relevant to this topic of reflexivity in oral history interviewing – particularly, the research on how the ways we think about ourselves influence our judgment of the narrator.[66] In any one-on-one situation, we are bombarded with many stimuli – so many that we have to focus on certain aspects of the other person's behavior and ignore others. We have to be selective and we may select according to what we value. What we value comes from thinking about our own experiences. Psychologists Hazel Markus and Jeanne Smith described the assumption researchers make about this phenomenon: the self-structure (sometimes referred to as the self-schema) is comprised of thoughts and feelings about the self in certain domains and influences the individual's perception of others in those domains.[67] This assumption has been tested and research results do indicate that 'self-relevant qualities (traits and behaviors) can figure in the description of others.'[68]

Furthermore, it appears from the research that we notice variation in the behavior of others in those areas of pre-defined importance to us. Markus and Smith explained: 'thus when some aspect of the stimulus (the person-to-be-perceived) is relevant to an area that is important to the perceiver, this aspect is likely to be focused on and elaborated with information from the individual's own self-structure.'[69]

The schema about the self is only the beginning. In the plural, there are constructs based on gender, class, age, race, ethnicity, and ideology which influence how the interviewer relates to the narrator. These schemata, or preconceived ideas about what a person or situation should be, are learned in the subculture we grew up in or live in as an adult.[70] Raymond Gorden gives the example of the interviewer who asked a narrator living in an urban slum about parenthood. Her views were unlike his middle-class views and his disapproval was subtly communicated. His narrator did not respond so candidly after that.[71]

Howard Sypher, Mary Lee Hummert, and Sheryl Williams concluded that this self-schema research provides a 'cautionary message' for the interviewer: 'As interviewers, we must attempt to move beyond our own self-schemas, focusing the interview not on what is important to us in our lives, but what is important to our interviewees – regardless of the accuracy with which they actually recall events.'[72]

Recently an example of this smacked me in the face. I was interviewing family members of a woman whose literary biography I was engaged in writing. I had read all of her published work, including her autobiography, and much of her documents collection in the archives. The first narrator came to my cottage to record. I was excited about finding the answers to the questions that had been flooding my mind. Soon I became aware of a feeling of great heaviness. By the end of the interview, although I managed to serve tea and express my gratitude to the narrator, I was depressed. I packed the tape away and did not listen to it for three months. When I did take courage and listened, I realized that I had wanted information on family relationships and on clues to this woman writer's internal life. The narrator recounted external events, purely factual information. I had had unrealistic expectations of the narrator: I wanted him to think out loud along the lines I was thinking. He did not say what I thought was important – he said what in his view was important.

Now there is a body of research literature in communication studies, especially sociolinguistics, on the effects of gender in conversation. Some of these studies, but not all, are applicable to the interview situation. For example, a male interviewer may begin to feel some competition with his male narrator;[73] or a woman who is interviewing may express empathy only to find it is received by the male narrator as condescension.[74] Expertise, if the interviewer is a woman, may come across differently to the narrator than if the interviewer is a man: men may use expertise to establish authority while women may use expertise to get a feeling of empowerment from being helpful.[75]

Age can also make a difference in what kinds of information the interviewer thinks is important. Attorney and historian Amy Tobol interviewed attorneys who had been active in a law school student organization which assisted southern civil rights attorneys in the 1960s and 1970s. She found that they were puzzled when she raised the question of whether they perceived of themselves as activists or lawyers and whether these roles seemed at odds with each other. She had trouble getting clear answers. She observed, 'It occurred to me, particularly after I interviewed people who participated during the late 1970s and 1980s that I was speaking in "nineties language" about "sixties" experiences.'[76] She had framed the question in terms of vital interests in her own life experience of the 1990s, but these were not terms they used to view their reality in the 1960s and 1970s.

Another facet of the interview situation is interviewer's need – whether instrumental or emotional. Barbara Erskine described her reaction to interviewing a man who had been a pilot during World War II. He talked about seeing his buddies in planes around him, dying. Suddenly his narration brought back to her own mind her father's death in a plane crash thirty years earlier. She said, 'Dad's face momentarily became that of my informant. I had to ask myself, "Whose story am I listening to?"' She had not allowed herself to cry at her father's funeral – the family needed her to be stoic and in control. Now she grieved with the narrator over losses. In this case, the sharing of a feeling, she believes, may have been 'a springboard to better interviewing.'[77]

Still, another possibility in the interaction of two people is the process by which a person infuses into a current personal situation feelings about someone from the past.[78] Transference usually operates on an unconscious level, but it does not have to remain an unconscious influence. Transferring past feelings onto a person in a present situation can go on in any interpersonal encounter, including the oral history interview. I do not merge here the distinctly different purposes and methods of the clinical interview and the oral history interview, but the concepts are of some practical value for the oral historian.

For example, an interviewer may take an instant dislike to the senior foreign service narrator because he evokes some feelings of injustice another authority figure has caused. If you feel at the beginning of the interview a real dislike of the narrator, transference may be one of the influences impinging. Here the interviewer's transference could set up a negative dynamic as he or she keeps challenging the narrator's every statement even when it is not warranted. If you can get a minute to think it over (for example, taking time to check the recording device), you can make yourself aware of the negative feeling and gain some control over it so that you do not unconsciously prejudice the interview. Later, when you have time for reflection, you can ask yourself some questions about what might be causing the negative feelings.

Another example of this occurs frequently, I suspect: a narrator may be consciously or unconsciously relating to a younger interviewer as a daughter or son. Not only may transference be influencing narrators' attitudes in the interview but there may be transference as the interviewer responds to this. Micaela di Leonardo in *Varieties of Ethnic Experience* said that her middle-aged narrators often thought of her as a daughter – they fitted her into 'an established role.' She enjoyed the warm rapport this infused into the interviewing. However, she was not so pleased when one narrator scolded her in a parental manner: 'You mean Mommy and Daddy *allowed* you to have Thanksgiving away from home?'[79]

When the feelings between narrator and interviewer are positive, the influence of this on the progress of the interview will usually be positive and you will have time later to muse over this. But I have found myself hesitating to ask some things of narrators for whom I felt affection lest my questions cause them discomfort. Awareness of this positive transference might help the interviewer to confront the narrator with the difficult questions that would have perhaps been avoided otherwise.

There is also the possibility that the interviewer can be too much invested in the topic, too closely identifying with a person or cause. In the interview mentioned above in which I sought information for a biography and became more and more dispirited, the narrator near the end said in his factual way that my subject's husband died without a will. All the money and property was divided equally, among his heirs so that at the end of her life, she had only her house and no money to heat it. He found her living in winter in one room of her house with only a little space heater for warmth. I had begun to identify with the subject of the biography so much that when he described her poverty, I felt such distress that his next words passed me by.

There is also the unique situation in oral history research with which psychological research is not concerned. In the oral history interview, just by virtue of the fact that you are recording the testimony means that both interviewer and narrator have in the back of their minds the presence of other audiences.[80] Both have a need to articulate a view of their reality consonant with the communities they identify with, an ideology they share. Ronald Grele described this as a 'particular vision of history' which provides a context for each participant. Grele analyzed an interview with Mel Dubin, a cutter in the garment industry, union organizer for the International Ladies Garment Workers Union, and later an officer. Grele said that the narrative interwove four different historical strands: 'his own autobiography, the history of the organization and success of the ILGWU, a history of the garment industry, and a brief history of the City of New York.'[81] People involved in labor struggles, especially in his union, were Dubin's imagined audience; his ideology was based on his conviction of the union's championship of the working person. Undoubtedly, the interviewer asked questions soliciting information of interest to a different audience — labor historians and other academics who would pass judgment on his work. The interviewer's ideology was similar to Dubin's in that there is shown sympathy to the struggles of working-class men and women.

This consideration of the influence of ideology leads to a closely allied one, the influence on the research process of the community the researcher is identified with. Michael V. Angrosino in his article 'Conversations in a Monastery' explained why he thought the monks were willing to talk to him. He was Catholic and he often stayed in the monastery for several days at a time, following the daily schedule of prayers and meals. They knew that he was 'sympathetic with their aims.' They must have identified him with the community of practicing Catholics and with people who appreciate the monks' way of life. He said, 'I believe that I was able to overcome (or, at least, to mitigate) these resistance factors mainly because I was perceived as something of a participant-observer, that I had attended retreats at the monastery and had been involved in various community programs that had brought me into contact with some of the monks, including the Abbot.'[82]

Consider how a *difference* in ideology can impinge. As long as we are interviewing people of similar ideology, there is no problem with empathy. (Possibly there is a tendency to make heroes of our narrators in this case.) Having empathy with someone whose values you abhor is difficult. Even if you repress an expression of disdain, body language and subtleties in the phrasing of the questions will reveal your attitude. William Sheridan Allen described his attitude about interacting with former Nazis in his research for *The Nazi Seizure of Power* — he needed to understand why and how people on all sides did what they did.[83] I think you would have to keep reminding yourself of this.

Sometimes, you simply cannot empathize with a narrator for good reason, but you have to be aware of what is happening to be in control of yourself and make a conscious decision about what to do. For example, you might explain briefly your point of view and respectfully remind the narrator that this is her or his opportunity to record for a wider audience. But expect the responses to be different from those the narrator would give a sympathetic listener. Interviewers who can respond to narrators with empathy can expect fuller answers, while an inability to have empathy may cut short the interview.[84]

In summary, liking or not liking, feeling repelled by difference in ideology or attracted by a shared world-view, sensing difference in gender or age or social class or ethnicity, all influence the ways we ask questions and respond to narrators and interpret and evaluate what they say. As analyst and fieldworker George Devereux argued nearly 30 years ago, we must view our difficulties (and I would add, pleasures as well) as important data in their own right.[85]

There are specific questions to ask so that we understand what is happening:

1. What am I feeling about this narrator?
2. What similarities and what differences impinge on this interpersonal situation?
3. How does my own ideology affect this process? What group outside of the process am I identifying with?
4. Why am I doing the project in the first place?
5. In selecting topics and questions, what alternatives might I have taken? Why didn't I choose these?
6. What other possible interpretations are there? Why did I reject them?
7. What are the effects on me as I go about this research? How are my reactions impinging on the research?

Now we have a paradigm that permits us awareness and use of the interactive process of interviewer and narrator, of interviewer and content. This kind of awareness is on the main stage – it's not the side show that it used to be.

Notes

1 Paul Rainbow 'Representations Are Social Facts: Modernity and Post Modernity in Anthropology', in J. Clifford and G.E. Marcus (eds), *Writing Culture: The Poetics and Politics of Ethnology*, Berkeley: University Of California Press, 1986, p. 253.
2 James Hoopes, *Oral History: An Introduction for Students*, Chapel Hill, N.C.: University of North Carolina Press, 1979, p. 127.
3 Ibid., p. 84.
4 Elliot Wigginton, *The Foxfire Book*, New York: Doubleday, 1972.
5 Ronald Grele (ed.), *Envelopes of Sound: The Art of Oral History*, Chicago: Precedent Publishing Company, 1973, p. 2.
6 Ibid., pp. 2–3.
7 Ibid., p. 35.
8 Ibid., p. 81.
9 Ibid., pp. 81–82.
10 Ibid., p. 85.

11   Grele, 'Movement Without Aim: Methodological and Theoretical Problems in Oral History', ibid., pp. 127–143, see p. 136.

12   Luisa Passerini, 'Work Ideology and Consensus Under Italian Fascism', *History Workshop Journal* 8 (Autumn 1979) pp. 82–118.

13   Oscar Handlin, *The Uprooted*, Boston: Little Brown, 1973.

14   Martin Duberman, *Black Mountain: An Exploration in Community*, London: Wildwood House, 1974, p. 12.

15   Theodore Rosengarten, *All God's Dangers: The Life of Nate Shaw*, New York: Avon, 1974, p. xix.

16   Theodore Rosengarten, 'Stepping Over Cockleburs: Conversations With Ned Cobb', *Telling Lives: The Biographer's Art*, ed. Marc Pachter, Washington, D.C.: New Republic Books, 1979, p. 113.

17   Robin George Collingwood, 'The Philosophy of History', *Essays in the Philosophy of History*, Austin: University of Texas Press, 1985, p. 137.

18   Peter Novick, *That Noble Dream. The 'Objectivity Question' and the American Historical Profession*, New York: Cambridge University Press, 1988, p. 593 and pp. 595–596.

19   Ibid., p. 596.

20   Kristin Langellier, 'Personal Narratives: Perspectives on Theory and Research', *Text and Performance Quarterly* 9/4 (Oct. 1989): p. 243. Clifford Geertz treats this topic and reminds readers of Clyde Kluckholm's statement that a degree for anthropologists is a license to poach (and for the rest of us as well). 'Blurred Genres', *American Scholar* 49 (1980): p. 167.

21   Novick, *That Noble Dream*, p. 596.

22   Both hermeneutics and phenomenology require us to question our own assumptions and prior understandings. According to the main tenet of hermeneutics, we as researchers must realize that the very questions we ask come from the world we live in, the scientific attitude that we assume is itself something we learned in our culture. The very language we use comes from a culture that we swim in as a fish in water. Phenomenologists also assert that we are in a dialectical relationship with the phenomenon we study: in this interactive process going on, we are influencing even while we are being influenced. See discussion by Lawrence C. Watson, 'Understanding a Life History as a Subjective Document: Hermeneutical and Phenomenological Perspectives', *Ethos* 4/1 (Spring 1976): p. 98, pp. 103–105.

23   Abraham Kaplan, *The Conduct of Inquiry: Methodology for Behavioral Science*, San Francisco: Chandler Publishing Company, 1964, p. 133 and p. 136.

24   See Barney Glaser and Anselm Strauss, *The Discovery of Grounded Theory: Strategies for Qualitative Research*, Chicago: Aldnie Publishing, 1967. James Spradley, *The Ethnographic Interview*, New York: Holt, Rinehart and Winston, 1979.

25   Rosalie H. Wax, *Doing Fieldwork: Warnings and Advice*, Chicago: The University of Chicago Press, 1971, p. 179.

26   Shulamit Reinharz, *On Becoming a Social Scientist: From Survey Research and Participant Observation to Experiential Analysis*, San Francisco: Jossey-Bass, 1979, p. 127, pp. 241–243.

27   Raymond Gorden, *Interviewing: Strategy, Techniques and Tactics*, Chicago: Dorsey Press, 1969, first edition.

28   Jack Douglas, *Investigative Social Research*, Beverly Hills: Sage, 1976.

29   Howard Schwartz and Jerry Jacobs, *Qualitative Sociology: A Method to the Madness*, New York: Free Press, 1979, p. 123. Anthony Giddens, *New Rules of Sociological Method: A Positive Critique of Interpretative Sociologies*, New York: Basic Books, 1976, p. 19 and see especially the chapter 'Some Schools of Social Theory and Philosophy', pp. 23–70, for a discussion of the impact of phenomenology on sociological theory.

30   Arlene Kaplan Daniels, 'Self-Deception and Self-Discovery in Fieldwork', *Qualitative Sociology* 6/3, (Fall 1983): p. 210.

31   Victor Turner, Foreword to Bennetta Jules-Rosette, *African Apostles*: *Ritual and Conversion in the Church of John Maranke*, Ithaca: Cornell University Press, 1975, p. 8.

32   Bob Scholte, 'Toward a Reflexive and Critical Anthropology', in Dell Hymes (ed.). *Reinventing Anthropology*, New York: Pantheon, 1969, p. 440.

33   Barbara Myerhoff, 'Telling One's Story', *Center Magazine*, March 1980, pp. 28–29.

34   Novick, *That Noble Dream*, pp. 548–549.

35   James Clifford, 'Introduction: Partial Truths', *Writing Culture: The Poetics and Politics of Ethnography*, (eds) James Clifford and George Marcus, Berkeley: University of California Press, 1986, p. 14.

36   Clifford Geertz, *The Interpretation of Cultures*, New York: Basic Books, 1973, see especially pp. 10 and 23.

37   Dennis Tedlock, 'The Analogical Tradition and the Emergence of a Dialogical Anthropology', *Journal of Anthropological Research* 35:4 (Winter 1979): pp. 387–399.

38   Robert A. Georges and Michael O. Jones, *People Studying People*: *The Human Element in Fieldwork*, Berkeley: University of California Press, 1980, p. 153.

39   George W. Stocking, Jr., (ed.), *Observers Observed*: *Essays on Ethnographic Fieldwork*, Madison: University Of Wisconsin Press, 1983.

40   Renato Rosaldo, *Culture and Truth*: *The Remaking of Social Analysis*, Boston: Beacon Press, 1989, see especially pp. 19–21.

41   Richard Lebeaux, 'Thoreau's Lives, Lebeaux's Lives', in *Introspection in Biography*: *The Biographer's Quest for Self-Awareness*, Samuel Baron and Carl Pletsch (eds), Hilldale, New Jersey: Analytic Press, 1985, p. 232.

42   Ibid., p. 238.

43   Ibid., p. 360.

44   Thomas Cottle, 'The Life Study: On Mutual Recognition and the Subjective Inquiry', *Urban Life and Culture* 2/3 (October 1973): pp. 349–350.

45   Ken Plummer, 'The Doing of Life Histories' and 'Theorizing Lives' in *Documents of Life*, no. 7 in the Contemporary Social Research Series, general editor M. Bulmer. London: Allen and Unwin, 1983, p. 84 and p. 103.

46   Dorothy Smith, 'Women's Perspective as a Radical Critique of Sociology', *Sociological Inquiry* 44/1 (1974): p. 12.

47   Marcia Millman and Rosabeth Moss Kanter (eds), *Another Voice*: *Feminist Perspectives on Social Life and Social Science*, Garden City, New York: Anchor Books, 1975.

48   Sherna Gluck, 'What's So Special About Women: Women's Oral history', *Frontiers*: *A Journal of Women's Studies* 2/2 (Summer 1977): p. 7.

49   Marcia Weskott, 'Feminist Criticism of the Social Sciences', *Harvard Educational Review* 49:4 (1979): p. 425.

50   Ibid. See also Ann Oakley, 'Interviewing Women: A Contradiction in Terms', in *Doing Feminist Research* (ed.), Helen Roberts, London: Routledge and Kegan Paul, 1981, pp. 30–61: and Judith Stacey, 'Can There Be a Feminist Ethnography?' in *Women's Words*: *The Feminist Practice of Oral History*, Sherna Berger Gluck and Daphne Patai (eds), London: Routledge and Kegan Paul, 1991, pp. 111–119.

51   Liz Stanley and Sue Wise, '"Back Into the Personal" or: Our Attempt to Construct Feminist Research', *Theories of Women's Studies*, Gloria Bowles and Renate Duelli Klein (eds), London: Routledge, 1983, pp. 194–195.

52   Susan Geiger, 'Women's Life Histories: Method and Content', *Signs* 11 (1986): p. 338.

53   Ilene Alexander, Suzanne Bunkers, and Cherry Muhanji, 'A Conversation on Studying and Writing about Women's Lives Using Nontraditional Methodologies', *Women's Studies Quarterly* 3 & 4 (1989): p. 99.

54   Kathryn Anderson et al., 'Beginning Where We Are: Feminist Methodology in Oral History', *Oral History Review* (Spring 1987): p. 109.

55   Daphne Patai, 'Ethical Problems of Personal Narratives, or Who Should Eat the Last Piece of Cake?' *International Journal of Oral History* 8 (February 1987): pp. 5–27.

56   Myra Marx Ferree and Beth Hess, *Analyzing Gender: A Handbook of Social Science Research*, Newbury Park, CA: Sage Publications, 1987; see also Marilyn Strathern, 'An Awkward Relationship: The Case of Feminism and Anthropology', *Signs: Journal of Women in Culture and Society* 12:2 (1987): pp. 276–292

57   Novick, *That Noble Dream*, p. 592.

58   See especially recent work such as the sociological text by Sherryl Kleinman and Martha Copp, *Emotions and Fieldwork*, Newbury Park, CA: Sage, 1993; the work of anthropologists like Renato Rosaldo, *Culture and Truth: The Remaking of Social Analysis*, Boston: Beacon Press, 1989; in collections of writers' observations of their process in writing biography, such as *The Challenge of Feminist Biography*, eds Sara Alpern, Joyce Antler, Elisabeth Perry, and Ingrid Scobie, Chicago: University of Illinois Press, 1992.

59   See especially articles in *The Oral History Review*, such as Blanca Erazo, 'The Stories Our Mothers Tell' *Oral History Review* 16/2 (Fall 1988): pp. 23–28; Micaela di Leonardo, 'Oral History As Ethnographic Encounter', *Oral History Review* 15 (Spring 1987): pp. 1–20: John Forrest and Elisabeth Jackson, 'Get Real: Empowering the Student Through Oral History', *Oral History Review* 18/1 (Spring 1990): pp. 29–44; Robert S. Newman, 'Objectivity and Subjectivities: Oral Narratives from Cambodia, Laos, and Vietnam', *Oral History Review* 21/2 (Winter 1993): pp. 89–95; Richard Candida Smith, 'Review Essay: Ronald Grele on the Role of Theory in Oral History', *Oral History Review* 21/2 (Winter 1993): pp. 99–103. See also the volume *International Annual of Oral History, 1990: Subjectivity and Multiculturalism in Oral History*, edited by Ronald Grele, Westport, Connecticut: Greenwood Press, 1992.

60   Allan Futrell and Charles Willard, 'Intersubjectivity and Interviewing', in *Interactive Oral History Interviewing*, Eva M. McMahan and Kim Lacy Rogers (eds), Hillsdale, NJ: Lawrence Erlbaum Associates, 1994, p. 84.

61   Turner, Foreward to *African Apostles*, p. 8.

62   George Devereux, *From Anxiety to Method in the Social Sciences*, The Hague, Mouton, 1967, p. xvii.

63   In the presentation of Louise Tilly's essay, 'People's History and Social Science History', and responses, 'Between Social Scientists: Responses to Louise A. Tilly', *The International Journal of Oral History* 6:1 (1985): pp. 5–46, definitions of objectivity in social science research were blurred but seem to refer to using subjective elements in the document as opposed to 'hard facts.' Louisa Passerini called attention to the fact that the two concepts, objectivity and subjectivity, cannot be separated, see pp. 22–23. And Ronald Grele noted that the selection of facts to present depends upon many factors, some of them subjective. 'Louise A. Tilly's Response to Thompson, Passerini, Bertaux-Wiame and Portelli. With a Concluding Comment by Ronald J. Grele', ibid., pp. 40–46.

64   Charles L. Briggs offers a critique of Durkheim's notion that 'social facts exist independently of the observer' and draws attention to the 'complex web' of interpersonal relations in the interview. Charles L. Briggs, *Learning How to Ask: A Sociolinguistic Appraisal of the Role of the Interview in Social Science Research*, Cambridge: Cambridge University Press, 1986, pp. 21–22.

65   Notable recent exceptions to this are articles in the *International Annual of Oral History, 1990: Subjectivity and Multiculturalism in Oral History*, Ronald J. Grele (ed.), New York: Greenwood Press, 1992. See Michelle Palmer, Marianne Esolen, Susan Rose, Andrea

Fishman, and Jill Bartoli, '"I Haven't Anything to Say": Reflections on Self and Community in Collecting Oral Histories', pp. 167–189, see especially pp. 176–177; LuAnn Jones, 'Voices of Southern Agricultural History', pp. 135–144.

66 E. Mintz, 'An Example of Assimilative Projection', *Journal of Abnormal and Social Psychology* 52 (1956): pp. 270–280. H.J. Goldings, 'On the Avowal and Projection of Happiness', *Journal of Personality* 25 (1954): pp. 50–57. See the volume, M. Sherif and C.I. Hovland, *Social Judgment: Assimilation and Contrast Effects in Communication and Attitude Change*, New Haven: Yale University Press, 1961.

67 Hazel Markus and Jeanne Smith, 'The Influence of Self-Schemata on the Perception of Others' in *Personality, Cognition, and Social Interaction*, eds Nancy Cantor and John F. Kihlstrom, Hillsdale, New Jersey: Erlbaum, 1981, see p. 234 for the section I paraphrase here.

68 Ibid., p. 237.

69 Ibid., p. 256.

70 Peter S. Andersen, 'Cognitive Schemata in Personal Relationships', in *Individuals in Relationships*, Steve Duck (ed.), Newbury Park, CA: Sage, 1993, pp. 16–18.

71 Raymond L. Gorden, *Interviewing: Strategy, Techniques and Tactics*, Chicago: Dorsey Press, 1987, p. 281.

72 Howard Sypher, Mary Lee Hummert, and Sheryl Williams, 'Social Psychological Aspects of the Oral History Interview', in *Interactive Oral History Interviewing*, Eva M. McMahan and Kim Lacy Rogers (eds), Hillsdale, New Jersey: Erlbaum Associates: 1994, p. 58.

73 Don H. Zimmennan and Candace West, 'Sex Roles, Interruptions and Silences in Conversation', in *Language and Sex: Difference and Dominance*, Barrie Thorner and Nancy Henley (eds), Rowley, MA: Newbury House, 1983, p. 125. H. M. Leet-Pellegrini, 'Conversational Dominance as a Function of Gender and Expertise', in *Language: Social Psychological Perspectives*, Howard Giles, W. Peter Robinson, and Philip M. Smith (eds), Oxford: Pergamon, 1980, p. 102. For discussion of these findings applicable to the in-depth interview, see Valerie Yow, *Recording Oral History: A Practical Guide for Social Scientists*, Newbury Park, CA: Sage, 1994, pp. 129–134.

74 Research findings summarized by Daniel N. Maltz and Ruth A. Borker, 'A Cultural Approach to Male-Female Miscommunication', in *Language and Social Identity*, John J. Gumperez (ed.), Cambridge: Cambridge University Press, 1982, p. 198.

75 Leet-Pellegrini, 'Conversational Dominance as a Function of Gender and Expertise', p. 98.

76 Amy Ruth Tobol, 'Talking to Advocates: Interviewing Law Students, Civil Rights Research Council Activists', paper delivered at the Annual Conference of the Oral History Association, Milwaukee, Wisconsin, October 19, 1995.

77 Barbara Erskine, 'Loss and Grief in Oral History', paper delivered at the Annual Meeting of the Oral History Association, Milwaukee, Wisconsin, October 19, 1995.

78 Karl Figli presents a discussion of transference in the oral history interview in 'Oral History and the Unconscious', *History Workshop Journal* 26 (Autumn 1988): pp. 120–132. In this issue, there is a Special Feature on psychoanalysis and history. Transference is difficult to measure and therefore researchers have shied away from this topic in empirical research. Most often the research literature contains case by case analysis of the way transference and countertransference have operated. See Charles J. Gelso and Jean A. Carter, 'Components of the Psychotherapy Relationship: Their Interaction and Unfolding During Treatment', *Journal of Counseling Psychology* 41/3 (1994): pp. 296–306. Charles J. Gelso and Jean A. Carter, 'Level of Generality and Clear Thinking in Theory Construction and Theory Evaluation: Reply to

Greenberg (1994) and Patton (1994)', *Journal of Counseling Psychology* 41/3 (1994): p. 414. See also Edward S. Bordin, 'Theory and Research on the Therapeutic Working Alliance' in *The Working Alliance: Theory, Research and Practice*', Adam O. Horvath and Leslie L. Greenberg (eds), New York: Wiley, 1994, pp. 13–37, see especially pp. 29–30 and pp. 33–34.

79   Micaela di Leonardo, *Varieties of Ethnic Experience: Kinship, Class and Gender Among Californian Italian-Americans*, Ithaca and London: Cornell University Press, 1984, p. 37.

80   Eva M. McMahan, *Elite Oral History Discourse: A Study of Cooperation and Coherence*, Tuscaloosa, Alabama: University of Alabama Press, 1989, p. 19. See brief discussion of Lacan's idea that in any two-person conversation, there is at least a third audience present, George E. Marcus and Michael J. Fischer, *Anthropology as Cultural Critique: An Experimental Moment in the Human Sciences*, Chicago: University of Chicago Press, 1986, p. 31.

81   Ronald Grele, 'Listen to Their Voices', in *Envelopes of Sound*, Ronald Grele (ed.), Chicago: Precedent Publishers, 1985, 2nd rev. ed., p. 213 and p. 216.

82   Michael V. Angrosino, 'Conversations in a Monastery', *Oral History Review* 19/1–2 (Spring–Fall, 1991): p. 60 and p. 71.

83   William Sheridan Allen, *The Nazi Seizure of Power: The Experience of a Single German Town, 1922–1945*, New York: F. Watts, 1984, see author's preface, p. x and p. xi.

84   Deborah Davis and William T. Perkowitz, 'Consequences of Responsiveness in Dyadic Interaction', *Journal of Personality and Social Psychology* 37: p. 544.

85   George Devereux, *From Anxiety to Method in the Behavioral Sciences*, p. xvii.

Chapter 6

Susan H. Armitage and Sherna Berger Gluck

REFLECTIONS ON WOMEN'S ORAL HISTORY
An exchange

In this email exchange, pioneering feminist oral historians Susan Armitage and Sherna Gluck discuss the development of women's oral history. They note the important turn to subjectivity from the late 1970s and the tensions between necessary but 'wearying' analytical sophistication and the naïve enthusiasm of pioneering 'recovery' history, and they argue that oral history retains an urgent political importance in many parts of the world where women's oppression is reinforced by the silencing of women's voices and histories. Susan Armitage is a Professor of History at Washington State University and was editor of *Frontiers: A Journal of Women's Studies* from 1995–2003. Sherna Gluck is the Director of the Oral History Programme at California State University at Long Beach, and co-editor of *Women's Words: The Feminist Practice of Oral History* (1991). Originally published in *Frontiers*, 1998, vol. 19, no. 3, pp. 1–11. Reprinted from S.H. Armitage with P. Hart and K. Weatherman (eds), *Women's Oral History: The* Frontiers *Reader*, Lincoln: University of Nebraska Press, 2002, pp. 75–86, by permission. © 2002 by the Frontiers Publishing, Inc.

IN 1977, SHERNA BERGER GLUCK opened the first *Frontiers* issue on women's oral history with an article about the interview process, 'What's So Special about Women? Women's Oral History.' In 1983, in the second *Frontiers* issue on women's oral history, Sue Armitage wrote 'The Next Step' about oral history projects.[1] This issue of *Frontiers* (in 1998) offered them an opportunity to consider current issues in women's oral history, which they did in the following electronic exchange.

Armitage: opening comments and questions

In preparation for this electronic dialogue, I reread the two earlier *Frontiers* issues on women's oral history (2:2 [1977] and 7:1 [1983]). I still think your 1977 article,

'What's So Special about Women? Women's Oral History,' is the best of all possible starting places. I think you write sensitively and thoroughly about the interpersonal aspects of the interview. For beginners, it is a great introduction. As you know from your own work with students, they commonly experience precisely the four goals you articulate: discovery, affirmation, communication, and continuity. My first direct question to you, then, is whether you would substantially change anything either in the article or in the interview guide in the light of your subsequent experience?

In 1983, as both you and I noted in our articles in that issue, those of us who had been interviewing for a while were beginning to sense that the oral history interview might be more complex than we had realized. And in my article 'The Next Step' I tried to lay out some of the issues involved in large projects and the hopes that I had then for the larger insights or generalizations that we might gain from group projects. Those hopes are still unfulfilled. What actually happened in the 1980s was that funding for large projects dried up and researchers' energies waned as the second wave of the Women's Movement ran into backlash. Today we have very little sense of what we might learn from larger projects because there have been so few of them since the early eighties, and there have been so few experienced practitioners who have stayed active. You are one of that small handful, so my second direct question to you is what you now think about the potential in large projects. What does your experience tell us about what we can learn and how we can learn it?

My larger feeling (and the place where I think we may disagree) is that we missed a huge opportunity in the 1980s. The reality today is that women's oral history is used in the classroom as a valuable discovery tool. Even when, as in my own case, a substantial number of student interviews have been done and archived, they are all just beginnings with no follow-through.[2] The other principal form of women's oral history is done by doctoral students as part of dissertation research. Usually the number of people interviewed is small, the interviewers are beginners, and the research is conducted under the time and other constraints of dissertation pressure. And because so much work is academic and is shaped by current academic styles, the emphasis is sometimes more on the interviewing interaction and its difficulties than on what the narrator actually says. I realize I'm on tricky ground here, but what I see in a lot of work looks a whole lot like academic self-absorption to me. In saying this I don't mean in any way to deny the importance of difference, nor even to dispute the serious difficulties of representation and the real perils of appropriation – but is that all? Isn't there still a forest out there that we're missing because we're so focused on the trees?

Gluck: introduction and dialogue

It is almost exactly twenty-seven years since I plunked my tape recorder down and interviewed Sylvie Thygeson, the 102-year-old suffragist and birth control activist from St Paul, Minnesota.[3] That interview remains one of my most profound oral history experiences. There I was facing one hundred years of U.S. history, captured in her poignant vignettes, like how she was named after the daughter of a runaway slave family that her father helped on the underground railway. As this centenarian spoke in incredibly measured words and elegant language, bingo numbers were being called out in the background to convalescent home residents who were three-quarters her age. I often refer to this first interview experience, trying to generate the kind of enthusiasm I had then about oral history. I rely on the anecdote about that experience because I don't want my subsequent, more critical questions about oral history to dampen my students' enthusiasm. In fact, as I looked at the students in my oral history methods class at our first class session this fall, I was thrown into a quandary once again. How do I strike a balance between the somewhat naive faith of the first-year college students in the class with the more sophisticated historiographic concerns of the graduate student members? The dilemma posed by the disparate composition of my class echoes the confusion with which I have been beset and the contradictions with which I have grappled for the past decade – and which, oftentimes, make me regret the loss of innocence that marked my earlier work, including the initial methodological essay that I penned for *Frontiers* in 1977.

These contradictory impulses, so evident in the volume on the feminist practice of oral history that Daphne Patai and I coedited almost ten years ago, get played out in a host of arenas.[4] At Oral History Association meetings I find myself avoiding the sessions where presenters focus uncritically on the narratives they have gathered, whether they present them as unmediated reflections or lay claim to a host of historical generalizations. On the other hand, as interested as I am in some of the more theoretical questions about memory, meaning, and representation, I also get impatient with what sometimes verges on navel-gazing – especially since I remain committed to the idea that oral history can be both a scholarly and an activist enterprise, that it can advance our knowledge but also empower people and contribute to social change.

Beset by this dilemma, for several years I drifted toward writing more methodological essays. Recently, however, I have returned to using excerpts from narratives in my own work, but using them to answer a very different set of questions than those with which many of us started. For instance, in an article that I wrote in collaboration with several former students, 'Whose Feminism, Whose History? Reflections on Excavating the History of (the) U.S. Women's Movement(s),' we discuss how our interviews with women who were involved in the Asian American, Chicano, American Indian, and welfare rights movements reveal that they were forging what we might now define as varieties of 'feminisms.'[5] We argue that this reinterpretation of their activism should place them squarely in the history of the contemporary Women's Movement. On the other hand, by questioning our interpretations of their narratives, we raise questions about the legitimacy and appropriateness of such conclusions. Pushing beyond our roles as historical interpreters, however, we engaged in dialogue with at least some of the narrators about our analysis and conclusions, and thus were able to explore the validity (for them) of our arguments.

In other words, this was exploration of meaning and a discussion of interpretive authority but at the same time it put some meat on the query with the use of narrative excerpts to illustrate the kinds of activities in which the women engaged and the ways in which they seem to express a feminist consciousness. So at the same time that we were grappling with these questions, we were providing important new source material for others to ponder and use.

Although I also explored meaning in the narratives from the earlier, larger scale, more systematic project of WWII women aircraft workers (Rosie the Riveter

Revisited), in that instance I was imposing my interpretation of the meaning of their experience for them, with little hesitation about the validity of my interpretation. In other words, I was playing the role of the conventional historian. I did try to engage the women in dialogue after I wrote my interpretive essays in order to register their reactions to my interpretation of their narratives. However, these working-class women saw me as the 'expert' and were reluctant to do much more than express trepidation about some of their revelations.

To conclude these preliminary remarks, I want to focus a bit on a recent paper I wrote that relied on several other sources of Palestinian women's narratives besides my own. In separate research projects focusing on the Women's Movement in Palestine, three of us interviewed some of the same members of the women's committees at different times. And although all of our interviews were conducted over a ten-year span, they have to be contextualized in very different historical moments. In some instances, both before, during, and after the Intifada, there was a fair amount of unity among different political factions with which the women's committees were aligned, and the espousal of a strong feminist consciousness, I argue, is tied directly to variations in the pressure for nationalist political conformity.[6] As a result, when I compared the different narratives recounting the founding meeting of the first women's committee in 1978, as well as the other expressions of concern about women, I had to revise my earlier conclusions about the evolving feminist consciousness of women activists, which were based on my own repeated interviews with the same group of women over a five-year period. Indeed, the changes that I thought were evident in 1991, in contrast to the discourse of 1989–90, were reflections of consciousness that some of the very same people had expressed some five years earlier in interviews with Joost Hiltermann.[7] In other words, what had changed was not their consciousness but the political environment in which it was revealed.

These preliminary comments on the current state of my thinking and the direction that my work has taken in the fifteen years since the 'Women's Oral History Two' (1983) issue of *Frontiers* was published lay the foundation for my side of our dialogue. Indeed, my responses to your comments and questions probably can be predicted based on these reflections.

Dialogue: Gluck to Armitage (1)

You ask if I would substantially change anything in the original 'What's So Special about Women? Women's Oral History' article. Given what I have said above and the criticism of our uncritical celebration of women's oral narratives in the early days of women's oral history, I am terribly embarrassed by the naive assumptions of gender solidarity that mark this article, much as they did a lot of our political and scholarly work in the early 1970s. Yet, when it comes to introducing new students to women's oral history, I would stand by much of the advice I gave in that article, including the topical outline appended to it. However, I wouldn't use the article by itself but would supplement it with more sensitive pieces that force the interviewer to be more self-reflexive. The advice about interviewing that you proffer in 'Women's Oral History Two' is precisely what I would add and, in fact, mirrors much of what I tell students, as does the piece by Kathryn Anderson and Dana Jack in *Women's Words*.[8]

In other words, most of my criticism of that early advice is based more on some of the political assumptions than on the practical tips. For instance, the complex and shifting relationship between interviewer and narrator cannot be captured in simplistic assumptions about 'insiderness.' In fact, sometimes the insider is severely disadvantaged, both by the assumptions she makes of shared meaning and by the assumptions that the narrator makes about her. The realization that any oral history narrative is only a partial history also leads to the recognition that each interviewer will get different partial truths, given her or his positionality. I would put considerably more faith in the ability of some of my male colleagues in oral history to apply what we have often referred to as feminist principles than I would some women who are more bound by race, class, gender, and sexual orientation.

So, when it comes down to the interview process, there is not a lot I would change, except to advise that we be aware of the complexity of the relationship and the interview moment and that, among other things, we attend to the performative aspects of the interview situation. It is when we move to the next step, using and/or presenting the narrative, that my advice would be different, as I alluded to earlier, and may well diverge from yours.

As you point out, by 1983 we were moving beyond the discovery phase and beginning to come to grips with the complexity of the oral history interview. In your 1983 advice about project design, however, I detect some of the same assumptions that guided us earlier about interpretation and use.

The Rosie the Riveter Revisited Project, initiated in 1979, is one of those larger scale, systematic projects to which you allude.[9] My own background in sociology came into play here, and the attempt to reflect a similar composition in our narrator pool to that of the women defense workers did, indeed, give me confidence in interpreting the interviews. I detected certain patterns as I tried to make sense of what the experience meant to different groups of women. And the regular discussion in which the three interviewers on the project engaged involved us in a continuous process: rethinking some of our early ideas, stimulating each other to ask new questions, and so on. The analyses resulting from this more systematic project focused on the meaning of the experience to the women who had worked in the aircraft industry, exploring how it affected their lives. Perhaps of even greater importance is that, regardless of my own analysis, we created a body of interviews that have been used widely and in different ways by a host of others. So my experience with this project does confirm for me the value of more systematic designs.

However, I don't think this is the only way to go, and I believe that I did not pay sufficient attention to exploring the meaning of the historical moment in which the interviews were collected. In other words, even with a more systematic design, much more historicizing about the interviews themselves is necessary. Conversely, as I hope I made clear in my initial remarks, even with a smaller number of interviews perhaps there is a way to both create accounts that yield insights yet simultaneously challenge the assumptions and interpretations we make about them. And while some of the self-reflexive discussions of oral history might do more of the latter, I do believe there is a way – and a need – to do both. Among other things, as I mentioned in talking about the attempt to write various forms of activism of women of color into the history of the contemporary feminist movement, don't we stand on shaky ground imposing our interpretations of the meaning of women's experiences if we are not in dialogue with them about it? This one is really tricky, and I must admit my own ambivalence. Am I willing to give up my analysis if the narrator doesn't agree with it? What is my responsibility to her? To scholarship? What do you think about this?

Dialogue: Armitage to Gluck

Let's see where we are: we agree about interviewing, the need for sensitivity and self-awareness but also on that sense of discovery and connection that really does happen sometimes, even across race and class lines. So we know how to start, how to do frequently excellent interviews that capture individual voices – and that are a pleasure to read almost in a literary sense, for the individuality of the voice. But I think we need to go beyond that. We live in a society that is a cacophony of individual voices and individualism. The collective, related ways we think and act, and the meanings that women (presumably men, too) draw from those connections is getting lost. Women's history is built on the notion of groups, of collective experience, of the ways in which women in similar but different ways have been kept subordinate. Oral history is the best method I know for understanding women's consciousness and their coping strategies. Besides, it provides access to huge populations of women from whom we would otherwise not hear. Surely there are meanings that go beyond individual coping strategies that we can understand. But – and this is what you asked – how and on whose terms?

We agree that there is no such thing as a transparent interview. The interaction and the 'positionality' (as we say) of both interviewer and narrator are a fundamental part of the process. We also agree that the interviewer, as historian or sociologist, can't simply lay her interpretation on what she's heard. This is the postmodern heart of it: We have to be faithful to the meanings the narrators give to their lives. But once we have, by whatever means, done our best to understand their lives in their terms, can we go beyond to deal with larger context?

The question I want to get to is what are the legitimate ways to draw meanings and generalizations from interviews. If, as you argue, they ought to be collaborative, how do you do it? One well-known way is the life history interview – a long series of interviews with the same person. The woman who does this best is Fran Leeper Buss.[10] She does, I think, arrive at what you might call a collaborative meaning because she gets to know the woman she interviews so very well. In group projects, I'm convinced that multiple interviewers are best, and the process you describe of frequent consultations among interviewers is essential. Differences in interpretation among the interviewers ought to keep everyone aware of biases – their own and others. The harder part is collaboration with the women who have been interviewed. I think that, as you point out, much of the effort to 'take it back to the community' or to the narrators has been superficial or condescending. We academic women are more formidable than we think!

Finally, this exchange has made me realize that the issue for me is still discovery/recovery. There is a world (and I do mean a global one) of women out there, and we've heard from very few of them. Our job is to get out there and find out what women say about their lives as sensitively as we can. I don't want postmodern cautions and concerns to stop us from interviewing women we haven't encountered before. I want the kind of shock and necessity to accept difference and the multitude of voices that have characterized international women's conferences, and I want to do it with tape recorder and video recorder.

So to summarize where I think we are: women's oral history is well established in the classroom as a discovery/connective tool. However, especially among long-time practitioners, the difficulties of interviewing are much better understood as a result of postmodernism and the recognition of the importance of difference. As a result, interviewers are much more self-conscious and narrators more wary. On the whole, this is a good thing and has led to more careful representation and much more cautious conclusions and generalizations. The biggest danger is academic navel-gazing, that is, the tendency for the interviewer to grab center stage.

We are still stuck with problems around meaning:

1.   We don't really know how collaborative meaning-making might occur because we don't do it. This is what got lost when we threw out 'sisterhood is powerful.' We don't think that we can achieve agreed meanings, or we don't know how to do it.
2.   Because few recent projects have been very large, the issue of generalization, the search for patterns, has receded from view. But surely the search for what in 1977 you called 'the rhythms of women's lives' is one we should continue.
3.   There is the really big problem of what all the interviews we've already done mean. Shouldn't we be thinking about what we can learn from all the archived tapes? Or is this a problem we should leave to future historians?

Dialogue: Gluck to Armitage (2)

Despite my own more critical self-reflexive stance and the changes in how I use oral history, I agree that we must still 'recover, recover, recover.' In fact, as suggested by the title of my recent essay on the history of contemporary women's move-ments, I think we still need to excavate. There are lots of stories out there – all over the world. Indeed, oral history is the major venue for women who have not had a formal education and/or who don't have access to channels of communication to have their voices heard. And it continues to empower women. Moreover, I still love reading a good oral narrative, though I am increasingly concerned about the authenticity of the voice as edited by the interviewer. So, I think we agree that collection is as urgent as ever. Furthermore, regardless of how we use the narratives ourselves – or today – the recorded interviews are invaluable primary documents.

The questions I have are more about use and interpretation. Perhaps because of my original background in sociology I am not sold on the notion that large-scale projects offer such a good solution. The problem is that our oral history narrators, for the most part, as we observed early on, are the survivors. They are the women who found what you refer to as 'coping strategies' that worked, the women whose families 'allow' them to speak, the women who are still alive. Those that have been battered, killed, silenced, or who have gone insane aren't around to tell us their stories. At a less dramatic level, the ones who don't volunteer, that is, agree to be interviewed, might also be among those whose coping skills didn't work.

What I am leading to, I guess, is that though we – and our narrators – might be uplifted by the hearing and telling of their successes, their ingenious coping mechanisms, and especially by their acts of daily resistance, is this really what women's history is about? It is a part of it, and an important part. But I still struggle with trying to achieve that balance about which I worried when I first began to teach women's history: how do we simultaneously understand and document women's subordination and resistance? This is where the issue of the larger context comes in, the need for the 'scholar' to historicize the narrative. By this I mean not only the conditions of women's lives but also the political and social contexts in which the narrative is collected, as well as the specific conditions relating to the narrator and the recording. Realizing that even a life history is only a partial truth, it is critical that we spell out the latter conditions to help us understand that partialness. That includes the question of performance, especially among women from cultures where the oral tradition, with all its drama, is still strong. I began to recognize the significance of understanding performance when I interviewed older Palestinian women. Where I had assumed that shifts in emotional tone among narrators in our culture might denote some special meaning for them, among these older Palestinian women these emotional high points did not necessarily reflect their individual state of mind but rather the cultural prescriptions for storytelling.

The construction of meaning is perhaps the most difficult challenge we face, and I guess we just all muddle along in our own way. I think what Daphne and I were trying to say in the afterword to *Women's Words* is that we should continue to muddle along and encourage others to do the same, regardless of all our doubts and questions. Nevertheless, we somehow have to try to figure out ways to collaborate with the narrators about meaning. Part of this requires that we do a lot of soul-searching, too. Are we willing to give up our interpretive authority? What if Katherine Borland's grandmother hadn't finally agreed with Borland's feminist interpretation of her narrative?[11] What if one of my Palestinian narrators – a woman in whose home I stayed repeatedly – had told me what she meant when she responded to a question of mine about what would change in a future Palestinian state? In 1989, when I asked her, she laughed and then said, 'Mahmoud [her husband] would be free to take another wife.' Unfortunately, for a host of reasons, I never had the opportunity to follow up and ask her what she meant by this, and years later she probably didn't remember the exchange. But because I stayed in their house repeatedly and saw her workload and his lack of domestic responsibility, I interpreted her earlier remark to mean, quite cynically, that perhaps she'd get more help, as co-wives in polygamous households often do.

Is our best advice to try and dialogue about meaning and, if we can't, at least explain the basis for our attribution of meaning? Some might still say, 'Let them speak for themselves.' But increasingly I find this a disingenuous stance. If we believe that the narrative is a partial story, is a representation, and is governed by a host of complicated determinants, then I think we have an obligation to historicize and contextualize.

This brings me to another point that you raised once again, as you did several years ago: What do we do about all of those archived tapes? Do we just leave them for future historians? Again, I am concerned about our ability to use all these archived tapes if we can't historicize the narratives themselves, that is, the personal as well as social and historical conditions under which they were collected. With the example I gave earlier about the use of some other Palestinian narratives, all of these were collected within a decade, and both the original interviewers and I were able to contextualize them. However, I don't believe that enough of this has been done with the interviews that have been collected and archived. At best, we have some interviewer notes. So perhaps we need to go beyond our earlier agreement that we should still be 'collecting, collecting, collecting.' Perhaps even the process of collecting requires more than our own self-consciousness and reflexivity, and interviewers need to go further in problematizing and historicizing the narratives they record.

Gluck: some closing thoughts

Inveterate editor that I am, as I looked over our exchange, I was tempted to do some reorganizing so that it 'flowed' better – exactly what publishers always try to get us to do with our oral history narratives and what we resist. It occurred to me that in some ways the quick, more spontaneous messages that we write and exchange in our e-mails (probably what has made many of us who are not letter writers become e-mail correspondents) reproduce some of the spontaneity of the oral history interview and pose some of the same questions about presentation to which we have alluded here. So, in keeping with that spirit, I have tried to do what we ask of our narrators – to leave the conversational tone intact.

Notes

1   Sherna Gluck, 'What's So Special about Women? Women's Oral History', *Frontiers: A Journal of Women's Studies* 2:2 (1977): pp. 3–17; and Susan H. Armitage, 'The Next Step', *Frontiers: A Journal of Women's Studies* 2:1 (1983): pp. 3–8.

2   Since 1979, I have deposited oral histories done by students in my women's history classes at Washington State University in the library archives. There are several hundred interviews in the collection, which is titled 'Women's Oral History Project, Washington State University.'

3   Sherna Gluck, ed., *From Parlor to Prison: Five American Suffragists Talk about Their Lives*, New York: Vintage Books, 1976.

4   Sherna Berger Gluck and Daphne Patai (eds), *Women's Words: The Feminist Practice of Oral History*, New York: Routledge, 1991.

5   Sherna Berger Gluck in collaboration with Maylei Blackwell, Sharon Cotrell, and Karen S. Harper, 'Whose Feminism, Whose History? Reflections on Excavating the History of (the) U.S. Women's Movement(s)', in *Community Activism and Feminist Politics: Organizing Across Race, Class, and Gender*, Nancy A. Naples (ed.), New York: Routledge, 1998, pp. 31–56.

6   It was Ted Swedenhorg's framing of his interviews on the 1936–39 revolt that inspired me to reexamine my earlier interviews and conclusions and to pay more attention to the varying environments of political pluralism and conformism.

7   Joost R. Hiltermann, 'Before the Uprising: The Organization and Mobilization of Palestinian Workers and Women in the Israeli-Occupied West Bank and Gaza Strip', Ph.D. diss., University of California, Santa Cruz, 1988.

8   Armitage, 'The Next Step'; and Kathryn Anderson and Dana C. Jack, 'Learning to Listen: Interview Techniques and Analyses,' in Gluck and Patai, *Women's Words*, pp. 11–26. An earlier version of the latter article, with comments about large-scale

projects and generalization by Sue Armitage and July Wittner, 'Beginning Where We Are: Feminist Methodology in Oral History', appeared in *Oral History Review* 15 (1987): pp. 103–27, and was reprinted in *Feminist Research Methods*: *Exemplary Readings in the Social Sciences*, Joyce McCarl Nielsen (ed.), Boulder, Colo.: Westview Press, 1990, pp. 94–112.

9   Sherna Berger Gluck, *Rosie the Riveter Revisited*: *Women, the War, and Social Change*, Boston: Twayne Publishers, 1987.

10   Fran Leeper Buss, *La Partera*: *Story of a Midwife*, Ann Arbor: University of Michigan Press, 1980, and *Forged under the Sun/Forjado bajo el Sol*: *The Life of Maria Elena Luca*, Ann Arbor: University of Michigan Press, 1993.

11   Katherine Borland, '"That's Not What I Said": Interpretive Conflict in Oral Narrative Research', in Gluck and Patai, *Women's Words*, pp. 63–75.

Daniel James

LISTENING IN THE COLD
The practice of oral history in an Argentine meatpacking community

This essay explores the challenges of recording, hearing and comprehending testimony influenced by the narrative forms available within a twentieth-century Argentinian industrial community, by the political and psychological identity of the narrator, and by an interview relationship that can enable or disable recollection. Daniel James also poses the problem of modern memory for working-class communities faced with deindustrialization and the destruction of sites for personal and collective memory. Daniel James is Mendel Professor of Latin American History at Indiana University. Extracted from Daniel James, *Dona María's Story*: *Life History, Memory and Political Identity*, Durham, NC: Duke University Press, 2000, pp. 119–156. © 2000, Duke University Press. All rights reserved. Used by permission of the publisher.

The trick is not to get yourself into some inner correspondence of spirit with your informants. Preferring like the rest of us to call their souls their own, they are not going to be altogether keen about such an effort anyhow. The trick is to figure out what the devil they think they are up to.
Clifford Geertz, *Local Knowledge*:
Further Essays in Interpretive Anthropology

I believe that we can promise to tell the truth, I believe in the transparency of language, and in the existence of the complete subject who expresses himself through it. . . . but of course I also believe the contrary. . . . 'In the field of the subject there is no referent.' . . . we indeed know all this. . . . we are not so dumb, but once this precaution has been taken, we go on as if we did not know it. Telling the truth about the self, constituting the self as a complete subject – it is a fantasy. In spite of the fact that autobiography is impossible, this in no way prevents it from existing.
Philippe Lejeune, *On Autobiography*

I FIRST MET Doña María Roldán in August 1985 in the house of Cipriano Reyes. I was beginning to study the origins of Peronist unionism in Berisso [in Argentina] and had made Reyes's acquaintance. He had introduced me to several of his old union and 'laborista' colleagues, and one day he announced we would be meeting the 'first female shop steward' in the Swift plant, and someone who had played an important part in the emergence of the union in Berisso. The meeting in Reyes's front room was a little formal. Doña María evidently had been told about the English professor who was researching the old days of Berisso's golden past, the emergence of the meatpacking union, the mobilization of 17 October 1945, the formation of the Partido Laborista, and, of course, the role of Cipriano Reyes. Although I don't think that there had been any formal prior arrangement of an appropriate script, it was clear that during our meeting Reyes, as he was in other similar meetings, was very much the master of ceremonies, and Doña María willingly, and convincingly, played her role. The meeting lasted perhaps forty minutes, and I filed it away as an interesting encounter, and I filed Doña María away, too, as a potential future source of information on Berisso's social and labor history.

I next met her eighteen months later when I returned to do a more prolonged stretch of research and began to seek out informants who could provide me with oral testimonies about Berisso's past, in particular its labor history and the history of work in the meatpacking plants. Although she had clearly kept to Reyes's script in our previous meeting, I had been impressed with her articulateness and apparently well-tuned memory. The fact that she had been among the first group of shop floor representatives in Swift drew me to her. She had been an active participant in the struggles of the 1940s, a militant in both the union and the Partido Laborista. I first went to her house in Berisso in January 1987, with the aim principally of obtaining from her empirical information that I was missing in my attempt to reconstruct the unionization drive within the plants. There was also a hope on my part that I would emerge with the difficult to define but always sought-after commodity – a 'feeling' for the period by way of some appropriate anecdotes Doña María might be able to recall for me. I assumed that our conversation, which I intended to record, would last a few hours. As it turned out, I ended up recording some thirty hours of interview over a nine-month period, visiting her house on average once a week to tape conversations, though I was frequently there more often.

One reason for the change in my intentions was clearly the self-evident one that I found Doña María's testimony of great interest. Yet this was not primarily for the reasons I had initially intended to interview her. The testimony, which came to over six hundred pages of typed script, is a rich, multilayered, often puzzling narrative. It does contain passages that add considerably to an understanding of many basic issues that I wished to document and understand better. Doña María's account, for example, of the difficulties encountered by the activists during the unionization drive of 1944–45, or her recounting of her experiences, and those of other women in her section, of the Taylorist system of work organization, the 'Standard,' adds considerably to our objective knowledge of these issues. Indeed, the collection of oral testimony can be of enormous help in constructing the history of a working-class community such as Berisso.

On the one hand, oral history can provide access to basic empirical information unobtainable from more traditional sources, such as newspapers, municipal archives, and company records. In Berisso, for example, knowledge of the early history of the union movement in the packing plants is difficult to obtain from sources such as union newspapers for the simple reason that until the 1940s there was no such thing. It is only in the 1940s that a union newspaper appears with any regularity. Many of the sources traditionally used for historical research in working-class communities are, therefore, not available in the case of Berisso.

It would scarcely seem necessary at this juncture to argue that oral history can offer important access to areas of historical knowledge. The debate on objectivity and empirical validity with its explicit privileging of the written document can no longer be sustained on the old terms. The shifting in the terms of the debate can be traced in the difference between a book such as Paul Thompson's *The Voice of the Past*, with its essentially defensive posture concerning issues such as objectivity, the failings of memory and representativity, and a text such as *The Myths We Live By*, published a decade later and edited by Thompson and Raphael Samuel with its explicit celebration of the unique status of the knowledge generated by oral sources.[1]

Oral sources can also take us beyond the limits of existing empirical data. Although we do know a considerable amount about the implementation of rationalization schemes within the plants from sources such as company archives, how the workers felt about these changes is far more difficult to deduce from this sort of material. Doña María's account addresses the issue of how these schemes were experienced and handled by historical actors. Oral testimony speaks far more directly to this domain of working-class experience. The usefulness of oral testimony goes, of course, beyond the working environment. We have, for example, the casual mention in conversation that it would be unthinkable in the Berisso of the 1920s, 1930s, and 1940s for a man to go out socially on a Saturday night without packing his revolver. It was simply part of his dress – a normative accompaniment. This opens up a social and cultural universe largely beyond the realm of official statistics. Where such statistics do surface in sources such as newspapers and police and judicial archives they refer to basic indices of criminality; or perhaps more precisely to those occasions when violence occurred. The oral statement, however, when contextualized, speaks to a far more mundane, taken-for-granted level of experience. In a related vein, the use of perfect, Oxford-intonated BBC English by Don Rodolfo Caride when I started to ask him questions – an English acquired entirely on the job from his English bosses in the time and motion department of the Swift plant – bespoke a world of deference and paternalism, cultural power and symbolic violence.

In the case of Doña María's narrative it became increasingly clear to me as we talked that although her testimony was a rich potential source of empirical information, it was both limited in this sense and also involved something else besides. The limits were, of course, partly to do with the problem of memory, its limits, its failing, and its distortions. But what of the 'something else' that I intuited as being involved in Doña María's narrative? One reason for the problems, the limits confronted in using this narrative primarily as a source of empirical knowledge, is that it involves a largely passive role for Doña María, as simply a repository of more or less coherent, more or less available, historical data. Yet it was clear to me before long that even in response to my most 'factual,' 'information-seeking' questions Doña María was narrating, telling me a story about her life, reconstructing her past in a selective way that would both legitimize it to me and make sense of it to herself.

Contemporary oral history now rarely invokes the kind of claim to having privileged access to hitherto ignored historical facts and experience based on the practice of a sort of 'naive realism.' Influenced by trends in literary criticism that emphasize the importance of narrative and the construction of texts – and that have tended by extension to see historical reality as another text – oral historians are increasingly aware of the limits of oral testimony as a source for expanding our stock of historical facts about the recent past. The form of oral narrative is often taken now to be as significant as the content.

Increasingly, oral historians such as Luisa Passerini, Ronald Grele, and Alessandro Portelli have begun to challenge us to treat the subjective, textual quality of oral testimony as unique opportunities rather than the obstacles to historical objectivity and empirical rigor they had seemed to an earlier generation of practitioners.[2] As the editors of *The Myths We Live By* contend: 'At the same time the individuality of each life story ceases to be an awkward impediment to generalization, and becomes instead a vital document of the construction of consciousness.'[3] Portelli is equally forthright. At the start of one of his essays he offers both a concession and an affirmation: 'The oral sources used in this essay are not always fully reliable in point of fact. Rather than being a weakness, this is, however, their strength: errors, inventions and myths lead us through and beyond facts to their meanings.'[4] In particular, oral testimony enables us to approach the issue of agency and subjectivity in history.

Yet once more we must beware of falling back on the assumptions of a naive realism, of presupposing a mimetic quality in oral narratives as they express consciousness and feeling. For the issue of using oral narratives to gain access to the domain of consciousness, of 'lived experience,' is one of the issues complicated by an attention to oral testimony as narrative. If oral testimony is indeed a window onto the subjective in history – the cultural, social, and ideological universe of historical actors – then it must be said that the view it affords is not a transparent one that simply reflects thoughts, feelings as they really were/are. At the very least the image is bent, the glass of the window unclear.

Thus the relationship between personal narratives and history – as indeed between autobiography in general and history – is complex and problematic. Life stories are cultural constructs that draw on a public discourse structured by class and gender conventions. They also make use of a wide spectrum of possible roles, self-representations, and available narratives. As such, we have to learn to read these stories and the symbols and logic embedded in them if we are to attend to their deeper meaning and do justice to the complexity found in the lives and historical experiences of those who recount them.

We also need to be aware of the tension that exists between the notion of oral testimony as an empirical information-gathering tool and the notion of the oral interview as the production of a joint narrative produced by the interviewer and the interviewed. The text produced by this 'conversational narrative' is not only structured by cultural conventions. It is also an essentially social construction, permeated by the interchange between the interviewer and her subject, and also permeated by other communal and national narratives. In addition, it has a profoundly ideological character.[5] If literary criticism has been instrumental in fostering a growing sensitivity of oral historians to the narrative qualities of the texts they study, we must also credit the influence of postmodernist anthropology for emphasizing the complex authority relations involved in the production of an oral text. The authorial shaping of ethnographic narratives and the attendant textual and rhetorical devices used to construct an apparently objective and authoritative account of another's life and society have now been firmly placed on the agenda, and oral historians ignore such warnings at their peril.[6]

The tension implicit in the production of this conversational text can indeed call into question the entire basis of the oral history project. The pitfalls attendant on this situation are partly epistemological in that they deeply affect the status of even the 'hard' empirical evidence garnered from such interviews, signaling as they do the existence of subtexts and silences, evasions and tropes, used to filter, to resist, to deal with, and to confess. A too literal 'realist' reading of the 'evidence' produced in these narratives can be both blind and deaf to the nuance implied in such strategies. Partly, too, the pitfalls involve a more personal domain – they have to do with differences in expectations between the interviewer and interviewed, about the different status and prestige involved, the different allocations of cultural capital implied in interactions between young and old, formally educated and uneducated, foreign and native. Ultimately, too, the pitfalls speak to our ability, talent, willingness, and commitment to listen.

Many of the issues raised here are, as I have indicated, increasingly present in writings on oral history. Yet I was only dimly aware of most of them in 1987 when I began interviewing Doña María and others in Berisso. My awareness of the methodological and epistemological problems grew, as I confronted issues emerging from my own practice as an oral historian in Berisso. In this sense theory clearly followed practice, as I was forced to seek understanding of problems that were confronting me daily in my interactions with informants. But theory is not something that oral historians would seem to take to with much enthusiasm. Indeed, the directness of the genre, the apparently self-evident status of the communication and knowledge produced in oral history texts, has a powerfully doxic effect, compounding the traditional claims of orality to provide unmediated access to self-knowledge and knowledge of another. The best-known texts of the genre have largely eschewed conscious reflection on the conditions of their own production, a fact that both derives from, and helps sustain, the populist appeal of such works.[7]

Now, in the case of Latin America it is true that by the time I had embarked on my project in Berisso there was a growing body of work of potential relevance for oral historians. The field of *testimonio* studies was already booming. Centered primarily on the texts produced by Mexican and Central American women, these studies were to problematize fundamental issues of voice and agency, memory and silence, and the nature of subaltern cultural production.[8] Yet much of this critical production remained within the fields of literary criticism and romance studies, and to a lesser extent cultural anthropology. Despite a few prescient voices, very little of this had affected Latin Americanist historians. Whatever other borders were being crossed in these endeavors, the frontiers between disciplines still remained remarkably impermeable.[9] The announced era of blurred genres and joyous interdisciplinary miscegenation was to be largely confined to the safely ghettoized terrain of cultural studies.

A defining moment for me came halfway through my stay in Berisso in 1987. I am tempted to call it a sort of epiphany, though I am aware of the temptation to construct myths of origin, parables that help retroactively rationalize paths that ended up being followed. At the very least, however, I can truthfully say that the incident forcefully confronted me with the limits of a historian's common-sense pragmatism in dealing with, and understanding, certain crucial dilemmas with which I was faced. The incident occurred in the middle of winter and involved a long inter-view I did with a middle-aged Peronist militant. Doña María had mentioned him to me, as had other friends and contacts I had already made – he was someone known for his militant past, he had been particularly active in the era known as the Peronist Resistance as a young, firebrand leader in the Armour plant and a leading protago-nist in several crucial mass meetings of that era that had ended in gunfights and general mayhem. Although his family was of an impeccable Peronist lineage, there was also something, more alluded to than explicitly spoken by my contacts and by Doña María, which suggested that this was someone whose personal and family history were beyond the normal. As I later learned, his father was famed for stop-ping non-Peronists in the street and haranguing them, two of his brothers had died in mysterious circumstances apparently related to their militancy, and he himself had been closely tied to a Trotskyist group when he was active in the plants. After an initial meeting over lunch he invited me to visit the following Saturday a group of which he was a leading member called Centro de Adoctrinamiento Justicialista. Our lunchtime conversation had whetted my appetite – he clearly had a lot to tell me about the Resistance period and the internecine battles within Peronism in the post-1955 era, especially as they related to the meatpackers union. So I went. The meeting was actually held over lunch on the site of a center they were building from scratch with their own labor. Over a *buseca* – a Genovese stew made of tripe – on a freezing day in the shell of this building and in the presence of other associates of the center he proceeded to give me a version of the history of the plants, his role in it, and a general evaluation of the importance of Perón and justicialism. It was a strange occasion, not least because I was freezing, eating something I didn't like, and because of the presence of some Paraguayan laborers who were being paid to build the place. During the meal some of them proceeded to get drunk, mostly at the times when my host was being most eloquent about Perón – this simply heightened an underlying tension that was really one of status within the working class between the core group of affiliates and new migrants into Berisso who were still largely marginal both geographically and socially within the community. After several hours of taping his monologue with the occasional Paraguayan interruptions we parted with an agreement to meet the following week at his house.

In reviewing later what had transpired I confirmed my initial impression that what I had got had been a particular story/narrative, a version of the past that had left out as much as it contained – it had been particularly evasive about the internal disputes. It seemed to me that the obvious reason had been the presence of an outsider and the desire not to wash dirty linen in public. At times indeed he had scarcely veiled his annoyance when I had pressed him for more details about disputes: he had said, 'I don't know why you want to go back over that, I've already explained it.' Yet he couldn't deny it altogether because he knew that I already had enough details – in fact, I had already interviewed one of the other protagonists. Also, he had to take into account the listening public. He was clearly the designated narrator of this group – by far its most articulate member, its intellectual core, guardian of its history, its official storyteller. And yet precisely because of his privileged status he was not free to invent, erase, elide at will. However much it may have seemed to me that I had listened to a monologue, what I had in fact witnessed was a dialogue between himself and his listeners/his public and, at a remove, with myself, the outsider. His story had to remain credible, and this credibility was rooted in several elements – among them notions of truth telling. As Henry Glassie asserts in his wonderful book *Passing the Time in Ballymenone*, both academic and local historians do much the same thing: 'Whether they teach at Oxford or wheel turf in Ballymenone, historians get the facts as accurately as they can get them, but since the past has passed they cannot get all the facts, or get them all right.'[10]

There was also some more profound referential pact between storyteller/local historian and the community and its needs, and this was something that went beyond my insight about his not wanting to wash dirty linen in public. The story he told me had to be based on the truth – but as in all effective storytelling, it also could be manipulated truth. Not at will, according to individual whim with arbitrary intent, but rather according to tacit, largely unspoken consensus between both audience and narrator about present needs, priorities, and imperatives. These were in turn arrived at through negotiation and concession with other alternative narratives within this community. As such, his annoyance with my desire to turn the narrative back to the details of past divisions, to center his recollections on the internal fights and the sad chronicle of the decline of the meatpacking plants in Berisso, was rooted in a different appreciation of the uses of history and the stories in which it is embodied. He wanted to use the story to draw wider conclusions about the sources of community strength, about survival, about the overcoming of differences, about the unifying power of Peronism and the role of Perón in achieving that. My insistence on the academicist notion of 'getting it right' of course threatened to open old wounds, to expose the more unseemly underbelly of Peronist unionism, but this was not the sole or even, I think, the main reason for his evasions and omissions.

Much of what I have just said is the result of later reflection. At the time I was convinced that with sufficient persistence I could come up with the goods. As with any good ethnographer or oral historian, effective questioning would track the beast of historical objectivity, the facts, down to its layer. Evasion would be ultimately useless. The informant could run, but faced with the array of devices at my disposal – along with a basic assumption that I was smarter than him – he could not ultimately hide. At the time I had not encountered postmodern anthropological speculations about the construction of ethnographic knowledge and authority. Later, as I reviewed the interview in the United States, I read James Clifford's essay, 'Power and Dialogue in Ethnography.' There, I found the following quote from Marcel Griault, drawn from his meditations about the practice of ethnography in Africa:

> Active ethnography is the art of being a midwife and an examining magistrate, by turns an affable comrade of the person put to cross-examination, a distant friend, a severe stranger, compassionate father, concerned patron, a trader paying for revelations one by one, a listener affecting distraction before the open gates of the most dangerous mysteries, an obliging friend showing lively interest for the most insipid family stories – the ethnographer parades across his face as pretty a collection of masks as that possessed by any museum.[11]

I was struck by how accurately this described what I had been engaged with in Berisso. It would be nice to be able to report that one of these masks had stood me in good stead in the interview at his home. In fact, the encounter, when it arrived, was both deeply disturbing and frustrating and also a humbling lesson in the pitfalls awaiting the overarrogant oral historian. When I attempted to take him back over the union story, he impatiently repeated the essence of his previous accounting. When I interrupted him to ask for clarification, he finally exploded: 'You just want to get things from me, but you don't tell me anything about yourself, about what you think, about your ideas. What do you value? What do you think of Perón?' I was taken aback but sufficiently astute to realize that the fact-finding, inquisitorial mode that I had adopted was in danger of self-destructing. I had to try another tack if only to maintain any open channels of communication. I had to embark on the terrain that he wanted to explore – which I was slowly coming to realize was his principal interest in me and in our relationship. He was, in fact, challenging the entire premise of my activity, the power relationship I had taken for granted and which underlay my sense of myself as the author, the constructor, the editor of the historical knowledge that would come out of our encounter. He wanted some form of genuine dialogue and interchange, but also, more than that, he wanted this to be the basis of my listening to what he most wanted to say. And what he wanted to say certainly had to do with the larger-scale social history data I was bent on acquiring, but it was framed within a personal key and had to do with his place in that broader history, his sense of himself, the meaning of his life.

I would like to be able to say that with my slow coming to awareness of what was happening I was able to construct some new, more adequate 'fable of rapport' and adopt a more appropriate mask. Unfortunately, the dialogue that followed was a fractured, deeply awkward encounter. He spoke of his life, of how he had attended college under Perón, how he had been involved in various drama groups, had written poetry, and of how all that had stopped with Perón's ouster, when access to education had been cut off and he had had to enter the plants. How he had been disoriented by Perón's overthrow, bitter about the changes in his life chances, hotheaded and hence drawn into non-Peronist left politics. How he had been blacklisted from the plants and during the 1960s had come to realize that he had been wrong, had been manipulated by the Trotskyists and had misjudged many of his former Peronist opponents. He had eventually sought reintegration into the movement, where he had become involved in something like cadre education, ending up in the early 1970s working for the Juventud Sindical Peronista – a union group closely tied with the Peronist right and José Lopez Rega. He had also continued to be involved in drama and poetry as well as propagating official justicialist ideology. He had produced several pageants about Perón and Justicialism and their relationship with Christianity. At one stage he recited a long excerpt from his major prose poem on the theme.

By this time in the interview I realized that I had totally misjudged my informant and that I was very much out of my depth. The life story he was telling me was a complex story of disillusion, youthful error, and ultimately redemption all told in a tone of great emotionality. At many times he would seem on the verge of breaking down, his voice would crack and his eyes fill with tears as he spoke in Christian terms of forgiveness, love, and Perón and recite the Veinte Verdades (twenty truths) of Peronism.[12] Interwoven into this narrative were obviously elements of remorse and pain associated with the deaths of his brothers and the internecine warfare within Peronism in the 1960s and 1970s. It was clearly important for him to make me understand, to engage me in a discussion among equals about the intellectual underpinning of his life, about the moral choices he had made, about the Great Tradition (Peronism) that made sense of the Little Tradition (Berisso) in which he had lived out his life.[13]

The problem was that I was unable to adequately live up to my part of the implicit bargain being proposed here. Although I knew that my initial pretence of uncovering the sordid, if exciting, untold story of rank-and-file Peronism was no longer viable, I could not bring myself to enter fully into the new arrangement. I would like to be able to say that this was due to my refusal to embrace the bad faith involved in adopting a new mask. It wasn't. It was, I think now, a mixture of many things. In part, it was ideological wariness, especially as he spoke of his associations with the extreme right wing of Peronism. It was also due to intolerance and impatience on my part, a lack of sensitivity about his core beliefs – the Veinte Verdades and all they implied.

Something else also underlay my reluctance to engage with this man, and this was, I think, a profound sense of discomfort. It was in one sense a physical unease. The day was bitterly cold, the sort of winter cold that distinguishes Berisso from even La Plata, a scant eight miles away. It is a damp cold that comes straight off the estuary and is borne on the wind and which can penetrate you to the bone. His house was typical of many in Berisso constructed during the Peronist regime; it was made of concrete, with a cold slab floor and a single gas-fired space heater to give a sparse warmth. The interview started at dusk as the temperature was dropping. So I was cold, but this is hardly the entire explanation for my discomfort. I was used to Berisso's winter by this time; I had conducted other interviews in similar conditions. Indeed, Doña María's house was if anything colder. My physical discomfort was intensified by a sense of gloom that permeated the house and that had much to do with the presence of his wife, who was in the house but who played no part in the interview. There was a palpable tension between them; her body language, her gestures, and her glances spoke of resignation and resentment that I intuited had to do with the poverty of the household, evident in ancient furniture, the lack of paint on the walls, and the lack of food in the kitchen. I read in her presence an ironic comment on her husband's performance for the outsider. It was as if she were used to his claims and his emotions, as though she had resigned herself to the fact these would never translate into anything substantial in terms of some minimal comforts and basic hopes. Whether he was a Trotskyist or a Peronist, their lot would not change.

This sense of intruding on an intimate drama compounded what was an instinctive wariness on my part, a reluctance to empathize with the emotionalism with which he imbued his story and its telling. I felt like a voyeur and found the sensation deeply disturbing. He, of course, noticed my reserve, and the interview wound down. I have never returned to formally interview him. We meet on the street, exchange greetings, but my chance of access to whatever the deeper meanings of his story could be has gone, and with it even my chance of uncovering, through him, the key to the empirical information I had so craved at the start.

I am not sure that I learned any immediate lessons from the encounter I have just recounted. Its status as a morality tale has been largely constructed with hindsight.

My interviews with Doña María continued, and although we had our good days and our bad days, nothing approaching this sort of breakdown ever occurred. My relationship with an elderly woman was, evidently, far more comfortable than that with a middle-aged man. I had established a degree of intimacy with her, I was welcomed by her family, and she had progressed from addressing me as 'professor' to calling me Danielito. And yet the incident lingered in some semi-conscious way as something that I realized I would have to analyze sooner or later. When I did permit myself to think about it aloud – always in Buenos Aires, with friends, at a bar, never in Berisso – the simplest answer to the question why I had not been able to rescue the interviewer/interviewee relationship with him was to state the obvious: I had found his brand of religiously intense right-wing Peronism impossible to empathize with. But although this answer allowed me to bask in the genuine rapport that I had with Doña María, it could not hide the fact that the experience had raised issues that went beyond an extreme individual case of empathic failure between historian and informant. Beyond my distaste for his brand of politics were there not other, more general issues raised about the practice of oral history?

One that certainly occurred to me on later reflection had to do with the notion of truth telling, so powerfully raised by this incident. It is by now a commonplace of narratology that stories are not iconic renderings of actual sequences of events; all narration involves reconstituting events concerning a narrator's life or the history of the wider community.[14] And yet the criteria upon which such reconstituting takes place are scarcely arbitrary and are, it would seem, in the Western world overwhelmingly linked to requirements of truth and factuality. Although we can be open to other cultural possibilities, Henry Glassie's conclusions about the mandate to tell the truth among his Northern Irish local historians in Ballymenone would seem to hold in Berisso, too. After telling us that Oxford historians and their colleagues who wheel turf in Ballymenone do much the same thing, Glassie goes on to elaborate: 'When they string facts into narratives, they will create something other than the factual past, if only by dint of omission, and the dynamics of presentation, but they do not do so to fool people but to help them by driving at a truth larger than that trapped in the factual scraps. . . . their joy is finding, holding, manipulating truth.'[15] Whether the narrative was being performed in the Centro de Adoctrinamiento Justicialista or in Doña María's kitchen, my informants showed a similar respect for the truth.

And yet it seems that this is more complicated than Glassie would allow. For a start we must distinguish between the different levels of narration produced in the oral transcript. At one level, certainly, we could say that our subjects are able and willing to adopt the dominant narrative form of professional historical discourse, framing their narrative within the canons of expository narration.[16] In this sense they largely adopt a version of the formal political and historical discourse of their interviewers. The sources of such a discourse are multiple, ranging from formal school curricula to televised historical documentaries to historical narratives embedded in political traditions, Doña María would often move into such a mode, as she recounted crucial events in the history of Peronism or events that had happened in the union. Such a narrative was normally marked by a phrase such as 'whether we like it or not, that's history and we can't ignore it.'

On another level, we find that much of oral testimony consists of a far more informal conversational narrative, framed as personal experience stories, anecdotes, gossip. The two levels cannot be artificially separated. Indeed, the commonest way in which History is recalled is precisely in this minor key. As James Fentress and Chris Wickham argue: 'No matter how keyed into historical culture one is, one's memories of major events – World War 2 for instance – can turn into simple exercises in day-to-day survival at home or at the front or sources of isolated anecdotes, whether terrifying, terrible, amusing or life affirming.'[17] Different types of memory – collective and individual – also correspond to these different levels. But to these different levels of narration, and memory, we can apply different evaluative criteria concerning truth telling.

It is clearly important to try and verify the factual accuracy of historical material found in oral interviews from other sources. Yet I think that very often this, too, is largely an exercise in professional glorification on the part of the academic historian. We frequently know 'the facts' better than our informants. And there is a price to be paid for the aggressive interrogation of factual accuracy. As Glassie observes, 'Dates alienate. They are a means to kill the past and bury it in irrelevance.'[18] Glassie's Northern Irish historians know this instinctively, though it is doubtful that their Oxford colleagues would agree. Indeed, it is part of our role as historians, our professional ideology, to enforce different criteria. My own propensity for aggressive intervention along these lines was evident in the case I have just recounted. My search not just for dates but for 'historical information' in general led me to endanger the entire relationship. With Doña María, too, rereading the transcript has brought home to me the frequency and insistence with which I would interrupt her to insist on dating or on other forms of categorizing.

The damage done by such insistence can go much further than burying the past in irrelevance. Ronald Grele has argued that there is a fundamental tension in the oral history interview between narrative and analysis:

> If oral history is a conversational narrative this conversation often takes place in opposition to the power of the narrative. . . . while we destroy narrative as such the interviewed rapidly try to reestablish it. . . . the role of the interviewer is crucial but we fulfill it by adding details, forcing memory to its limits, destroying its very narrative capacity. We don't treat it like a story that keeps developing and that carries us along, rather we treat it like an object of analysis and deconstruction.[19]

If we add to this the fact that there are frequently great discrepancies of cultural and social capital involved, too, in the social field within which the interview is structured, then we can appreciate the very real potential for symbolic violence that could result from the insistence on the professional ideology of the historian.[20]

If the rigid application of criteria central to the professional ideology of historians has serious implications for the knowledge produced at this level of narrative discourse, its impact at the level of conversational discourse is even more problematical. Perhaps a comparison of oral history and autobiography can help us appreciate this issue. Philippe Lejeune in his analysis of autobiography as a genre emphasizes the importance for autobiography of what he calls the referential pact, the commitment on the part of the teller to 'tell the truth, the whole truth and nothing but the truth' about her life. It is this that marks autobiography as a referential text exactly like scientific and historical discourse and that distinguishes it from fiction. The oath that underlies the autobiographer's pact is along the lines of 'telling the truth as it appears to me, in as much as I can know it, making allowances for lapses of memory, errors, involuntary distortions etc.'[21] Yet there is, according to Lejeune, a fundamental difference between the pact of the historian or journalist and that which underwrites autobiography: 'In autobiography it is essential that the referential pact be *drawn up*, and that it be *kept*; but it is not necessary that the result be of the order of strict resemblance. The autobiographical pact can be, according to the criteria of the reader, badly kept without the referential value of the text disappearing (on the contrary) – this is not the case for historical and journalistic texts' (22–23). I would only add that on the contrary it *is* the case for oral history texts, or at least those predominantly framed within conversational narrative discourse. What test of verification could we possibly think of applying to the subjective experience recalled at this level? As Lejeune notes, 'Autobiography tells us precisely, here is the advantage of its narrative, what it alone can tell us' (22). We are not talking about criteria of resemblance measured against an externally verifiable referent. The referential pact associated with the oral history text is likely to be, as with autobiography, premised on notions of fidelity to meaning rather than to criteria of strict accuracy associated with information.

We could perhaps also think of the distinction I am making in terms of the growing body of work on life story as a fundamental sociocultural practice focused on the narrative shaping of personal experience. In contrast to the more traditional model of life history 'focused mainly on diachronic change within anthropology's traditional paradigm of naturalism or realism,' life-story research 'focuses on the cultural scripts and narrative devices individuals use to make sense of experience. [It] emphasizes the truth of the telling versus telling the truth.'[22] Charlotte Linde, one of its foremost theorists, has defined the life story as consisting 'of all the stories and associated discourse units, such as explanations and chronicles, and the connections between them, told by an individual in his/her lifetime.'[23] This clearly directs us, once more, toward oral sources as narrative and the appropriate analytical procedures needed to interpret them. [. . .]

Oral history texts are made up in varying degrees of both of these models, and each requires its own careful listening, the careful application of criteria of evaluation concerning truth and accuracy. Informants themselves are frequently aware of the distinction and the different expectations this generates are part of the, often implicit, bargaining that goes on within any interview situation. The abrupt interjection that transformed and ultimately unraveled my relationship in the cold house in Berisso was, I think, in large part occasioned by my informant's sense that I had failed to recognize such distinctions. He had told me the 'true' history of Berisso, the union and his role in it in the public setting of the Centro de Adoctrinamiento Justicialista. Now, in his home, he expected that his life story would elicit another sort of attention and judgment on my part.

The issue of truth telling in oral testimony is, then, intimately related to the question of the nature of the relationship between the oral historian and her subject and the status of the knowledge produced by that relationship. Despite the rapport that existed between myself and Doña María, was the basic drive of what I was attempting to do with her all that different from what I had attempted to do, but failed, with my male informant? Despite the lesson that this parable told about the pitfalls awaiting the overly arrogant oral historian, the basic metaphor that informed my approach continued to be that of the detective uncovering secrets, breaking codes, tracking down beyond the grave the hidden meanings of Doña María's life. The chapters [of my book] stand as testimony to that enduring passion, which is in some fundamental way basic to the analytical function of historical discourse. It is simply what historians do. But what are the presuppositions of this approach and the strategy of representation associated with it?

In the first place it seems important to recognize what is going on when the oral historian produces a text that claims to speak about, and for, another. To bridge the gap between two radically heterogeneous fields of experience, between the historian and the other, between myself and Doña María, is to engage in what Alberto Moreiras has called prosopopeic representation. In an essay on testimonio autobiography Moreiras defines prosopopeia as 'a mask through which one's own voice is projected onto another, where that other is always suffering from a certain inability to speak.' As Moreiras goes on to argue, 'The relational mediation is then always unequal and hierarchical, even at its most redemptive.'[24] This would seem to be an unavoidable truth that no claims to empathic identification on the part of ethnographer or oral historian can fully offset. In recent times the figure of the 'redemptive ethnographer' giving voice to the oppressed other in a process of reciprocal text production has appeared in various guises. Certainly, oral history's fundamental claim to distinguish itself by giving a voice to the voiceless, to those who do not enter the dominant narrative of history, shares this redemptive urge.

An implicit part of this trope is also the claim to a sort of 'horizontal affinity' between the two sides engaged in the ethnographic relationship.[25] I personally find it hard to imagine such a claim of affinity between myself and Doña María. Clearly it could not have a gender basis. I could, perhaps, claim a class-based affinity. My parents were workers, both from mining communities. I grew up in a household permeated by a union and left-wing culture. I was frequently struck by parallels between Doña María and my mother. But I have spent my adult life moving ever further away from those roots, and the cultural alienation of social mobility has done its work. I admired Doña María and felt a deep affection and respect for her, but this falls far short of the sort of emotional fusion through which a self is apparently projected onto an alter ego. Whatever the innate attraction of the 'passion to swim in the stream of their (the native's) experience' may be, this is, as Clifford Geertz warns us, ultimately an illusion.[26]

It may, of course, be a necessary and productive illusion, a powerful heuristic weapon. In an extraordinary scene from the documentary film *Number Our Days*, in which she speaks of her work among the elderly members of a Jewish cultural center in Venice, California, the anthropologist Barbara Myerhoff speaks of her move away from research on the Huichol Indians of Northern Mexico to the study of elderly Jews by explaining that 'after all I will never be a Huichol Indian, but I will be a little old Jewish lady.' It was very probably this conviction that enabled her to produce the profound ethnographic representations embodied in the book of the same title. At the very least this gesture may provide the basis for an effective 'hermeneutics of solidarity,' which is certainly preferable to the objectivizing appropriation of much traditional analysis. It may be, too, that there are reasons to question the overemphasis on the dire consequences of the hierarchical and unequal character of prosopopeic representation. Although we might agree that at a level of abstraction this is unavoidable, at the concrete level of the interview situation we may find countervailing tendencies.

One presupposition of the pathos of pessimism that informs much postmodernist ethnographic speculation concerning representation is the figure of the interviewee/informant as victim whose memory and identity are appropriated and exploited. I would suggest that this seriously underestimates the power of the interviewee to negotiate the conditions under which communication takes place in the interview situation. Let me give an example. Very early in our interviews Doña María and I had the following exchange:

> DJ: How did the strike of ninety-six days come about?
> DM: Because this woman, this one, that one all said to themselves.
> . . . Me, for instance, who taught me? The book of life, not the university, pardon me, professor, the university is the best that humanity has because there you learn and the shadows of the mind disappear and wisdom emerges but you know that the university of life is beautiful. When I put my children to bed at night many times with only a warm tea and a piece of bread and then cried and wet the pillow and my husband would say to me, this will get better, don't cry, that's where I learned. . . . pain taught me to free myself.

In the months that followed she frequently repeated this claim. We could interpret this in several ways. It is certainly a claim to establish footing, to equalize the gap in cultural status between a university professor and a meatpacking worker. The recent work on life-story construction has alerted us to the fact that there is generally an underlying mandate that life stories achieve coherence through a cooperative effort between teller and addressee.[27] [. . .] However, here I want to stress the fact that I present particular problems for Doña María as the addressee of last resort in our relationship. In the first place, she had to make the assumption that I, as many outsiders were, would be critical if not hostile toward Perón and Peronism. Many of her stories had already been negotiated within Berisso with other addressees in mind. This fact is not necessarily a handicap. Indeed, it is precisely one of the preconditions of any possibility that the historian/interviewer can move from the individual to collective questions of agency and consciousness in later analysis.

Beyond this, the claim is also an assertion that there is a level of experience and knowledge to which I do not have access. And this is because I haven't lived it and had the experiences on which it has been based and because it is of a fundamentally different status. It comes from the heart, from the emotional core of a person, from the pain of life, which are radically different criteria from the book-learning criteria of the university professor. Without knowing or caring about it, Doña María is expressing the distinction between emic and etic, experience-near and experience-distant ways of knowing.[28] She is also, of course, telling me about the limits of empathy and prosopopeic representation, that there are things that I cannot understand or perhaps should not know. What would the most adequate response to such a claim be on the part of the oral historian? One possibility is that offered by Doris Sommer in an influential essay within testimonio criticism, in which she enjoined the reader/critic to respect the secret, to treat the claim as an ethically unpassable border that no form of interpretative representation should seek to cross. In her terms the reader should remain 'incompetent' in the face of this 'resistant text.'[29]

Yet I do not think that Doña María is claiming an absolutely unbridgeable gap. Far from radically problematizing communication, we could interpret her claim as the first step in negotiating the conditions under which it might take place. Such conditions would ideally allow her to both posit her secret, the uniqueness of her suffering-based experience, and articulate her interpretation of her life and world-view. The possibility that the conditions for such an outcome can be negotiated in any interview situation is an uncertain one. Certainly, my experience in Berisso is a warning against overconfidence regarding this wager. And yet it might also offer a clue as to what might be needed. In my story of a failed encounter in a cold house the fundamental failure in my mind was my failure to listen, my refusal to submerge myself and my criteria in a gesture that would have signaled my willingness to engage my interlocutor on his own terms.

Although we might express this in semiotic terms I think that at root it is best framed as an ethical issue. Indeed, it is striking to note how some of the most profound meditations on this issue have been framed in these terms. Marc Kaminsky, the editor of Barbara Myerhoff's posthumously published collected essays, speaks of her concern for what she called the 'pathos of the absent listener.' Filling the void left by such absence was one of the fundamental roles of the ethno-grapher. In Myerhoff's own personal case Kaminsky assures us that listening was 'a sacralization of a secular vocation' that was based on a unique 'gift as a listener':

> Immersed in this full and unusually intense attentiveness, received by a listener who offered herself as a 'partner in security' . . .; met more-over by someone whose steadiness of attention by turns offered a supple, accepting, lucid, brilliant auditor, Myerhoff's interlocutors felt free to think and feel through dimensions of their experience that they had not owned or connected before. She was often present at the saying out loud for the first time of something often lived with, subliminally. The inter-view felt emancipatory. The gathered material registered the sense of discovery.[30]

The tone of these observations is strikingly similar to remarks made by Pierre Bourdieu in his meditation on the interviewing practice drawn from the interviews collected in *La Misère du Monde*. Although he maintains that 'there are limits to the procedures and subterfuges that we have been able to think up to reduce the distance' between interviewer and interviewed, Bourdieu claims in the end that any 'true comprehension' must be based on 'attentiveness to others and an openness toward them.' This sort of attention would be the opposite of the 'ritualized small talk' and 'inattentive drowsiness' normal in social conversation. For Bourdieu the interview that arrives at true comprehension 'can be considered a sort of spiritual exercise, aiming to attain, through forgetfulness of self, a true transformation of the view we take of others in the ordinary circumstances of life.' He concludes that 'the welcoming disposition, which leads one to share the problems of the respondent, the capacity to take her and understand her just as she is, in her distinc-tive necessity, is a sort of intellectual love.'[31]

Fifty years earlier, in a text that struggled in a uniquely powerful way with the problems of representation and that has been strangely forgotten in the current spec-ulations on the theme, James Agee spoke in a similar vein. Although the 'nominal subject' of *Let Us Now Praise Famous Men* is 'North American cotton tenantry as examined in the daily living of three representative white tenant families,' Agee goes on to affirm: 'Actually, the effort is to recognize the stature of a portion of unimagined existence, and to contrive techniques proper to its recording, communication, analysis and defence. More essentially, this is an independent inquiry into certain normal predicaments of human divinity.'[32] Agee brought love, passion, guilt, anger, and an extraordinary ear for listening to his tortured effort to translate a 'portion of unimagined existence' for his educated Northern audience. [. . .]

The memory recovered in the oral history project is not the invention of the historian, though she certainly helps shape it and can perfectly well disrupt it. The issue of memory is not uninteresting for many respondents; indeed, it is often at the root of their desire to participate. For the elderly in particular, remembering can be both a moral and a psychic priority. On a cold, bright day in mid-June, six months after we started our interviews, Doña María and I took a bus down to the calle Nueva York, the street that led to the two packing houses. As we walked along the dock that ran along the two plants, we could see the empty shell of the Swift plant and we could survey the overgrown field that had been the site of the Armour plant. After a long silence Doña María spoke:

> You know this used to be like a city within a city. It was lit up twenty-four hours a day. I worked over there for many years, and my husband worked here. . . . but my grandson said to me the other day, 'You know, abuela, grandfather gave his whole life working over there and now there isn't a brick left. When they pull Swift down there will be nothing to remind us of what you did in there.' You know he's right. . . . When I die my great-grandchildren will have no memory of our struggles and our lives.

I took it as both a statement of fact and of implicit desire. It was the nearest we ever got to discussing what she wanted out of our interviews.

No one has addressed the issue of the process of 're-membering' among the elderly as passionately as Barbara Myerhoff. Marc Kaminsky summarized the meaning of this notion for her: 'Through "re-membering" the old people's rituals, storytelling and other cultural performances become forms for constituting a collective subject, a social individual in whom the ancestors live on renewed.'[33] This powerful redemptive claim centers on the notion of 'remembering' as a practice of memory distinct from ordinary recollection and is embodied in cultural practices such as storytelling, which are vital to the psychological health of the elderly. The importance of re-membering lives is nowhere more explicitly stated than in the words of Shmuel, the taylor and central character of *Number Our Days*. In his last conversation with Myerhoff, Shmuel laments that his village and the Jewish culture of eastern Europe have all been erased by the Holocaust and other cruelties of history. That past and his loved ones exist now only in his stories – 'all those people and all those places, I carry them around until my shoulders break.' But even this burden does not suffice:

> Even with all that poverty and suffering it would be enough if the place remained, even old men like me, ending their days would find it enough.

> But when I come back from these stories and remember the way they
> lived is gone forever, wiped out like you would erase a line of writing,
> then it means another thing altogether for me to accept leaving this life.
> If my life goes now, it means nothing. But if my life goes, with my
> memories, and all that is lost, that is something else to bear.[34]

Now it may be the case that Myerhoff exaggerates her claim. Certainly, we need
to be aware of the process of forgetting, which can be of as much interest to the
oral historian as the culturally creative process of re-membering lives that Myerhoff
celebrated. Indeed, any process of remembering is inevitably shaped by what is
omitted, silenced, not evoked. More than that, it is also clear that for some old
people the ethical imperative not to forget is more than offset by the pain associated with certain memories. One woman, who had worked in the Armour plant
and attended the slide show [a public commemorative event in 1984 combining
photographs of the factory before it was pulled down and a narrative sound track],
turned down my request to interview her about it. Her life in the plant had been
'a very sad time,' and she didn't want to be 'forced to remember things that would
cause me pain.' She would later prove to be more than happy to talk about her
participation in the social and cultural life of the Ukrainian ethnic association. The
Armour commemoration had, in her case, simply provoked a memory that she did
not wish to share, an experience she did not wish to transmit.[35]

In part Shmuel's legacy – the fate of his memories – depends on Myerhoff, his
brilliant auditor and cocreator of his 're-membered' life. In a similar way the survival
of Doña Maria's memories also depends on my good faith and skill as a listener. I
suspect that all of us who undertake to record these sorts of extended life stories
share, at some level, Myerhoff's contention that 'such re-membered lives are moral
documents and their function is salvific, inevitably implying, "All this has not been
for nothing."'[36] Such a belief provides the ethical basis for the project we have
embarked on. But there is also an element that inevitably escapes the dimension of
the individual listener, and the efficacy and ethical content of the narrator/listener
relationship. And that element has to do with the problematic status of modern
memory.

In part we have already alluded to one source of this problematic status. We
have spoken of the process of mourning for a past that is inevitably slipping away,
as orality tries to stem the consequences of its own impermanence. It can do this
by mobilizing the mnemonic resources available in the photographic image and the
written narrative. Yet both of these imply a degree of distantiation. Orality presup-
poses a certain level of communal, social negotiation and control of meaning –
though this certainly has its limits. The written document – the transcribed oral
text – and the visual image will be ultimately controlled by others and escape the
control of community interpretation. Beyond this, however, there lies the broader
issue of the transmission of collective memory. As Andreas Huyssen notes, a central
paradox of the postmodern West is that the society of 'mnemonic convulsions' is
also a society permeated by a 'culture of amnesia.'[37] Part of this culture of amnesia
is precisely the crisis of collective transmission of social memory. We could express
this by asking the question: what are the sites and social practices of remembering
that could carry out the social transmission of memory in the contemporary era?
Both [Walter] Benjamin and Myerhoff confronted this question, and both sought

answers in the collective realm. Benjamin offers us the brief clue that individual and collective memory could be triggered through rituals, ceremonies, and festivals produced by society.[38] For Myerhoff the ability to re-member could be fostered by providing the social space within which individuals could perform the cultural practices that give access to deep memory. Part of the crisis of contemporary memory in working-class communities is precisely the crisis of such social spaces that have fallen victim to the destructive power of de-industrialization, social dislocation, and simple irrelevance. In Berisso we might say that the fate of memory still hangs in the balance. It certainly still possesses resources that can underwrite social memory. We would, however, be foolish to ignore other tendencies. Even the vibrant memory of lives of labor centered on the *lieux de mémoire* of the packing house has a very tenuous purchase on contemporary memory, as the generations of packing-house workers rapidly dwindle in numbers.

Notes

1   Paul Thompson, *The Voice of the Past*, Oxford: Oxford University Press, 1990; Raphael Samuel and Paul Thompson, *The Myths We Live By*, New York: Routledge, 1990.

2   Luisa Passerini, *Fascism in Popular Memory: The Cultural Experience of the Turin Working Class*, Cambridge: Cambridge University Press, 1987; Ronald Grele, 'Listen to Their Voices: Two Case Studies in the Interpretation of Oral History Interviews', *Oral History* 7, no. 1 (1979): pp. 33–42; Alessandro Portelli, *The Death of Luigi Trastulli and Other Stories: Form and Meaning in Oral History*, Albany: State University of New York Press, 1991.

3   Samuel and Thompson, *Myths We Live By*, p. 2.

4   Portelli, in *Death of Luigi Trastulli and Other Stories*, p. 2.

5   The phrase is Ronald Grele's, in 'La historia y sus lenguajes en la entrevista de historia oral: Quién contesta a las preguntas de quién y porqué', *Historia y Fuente Oral* 20, no. 3 (1989), pp. 63–83.

6   See James Clifford and George Marcus, *Writing Culture: The Poetics and Politics of Ethnography*, Berkeley: University of California Press, 1986; George E. Marcus and Michael M.J. Fischer, *Anthropology as Cultural Critique: An Experimental Moment in the Human Sciences*, Chicago: University of Chicago Press, 1986.

7   See, for example, Theodore Rosengarten, comp., *All God's Dangers: The Life of Nate Shaw*, New York: Knopf, 1974; and Jacquelyn Dowd Hall et al., *Like a Family: The Making of a Southern Cotton Mill World*, Chapel Hill: University of North Carolina Press, 1987.

8   See especially John Beverley and Marc Zimmerman, *Literature and Politics in the Central American Revolutions*, Austin: University of Texas Press, 1990.

9   See Passerini, *Fascism in Popular Memory*, and Portelli, *Death of Luigi Trastulli and Other Stories*.

10 Henry Glassie, *Passing the Time in Ballymenone: Culture and History of an Ulster Community*, Philadelphia: University of Pennsylvania Press, 1982, p. 620.

11 Quoted in James Clifford, *The Predicament of Culture: Twentieth Century Ethnography, Literature, and Art*, Cambridge, Mass.: Harvard University Press, 1988, p. 75.

12 The twenty truths of Peronism refer to a set of basic maxims that were meant to guide the social and political behavior of Peronist affiliates.

13   The concept of a Great Tradition and a Little Tradition was originally developed by the anthropologist Robert Redfield. For its usage in an oral interview context see Barbara Myerhoff, *Number Our Days*, New York: Simon and Schuster, 1978, p. 256.

14   See Barbara Johnstone, *Stories, Community, and Place: Narratives from Middle America*, Bloomington: Indiana University Press, 1990, pp. 99–101.

15   Glassie, *Passing the Time in Ballymenone*, p. 651.

16   See Gillian Bennett, 'Narrative as Expository Discourse', *Journal of American Folklore* 99, no. 394 (October-December 1986): pp. 415–35.

17   James Fentress and Chris Wickham, *Social Memory*, Oxford: Blackwell, 1992, p. 101.

18   Glassie, *Passing the Time in Ballymenone*, p. 664.

19   Grele, 'La historia y sus lenguajes en la entrevista de historia oral', p. 74.

20   On the notion of symbolic violence see Pierre Bourdieu, *Outline of a Theory of Practice*, Cambridge: Cambridge University Press, 1983.

21   Philippe Lejeune, *On Autobiography*, Minneapolis: University of Minnesota Press, 1989, p. 22.

22   Gelya Frank, 'Anthropology and Individual Lives: The Story of Life History and the History of the Life Story', *American Anthropologist* 97, no. 1 (March 1995): pp. 145–49.

23   Charlotte Linde, *Life Stories: The Creation of Coherence*, Oxford: Oxford University Press, 1993, p. 21. See also George C. Rosenwald and Richard L. Ochberg, eds, *Storied Lives: The Cultural Politics of Self-Understanding*, New Haven, Conn.: Yale University Press, 1992.

24   Alberto Moreiras, 'The Aura of Testimonio', in *Testimonial Literature and Latin America*, ed. George M. Gugelberger, Durham, N.C.: Duke University Press, 1996.

25   The phrase 'redemptive ethnographer' is Ruth Behar's, in *Translated Woman: Crossing the Border with Esperanza's Story*, Boston: Beacon Press, 1993, p. 269.

26   Clifford Geertz, 'From the Native's Point of View: On the Nature of Anthropological Understanding', in *Local Knowledge: Further Essays in Interpretive Anthropology*, New York: Basic, 1983, p. 8.

27   Linde, op. cit.

28   Geertz, op. cit.

29   Doris Sommer, 'Resistant Texts and Incompetent Readers', *Latin American Literary Review* 4 (1992): pp. 104–8.

30   Marc Kaminsky, introduction to *Remembered Lives: The Work of Ritual, Storytelling, and Growing Older*, Barbara Myerhoff, Ann Arbor: University of Michigan Press, 1992, p. 13.

31   Pierre Bourdieu, 'Understanding,' *Theory, Culture, and Society* 13, no. 2 (1996): p. 24. Translation of Bourdieu, *La Misère du Monde*, Paris: Seuil, 1993, pp. 903–25.

32   James Agee and Walker Evans, *Let Us Now Praise Famous Men*, New York: Houghton Muffin, 1988, p. xlvi.

33   Kaminsky, op. cit., p. 66.

34   Myerhoff, op. cit., p. 74.

35   See Kaminsky's critical comment on Myerhoff's essay, 'Life History as Integration', in Myerhoff, *Remembered Lives: The Work of Storytelling, Ritual, and Growing Older*, Ann Arbor: University of Michigan Press, 1992, p. 254.

36   Myerhoff, ibid., p. 240.

37   Andreas Huyssen, *Twilight Memories: Marking Time in a Culture of Amnesia*, New York: Routledge, 1995.

38   Walter Benjamin, 'On Some Motifs in Baudelaire', in *Illuminations: Essays and Reflections*, New York: Schocken, 1969, p. 159.

Chapter 8

Michael Frisch

ORAL HISTORY AND THE
DIGITAL REVOLUTION
Toward a post-documentary sensibility

Michael Frisch argues that digitization of sound and image is challenging the current dominance of transcription and will return aurality to oral history, and that non-text-reliant digital index and search mechanisms will enable imaginative, unforeseen uses for oral history. He concludes that 'new digital tools and the rich landscape of practice they define may become powerful resources in restoring one of the original appeals of oral history – to open new dimensions of understanding and engagement through the broadly inclusive sharing and interrogation of memory.' Michael Frisch teaches History and American Studies at the State University of New York, Buffalo and has a consulting office, The Randforce Associates, in the University at Buffalo's Technology Incubator. An earlier version of this paper was presented at the XIIIth International Oral History Conference, Rome, June 2004.

Putting the oral back in oral history

EVERYONE RECOGNIZES THAT the core audio-video dimension of oral history is notoriously underutilized. The nicely cataloged but rarely consulted shelves of audio and video cassettes in even the best media and oral history libraries are closer than most people realize to that shoebox of unviewed home-video camcorder cassettes in so many families – precious documentation that is inaccessible and generally unlistened to and unwatched. The content of these collections is rarely organized, much less indexed in any depth, and the actual audio or video is generally not searchable or browsable in any useful way. As a result, the considerable potential of audio and video documents to support high-impact, vivid, thematic, and analytic engagement with meaningful issues, personalities, and contexts is largely untapped.

We all know, as well, that in most uses of oral history the shift from voice to text is extensive and controlling. Oral history source materials have generally been approached, used, and represented through expensive and cumbersome transcription into text. Even when the enormous flattening of meaning inherent in text reduction is recognized, transcription has seemed quite literally essential – not only inevitable but something close to 'natural.' The assumption in this near-universal practice is that only in text can the material be efficiently and effectively engaged – text is easier to read, scan, browse, search, publish, display, and distribute. Audio or video documents, in contrast, inevitably have to be experienced in 'real time.' And paraphrasing Bob Dylan, 'Time passes slowly up here on the audio/video deck.' Even when there are any guides, finding aids, indexes, or descriptions of the actual video or audio, these are likely to be in text disconnected from and not easily linked to the actual media, with particular points and passages cumbersome to locate for auditing or viewing.

The basic point could not be simpler: everyone knows that there are worlds of meaning that lie beyond words; nobody pretends for a moment that the transcript is in any real sense a better representation of reality than the voice itself. Meaning inheres in context and setting, in gesture, in tone, in body language, in expression, in pauses, in performed skills and movements. To the extent we are restricted to text and transcription, we will never locate such moments and meaning, much less have the chance to study, reflect on, learn from, and share them.

But we have, for decades if not centuries, operated under the sometimes explicit, sometimes implicit, sometimes simply unexamined assumption that the gains from transformation into text – in everything from analytic access to ease of casual use and broader public sharing – are worth the price of lost meaning and texture rendered inaccessible. We have also known that there are, at least, other compensating ways, mainly through documentary as will be discussed shortly, for retrieving and making use of those realms of meaning.

All of this proceeds from the core assumption that oral and film or video documents are next to impossible to work with, especially when they involve extensive collections and broader groups of imagined users who might be interested in the material.

But what if this assumption can be discarded? The digital revolution has two simple but profound ground-level implications. First, digitization means that in crucial respects all information can be considered the same – in digital form, there is simply no difference between text, photographs, drawings and models, music, speech, and visual information: all can be expressed as digital information that can be organized, searched, extracted, and integrated with equal facility. And second, as every user of a CD or DVD knows, digitization means that any point in the data can be accessed instantly; one can move from point to point, anywhere in the data, without having to scroll or play forward or backward through the documentation in a linear way, as with tapes.

Together, these considerations help define the threshold on which we stand: digital technologies are opening new ways to work directly and easily with audio and video documents. Oral history audio and video can now be placed in an environment in which rich annotation, cross-referencing codes, and other descriptive or analytic 'meta-data' can be linked to specific passages of audio-video content. By searching or sorting by means of these reference tools, the audio-video materials themselves – not the transcribed text version – can be searched, browsed, accessed, studied, and selected for use at a high level of specificity. Indeed, with many of the emerging tools for providing such access, users and researchers themselves can mark, assess, analyze, select, and export meaningful audio and video passages for a range of customized research, presentational, and pedagogic uses. On this software frontier, audio and video documentation becomes as richly and easily accessible as a well-organized text-based reference book, and far more easily usable. The actual voice (orality, in all its meanings), and embodied voices and contexts in even richer video documentation, returns to the centre of immediacy and focus in oral history, as in the experiential interview or field documentation setting.[1]

Approaches to mapping or indexing audio-visual documents

The frontier I am describing is moving and changing very quickly, as is true with all software approaches, especially those being developed for working directly with media documents. By the time this chapter appears in print, the particular tools available today, including those with which I have been working directly in a broad range of applied contexts, will seem very primitive. Newer approaches will certainly transform profoundly our sense of what is possible, and the choices before us.

It is therefore perhaps less than useful to discuss current work or modes in great detail, and it may be correspondingly more useful to describe this moving frontier in broad terms so as to get a better sense of the forces propelling it – in terms of needs, objectives, software approaches, and emerging modalities. This can suggest some of the directions in which the field is headed, and these in turn inform directly the opportunities for new uses of oral history that I explore in the balance of this chapter.

Broadly speaking, the challenges in searching and exploring audio-video digital materials are less technical than they are intellectual and even philosophical. Technically, the problem is straightforward, though there are many evolving and competing ways of addressing it. Essentially, digital audio or video carries precise time stamps that mark the audio or video stream, like markers on a highway. Passages can be defined by identifying start and stop time codes for a particular passage or segment or even a word, and a program can then go to and play such passages simply by locating the appropriate points. When particular identifiers or combinations of identifiers have been associated with points in the data stream, the program can use these for searching the audio-video content in order instantly to locate and play the audio or video associated with those selected reference terms, whether these identifiers be subject headings, cross-reference codes, or words in a transcript.

Given the central dilemma of working with audio and video noted above – the need to watch or listen in real time, and the consequent difficulty of rapidly skimming through documentation as easily as the eye can move over pages of text – the real test of these tools is the ability to bring the user to relevant material, and to permit this material to be explored efficiently and used easily. The underlying challenge is the organization and practicality of the cross-referencing, and how this is connected to precise passages in the audio or video documentation – how the optimal qualities of access are defined, and then how these can best be served by software tools.

In this light, current and emerging approaches to cross-referencing and accessing audio oral history documentation, and to a lesser extent video documentation, can be helpfully organized – as on a literal map – as choices arrayed along a number of intersecting axes or dimensions. Before identifying and discussing these, it will be helpful to recognize the degree to which they are driven by what might be imagined as the scale or granularity of the map itself.

The most dramatic and comprehensive approaches to oral history audio-video documentation deal with very large collections and seek to make them accessible at a meaningful level to the widest extent possible, increasingly through website access. Perhaps the best-known and most instructive example is the *Survivors of the Shoah Visual History Foundation*, the massive Holocaust survivor oral history project initiated by film director Stephen Spielberg (www.vhf.org/). Confronting a body of documentation amounting to hundreds of thousands of hours, the Foundation has invested very extensively in technologies for organizing and navigating a colossal, multi-language archive. Its website offers rich insights into what it has done and how – and the many ways in which this material is now open for exploration and use, much of it in video form.

Other illustrative award-winning large-scale projects include *The Virtual Oral/Aural History Archive* at California State University, Long Beach (http://salticid. nmc.csulb.edu/cgi–bin/WebObjects/OralAural.woa/), led by Sherna Berger Gluck, in which extensive audio interviews have been put online in a uniquely interactive, highly searchable format, and the Kentucky Historical Society's *Kentucky Oral History Commission* (http://history.ky.gov/Programs/KOHC/index.htm), which has recently won a major Oral History Association award for its pathbreaking approach to turning a broad archival collection into an explorable online resource.

And finally, there is the imposing Alexander Street Press project *Oral History Online* (http://alexanderstreetpress.com/products/orhi.htm), offering a huge cross-collection union catalog of oral histories internationally, which even in its early form includes capacities to locate and access a considerable amount of audio documentation.

At the other end of this spectrum are tools for working closely with more discrete collections, by individual or team researchers, community projects, and the like. Here the interest is less likely to be with wholesale web access for open-ended exploration, and more likely to involve user-driven hands-on engagement with particular bodies of material. The work I have been doing with The Randforce Associates (www.randforce.com) stands closer to this pole. Using *Interclipper* (www. interclipper.com/) software developed initially for focus-group recording and analysis in the market research industry, one of our small-scale projects, for example, involves a collection of African-American childhood stories being cross-referenced for use in community and classroom settings. Another is a law school alumni association's oral history project seeking to document educational and legal change as well as to develop a 'memory bank', useful in alumni relations and fund-raising. A third involves content analysis of a discrete collection of researcher interviews conducted for a social-science project assessing group dynamics. All of these examples involve discrete collections that require descriptive and cross-referencing tailored to specific project content, needs, and intended uses.

Scale tends to drive choices in tools and approach as well. The larger and more diverse the collection, the more overwhelming and complex the task of cross-referencing, annotation, and indexing becomes. Accordingly, large archival projects have tended to rely on approaches that can be standardized – through controlled vocabulary thesauri and standardized subject-headings – to the greatest extent possible. Their finding and navigation tools have tended to rely on full-text searches of pre-existing transcripts, which then lead directly, via embedded time codes, to passages in the audio or video files.

Many have been experimenting with various forms of 'artificial intelligence' (AI) to model the thinking process of searchers. This can make it possible to process immense volumes of material more efficiently, and to narrow dramatically the counterproductively large number of 'hits' that cruder word or term searches tend to produce, even when narrowed through familiar Boolean query combinations. Such AI approaches are also increasingly significant in video work, where vast bodies of material can be automatically organized by analysis of visual qualities such as shot changes and rendered searchable by GPS location, face recognition, or other visual content tags.

There have been relatively fewer oral history applications to date of these tools from what in the business, media, and governmental world is coming to be known as 'digital asset management.' But the implications and potential uses of techniques developing there are substantial. The large-volume video analysis offered by *Streamsage* software (www.streamsage.com/index.htm) is one good example; another is the *Informedia Project* at Carnegie Mellon University, (www.informedia. cs.cmu.edu/). In fact, *The History Makers, Inc.* (www.thehistorymakers.com/), an ambitious Chicago-based project documenting African-American culture and history and our partner in the focused childhood story project noted above, is also working with CMU's *Informedia* to build an accessible video archive of the thousands of hours of video life-history interviews collected to date.

Tools for smaller-scale work tend to share the characteristics of qualitative analysis approaches familiar in the social sciences. Well-known software like *N6* (formerly *NUD*IST*: www.qsr.com.au/products/productoverview/product_overview.htm) and *Ethnograph* (www.qualisresearch.com/) have for some time provided sophisticated software for mapping complex interview or other data through marking text with a range of researcher-driven observational, thematic, or categorical organizers, flexible and capacious database tools for helping to meet age-old researcher needs to organize, sort, and rearrange information, whether reading notes or more structured research data. The *Interclipper* software I have been working with is one of the first tools to permit this kind of qualitative analysis of video and audio directly. It allows us to note and cross-reference – as easily as we cross-reference the place, names, or explicit content of a story – the emotional intensity, body language, thematic meaning, or pedagogic uses observable by watching the video of a narrator telling that story.

These descriptions of scale imply somewhat more general distinctions in approach that are worth identifying as independent variables – as axes for mapping contemporary practice – since they are found to varying degrees and combinations even in similarly scaled projects.

Drawing on a comfortably old-fashioned library frame of reference, one basic axis has cataloging at one end, and indexing at the other. Generally speaking, the purpose of a catalog is to help you find a needed or relevant book, and the purpose of an index is to help locate content of interest within that book once you have found it. But modern information tools are narrowing the distance between these functions, opening up an intriguing middle ground between them.

No longer limited to the one or two subject headings of the old card catalogs, modern tools permit cataloging to reach more deeply into the content of books, locating sources where there is material of interest even when this is not likely to be identified with the book's major subject-heading identifiers. In doing this, however, such descriptors still necessary tend to be relatively general subject headings, and do not necessarily identify or connect to specific passages.

Conversely, passage-specific indexing once limited to discrete individual works is now coming to reach beyond the particular book. Everyone is familiar with this from working with keywords and search engines, but the concept is more open-ended than that. The idea basic to indexing from the beginning – that it can include anything worth noting, from explicit nominal references to broader umbrella ideas to abstract themes – is more responsive to a user's or researcher's approach to analysis, in which particular avenues of inquiry not reducible to content alone can be the basis of cross-sectional searching and navigation. This has particular significance, as we will see, when working with audio and video data that is not always best approached by its explicit content – for example, an anecdote about a friend or a conversation that is really a story about relationships or personal life decisions – or where the data is simply not lexical at all.

Following this thread suggests the value of identifying as an overlapping but yet distinct dimension, the distinction between content-driven mapping and exploration, and what might be called meaning-driven, analysis-driven, or inquiry-driven mapping and exploration. This distinction has broader implications for describing and conceptualizing the range of contemporary approaches to mapping information in general, and audio-video documentation in particular.

Many archivists and librarians have traditionally assumed this distinction to be central and controlling – it is the job of archivists to map content broadly, mainly by focusing on whole units such as collections, or perhaps specific interviews, rather than particular passages within documents. Archivists have generally been reluctant to privilege any particular approach to meaning or inquiry, much less to incorporate it in their taxonomies. In a recent discussion on the H-Oral electronic oral history discussion forum, for example, an American archivist termed anything other than collection or interview-level indexing to be 'ethically problematic':

> As an archivist it's not my job to create new meaning, it is just to try to stabilize the meaning of a recording or document in relation to the larger grouping from which it comes – to maintain it as best as possible within the intellectual context of its creation and use. Making new meaning is the job of a researcher using the materials.[2]

This is an understandable posture in traditional archiving, but its limitations in dealing with oral history audio and video documentation are manifest since, as noted earlier, without being able to get closer to passages of interest, researchers simply are not able to explore collections given the time demanded by listening to or viewing tapes – which is exactly why most audio and video archives are so under-utilized. It is a limiting notion even in traditional terms, since indexing, for hundreds of years, has offered flexible tools for identifying meaning as well as content, with no privileging or narrowing of opportunities in the process: when the index of a book directs readers to page 312 they have access to the full text surrounding the identified point or passage. The traditional book index is, in this sense, less a restrictive filter or funnel than it is a kind of hyper-textual alternative to linear reading. Minimally, it can be said that a broad middle ground between, and combining indexing and cataloging, content and meaning – a zone very much supported by new information tools and capacities – is only beginning to be recognized and understood as it applies to oral history collection management and use.

In oral history, the major response to this challenge in many of the leading archives managing digital audio-video collections has been the general reliance on text as the route to more specific passages of audio and video data, through embedded time-coded links between transcription and particular portions of videos. Word-based searches speak to some of the archivists' concerns in that they remain content-based, rather than driven by researcher-imposed themes, inquiries, or categories. And increasingly sophisticated word-search tools move beyond the overly literal clumping of 'hits': context and proximity links, for example, can help distinguish a search interested in 'bomb' and 'airplane' from one focused on 'bomb' and 'Broadway.'

But the limits of this approach are clearly the inverse of its strengths, which is why many approaches, including a number of those referenced above, have been seeking to transcend the limits of text for reaching both non-lexical content and information, and dimensions of meaning or cross-referencing not explicit in the words of an interview. In this regard, the degree and form of text-reliance in searching and organizing can be identified as a third axis along which current approaches are arrayed. At one end of this spectrum is total reliance on text – all searches based on the words in transcripts synchronized seamlessly to the audio or video stream. At the other end is no reliance on transcription – with searching or navigation based on cross-referencing independent of interview transcripts. Most approaches are coming to be located somewhere in between these poles, with various combinations of transcript-based and transcript-independent cross-referencing.

There is one final dimension useful to appreciate in considering the way approaches to working with audio and video documentation have been evolving. Imagine a spectrum at one end which is the essentially linear, funnel-like nature of search-engine queries, in which all possible references are treated similarly and the search is narrowed or particularized by restrictive or inclusive combinations that can zoom in on a more and more manageable group of 'hits.' At the other end of the spectrum is the multi-dimensional or multi-field approach of a relational database, in which any piece of data can be identified in an unlimited number of discrete fields each of which can offer a range of values or choices in relation to a given object.

A neighborhood, for instance, can be identified as having a particular ethnic composition, a particular socio-economic status, an architectural character, a density level, or a value of whatever variable might be of interest – it is the same neighborhood, but it can be identified in terms of its particular value in any of these variable fields. What can seem new and intimidating when terms like 'relational database' are used has actually been quite common for a long time in common-sense usage. In book indexes, for instance, a passage may be given a range of identifiers that in turn may be listed both individually and under broader subheadings. A cookbook might have a recipe for a Greek lamb stew indexed by ethnic origin, by type of dish, and by both the general 'meat' and the specific 'lamb' – the variables are completely independent, and the book can be explored by initiating searches through any of them, in any order, which reveals how they are related and combined in the attributes of each recipe. Such notions apply to meaning-mapping as well. In confronting demanding academic or scholarly books, I've told my students for years, it's always a good idea to study the index, which can be seen as offering an overview of the book's central concerns and approach. These are made particularly vivid in the way master-idea headings jump out at the reader via the long indented lists of references and sub-references that such headings – and not others less central to the argument – command.

These approaches require notions of generality and categorization that are necessarily other than literal, and rarely found by word searches. In electronic form, such approaches become more and more powerful, as if the entire book were being re-indexed on demand – with its content displayed and organized through the lens of any particular field or combination of fields. The ease of manipulation and navigation, and the analytic capacity these confer, is one reason why contemporary information tools have so dramatically advanced the power of fluid, relational approaches to information. It means the same content can easily be explored from a variety of contrasting directions. In our childhood story project, for instance, the same anecdote might be located by searching choices in a typology of biographical stories (say, conflict with parents), or by searching a typology of historical or cultural topics (say, the Civil Rights movement). And unlike random searches that might combine such explicit terms, in these modes a richer exploration is possible – for instance, we could select all stories about conflict with parents sub-sorted by historical topic, or, alternatively, we could select all stories about the Civil Rights movement sub-sorted by biographical theme. Either route would lead to our selected combination – conflict with parents and the Civil Rights movement – but in getting there we would also have a chance to discover and explore a wide range of combinations we might never have thought to look for.

Taken together, then, our map of emergent approaches to working with audio-video materials involves four overlapping, interrelated, but conceptually and operationally distinct dimensions, or axes: (1) from cataloging to indexing; (2) from content-referencing to meaning or qualitative analysis referencing; (3) from text-transcript based audio or video access to direct or observational cross-referencing of audio or video as such; and (4) from linear search-engine tools to relational databased mapping of audio and video documentation.

At the current moment, many leading approaches to digital oral history collections in general, and to accessing their audio and video content in particular, remain closer to the first-mentioned end of each of these dimensions: they are closer to cataloging than indexing, to content-mapping than to meaning-mapping, to transcript-driven searches than to non-transcript or observational referencing, and to linear searches rather than relational database approaches to organization and navigation. These preferences are driven to a certain degree by scale, to an additional degree by the archival and library collection-management auspices of most of these projects, and to some extent as well by the state of current technology.

Those software approaches originating in researcher or user-driven qualitative analysis, or outside oral history in fields such as digital asset management or market research, have been exploring the other end of each of these dimensions, as illustrated by some of the examples from my own practice previously discussed.

I think it can safely be said that these distinctions are all very much in motion – much of the 'action' in current software development for oral history applications involves seeking various ways in which the capacities of every approach can be combined and more effectively mobilized for working with the audio-video documentation at the heart of all oral history.

And what all of these approaches have in common, what defines the current and prospective development of the field in this regard, is that one way or the other, from large-scale archive to small community project to home and family collections, it is going to be more and more feasible to hear, see, browse, search, study, refine, select, export, and make use of audio and video extracts from oral histories directly – through directly engaging the documentation itself. In the future that is rapidly unfolding I can claim with considerable confidence that this mode, rather than piles or even files of text transcription, will become the primary, preferred way to explore and use oral history. And that returns us to the problem with which this chapter began – the implications of 'putting the oral back in oral history,' in terms of theory, practice, and most especially use, that flow from this profound reorientation to the core orality, voice, and embodiment found in oral history documents.

Beyond raw and cooked: documentary and oral history in the digital age

Documentary has been the mode in which oral history has most generally, and usefully, been mobilized for communicative, historical, and political purposes. As such, documentary has been in effect the long-standing solution of choice to the problem I have identified here. It has been the main resource for engaging and presenting those realms of meaning embodied in oral and embodied performance, the realms and dimensions that make our oral history collections valuable as such. Whatever the particular approach or format, documentary involves, virtually by definition, an exploration of a broader body of documentation in search of desired qualities or content, which leads in turn to a evocative product – some selection, arrangement, incorporation, and presentation of meaning grounded in that documentation, which takes the form of a presentation – whether film, video, exhibit, book, radio presentation, CD, or DVD.

In documentary, of course, the 'naturalness' or inevitability of text transcription is not the unexamined core assumption, though neither is its opposite, the subordination of text, since the documentary approach can be similar whether the object is a film or a book such as Theodore Rosengarten's *All God's Dangers: The Life of Nate Shaw* or my own *Portraits in Steel* in which oral histories were combined with Milton Rogovin's photographs so that images and text could represent parallel and resonant modes of documentary portraiture.[3]

Rather, the central assumption in documentary is the inevitability and indeed – as I have argued elsewhere – the indispensability of editorial intervention, selection, shaping, arrangement, and even manipulation. Documents may be found, even if this is perhaps less straightforward a matter than it can seem. But everyone understands that documentaries are not found – they are made, although it is also easy to avoid thinking carefully about what is involved in the process. Rather than mediating oral history through text, documentary requires the mediating of the oral history as a whole through some critical intelligence – the editor's, the artist's, the director's, the curator's, the producer's.

Put differently, if audio-video oral history content itself has characteristically been seen as 'raw' documentation almost impossible to search or navigate analytically, oral history documentation has become meaningful, shareable, and usable only when it is 'cooked' in the form of a documentary selection or arrangement and then served up to consumers. This 'cooking' has seemed as necessary, natural, and inevitable in documentary as text transcription has seemed in working with oral history collections. Whatever the uses, political content, community purpose, or artistic and expressive intent, documentary has always presumed this kind of culinary role.

But what happens if that assumption, too, can be dramatically recast, or discarded altogether, when the potential of new technological tools is fully unfolded? Let me suggest two lines of approach that describe what is, in fact, happening already, each of which speaks to this question.

One – the more obvious and visible to date – involves the crucial issue of access and privilege, where new modes are so dramatically democratizing access to the tools and processes of documentary production as to transform the approach profoundly. The most immediate and dramatic effect of new tools and techniques is to distribute widely the capacity for documentary production. The digital revolution has taken film from the darkroom and the movie studio into anyone's computer and elementary school classroom. It is redistributing to students, families, teachers, artists, social scientists, and activists the capacity to manage and exploit extensive bodies of documentation, and to produce meaningful versions of it. All now have, easily at hand, exciting and increasingly affordable tools for consolidating and communicating the meanings they find in materials that matter to them, and for purposes that matter to them.

The radical simplification and distribution of what had been highly restricted skills and equipment is, in this sense, surely transforming what up to now has been the privilege of the documentary producer – a transformation with political implications that are as unbounded as they are straightforward. A wide-open door changes not only access, but the very nature of what takes place within, of what can be done, by whom and for what purposes.

However, there is another implication of new technology that is far less obvious, but potentially even more powerful and transformative. Here I refer to the implicit challenge posed to the assumption of pathed linearity, an assumption embedded in documentary production.

Most documentaries, even experimental ones that challenge the form, are necessarily versions – a selection out of a broader body of material. They represent a linear product: a path, through the material that embodies, supports, represents, or evokes a story being told, a point being made, a context or mood or texture being evoked and conveyed. This is the definitional difference between documentation and documentary. But it is precisely this distinction, as such, that new tools are subverting in some potentially very exciting ways.

Consider that fundamental quality of digital media noted earlier, and familiar to anyone who has made the shift from tapes to listening to CDs or watching DVDs: in digital modes, all information is instantly accessible, at will. One can get anywhere, and go anywhere, instantly. Capacities in this regard are limited or expanded only by the modes in which the digital content is organized and mapped.

Almost all production in film and video now is taking place in such digital modes, and oral history editing is rapidly moving into this realm as well: it can safely be predicted that in ten years tape will not be used at all in any form, whether magnetic or DAT. There will be little use for and of CD-ROMs. All material will be in digital file formats for editing, and for recording as well, as witness the new generation of recorders that continue, quaintly, to look like tape recorders but in actuality are small computers with enhanced audio- and video-recording capacity.

This digital transformation has only begun to be appreciated, even – perhaps especially – by those who work with these media routinely. Michael Haller, developer of the indexing software *Interclipper*, began as a documentary film-maker, and he likes to observe that while everyone is now doing their editing and production in non-linear digital editing modes they still approach what they are producing in linear, analog terms: as a documentary that will begin here and end there, telling its story through a sequential arrangement of whatever materials are selected and refined through the digital editing process, and leaving everything else behind, obscured in the archive or collection or left as out-takes from which the selection emerged.

Towards a post-documentary sensibility

What would a contrasting approach to documentary be like, one that proceeded from the fluid, flexible, multi-pathed non-linear access to core documentation? The new modalities for working with oral history documentation discussed in the first part of this chapter all suggest powerfully that emphasis can and will shift from the final documentary to a notion at the core of which is located the body of documentation in a searchable and easily navigated and used database environment – a platform for the generation of paths and versions on a far more fluid, ongoing basis. In such modes, every search and inquiry can lead to a different focus, or material for a different story, and each one is as instantly and continually as accessible and easily constructed as any other.

To take a prosaic but instructive example, imagine the family video collections that millions are now being encouraged to transform, via their iMacs or the like, into little documentary movies. And ask whether instead of one, two, or even a file folder full of such pre-cast movies it wouldn't be more interesting to imagine the material so organized and accessible that such a path could be instantly generated in response to any visiting relative, or a child's birthday, or a grandparent's funeral, or the sale of a house in the hometown, or whatever might be occasioning interest in the relevant resources found in the video record. Such a located selection could easily be displayed, saved, and worked into a presentational form, if it proved interesting, or, it could be released to return to the database, awaiting some later inquiry or use.

Such notions apply to more complex settings and to more complex collections of documentation, wherein accessibility for very different dimensions of question, evaluation, and application would make an easily navigable map far more useful and interesting than a pre-selected itinerary. This is precisely what new modes offer, and, as this is realized, so too is the potential to imagine documentary itself as a natural extension of such non-linear modes rather than as a linear path and destination. In this way, the documentary impulse and intelligence becomes more responsive, contingent, and shareable. This is not a new idea by any means, and in fact its ancient provenance offers yet another dimension in which new tools ought best be seen as permitting a return and rediscovery, rather than an invocation to invention. Any reference work is a compilation of answers awaiting questions as, indeed, is any book – the instantly and fluidly navigable book being in this sense the mother of all hypertext instruments in contrast to the scrolls it so easily superseded centuries ago. In this very same sense, new tools need only mean that audio and video documentation can become a similarly liberating, flexible resource for whatever questions and uses, situationally, are presented, and by whatever diversity of users.

It seems to me the implications of such a reorientation of our relation to documentary source material are suggestive, and potentially quite profound in practice. Beyond returning the power of 'voice' in oral history, digital indexing of audio and video thus speaks to political questions central to oral history discourse. The much-touted democratic promise of oral history has been in fact usually restricted either to the 'input' into collections, or to the audience receipt of 'output.' In between has been the author, the mediator, the documentary film-maker, the TV or radio producer – the shapers of whatever is selected from those oral histories for representation in public forms, whether through films, exhibits, books, radio and TV documentaries, and the like.

I am arguing here that new digital tools open the significant non linear, fluidly multi-pathed ground between these poles. Because audio-video indexing means the entire content can be usefully, intelligently, instrumentally searched and accessed at a rich level, it becomes a great deal more than a 'raw' collection. And the same tools providing that access permit anyone, continually, to 'cook' – to explore a collection and select and order meaningful materials. In other words, documentary representation becomes a democratically shareable process. Implicit in this approach are whole new modes of publication and public access. Imagine, for example, the value of producing a broadly distributed collection of richly mapped and thoroughly searchable interviews, music, and performance, or other field documentation, in which users might find and make their own meanings. In producing such a documentary source, authorship would reside not in fixed path-making but rather in the richness and openness of the mapping coordinates, codes, and finding tools offered to users.

Such modalities suggest something even more significant and potentially transformative in our relationship to audio and video documentation itself – a deeply and essentially non-linear orientation that I will term a post-documentary sensibility. With accessible, meaningful, fluid, and non-privileged access to the content of oral history, the authority of the mediating intelligence or documentary authorship is displaced by a shareable, dialogic capacity to explore, select, order, and interpret.

In this mode, the privilege of a fixed documentary version that necessarily marginalizes other meanings or stories in the material – the very notion of documentary as product – is displaced by a notion of documentary as process; that is, as an ongoing, contextually contingent, fluid construction of meaning. In so doing,

I suggest, new digital tools and the rich landscape of practice they define may become powerful resources in restoring one of the original appeals of oral history – to open new dimensions of understanding and engagement through the broadly inclusive sharing and interrogation of memory.

Notes

1   References discussing history, oral history, and the digital revolution include: T.J. Bond, 'Streaming audio from African American oral history collections', *OCLS Systems & Services*, 2004, vol. 20, no. 1, pp. 15–23; G.A. Crothers, '"Bringing history to life": oral history, community research, and multiple levels of learning', *Journal of American History*, 2002, vol. 88, no. 4, pp. 1446–1451; T. Fogg, 'Using new computer technology for oral history interviews and archival research', *American Educational History Journal*, 2001, vol. 28, pp. 135–141; M. Larson, 'Beyond the page: non-print oral history resources for educators', *Oral History Review*, 1998, vol. 25, nos 1–2, pp. 129–135; D.A. Ritchie, 'The changing current of oral history', *History News*, 2004, vol. 59, no. 1, pp. 7–10; D.A. Ritchie, *Doing Oral History: A Practical Guide*, Oxford: Oxford University Press, 2003, pp. 79–84, 171–179 and 245–251; R. Rosenzweig, A. McMichael, *et al.*, 'Historians and the web: a guide', *Perspectives: American Historical Association Newsletter*, 1996, vol. 34, no. 1, pp. 11–15; R. Rosenzweig, 'Scarcity or abundance: preserving the past in a digital era', *American Historical Review*, 2003, vol. 108, no. 3, pp. 735–762; E.D. Swain, 'Oral history in the archives: its documentary role in the twenty-first century', *American Archivist*, 2003, vol. 66, no. 1, pp.139–158; T.M. Weis, R. Benmayor, *et al.*, 'Digital technologies and pedagogies', *Social Justice*, 2002, vol. 29, no. 4, pp. 153–168; C. Wilmsen, 'For the record: editing and the production of meaning in oral history', *Oral History Review*, 2001, vol. 28, no. 1, pp. 65–85.
2   A. Kolovos, posting to H-Oral Discussion List, 17 November, 2004.
3   T. Rosengarten's *All God's Dangers: The Life of Nate Shaw*, New York, Knopf, 1974; M. Frisch and M. Rogovin, *Portraits in Steel*, Ithaca, N.Y.: Cornell University Press, 1993.

PART II

Interviewing: introduction

EXACTLY WHEN HISTORIANS BEGAN TO USE interviews to gather information, and whether this can be characterized as 'oral history interviewing', has been much debated. As early as the fifth century BC Greek historian Herodotus was questioning eye witnesses, and in early eighth-century England the Venerable Bede, author of the *History of the English Church and People*, often valued oral evidence over hagiographic paper records. At the end of the eighteenth century Samuel Johnson argued, in the absence of documentary sources, for a series of interviews with participants in the 1745 Scottish rebellion against the English, remarking that 'all history was at first oral'.[1] Yet these were perhaps exceptions as interviewing was not until recently a technique routinely embraced by a historical profession largely fixated on paper-based research and frequently hostile to eye-witness and interview data. In other spheres, we know that journalists were routinely using interviews from the middle of the nineteenth century onwards, and by the turn of the twentieth century anthropologists and social investigators were valuing interview evidence.[2] Both were influences on the emergence of the modern oral history movement that forced the reassessment by historians of the interviewing methodology, as Part I of this volume has shown. The invention of recorded sound at the end of the nineteenth century, and particularly the advent of portable tape-recorders in the 1950s, liberated researchers from laborious note-taking, at the same time focusing attention on the *process* of recording memory.[3] That initial *frisson* of hearing the authentic voice and the excited discovery of previously undocumented memory has given way to more acute reflection about the interview relationship. It is this that we explore in this section.

Fittingly, it is an interview about interviewing that opens the section, as two masters of the tape-recorded interview discuss technique. Studs Terkel, an icon of US radio talk shows and the author of many best-selling oral history books, talks to Tony Parker, often described as Britain's own 'Studs Terkel', who made his reputation writing interview-based books about prisoners and offenders.[4] It is an invigorating encounter. Terkel starts by characterizing the interviewer as an explorer, making up the rules, but nonetheless outlines the kind of practical advice which is to be found in a plethora of oral history handbooks: not appearing too obsessed by the equipment; the importance of establishing rapport and intimacy, of listening and of asking open-ended questions; not interrupting; allowing for pauses and silences; informality; probing, and above all remembering that 'people aren't boring'.[5]

The essential skill of listening is explored further by Kathryn Anderson and Dana Jack who argue that in 'uncovering women's perspectives' the interviewer needs to shift from 'information gathering to interaction', moving beyond facts to subjective feelings, by listening more carefully not only to what is said but what is meant.[6] When interviewing women we need to learn to listen 'in stereo', they argue, to both women's dominant and muted channels of thought.[7] Although as interviewers we are active participants in the process, we need to set aside preconceived structures and interpretations of our own. We must be vigilant to discrepancies between what is said through the conventions of ordinary social conversation and the meanings that lie beneath. Listening for 'meta-statements' or reflections, for silences and for internal inconsistency, becomes vital.

Dana Jack's background as a psychoanalyst encourages different kinds of readings of one-to-one interviews that have since been developed by other oral historians, raising notions of transference, counter-transference and 'collaboration'. They argue that too much attention has been placed on analysing the actual words spoken in an interview, which is not merely a narrative but a relationship with two subjectivities at play and informed by unconscious dynamics.[8] As Valerie Yow's chapter in Part I outlines, this 'conceptual shift' towards a recognition of the interviewer's own subjective reactions to, and involvement in, the interview encounter has informed the way we have been thinking about oral history over the past two decades.

As oral history techniques have been adopted all over the world, there has been a growing awareness that interviewing is significantly more both complex and culturally specific: that the methods taken for granted by oral historians in the 'developed world' of the North can be wholly inappropriate for researchers in the South. This is the focus of the chapter by Slim and Thompson on collecting oral testimony in developing countries, in which they characterize the one-to-one interview as a 'dangerously intimate encounter' and emphasize the value of group remembering. Drawing on the work of anthropologists, they point out that in certain societies storytelling has a season (often winter) and that researchers need to be aware of local hierarchies and 'norms relating to turn-taking' which differ markedly from interviewing in the North.[9] Whilst other oral historians have written of eliciting memories through introducing photographs[10] and objects[11] into the interview, Slim and Thompson highlight the value of visual techniques when gathering testimony in communities unfamiliar with the interview form: time-lines, maps and diagrams become expressions of personal and collective memory. They also explore alternative, and equally valid interview approaches: family-tree interviewing, single-issue testimony, diary interviewing, focus groups and community interviews. In Part V of this volume we explore how the context for the conduct of interviews, for example a legal tribunal investigating land rights or reconciliation, might affect the stories that are told and how they are understood.

In an extract from *Women of Phokeng*, a study of black South African women which seeks to assess the 'consciousness of the powerless' in a society of 'inequality and brutality', Belinda Bozzoli picks up the issues around culturally specific interviewing raised by Slim and Thompson and goes on to argue that her colleague Mmantho's successful interviewing was due to her 'insider' status as a local, black female, speaking the same dialect as her interviewees and from the same class. Whilst some historians believe 'outsider' status accords objectivity and detachment, an 'insider' perspective has the benefits of special insight otherwise obscure to outsiders. Bozzoli observes that a spontaneous and unstructured questioning approach of informal exchanges had yielded the most subjective and revealing results.[12] Yet she also found that there was a clear interaction between interviewer and interviewee that shaped the latter's perception of self-identity, highlighting the need for an acute self-awareness by the interviewer of his or her own agenda.

Cross-cultural interviewing is the focus of Susan Burton's reflections as an English woman interviewing Japanese women living in England. In this case she explores the insider/outsider debate in the context of language and notes the cultural differences between languages: that Japanese is, she argues, an intrinsically hierarchical and gendered language, better at creating context and mood, and avoiding conflict, than arriving at clear conclusions.[13] Ultimately, 'Perhaps the true strength of cross-cultural interviewing is that it can help to represent the real cultural and linguistic contradictions of the Japanese women's migration experiences.'[14]

Whilst there has been critical writing about cross-cultural interviewing in recent years, this has been less obvious in the case of family history interviewing, frequently assumed by novice interviewers to be a good starting point but in fact a type of interviewing fraught with problems.[15] There are thorny issues around family myth and memory; there are pitfalls in using the interview technique alongside paper-based family records such as parish records and census returns; and there are practical considerations about whether or not to interview a husband and wife together. Ruth Finnegan draws on her own family's migration experience to reveal the challenges of recording conflicting versions of the 'same' family story. She notes how seemingly simple stories might have a mythic status within the family as key 'turning points': the origin of bitter quarrels or love-matches.[16] The value of oral testimony for family historians is not in doubt, but the complexities of the family context need careful evaluation.

Moving to another mode of interview practice, oral history with people with learning disabilities, Jan Walmsley interrogates the life story or 'biographical chronology' form of interviewing that many oral historians now espouse as the most effective means of contextualizing specific disability experiences. Like Joanna Bornat and Daniel Kerr in Part V she draws lessons from the use of reminiscence or life review in a caring, 'therapeutic' context, and in interviewing vulnerable and less verbally articulate groups. For Walmsley, life story interviews with people with learning difficulties present a challenge, and she emphasizes that adaptations have to be made to the research process if the interviewer's aims are to be fully explained and disempowered people are to have a voice.[17] She found that one-to-one interviews are not always possible and that her interviewees often have carers functioning as participant intermediaries, who in some cases try to control the content and circumstances of the interview.

Ensuring 'informed consent' is never straightforward in any interview context and oral history groups and associations around the world have attempted to address the moral issue of ownership by rendering the power relationship inherent in the interview situation into codes of ethics and interview guidelines.[18] These have, of course, been made more and more complex as interview extracts and transcripts are digitized, packaged and made available to new world-wide audiences via the internet.[19] Only recently have oral historians begun to consider the possible impact of this new open-ended, uncontrolled dissemination on the interview relationship itself.[20]

We close Part II with a piece about an aspect of interviewing which has preoccupied novice and experienced interviewers alike: traumatic remembering. Mark Klempner draws on his own interviews with Holocaust survivors, and writings from psychology and 'traumatology', to offer advice to interviewers in grappling with traumatic narratives. He argues that interviewers need to accept a role in the narrator's quest for 'closure' and prepare themselves to exhibit 'a greater degree of both sensitivity and sturdiness than is normally brought to a life review'. He cautions us not to resist or deny what we are hearing, but also to be mindful that the interviewee might have better-developed coping mechanisms in place than the interviewer.[21] Like Mark Roseman in Part III, Klempner highlights the impact that trauma has on narratives and how they are shaped over time.

Some writers, including Elie Wiesel, have suggested that the Holocaust is so traumatic and so utterly removed from 'normal' human experience that it can never be spoken about directly, and that it can only be evoked through silence.[22] Listening for silences, as much as for words, thus becomes central to the interviewing relationship; they provide new layers of meaning. As Luisa Passerini has remarked, 'There is no "work of memory" without a corresponding "work of forgetting".'[23] Yet amongst at least some survivors of trauma this is complicated by a compelling desire to 'bear witness' (examples include survivors from the Soviet 'Gulag' and Central America in Part V). The need to speak out to prevent similar atrocities from happening again tests our understanding of the relationship between what is remembered but not verbalized, and what becomes public memory through being shared.

We have travelled a long way from those early oral historians who tended to see themselves as slightly aloof from the data-gathering process, who believed that merely asking sensible questions could extract useful information which they could use themselves for their own research. Not only is the interview now viewed as a co-construction, a dynamic process of interactivity where there is a recognition that the interviewer takes a major role in shaping the interview, but we now recognize that there is a complex multiplicity of gendered, cultural and identity-specific variables that we must negotiate as interviewers.

Notes

1   For example: P. Thompson, *The Voice of the Past: Oral History*, Oxford: Oxford University Press, 3rd edition, 2000, chapter 2; C. Morrissey, 'Why call it oral history?

Searching for early use of a generic term', *Oral History Review*, 1980, vol. 8, pp. 20–48.

2   C. Silvester (ed.), *The Penguin Book of Interviews*: *An Anthology from 1859 to the Present Day*, London: Viking, 1993; H. Mayhew, *London Labour and the London Poor*, London, 1851, is a good early example. Also A. Fontana and J.H. Frey, 'The interview: from neutral stance to political involvement', in N.K. Denzin and Y.S. Lincoln (eds), *The Sage Handbook of Qualitative Research*, Thousand Oaks, Calif.: Sage, 3rd edition, 2005.

3   The advent of video recording was expected to have a major impact on oral history but in actual fact the vast majority of oral history practitioners continue to use audio only, and there have been some fears expressed about the impact of a camera (and additional staff) on the intimacy of the interview encounter, although this has been very little written about, important exceptions being D. Ritchie's good overview, 'Videotaping oral history', chapter five in his *Doing Oral History*: *A Practical Guide*, New York: Oxford University Press, 2nd edition, 2003; T.A. Shorzman, *A Practical Introduction to Videohistory*: *The Smithsonian Institution and Alfred P. Sloan Foundation Experiment*, Krieger, 1993, which surveys the field; Brad Jolly, *Videotaping Local History*, Nashville, Tenn.: American Association for State and Local History, 1982; S. Humphries, 'Unseen stories: video history in museums', *Oral History*, 2003, vol. 31, no. 2, pp. 75–84; A. Lichtblau, 'Facing audiovisual history', paper presented to the XIIIth International Oral History Association conference, Rome, June 2004; and Dan Sipe's chapter in Part IV.

4   Studs Terkel (1912–) published his first book in 1956, and since then: *Division Street*: *America*, 1967; *Hard Times*: *An Oral History of the Great Depression*, 1970; *Working*: *People Talk About What They Do All Day and How They Feel About What They Do*, 1974; *The 'Good War'*: *An Oral History of World War Two*, 1984; *Race*: *How Blacks and Whites Think and Feel About the American Obsession*, 1992; *Will the Circle Be Unbroken?*: *Reflections on Death and Dignity*, 2001. Tony Parker (1923–96): *Five Women*, London: Hutchinson, 1965; *The Frying Pan*: *A Prison and its Prisoners*, London: Hutchinson, 1970; *Lighthouse*, London: Hutchinson, 1975; *The People of Providence*: *A Housing Estate and Some of its Inhabitants*, London: Hutchinson, 1983; *Soldier, Soldier*, London: Heinemann, 1985; *Life after Life*: *Interviews with Twelve Murderers*, London: Secker & Warburg, 1990; *Russian Voices*, London: Jonathan Cape, 1991; *The Violence of Our Lives*: *Interviews with Life-Sentence Prisoners in America*, London: HarperCollins, 1995. His last book was *Studs Terkel*: *A Life in Words*, London: HarperCollins, 1997, from which our opening chapter in Part II is taken. See also P. Thompson, 'Tony Parker: writer and oral historian', *Oral History*, 1994, vol. 22 no. 2, pp. 64–73.

5   For example: V.R. Yow, *Recording Oral History*: *A Guide for the Humanities and Social Sciences*, Walnut Creek, Calif.: AltaMira Press, 2nd edition, 2005; D. Ritchie, *Doing Oral History*; R. Perks, *Oral History*: *Talking about the Past*, London: The Historical Association, 1995; P. Hayes, *Speak for Yourself*, Namibia: Longman, 1992; E.D. Ives, *The Tape-Recorded Interview*: *A Manual for Field Workers in Folklore and Oral History*, Knoxville: University of Tennessee Press, 1980; K. Kann, 'Reconstructing the history of a community', *International Journal of Oral History*, 1981, vol. 2 no. 1, pp. 4–12. For research-based life story and biographical interviewing in other disciplines see: E.G. Mishler, *Research Interviewing*: *Context and Narrative*, Cambridge, Mass.: Harvard University Press, 1986; C.L. Briggs, *Learning How To Ask*: *A Sociolinguistic Appraisal of the Role of the Interview in Social Science Research*, Cambridge: Cambridge University Press, 1986; R. Atkinson, *The Life Story Interview*: *Qualitative Research Methods Series 44*, London: Sage, 1998; R. Legard, J. Keegan and K. Ward, 'In-depth interviews', in J. Ritchie and J. Lewis (eds), *Qualitative Research Practice*: *A Guide for Social Science Students and Researchers*, London: Sage, 2003, pp. 139–169; B. Roberts, *Biographical Research*, Milton Keynes: Open University

Press, 2002; C. Seale, G. Giampieto, J.F. Gubrium and D. Silverman, *Qualitative Research Practice*, London: Sage, 2004. C. Morrissey, 'On oral history interviewing', in L.A. Dexter (ed.), *Elite and Specialised Interviewing*, Evanston, Ill.: Northwestern University Press, 1970, pp. 109–118, remains an excellent overview, and he offers a valuable and amusing blow-by-blow critique of an interview in 'John Hawkes on tape: the paradox of self-identity in a recorded interview', *International Journal of Oral History*, 1985, vol. 6, no. 1. A. Seldon and J. Pappworth, *By Word of Mouth: 'Elite' Oral History*, London: Methuen, 1983, surveys the field of elite interviewing very effectively. On the challenges of political interviewing see Blee in Part III this volume, and C. Romalis, 'Political volatility and historical accounts: tiptoeing through contested ground', *Canadian Oral History Association Journal*, 1992, vol. 12, pp. 25–29.

6   On feminist interviewing, see Armitage and Gluck in Part I for an overview, and other essays in both S.H. Armitage with P. Hart and K. Weatherman (eds), *Women's Oral History: The Frontiers Reader*, Lincoln: University of Nebraska Press, 2002; and in the excellent anthology by S.B. Gluck and D. Patai (eds), *Women's Words: The Feminist Practice of Oral History*, London: Routledge, 1991. Also A. Oakley, 'Interviewing women: a contradiction in terms', in H. Roberts, *Doing Feminist Research*, London: Routledge, 1981, pp. 30–61; R. Edwards, 'Connecting method and epistemology: a white woman interviewing black women', *Women's Studies International Forum*, 1990, vol. 13 no. 5, pp. 477–490; J. Scanlon, 'Challenging the imbalances of power in feminist oral history: developing a take-and-give methodology', *Women's Studies International Forum*, 1993, vol. 16, no. 6, pp. 639–645; A. Janson, 'Respecting silences: recording the lives of immigrant women', *Oral History in New Zealand*, 1990/1, no. 3, pp. 11–13; P. Atkinson, A. Coffey and S. Delamont (eds), *Key Themes in Qualitative Research: Continuities and Change*, Walnut Creek, Calif.: AltaMira Press, 2003; T. Cosslett, C. Lurie and P. Summerfield (eds), *Feminism and Autobiography: Texts, Theories, Methods*, London: Routledge, 2000, pp. 154–166.

7   I. Bertaux-Wiame, 'The life story approach in the study of internal migration', *Oral History*, 1979, vol. 7, no. 1, pp. 26–32, discusses how men and women reminisce in different ways. Also C. Daley, '"He would know, but I just have a feeling": gender and oral history', *Women's History Review*, 1998, vol. 7, no. 3, pp. 343–359.

8   M. Roper, 'Analysing the analysed: transference and counter-transference in the oral history encounter', *Oral History*, 2003, vol. 31, no. 2, pp. 20–32; P. Summerfield, 'Dis/composing the subject: Intersubjectivities in oral history', in T. Cosslet, C. Lurie and P. Summerfield (eds), *Feminism and Autobiography. Texts, Theories, Methods*, London: Routledge, 2000; A.J. Rouverol, '"I was content and not content": oral history and the collaborative process', *Oral History*, 2000, vol. 28, no. 2, pp. 66–78; A. Turnbull, 'Collaboration and censorship in the oral history interview', *International Journal of Social Research Methodology*, 2000, vol. 3, no. 1, pp. 15–34.

9   See, for example, E. Tonkin, *Narrating Our Pasts: The Social Construction of Oral History*, Cambridge: Cambridge University Press, 1992; and R. Finnegan, *Oral Tradition and the Verbal Arts*, London, Routledge, 1991; T. Giles-Vernick, 'Lives, histories, and sites of recollection', in L. White, S.F. Miescher and D.W. Cohen (eds), *African Words, African Voices: Critical Practices in Oral History*, Bloomington: Indiana University Press, 2001, pp. 194–213.

10   J. Modell and C. Brodsky, 'Envisioning homestead: using photographs in interviewing', in E.M. McMahan and K. Lacey Rogers (eds), *Interactive Oral History Interviewing*, Hillsdale, N.J., Erlbaum, 1994, pp. 141–161; R. Samuel, *Theatres of Memory*, London: Verso, 1994; A. Kuhn, *Family Secrets: Acts of Memory and Imagination*, London: Verso, 1995; M. Hirsch, *Family Frames: Photographs, Narrative and Postmemory*, London: Routledge, 1997; D. James, 'Listening in the cold: the practice of oral history in the Argentine meatpacking community' – in his book *Dona María's Story: Life History, Memory and Political Identity*, Durham, N.C.: Duke University Press, 2001, pp. 119–142.

11 For example G.E. Evans, 'Approaches to interviewing', *Oral History*, 1973, vol. 1, no. 4, pp. 56–71; P. Denis and N. Makiwane, 'Stories of love, pain and courage: AIDS orphans and memory boxes', *Oral History*, 2003, vol. 31, no. 2, pp. 66–74.

12 Whether it is helpful to have a questionnaire or question structure has been much debated. See Thompson, *The Voice of the Past*, chapter 7, for a summary.

13 The issue of interviewing in a second language and through an interpreter is explored in M. Andrews, 'A monoglot abroad: working through problems of translation', *Oral History*, 1995, vol. 23, no. 2, pp. 47–50; and N. North, 'Narratives of Cambodian refugees: issues in the collection of refugee stories', *Oral History*, 1995, vol. 23, no. 2, pp. 32–39.

14 Other key writings on cross-cultural interviewing include J. Cruikshank, *The Social Life of Stories*: *Narrative and Knowledge in the Yukon Territory*, Lincoln: University of Nebraska Press, 1998; Y.J. Kopijn, 'The oral history interview in a cross cultural setting: an analysis of its linguistic, social and ideological structure', in M. Chamberlain and P. Thompson (eds), *Narrative and Genre*: *Contexts and Types of Communication*, New Brunswick, N.J.: Transaction Publishers, 2004 (previously Routledge, 1998); B. Sansome, 'In the absence of vita as genre. The making of the Roy Kelly story', in B. Attwood and F. Magowan (eds), *Telling Stories*: *Indigenous History and Memory in Australia and New Zealand*, Crows Nest, New South Wales: Allen & Unwin, 2001, pp. 99–122; R.J. Grele, 'History and the languages of history in the oral history interview: who answers whose questions and why', in McMahan and Lacey Rogers, *Interactive Oral History Interviewing*, 1994, pp. 141–161; E.M. McMahan, *Elite Oral History Discourse*: *A Study of Cooperation and Coherence*, Tuscaloosa: University of Alabama, 1989.

15 For a good overview of the issues involved in family interviewing see V.R. Yow, *Recording Oral History*, 2005, chapter 9; also L. Shopes, 'Using oral history for a family history project', in D.K. Dunaway and W.K. Baum (eds), *Oral History*: *An Interdisciplinary Anthology*, Walnut Creek, Calif.: AltaMira, 1996, pp. 231–240; A. Kikumura, 'Family life histories: a collaborative venture', *Oral History Review*, 1986, vol. 14, pp. 1–7; *Oral History Association of Australia Journal*, 1981–2, vol. 4: special issue on 'Family and local history'; C. Parekowhai, 'Korero taku whaea: Talk my aunt. Learning to listen to Maori women', *Oral History in New Zealand*, 1992, no. 4, pp. 1–4; R.L. Miller, *Researching Life Stories and Family Histories*, London: Sage 1999. On interviewing friends see M. Zukas, 'Friendship as oral history: a feminist psychologist's view', *Oral History*, 1993, vol. 21, no. 2, pp. 73–79; P. Cotterill, 'Interviewing women: issues of friendship, vulnerability and power', *Women's Studies International Forum*, 1992, vol. 15, nos 5/6, pp. 593–606; M. Stuart, 'And how was it for you Mary? Self identity and meaning for oral historians', *Oral History*, 1993, vol. 21, no. 1, pp. 80–83; D. Treleven, 'Interviewing a close friend: First Amendment activist Frank Wilkinson', *Journal of American History*, 1998, vol. 82, no. 2, pp. 611–619. More generally, see J. Stanley, 'Including the feelings: personal political testimony and self-disclosure', *Oral History*, 1996, vol. 24, no. 1, pp. 60–67; O. Thomas, 'Voices of the past', *Family History Monthly*, July 2005, no. 119, pp. 18–23.

16 R. Samuel and P. Thompson, *The Myths We Live By*, London: Routledge, 1990.

17 For the US context for oral history and disability see K. Hirsch, 'Culture and disability: the role of oral history', *Oral History Review*, 1995, vol. 22, no. 1, pp. 1–27. For the British context see S. Humphries and P. Gordon, *Out of Sight*: *The Experience of Disability 1900–1950*, Plymouth, Northcote, 1993; M. Potts and R. Fido, *A Fit Person To Be Removed*, Plymouth: Northcote, 1991; D. Atkinson, M. Jackson and J. Walmsley, *Forgotten Lives*: *Exploring the History of Learning Disability*, Kidderminster: Bild, 1997; S. Rolph, 'Ethical dilemmas: oral history work with people with learning difficulties', *Oral History*, 1998, vol. 26, no. 2, pp. 65–72; M. Atherton, D. Russell and G. Turner, 'Looking to the past: the role of oral history research in recording the visual history of Britain's deaf community', *Oral History*, 2001, vol. 29, no. 2, pp. 35–47.

18   Oral History Association, *Oral History Evaluation Guidelines*, revised 2000, (www.dick-inson.edu/oha/pub_eg.html); Oral History Society/A. Ward, 'Is your oral history legal and ethical?', (www.ohs.org.uk/ethics); Oral History Association of Australia, *Guidelines of Ethical Practice*, (www.ohaa.net.au/guidelines.htm); National Oral History Association of New Zealand (NOHANZ), *Code of Ethical and Technical Practice*, (www.oralhistory.org.nz/Code.htm). See also V.R. Yow, 'Ethics and interpersonal relationships in oral history research', *Oral History Review*, 1995, vol. 22, no. 1, pp. 51–66; Yow, *Recording Oral History*, 2005, chapter 5; A. Lynch, 'The ethics of interviewing', *Canadian Oral History Association Journal*, 1979, vol. 4, no. 1, pp. 4–9; L. Hall, 'Confidentially speaking: ethics in interviewing', in A. Green and M. Hutching (eds), *Remembering*: *Writing Oral History*, Auckland: Auckland University Press, 2004, pp. 152–67.

19   K. Brewster, 'Internet access to oral recordings: finding the issues', Alaska: University of Fairbanks, 2000, (www.uaf.edu/library/oralhistory/brewster1/); M.A. Larson, 'Potential, potential, potential: the marriage of oral history and the world wide web', *The Journal of American History*, 2001, pp. 596–603.

20   R. Perks and J. Robinson, '"The way we speak": web-based representations of changing communities in England', *Oral History*, 2005, vol. 33, no. 2, pp. 79–90.

21   W. Rickard, 'Oral history: "More dangerous than therapy?" Interviewees' reflections on recording traumatic and taboo issues', *Oral History*, 1998, vol. 26, no. 2, pp. 38–48; D. Jones, 'Distressing histories and unhappy interviewing', *Oral History*, 1998, vol. 26, no. 2, pp. 49–56.

22   E. Wiesel, *One Generation After*, New York: Simon & Shuster, 1970. L.L. Langer, *Holocaust Testimonies*: *The Ruins of Memory*, New Haven: Yale University Press, 1991, is an essential text on the Holocaust and oral history. Also G. Rosenthal, *The Holocaust in Three Generations*: *Families of Victims and Perpetrators of the Nazi Regime*, London: Cassell, 1998; D. Laub, 'Bearing witness or the vicissitudes of listening', in S. Felman and D. Laub (eds), *Testimony*: *Crises of Witnessing in Literature, Psychoanalysis and History*, New York: Routledge, 1992, pp. 57–74; N.R. White, 'Marking absences: Holocaust testimony and history', *Oral History Association of Australia Journal*, 1994, no. 16, pp. 12–18; J.E. Young, *Writing and Rewriting the Holocaust*: *Narrative and the Consequences of Interpretation*, Bloomington: University of Indiana Press, 1990; H. Greenspan, *On Listening to Holocaust Survivors*: *Recounting and Life History*, Westport, Conn., Praeger, 1998; G. Hartman (ed.), *Holocaust Remembrance*: *The Shapes of Memory*, Cambridge, Mass.: Basil Blackwell, 1994.

23   L. Passerini, 'Memory', *History Workshop Journal*, 1983, no. 15, p. 196. Also on how 'gaps, omissions and silences . . . play as important a role in identity formation as that which is included, spoken, and discussed in rich detail', see N. Norquay, 'Identity and forgetting', *Oral History Review*, 1999, vol. 26, no. 1, pp. 1–21; K.L. Nasstrom, 'Beginnings and endings: life stories and the periodization of the Civil Rights Movement', *Journal of American History*, 1999, vol. 86, no. 2, pp. 700–711; E.F. Xavier Ferreira, 'Oral history and the social identity of Brazilian women under military rule', *Oral History Review*, 1997, vol. 24, no. 2, pp. 1–33.

Chapter 9

Studs Terkel, with Tony Parker

INTERVIEWING AN INTERVIEWER

Studs Terkel, iconic US oral historian and broadcaster, the author of many best-selling books, is here interviewed by Tony Parker, often described as Britain's own 'Studs', in an extract from Parker's oral biography, *Studs Terkel: A Life in Words* (1997, pp. 163–170), published after Parker's death in 1996. With a century of experience between them, two veterans of the tape-recorded interview reflect on good technique: asking questions, establishing rapport, the importance of silences and of listening. The style is discursive and vibrates with the shared enthusiasm of unobtrusive and respectful listening. Copyright © 1997 HarperCollins. Reproduced by permission of the author c/o Rogers, Coleridge & White Ltd, 20 Powis Mews, London W11 1JN.

YOU'RE COLUMBUS, YOU'RE SETTING out onto the unknown sea. There are no maps, because no one's been there before. You're an explorer, a discoverer. It's exciting – and its scary, it frightens you. It frightens the person you're going to interview too. Remember that. Where in the radio interview you start level in confidence, in knowing where you're going, in the one-to-one interview you start level in the unconfidence, in not knowing where you're going.

There aren't any rules. You do it your own way. You experiment. You try this, you try that. With one person one way's the best, with another person another. Stay loose, stay flexible. Think about your lead-in, about whether it's going to be into the person or into the subject. One I sometimes use is 'Tell me where I am, and who I'm talking to.' That's quite a good one, because it lets me follow up. When they've said where we are 'and you're talking to John Doe,' I say 'And who's John Doe?' And if they start telling you, well then you're on your way.

I don't know how a tape recorder works. Not even the simplest one that's ever been invented. And I don't mean the machinery inside it either, I mean all of it. I don't know how to open it, I don't know how to put in the cassette, which way up it goes, how to close the lid when it's in, which is the button to press to get it to start recording, which is the button to press to make it stop. None of it, I don't know any of it. Some people say to me 'Why don't you learn?'

Asking me why I don't learn is missing the point, I don't learn because I'm nervous of the machine. If I press the button and the wheels are going round and I can see the tape's moving, that doesn't make any difference, I'm still nervous because I don't know whether it's recording what's being said, or whether I'm recording over something else that's already there and losing that, or what.

Are you with me? What am I describing? I'm describing one of my biggest assets. Its name is ineptitude. Why's it an asset? Well, would you be frightened of a little old guy who wants to tape-record a conversation with you – *and he can't even work his tape recorder*? We won't go into what you might feel about him, but the one thing you wouldn't for sure feel is scared.

So it's a bonus. I'm not up there on Mount Olympus, I'm not the Messiah with the microphone, I'm just another human being. I don't want anyone to be in awe of me. I don't mind what they feel so long as it's not scared.

Sometimes that way I can get more out of it too. I don't overplay it, but I'll often accompany the fumbling around with a question. 'Heh, can you tell me if I've got this OK now, is this thing working OK?' That helps to ease the tension. It might even bring a smile or a laugh. So what's being done by that is this: you're asking for help, making it into you-and-them-together on the same side against the machine. You can't pretend though, it's got to be genuine: no tricks, no deceits. You've really not got to know what you're doing. That's why I'm always going to stay that way. Blessed be the ignorant: they'll often get the breaks.

So now we come around to the questioning. The first thing I'd say to any inter-viewer is . . . 'Listen.' It's the second thing I'd say too, and the third, and the fourth. 'Listen . . . listen . . . listen . . . listen.' And if you do, people will talk. They'll *always* talk. Why? Because no one has ever listened to them before in all their lives. Perhaps they've not ever even listened to themselves. You don't have to agree with them or disagree with them, all of that's irrelevant. Don't push them, don't rush them, don't chase them or harass them with getting on to the next ques-tion. Take your time. Or no, let's put it the right way: let them take *their* time.

And I'll tell you something else you should always have in your mind, and remind yourself constantly about it – they're doing you a favor. This person you're talking to is entrusting you with their memories and their hopes, their realities and their dreams. So remember that, handle them carefully, they're holding out to you fragile things.

I'm thinking of two quotations. One of them's from James Joyce, the other one's from Thomas Hardy. James Joyce's is from *Portrait of the Artist as a Young Man*, I think. 'Tell me about Anna Livia. . . .' How does it go? 'Tell me about Anna Livia, I want to hear all about Anna Livia. We all know Anna Livia, tell me all, tell me now.' Anna Livia – the River Liffey running through Dublin, the river of life. Tell me about the river of life. The Thomas Hardy one, I'm not sure which of his books it's in. 'This man's silence is wonderful to listen to.'

So there we have our two basic texts for interviewers, don't we? Tell me about the river of life, and listen to the silence. I'd say listen and wait are the two essen-tials, with watch and be aware a close third. A laugh can be a cry of pain, and a silence can be a shout. And God knows how many different meanings there are to a smile. It's what a person says and how they say it, and where they're saying it to

– to you, to themselves, to the past, the future, the outside world. Those are the basics.

If you've lost touch, or you're unsure of where you're at and how things stand, I think a 'How?' or a 'Why?'' question can be very harmful and destructive: and hurtful too, too much of a jolt. I said when we talked about radio, this isn't an inquisition. It's an exploration, usually an exploration into the past. So I think the gentlest question is the best one. And the gentlest is 'And what happened then?' Maybe you'll get an answer, maybe you'll get a shrug. And boy, what an answer that is! A shrug means I don't know – or I don't care – or I don't care to know – or what the hell does it matter anyway? But it's a signal, isn't it? And what does the signal say? It says 'Shut up and keep still.'

Interviewing? Easy? Ask me another one? Exciting? Ah, you're right on the button with that one. Is it exciting? I'll say it is, yes!

– Why me? That's what they say, isn't it? Why me, why'd you want to talk to me, I'm not important? I like that, I like to hear it, it's a good start. The uncelebrated person – oh boy, how many of those have we missed! There weren't any guys around with tape recorders when they were building the pyramids, when they sailed the Spanish Armada, when they fought the battle of Waterloo. We've spoken of this before haven't we, yeah, about how much we've lost? Bertolt Brecht said it, in *Mother Courage* was it, 'Who built Thebes?' What we've lost. We'll do the best we can, right, to make up for the epiphanic moments, the things that really mattered, that are gone forever. What was it like to be a certain person then? What's it like to be a certain person now? That's what I'm trying to capture. I'm looking for the uniqueness in each person. And I'm not looking for some such abstraction as *the* truth, because it doesn't exist. What I'm looking for is what is the truth for *them*.

The word I'm looking for is 'curious.' I don't have to stay curious, I *am* curious, about all of it, all the time, 'Curiosity never killed this cat' – that's what I'd like as my epitaph. It won't kill me, no sir. I breathed it, it's what gave me life, the older I got the more curious I became. What's happening, what's going on, what's it like, what does it mean? They're big questions for everyone.

'Do you work to a framework?' they sometimes ask me. And sometimes I answer yes and sometimes I answer no. What I'm trying to put over is that there aren't any rules, each tune's a new beginning, right? That's what's exciting about it. Isn't it, isn't that what's exciting about it? If it wasn't, then you'd be better working for a market research company so that at the end you could say 'I asked a hundred people the same questions, and these are the results.' It's the uncertainty, the not knowing where you're going that's the best part of it. People aren't boring. Interviewing people is discovering people, and one of the biggest thrills you can get is discovering that somebody who sounds boring isn't boring at all.

One thing I'll never do is write my questions down. I'll not do it because it's false and it's unnatural and it's not what you do when you're having a conversation and it'll make them feel – here's that word again – interrogated. I want them to talk about what they want to talk about in the way they want to talk about it, or not talk about it, in the way they want to stay silent about it. I'll keep them to the theme – age or the Depression or work or whatever – but that's all.

How do you get someone started? I suppose that's the one people ask me most often. Where do you begin? Well, childhood's a good place sometimes, that'll often

open the sluice gates. But you've got to think out the wording first if you're going to use it, it's got to be something that requires a bit of thought from them to answer it. 'How was it when you were a kid?' I think that's quite a good one. I think it's better than something more simple like 'Did you have a happy childhood?' which they can answer yes or no. I try not to use questions which can be answered that way, you know, with a yes or no. I try to use ones that'll lead to a follow-up. An example? OK, off the top of my head. 'Do you like Chinese food?' 'Yes,' 'Do you like Indian food?' 'No.' So where's that got you? Nowhere. What's better is 'Which do you like better, Chinese food or Indian food?' Because whatever the answer is, even if it's 'I don't like either of them' you're straight in then with your follow-up – 'Why?''

And people's answers aren't always direct. So don't be admonishing about it. Accept it, and think about it afterwards. We've talked another time, haven't we, about silences and nods and shrugs and things of that kind? Well sometimes the indirect answer that the person *thinks* is the answer is more informative than the straight answer. I said to a guy once, he was a retired meat boner in a factory, and he was telling me how he started work there when he was thirteen, and he said something like 'And I tell you, when I was eighteen, I was in charge of a whole production line.' And the way he said it made me say 'You sound like it surprised you, why was that?' And he said 'Well, me!' So I let it go. Then he said it again about something else – 'Well, me!' And a third time 'Well, me!' I was young in those days, and I didn't realize what he was telling me – until he added two more words to it, and then I knew what it was. 'Well, me – a darkie!'

People's questions too, they can be signals to you. If you can answer them, do. Demystify the experience in advance for them, if they ask you what you want to talk to them about. But they might be saying there's something *they'd* like to talk about, something they *hope* you're going to ask about, so ask them if there is. And the best part's the detail that comes out, that you couldn't imagine because you never knew it was there. Perhaps the person didn't know it was there either.

The questioning's important – but what's the most important is that it shouldn't *sound* like questioning. What time did you get up yesterday morning, what time did you go to bed, what did you do in between – none of that. So tell me, how was yesterday, that's the right way of doing it. Making it sound like you're having a conversation, not carrying on an inquisition, right? There's that word 'inquisition' again. I'd say that to everyone and go on saying it – keep away from it, don't be the examiner, be the interested enquirer.

There was this black woman one time, I saw her standing in the street, with two or three of her kids round her and she was looking in a shop window. And as I'm walking by, I look to see what it is she's looking at – and you know what? There's nothing in the window, she's looking in an empty shopwindow – looking at nothing. So naturally I'm curious – *naturally* I'm curious – so I say 'Excuse me ma'am – but what are on looking at?' She doesn't seem to mind being spoken to by a stranger, and she doesn't turn her head around to see who's asking her or anything, and after a moment or so she says 'Oh' she says, 'Oh, dreams, I'm just looking at dreams.' So I've got my tape recorder and I switch it on and I say 'Good dreams, bad dreams . . .?' And she starts to talk. Then she talks a little bit more, and a little bit more. And her kids are playing around her, and they can see I'm tape-recording what their mom is saying, and when she stops talking after eight, maybe ten minutes or so, one of them says 'Heh mom, can we listen to what you said?' And I ask her if it's OK with her and she says yes, so I play it back and she listens to it too. And when it's over, she gives a little shake of her head and she looks at me, and she says 'Well until I heard that, I never knew I felt that way.' 'I never knew I felt that way!' Isn't that incredible? The way I look at it, it's like being a gold prospector. You find this precious metal in people when you least expect it.

And the contrasts and the rewards, well those come in all different shapes and sizes. I remember one week I was in Pittsburgh, I'd gone there to get material for a series of interviews I was doing on how working people spent their days. I'd two introductions – one to a college lecturer and the other to a guy who worked in an auto plant and lived in a mobile home with his wife on the outskirts of a small town nearby.

I met him in a cheap diner, we had something to eat, and then we sat outside on a bench under some trees because it was summer and warm. All I said to him was something like 'Tell me about a typical working day for you, how it would begin.' I don't remember now why I used those particular words: they felt right, I guess.

'OK sir' he said, 'well I'll tell you. I have one of those little electric radio alarm clocks, and when it goes off and I hear the music playing, my wife's lying beside me and she's still asleep so I give her a kiss. That's routine you understand. Then I get out of bed and I go to the bathroom, and I wash and I comb my one hair and I clean my teeth and I shave. Routine again you understand. When I step out of the bathroom by this time the radio's woken my wife up, and she has a cup of coffee waiting for me. Some days I drink it, and some days I drink only a half of it. All depends on my mood you see. Then I get myself dressed and my wife makes me two pieces of toast. So I eat the two pieces of toast, but some days I only eat the one. All depends on my mood again you see. Then I kiss my wife again, that's more routine you understand. My wife gives me my lunch bucket, I get into my car and I set out to drive to the plant. And I've got to get there on time, because you see sir, if you get one minute late, they dock you for one whole hour. And well sir, between my home and the plant there's nine railroad tracks I have to cross – and at that time of morning there's a lot of freight trains go by. So if get to any one of those tracks at just a half a minute off the wrong time, I have to wait maybe fifteen twenty minutes or so while a hundred cars go by. And that means I am late for my work.' Well the way he told that me, by the time he'd finished I'm sitting on the edge of the bench! So I thought boy, that's some way of getting a guy started, I'm going to use exactly those same words again tomorrow with the college professor.

Which I did. I said to him 'Tell me about a typical working day for you, how it would begin?' You know what he said? He said 'Well, a typical day would be I'd get up, have my breakfast, go to my class, and since it's Aristotle's *Poetics* we're studying, I'd talk about it.' I said 'You'd talk about it? What would you say?' He said 'Oh this and that.' And that was all I got out of him! That was it! Nothing!

I guess the guy who lived in the mobile home had spoiled me. You can't be too prepared for an interview, because you don't know what the person you're talking to's going to say. But you've got to be ready for anything – and I wasn't ready for the unloquacious professor. In a way it's like jazz, you've got to improvise. Have a skeletal framework, but be ready to improvise within that.

The third, and it's *the* most important part of the work, is the editing of the transcripts of the recorded material, the cutting and shaping of it, into a readable result. The way I look at it is I suppose something like the way a sculptor looks at a block of stone: inside it there's a shape which he'll find and he'll reveal it by chipping away with a mallet and chisel. I've got a mountain of tapes, and somewhere inside them there's a book. But how do you cut without distorting the meaning? Well, you've got to be skillful and respectful and you can reorder and rearrange to highlight, and you can juxtapose: but the one thing you can't do is invent, make up, have people say what they didn't say.

I work from transcripts, but all the way through I keep on playing back sections of each interview so I'll have a constant reminder in my head of how they sounded when they said what they said. The most painful choice to make always is not who you're going to have in the book, but who you're going to cut out. Sometimes it feels like casting a play – you've got four equally good people for one character – only in the case of a book its four people representing one point of view. It's a tough decision to make.

Some things are easy to remove, like 'ums' and 'ers,' or you think they're going to be until you listen to them and you realize that that's how that person talks, and if you take all of them out, you lose the reality of the speech pattern of that person. Or someone else'll have a habit of repeating phrases – 'Yes, that's how it was, that's how it was,' say – and you've got to watch out that you keep those.

And length too of course, that's another crucial thing. You might think what the person's saying is very interesting. It might be to you. But it's got to be interesting to the reader, so keep an eye on that. I want a reader to feel they'd like to hear more, so the principle I try and hold on to is when in doubt, cut.

From sixty pages of transcript I reduce to eight. I talk while I'm writing: I talk *what* I'm writing. That way I try and get the sound and the tempo and the rhythm. I take out nearly all my questions because I don't want to stand in the way between the reader and the person who's talking. People aren't boring. When you talk to them, they may have a monotonous voice and you think they sound boring. But when you see their words transcribed, they read great. Other times it's the other way round – they're lively when they talk, but it doesn't come out that way on the printed page. So you have to exercise care. Oh boy – interviewing – isn't it great?

Chapter 10

Kathryn Anderson and Dana C. Jack

LEARNING TO LISTEN
Interview techniques and analyses

This piece focuses on the need to listen more carefully, and, in particular with women's perspectives, to 'listen in stereo' to both the facts and the feelings. The authors reflect on the essential subjectivity of the interview encounter and raise issues around the 'collaborative' or 'co-constructive' nature of oral history arising out of a growing awareness of the role of the interviewer. Kathryn Anderson and Dana Jack are both professors at Fairhaven College, Western Washington University. Reprinted from Sherna Berger Gluck and Daphne Patai (eds), *Women's Words: The Feminist Practice of Oral History*, London: Routledge, 1991, pp. 11–26, with permission.

ORAL HISTORY INTERVIEWS provide an invaluable means of generating new insights about women's experiences of themselves in their worlds. The spontaneous exchange within an interview offers possibilities of freedom and flexibility for researchers and narrators alike. For the narrator, the interview provides the opportunity to tell her own story in her own terms. For researchers, taped interviews preserve a living interchange for present and future use; we can rummage through interviews as we do through an old attic – probing, comparing, checking insights, finding new treasures the third time through, then arranging and carefully documenting our results.

Oral interviews are particularly valuable for uncovering women's perspectives. Anthropologists have observed how the expression of women's unique experience as women is often muted, particularly in any situation where women's interests and experiences are at variance with those of men.[1] A woman's discussion of her life may combine two separate, often conflicting, perspectives: one framed in concepts and values that reflect men's dominant position in the culture, and one informed by the more immediate realities of a woman's personal experience. Where experience does not 'fit' dominant meanings, alternative concepts may not readily be available. Hence, inadvertently, women often mute their own thoughts and feelings when they try to describe their lives in the familiar and publicly acceptable terms of prevailing concepts and conventions. To hear women's perspectives accurately, we have to learn to listen in stereo, receiving both the dominant and the muted channels clearly and tuning into them carefully to understand the relationship between them.

How do we hear the weaker signal of thoughts and feelings that differ from conventional expectations? Carolyn Heilbrun urges biographers to search for the choices, the pain, the stories that lie beyond the 'constraints of acceptable discussion'.[2] An interview that fails to expose the distortions and conspires to mask the facts and feelings that did not fit will overemphasize expected aspects of the female role. More important, it will miss an opportunity to document the experience that lies outside the boundaries of acceptability.

To facilitate access to the muted channel of women's subjectivity, we must inquire whose story the interview is asked to tell, who interprets the story, and with what theoretical frameworks. Is the narrator asked what meanings she makes of her experiences? Is the researcher's attitude one of receptivity to learn rather than to prove preexisting ideas that are brought into the interview? In order to learn to listen, we need to attend more to the narrator than to our own agendas.

Interview techniques: shedding agendas

Kathryn Anderson

My awareness of how both personal and collective agendas can short-circuit the listening process developed while scanning oral histories for the Washington Women's Heritage Project. This statewide collaborative effort received major support from the National Endowment for the Humanities and the Washington Commission for the Humanities to develop educational workshops and to produce a traveling exhibit documenting women's lives in interviews and historical photographs. The first stage of the project involved training dozens of interviewers in a series of oral history workshops held throughout the state. A typical workshop provided information on equipment, processing tapes, interviewing techniques, and a crash course in the new women's history scholarship. Prospective interviewers left with a manual, which included Sherna Gluck's 'Topical Guide for Oral History Interviews with Women'.[3]

To select excerpts for the exhibit, we reviewed dozens of interviews produced by project staff and workshop participants along with hundreds of interviews housed in archives and historical societies. We found them filled with passages describing the range and significance of activities and events portrayed in the photographs. To our dismay and disappointment, however, most of them lacked detailed discussions of the web of feelings, attitudes, and values that give meaning to activities and events. Interviewers had either ignored these more subjective dimensions of women's lives or had accepted comments at face value when a pause, a word, or an expression might have invited the narrator to continue. Some of us found discrepancies between our memories of interviews and the transcripts because the meaning we remembered hearing had been expressed through intense vocal quality and body language, not through words alone.

We were especially confused that our interviews did not corroborate the satisfactions and concerns other historians were discovering in women's diaries and letters, or the importance of relationships social scientists were uncovering in women's interviews. To understand why, I scrutinized the interviews with rural women that I had done for the project, paying special attention to interview strategies and techniques. My expectations that the interviews would give rural women a forum to describe their experiences in their own terms and to reflect on their experiences as women in the specific context of Washington state were thwarted to some extent by three factors: the project's agenda to document women's lives for the exhibit; an incomplete conversion from traditional to feminist historical paradigms; and the conventions of social discourse.

While the project's general goal was to accumulate a series of life histories, my special task was to discover women's roles in northwest Washington farming communities. Project deadlines and the need to cover a representative range of experiences combined to limit interviews to no more than three hours. In retrospect, I can see how I listened with at least part of my attention focused on producing potential material for the exhibit – the concrete description of experiences that would accompany pictures of women's activities. As I rummage through the interviews long after the exhibit has been placed in storage, I am painfully aware of lost opportunities for women to reflect on the activities and events they described and to explain their terms more fully in their own words.

In spite of my interest at the time in learning how women saw themselves as women in specific historical contexts, the task of creating public historical documents as well as the needs of the project combined to subvert my personal interests and led to fairly traditional strategies. As a result, my interviews tended to focus on activities and facts, on what happened and how it happened. They revealed important information about the variety of roles women filled on Washington farms, and how they disguised the extent and importance of their contributions by insisting that they were just 'helping out' or 'doing what needed to be done'. Left out, however, was the more subjective realm of feelings about what made these activities fun or drudgery, which ones were accompanied by feelings of pride or failure. The resulting story of what they did tells us something about the limitations under which they operated but less about the choices they might have made. My interests were not incompatible with the project's goals but my methods often failed to give women the opportunity to discuss the complex web of feelings and contradictions behind their familiar stories.

My background included both women's history and interpersonal communication, but no specific training in counseling. My fear of forcing or manipulating individuals into discussing topics they did not want to talk about sometimes prevented me from giving women the space and the permission to explore some of the deeper, more conflicted parts of their stories. I feared, for good reasons, that I lacked the training to respond appropriately to some of the issues that might be raised or uncovered. Thus, my interview strategies were bound to some extent by the conventions of social discourse. The unwritten rules of conversation about appropriate questions and topics – especially the one that says 'don't pry!' – kept me from encouraging women to make explicit the range of emotions surrounding the events and experiences they related. These rules are particularly restrictive in the rural style I had absorbed as a child on an Iowa farm. In a context where weather, blight, pests, and disease were so crucial to productivity and survival, conversation often tended towards the fatalistic and pragmatic; we certainly did not dwell on feelings about things beyond our control. As I interviewed rural women, the sights, sounds, and smells of a farm kitchen elicited my habits of a rural style of conversation and constrained my interview strategies.

Another interviewer experienced tensions between project goals and rules of conversation in a different context for different reasons. As she interviewed Indian women from various Washington tribes, she felt torn between a need to gather specific information and an awareness of appropriate relationships between young and old: the rules she had learned as an Indian child prohibited questioning elders, initiating topics, or disagreeing in any form, even by implying that a comment might be incomplete. When, as in these instances, interviewer and narrator share similar backgrounds that include norms for conversation and interaction, interview strategies must be particularly explicit to avoid interference.

Although I approached the interviews with a genuine interest in farm women's perceptions of themselves, their roles, and their relationships in the rural community, I now see how often the agenda to document farm activities and my habit of taking the comments of the farm women at face value determined my questions and responses. Both interfered with my sensitivity to the emotionally laden language they used to describe their lives. My first interview with Elizabeth illustrates a lost opportunity to explore her discussion of the physical and mental strains of multiple roles.[4] We had been talking about her relationships with her mother and half-sister when she offered the following:

> I practically had a nervous breakdown when I discovered my sister had cancer, you know; it was kind of like knocking the pins [out from under me] – and I had, after the second boy was born, I just had ill health for quite a few years. I evidently had a low-grade blood infection or something. Because I was very thin, and, of course, I kept working hard. And every fall, why, I'd generally spend a month or so being sick – from overdoing, probably.

Instead of encouraging further reflection on the importance of her relationship with her sister or on the difficulties of that period in her life, my next question followed my imperative for detailing her role on the farm: 'What kind of farming did you do right after you were married?'

Elizabeth was a full partner with her husband in their dairy farm and continued to play an active role as the farm switched to the production of small grains. Her interview has the potential of giving us valuable information about the costs incurred by women who combined child-rearing and housework with the physical labor and business decisions of the farm. It also suggests something of the importance of relationships with family and close friends in coping with both roles. The interview's potential is severely limited, however, by my failure to encourage her to expand upon her spontaneous reflections and by my eagerness to document the details of her farming activity. Not until later did I realize that I do not know what she meant by 'nervous breakdown' or 'overdoing'. The fact that other farm women used the same or similar terms to describe parts of their lives alerted me to the need for further clarification. I now wish I had asked her to tell me in her own words of the importance of the relationship with her sister and why its possible loss was such a threat.

Later in the same interview I was more sensitive to Elizabeth's feelings about the difficulty of combining roles, only to deflect the focus from her experience once again. She was telling me how hard it was to be a full partner in the field and still have sole responsibility for the house:

> This is what was so hard, you know. You'd both be out working together, and he'd come in and sit down, and I would have to hustle a meal together, you know. And that's typical.
>
> *How did you manage?*
>
> Well, sometimes you didn't get to bed till midnight or after, and you were up at five. Sometimes when I think back to the early days, though, we'd take a day off, we'd get the chores done, and we'd go take off and go visiting.
>
> *Was that typical? Neighbors going to visit each other after the chores were done?*

While Elizabeth was telling me how she managed, I was already thinking about patterns in the neighborhood. My first question had been a good one, but, by asking about what other people did, my next one told her that I had heard enough about her experience. The two questions in succession have a double message: 'Tell me about your experience, but don't tell me too much'. Part of the problem may have been that even while I was interviewing women I was aware of the need to make sense of what they told me. In this case, the scholar's search for generalizations undermined the interviewer's need to attend to an individual's experience. Ideally, the processes of analysis should be suspended or at least subordinated in the process of listening.

If we want to know how women feel about their lives, then we have to allow them to talk about their feelings as well as their activities. If we see rich potential in the language people use to describe their daily activities, then we have to take advantage of the opportunity to let them tell us what that language means, 'Nervous breakdown' is not the only phrase that I heard without asking for clarification. Verna was answering a question about the relationship between her mother and her grandmother when she said:

> It was quite close since my mother was the only daughter that was living. My grandmother did have another daughter, that one died. I didn't know it until we got to working on the family tree. My mother was older than her brother. They were quite close. They worked together quite well when it would come to preparing meals and things. They visited back and forth a lot.

Her answer gave several general examples of how the closeness was manifested, but what did Verna mean when she described a relationship as 'close' twice in a short answer? What did her perception of this relationship mean to her? My next question asked, instead, for further examples: 'Did they [your grandparents] come to western Washington because your parents were here?'

Even efforts to seek clarification were not always framed in ways that encouraged the interviewee to reflect upon the meaning of her experience. Elizabeth was answering a question about household rules when she was a child and commented: 'My mother was real partial to my brother because, of course, you know that old country way; the boy was the important one.' My question 'How did her partiality to the brother show?' elicited some specific examples, but none of a series of subsequent questions gave her an opportunity to reflect upon how this perception affected her understanding of herself and her place in the family.

A final example from Verna's interview illustrates the best and the worst of what we are trying to do. Her statement is a powerful reflection upon her roles as a mother; the subsequent question, however, ignores all the emotional content of her remarks:

> Yes. There was times that I just wished I could get away from it all. And there were times when I would have liked to have taken the kids and left them someplace for a week – the whole bunch at one time – so that I wouldn't have to worry about them. I don't know whether anybody else had that feeling or not, but there were times when I just felt like I needed to get away from everybody, even my husband, for a little while. Those were times when I would maybe take a walk back in the woods and look at the flowers and maybe go down there and find an old cow that was real gentle and walk up to her and pat her a while – kind of get away from it. I just had to, it seems like sometimes.

Were you active in clubs?

As the above portion of her remarks indicates, Verna was more than willing to talk spontaneously about the costs of her choice to combine the roles of wife, mother, and diligent farm woman. Perhaps she had exhausted the topic. If not, my question, even though it acknowledged the need for support at such times, certainly did not invite her to expand upon the feelings that both she and I knew might contradict some notion of what women ought to do and feel. She was comfortable enough to begin to consider the realities beyond the acceptable façade of the female role, but my question diverted the focus from her unique, individual reflections to the relative safety of women's clubs and activities, a more acceptable outlet for such feelings. In this case, my ability to listen, not Verna's memory, suffered from the constraints of internalized cultural boundaries. Until we can figure out how to release the brakes that these boundaries place on both hearing and memory, our oral histories are likely to confirm the prevailing ideology of women's lives and rob women of their honest voices.

What I learned by listening carefully to my interviews is that women's oral history requires much more than a new set of questions to explore women's unique experiences and unique perspectives; we need to refine our methods for probing more deeply by listening to the levels on which the narrator responds to the original questions. To do so we need to listen critically to our interviews, to our responses as well as to our questions. We need to hear what women implied, suggested, and started to say but didn't. We need to interpret their pauses and, when it happens, their unwillingness or inability to respond. We need to consider carefully whether our interviews create a context in which women feel comfortable exploring the subjective feelings that give meaning to actions, things, and events, whether they allow women to explore 'unwomanly' feelings and behaviors, and whether they encourage women to explain what they mean in their own terms.

When women talk about relationships, our responses can create an opportunity to talk about how much relationships enriched or diminished life experiences. When women talk about activities or events, they might find it easy to take blame for failures, but more sensitive responses may also make it possible to talk about feelings of competence or pride, even for women who do not consider such qualities very womanly. When women talk about what they have done, they may also want to explore their perceptions of the options they thought they had and how they feel about their responses. We can probe the costs that sometimes accompany choices, the means for accommodating and compensating for such costs, and how they are evaluated in retrospect. We can make it easier for women to talk about the values that may be implicit in their choices or feelings. When women reveal feelings or experiences that suggest conflict, we can explore what the conflict means and what form it takes. We can be prepared to expect and permit discussion of anger. If our questions are general enough, women will be able to reflect upon their experience and choose for themselves which experiences and feelings are central to their sense of their past.

The language women use to explore the above topics will be all the richer when they have ample opportunity to explain and clarify what they mean. When they use words and phrases like 'nervous breakdown', 'support', 'close', 'visiting', and 'working together', they should have an opportunity to explain what they mean in their own terms. With letters and diaries we can only infer what individuals mean by the language they use; with oral interviews we can ask them. As they discuss examples, the particularities of their experiences often begin to emerge from behind the veil of familiar and ambiguous terms.

As a result of my discussions with Dana, a trained therapist, I have developed a new appreciation for oral history's potential for exploring questions of self-concept and [self]-consciousness, for documenting questions of value and meaning in individuals' reflections upon their past. Important distinctions remain between oral history and therapeutic interviews, but as we shed our specific agendas the women we interview will become freer to tell their own stories as fully, completely, and honestly as they desire.

Interview analyses: listening for meaning

Dana Jack

I have been using oral interviews in research on depression among women and on moral reasoning among practicing attorneys.[5] In broad terms, both studies examine the interactions among social institutions, social roles, and women's consciousness. The women I interviewed are grappling with ideas about relationships, self-worth, career, and personal integrity in the context of society-wide changes in women's roles. As I listened to a woman's self-commentary, to her reflection upon her own thoughts and actions, I learned about her adaptation to her particular relationships and historical circumstances, especially her adaptation to the ideas of 'good lawyer', 'good wife', 'good woman', to which she tried to conform.

I listened with an awareness that a person's self-reflection is not just a private, subjective act. The categories and concepts we use for reflecting upon and evaluating ourselves come from a cultural context, one that has historically demeaned and controlled women's activities. Thus, an exploration of the language and the meanings women use to articulate their own experience leads to an awareness of the conflicting social forces and institutions affecting women's consciousness. It also reveals how women act either to restructure or preserve their psychological orientations, their relationships, and their social contexts. This was true for two very different studies and populations – depressed women and practicing lawyers.

The first, and the hardest, step of interviewing was to learn to listen in a new way, to hold in abeyance the theories that told me what to hear and how to interpret what these women had to say. Depressed women, for example, told stories of the failure of relationships, an inability to connect with the person(s) with whom they wanted to experience intimacy. These were the expected stories, predicted by existing models, and the temptation was to interpret the stories according to accepted concepts and norms for 'maturity' and 'health'. Because psychological theories have relied on men's lives and men's formulations for these norms, they explain women's psychological difference as deviant or 'other'.[6] The interview is a critical tool for developing new frameworks and theories based on women's lives and women's formulations. But we are at an awkward stage: old theories are set aside or under suspicion and new ones are still emerging. We must therefore be especially attentive to the influences that shape what we hear and how we interpret. How do we listen to an interview when we have rejected the old frameworks for interpretation and are in the process of developing new ones? How can an interview pull us beyond existing frameworks so that we stretch and expand them?

First, we must remember that the researcher is an active participant in qualitative research. My initial training was as a therapist, and the practice of listening to others while also attending to my own response to them has helped in conducting interviews. Theodore Reik calls this quiet involvement of the self 'listening with the third ear'.[7] As a researcher, I have learned that critical areas demanding attention are frequently those where I think I already know what the woman is saying. This means I am already appropriating what she says to an existing schema, and therefore I am no longer really listening to *her*. Rather, I am listening to how what she says fits into what I think I already know. So I try to be very careful to ask each woman what she means by a certain word, or to make sure that I attend to what is missing, what literary critics call the 'presence of the absence' in women's texts – the 'hollows, centers, caverns within the work-places where activity that one might expect is missing . . . or deceptively coded.'[8]

And what is it that is absent? Because women have internalized the categories by which to interpret their experience and activities, categories that 'represent a deposit of the desires and disappointments of men',[9] what is often missing is the woman's own interpretation of her experience, or her own perspective on her life and activity. Interviews allow us to hear, if we will, the particular meanings of a language that both women and men use but that each translates differently. Looking closely at the language and the particular meanings of important words women use to describe their experience allows us to understand how women are adapting to the culture within which they live. When their behavior is observed from the outside, depressed women are called passive, dependent, masochistic, compliant, and victimized by their own learned helplessness. Yet, when I listened to the women's self-reflection, what became clear was that behind the so-called passive behavior of depressed women was the tremendous cognitive activity required to inhibit both outer actions and inner feelings in order to live up to the ideal of the 'good' woman, particularly the good wife. Statements such as 'I have to walk on eggshells in dealing with my husband', and 'I have learned "don't rock the boat"' show awareness of both their actions and their intended effects: not to cause discord.[10]

How do we listen to interviews without immediately leaping to interpretations suggested by prevailing theories? The first step is to immerse ourselves in the interview, to try to understand the person's story from her vantage point. I found that three ways of listening helped me understand the narrator's point of view. The first was to listen to the person's *moral language*. In the depression study, I heard things like: 'I feel like I'm a failure', 'I don't measure up', 'I'm a liar, a cheat, and I'm no good.' In the lawyer study, when lawyers were describing fulfilling the obligations of role, we heard statements such as: 'It's like being forced into a sex relationship you didn't anticipate. It's a screw job. It feels horrible to do something that you wouldn't do normally.' Or 'I have to contradict myself depending on what role I'm taking . . . it's sort of professional prostitution.' Or finally, 'Sometimes you feel almost like a pimp or something . . . [I]t felt sleazy to cut the truth that finely.'

Although very different in tone, these moral self-evaluative statements allow us to examine the relationship between self-concept and cultural norms, between what we value and what others value, between how we are told to act and how we feel about ourselves when we do or do not act that way. In a person's self-judgement, we can see which moral standards are accepted and used to judge the self, which values the person strives to attain. In the depression study, this was the key to learning about gender differences in the prevalence and dynamics of depression. Negative self-judgement affecting the fall in self-esteem is considered to be one of the key symptoms of depression. Research by Carol Gilligan and her colleagues indicates that women and men often use differing moral frameworks to guide their perception and resolution of moral problems.[11] Listening to the moral language of depressed women illuminated both the standards used to judge the self and the source of their despair. The women considered the failure of their relationships to be a *moral* failure; their sense of hopelessness and helplessness stemmed from despair about the inability to be an authentic, developing self within an intimate marriage while also living up to the moral imperatives of the 'good woman'.

Attending to the moral standards used to judge the self allows the researcher to honor the individuality of each woman through observing what values she is striving to attain. An oral interview, when structured by the narrator instead of the researcher, allows each woman to express her uniqueness in its full class, racial, and ethnic richness. Each person is free to describe her idiosyncratic interaction between self-image and cultural norms. Each person can tell us how she comes to value or devalue herself. During the interview, the researcher's role is to preserve and foster this freedom, and to restrict the imposition of personal expectations. When the woman, and not existing theory, is considered the expert on her own psychological experience, one can begin to hear the muted channel of women's experience come through.

In analyzing the depression study, for example, I heard how women use the language of the culture to deny what, on another level, they value and desire. A key word for depressed women is 'dependency'. Psychologists consider depressed women to be excessively dependent upon their relationships for a sense of self and self-esteem. But when I looked at how depressed women understand dependence, and how their negative evaluation of themselves as dependent affects their self-perception and their actions, the concept was cast in a new light.

In a first interview with a thirty-three-year-old depressed woman, the issue of dependence was central and problematic: 'You know, I'm basically a very dependent person to start with. And then you get me married and tied down to a home and start not working . . .'

Asked what she meant by dependent, she responded:

> I like closeness. I like companionship. I like somebody, an intimate close-ness, even with a best friend. And I've never had that with my husband . . . Sometimes I get frustrated with myself that I have to have that, you know. I look at other people that seem so self-sufficient and so inde-pendent. I don't know – I just have always needed a closeness. And maybe I identified that as dependency.

> . . . [S]ince I've been married I realize it's kind of a negative thing to be that way. I've tried to bury that need for closeness. And so I guess that has also contributed to a lot of my frustrations.

Saying that she 'had been feeling that my need for intimacy and my need for that kind of a deep level of friendship or relationships with people was sort of bad', this woman began 'to believe there was something the matter with me'. In her attempt to bury her needs for closeness, she revealed the activity required to be passive, to try to live up to self-alienating images of 'today's woman'.

This interview contains an implicit challenge to prevalent understandings of dependence. Looking closely, we are able to see how this woman has judged her feelings against a dominant standard that says to need closeness makes one depen-dent, when one should be able to be self-sufficient and autonomous. Further, she reflects upon her own experience, her capabilities, and her needs not from the basis of who she is and what she needs but in terms of how her husband and others see her. Her capacity for closeness and intimacy goes unacknowledged as strength. Rather than a failure of the husband's response, the problem is identified as her 'neediness'. If a researcher went into this interview with the traditional notion of dependence in mind, s/he would find the hypothesis that depressed women are too dependent confirmed. But if one listens to the woman's own feelings about depen-dence, her confusion about what she knows she needs and what the culture says she *should* need, one begins to see part of the self-alienation and separation from feelings that is a key aspect of depression.

The second way of listening that allowed me to hear the voice of the subject instead of my own preconceptions was to attend to the subject's *meta-statements*. These are places in the interview where people spontaneously stop, look back, and comment about their own thoughts or something just said.

For example, in the lawyer study, a woman is answering the question, 'What does morality mean to you?':

> [I]t seems to me anything that raises to mind hurting other people or taking things away from other people or some sort of monetary gain for oneself . . . And I suppose just how we interact with each other, if there's a contentiousness or bad feelings or bad blood between some people, that raises some moral issues because I guess I see us all as having a bit of a moral obligation to be nice to each other and to get along. *So – do I sound much like a litigator?*

Meta-statements alert us to the individual's awareness of a discrepancy within the self – or between what is expected and what is being said. They inform the interviewer about what categories the individual is using to monitor her thoughts, and allow observation of how the person socializes feelings or thoughts according to certain norms.[12] Women lawyers made many more meta-statements than men, indicating they were 'watching' their own thinking. Because women have come into a legal system designed by men, for men, and because they still face discrimination, it is easy for them to develop an 'onlooker' attitude of critical observation toward themselves.[13] This woman looks at herself being looked at in law and notices the difference. Second, these remarks show how powerfully a stereotypic image of the successful, adversarial lawyer divides them from their personal experience and makes some women, early in their careers, question their ability within law. Finally, such comments reveal the lack of public validation of frameworks that women use to understand and value their own feelings and experiences.[14]

The third way of listening was to attend to the *logic of the narrative*, noticing the internal consistency or contradictions in the person's statements about recurring themes and the way these themes relate to each other. I listened to how the person strings together major statements about experience so I could understand the assumptions and beliefs that inform the logic and guide the woman's interpretation of her experience.

A woman I call Anna, age fifty-four, hospitalized twice for major depression, provides an example of a contradiction within the logic of her narrative, a contradiction that points to conflicting beliefs. Anna says:

> I was telling my daughter-in-law, 'I guess I was just born to serve others.' But we shouldn't be born to serve other people, we should look after ourselves.

Anna constructs the most important issues in her life – how to balance the needs of her self with the needs of others – as an either/or choice that presents her with loss on either side. The choice is either loss of self or loss of other. Such dichotomous thinking leaves Anna with feelings of hopelessness about how to resolve the conflicts in the relationships, and restricts her perception of choice.

On the surface, Anna's statement simply pits the traditional female role against the new 'me first' ethic of self-development. But, looking more deeply, one sees that she describes two visions of relationship: either isolation or subordination. Through Anna's construction of her possibilities in relationship, one gains a glimpse of how specific historical ideas about women's roles and women's worth affect her own depression. Anna's vision of her self in relationship as either subordinated or isolated is profoundly influenced by a social context of inequality and competition. When unresolved personal issues intersect with conflicting social ideals that limit women's lives, that intersection increases the difficulty of forming a positive and realistic vision of self toward which one can strive.

Rather than conclude, as do cognitive theories of depression, that cognitive errors 'cause' depression, observing this dichotomous thinking led me to see how the female social role is structured in thought and works to constrict women's perceptions of their relationships and their choices. Such logic of the narrative allowed me to see how a woman deals with conflicting cultural ideas, and how easy it is to feel depression as a personal failure rather than to recognize its social and historical aspects.

Conclusion

The process of sharing and critiquing our interviews has helped us sharpen our listening skills and improve our interviewing methods so that narrators feel more free to explore complex and conflicting experiences in their lives. Because of our divergent disciplinary interests, we have changed in different ways. The historian has become more alert to the subjective dimensions of events and activities; the psychologist has gained greater awareness of how the sociohistorical context can be read between the lines of a woman's 'private' inner conflict. Both are more deter-mined to discover how individual women define and evaluate their experience in their own terms.

Realizing the possibilities of the oral history interview demands a shift in methodology from information gathering, where the focus is on the right questions, to interaction, where the focus is on process, on the dynamic unfolding of the subject's viewpoint. It is the interactive nature of the interview that allows us to ask for clarification, to notice what questions the subject formulates about her own life, to go behind conventional, expected answers to the woman's personal construc-tion of her own experience. This shift of focus from data gathering to interactive process affects what the researcher regards as valuable information. Those aspects of live interviews unavailable in a written text – the pauses, the laughter – all invite us to explore their meaning for the narrator. The exploration does not have to be intrusive; it can be as simple as 'What did that [event] mean for you?'

This shift in focus, from information (data) gathering to interactive process, requires new skills on the researcher's part. In our view, it stimulates the develop-ment of a specific kind of readiness, the dimensions of which have been sketched in this paper. As Anderson has suggested, its most general aspects include an aware-ness that (1) actions, things, and events are accompanied by subjective emotional experience that gives them meaning; (2) some of the feelings uncovered may exceed the boundaries of acceptable or expected female behavior; and (3) individuals can and must explain what they mean in their own terms. Jack described three ways of listening during the interview that sharpen the researcher's awareness of the feelings and thoughts that lie behind the woman's outwardly conventional story: (1) listen-ing to the narrator's moral language; (2) attending to the meta-statements; and (3) observing the logic of the narrative. Incorporating these insights has helped us learn how to remain suspended and attentive on a fine line between accomplishing our research goals and letting the subject be in charge of the material in the interview.

While by no means conclusive or inclusive, the following points suggest further ways to sharpen our attentiveness to the interactive process of the interview:

A.   Listening to the narrator
   1   If the narrator is to have the chance to tell her own story, the interviewer's first question needs to be very open-ended. It needs to convey the message that in this situation, the narrator's interpretation of her experience guides the interview. For example, in the depression study, Jack started with, 'Can you tell me, in your own mind what led up to your experience of depression?'
   2   If she doesn't answer the interviewer's question, what and whose questions does the woman answer?
   3   What are her feelings about the facts or events she is describing?
   4   How does she understand what happened to her? What meaning does she make of events? Does she think about it in more than one way? How does she evaluate what she is describing?
   5   What is being left out, what are the absences?

B.   Listening to ourselves
   1   Try not to cut the narrator off to steer her to what our concerns are.
   2   Trust our own hunches, feelings, responses that arise through listening to others.
   3   Notice our own areas of confusion, or of too great a certainty about what the woman is saying — these are areas to probe further.
   4   Notice our personal discomfort; it can become a personal alarm bell alerting us to a discrepancy between what is being said and what the woman is feeling.

Oral history interviews are unique in that the interaction of researcher and subject creates the possibility of going beyond the conventional stories of women's lives, their pain and their satisfactions, to reveal experience in a less culturally edited form. But despite the value of this focus on the oral history interview in its dynamic, interactive form, we must offer one word of caution. The researcher must always remain attentive to the moral dimension of interviewing and aware that she is there to follow the narrator's lead, to honor her integrity and privacy, not to intrude into areas that the narrator has chosen to hold back.[15] This is another part of the specific kind of readiness the researcher brings to the interview: a readiness to be sensitive to the narrator's privacy while, at the same time, offering her the freedom to express her own thoughts and experiences, and listening for how that expression goes beyond prevailing concepts.

Notes

Public discussion of this collaborative work began at the National Women's Studies Association Conference held in Seattle, Washington, in June 1985 and continued with coauthors Susan Armitage and Judith Wittner in the *Oral History Review*, 1987, vol. 15 (Spring), pp. 103–127.

1   See S. Ardener (ed.), *Perceiving Women*, New York: John Wiley & Sons, 1975, pp. xi–xxiii. In that volume see also E. Ardener, 'Belief and the problem of women', pp. 1–27, and H. Callan, 'The premise of dedication: notes towards an ethnography of diplomats' wives', pp. 87–104.

2   C. Heilbrun, *Writing a Woman's Life*, New York: W.W. Norton & Company, 1988, pp. 30–31.

3   'Women's oral history resource section', *Frontiers*, 1977, vol. 2 (Summer), pp. 110–118.

4   K. Anderson and others, interviews for the Washington Women's Heritage Project, Center for Pacific Northwest Studies, Western Washington University, Bellingham, Washington. In the following account, two interviews from the collection are cited: interview with Elizabeth Bailey, 1 July 1980; interview with Verna Friend, 31 July 1980.

5   D.C. Jack, 'Clinical depression in women: cognitive schemas of self, care and relationships in a longitudinal study', unpublished doctoral dissertation, Harvard University, 1984; and D.C. Jack, 'Silencing the self: the power of social imperatives in female depression', in R. Formanek and A. Gurian (eds), *Women and Depression: A Lifespan Perspective*, New York: Springer Publishing Co., 1987. The lawyer study is in R. Jack and D.C. Jack, *Moral Vision and Professional Decisions: The Changing Values of Women and Men Lawyers*, New York: Cambridge University Press, 1989.

6   C. Gilligan, *In a Different Voice*, Cambridge, Mass.: Harvard University Press, 1982.

7   T. Reik, *Listening with the Third Ear*, New York: Farrar Straus Giroux, 1948.

8   C. Jeilbrun and C. Stimpson, 'Theories of feminist criticism: a dialogue', in J. Donovan (ed.), *Feminist Literary Criticism*, Lexington, Ky.: The University Press of Kentucky, 1975, pp. 61–73.

9   K. Horney, *Feminine Psychology*, New York: W.W. Norton & Company, 1967, p. 56.

10 Jack, 'Clinical depression in women', p. 177.

11 Gilligan, *In a Different Voice*. See also C. Gilligan, J. Taylor and J. Ward (eds), *Mapping the Moral Domain*, Cambridge, Mass.: Harvard University Press, 1989.

12 See A. Russell Hochschild, 'Emotion work, feeling rule, and social structure', *American Journal of Sociology*, 1979, vol. 85 (November), pp. 551–575.

13 The onlooker phenomenon is described by M. Westkott, *The Feminist Legacy of Karen Horney*, New Haven, Conn.: Yale University Press, 1986.

14 J. Baker Miller, *Toward a New Psychology of Women*, Boston, Beacon Press, 1976, writes 'When . . . we can think only in terms given by dominant culture, and when that culture not only does not attend to our own experiences but specifically denies and devalues them, we are left with no way of conceptualizing our lives. Under these circumstances, a woman is often left with a global, undefined sense that she must be wrong' (p. 57).

15 The American Psychological Association (APA) has adopted ethical standards for the treatment of research subjects that provide some guidelines for thinking through issues of researcher intrusiveness. A copy of the APA Ethical Principles may be obtained from the APA Ethics Office, 1200 17th Street NW, Washington, DC 20036.

Chapter 11

Hugo Slim and Paul Thompson, with Olivia Bennett and Nigel Cross

WAYS OF LISTENING

The book from which this chapter is drawn was published as part of the Panos Institute's Oral Testimony Programme, which explores and illustrates the potential of oral testimony in the development process, and gathers, publishes and amplifies the views and experiences of individuals and communities in the South on specific development themes. Mindful of the culturally (and historically) specific prevalence of the one-to-one interview in the North, this chapter explores a variety of other approaches, from group interviews to the use of visual techniques. Hugo Slim was Senior Overseas Research Officer for Save the Children Fund, and is now Co-Director, Centre for Development and Emergency Planning (CENDEP) at Oxford Brookes University. Paul Thompson is Research Professor at the University of Essex. Olivia Bennett was Director, Oral Testimony Programme, Panos Institute, London until 2004. Nigel Cross was Research Director of the Sahel Oral History Project. Reprinted with permission from Hugo Slim and Paul Thompson, with Olivia Bennett and Nigel Cross (eds), *Listening For Change: Oral History and Development*, London: Panos, 1993, pp. 61–94.

[. . .]

WHILE THE INTERVIEW is now a common form of enquiry and communication in the West – where a job interview is a prerequisite for most employment, the media feature endless interviews, both informative and entertaining, and few people escape having to take part in polls and questionnaires – this is by no means a universal experience. As British anthropologist Charles Briggs has observed, in some societies the interview is not an established type of speech event, and there can often be an incompatibility between standard interview techniques and indigenous systems of communication.[1] This incompatibility can create problems for people who, as interviewees, are forced to express themselves in an unfamiliar speech format. In particular, the interview form has a tendency to put unnatural pressure on people to find ready answers, to be concise and to summarise a variety of complex experiences and intricate knowledge.[2] It may also mean that researchers and interviewers unwittingly violate local communication norms relating to turn-taking, the order of topics for discussion or various rituals attached to storytelling. In some societies, individual interviews are considered dangerously intimate encounters. In others, the recounting of group history can be a sacred ritual and certain people must be consulted before others. Sometimes a number of clearly prescribed topics should be used to start proceedings, while other topics may be taboo, or should not be introduced until a particular level of intimacy and trust has been achieved.

In many societies, community or clan history is the vested interest of particular people or a designated caste, such as the *griots* of West Africa. They will often adapt their account to a particular audience, tailoring it to focus on the ancestors of their listeners. Alongside the right to tell, there is often a reward: payment in cash or kind for the teller. Storytelling may also have a seasonal dimension. In Ladakh, for example, winter is the time for telling stories. It is considered an inappropriate activity during the busy summer months when the agricultural workload is at its peak, as a local saying makes clear: 'As long as the earth is green, no tale should be told.'[3] It would be an ill-prepared and disappointed oral testimony project that set out to collect traditional stories in Ladakh during the summer!

There may also be special rituals of rendition which require certain elders to act as witnesses and checks on the history or stories being recounted. The proper setting for the recounting of a community history may be a feast with a minimum number present. Such conditions affect the collection of oral history and can sometimes even make it impossible, as Lomo Zachary, a Sudanese researcher, found when he tried to gather information about the origins and relations of various Ugandan clans living as refugees in South Sudan:

> I approached several clan historians but all were asking me for a 'Calabash' – meaning some liquor . . . After requesting some liquor most told me that they were unable to narrate me any stories because there were no esteemed witnesses or observers. Usually when such clan histories are told to clansmen or a group of interested young clansmen there is someone also well versed in the clan history who makes corrections when necessary. Sometimes they have long debates on a controversial item in the history. For example, the storyteller might skip or include a false family line of a particular clansman. Here the observer or witness has to interpose immediately with concrete proofs . . . So all gave me a similar response: 'My son, I am indeed grateful for your wise request for knowing where we originated from, how we have come to be separated and how we handle our affairs. I could have given you an elaborate history of our people but as you know, we are all scattered at this time. We have lost all our animals. There are no more tribal palavers where our people could be gathered . . . It could be during such sittings that our wise children could now put down all our cultures and traditions. Please accept my sincere apologies.'[4]

It is critically important to be aware of these different conceptual and cultural dimensions to interviewing and to historical information. A vital part of any preparation for an oral testimony project should involve learning about the norms of what Briggs describes as people's 'communicative repertoire': its particular forms, its special events, its speech categories and its taboos.[5] The most fundamental rule is to be sensitive to customary modes of speech and communication and allow people to speak on their own terms.

Methods of collection

There are a number of different kinds of interview. The most wide-ranging form is the individual life story. This allows a person to narrate the story of his or her whole life in all its dimensions: personal, spiritual, social and economic. Another kind is the single-issue interview which seeks to gain testimony about a particular aspect or period of a person's life. The object might be to hear about someone's working life, perhaps with an emphasis on indigenous knowledge, or to listen to their experiences during an event or episode such as a famine or a time of conflict or displacement. In addition to individual interviews, oral testimony can also be collected in focus group discussions, community interviews or by diary interviewing. When choosing the method(s) to be employed, it is important to bear in mind the objectives of the project and the kind of testimony required.

Life story interviews

These are normally private, one-to-one encounters between interviewer and narrator. Sessions should be held at a time convenient to the interviewee and in a suitable location, preferably somewhere which offers seclusion, comfort and familiarity. There is often no better place than the narrator's home.

In some societies, a one-to-one interview may not be acceptable, particularly for women, and one or more observers will need to be present. This can serve the additional function of testing and cross-checking information as observers interrupt to challenge or correct the interviewee. However, it can also mean that information is distorted. In some situations observers can act as censors and indeed may be there specifically to intimidate: husbands observing wives; parents observing children; or officials observing a community living in fear or repression.[6] While it is important to conform to the communicative repertoire of the people being interviewed, it pays to be aware that there may be more dubious aspects to observation and extra participation. Gender can also be an inhibiting factor and as a general rule interviewer and narrator should be the same sex.[7] [. . .]

An average life story interview may need two or three sessions and can take anything from one to eight hours. Breaking up the interview into separate sessions gives people time to remember and explore the past and makes recollection more of a process than an occasion. It takes the pressure off a single session, when the narrator might feel obliged to cram everything in. Things triggered in one session can be reflected upon by the narrator in peace and then brought to the next. The interviewer can similarly benefit from the pause between sessions.

It is important to remember that a life story interview can often have a profound effect on the interviewee, who may never have told anyone their memories before and certainly is unlikely to have recalled their whole life in the course of a few

hours. For most people, recounting their life story is a positive, if emotional, experience from which they can gain much satisfaction and a renewed sense of perspective,
but the listener should always ensure that the narrator is comfortable at the end of
the interview and is surrounded by the support they need, whether from family or
friends.

Family-tree interviewing

In the course of a life story interview, the narrator will describe many members of
his or her family from contemporary or previous generations. These people will
obviously be mentioned largely in terms of their impact on the narrator. However,
it is possible to focus on these other family members in more depth by asking the
narrator to supply second-hand accounts of their relatives' lives. This technique is
perhaps best described as family-tree interviewing. [. . .]

It obviously takes up much more time, but it does give an interesting ripple
effect to any study. It is perhaps most useful when one is looking for trends, rather
than the specific detail of direct personal experience. An alternative, which is still
more time-consuming but also a more direct measure of change, is to interview
two generations from the same family.

Single-issue testimony

Single-issue interviews may be carried out on a one-to-one or group basis, and focus
on a specific aspect of the narrator's life. As such they can be shorter than a life
story, but more detailed. Single-issue interviews can yield valuable insights for many
development and relief activities. They are the main method of learning about a
particular event, such as drought, or for an investigation into a particular area of
knowledge or experience. For example, they might involve interviewing farmers
about land use and water conservation methods, or a traditional healer about botany
and plant use. They require the interviewer to have more detailed background or
technical knowledge of the subject matter than is necessary for a more wide-ranging
life story.

Diary interviewing

Diary interviewing is a method which is increasingly being used by social scientists.
It involves selecting a sample of people who contribute regular diary entries as part
of a continuing and long-term study of social trends. Such a study might ask people
to report on specific issues or it might seek more general life story material. The
participants make a commitment to keep a written or oral, tape-recorded diary.
Entries might be made on a daily, weekly, monthly or annual basis, and are then
sent in and analysed centrally, over time.

Alternatively, diary interviewing can involve a less rigorous procedure whereby
the participant is interviewed at key moments over a period of time. In a study of
indigenous agricultural practices, for example, these might include particular times
during the cropping calendar such as land preparation, sowing, weeding, harvesting
and threshing. In a more general life story study, such moments might include religious festivals, rites of passage or different stages of educational or working life.

The objective of diary interviewing is therefore to collect a running progress of a person's experience over time and not just retrospectively.

Group interviews

Oral testimony can also be collected through group work. Indeed, in many societies, group interviews may be more in keeping with the customary ways of communicating. If the concept of a one-to-one interview seems unusual or unnatural, the format of group discussions or public meetings may be more familiar and oral testimony collection can be adapted accordingly.

Groups can bring out the best and the worst in people. Sometimes, by taking the focus off individuals, they make them less inhibited, but the opposite can occur just as easily. A group may subtly pressurise people towards a socially acceptable testimony or a mythical representation of the past or of a current issue which everyone feels is 'safe' to share and which may be in some sense idealised. Communal histories gathered in this way can involve a powerful process of myth construction or fabulation which misrepresents the real complexity of the community. At worst, this can develop into a persistent false consciousness which can only tolerate the good things, and remembers 'how united we all were', or which exaggerates the totality of suffering and recalls 'how bad everything was'.[8] The voices of the less confident, the poorer and the powerless, are less likely to be heard, and so the variety of experience and the clashes and conflicts within a community may well remain hidden.

But groups can also be especially productive, as members 'spark' off one another. Memories are triggered, facts can be verified or checked, views can be challenged and the burning issues of the past can be discussed and argued about again in the light of the present. Group work can also increase rapport between project workers/interviewers and the community, encouraging people to come forward for one-to-one sessions if appropriate. Two kinds of group work are appropriate to oral testimony collection: small focus group discussions and larger community interviews.

Focus group discussions developed as an important part of market research, but are now used widely on an inter-disciplinary basis as a means of assessing attitudes and opinions. In this context, they are a particularly useful forum for discussing both the past and the major issues of the day. Focus groups are particularly appropriate for collecting testimony from people who may be very reserved on a one-to-one basis, but draw confidence from being in a familiar group. Children are a good example of this.

The idea is to bring a group together – preferably between five and twelve people – to discuss a particular issue or a number of issues. They should be a homogeneous group made up of participants of the same sex and largely equal in social status, knowledge and experience so that confidence is generally high and no-one feels threatened. The discussion should last for one to two hours, with the participants sitting comfortably and facing each other in a circle. Several consecutive sessions can be held if necessary.

Social scientist Krishna Kumar notes that the main emphasis on a focus group is the interaction between the participants themselves, and not that between participants and interviewer.[9] Focus groups are therefore guided by a 'moderator' rather than an interviewer, whose role is to steer the discussion and ask some probing questions by adopting a posture of 'sophisticated naïveté'. This encourages the group to talk in depth with confidence, but also to be ready to spell things out for the outsider. The moderator's role also involves countering the two main constraints on a focus group: dominance of the proceedings by so-called 'monopolisers'; and a sense of group pressure which can build up from a majority viewpoint and which then discourages a minority of participants from expressing their views.

Community interviews involve larger groups and may resemble public meetings more than group discussions. Their emphasis is different, too. The main interaction of a community interview is between the interviewer and the community. The ideal size is around thirty people, but no more, and two interviewers will be needed for such an event. Their role is a directly questioning one, but they must still take responsibility for balancing participation in the meeting with guiding the interview. Having two interviewers can be confusing and their respective roles should be well defined in advance of the interview, to ensure that they do not speak at the same time or interrupt each other's train of enquiry.

The advantage of a community interview is the opportunity it provides for gathering a wide cross-section of people together at one time. This is particularly useful at the outset of a project, for example, when background information is being collected or future interviewees are being sought and selected. It is also useful midway or at the end of the process of collecting interviews, when certain details or views need to be tested or checked. It can provide the occasion for a number of 'straw polls' and hand counts in order to learn how many people share experiences or hold similar views. Finally, both group and community meetings are especially useful for the 'return' of oral testimony. They can act as a review mechanism and can encourage decision-making based on the testimonies collected. [. . .]

Props and mnemonics

Questions are not the only way to inspire a narrator and jog the memory. Physical objects, such as old tools, photographs and traditional costumes or artefacts, can provide the focus for a more detailed testimony or group discussion. A farmer will often be more eloquent when holding an implement and describing its function. A refugee may find much more to say when looking at a picture of home. However, any prop should be carefully chosen, otherwise they will tend to distract the narrator and divert the interview instead of giving it depth.

One prop which is central to the communicative repertoire of Native Americans is the talking-stick.[10] This is a ritual stick which lies in the centre of any group of people who are there to talk or listen, whether it be at a political meeting or a storytelling session. In order to speak a person must go into the centre of the circle and pick up the stick. The speaker must then hold it while they talk and replace it when they stop. The stick places certain responsibilities upon speaker and listeners alike. It requires the latter to listen actively and patiently, but also tends to curb excessive talkativeness on the part of garrulous speakers and gives courage to the shy. Similar indigenous speech rituals should be employed wherever they exist.

Revisiting a place and conducting an interview *in situ* or during a 'walkabout' can also free the mind and allow someone to recall the past more easily. Such walkabouts might include: visiting a sparsely wooded watershed which used to be a forest, in order to discuss environmental history and change; returning to a mine or factory which used to be a place of work, to discuss child labour; or examining an abandoned and broken pump, to discuss irrigation techniques and land use.[11]

Role play can also be useful as a mnemonic or memory aid, particularly in groups, but also in one-to-one interviews (if you had been the elder what would you have done?). Role play not only releases memory through the re-enacting of situations or events (a certain dance, a typical working day, a particularly important meeting), but also allows people to be less inhibited as they narrate events under the cover of a different persona. Hearing old stories is another good way to jog the memory, and a song or tune from the past can be particularly evocative, taking the mind right back to the time the interviewer is investigating.

Visual techniques

While props and mnemonics help to jog people's memories, some visual techniques may assist them to express the past more clearly. Many oral testimony projects rely on straightforward interviewing alone, but additional visual methods can be helpful when testimony is being gathered among groups unfamiliar with the interview form. Creating a diagram or making a model can take the place of a potentially awkward persona interaction between interviewer and narrator; or may complement, assist or encourage people's verbal performance. Such material can then be displayed alongside the testimony in any report, exhibition or book resulting from a project.

Robert Chambers has described a range of techniques which can be used by rural people and development workers to give expression to various aspects of the past or recent past. These include time lines and biographies (including ethno-biographies); historical maps and models; historical transects; and trend diagrams and estimates.[12] Older people in the community usually play a key role in providing and shaping the relevant historical information in these techniques.

A *time line* is a list of key events, changes and 'landmarks' in the past, written up in chronological order on a large sheet of paper. It is often a useful way of putting an individual's or a community's history into perspective by identifying the broad framework of events which shaped their past. It can therefore be a good way into a life story interview or focus group discussion and may also provide the basis for the interview map. Figure 1 shows a time line produced by a village in Tamil Nadu, India, stretching from 1932 to 1990.[13]

A visual *biography* is a similar kind of chart which traces the 'life' of a particular phenomenon, whether it be a famine, a certain crop or diet, or the development of a kind of technology. These biographies are particularly useful for single-issue histories and can form the framework for the interview.

Maps can be drawn on paper or on the ground with sticks, chalks, pens or paints. Those worked on the ground can be photographed or transcribed on to paper before they are destroyed. Maps of the past are particularly useful in illustrating ecological histories and showing previous land-use patterns, plant and animal coverage. Figure 2 shows the landscape change over the past twenty-five years in Abela Sipa Peasant Association in Ethiopa.[14]

1932	–	TANK UNDERTAKEN BY GOVT
1935–1946	–	ESTABLISHMENT OF VERANDA SCHOOL BY GOVT
1947	–	INDEPENDENCE
1948	–	16 WERE DIED DUE TO CHOLERA, FAMINE
1954	–	ROAD, RHATCHED SCHOOL
1956–1964	–	CYCLONE, FLOODS
1966	–	NEW SCHOOL BUILDING
1968	–	AGAIN CHOLERA, 4 WERE DIED
1970	–	ELECTRICITY FACILITY, BRIDGE 100 FAMILIES MIGRATED BECAUSE OF SEVERE DROUGHT
1977	–	ESTABLISHMENT OF NOON-MEAL CENTER
1978	–	COMMUNITY WELL, 2 BORE WELL FOR DRINKING PURPOSE
1983	–	TIN P
1984	–	ELECTION BOYCOTT. ONE MORE BORE WELL. DRINKING WATER OVERHEAD TANK. STREET TAPS BY GOVT
1984–1985	–	NON FORMAL EDUCATION BY GOVT
1987	–	SPEECH
1989	–	GROUP HOUSES FOR 20 HARIJANS
1990	–	HEAVY CROP DAMAGE BECAUSE OF FLOOD

Figure 1 Time line: Tamil Nadu, India, 1932–1990

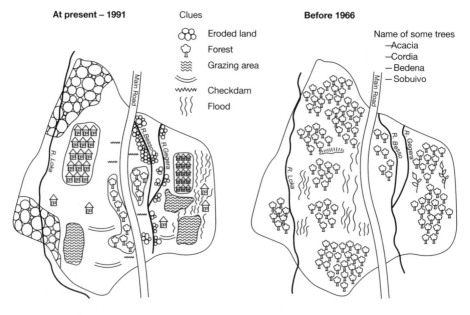

Figure 2 Landscape change: Abela Sipa Peasant Association, Ethiopia

Three-dimensional *historical models* using local materials have aided discussion on erosion and other environmental and agricultural concerns. In another example described by Chambers, villagers from Seganahalli in Karnataka, India, made two models on the ground. One showed their watershed as they remembered it fifty years earlier with trees growing on the rocky hills, and the other as they saw it now, with no trees and serious erosion. The striking difference between the two models began an important debate about what should be done, in which the models were used to present and explore the various options.[15] Thus historical analysis can be the trigger to development debate and it can also be used to generate so-called 'dream' models and maps, expressions of people's hopes for the future which can then form the basis of development action. *Historical transects* are another kind of diagram which represent changing conditions through time. Again they have traditionally been used in agro-ecosystem analysis and are usually compiled by walking through an area with some of the older inhabitants and recording their recollections of various conditions at key moments identified by the time line. Figure 3 is a transect through time illustrating land-use trends in a village in East Java.[16]

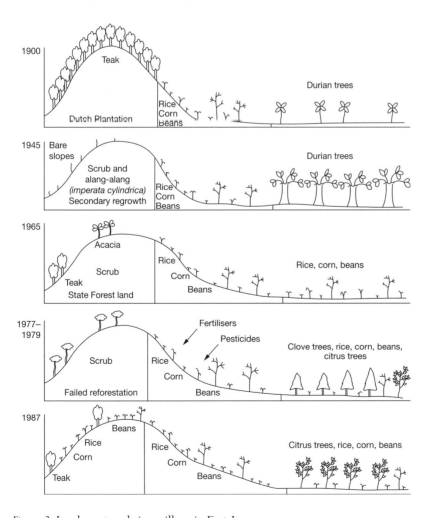

Figure 3 Land-use trends in a village in East Java

Three main kinds of chart have been used by rural people to estimate or measure change and historical trends: counters, pie charts and straightforward trend lines. Stones, seeds or pieces of stick can be used as *counters* representing absolute or relative values. People can pile up these counters along a simple time line to express absolute values for things like harvest yields, price changes or population changes. They can also place counters in a matrix diagram to express relative values or scores which indicate certain differences over time. For example, one matrix might allow a narrator to express her preferences for certain crops and income-generating activities during five key years in the past.

Pie charts drawn on paper or the ground are another useful way by which people can express relative values and how these changed over time. Figure 4 shows two pie charts made by three elderly farmers which illustrate changing cropping and land-use patterns in a village near Dehra Dun, Uttar Pradesh, India, between 1950 and 1990.[17]

Trend lines are simple graphs in which people use a curved line to illustrate historic trends. A normal histogram or bar-chart can be used for the same purpose. Figure 5 shows a trend line drawn in the dust by an old farmer in Mahbubnagar district, Andhra Pradesh, India. The lines illustrate the increasing and decreasing trends relating to farmyard manure, pests, soil fertility, fertiliser and yields over forty years.[18] Participatory diagrams are another way in which people can describe a past event and the processes it generated (flow diagrams) or the effect it had on their lives (impact diagrams).[19]

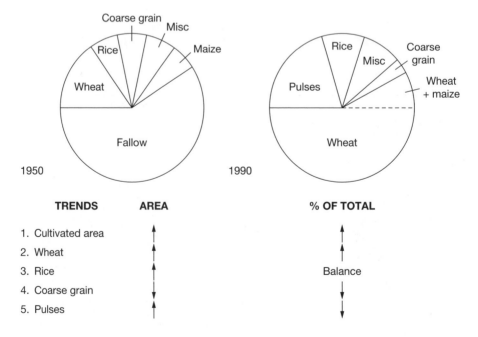

Figure 4 Cropping and land-use patterns in a village near Dehra Dun, Uttar Pradesh, India, 1950–1990

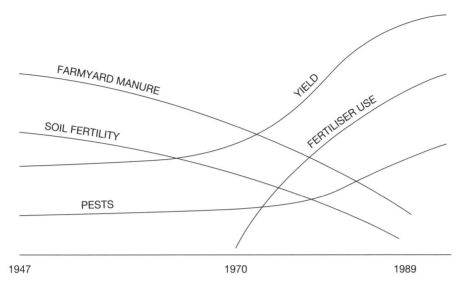

FARMYARD MANURE

SOIL FERTILITY

YIELD

FERTILISER USE

PESTS

1947   1970   1989

Figure 5 Trend line for Mahbubnagar district, Andhra Pradesh, India, 1947–1989

Notes

1   C. Briggs, *Learning How to Ask*: *A Sociolinguistic Appraisal of the Role of the Interview in Social Science Research*, Cambridge: Cambridge University Press, 1986.

2   J. Mitchell and H. Slim, 'Listening to rural people in Africa: the semi-structured interview in rapid rural appraisal', *Disasters*, 1991, vol. 15, no. 1.

3   H. Norberg-Hodge, *Ancient Futures*: *Learning From Ladakh*, London: Rider Books, 1991, p. 36.

4   Lomo Zachary in a letter to Ken Wilson, Refugee Studies Programme, Oxford, 1987.

5   Briggs, *Learning How to Ask*.

6   J. Mitchell and H. Slim, 'Interviewing amidst fear', unpublished paper, Rural Evaluations, 1990.

7   See also the introduction to N. Cross and R. Baker (eds), *At The Desert's Edge*: *Oral Histories from the Sahel*, London: Panos Books, 1991.

8   See J. Bornat, 'The communities of community publishing', *Oral History*, 1992, vol. 20, no. 2.

9   K. Kumar, 'Conducting group interviews in developing countries', AID Program Design and Evaluation Methodology Report No. 8, US Agency for International Development, Washington, 1987.

10 The details about the Native American talking-stick are taken from a talk given by the American storyteller, Richard Cupidi, at Intermediate Technology's 1992 Annual Public Meeting, London.

11 See R. Chambers, 'Shaping the past: people's maps, models and diagrams in local historical analysis and planning', a paper presented to the National Life Story Collection's conference on Oral History and Development, London, November 1991.

12 See, for example, R. Chambers, 'Rural appraisal: rapid, relaxed and participatory', IDS Discussion Paper 311, Institute of Development Studies, Sussex, England, 1992.

13　J. Devararam, *et al.*, 'PRA for rural resource management', *RRA Notes*, 1991, no. 13, cited in Chambers, 'Shaping the past'. IIED training materials and *RRA Notes* are useful sources of information on PRA and RRA methods in practice.

14　'Farmer participatory research in north Omo, Ethiopia', a report on a training course in Rapid Rural Appraisal, Soddo, July 1991, IIED and FARM Africa, London, cited in Chambers, 'Shaping the Past'.

15　Chambers, 'Shaping the Past'.

16　J.N. Pretty, J.A. McCracken, D.S. McCauley and C. Mackie, *Agroecosystem Training and Analysis in Central and East Java, Indonesia*, London: IIED, 1988.

17　A. Venu Prasad, in Chambers, 'Shaping the Past'.

18　Chambers, 'Shaping the Past'.

19　See J. Theis and H. Grady, 'PRA for community development', IIED and SCF (UK), 1991; and R. Leurs, 'A resource manual for trainers and practitioners of PRA', Overseas Aid Group, Birmingham University, UK, 1993.

Chapter 12

Belinda Bozzoli

INTERVIEWING THE WOMEN
OF PHOKENG

Through a study of twenty-two black South African women migrants from one small town in the Western Transvaal, Belinda Bozzoli, working with black colleague Mmantho Nkotsoe, reflects on the impact of 'insider' and 'outsider' interviewer status: the effects of shared cultural value and rapport on the interview process. Bozzoli is Deputy Vice-Chancellor (Research) at the University of Witwatersrand, South Africa. Extracted from Belinda Bozzoli, with Mmantho Nkotsoe, *Women of Phokeng*: *Consciousness, Life Strategy and Migrancy in South Africa, 1900–1983*, London: James Currey, 1991, by permission of Ravan Press.

My name is Nkotsoe. I am a girl from Mabeskraal, the nearby village. I think you know that village.

Yes I do. My name is Ernestina Mekgwe. I was born here in Phokeng and brought up here also.[1]

THE TWENTY-TWO women whose interviews are analysed [in *Women of Phokeng*] were all residents of Phokeng, an old and typically Tswana settlement, now in the officially designated and legally 'independent' homeland of Bophuthatswana. Their stories exemplify some of the complexities involved in the formation of modern South Africa. Born at the turn of the century, they grew up in a rural economy that was both viable and resilient, but one that had already had to make significant adaptations to survive the newly emerging order of the times. Many of them became migrants to the city, however, in their early twenties, as migrancy became both an economic necessity and an institutionalised expectation. For many, what were planned as temporary sojourns in the city lasted for up to forty years, during which they lived a life defined by family, work, and community, a life that was only partially proletarian in character. In the end, they returned to their village to live as pensioners and grandmothers in the 'homeland' of Bophuthatswana.

The women were interviewed, up to four times each, by Mmantho Nkotsoe – also a black South African woman – who, as she says, was born in a 'nearby village'. The conversations between Mmantho and the women were recorded as part of a larger oral history project (the Oral Documentation Project, or ODP) initiated at the University of the Witwatersrand in 1979. Some one thousand oral histories of black and some white South Africans, mainly from the countryside of the Transvaal, have been collected since the project began.

The ODP has focussed on the life experiences of rural black South Africans in the Transvaal, and has a variety of analytical and geographical focal points. Methodologically, it adopted a pragmatic and eclectic approach.[2] No fixed procedure for obtaining life stories was decided upon in advance; researchers and interviewers worked together to construct a viable set of ground rules as the material was being collected and problems emerged. Fundamental to the ODP was the initial decision that interviews with rural people, often barely literate and certainly unfamiliar with the English language, needed to be undertaken in the vernacular, preferably without the presence of a translator or other intervening party. Setswana- or Sesotho-speakers were the obvious candidates for the role of interviewer in the case of the Transvaal, and the ODP has over the years employed a succession of interviewers fluent in either or both of these languages, who would undertake interviews in collaboration with a researcher or team of researchers, and then transcribe the tapes and translate them into English. The ODP archives have been used by a variety of authors and interpreted in a range of different ways. Some have used them as a source of information not obtainable elsewhere;[3] others have used selected interviews as the basis for essays on individual life experiences;[4] and a major biography of the ODP's most loquacious informant is under way.[5] This study has chosen a different means of interpreting the material, which was generated as a result of specific choices over time about the direction the interviewing should take.

Mmantho Nkotsoe, a university graduate, was trained by the ODP, and she and our initial research team – Tim Couzens, Charles van Onselen, and I – worked cooperatively on the project during 1981–1983. Her mandate was to find interesting elderly women who lived in the countryside and to record the stories of their lives. At first, the intention of the study was simply to record the stories of those whose lives are hidden from history; Mmantho was asked to travel around the Transvaal from village to village, and enquire whether any of the elderly women of the village would be willing to talk to her. She was working together with the other similarly trained oral historians in the ODP, but she alone has been asked to interview only women (the others interviewed men or women). Mmantho was given guidance as to the kinds of sociological questions which the study of the lives of African women in South Africa might involve. She was introduced to modern feminist literature, to the comparative literature on African women, and to the history of women in South Africa. She was trained to record life stories in roughly chronological sequence, and to prompt her informants with indirect questions about issues that she and we considered to be particularly interesting or informative. She was not, however, asked to administer anything like a structured interview schedule in the early stages of the project; when appropriate, she was to allow her informant to guide the interview.

In the early part of the project, Mmantho interviewed women from Potchefstroom, Kuruman, Vryburg and Phokeng.[6] But she developed a particularly striking rapport with the Phokeng women. Using her native Setswana to speak to Setswana-speaking informants, she elicited from the first few women from this particular place life stories and statements of world views that rang with intimacy. One obvious reason for this was Mmantho's own background in the neighbouring village. Now, of course, she was a university-trained historian and sociologist. But to the women she was interviewing, as will become evident in the body of this study, she was almost a kinswoman, a young girl, a child to some, who wanted to know the stories of the past. Thus, what to positivists might seem to be Mmantho's weakness (her subjective involvement in the lives of the informants, and their perception of her as having a particular meaning in their lives) proved to be her greatest strength. It was in the light of this that Mmantho was then asked to continue her interviewing only with women from Phokeng, and to focus her questions more directly on their specific experiences. In the subsequent months, the full twenty-two life stories of women living in Phokeng, in their late seventies and early eighties, were collected. These provide the basis for this study, a remarkably coherent collection of stories with a similarity of context that enabled this 'cohort' of women to be examined using sociological more than biographical tools.

This collection of stories has been both reported and interpreted somewhat unconventionally. The life stories have been treated as texts, imperfectly reflecting lives, and more accurately revealing 'cultural and psychological myth',[7] rather than as sources or 'gobbets' of useful answers to key questions, as the positivist approach might have it. While the 'texts' have not been given full priority over the 'context' in poststructuralist fashion, literary methods of analysis have certainly been brought to bear upon them.[8] The seventy or so bare transcripts that make up the twenty-two life histories have been subjected to a variety of different readings; they have been treated variously as documents, narratives, stories, histories, incoherent ramblings, interlinked fragments of consciousness, conversations, and/or recitals of fact.[9] Each of these ways of looking at them has revealed a different set of meanings.

The first, and most conventional, use to which they have been put has been as reflections of the history of the places and times experienced by the women interviewed – they have indeed provided us with 'more history'. The history of Phokeng – a relatively unknown village, in an underresearched part of South Africa – is undoubtedly illuminated by the recollections of the women who have lived there.[10] The conversations throw light on the way of life in early peasant and sharecropping households, the standard of living attained, the sexual division of labour that prevailed, the history of schooling, family relations, ethnic divisions, and particular Bafokeng struggles, for example. As the women migrate, they are drawn into relationships that are far better documented by other researchers. But we may still see their stories as sources of information about the conditions of labour in domestic service, wages, networks of support, and social relations, as well as about the nature of life in freehold townships such as Sophiatown and Alexandra during the interwar years in particular. Of course the interviewees tend to romanticise their childhood, to get dates wrong, to abandon all chronology, and simply to forget. The reading of these transcripts has involved the craft of sifting the valid piece of information from the invalid, the weak informant from the strong one. But what source of sociological and historical information does not involve these processes? Can we assume that the witnesses to government commissions of enquiry, or the government officials and public figures who write official letters to one another – sources that have all the grave respectability required of historians' footnotes – are freer of the sins of bias and distortion than the women of Phokeng? Thus, as with any source of information, there are crucial times and places where the informants interviewed here can and do provide valid, important, and useful insights, which might emerge as much in spite of their intentions as because of them. Of course these testimonies need to be read with a critical eye and with enough knowledge of the context to make it possible to sift the gold of true evidence from the bulk of ideology, poor memory, and wilful misleading that occurs. But it would be a poor researcher who did not perform this sifting process with every source available to her.

[Women of Phokeng] will have failed, however, if it is read as yet another contri- bution to the detailed understanding of 'what happened' – whether in Phokeng, Parkview, or Pimville. It is not designed to add, in incremental fashion, to our store of information about sharecroppers or peasants, servants or beerbrewers, although it does reveal a lot of interesting detail about these things. But more importantly, these texts have revealed themselves to be unsurpassed sources for revealing other- wise hidden forms of consciousness. In the case of interviews such as these, which take the form of a dynamic conversation, expressions of consciousness and social identity are evident which do not normally find their way into the kinds of sources and methods conventionally used – where black South Africans are in any case thinly represented, and women hardly at all.[11] How has this aspect of interpretation of the texts occurred?

The very intimacy and interactiveness of the interviews has lent them a special character, and the study has not pretended that these life stories were obtained through the sterile means of removing the interviewer as far as possible from any involvement in the interaction, and turning her into the 'absent' listener. Instead, the interaction itself is analysed here,[12] and the book acknowledges the transcripts of these interviews for being precisely what they are – records of conversations between black South Africans of differing backgrounds and levels of education, but with sufficient similarities between them to lend authenticity, richness, and depth to what is being said. As such, the interviews reveal things about the women and their mentalities that would otherwise remain opaque. Mmantho's questions as well as the women's answers are usually included, as are fairly lengthy extracts in which the full flow of their interaction is revealed. We see how even the most canny of informants tells Mmantho, the educated young girl from the nearby village, a little about her childbearing and marital experiences. Mmantho allays the suspicions of most of her informants about her political credentials in a culture riddled with suspi- cion and fear. It is Mmantho who draws out of her subjects stories of home and work that many white, or male, or 'outsider' researchers might struggle to obtain, even using the most 'scientific' of methods. Let us examine more carefully the various components of this process of interaction, in order to help us understand what precisely it is that these interviews are capable of yielding.

The interviews are not treated as having a clearly defined beginning and end, as perhaps a pseudoscientific interpretation of them might suggest.[13] Of course they have boundaries – between the 'formal' period of actual interviewing, where ques- tions are asked and answers recorded, and the 'informal' preliminaries, interludes, and lengthy farewells which surround and cushion what some think of as the 'actual' interview. But both the informal and the formal parts of the interaction have their functions, and are interpreted as part of the text – again providing us with insight into the kinds of people being interviewed. In the former, for example, Mmantho establishes the crucial rapport discussed above; in the latter, she requires the interviewee to respond to her questioning initiatives, to submit to a certain degree to the authority she claims to possess. In these conversations it becomes clear that what is formally recorded is informed and indeed inspired by what is not. Many of the insights these interviews give us are not derived from any clear-cut and formalised set of interview questions; nor are they insights that any interviewer, administering the same set of questions, could have gained. Rather, they are a product of the unique formal and informal exchanges between this particular interviewer and her interviewees.

Mmantho herself brings particular characteristics to bear upon the situation. The fact that she is 'a girl from Mabeskraal, the nearby village' is perhaps the most important of these[14] – the focus on Phokeng was selected at an early stage in the study precisely because of Mmantho's ability to call upon common understanding between herself and her interviewees from this particular place. As the 'local girl', Mmantho can appeal to common conceptions of space, community, boundary, property, history, hierarchy and culture, both on the broad level (she is a Tswana too) and on a local level (she knows Mrs X who lives down the road; her sister went to Y school, which Mrs J's daughter went to, or of which Mrs M has heard). These are areas where her knowledge of the society is more experiential and intuitive than learnt. On the level of class, too, Mmantho is not an outsider – for she shows great sensitivity to and empathy for those whom she interviews, in spite of her better education. Mmantho 'knows what is going on' in Phokeng. The interviews display a sense of conversation and intimacy between interviewer and interviewee, which is obviously aided by Mmantho's fluent use of rural Setswana. The interviews are replete with references to Tswana words, some with a local meaning, to surnames, clan names, and regional realities.[15] Her local origins allow a particular type of interview to emerge, one rich in local detail, and one which allows us to 'overhear' interactions. This means that what is taken for granted between Mmantho and her interviewee is often of as much significance as what is regarded as of unusual and extraordinary value by both of them. The structure that both parties almost unconsciously attribute to Bafokeng society and the world around it is one that contains categories which are of great interest to the sociologist. Often, as suggested earlier, social scientific categories of analysis prove inappropriate for, or have to be adapted to fit, reality as it is perceived locally. This is not to say there are not hidden, invisible structures that common consciousness does not perceive. Of course there are – and part of Mmantho's quest was to discover them. But often these hidden forces are better understood by starting with the common consciousness of existing forces, than by assuming that categories derived from other contexts are appropriate by virtue of their theoretical pedigree. In the interviews, the women assume that Mmantho is aware of such matters as the boundaries of the community, its inner workings, and the roles it attributes to its members, as well as a whole range of other matters they feel she 'knows', assumptions that give us a lot to work with. Sometimes this rapport fails, and the interviewee gets irritated with Mmantho because she hasn't indicated the common ground the subject thought they both possessed; or Mmantho finds her question gets the 'wrong' answer, because she has assumed common ground that does not exist.

Mmantho is also black, and to the white outsider, the interviews sometimes read like private conversations.[16] Interviewees will sometimes express a hostility towards whites that they feel Mmantho will understand. At other times they confide in her, with a sense of amazement, about the extraordinary behaviour displayed by whites. Elsewhere, they show simple interest, treating her as a source of potentially important and useful information about whites – what can you tell me about these people? The impression given is that whites are mysterious, they come in a variety of different 'types',[17] and their behaviour requires constant explication. There are, it is assumed, nice whites and not-so-nice ones.[18] Whites are the outside category in these interviews, blacks the inside one. 'We blacks' is a commonly used phrase, for example. Mmantho herself does not indulge in exchanging information about 'good' and 'bad' whites. But her interviewees assume she is a ready listener to such information because of the assumption of a common universe.

Thirdly, Mmantho is also a woman. Common womanhood is appealed to less frequently than Tswana-ness or blackness as a basis for mutual understanding. But Mmantho was trained to ask questions about the female experience, and about relations between men and women. Although the sociological categories she brings to bear on the interviews do not always 'work',[19] there are few examples of places in the interviews where such questions are brushed off or ignored. Rather, interviewees participate eagerly in discussions of such matters as how 'women get rich through farming',[20] how 'men do not worry about women who dislike arranged marriages',[21] or how women took out their breasts and showed them to the police, shouting 'you were fed from this breast'.[22] Perhaps the fact that Mmantho is a good fifty to sixty years younger than her informants made them less than forthcoming about the details of childbirth, or about the role of prostitution in township life – and the study is unable to pursue the issue of sexuality beyond a limited sphere. Still, childbirth rituals, fears of rape, and the difficulties of arranged marriage are issues raised by several of the women.

Mmantho's youth often causes her to be subjected to the older women's homilies about the evils of the younger generation, the virtues of the good old days, and the decline of moral and ethical standards. They like Mmantho because she shows respect towards them, and because she does not objectify them as 'old people'. Reminiscences are often treated by the women as opportunities for them to educate the younger girl about the culture, history, and achievements of her own people, and to draw her into an acknowledgement of the failures of the present. Her high level of education, while often treated as something to be valued, is assumed by some of the women to render Mmantho ignorant of local history and culture. She combines, therefore the roles of a learned authority, whose questions must be answered, and an ignorant junior, who must be told about reality. At the same time, some of the women prefer to present themselves to Mmantho in terms they know will be understood by a younger, modern person.

The very interviewing technique used by Mmantho – the pursuing, in as near chronological order as possible, of the trajectory of the life of each woman through her experiences as a young girl, a married woman, a peasant and an urban worker, a mother and a churchgoer – also contributed to the special character of the interviews. Mmantho was sensitive, for example, to the fact that most 'ordinary people', especially less educated ones, do not think of their lives as an elaborate curriculum vitae, arranged in chronological order and divided up into neat compartments such as work, home, and leisure.[23] Her interviewing technique adapted itself to the rambling style of many interviewees, to the fact that personal histories are a jumble and that they contain inconsistencies; or to occasions when the interviewee herself would wish to lead the discussion at certain crucial points rather than allow herself to be led – all of which would be anathema to the positivist. The consciousness of the interviewees is most often revealed, here, where they are not necessarily being 'led' by Mmantho, but when they make unsolicited or seemingly irrelevant statements, in the 'wrong' chronological order, about matters they consider to be important. Often it is what is spontaneous about the interviews that is most revealing.[24]

Some of these special characteristics of Mmantho as an interviewer were very clearly highlighted when, after the first thirty or so interviews were completed, we decided to 'advance' to a more 'scientific' stage in the research, by devising and administering a more formal questionnaire, based on the findings of the first interviews. The questionnaire was designed to overcome the problems of inconsistency between the interviewees – all would now be asked the same set of questions in the same order – and of major gaps that existed in the testimonies. The resulting more tightly structured interviews were factually informative, and probably, in case it appears that this book lacks any commitment to structure whatsoever, essential in giving us a bank of information common to all members of this 'cohort' of women. But they lacked qualitative insights. They told us about the ages and dates of birth of each member of the informants' families, for example, but informants failed to take the opportunity to make their own statements, answer their own questions, lead the interview, or give their own opinions. The interviews became less interactive, more one-sided. Subjectivity vanished. The terms of reference were dictated by myself; Mmantho became simply the channel of my structured views, and the resulting words of the informants were often static and shallow, although Mmantho managed to make more imaginative use of the questionnaire than seemed possible.

This problem became even more obvious when Mmantho left the project, and the final round of questionnaires was administered by a second interviewer who, although black and with every intention of sympathy, was male, from an entirely different region and social class from the Phokeng women, and not a native Setswana speaker. The women failed to respond to the questions with more than yes or no answers in some cases; and some expressed feelings of resentment and anxiety about being interviewed. The rapport was lacking, the women became reticent, and they presented themselves to him in less open a manner.

Thus when we look at each interview as the text of a conversation between Mmantho and another woman, we are able to ask questions about the self-perception of older Tswana women *vis-á-vis* the younger generation, or about the boundaries of common identity established between interviewer and interviewee, which suggest something about the meaning of being a 'Tswana', a woman, a black, or a Mofokeng. We can probe how the relating of historical tales and details is seen as an important and socially underestimated activity, or how complex is the matter of the value given the high level of education of a woman like Mmantho.

Besides the process of interaction that produced the texts, the interviewees themselves have brought certain personal and individual qualities to the interviews, which add to their value. It should be said that the interviewees here were all informed that their stories were to be recorded, translated, and made fully available to scholars. The women who agreed to participate did so for a variety of reasons, each of which leaves its mark on the kind of interview they give. Some agreed because they believed they had an interesting and important story or series of stories to tell. They show a sense of their place in history, and their significance as historical actors. Naomi Setshedi, for example, stops Mmantho and changes the direction of the interview completely at times, with the sense that she knows important things that Mmantho is not particularly good at getting at. Others believe that by participating in the interview some aspect of their lives will perhaps be bettered. One woman refused to be reinterviewed, claiming that 'nothing had come' of her previous interviews, so why, she asked, should she be interviewed again. Some treat the interview as an occasion to tell Mmantho all the things they have been longing to convey to the younger generation – either about the lost past, their own lost dignity, or about the lost struggles that achieved things which the younger generation now take for granted. The women regard themselves 'as stores of information and history'. They talk about times long ago, and about old practices, sometimes patronising Mmantho with a cultural heritage she 'should' know about, but at other times simply telling her that there are things she has not heard of.

The women are almost all keen to be interviewed. They wish their village and their people to be known. They place a value on history, on recording the deeds of people, and on genealogy. They display a feeling that the past contains truths and inspirations that the present has crushed. As 'ordinary' women, few interviewees give Mmantho the sense that they might think they are not worthy of being interviewed,[25] although it might be Mmantho's special status as an interviewer that brings their self-confidence and assertiveness to the fore.

Each interviewee constructs her life story in a different way. The different personalities of the interviewees of course affect their responses. But there are also ideological and cultural perceptions that have a social determination, varying from person to person. While the least successful interviewees treat the interview as something rather official, answering questions in a static, monosyllabic way and giving even Mmantho the status of an outsider, denied access to the interviewee's inner feelings, the best become storytellers, creating a series of well told anecdotes.[26] In telling stories, the informants construct the past in ways that place them at the centre of important events, and convey to us what they think is important about their lives – the pleasure or horror of living in Sophiatown, their courage, or their trauma, in difficult circumstances; and what type of person they wish to present themselves as being. Certain character 'types' emerge, whether by the artful design of the interviewee or as a reflection of different social patterns of identity. The 'Mayibuye' woman, who saw Christianity and education as a means to other ends, who took part in social protest, rebelled against arranged marriage, and has a coherent sense of her reasons for her various dissatisfactions, may be distinguished from the more conservative church-going woman, who tends to accept authority, to be overwhelmed by defeat, and to show a suspicion of social movements, for example. The study does not often try to label each individual woman as such. It is difficult to do so without obscuring the way in which the women's stories are also repositories of different fragmented components of consciousness and identity; the same woman who presents herself as having a rather clear sense of herself as a 'Mayibuye' woman, also reveals aspects of her identity as a tribeswoman, churchgoer, wife, mother, daughter, township dweller, and so on. What the study attempts to reveal are the patterns of interplay between the consistent and fragmented aspects of identity, the myriad building blocks out of which a particular individual is constructed, and the larger patterns she might try to present. We ask when and why it is that at certain times, identity appears to cohere. Does it have to do with the presence of an 'organic intellectual' (in Gramsci's terms) who seeks to and is able to organise consciousness?[27] The study does not seek to suggest that the presence of a variety of aspects of identity confirms the currently fashionable view that all subjectivity is 'decentred', but suggests that there is an interplay between the self and its multiple components, an interplay that may be historically examined, and which involves processes of social interaction and ideological creativity. [. . .]

Notes

1   Ernestina Mekgwe, interviewed by Mmantho Nkotsoe (MN) on 11–9–1981, p. 1, University of the Witwatersrand African Studies Institute Oral Documentation Project, Womens' Project [hereafter ODP WP].

2   As far as its theoretical background is concerned, in the early stages of the Oral Documentation Project, authors such as P. Thompson, *The Voice of the Past: Oral History*, Oxford: Oxford University Press, 1978, and T. Rosengarten, *All God's Dangers*, New York: Avon Books, 1974, proved influential – more so, perhaps, than the existing Africanists who had worked with oral sources. The women's project in particular was influenced by the work of such Western scholars as Ann Oakley and Lillian Rubin, both of whom gave the voices of ordinary women a prominent place earlier than most.

3   Perhaps using the 'more history' approach. See, for example, H. Bradford, *A Taste of Freedom: the ICU in Rural South Africa, 1924–1930*, New Haven: Yale University Press, 1987.

4   See, for example, T. Keegan, *Facing the Storm: Portraits of Black Lives in Rural South Africa*, Cape Town: David Philip, 1988; M. Nkadimeng and G. Relly, 'Kas Maine: the story of a black South African agriculturist', in B. Bozzoli (ed.), *Town and Countryside in the Transvaal*, Johannesburg: Ravan Press, 1983; and T. Matsetela, 'The life story of Nkgona Mma Pooe: aspects of sharecropping and proletarianisation in the northern Orange Free-State 1890–1930', in S. Marks and R. Rathbone (eds), *Industrialisation and Social Change in South Africa*, London: Longman, 1982.

5   C. van Onselen is writing a biography of Kas Maine, who was a sharecropper.

6   Tapes of these early interviews are lodged in the ODP, but, with the exception of the Phokeng tapes, do not form part of this study.

7   D.E. Faris, 'Narrative form and oral history: some problems and possibilities', *International Journal of Oral History*, 1980, vol. 1, no. 3, p. 172.

8   I am grateful to Isabel Hofmeyr and Stephen Clingman for having drawn me into these analytical approaches, although they bear no responsibility for my failings in this respect.

9   R. Grele suggests that oral history interviews are in fact 'conversational narratives' – a useful notion which approximates that used here, although perhaps it does not capture quite the range of ways in which the text of an oral history may be used. See R. Grele, 'Movement without aim: methodological and theoretical problems in oral

history', in R. Grele (ed.), *Envelopes of Sound: Six Practitioners Discuss the Method*, *Theory and Practice of Oral History and Oral Testimony*, Chicago: Precedent Publishers, 1985.

10   There are a few studies of Phokeng and the surrounding area. N. Mokgatle's *Autobiography of an Unknown South African*, London: University of California Press, 1971, includes important material on the oral traditions and early history of Phokeng.

11   See L. Passerini, 'Italian working class culture between the wars: consensus to fascism and work ideology', *International Journal of Oral History*, 1980, vol. 1, no. 1, pp. 8–10. Discussions of method are all too rare in Southern African studies.

12   I am not a symbolic interactionist, although this approach has proved useful – the ideas of Erving Goffman in particular have helped in the treatment of the 'conversations'.

13   However, in the physical sciences, too, we are told that great innovations and discovery often occur outside of what is formally defined as the 'experimental situation'.

14   This is one of many examples of the interviewees mentioning Mmantho's background, some of which appear in the body of the study. In another, Rosinah Setsome says to Mmantho, 'You come from a local area' (ODP WP, MN interview with Rosinah Setsome, 12–9–1981, p. 17), while elsewhere mention is made of Mmantho's school, her surname, and the likelihood that she will know some of the people being discussed.

15   Mrs Setshedi engages in a long discussion with her about the Setshedi clan, in which she assumes Mmantho has a knowledge of African history, and particularly of the Difaqane (early nineteenth-century wars between the Nguni and other ethnic groups in Southern Africa), and of its effects upon the Bafokeng.

16   It should be stressed that at no stage was the impression given to the interviewees that these conversations were, or would remain, private. They knew full well their purpose. The tone of intimacy simply arises as a result of Mmantho's skill and acceptability to her subjects.

17   Jews, Germans, Boers, English, and policemen are the main ones.

18   See, for a comparative example, P. Mayer's analysis of the attitudes of a sample of Sowetan blacks, in his '"Good" and "Bad" Whites', a paper presented to the Conference on South Africa in the Comparative Study of Class, Race and Nationalism, New York, 1982.

19   It was most frequently Western-derived feminist categories of analysis that proved difficult to transfer into this African setting – but more generally it was a case, as Passerini suggests, of existing social scientific concepts needing to be re-thought in the light of oral evidence.

20   ODP WP, MN interview with Ernestina Mekgwe, 11–9–1981, p. 2.

21   Ibid., pp. 14–15.

22   Ibid., p. 46.

23   It is important for positivistically inclined sociologists to recognise that questionnaire/survey methods of research were devised and evolved in Western settings, with high levels of literacy, good basic data from which to draw samples and construct questions, and the incorporation of even the poorer strata into a technocratic culture. People are used to filling in forms and ordering their perceptions. Even in those settings such methods have severe limitations. One of the reasons why sociological studies in South Africa have so often confined themselves to the white, middle class, literate, or dominant populations is that the discipline's own major heritage is faulty. These flawed instruments can barely be used amongst non-Western, peasant peoples, about whom basic raw data are almost entirely unknown, with low levels of literacy

and a low level of absorption of technocratic values. African sociologists would do well to look to the discipline's non-positivistic heritage, and its social anthropological offshoot, for insight into performing research in such settings.

24   Luisa Passerini found it significant in the 'spontaneous' part of her interviews with Italian workers who had lived through Fascism, that they remained silent about the fact of Fascism itself – an important form of self-censorship which, she says, is 'evidence of a scar, a violent annihilation of many years in human lives and memories, a profound wound in daily experience' (Passerini, 'Italian working-class culture', p. 9).

25   This is in strong contrast with the experiences of interviewers in many Western settings, where the kind of silences Passerini refers to appear to be common amongst poorer people who may have experienced harsh repression or taken part in strikes or other forms of protest without a sense of pride. See, for example, L. Shopes, 'Oral history and community involvement: the Baltimore Neighbourhood Heritage Project', in S.P. Benson et al. (eds), Presenting the Past, Philadelphia: Temple University Press, 1986.

26   I am grateful to Mike Kirkwood for first pointing out the rich storytelling capacities of particular interviewees, and for his creative editing of one of the woman's stories. See 'The story of Mrs S', Staffrider, 1984, vol. 6, no. 1. For an analysis of this essay and other life stories run in Staffrider see A. Oliphant, 'Staffrider magazine and popular history: the opportunities and challenges of personal testimony', Radical History Review, 1990 (Winter), pp. 46–47.

27   This concept is linked to those of 'inherent' and 'derived' ideologies mentioned above; Gramsci's idea was that particular knowledgeable and educated thinkers close to the working and poorer classes – the organic intellectuals – would be able to transform the incoherent 'inherent' set of ideas into a more coherent and socially useful ideology.

Chapter 13

Susan K. Burton

ISSUES IN CROSS-CULTURAL INTERVIEWING
Japanese women in England

This chapter explores cross-cultural interviewing and the insider/outsider debate in the context of language, arguing that language can shape identity and noting how some migrants seem to occupy a 'third culture' somewhere between their own and the host culture. Susan Burton completed a Ph.D. at Sussex University and is now a Lecturer in the Faculty of Foreign Languages and Asian Studies at Nagoya University, Japan. Reprinted with permission from *Oral History*, 2003, vol. 31, no. 1, pp. 38–46.

SINCE 1999 I HAVE BEEN researching the lives of Japanese women who live long-term (two years or more) in England. I have talked with sixteen so far: students, career women, women married to Japanese men, and women married to or divorced from British men. Having lived in Japan for several years, I speak passable Japanese and so conducted the interviews in whichever language the women preferred. I had no agenda and only one prepared question, 'Tell me how you come to be living in England'. The transcripts of these interviews form the basis of my, as yet unsubmitted, D.Phil. thesis. However, it is the methodology behind the interviews which has come to interest me more. There are currently three (that I know of) Japanese scholars researching aspects of Japanese women's lives in England: Toshie Habu, Keiko Itoh and Junko Sakai. They are interviewing in Japanese. As I began my research I wondered what I, as a foreigner, could bring to this subject through cross-cultural interviews that a native speaker could not easily do better. In this paper, I'd like to consider three of the issues I faced in my cross-cultural research: the insider/outsider debate, the pros and cons of interviewing in English or Japanese, and whether cross-cultural interviews add anything of significance to research on Japanese women in England.

Insider or outsider?

One of the first things a foreign student learns about Japanese society is that it is an insider/outsider culture, based on memberships of various groups including family, university, company and nationality. This encourages a strong Japanese identity and a clear perception of the foreign. Indeed, the commonly used word for foreigner, *gaijin*, means 'outside person'. Masao Miyamoto notes, 'no matter how deep their understanding of Japanese culture or how similar their lifestyle to that of the Japanese around them, foreigners are always "outside"'.[1] Clearly if, as has been suggested,[2] a perceived identity as an insider may be a prerequisite for a successful interview, then I was wasting my time.

However, it has also been noted that, just as it is often easier to talk to a stranger on a train, Japanese people sometimes find it easier to talk to foreigners about personal matters.

> Foreigners are, indeed, at a peculiar advantage in that respect. We are not part of the circle of evaluators and expecters, we are outside the ring of gossipers and colleagues and relatives, and so we may have confessions blurted out to us, sometimes embarrassingly.[3]

Being an outsider has its advantages in Japanese society. As Donald Ritchie writes, 'The foreigner is chosen precisely because telling him makes no difference'.[4] Yet could it even be so readily accepted that I would be viewed as an outsider? After all, although I was the *gaijin*, they were now living in my native country.

I felt I had a good chance of success and began looking for interviewees. It was suggested that I advertise in Japanese and English in some local Japanese language newsletters. This approach is generally very successful in the West but I didn't think this would work and so it proved; I didn't get a single reply. Partly this was due to the fact that oral history is largely unknown in Japan; in academic circles the attitude endures that it is amateurish, and there remains a heavy reliance on written evidence. Professor Shiozawa notes that oral history is usually written for a popular market by freelance writers: 'academic historians don't use such a style'.[5] But it was also the case that the direct approach is more of a Western concept. In Japan, as in much of Asia, there is greater reliance on personal connections, and relationships are established in a roundabout way. Have you ever noticed that at gatherings some Japanese people tend to stand alone perhaps not talking to anyone? It's not, as most Westerners think, shyness; they are waiting for someone they know to introduce them to somebody else. In Japan if you want to meet a particular person you ask a mutual friend to make the introductions.

I was very fortunate to have several long-time Japanese friends who were happy to introduce me around, explain my project, vouch for my trustworthiness, and even set up interviews for me. One even drove me to and picked me up from the interviews she had arranged. Through these initial introductions I was able to meet more women and indeed, in one town, it happened that once I'd interviewed one woman, one of her friends wanted interviewing too. (Of course, I didn't hear this directly. She called a mutual friend who then called me.) So it was the case that as an outsider, I needed the help of an insider to act as my 'sponsor'.

That I was heavily reliant on my Japanese friends was reinforced in the interviews. When asked, most interviewees admitted that they would not have agreed to see me if I had approached them directly. After all, how could they have known if I was reliable? Married women would also not have allowed me into their homes if I had been a man, Japanese or English. They said their husbands would not have approved. As a woman, my visits were viewed more as socialising than research. Since in Japan it is impolite to visit someone's home without a small gift, I usually took cake or biscuits and we drank and ate while we talked. They in turn had questions about English society they wished to ask or school newsletters they wanted explaining. For a couple of expatriate women whose husbands worked in local Japanese companies, I was the first English person they'd had a conversation with. After initial nervousness about the tie-pin microphones, the complete informality of the interviews seemed to help them relax and many later said they were surprised at what they had said. Some felt they had more to say and I interviewed a number of women twice. Two women cried over their loneliness. Overall they seemed to have enjoyed the opportunity to talk about themselves in a personal way.

> Thanks to speaking to you, I was able to organise my mind and feel more able to take appropriate steps in my life – which I am very grateful. It helps a lot to look back, particularly in my age.[6]

The pros and cons of interviewing in Japanese or English

It is obviously easier to speak freely in your native language. Your vocabulary is wider, you don't need to worry about whether your grammar is correct and you can be confident that you are saying what you mean to say. The onus is on the listener to understand. So why were all but four of the interviews carried out in English?

The obvious answer is that I must have asserted some form of pressure on the interviewees. It may have been the case that they felt they should speak English since they were living in England and I was an English guest in their home. However, my long-time friends rarely speak to me in English. More likely, it was the pressure all Japanese seem to feel when they encounter a foreigner anywhere in the world that, having spent six years studying English at school, they should make the effort to use it. Most *gaijin* in Japan have had the experience of asking a question in Japanese and getting the answer in English. But it was also the case that some of the interviewees, especially those who did not have contact with foreigners in their daily lives, wanted to use the interview as an opportunity to practise their English. When their English was weak, admittedly the interviews were not always as successful. However, instances when we both had to resort to our respective dictionaries proved to be useful 'bonding' experiences.

So that the interviewees didn't worry that they would be forced to speak English, I made it clear beforehand (or had my 'sponsor' assure them) that either language was acceptable, or any mixture of the two. In one case, a graduate student decided beforehand that she wanted to speak Japanese and that is how the interview began. As it progressed I noticed more and more English creeping into her conversation. After thirty minutes, I realised that I was speaking Japanese and she was speaking English. Why? One immediate answer is that the interviewees were talking about their lives in England, and recounting incidents that had happened to them in English.

> If I really need to speak about some unique aspect of Japanese culture I need to probably use Japanese words, but we have been talking about my background, my education mainly and work [in England], so my thinking system automatically switches in favour of English I suppose because that's what I was doing, using English teaching English and translating and then doing Ph.D. Everything is in English.[7]

The other reason lies in the nature of the Japanese and English languages. Japanese can be more suited to conveying things that are vague or intuitive, and English for things that are logical and direct.

> Perhaps Japanese language itself is not cut out for direct way of communication. As you know, we traditionally don't present any key ideas or issues, let alone your view of it, at first; instead, we have to pick up some irrelevant topics to create a certain mood which the audience can easily share. Then we go on to get close to the topic we want to talk about, trying all the time not to sound aggressive, without thinking a bit about logic or coherence. In English, you must try to present your main point clearly; but in Japanese, you must try to evoke some emotions.[8]

Indeed, having become used to speaking directly, some interviewees had experienced communication problems on trips back home.

> Japanese style is very fuzzy and you need to interpret what he is or what she is actually expecting you [to do, to say] but I get used to more direct ways of addressing things . . . I sometimes thought it's so straightforward dealing with foreigners but why it's not the case with Japanese people?[9]

It is also the case that Japanese is a hierarchical language, having several different levels of politeness. This is one reason why you cannot introduce yourself directly to someone; if you do not know whether they rank higher or lower than yourself you cannot know what level of politeness to use, hence the reliance on a mutual friend and the popularity of business cards. Indeed, one expatriate wife told me that she avoided wives' group gatherings because she could not know in advance the ranking of the other attendees. I did not think this would apply to oral history interviewing but apparently it did. When asked, the women said they would have talked to me if I had been a Japanese woman but that the interview would naturally have been bound by linguistic and cultural values. By switching to English they were able to avoid these.

> If I have to talk to a Japanese woman in Japanese, different, because some kind of things back of my brain like have to be modest all the

time and have to be polite so those things is part of my education . . .
So English speaking is good for me to express my real, natural thinking.[10]

Japanese is also a gendered language with male speech normally more authoritative and female speech soft, polite, indirect and, generally, powerless.[11] Although women, especially those in the workplace, are increasingly finding ways to overcome these linguistic conflicts, it is still the case that some women find it difficult to express themselves freely in Japanese – to 'defeminise' their speech – without sounding rude or odd. Because of this, James Stanlaw notes the prevalence of English or English loanwords in the songs of female songwriters which enable them to avoid gendered linguistic restrictions as well as making it easier for them to express strong personal emotions which can be difficult to do in Japanese.[12]

> They provide Japanese women not only with another 'voice', an additional and different symbolic vocabulary with which to express their thoughts and feelings, but also with a rhetorical power that was unknown to them previously, and that is suited for the growing power and stature that women are gaining in Japanese society.[13]

English, as Joy Hendry notes, is 'evidently associated with an informal level of communication, perhaps influenced by the idea that Westerners, typically Americans, are supposed to be frank with each other'.[14]

> [This] may explain the phenomenon several foreigners visiting Japan have noticed, namely that Japanese friends sometimes reveal the most intimate secrets about themselves when they are speaking English.[15]

I feel there is a lot of truth in this statement. However it should not be overlooked that due to the nature of the languages it is often easier to reveal secrets in English and just as easy to hide them in Japanese.

> I think partly the language, English, makes me act in a different way, yeah, act more freely and say what I like to say because English itself is much more direct than Japanese language so it's difficult to kind of hide my opinion with English while in Japanese it's much easier to be vague and ambivalent about things. Yeah, so partly because language affects how you behave and what you say.[16]

English loanwords are increasingly popular in Japan. The average Japanese person uses 3–5,000 of them – up to ten per cent of their daily vocabulary[17] – many of them replacing perfectly acceptable Japanese words because they sound more fashionable, more Western and consequently less traditionally Japanese. Thus hip, young Japanese might use the word *moodo* (mood) to describe an atmosphere whereas the older generation might prefer the word, *fun'iki* (same meaning). In this way, their choice of English can demonstrate a desire to be perceived as more international and less traditional. As a Japanese colleague noted, English is a form of brand goods, like a Prada bag or a Rolex watch. Acquiring a level of proficiency in it brings the speaker status and power, a very important asset for Japanese women within Japan's patriarchal society.

There is also a link here to identities, theirs and mine. How they viewed themselves and, in relation, how they viewed me tended to decide which language we spoke as well as the tone of the interview. For example, proficiency in English can give female academics status which they may rarely enjoy in Japan. Through English they can access a wider academic community and consequently their conversations with me, a fellow female academic, seemed to flow better in English. However, my interview with the wife of a high-ranking company president was conducted entirely in very polite Japanese with the wife, as the older woman and therefore my senior, dictating the entire flow of the interview and 'teaching' me about expatriate life, with myself saying very little. In fact, she spoke so fast that I lost the thread after about forty-five minutes and so couldn't direct the interview in any way. It was one of the best interviews I did. The wife, having lived in America and Britain for over twenty years, was apparently fluent in English but she never spoke it in front of me because I had been introduced to her by a lower-ranking wife, in front of whom she could not speak English because if she had made a mistake she would have lost face.

And there was always a middle ground. With friends or academic colleagues who knew I could understand Japanese, conversations switched from Japanese to English and back again depending on what was being said and which language was better at conveying it. Tiredness was also a factor. When the interview was in Japanese, after one hour I was exhausted and they were exhilarated. It was the opposite in English. So some interviews started in one language and ended in another. It was hell to transcribe.

Of course, like Molly Andrews[18] and Nicola North[19], I could have used a translator. Certainly two native Japanese speakers could have chatted much more freely, however, they would have been bounded by the Japanese linguistic and culture values previously mentioned. For example, in front of a translator, the interviewee may have hesitated to voice criticisms about other Japanese, to reveal personal traumas or weaknesses, and she could very well have felt ashamed that her lack of proficiency necessitated the presence of a fellow Japanese, and one whose English was superior to hers. Although my Japanese is not perfect, it is conversational, and I preferred to struggle on with my dictionary when necessary, and to preserve the casual, informal atmosphere of our chats. Also since I was already friends or on friendly terms with most of the women before the interviews, turning up with an interpreter (even pleading my poor Japanese) would have seemed odd. 'Muddling through' is a Japanese trait. Indeed, while in the West hesitancy is considered poor conversational style and perhaps rather amateurish in an oral historian, they are an essential component in Japanese conversation:

> Because hesitancy is interpreted in Japan as a sign of good social manners, not as in indication of inadequate knowledge, foreigners need not worry about speaking slowly and deliberately . . . polite hemming and hawing can often prevent bad will.[20]

Whilst one researcher during her work on the banking community[21] felt that her lack of English proficiency was an obstacle in gaining the trust of potential British interviewees, I never felt that proficiency and trust were ever linked in this way. In fact quite the opposite. Language proficiency is perceived as one of the components of the Japanese cultural identity, therefore there remains a common belief that foreigners can never master it.[22] To do so is a violation of Japanese sociolinguistic territorial integrity which many Japanese refuse to accept.[23] Moreover, both Roy Miller and Joy Hendry note experiences of being told that for a foreigner to speak fluent Japanese is 'an unnatural act'[24] and can be 'like a kind of psychological torture'[25] for the Japanese listener. As a British scholar of Japanese literature was once told, 'the better you speak Japanese, the worse impression we Japanese have of you'.[26] Therefore a foreigner who speaks less than perfect Japanese is not regarded as a threat and 'may invade this sociolinguistic territory with relative impunity'[27] whilst the fluent speaker may be viewed with some suspicion.[28] Although such a view is slowly disappearing in Japanese cities where foreigners are more visible, it can be seen that whilst one researcher's struggles with English may have been viewed as unprofessional, my own may have been regarded as quite natural and even rather comforting.

Cross-cultural interviews – of value to research?

So can the interviews add anything of value to research on Japanese women in England? I think it is fair to say that the interviews lose and gain something from being cross-cultural.

What they lose is that, whether I like it or not, the women probably made allowances for the fact that I am not Japanese. For example, although one woman, Rie, spoke in English, towards the end of the interview she said:

> I find I'm more comfortable with myself when I'm speaking in Japanese. That's because there's no language barrier, and because I think when you're more eloquent in a certain language you're more confident and when you're more confident you say different things from when you're not confident so naturally you sometimes have completely different things that comes out from your mouth.[29]

Moreover, although Japanese can be vague, meaning can be conveyed in other ways such as tone of voice and silence, which as a non-native speaker I may have missed. As another woman noted:

> One thing you find with Japanese people is that we can't label our emotions . . .you sort-of know from the tone of their voice that they're very upset or they're very angry. But they won't ever say, 'I'm really cross because . . .' or 'I'm really hurt because so-and-so said something' so you sort-of have to read between the lines.[30]

Indeed, many times I had to refer back to the original Japanese language recordings because the written transcript alone did not adequately convey the meaning. In English it was quite the opposite. Japanese women tend to speak very quietly and in high-pitched voices, seeming to lack gravity. However, once I had transferred their words into a written transcript I was surprised to discover that they had voiced some very strong views.

One other problem is how to present vague Japanese concepts and views in direct and logical English. Japanese is more of a contextual language; as previously noted you need to create a mood, but this doesn't translate well into an English language thesis for an English-speaking readership who expect in-depth analysis and rational conclusions.

> Written Japanese is OK but spoken language is little bit more problem
> . . . I think you need to locate a particular expression in the context so
> in order to specify this meaning you cannot lose the context any time,
> so it could be interpreted in maybe three or four ways so you always
> need to check it with the listener.[31]

It can also be difficult to present Japanese extracts in a short and comprehensible form. Most of the extracts in this article are from interviews conducted in English.

What the interviews gain is that I may have learned things that Japanese interviewers may not have been told.

> Oh, but you have advantage. Some Japanese women, maybe Japanese
> speaker, they will tell you the truth because you don't look like Japanese.
> And if Japanese woman interviewed other Japanese women, of course,
> they do in Japanese. So you have really good advantage.[32]

Speaking with a foreigner, many women also felt free of cultural and linguistic restrictions, and consequently were more prepared to state their own opinions and disagree with accepted wisdom. Whereas in Japan, you don't contradict someone who ranks higher than yourself:

> In Japan, if I talk with elderly man, if elderly man is very traditional
> Japanese man, I have to be careful because if he says, 'This is black'
> [pointing to something white] I have to say, 'Maybe'.[33]

Moreover, women who have lived and worked long-term in England often felt more comfortable in English:

> It's funny isn't it because my English is far from perfect but when I'm
> talking in Japanese I think, 'Oh gosh, I could explain better in English'.
> Probably I'm here too long.[34]

I only ever had one refusal for an interview, and that was from a woman whose husband had apparently just been hospitalised. Having said that, I don't know how many refusals my 'sponsors' received. But it seems that the women were happy to be interviewed and I have no reason to suspect that they told me any less of the truth than they would have told a Japanese interviewer. The fact remains, however, that what constitutes a truth in Japanese may well be different, or at least differently voiced, than one in English. There are two reasons for this. Firstly, for linguistic and cultural reasons, one might voice differing views in different languages. Indeed, the interviewees sometimes contradicted themselves, for example, being self-critical and pessimistic in Japanese but self-confident and optimistic in English. This is not uncommon. Ervin-Tripp[35] asked bilingual Japanese women the same question on different days in Japanese and English and received different answers depending on the language spoken. This, as William Gudykunst and Tsukasa Nishida[36] note, 'clearly indicates that different approaches to the world emerge when Japanese bilinguals think in Japanese and English'. It therefore has to be acknowledged that what the women said to me in English may well have been different to what they would have said to a Japanese interviewer in Japanese. As Rie previously noted, 'You sometimes have completely different things that comes out from your mouth'.[37]

Secondly, when you come to view the world from a different linguistic and cultural perspective, you must also reevaluate your own identity within it. When Japanese women come to England they find themselves in a new hybrid community known as the 'third culture'[38] which expatriates and long-term overseas sojourners create whilst abroad. Through this third culture they find new voices and new identities and must learn to reconcile them with their previous selves.

> You start thinking, 'So which one's my true self? A Japanese self that speaks in Japanese language or the one that speaks in English?'.[39]

Speaking English, I was told time and time again, is like wearing a mask at a masked ball, not for the purpose of concealing identity but to give them the freedom – if they wish it – to be *more* themselves, to express facets of their personalities that must remain hidden within Japanese culture, where their faces are known.

> Now I come to think of it, it's really interesting the way language plays the part of conditioning your performance in life, it's very interesting.[40]

Whatever the level of English language proficiency or the length of time spent in England, to a greater or lesser extent all interviewees displayed some 'third culture' confusion but whether they adapted successfully or not seemed to depend on their level of English proficiency and whether or not it was their decision to immigrate here.

Conclusion

Over time, I came to realise that the variables within a cross-cultural interview: the cultural context, the choice of language, the use of English or Japanese communicative styles, were largely dependent on how the women viewed themselves and how they chose to express their own cultural identities in conversation with a non-Japanese interviewer. It determined what they chose to say and how they preferred to express it. This is something that a Japanese interviewer, who is likely to interview in Japanese with a Japanese cultural style, would not be concerned with. Perhaps the true strength of cross-cultural interviewing is that it can help to represent the real cultural and linguistic contradictions of the Japanese women's migration experiences.

Notes

1 Masao Miyamoto, *Straightjacket Society, An Insider's Irreverent View of Bureaucratic Japan*, English Language Edition, Tokyo: Kodansha International, 1994, p. 129.

2 See A. Kikumura, 'Family Life Histories: a Collaborative Venture', in R. Perks and A. Thomson, *The Oral History Reader*, London: Routledge, 1998.

3 Jonathan Rauch, *The Outnation: A Search for the Soul of Japan*, Boston: Harvard Business School Press, 1992, p. 17.

4 Donald Ritchie quoted in Rauch 1992, p. 17.

5 Professor Shiozawa's quotation taken from the News from Abroad section of *Oral History* (UK), vol. 20, no. 2, Autumn 1992, p. 16.

6 Interview with Ikumi, a divorcee (from a British man) who has lived in England for ten years.

7 Interview with Rimika, a single academic who completed her Masters and Ph.D. in England.

8 Private correspondence with Gen'ichiro Itakura of Chukyo University, Japan.

9 Interview with Mitsuko, a single academic who completed her Ph.D. in England and now works in Europe.

10 Interview with Sachiko, an English teacher and divorcee now married to a British man.

11 Janet Smith, 'Women in Charge: Politeness and Directives in the Speech of Japanese Women', in *Language in Society*, vol. 21, 1992, pp. 59–82.

12 James Stanlaw, 'Open Your File, Open Your Mind: Women, English and Changing Roles and Voices in Japanese Pop Music', in Timothy J. Craig (ed.), *Japan Pop! Inside the World of Japanese Popular Culture*, New York: Armonk, and London: M E Sharpe, 2000.

13 Stanlaw in Craig, 2000, p. 99.

14 Joy Hendry, *Wrapping Culture: Politeness, Presentation and Power in Japan and other Societies*, Oxford: Clarendon Press, 1993, p. 144.

15 Joy Hendry, 1993, p. 144.

16 Interview with Naomi, a single ex-OL (Office Lady) who completed her Masters in England and is now working in Africa.

17 Stanlaw in Joseph J. Tobin, *Remade in Japan: Everyday Life and Consumer Taste in a Changing Society*, London: Yale University Press, 1992, p. 61.

18 Molly Andrews, 'A Monoglot Working Abroad: Working through the Problems of Translation', in *Oral History* (UK), vol. 23, no. 2, Autumn 1995.

19 Nicola North, 'Narratives of Cambodian Refugees: Issues in the Collection of Refugee Stories', in *Oral History* (UK), vol. 23, no. 2, Autumn 1995.

20 Ann Kaneko, *Japanese for All Occasions*, Tokyo: Tuttle Publishing, 1995, p. 14.

21 Junko Sakai, 'Narrating out Cultures in the Floating World: Working Lives in Japanese Banks in the City of London since the 1970s', Ph.D. thesis no. DX201697, University of Essex, 1997, p. 28.

22 Mizutani in William B. Gudykunst and Tsukasa Nishida, *Bridging Japanese/North American Differences*, Sage Publications, California: Thousand Oaks, 1994, p. 56.

23 Roy Andrew Miller, *The Japanese Language in Contemporary Japan: Some Sociolinguistic Observations*, Stanford: Hoover Institute, 1977.

24 Miller, 1977, p. 84.

25 Joy Hendry, *An Anthropologist in Japan: Glimpses of Life in the Field*, London: Routledge, 1999, p. 95.

26 Miller, 1977, p. 80.

27   Miller, 1977, p. 82.
28   See also Gudykunst, 1994, pp. 58–59.
29   Interview with Rie, a married (to a Japanese man) student currently completing her Ph.D. in England.
30   Interview with Sayuri, an expatriate wife and full-time mother living in London.
31   Interview with Mitsuko.
32   Interview with Sachiko.
33   Interview with Sachiko.
34   Interview with Rimika.
35   Cited in Gudykunst, 1994, p. 55.
36   Gudykunst, 1994, p. 55.
37   Interview with Rie.
38   For an overview of the Third Culture experience, see David C. Pollack and Ruth E. Van Reken, *Third Culture Kids: The Experience of Growing Up Among Worlds*, London: Nicholas Brealey Publishing, in association with Intercultural Press Inc., 2001.
39   Interview with Rie.
40   Interview with Rie.

Chapter 14

Ruth Finnegan

FAMILY MYTHS, MEMORIES
AND INTERVIEWING

This extract, from a distance-learning textbook about family and community history, highlights the challenges of family history interviews, in particular negotiating myth and folklore, and the comparison of oral evidence with paper-based family records. Ruth Finnegan is a Visiting Research Professor and Emeritus Professor at the Open University, well known for her publications on the anthropology of oral tradition, literature, and orality. Edited extract from Ruth Finnegan and Michael Drake (eds), *Studying Family and Community History: 19th and 20th Centuries. Volume 1: From Family Tree to Family History*, Cambridge, Cambridge University Press in association with The Open University, 1994, pp. 117–122, reproduced with permission.

> From countless incidents, families choose a few stories to pass on, the funniest or perhaps the most telling. From all of the garbled baby talk, a single utterance may become a family expression. Yet these time-honored images do more than recall scattered people and events; they come to represent the unremembered past, the sum total of a family's heritage.
>
> (Zeitlin *et al.*, 1982, p.2)

MOST FAMILIES have their own stories and traditions, selected from their many memories. Perhaps tellers are not fully conscious that they are crystallizing their family's heritage, telling and retelling stories that express that family's being. Yet this is a common feature of family experience.

The stories and sayings that have come to represent a family's tradition may not look 'deep' at first sight, nor are they always told consistently. Some may be just about everyday episodes like a funny misunderstanding by an ancestor or a now-grown-up child, or an amusing incident experienced by a grandparent, but they have gradually taken on a symbolic depth. Others may centre on a 'last straw' incident which pushed someone into a momentous course – emigration perhaps. Courtship is another focus, often woven around the motifs of 'love-at-first-sight' or of a test between competing suitors. Quarrels too may get highlighted, or a story built on 'the rogue' theme:

> My grandfather mentioned that his ancestors had been, perhaps, for the most part honest – traveling peddlers and merchants – but perhaps with a little bit of piracy. They were in Latvia and Lithuania on the Baltic Sea. I'd like to think they were pirates, but when I think about it seriously, they were probably all hard-working people, to be perfectly honest.
>
> (John Bishop, quoted in Zeitlin, *et al.*, 1982, p. vii)

Traditions often emerge or become more formulated in situations of change or crisis. Migration can separate family members drastically, but can also add all the more symbolic depth to selective memories. Stories and images can become especially poignant as a vehicle of family (and ethnic) identity when people make their way against the odds or face discrimination.

The explicit crystallization of a family's shared memories also results from a family history or individual autobiography being written or recorded. Take my own family. I grew up learning many traditions from my parents but did not consciously recognize how these images had moulded my own experience of the world until they were actually verbalized in my mother's autobiography. She repeats there those same stories that I now recall she had told us as children, of the missionaries, scholars and naturalists in her own family, as well as of their close ties to the beauties and battles of the Irish countryside. She symbolizes some of this in her tale of her great-grandfather's father, a nationalist and a Protestant in the United Irishmen's 1798 rebellion, who fled to America from the English soldiers, leaving his unborn son behind in Ulster.

> The vision must somehow have entered into the genes of succeeding generations for surely inheritance is not only in bone structure but also in an inclination towards freedom of conscience and the right to revolt against any form of improper power . . . The qualities in the succeeding generations might be attributed to the momentum of the past.
>
> (Finnegan, 1991, p. 5)

Not everyone in the family may see it exactly the same way, of course: there can be competing images. But still the formulation of such symbols – different for different families or for different people within them – provides the background, the mythic sense of continuance, that can have hidden, deep effects on one's own sense of identity and experience.

Such tales do more than just express a particular sense of history and of one's place in it, they also help shape that experience. Those who enunciate and guard the traditions are thus not just passive transmitters but also in a way active creators of a family's ethos. Often a particular member of a family takes a central role, someone accepted as 'knowing everything about the family'. Stories about the past are also told by their elders to younger family members, sending their influence down the generations. There is often a special bond between grandparents and their grandchildren, an emotive channel through which traditions and identities become formulated between the generations. They result in the 'myths', which, whether or not accurate in factual terms, play a part in moulding a family's views of themselves and their experience.

Such traditions are not necessarily agreed in every detail nor always expressed in textual form. They may even be the focus of dispute, symbolizing feuds among different individuals or different branches of the family. Sometimes there are joint family traditions: relations may have been separated in their youth, or gone in different directions in their adult lives. But memories in such situations may also be more valued, or even romantically exaggerated; or new families may be created and their shared memories developed. Fragmentation or disputes may not mean an absence of shared traditions. Indeed these may surface long after the individuals thought they had shed their earlier family connections and remain a deep influence on how they experience their lives.

Traditions may not be fully conscious but still have an effect on family memories and actions. This is more controversial perhaps. But it is interesting to consider a psychiatrist's assessment of 'the power of family myths', images that recur through the generations.

> People have told me of terrible events, tragedies and deaths, which they had not told their spouses or their children: yet nevertheless the theme behind the tragedy is re-enacted by the children . . . Somehow the imagery is so powerful for the person who holds it that the rest of the family picks up that imagery and ends by re-enacting it.
>
> (Byng-Hall, 1990, p. 223)

There are further questions to explore. These concern not just what goes on *inside* a family, but also the influence of external ideas and conventions.

Myths and images current in particular epochs or in particular cultures themselves affect family and individual memories, and shape the ways they represent the past, even their own experiences. In nineteenth-century autobiographies, for example, stock themes, like the pursuit of knowledge or progress towards greater freedom, recur again and again (Vincent, 1981). Similarly, life histories among immigrants – Irish, Jews, Italians, Poles, Pakistanis – may each in one way be unique, but also commonly draw on the 'classic' tale of the upward social mobility of an ethnic minority group, so that 'the rise to fortune or success is in fact a favourite tale about immigrants by immigrants' (Werbner, 1980, p. 46). Thus personal and family memories are often inspired by the familiar conventions in our culture for expressing and narrating stories about, say, courage or loss or success. Luisa Passerini (1990) illustrates this process from her recordings of Italian women imprisoned for belonging to terrorist organizations in the 1970s and 1980s. Shared images formed part of their collective experience, with only a shadowy distinction between the imaginary and the real. Their memories drew on deeply symbolic themes like

> the legend of the hero or heroine who leaves home to help the oppressed against the oppressors . . . the ideal of a small community united against the world, united beyond separation induced by exile and gaol, even beyond death; fables of the loyalty of mothers who do not abandon their defeated daughters, but are ready to give their lives for them.
>
> (Passerini, 1990, p. 54)

It is too simple to dismiss such images as 'fantasy', for they have their reality in people's lived experience. So in analysing the memories of individuals, whether or not expressed in a family context, we also have to take account of themes and narrative models current in the culture of the time.

Such themes emerge in many stories about family experiences. Ideals like 'motherhood' or the triumph of the youngest child form ready moulds within which experiences can be understood or memories formulated. So too do the motifs running through so many family tales: narratives of adventure, lost fortunes, survival from defeat or humiliation, triumphs, migrations, the odd one out, or the antics of heroes or of rogues and tricksters. The image of 'the stepmother' is another potent symbol, as Natasha Burchardt (1990) illustrates in her analysis of step-children's memories: 'myth weaves a thread, helping to shape the memories' (p. 249).

Equally influential is the image of 'the Golden Age of the family', the story that in the past 'the family' was stable and united, held together by unstressed love and harmony. This myth may have little support in literal historical fact, but that does not prevent its being a powerful influence on our self-images and life stories. How many of our spoken or written memories focus on the united family, free from conflicts or everyday annoyances? Does this wished-for ideal – or indeed the 'shocking' reminiscences from reacting against that myth – sometimes unconsciously affect our remembered experience? When we analyse family memories, our own or another's, we need to be aware that they are shaped by such images and counter-images, and not just a simple 'factual recall'.

Whether or not you pursue research in this area, there is a more general point to notice about both memory and the use of sources, namely the relevance of this discussion not just for the analysis of family stories but for all the products of memory. This includes written documents which themselves ultimately depend on people's memories. It is not so much that memory is fallible, both over short periods and, more especially, over long time spans. This is an obvious enough point, well illustrated in the simple but telling hints in the table.

What is harder to grapple with, but even more important, is how our memo-ries are built up through myth and images, by the conventions and ideologies around us. In a way our narrative models, drawn from the culture we live in, shape even our own first-hand experience and expression. To understand who we are and what we have done we 'narrate our lives' following out those models.

So when we look at the products of memories, whether autobiographies, life stories, or the records of oral interviews, we should also reflect on how they have been generated and expressed. We can certainly value them as rich sources for our understanding of family and personal history, and for the experiential spheres some-times neglected in other approaches. But we must also remember that they are not limpid empirical data, transmitted by some mechanical process.

This does not mean that research drawing on oral sources is to be dismissed. On the contrary, it is one of the recognized and growing research methods in family and community history. It does need to be employed critically, however, and in full awareness of the complexities of remembering: the way people's memories and experiences – not least their experience of family and community – are in part moulded by a series of existing myths, images and ideologies.

Table   Can we believe these facts from oral evidence?[1]

Place name	Yes – the most accurate item because it is the longest-lasting. Very unlikely to be wrong. Watch spelling, might be spelt as said by illiterate ancestor, or might be confused with another place name familiar to a later ancestor.	*Check*: Ordnance Survey map Census returns
Occupation	Yes – usually at least partly right. Watch: (a) ancestor having different jobs at different times in his life; (b) 'family promotions' – many farmers and master craftsmen turn out to be labourers and journeymen.	*Check*: Trade directories Census returns Parish registers St Catherine's House
Surname	Yes – few lies but many pitfalls. Watch: (a) spelling: might be spelt as said by illiterate clerk/ancestor; (b) ancestor using more than one name interchangeably: maiden and married, mother's and father's, first husband's and second husband's; (c) illegitimate ancestor might use father's, mother's or stepfather's name, or all three; (d) woman using her lover's name (common)	*Check*: Census returns Parish registers St Catherine's House *London Gazette*
First name	No – can be great confusion. Watch: (a) nicknames (very common); (b) use of middle name; (c) use of similar name that ancestor thought was same name; (d) parents giving same name to more than one child (often because earlier child died); (e) ancestor being confused with close relative (parent, sibling).	*Check*: Parish registers St Catherine's House
Date	No – least accurate fact. Never trust a date. Watch: (a) women reducing their age; (b) adding years, especially on marriage certificates; (c) wrong age on census; (d) baptism doesn't mean birth; (e) birth/ marriage dates adjusted to mask pre-wedding pregnancies.	*Check*: Parish registers St Catherine's House Family bible

1   This table was originally compiled to enable family tree researchers to check oral evidence through written sources in record offices etc., but it can also serve as a reminder of points that need checking by consulting whatever sources you have access to (including further oral sources). Such cautions apply to any source: official documentary records too can rely in part on fallible human memory.

Source: Based on Pearl (1990) p. 7.

References and further reading

Note: *suggestions for further reading are indicated by an asterisk.*

Abrahams, R.D., 'Our native notions of story', *New York Folklore*, 11, 1985, pp. 37–47.

Abrams, M., *Beyond three score years and ten*: *a first report on a survey of the elderly*, London: Age Concern, 1978.

Anderson, M., *Approaches to the history of the western family 1500–1914*, Basingstoke: Macmillan Educational, 1980. See especially Chapter 4.*

Anderson, M., 'What is new about the modern family?', Occasional Paper 31, *The family*, London: OPCS, 1983, pp. 2–16. Reprinted in Drake (1994).*

Bigger, D. and McDonald, T., *In sunshine or in shadow*: *photographs from the Derry Standard 1928–1939*, Belfast: Friar's Bush Press, 1990.

Bornat, J., 'Oral history as a social movement: reminiscence and older people', *Oral History*, 17, 1989, pp. 16–24.

Bornat, J. and Kirkup, G., 'Oral history interviews', audio-cassette 1B in Braham, P. (ed.) *Using the past*: *audio-cassettes on sources and methods for family and community historians*, Milton Keynes: The Open University, 1993.

Burchardt, N., 'Stepchildren's memories: myth, understanding, and forgiveness', in Samuel and Thompson, 1990.

Byng-Hall, J., 'The power of family myths', in Samuel and Thompson, 1990.

Collins, B. (1982) 'Proto-industrialization and pre-famine emigration', *Social History*, 7, 2, 1990, pp. 127–46.

Davidoff, L., 'The family in Britain', in Thompson, F.M.L. (ed.) *Cambridge social history of Britain*, vol. 2, Cambridge: Cambridge University Press, 1990.*

Davin, A. , 'When is a child not a child?', in Corr, H. and Jamieson, L. (eds) *Politics of everyday life*, Basingstoke: Macmillan, 1990.

Drake, M. (ed.), *Time, family and community*: *perspectives on family and community history*, Oxford: Blackwell in association with The Open University (Course Reader), 1994.

Elliott, B., 'Biography, family history and the analysis of social change', in Kendrick, S. *et al.* (eds) *Interpreting the past, understanding the present*, Basingstoke: Macmillan. Reprinted in Drake, 1994.

Finch, J., *Family obligations and social change*, Cambridge: Polity Press, 1989. Extract reprinted as 'Do families support each other more or less than in the past?', in Drake (1994).*

Finnegan, A., *Reaching for the fruit*: *growing up in Ulster*, Birmingham: Callender Press, 1991.

Finnegan, R., 'Working outside formal employment', in Deem, R. and Salaman, G. (eds) *Work, culture and society*, Milton Keynes: Open University Press, 1985.

Goody, E.N. and Groothues, C.M., 'The West Africans: the quest for education', in Watson, J.L. (ed.) *Between two cultures, migrants and minorities in Britain*, Oxford: Blackwell, 1977.

Hair, P.E.H., 'Children in society 1850–1980', in Barker, T. and Drake, M. (eds) *Population and society in Britain 1850–1980*, London: Batsford, 1982.

Hareven, T.K., 'The history of the family and the complexity of social change', *American Historical Review*, 96, 1, pp. 95–124. Reprinted in an abridged form as 'Recent historical research on the family' in Drake, 1991.*

Holley, J.C., 'The two family economics of industrialism: factory workers in Victorian Scotland', *Journal of Family History*, 6, 1, 1981, pp. 57–69.

Howes, D., 'Residential mobility and family separation in retirement', Occasional Paper 22, Kings College London: Department of Geography, 1984.

Hudson, P. and Lee, W.R. (eds), *Women's work and the family*: *economy in historical perspective*, Manchester: Manchester University Press, 1990.

Jamieson, L., 'Theories of family development and the experience of being brought up', *Sociology*, 21, 1987, pp. 591–607. Reprinted in Drake (1994).*

Kiernan, K. 'The British family: contemporary trends and issues', *Journal of Family issues*, 9, 3, 1988, pp. 298–316.

Levine, D., *Reproducing families the political economy of English population history*, Cambridge: Cambridge University Press, 1987.

Pahl, J., *Money and marriage*, Basingstoke: Macmillan, 1989.

Pahl, J., 'Household spending, personal spending and the control of money in marriage', *Sociology*, 24, 1990, pp. 119–38.

Pahl, R., *Divisions of labour*, Oxford: Blackwell, 1984. See especially Chapters 2–4.*

Passerini, L., 'Mythobiography in oral history', in Samuel and Thompson, 1990.

Pearl, S., 'Fact from fiction', *Family Tree Magazine*, August, 1990, p.7.

Pennington, S. and Westover, B., *A hidden workforce: homeworkers in England 1850–1985*, Basingstoke: Macmillan Education, 1989.

Roberts, E., *A woman's place; an oral history of working class women 1890–1940*, Oxford: Blackwell, 1984.

Roberts, E., 'Women and the domestic economy 1940–1970: the oral evidence', in Drake (1994)*, 1993.

Rogers, P. (ed.), *Daniel Defoe, a tour through the whole island of Great Britain*, abridged, Harmondsworth, Penguin, 1971 (first published in 1724–6).

Rosser, C. and Harris, C., *The family and social change a study of family and kinship in a South Wales town*, London: Routledge & Kegan Paul, 1965.

Samuel, B. and Thompson, P. (eds), *The myths we live by*, London: Routledge, 1990.*

Thompson, P., *The voice of the past: oral history*, Oxford: Oxford University Press, 2nd edition, 1988.

Tilly, L.A. and Scott, J.W., *Women, work and family*, New York: Holt, Rinehart & Winston, 1978.

Townsend, P., *The family life of old people: an inquiry in East London*, London: Routledge & Kegan Paul, 1957.

Vincent, D., *Bread, knowledge and freedom: a study of nineteenth-century working-class autobiography*, London: Europa Publications, 1981.

Wall, R., 'Work, welfare and the family: an illustration of the adaptive family economy', in Bonfield, L., Scott, R.M. and Wrightson, K. (eds) *The world we have gained: histories of population and social structure*, Oxford: Blackwell, 1986.

Wall, R., 'Relationships between the generations in British families past and present', in Marsh, C. and Arber, S. (eds) *Families and households: divisions and change*, Basingstoke: Macmillan, 1992.

Wallman, S., *Eight London households*, London: Tavistock, 1984.

Warnes, A.M., 'The residential mobility histories of parents and children, and relationships to present proximity and social integration', *Environment and Planning* 18, 1986, pp. 158–94.

Werbner, P., 'Rich man poor man – or a community of suffering: heroic motifs in Manchester Pakistani life histories', *Oral History*, 8, 1, 1980, pp. 43–51.

Young, M. and Willmott, P., *The symmetrical family*, Harmondsworth, Penguin, 1973.

Zeitlin, S.J., Kotkin, A.J. and Baker, H.C. (eds), *A celebration of American family folklore*, New York: Pantheon Books for Smithsonian Institution, 1982.

Chapter 15

Jan Walmsley

LIFE HISTORY INTERVIEWS WITH PEOPLE WITH LEARNING DISABILITIES

Drawing on work in the 'therapeutic' environment of reminiscence and life review, Jan Walmsley offers different models for interviews with disabled and disempowered people, placing an emphasis on clarity of purpose, negotiated ownership, and visual techniques. Walmsley was a Senior Lecturer at The Open University and is now Assistant Director of the Health Foundation, an independent charity that aims to improve health and the quality of healthcare for the people of the United Kingdom. Reprinted with permission from *Oral History*, 1995, vol. 23, no. 1, pp. 71–77.

THIS PAPER DESCRIBES a life history research project with people with learning disabilities (mental handicap). I discuss the methods adopted for the research, and compare them with other approaches in life history research. I argue that because most people with learning disabilities have minimal literacy skills certain adaptations of method have to be made. These adaptations may have insights to offer other researchers because they highlight important and problematic issues: explaining the research, enabling people to 'have a voice', and offering feedback and a final say to research participants. Sally French[1] suggests that improvements to the environment to give access to disabled people can be of benefit to all. Similarly, some of the issues raised in this research can inform life history research with a wide range of people.

The aim of the research was to discover what experiences people with learning disabilities have, and have had, of caring and being cared for.[2] A life history approach was chosen as people's experiences of care are related to their biographies. Their circumstances influence their opportunities to care for others, as well as determining the kind of care they have received in their lives. People with learning disabilities are often portrayed as people who receive care, not people who give it. Yet this is not always the whole picture. Some people with learning disabilities give care, as well as receive it. Through personal testimony it is possible to challenge the myth of dependence, and demonstrate that they see themselves as giving, taking and reciprocating care, support and help.

Life histories in research with disabled people

Disabled people have been marginalised in biographical research, in particular in oral history. Humphries and Gordon write: 'The experience of physical disability in Britain during the first half of the century is almost completely undocumented'[3] and Joanna Bornat found few disabled people represented in the 'communities of community publishing'.[4] No examples of work with people with learning disabilities are mentioned in Paul Thompson's extensive review of the practice of oral history.[5] Yet it is important to recognise the experiences of disabled people as distinctive, and to add their voices to those of other 'outsiders' whose viewpoints have not appeared in conventional histories. A beginning has been made. Some anthologies exist, compiled and edited by disabled women, in particular.[6] These focus on the experience of being disabled, rather than on the historical contexts in which people have lived.

Gerber[7] dates the tradition of asking people with *learning* disabilities to speak to researchers about their lives to Bogdan and Taylor's life history of Ed Murphy, a man labelled as mentally retarded.[8] He describes this as 'an essential step in recasting social welfare policy' and links it to a process in which minority or oppressed groups are finding a voice.[9] Bogdan and Taylor drew radical conclusions from this work, concluding, 'Our research suggests . . . that the concept of mental retardation is not just less than useful, it is seriously misleading.'[10]

Three recent examples of work which draws on the personal testimonies of people with learning disabilities demonstrate the variety of work now being undertaken. The first of these, *Know Me As I Am*,[11] is an anthology, similar to the anthologies compiled by disabled women described above. The editors discovered that people's common human experiences override the label they have been given, 'It challenges our assumptions and stereotypes even when we think we have none.'[12] The second example, *A Fit Person to be Removed*,[13] draws on oral history accounts from patients to reconstruct the experience of being in a mental handicap hospital (colony) in the twentieth century. The emphasis is on being labelled and the consequences of that; spending long periods in an institution shut away from the rest of the world. The third example, *Parenting under Pressure*,[14] uses a life story approach to explore the lives of parents with learning disabilities. The authors found this approach altered their perceptions of parents with learning disabilities, and conclude that the problems they experience are as much to do with poverty and prejudice as they are due to their individual deficits.

In trying to categorise these approaches Armstrong's summary is useful: 'The complete life history attempts to cover the entire sweep of the subject's life experience. It is inevitably long, many sided and complex . . . The multiple biographies approach, by abstracting dominant themes, makes it possible to generalise to one type by showing that certain biographies have, for all the idiosyncrasy, some common elements.'[15]

Oral history tends to focus on a historical question, and use oral evidence to help answer it. It is, in its pure form, a more focused approach than the life history.[16]

Potts and Fido's *A Fit Person to be Removed* is oral history in a way that other research cited here is not, because it seeks to answer an essentially historical set of questions about life in an institution through the testimonies of those who lived there.

Placing my own research within the rich context of work which draws on people's life stories is complex. It has most in common with multiple life histories like Booth and Booth's *Parenting under Pressure*, where the stories are used to contribute to an analysis which abstracts dominant themes, but it also draws on oral history in that there is a 'focus on the way in which historical time and place and personal experiences are lived out by individual(s)'.[17]

Particular challenges in learning disability research

Compiling life histories of people with learning disabilities is unlike superficially similar projects such as the Jewish Women in London Group's *Generations of Memories*[18] and the Hall Carpenter Archive's *Inventing Ourselves: Lesbian Life Stories*.[19] In these collections, the contributors wrote their own stories, a task few adults with learning difficulties can undertake unaided. In addition, learning disability is an ascribed characteristic which, at least at present, has negative overtones. It is not a label people bear with pride, unlike, say, being a Jewish woman or, sometimes, being a lesbian. Some researchers cited here concluded that being a person with a learning disability is most akin to being a human being.[20] Yet people are labelled, and it does affect their lives, as Potts and Fido's book shows. There is an argument, well rehearsed amongst oppressed groups, that reclaiming one's history is an important step in understanding and learning to celebrate one's identity.[21] Joanna Ryan wrote of people with learning disabilities, 'What history they do have is not so much theirs as the history of others acting either on their behalf or against them'.[22] Reclaiming that history is important in enabling people to set their lives in a broader context and to comprehend them; it is a step towards empowerment.

In undertaking this research I faced distinct challenges. One of these was working as a non-disabled researcher. A strong theme in disability research currently is the importance of disabled people setting the agenda.[23] This poses an additional challenge, especially in learning disability. It would, I believe, be unrealistic at this time to expect people with learning disabilities to record their history unaided. Even to scholars it is a relatively unexplored field, lacking the glamour of mental illness which is now well researched. People with learning disabilities lack the formal skills required of historians, often even basic ones such as literacy. Oral history and personal testimonies are one way, but without a basic map it is hard to make sense of them. As Patricia Hill Collins observed in relation to Black people, 'groups unequal in power are correspondingly unequal in their ability to make their standpoint known to themselves and others'.[24]

A second challenge is related to the question 'what history?' It is possible to reconstruct the history of mental handicap services through documentary sources, both primary and secondary. Yet this history is not known to people with learning disabilities, often even at a basic level. No one I interviewed had heard of the 1913 Mental Deficiency Act, the legislation to have attracted most attention from historians. It remained in force until 1959, and was the legislative framework which influenced people's early lives, but its existence was unknown to them. This made relating people's accounts to the history, and using one's own knowledge of that history to prompt questions somewhat problematic, though this is recommended in all basic oral history texts.[25]

A third challenge was that most methods employed in oral history and life history research rely on respondents having literacy skills: the introductory letter; the return of the transcript for correction; the provision of the finished account. In working with people with learning disabilities different approaches were required, based on tape recordings and face-to-face meetings. It is this challenge that is the main focus of this article.

Research methods

In carrying out life history interviews with people with learning disabilities I struggled to adapt mainstream research methods advocated by oral historians and life history researchers to make it possible for them to relate their own life stories. In this article I focus on four main aspects: explaining the research; power and involvement in the interview; the interview process; and negotiating meanings.

None of these issues are new to life history or oral historians, though working with people with learning disabilities presented them in quite a stark way.

Explaining the research

Actually finding people to interview and telling them about the project was a taxing process. Surprisingly little is written about this in standard texts. The advice is often confined to construction of sampling frames and the virtues of insider or outsider status for the researcher. Advice also includes sending an introductory letter, or making a preliminary phone call.

People with learning disabilities often are not on the phone, and may be unable to read letters and notices. I am based in a university and do not have direct access to service users. Making contact was not straightforward. On the whole, people taking part were contacted and briefed through intermediaries (MENCAP, Adult Training Centre workers, friends, social workers, adult education tutors). This meant that I was not fully in control of the circumstances in which people were approached, with problematic results. For example, I planned to interview people in their forties, but eventually extended my sampling frame to include thirty to seventy year olds because intermediaries either forgot the age bracket, or were not sure of people's ages.

Working through intermediaries extended the chain of communication about the research. In one instance the project had to be explained to five people before I got to speak to Eileen, the interviewee. The original contact was an adult education tutor who referred me to the Adult Training Centre where I spoke to the receptionist, the key worker, the deputy manager who in turn consulted with the woman's family. Only then was Eileen herself asked, by her key worker.

After some pilot interviews I decided that an information sheet was needed as the process of explaining to intermediaries was both time consuming and somewhat erratic. Using some data obtained in pilot interviews, I drew up an illustrated information sheet. This sheet gave intermediaries information about the research which they could show to potential interviewees and provided a starting point for discussion in the interview itself. It also found another unexpected use as participants showed it to other people to explain what they were doing. One interviewee, Gary, took it away to show his mother.

The information sheet also had limitations. It may have constrained the research, giving people a set of fairly concrete ideas to respond to which may not correspond with their experiences. In one instance it appeared patronising. Alison, for example, was critical of the way she had been approached and argued that she would have preferred to respond in writing to a set of pre-set questions, rather than in a face-to-face interview where she had felt exposed and vulnerable. This throws an interesting light on the school of thought, associated with feminist research, which advocates free-ranging interviews where the interviewee sets the research agenda.[26]

There was a tension between allowing interviewees free rein, and at the same time informing them about the research to the extent that they could make an informed choice about consent. This tension was made more acute when the approach was made through others. Alison (see above) in reflecting on why she had agreed to be interviewed said, 'I didn't want to let Hazel (tutor) down.' In using Hazel to make contact with Alison I had unwittingly compromised her. When Alison subsequently became distressed about our initial interview it was Hazel who bore the brunt of her distress, not I.

It was not always clear that the person involved was actually consenting to be interviewed, so much as feeling she had no choice. It is a pitfall in research with people with learning disabilities that interviews for assessment and other purposes are fairly commonplace. Bercovici observes: 'It took many months to convince "natives" of this system that the researcher was not part of the collaborative network they saw as an immutable part of life . . . they had no social type in their classification system that corresponded to the identity the researcher wanted them to perceive and understand.'[27] Atkinson, describing her research interviews, furnishes some insights into her interviewees' perceptions of her: one said to his social worker, 'She must be very important, asking us all these questions.'[28] After I had consulted five people about interviewing Eileen it might have been hard for her to refuse.

The information sheet was no guarantee of avoiding the researcher being viewed as a professional service provider. It did serve to differentiate the research from other interview situations, and to set out a contract specifying how many meetings, the choice of confidentiality, and the type of feedback people could expect.

However, consent issues remained problematic, especially where, as was often the case, people had little idea of what research is, and what use it may be put to. Of the twenty-two people I interviewed only Alison challenged me beyond the polite, 'you doing a project?' level of query.

The practicalities of working with many people with learning disabilities are currently such that far from undertaking 'emancipatory research',[29] the researcher must police her own ethical stance. To achieve a level of understanding of research to the extent that people could challenge the researcher directly was beyond the scope of a small-scale research project such as this, though might be a worthy enterprise in its own right.

Except for a few cases I am certain that people were very hazy about my intentions in interviewing them, though this may not be unique to adults with learning difficulties. As McCall and Simmonds observed, 'What motives, what alien causes, would lead a man to turn on his brethren with an analytic eye?'[30] How many people invited to take part in any research really know what is going on? Perhaps it is not just people with learning disabilities who are confused by this esoteric activity.

Involvement and power in the interview relationship

The importance of developing rapport with informants has been well documented both in research relating to learning disability and in qualitative research more generally.[31] In this research some strategies were particularly helpful with people with learning disabilities.

Like others, I found that it took time to build trust. The first time I met Anna, a woman in her fifties, I obtained little information as it was the first time she had been tape recorded and she asked me to play back our taped conversation seven times within fifty minutes. The interview ended with my promising to let her have a copy of the tape, and she insisted that I name the time I would return with it, despite some reluctance on my part. When I returned as agreed she was ready to show me her photos, and she rewarded me with as much information as she could recall.

On one occasion I felt I may have been too successful in establishing rapport. Janet Finch recounts how easy it was for her to gain the confidence of the clergy wives she interviewed. They were lonely, and welcomed the chance to talk.[32] Alison confided more in me than she subsequently felt was good for her, and became quite distressed. Why this happened I can only guess, but one reason may be that as an experienced counsellor I knew how to establish rapport quickly, and to persist with subjects that appear to be sensitive. And Alison herself was an experienced counsellee; she knew the role well.

Most texts on interviewing recommend that the interviewee is seen alone: 'Nearly always it is best to be alone with an informant.'[33] I found that this was not always possible, and adopted a policy of involving other people at the request of the interviewee. The first person I interviewed, Isobel, had been briefed by her adult education tutor in advance, but was very nervous when we met, and made an excuse to end the interview after thirty minutes. However, after I'd switched off the tape, she hinted that she'd like her boyfriend there next time. I duly collected Barry before our next interview and the conversation flowed, they were reluctant to end the interview, and Barry subsequently became an interviewee in his own right. He commented on his importance: 'she might feel better when I'm here, more confident' and Isobel added, 'keep me company'.

Involvement of a third person undoubtedly adds a new dimension to the interview. The researcher can observe a social relationship which casts light on the interviewee's situation. Beryl sat in on two interviews with her friend Eileen. Eventually I realised that Beryl, no less than staff and family, was determined that Eileen stay in the Adult Training Centre she had attended for twenty-five years. When Eileen and I discussed the possibility of her doing some voluntary work with children Beryl intervened with a series of good reasons why she should not: 'children can be horrible, hit you', 'your dad would be upset', 'you're better off in the Centre'. I realised how hard it was for Eileen to make any changes in her life when her friend joined the chorus of voices keeping her where she was.

It is important that the choice of companion is made by the interviewee. Jacqueline, a woman in her forties living with her widowed mother, was contacted through her mother who was present at both interviews. I could not persuade Mrs M to allow me to speak to her daughter alone, and Mrs M's voice was the only one I heard.

The social relations of research have been a preoccupation in feminist research for many years. Mies argues that when people from 'underprivileged groups are being interviewed by people from a socially higher stratum it has been observed that the data thus gathered often reflect "expected behaviour" rather than "real behaviour".'[34] More recently disabled people have begun to challenge traditional research into disability as being oppressive rather than enlightening.[35]

I belong to a higher social stratum than the interviewees, and I am not disabled. I was aware that this could influence the research, and that the relative powerlessness of the interviewees could distort their perception of me. It is hard to document this. One instance, however, is indicative. Lynne lived with her father, and emphasized in our interviews how much she wanted to move into her own place. This was such a strong theme that I am convinced she perceived me as someone who could help her achieve such a move. It was so powerful a message that after our second interview I contacted an acquaintance in the Social Services Department to ask whether Lynne could get any help. In a sense Lynne was right; I was powerful enough to pick up the phone to someone who could help her.

Ethics aside, I am uncertain how problematic such misunderstandings are. Dean and Foot Whyte argue that there is no such thing as truth telling in interviews; whatever the interviewee tells you is informative.[36] Stimson[37] proposes that 'life histories will be influenced by the social situation in which they are told'. The problem lies more in not always knowing what social situation people think they are in, in an interview; what kind of impression are they trying to convey; and why.

Within limits interviewees did exercise power. Anna had me switching the tape recorder on and off for her which was not behaviour I had chosen. Isobel arranged for me to collect Barry and take him to her house for an interview. When we arrived she was having a personal review meeting with her social worker. Barry was ushered in to join her and I was left sitting outside the house. I was told later that she had probably used me as a means of getting Barry to the review! In that situation she had exercised power, and I was thwarted. These instances correspond with Stimson and Webb's findings[38] that in doctor–patient interactions the patient exercises power: to ignore the doctor's advice, to recast the story in a light favourable to them, to withhold information. The doctor, like the researcher, apparently is the one with the power; but it is not as straightforward as it appears.

The interview process

In order to ensure that people were aware of the research focus and its purpose I tried to support the process throughout with concrete information. With a fairly abstract research question it is not as straightforward as it was for George Ewart Evans who used to take along a work tool to stimulate memory.[39]

My starting point was the illustrated information sheet. The first interview was loosely structured, using prompts from the information sheet. After this I transcribed the tape and developed two diagrams, a 'life map' (Figure 1) and a 'network

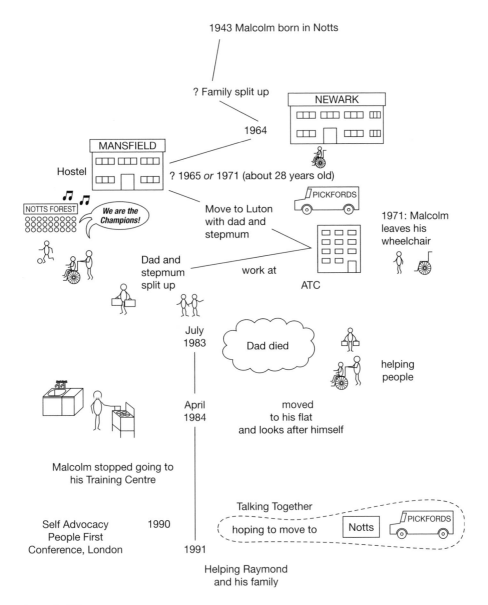

Figure 1 Life map

diagram' (Figure 2). The life map illustrates key points in the individual's biography, for example date of birth, schooling, changes of residence. The network diagram contains information about the people currently in the participant's social networks, with an indication of the degree of reciprocity. If a relationship is primarily one in which the participant receives care an arrow points towards the participant, and vice versa. Two-way arrows indicate a reciprocal relationship.

These 'life maps' and 'network diagrams' provided a basis for the follow-up interview. I talked through the diagrams with the interviewees and pursued any omissions, ambiguities or contradictions. The advantage of diagrams was that they

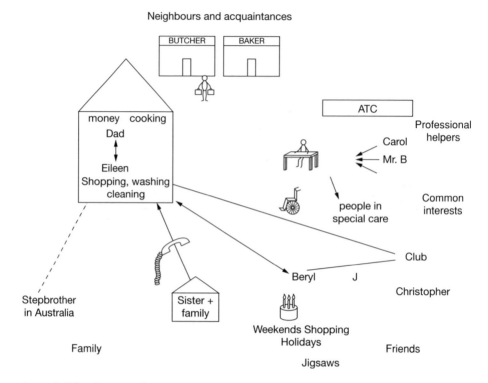

Neighbours and acquaintances

Figure 2 Eileen's network

could be shown to participants to see what information has been derived from their words. I saw them as research tools, forcing me to summarise data, and to try to make sense of it in a way people could understand.

In this way I was able to clarify points which were unclear in the first interview, and to make corrections. People's inability to read once more put the onus on me to be painstaking in checking understanding; yet it was valuable because it gave the opportunity to elaborate on points touched on in the first interview. For example, Gary had glossed over the reasons for his going into hospital in our first interview, but it appeared on the 'life map'. As we went over this he explained further:

> I stayed at home for quite a long time and then I went on there (the ATC), and then I went to Bromham (hospital) for me fits. It's a long story really because where me fits are, with all the tablets I used to take, I used to take more tablets than I do now and I used to get very bad tempered and shout and swear and turn nasty so they sent me to Bromham for me medication and me tempers. I was only supposed to be there for seven weeks but I was there for quite a long time.
>
> (GH Interview September 1992)

Photographs were a good support. If we met in people's own homes they showed me the photos on the walls, and talked about them. If we were in another setting I encouraged people to bring photos to our second meeting, and to talk about who was in them, where they were when they were taken, and what was going on. Anna was vague about her past life, but the photos helped establish some kind of chronology, and introduced new people, like her neighbour's daughter. They also corroborated some of the things she had told me, for example the importance of her friend Helen whom she sees infrequently. There were photos of Anna and Helen smiling as they exchanged Christmas gifts, and Helen was present at Anna's birthday celebration.

Concreteness was also expressed verbally. 'Care' and 'caring' are jargon words. People did not ever use them in describing relationships. Instead they used the terms 'helping' or, less often, 'looking after'. I tried to reflect this in the information sheet, following the pilot interviews. This practice, of using people's own terms rather than imposing language from an academic culture, is based on Glaser and Strauss's concept, 'grounded theory'.[40]

A final prompt was the 'story'. To end the relationship I compiled a brief life story based on the interview data using, as far as possible, the informant's own words. Once more, this was usually delivered face to face. The utility of the 'story' as a means of checking accuracy varied. Eileen, for example, used the opportunity to correct one or two names, and the date when she left school. By contrast, Alanna used the opportunity to say what she wanted for the future:

> *Jan*:   What about the ending? I didn't know how to end it, what about the future?
> *Alanna*:   I'd like mum if she lives that long to get to know me better . . . I don't know, I think other mothers let their daughters do what they want to do and I think I'm a bit left behind if you know what I mean. I'm doing what my mum wants me to do.

In effect, Alanna was saying something very important about herself and her wish to assert her adult status to her mother, providing an important insight with which to end our relationship.

Research interviews with people with learning disabilities throw up similar issues to other research relationships. All interviewers have to develop rapport, to ponder how they are perceived by the interviewee, and to check accuracy. The relative powerlessness of many people with learning disabilities and their inability to read forced me to tackle those issues in a slightly different way. These lessons may have wider implications.

Negotiating meanings

Finally, my research gave me cause to consider negotiated meanings. Much research literature recently has emphasised the importance of leaving the 'ownership' of the research with the participants: 'Recently the practice has developed, particularly amongst anthropologists, of giving a draft of the report to research participants and asking them to comment on its validity'.[41] In my own research I did this by drawing up life maps and network diagrams, summarising the research information in a 'story', and working through it with them.

I consciously omitted the normal oral history practice of returning the transcript to people[42] because of the weight of reading, though I gave a copy of the tape as a memento.

The 'story' has limitations as a way of giving 'ownership' to the interviewees because only the individual's account is available. I, as researcher, had an overview of all the interviews. The individual only knew of her own contribution and the guarantee of confidentiality requires that this remains the case. I have discussed elsewhere the difficulties of feeding back research findings to a group of research participants who know one another.[43] Opie identifies another difficulty: 'such a (co-authorship) relationship is difficult to achieve when participants, while constituting a community of interest, do not form a close knit physical community'.[44] Only some interviewees knew one another, and to constitute them as a group for the purpose of sharing research findings would be impractical as well as presenting a major challenge to my powers of explaining. Overall, although interviewees had the final word on their own 'story', they had no means of controlling the interpretations I subsequently made of their experiences as related to me. They have had no direct say in this paper, for example.

A second limitation is more personal. The Jewish Women in London Group comment in their introduction: 'For most of the women being presented some time later with, as one of us put it, an "autobiography that they had not written" was a disturbing experience and added another dimension to the vexed question of "finding a voice".'[45] Only one of my interviewees, Alison, expressed reservations about having her 'story' presented to her. Because she can read I posted it to her in advance of our meeting. She described graphically the experience of reading it for the first time; finding a private moment, making herself a coffee, taking a deep breath, and . . . In the end, she rewrote it for me and we jointly finalised the draft. Alison asked why she could not have written it herself. There is no doubt she could have done so, but she alone of the twenty-two had the writing skills to produce such an account. The others relied on me to do so, and questioned little. The 'story' was already one step removed from the immediate interview account. It had the authority of the written word, albeit mediated by a face-to-face meeting. Perhaps it required more confidence than most people had to challenge the authority of print.

Summary

In this research I adapted tried and tested methods in life history research to suit the interviewees. How far are these generalisable to other research of this nature?

The main contribution is, I believe, the commitment to clarity about the research in explaining it to interviewees. The particular circumstances of many people with learning difficulties mean that questions about their lives are both familiar, in the form of assessment interviews, case conferences and reviews, and unfamiliar, in that they are unlikely to have a concept of 'research' as an activity. I am not satisfied that I achieved a high level of understanding of my research, or its goals but I began to move towards that. If an interview is seen as a social situation in which both participants work to construct a version of the 'truth', then the importance of the interviewee understanding her role becomes paramount. Otherwise, the researcher may see a version of the truth, but she is unclear about what has influenced that particular portrayal.

A second important observation relates to the current orthodoxy that research must be owned by those researched. In principle, this is a worthy goal; in practice I found it almost impossible to achieve. I am certain that none of the people I interviewed would have thought of asking the questions which I sought to answer, questions about how biography and history have interacted to produce their unique experiences. Yet I believe that it is important to ask those questions so that in the longer term people may come to have an understanding of the 'life course', the subtle interaction of accident of birth, specific historical time and social policy which have combined to produce a set of unique experiences. The challenge will be to find ways of telling people what I discovered in a way that they can comprehend. It is a challenge I have yet to tackle.

Notes

1   Sally French in Workbook 3 of *The Disabling Society*, Buckingham: Open University, 1993.

2   Some of the research findings are published in J. Walmsley, 'Contradictions in Caring', *Disability, Handicap and Society*, 1993, vol. 8, no. 2.

3   S. Humphries and P. Gordon, *Out of Sight*: *The Experience of Disability 1900–1950*, Plymouth: Channel Four/Northcote Press, 1992, p. 9.

4   J. Bornat, 'The communities of community publishing', *Oral History*, 1992, vol. 20, no. 2, pp. 23–31.

5   P. Thompson, *The Voice of the Past*, second edition, Oxford: Oxford University Press, 1988.

6   J. Campling, *Images of Ourselves*, London: Routledge & Kegan Paul, 1981; J. Morris, *Able Lives*, Women's Press, 1989, are examples.

7   D. Gerber, 'Listening to disabled people: the problem of voice and authority' in R.B. Edgerton's 'The Cloak of Competence', *Disability, Handicap and Society*, 1990, vol. 5, no. 1, pp. 3–23.

8   R. Bogdan and S. Taylor, 'The judges not the judged: an insider's view of mental retardation', *American Psychologist*, 1976, vol. 31, pp. 47–52.

9   Gerber, 'Listening to disabled people', p. 4.

10   R. Bogdan and S. Taylor, *Inside Out*: *The Social Meaning of Mental Retardation*, University of Toronto Press, 1982.

11   D. Atkinson and F. Williams (eds), *Know Me As I Am*, London: Hodder & Stoughton, 1990.

12   Ibid., p. 7.

13   M. Potts and R. Fido, *A Fit Person to be Removed*, Plymouth: Northcote Press, 1991.

14   T. Booth and W. Booth, *Parenting under Pressure*: *Mothers and Fathers with Learning Difficulties*, Buckingham: Open University Press, 1994.

15   P. Armstrong, *The Use of the Life History Method in Social and Educational Research*, Newland Papers no. 7, University of Hull, 1982, p. 10.

16   Thompson, *The Voice of the Past*, p. 72.

17   Jewish Women in London Group, *Generations of Memories*, London: Women's Press, 1989, p. 9.

18   Jewish Women in London Group, *Generations of Memories*, 1989.

19   Hall Carpenter Archives, *Inventing Ourselves: Lesbian Life Stories*, London: Routledge, 1989.

20   Bogdan and Taylor, 'The judges not the judged', and *Inside Out*; Atkinson and Williams, *Know Me As I Am*.

21   See, for example, S. Rowbotham, *Hidden from History*, London: Pluto, 1981, and Jewish Women in London Group, *Generations of Memories*.

22   J. Ryan and F. Thomas, *The Politics of Mental Handicap*, London: Free Association Books, 1987, p. 85.

23   G. Zarb, 'On the road to Damascus: first steps towards changing the relations of disability research production', *Disability, Handicap and Society*, 1992, vol. 7, no. 2, pp. 157–166.

24   P. Hill Collins, *Black Feminist Thought: Knowledge, Consciousness and the Politics of Empowerment*, Unwin Hyman, 1990.

25   Thompson, *The Voice of the Past*.

26   Such advice is current orthodoxy in feminist research; see K. Anderson and D. Jack, 'Learning to listen: interview techniques and analysis', in S. Gluck and D. Patai (eds), *Women's Words*, London: Routledge, 1991.

27   S. Bercovici, 'Qualitative methods and cultural perspectives in the study of deinstitutionalisation', in R. Bruininks, C. Meyers, B. Sigfold and C. Lakin (eds), *Deinstitutionalisation and Community Adjustment of Mentally Retarded People*, Monograph of the American Association of Mental Deficiency, 1981, no. 4, p. 139.

28   D. Atkinson, 'Research interviews with people with mental handicaps', in A. Brechin and J. Walmsley (eds), *Making Connections*, London: Hodder & Stoughton, 1989.

29   M. Oliver, 'Changing the social relations of research production?', *Disability, Handicap and Society*, 1992, vol. 7, no. 2, pp. 157–166.

30   G. McCall and J. Simmonds, *Issues in Participant Observation*, Addison Wesley, 1969.

31   R. Bogdan and S. Taylor, *An Introduction to Qualitative Research Methods*, John Wiley, 1984; J. Cornwell and B. Gearing, 'Biographical interviews with older people', *Oral History*, 1990, vol. 17, no. 1, pp. 36–43.

32   J. Finch, 'It's great to have someone to talk to', in C. Bell and H. Roberts (eds), *Social Researching: Politics, Problems and Practice*, London: Routledge & Kegan Paul, 1984.

33   Thompson, *The Voice of the Past*, p. 205.

34   M. Mies, 'Towards a methodology for feminist research', in G. Bowles and R. Duelli Klein (eds), *Theories of Women's Studies*, London: Routledge & Kegan Paul, 1983, p. 123.

35   Oliver, 'Changing the social relations of research production', and Zarb, 'On the road to Damascus'.

36   J. Dean and W. Foot Whyte, 'How do you know if the informant is telling the truth?' in J. Bynner and K. Stribley (eds), *Social Research: Principle and Procedures*, London: Longman, 1978.

37   G. Stimson, 'Biography and retrospection: some problems in the study of life histories'. Paper delivered at the British Sociological Association's Conference, 6–9 April, 1976.

38   G. Stimson and B. Webb, *Going to see the Doctor*, London: Routledge & Kegan Paul, 1975.

39   Thompson, *The Voice of the Past*, pp. 204–205.

40   B. Glaser and A. Strauss, *The Discovery of Grounded Theory*, Aldine Press, 1967.

41   A. Opie, 'Qualitative research, appropriation of the "other" and feminism', *Feminist Review*, 1992, no. 40, pp. 52–69.

42   Thompson, *The Voice of the Past*, p. 216.

43   J. Walmsley, 'Adulthood and people with mental handicaps: report of a research project', *Mental Handicap Research*, 1991, vol. 4, no. 2, pp. 141–154.

44   Opie, 'Qualitative research', p. 63.

45   Jewish Women in London Group, *Generations of Memories*, p. 15.

Chapter 16

Mark Klempner

NAVIGATING LIFE REVIEW INTERVIEWS WITH SURVIVORS OF TRAUMA

Traumatic memory is a theme that recurs throughout this volume. Here Mark Klempner offers some guidance to interviewers encountering traumatic narratives: the need for sensitivity and a preparedness to listen for silences, but also the notion of the interview as 'closure'. Klempner is the son of a Holocaust survivor and the author of an oral history about Dutch rescuers. Reprinted from *Oral History Review*, 2000, vol. 27, no. 2, pp. 67–83. © 2000, Oral History Association. All rights reserved. Used by permission.

I'M SITTING WITH a Holocaust survivor listening to her recount the murder of her entire family. To hear about such devastation is difficult. I go blank and numb, not knowing how to respond to suffering of such magnitude. I feel cheap somehow, that I am hearing these things so casually, that is, upon having just met her. In these few seconds, as the depth of her loss continues to sink in, I say, 'These must be very painful memories for you.' Her response sounds dissonant and almost bizarre: 'It's not very pleasant,' followed by a cheerful laugh. I feel a sinking sensation as she explains to me that it came at a 'perfect' time since she was already seventeen and would have soon left home anyway.

Conducting a life review interview with a person who has experienced severe trauma presents many dilemmas.[1] What if hearing the narrative is overwhelming to the interviewer? What if telling the narrative puts the interviewee at risk emotionally? Are there special responsibilities interviewers must assume when they are taken into the confidence of someone who recounts traumatic memories? How must an interview involving such memories be conducted differently from an ordinary interview?

John Robinson, writing on narrative in the *Journal of American Folklore*, notes that many narratives of trauma are never told because 'such experiences produce shame, anger, often guilt in the victim, and are regarded as secrets rather than as stories to tell.' He adds, 'Such narratives may be qualitatively different in structure and function from more conventional and public narratives.'[2]

The growing body of research that specifically addresses the issues of trauma narrative tends to confirm Robinson's conjectures. Within psychology, the rapidly developing field of traumatology, the study of traumatic stress, displays a marked concern with narrative as a resource in diagnosis and an arena for therapeutic intervention.[3] Much qualitative research has been undertaken with those who were traumatized as soldiers, such as Vietnam veterans.[4] Other work has been done with women who have been abused through rape and battering. By drawing extensively on their narratives, researchers have attempted to unravel the skein of shame and stigma that often characterizes such trauma.[5]

At the same time, there are over thirty ongoing oral history projects being carried out by Holocaust organizations throughout the world to record the narratives of survivors and witnesses.[6] In the early 1970s, Professor Yaffa Eliach began to record survivor testimony for the purpose of filling gaps in the historical record. Her *Center for Holocaust Studies* in New York now contains a growing collection of over 2,000 audio interviews. The *Fortunoff Video Archive* currently houses a collection exceeding 3,800 videotaped interviews.[7] Originally known as the *Holocaust Survivor's Film Project*, it was founded in 1979 by Dori Laub, Associate Clinical Professor of Psychiatry at Yale University, and Laurel Vlock, a television specialist.

In 1994, Stephen Spielberg, using revenues generated by *Schlinder's List*, launched the massive *Shoah Visual History Foundation*.[8] The mission of this conspicuous project seems to be to preserve the testimony of all living Holocaust survivors. To date, the Foundation has collected over 50,000 testimonies in 57 countries, with interviews conducted in 32 languages. It plans eventually to make its digitized collection available to various history museums and archives.

Concurrently, the curricula for middle school and high school in the United States includes the Holocaust, and some teachers are engaging their students in oral history projects involving survivors, or are inviting survivors into the classroom to share their testimony.[9] At colleges and universities, scholars within the newly established discipline of Holocaust studies are rapidly producing a literature based on recorded survivor testimony, which offers new perspectives on trauma narrative.[10]

My own involvement with trauma narrative came as a result of my interviews with 30 Holocaust survivors as part of a research project conducted under the auspices of the Institute for European Studies at Cornell University in cooperation with Y'ad Vashem in Israel. In this article I will explore what took place at certain critical moments in the interview process when the intensely emotional nature of the encounter came to the fore and I found myself and my interview subjects responding in unanticipated and sometimes disturbing ways. To assist me in an analysis of the underlying issues involved in such occurrences, I will utilize a theoretical model framed by Dori Laub. Dr Laub, an authority on traumatology as well as an applied oral historian, has achieved a perspective that spans both disciplines. As a Holocaust survivor who devotes his private practice to treating other survivors, he has become adept at spanning emotional worlds as well. In my fitful struggles to work through the emotional issues which arose in the course of my fieldwork, his writings spoke eloquently to my need for a practical yet profound approach. All the passages I will be using from Dr Laub are excerpted from the book *Testimony: Crises of Witnessing in Literature, Psychoanalysis, and History*, which he co-authored with Shoshana Felman.[11]

The recounting of a trauma narrative can be a psychically charged event entailing great vulnerability. Unlike ordinary narratives, trauma narratives almost always engage the narrator in an attempt to find closure. Closure is signaled by a sense of completion, the feeling that one does not *have* to dwell on the distressing event from the past. It is experienced as a resolution which allows the event to become integrated into the psyche. However, it may come in increments, and the concept is best conceived of in a flexible way, allowing for the many different ways and degrees it can manifest.

Those who conduct life review interviews sometimes sense their interviewees attempting to come to terms with experiences from their past.[12] However, survivors of trauma encounter a special challenge. In the view of Dori Laub, people who undergo severe trauma are unable to register such experiences for they exceed 'the human cognitive capacity to perceive and to assimilate the totality of what was really happening at the time.'[13] As he explains:

> The victim's narrative – the very process of bearing witness to massive trauma – does indeed begin with someone who testifies to an absence, to an event that has not yet come into existence . . . the trauma – as a known event and not simply as an overwhelming shock – has not been truly witnessed yet, not been taken cognizance of. The emergence of the narrative which is being listened to – and heard – is, therefore, the process and the place wherein the cognizance the 'knowing' of the event is given birth to.[14]

Laub's conceptions give tremendous importance to the listener and he goes so far as to say that the listener becomes a 'participant,' even a 'co-owner' of the traumatic event. In Laub's therapeutic framework, healing of the trauma lies in the victim's act of narrating the event. In the excerpt that follows, he capsulizes the dilemma the survivors face, and outlines, as he sees it, the process through which healing can occur:

> Trauma survivors live not with memories of the past, but with an event that could not and did not proceed through to its completion, has no ending, attained no closure, and therefore, as far as its survivors are concerned, continues into the present and is current in every respect. The survivor, indeed, is not truly in touch either with the core of his traumatic reality or with the fatedness of its reenactments, and thereby remains entrapped in both.[15]

> To undo this entrapment in a fate that cannot be known, cannot be told, but can only be repeated, a therapeutic process – a process of constructing a narrative of reconstructing a history and essentially of *re-externalizing the event* – has to be set in motion.[16] This re-externalization of the event can occur and take effect only when one can articulate and transmit the story, literally transfer it to another outside oneself and then take it back again, inside. Telling thus entails a reassertion of the hegemony of reality, and a re-externalization of the evil that affected and contaminated the trauma victim.[17]

As oral historians we are not psychotherapists, yet we hear narratives as miasmic as any that might surface in a therapist's office. Our interview subjects may never visit a psychiatrist yet they *will* talk to us, and, in some cases, disclose things they have never shared with another human being. Any attempt at carrying out a life review interview with a survivor of trauma puts the interviewer in a position where he or she may precipitate the re-externalization of the event. As the survivor thus processes a piece of the trauma, the atmosphere of the interview becomes charged, and may trigger unexpected emotional reactions, both in the narrator and in the interviewer.

The term 're-externalization' may require some explanation as Laub seems to be using it in an idiosyncratic way. The event was originally external, but the trauma victim 'took it in,' that is, internalized the traumatic event. Through the therapeutic process of constructing a narrative and telling it to a listener, the event may be externalized once again, that is, re-externalized. In the process, its meaning changes, due in part to the empathy of the listener and the safety of the setting in which the narrative is shared. This allows for a re-evaluation of the event by the narrator. The listener contributes to this process, even if no words are spoken. As Laub explains, the victim may have felt personally responsible for the traumatic event, or guilt over it having happened. Re-externalization means that one 'puts it back into the outside world where there is a perpetrator who one has not provoked, and who has carried out the atrocity, and should be held responsible and guilty for it. And it is no longer in one's personal domain. There can be anger directed at the perpetrator, and no sense of guilt or responsibility for having taken part in it. It is making it into an objective outside event at a certain time in history.'[18] What is implied here is that by telling the narrative, the traumatic event becomes drained of some of its toxicity. The teller may then 'take it back again, inside' in a new version with a new frame. Of course, the memory can never become completely 'objective,' yet some of the distortions that tend to characterize traumatic memory can be undone.[19]

Both of the interview subjects I quote below, Gertrude P. and Martine N., are Holocaust survivors who immigrated to the United States after the war. Both are articulate and well educated. Martine was a social worker and child psychologist, while Gertrude had a prestigious career in the arts. They have been interviewed previously by staff from the United States Holocaust Memorial Museum and have clearly done a lot of thinking, feeling, talking, and processing regarding the traumatic experiences they went through during World War II. Still, there was a lot of emotional intensity to the interviews which I conducted with them; neither one found them 'easy'.[20]

Both interviewees made reference to the effects of the trauma, Martine N. spoke several times about having 'holes in her memory.' I asked her what she meant:

MN: What I mean is that there are some things I have no memory of.

MK: Do you think you've forgotten them, or have you blocked them out?

MN: No, I think there are some things I have blocked out because they were very painful. This happened to all of us –

MK: Do you have any idea why that is?

MN: We have a comfort zone with the kind of memories we live with. You know, people were dying around me. When I distributed food in this cabin, we had bread and we divided it in eight parts and put it on the table. People were so starved they would rush and try and grab the biggest piece. We put numbers on these eight parts; it was like a

lottery so that people wouldn't fight over it. A piece of bread! I
handed a piece of bread one day to a man, and he fell back in the bed
and he was dead. That I remember, other things I don't. It's very
painful memories of this experience.

Gertrude P. did not make mention of having blocked things out, but she exhibited
another common characteristic of the trauma survivor, which comes through in the
following excerpt. This is the point in the interview that I described at the opening
of this article. She had been recounting her early childhood in Germany: what it
was like to be a Jewish girl growing up there during the 1920s. I had been asking
her about her relationship with her family, which included her father and mother,
maternal grandmother, and sister. She went on to say that when anti-Semitism
reached a certain level, her father moved the family out of Germany and into the
Netherlands. Seven years later, during World War II, the Germans occupied the
Netherlands.

> GP: Well, you know, we were there and I came in '33, and it took seven
> years 'till the Germans walked in, so we had seven years. My father
> sort of 'saved' seven, eight years of life. And then of course when the
> Germans came into Holland they did get taken away and they died in
> Auschwitz. My parents and my sister. And my grandmother died in
> Bergen-Belsen –.
>
> MK: I'm sorry.
>
> GP: And I managed to escape. By that time I was seventeen. This was two
> years –. When the Germans walked in I was fifteen and when all this
> disaster happened I was seventeen. And so –.
>
> MK: These must be very painful memories for you.
>
> GP: It's not very pleasant. [Laughs] But it has, you know, I was very lucky
> because seventeen was perfect. Eighteen would have been better,
> but, you know, seventeen already I was a person; I probably would
> have left home at eighteen, you know? I had many friends my age, a
> little bit older, like up to three years older, and I often think, if I had
> been younger it would have been much harder. I would have been
> handed from one person to the other.

A key to understanding both my behavior and her behavior can be found in Terrence
Des Pres's essay, 'Holocaust Laughter?':

> The testimony of survivors often requires a detachment that keeps them
> at a distance from self-pity, whereas for us the pathos of their stories,
> and sometimes the mere telling of such stories, is nearly over-
> whelming.[21]

Des Pres articulates one of the primary disparities that arises during interviews with
people who have experienced severe trauma. The survivor has somehow managed
to cope with what has happened, and recounts it in a way that utilizes these coping
mechanisms. The interviewer gets to hear the recounting of experiences involving
a tremendous amount of suffering, often told in a way that is either without any

emotion, or with seemingly inappropriate affect. At the same time, the interviewer experiences his or her own emotional reactions to the events recounted.

There are several points to be made here. One is that our interviewees will have defense mechanisms in place that might make their responses sound strange or 'off.' We have to be prepared for that, even expect it. The second point is that the interviewer, not having been through the trauma, does not have such defense mechanisms in place. Hearing the traumatic material could invoke acute emotional reactions. Because the interviewer does not have the defensive structures, and the interviewee does, a situation might arise where the interviewer begins to feel acute distress while the interviewee maintains apparent composure.

In other cases, the coping mechanisms of the narrator are not so strong, and his or her emotions and vulnerability are more on the surface. I felt this to be the case with Martine N., who talked to me about her experiences as a young Jewish woman in Nazi-occupied France. At a certain point during the war, after having secured excellent false identification papers which represented her as being of Aryan descent, she became involved in taking care of Jewish children whose parents had been deported to concentration camps. She worked with many children during the war, mothering them, educating them, organizing activities for them, and trying to help them cope during this difficult period. When liberation came and the war ended, she was given support to open a children's home. In the excerpt that follows, she tells me about the great opportunity that the home presented:

> We got *carte blanche* to establish this magnificent home for pre-school age children. And, um, at the same time, the girls, the staff, looked after the kids, we trained them as early childhood educators so that they would be able to go and work with the children. We little by little –. But we didn't know just what happened to the parents. And it's not until [begins to cry] –. This is always the hardest part. [Pauses.] It's not until the allies actually got to the concentration camp that we could find out what happened to the parents. We had had rumors, but it was so horrible that nobody could really –. And it's only then that we really found out what happened. And we had to help the children get over this. I remember in Paris having these young children, and having a Montessori atmosphere for them and training these teenage girls, and having a birthday party for this little boy and giving him some presents. And he got so angry, he says, 'I don't want any of your presents. I want my mommy and my daddy.'

The way an interviewer responds – verbally and nonverbally – during moments like these is critical. The less guarded the narrator, the more careful the interviewer has to be. Empathy, 'the capacity to put oneself into the psychological frame of reference of another and thereby understand his or her thinking, feeling, and behavior,' is essential.[22] Martine N. had this to say about her early experiences of trying to talk to others about what she had gone through during the war:

> I really felt that people didn't understand it. I felt like people in the United States could not empathize, could not understand. Their questions put me on edge. It was very difficult.

I would like to explore further the vulnerability of the interviewer. Hearing a person talk about trauma can stir up nearly every fear to which human beings are subject. In her book *Living Beyond Fear*, psychologist Jeanne Segal discusses fear and summarizes the basic fears human beings experience:

> Fear is a bottom line emotion . . . and the source of compulsive and numbing behaviors. It's the good reason behind our reflexive and protective patterns. What do we protect ourselves from? What do we fear? We fear the loss of love, the loss of purpose and meaning in our lives, we fear physical degeneration, disease, loss of energy. We fear pain. We fear the loss of our loved one, loss of status, loss of job, loss of material possessions, especially if we believe that our identity is attached to these things. We fear being wrong, looking foolish, being stupid. We fear the loss of control, the possibility of insanity. We fear death. We fear the unknown, the uncertain, and the untried. We fear life – its unpredictability, and its responsibility.[23]

All trauma victims have experienced some or all of these things, and when we talk to them we sense in a very direct way that these things could happen to us as well. Perhaps one definition of trauma could be the realization of one's worst fears, the experiences that every human being would never want to have. Dori Laub approaches this same issue of the vulnerability of the listener in a more philosophical way:

> There are hazards to the listening to trauma. . . . As one comes to know the survivor, one really comes to know oneself; and this is not a simple task. The survival experience . . . is a very condensed version of most of what life is all about. . . . The listener can no longer ignore the question of facing death; of facing time and its passage; of the meaning and purpose of living; of the limits of one's omnipotence; of losing the ones that are close to us; the great question of our ultimate aloneness; our otherness from any other; our responsibility to and for our destiny; the question of loving and its limits; of parents and children; and so on.[24]

I find it interesting that some of the items on Laub's list are also found on Segal's. It appears that we fear the existential questions, and the existential questions are bound up with some of our deepest fears.[25]

In his essay, Laub implies that it is a valuable process to face these questions, and Segal, in her book, affirms that fear can be harnessed and used as a positive force. In an interview situation, the presence of strong emotions such as fear might help the interviewer to empathize with and understand the speaker. Problems arise, however, when the interviewer has defensive reactions in an effort to protect himself or herself from the 'onslaught of the images of trauma,' and the intensity of emotion those images generate. Laub lists six defensive positions to which the listener might succumb.[26] Two of them are obviously fear-driven:

- A sense of total paralysis, brought about by the threat of flooding – by the fear of merger with the atrocities being recounted.

- A flood of awe and fear; we endow the survivor with a kind of sanctity, both to pay our tribute to him and to keep him at a distance, to avoid the intimacy entailed in knowing.

If we are to concur with Jeanne Segal that fear is at the root of compulsive and numbing behaviors, then two more of Laub's defensive positions could be considered fear-driven:

- A sense of total withdrawal and numbness.
- Foreclosure through facts; through an obsession with fact-finding; an absorbing interest in the factual details of the account which serve to circumvent the human experience. Another version of this foreclosure, of this obsession with fact-finding, is a listener who already 'knows it all,' ahead of time, leaving little space for the survivor's story.

Laub lists projected anger as another defensive position:

- A sense of outrage and of anger, unwittingly directed at the victim – the narrator. When we meet a friend who has a malignant disease, we often feel angry at that person. We are torn apart by the inadequacy of our ability to respond properly, and inadvertently wish for the illness to be the patient's responsibility and wrongdoing.

This kind of projection often operates with much greater subtlety than Laub describes, although it can be at least as pernicious. Catharine MacKinnon gives an example in her analysis of the Clarence Thomas–Anita Hill hearings:

> What happens when you put the real language of sexual abuse in a Senate confirmation hearing? It is a lot like putting a videotape of your rape in your rape trial. It, and you, are treated as if you do not belong, as if you pulled down your pants and defecated in public. You are lowered by proving your injury. He is not. He allegedly said these things. If they were said, they were *his* words. She said them in quotation marks. But it is the woman to whom they are attributed when she speaks them. When she says them, it is believed they are true *of her* somehow, but not believed of him. Senator Grassley called it 'an offensive story.' Elise Norville, a radio commentator, 'left feeling dirty somehow.' President Bush 'felt unclean watching it.' The offensiveness, the dirt, the uncleanness stick to the woman, the woman of color in particular.[27]

MacKinnon's point has to do with feminism and sexual politics, but the excerpt expresses how negative feelings such as shame can – in the mind of the listener – attach themselves to the person recounting a traumatic event. The speaker – whether in a courtroom setting or during a life review interview can become the repository of the negative emotions that the narrative evokes in the listener. Though counselors are sensitized to the phenomenon of blaming the victim, oral historians need to be as well.[28]

Another listener reaction MacKinnon discusses in reference to the Anita Hill hearings is denial. Denial can be a protective mechanism against fear, anger, outrage, and possibly other emotions:

> We heard the spoken voice of a woman uttering the sounds of abuse, the moment in which silence breaks on the unspeakability of the experience, the echo of what had been unheard. Much of the response was disbelief, the reaffirmation of the silence of 'nothing happened,' the attempt to push the uncomfortable reality back underground through pathologizing dismissal.[29]

Oral historians are not politicians or lawyers. Yet, this same mechanism of denial can take place in interviews conducted by oral historians. Lawrence Langer gives an example from a videotaped interview with a Holocaust victim who had survived two deportations to Auschwitz. The interview was conducted for the Fortunoff Video Archive by trained interviewers from Yale University. The following is Langer's own transcription of one segment of a videotaped interview:

Interviewer: You survived because you were so plucky. When you stepped back . . .

Hanna F: No, dear, no dear, no . . . no, I had no . . . [*meanwhile, the two interviewers are whispering with each other audibly off-screen about this exchange, ignoring the survivor, who wants to reply*] how shall I explain to you? I know that I had to survive; I had to survive, even running away, even being with the people constantly, especially the second part, the second time, being back in Auschwitz. This time I had determined already to survive and you know what? It wasn't luck, it was stupidity. [*At this moment, the two interviewers laugh deprecatingly, disbelievingly, overriding her voice with their own 'explanation,' as one calls out, 'You had a lot of guts!'*]

Hanna F: [*simultaneously*]: No, no, no, no, there were not guts, there was just sheer stupidity. No . . . [*More laughter from the interviewers, one of whom now stands up between camera and survivor, blocking our vision, silencing her voice, terminating the interview. Why?*][30]

In this case, the interviewer refuses to 'admit' what the interviewee is saying. It is too threatening, too disruptive, too fear-producing, or anger-provoking for the interviewers to really *listen* to and accept what Hanna F. is saying. As a result, their frame overpowers her frame and, since the interviewers are in control, they cut the interview short.

I have never felt the need to resist my interviewees so vigorously, but I have enough investment in my expectations to understand how this kind of thing could take place. In my interview with Gertrude P., I wanted her to give me a profound and meaningful answer to the question 'What did you learn from the war?' Instead I got a long and somewhat eerie peal of laughter, followed by the sobering comment, 'You don't learn from a war.' I tried again, asking the question in another way, but eventually dropped the line of inquiry, accepting that, at least for this individual, the war provided no lessons, possessed not a shred of redeeming value.

Dori Laub's final category in his list of defensive positions is an interesting one:

- Hyperemotionality which superficially looks like compassion and caring. The testifier is simply flooded, drowned and lost in the listener's defensive affectivity.

I suppose that he means that the interviewer becomes so emotionally expressive – crying perhaps – that the interview is derailed. No doubt the interview subject reacts to the interviewer's emotional expression, probably in kind. The implication is that by a display of emotion, the one who asks the questions is able to escape the uncomfortable experience of having to listen to the answers. I have witnessed this in romantic relationships, so I surmise it is possible in an interview setting as well. I would add that there are other ways for interviewers to get away from material that makes them uncomfortable. A not-so-subtle example took place during my interview with Gertrude P.

At one point she was telling me about what happened in her Jewish neighborhood when the Germans marched into the Netherlands. To give some context as to what this information meant to me, I was well aware of criticism – both within and outside Jewish circles – that many Jews went to their death 'like lambs.' My grandfather had ten brothers, all of them rabbinical students, who perished in Hungary during the Nazi occupation. I always pictured these kin as being too wrapped up in reading the Torah and performing *mitzvahs* to have mounted a militant offensive. I had heard stories of Jews about to be shot who meekly recited the *shema* as they stood in front of the trenches that would become their graves, trenches that they themselves had been forced to dig. But I had never heard of mass suicide within the Jewish community in response to the arrival of the German army. This disturbing narrative took me by surprise and I suddenly wanted to change the subject. Gertrude P. would not let me. My emotional reaction and my defensive need to change the subject all occurred in less than half a minute.

GP: When the Germans walked in I was fifteen, and I remember standing at the window, we had a third floor apartment with double deckers, and we looked down and they were marching in singing. . . . And my father said to me, 'Take care of your mother. They're gonna get me tomorrow.' Because he was German, and he figured they're coming but it took a year and a half or so, or more. OK, so I was fifteen and people were jumping off the balconies in the back, killing themselves right and left, and gassing themselves, and using gas, you know we had gas –

MK: These are Jewish people.

GP: And I remember standing in the back while they were bombing Rotterdam. You could hear the sound of the bombing of Rotterdam. Holland is so flat the sound carries.

MK: All the way in Amsterdam?

GP: Oh yeah.

MK: Really.

GP: And, and, maybe a few bombs were dropped also close, but that's how I remember it; it might not be the truth. But –

MK: Wh – I'm sorry to interrupt. When you left, you came to the United States? When you left the Netherlands you came straight here?

GP: Yeah, I'll tell you how that happened. Anyway, we stood in the back there and we wanted to talk to our neighbors. And there were people screaming and crying and jumping off the balconies from the third floor and then there were people being revived who'd put their head in the oven, uh, or whatever, over the gas flame, and I kept saying to my father, 'Why would he do that? Why would he do that?' My father, 'Well, [unintelligible] terrible things *might* happen.'

Clearly, an interview with a trauma survivor makes special demands on both interviewer and interviewee. The interviewer must be prepared – if necessary – to serve as a midwife in the narrator's ongoing attempt to attain closure in regards to the traumatic material. The interviewer must also be prepared for unusual defensive behavior in the narrator, as well as the possibility of extreme vulnerability and pathos. In addition, the interviewer must be aware of his or her *own* emotional reactions to the narrator and to the material. This leads to the question posed by Inger Agger: 'How do we, supposedly the victims' helpers, contain their stories and simultaneously manage our own pain?'[31] Interviewing a trauma survivor requires a greater degree of both sensitivity and sturdiness than is normally brought to a life review.[32] The interviewer becomes a part of the trauma survivor's process by hearing the stories and being a witness to them. The narrator's emotional, mental, and spiritual well being must be put first, for it is never advisable to push for material that might lead to an internal re-enactment of the trauma rather than its re-externalization.[33] The principle of reciprocity, of giving back to the interviewee must be honored. In this case, if the interview is conducted with sufficient skill and sensitivity, it might be possible to give the narrator back a piece of his or her soul. Allowing the expression of the traumatic material in an atmosphere of empathy, free from distorted reactions, maximizes the possibility that some degree of closure will emerge out of the fragmentation and dissociation that trauma inflicts upon the human psyche.

Notes

1   Psychologist Charles R. Figley, summarizing the diagnostic criteria of the American Psychiatric Association, explains that 'a traumatic event occurs when a person experiences an event outside the range of usual human experience that would be markedly distressing to almost anyone: a serious threat to one's life or physical integrity; serious threat or harm to one's children, spouse, or other close relatives or friends; sudden destruction of one's home or community; or seeing another person seriously injured or killed in an accident or by physical violence.' *Burnout in Families: The Systemic Costs of Caring*, New York: CRC Press, 1998, p. 7

2   John A. Robinson, 'Personal Narratives Reconsidered', *Journal of American Folklore* 94, no. 371 (1981), p. 63.

3   See Rolf J. Kleber, ed., *Beyond Trauma: Cultural and Societal Dynamics*, New York: Plenum Press, 1995; Mary Beth Williams and John F. Sommers, *Handbook of Post-*

Traumatic Therapy, Westport: Greenwood Press, 1994; Gerald D. French and Chrys J. Harris, *Traumatic Incident Reduction (TIR)*, New York: CRC Press, 1999.

4 See H.W. Chalsma, *The Chambers of Memory: PTSD in the Life Stories of U.S. Vietnam Veterans*, London: Jason Aronson, Inc., 1998; Jonathan Shay, *Achilles in Vietnam: Combat Trauma and the Undoing of Character*, New York: Atheneum, 1994; L. Lewis, *The Tainted War: Culture and Identity in Vietnam War Narratives*, Westport: Greenwood, 1985; Robert Jay Litton, *Home from the War: Vietnam Veterans: Neither Victims nor Executioners*, New York: Simon & Schuster, 1973.

5 Highly recommended are Inger Agger, *The Blue Room: Trauma and Testimony among Refugee Women, A Psycho-Social Exploration*, London: Zed Books, 1994; Judith Herman, *Trauma and Recovery: The Aftermath of Violence, from Domestic Abuse to Political Terror*, New York: Basic Books, 1993.

6 William Shulman, ed., *2000 Directory: Association of Holocaust Organizations*, New York: Holocaust Resource Center and Archives, 2000.

7 www.library.yale.edu/testimonies

8 www.vhf.org/

9 Facing History and Ourselves Foundation (16 Hurd Road, Brookline, MA 02146) teaches secondary school teachers how to teach the Holocaust. They have produced *Elements of Times*, a very readable overview of different perspectives on Holocaust testimony (www.facing.org).

10 See James Young, *Writing and Rewriting the Holocaust*, Bloomington: Indiana University Press. 1988; Lawrence Langer, *Holocaust Testimony: The Ruins of Memory*, New Haven: Yale University Press, 1993; Efraim Sicher (ed.), *Breaking Crystal: Writing and Memory After Auschwitz*, Champaign, University of Illinois Press, 1998.

11 New York: Routledge, 1992. Other authoritative voices within the field of traumatology include Charles R. Figley (ed.), *Trauma and Its Wake*, Volume 1 and II, New York: Bruner/Mazel, 1985 and 1986; Inger Agger, *The Blue Room*; Cathy Caruth, *Unclaimed Experience: Trauma, Narrative, and History*, Baltimore: Johns Hopkins University Press, 1996; *Trauma: Explorations in Memory*, Baltimore: Johns Hopkins University Press, 1995.

12 Robert N. Butler, 'The Life Review: An Interpretation of Reminiscence in the Aged', *Psychiatry*, 26 (1963), pp. 65–76.

13 Laub and Felman, pp. 84–85.

14 Laub and Felman, p. 57.

15 Laub and Felman, p. 69.

16 See Linda Williams and Victoria Banyard eds, *Trauma and Memory*, Thousand Oaks: Sage Publications, 1999.

17 Laub and Felman, p. 69.

18 Personal communication with the author, 9/2/99.

19 Thank you to Lisa Bennett for her help with this interpretation. Laub's conception of re-externalization parallels what Elisabeth Kübler-Ross refers to, more simply, as 'externalization.' See Kübler-Ross, *Working it Through*, New York: Macmillan, 1982.

20 Pseudonyms were used to safeguard the privacy of the interviewees. The original interview cassettes recorded in December 1997 remain in my possession as each of the women requested they not be archived or used for purposes other than my research.

21 Terrence Des Pres, 'Holocaust Laughter?', in *Writing and the Holocaust*, (ed.) Berel Lang, New York: Holmes and Meier, 1986, pp. 229–230.

22 Harold Kaplan and Benjamin Sadock, *Synopsis of Psychiatry*, 7th edn, Baltimore: William and Wilkins, 1994.

23   Jeanne Segal, *Living Beyond Fear*, New York: Ballantine, 1989.

24   Laub and Felman, p. 72.

25   Roger Perilstein, M.D. informs me that a more accurate word than 'fear,' according to psychiatric terminology, would be 'anxiety.'

26   Laub and Felman, pp. 72–73.

27   Catharine MacKinnon, *Only Words*, Cambridge: Harvard University Press, 1993, pp. 65–66. See also Judith Herman, *Trauma and Recovery*, p. 2, who writes 'To speak publically about one's knowledge of atrocities is to invite the stigma that attaches to victims.' I have not been able to find any writings that address gender issues in interviewing. Regarding the many issues involved in interviewing those of other ethnicities and cultures see C.E. Vontress, 'Racial and Ethnic Barriers in Counselling', in P.B. Pederson, J.G. Draguns, W.J. Lonner and J.E. Trimble (eds), *Counselling Across Cultures*, revised and expanded edition, Honolulu: University Press of Hawaii, pp. 87–107; Derald and David Sue, *Counseling the Culturally Different*, New York: J. Wiley & Sons, 1999.

28   For this I would suggest turning to the extensive literature on counseling victims of sexual abuse, i.e. Ann Burgess (ed.), *Rape and Sexual Assault: A Research Handbook*, New York: Garland Press, 1985.

29   Catharine MacKinnon, *Only Words*, p. 65.

30   Lawrence Langer, *Holocaust Testimonies: The Ruins of Memory*, New Haven: Yale University Press, 1991, pp. 63–64. The original video is #HVT-18 in the Fortunoff Video Archive for Holocaust Testimonies, Yale University.

31   Inger Agger, *The Blue Room*, p. 5.

32   Information available to therapists to assist them in these difficult processes may be well utilised by oral historians. Try Charles R. Figley, *Compassion Fatigue. Coping With Secondary Traumatic Stress Disorder in Those Who Treat the Traumatized*, New York: Bruner/Mazel, 1995; Stuart D. Perlman, *The Therapist's Emotional Survival: Dealing with the Pain of Exploring Trauma*, London: Jason Aronson, Inc., 1999.

33   Flashbacks and other such manifestations of dissociation are not unusual among people who have experienced severe trauma. At such times, 'the person feels as if he or she is actually reliving the event and loses contact with their current environment, usually for a few seconds or minutes.' Alan Stoudemire, *Clinical Psychiatry for Medical Students*, third edition, Philadelphia: Lippincott-Raven, 1998 p. 328.

PART III

Interpreting memories: introduction

$\mathbf{M}$EMORY HAS BEEN A CONTENTIOUS HISTORICAL source and oral historians have been especially self-critical – perhaps more than most historians – about the nature of their source and approaches to its interpretation. The introduction to Part I, 'Critical developments', noted how the first generation of oral historians contested the claim that memory offered unreliable historical evidence, and at first adapted conventional guidelines for source evaluation such as checking for internal consistency and 'triangulation' with other sources.[1] By the late 1970s Alessandro Portelli's article 'What makes oral history different' (reproduced in Part I), typified a more positive and assertive defence of the 'peculiarities of oral history'. Memory *was* partial and selective, shaped into meaningful accounts, affected by the subjectivity of the speaker and the audience for the story, and influenced by the passage of time and by 'collective' memory. Underpinning this new approach was a model of memory as 'an active process of creation of meanings' rather than a 'passive repository of facts'.[2] In order to use oral testimony and interpret the experience and meaning of past events, researchers need to understand this active process through which a narrator creates meaningful stories about that past. Conversely, oral historians now agree that their memory sources are not only about the past but can also be used to examine the nature of historical memory and the meanings of the past in the present for individuals and society. Memory is thus the subject as well as source of oral history, and oral historians draw upon an exhilarating multi-disciplinary array of approaches to memory and its interpretation. The authors in Part III – historians, folklorists and anthropologists – use rich oral history case studies to demonstrate a wide variety of approaches to analysis and interpretation. References in this introduction direct readers to the wider literature of interpretative oral history.[3]

In 'Remembering a Vietnam War firefight', Fred Allison contrasts a US war veteran's memories of a brutal firefight – as recorded in an oral history interview in 2002 – with the account related by the same soldier in a debriefing interview conducted by the unit intelligence officer in 1968, two days after the event. The detailed but disjointed initial account contrasts markedly with the more dramatic, colourful and coherent oral history recorded by Allison. The earlier version reflects the narrow viewpoint of the soldier and the difficulty of making sense so close to a traumatic event, though it is not necessarily a more 'pure' or accurate rendition and is itself shaped by the context and audience of the wartime debriefing session. Drawing upon Charlotte Linde's notion that life story narrative enables the 'creation of coherence',[4] Allison shows how this war veteran developed a story – without altering the basic factual details – that makes sense of a significant and traumatic event, both for himself and for a modern audience that has not experienced war. Readers might consider other interpretations of the oral history interview. For example, the veteran might have told a different story to an interviewer who was not a former Marine officer; and to what extent did a continuing loyalty to his wartime 'band of brothers' nullify criticism of fellow soldiers or of the war itself?[5]

The Holocaust has probably generated more oral history interviews than any other single subject, and analysis of Holocaust survivor testimony has certainly made a major contribution to understandings of memory – especially memory of traumatic events.[6] In 'Surviving memory: truth and inaccuracy in Holocaust testimony', Mark Roseman notes 'an understandable reluctance to challenge the testimony's accuracy or veracity'. Through his biography of the German-born Jewish survivor Marianne Ellenbogen, Roseman shows that 'on the fundamentals, Marianne's memories were almost entirely borne out by other sources' and, indeed, that her memories often proved the inaccuracies and deceit of wartime Nazi records. Yet comparison of contemporary and retrospective accounts, including letters and diaries as well as interviews,[7] uncovered significant patterns of discrepancy in Marianne's memory. Roseman argues that a 'concern with accuracy' shows no disrespect to survivors, and that 'on the contrary, it helps to illuminate the very processes of memory which we are seeking to understand'. The minor inaccuracies concerned events that continued to generate terrible pain and guilt for Marianne, and 'the trauma resulted in an inability to cope with memory as it was, a pressure that led, on the one hand, to an unwillingness to communicate about it to the outside world, and, on the other, to the process of subtle modification'. Roseman's study conveys the psychic difficulty of remembering 'unbearable reality' and the need to 'impose *control* on memory and on the moments that caused such pain'.[8]

In 'Anzac memories' Alistair Thomson offers the notion of memory 'composure' as one model for understanding the psychological and social processes of remembering, and suggests a 'popular memory' approach to interviewing that might unravel the complex strands of memory.[9] Thomson argues that remembering often involves a psychic struggle to 'compose' a past that we can live with, and he highlights the symbiotic relationship between memory and identity throughout the life of Australian First World War veteran Fred Farrall. Farrall's identity – as a man and a soldier – was shaped by his war memories and, in turn, his changing personal identity affected how he was able to remember the war. Thomson also shows how remembering is a social as well as psychological process, that we draw upon the language and meanings of our culture in order to articulate our experience and seek social 'recognition' and affirmation of our memory stories from family, peers, community or nation. Throughout his life, and even as an old man reviewing his life,[10] Fred Farrall struggled to relate his own war memories to the powerful national collective memory of Australians at war. Since the 1980s – as noted in the Introduction to Part I – cultural or 'collective' memory has been a primary focus of memory studies in many disciplines.[11] Such studies have not always distinguished the processes of individual memory from the very different ways in which representations of the past ('collective memories') are created, institutionalized and contested in society. Cultural memory studies have tended to neglect individual memory and overstate the extent to which collective memories shape personal memories.[12] Oral historians have made important theoretical contributions to memory studies by interpreting interview evidence about the relationship between personal and cultural memory.[13]

In 1998 Sherna Gluck noted (in the email exchange reproduced in Chapter 6) that 'because few recent [oral history] projects have been very large, the issue of historical generalization, the search for patterns, has receded from view'.[14] It is certainly true that most of the theoretical and methodological writing about oral history interpretation since the 1980s has focused upon the analysis of individual interviews. Perhaps the focus is beginning to change, not least because there are now vast sets of oral history interviews available in archives throughout the world and researchers increasingly recognize the value of such collections for 'secondary analysis'. Two articles in Part III consider approaches to the interpretation of sets of oral history interviews.

In 'Structure and validity in oral evidence', Trevor Lummis argues that 'the problem at the heart of using the interview method in history still remains that of moving from the individual account to a social interpretation'. Writing in 1981, Lummis was responding to contemporary criticisms about the representativeness and generalizability of oral evidence, but his ideas about aggregation and tabulation of oral history data sets are useful, perhaps surprisingly so, for a new generation of researchers. Lummis recognizes that oral history interview sets are unlikely to comprise a 'representative sample' and shows how interviewee characteristics can be compared with the wider group under study in order to explore 'congruence' between a 'small accidental sample of elderly informants' and 'wide historical trends'. The structured evidence that Lummis produced by aggregating and tabulating data within interviews from British fishing communities reveals 'stratified distinctions in behaviour and attitudes which were not apparent from perusing the qualitative evidence of individual interviews'. Perhaps most intriguingly, Lummis shows that 'structuring a number of interviews can contribute to understanding memory – even in the shape of structured silences'.[15]

In the context of 'Oral history and the study of communities', Linda Shopes also considers the interpretation of extant sets of interviews. Shopes shows how to find relevant interview collections and reminds users to consider how the provenance of archived interviews shaped the recorded stories. She urges researchers to immerse themselves in the interviews – and to heed the aural recordings as well as the written transcript – so that they can begin to uncover patterns and develop social or historical generalizations. For example, one of the great values of oral testimony is that it can reveal how cross-cutting factors such as race, class and local identity influence attitudes and behaviour in complex ways, but 'such insights, however modest, do not come from quickly scanning interview transcripts. Only slowly do underlying strands of a community's culture reveal themselves, as interview after interview sounds the same themes.' Shopes argues that an awareness of interpretative possibilities should also influence the creation and use of new oral history records. A community oral history project should seek answers to conceptual problems; it should include a broad sample of interviewees and not just the usual suspects amongst community leaders and insiders, and it should ask difficult questions that challenge cosy assumptions about 'community'.[16]

In recent years narrative studies has emerged as a buoyant field of inter-disciplinary research that considers questions with particular relevance to oral history. How do individuals (and communities) tell stories that make sense of their lives? What is the relationship between personal narrative and identity? What can we learn from analysis of the language and form of oral narratives, from the patterns of speech and of silence? How do narrators both draw upon and create cultural genres of story-telling?[17] Two contributors to Part III focus upon approaches and issues in narrative analysis.

In 'Telling tales', Elizabeth Lapovsky Kennedy's analysis of 'the structure and style of storytelling' by working-class lesbians in New York State illuminates pre-Stonewall lesbian life.[18] The exquisite storytelling styles of her informants revealed the significance of storytelling in a vibrant but marginalized community that needed to create alternative identities and 'guidelines for living'. By embracing 'the uniquely subjective nature of life stories', Kennedy could explore how her narrators coped with and resisted heterosexism and homophobia, and how individuals 'decide to construct and express their identity'. Cases where narrators' memories were internally contradictory or in conflict with each other 'conveyed precisely the freedom and joy and the pain and limitation that characterized bar life in the mid–twentieth century'. Differences between gay male and lesbian memories of the Stonewall riots (a key event in gay liberation), and the ways in which only some stories were inscribed in the myth or meta-narrative of Stonewall, expressed 'the ambiguous position of women in gay culture' and captured 'the cultural processes of making lesbians and women invisible in history'. Kennedy demonstrates that 'there is a tremendous amount to be learned by fully exploring the subjective and oral nature of oral histories', but her conclusion – that the empirical and subjective values of oral evidence are 'fully complementary to one another' and should not be 'falsely polarized' – is an essential recommendation for all oral historians.

By contrast with the vibrant life stories of New York lesbians, the interviews with former servants of Dutch colonialists recorded by anthropologists Ann Laura Stoler and Karen Strassler produced rather 'flat', muted accounts that 'pointed us repeatedly to '"the content of the form"': to how and why former servants talk without sentimentality about sentiment and recollect the colonial past without telling scripted, storied narratives'. Stoler and Strassler challenge colonial memory studies that naively expect 'subaltern' anti-colonial memory stories. They show how the reticence of former servants is in part explained by a tension between their personal memories and the cultural memory of twentieth-century Indonesian history, and they note that the apparent lack of sentiment might also reflect a Javanese aversion to emotional display – thus reminding researchers to be alert to the expressive forms and historical world-view of the group under study.[19] But by following 'the surface grain' of their interviews Stoler and Strassler realized that 'concrete and sensory memories' about cooking, cleaning and child care – articulated through gestural and aural clues and distinctive word use and repetition – evoke 'sensibilities that other ways of telling do not' and illuminate the 'intimate landscape of affective ties and asymmetric relations'.[20]

Several of the articles in Part III note in passing the ethical and personal challenges of interpreting other people's lives. Stoler and Strassler describe their awkward interview with Ibu Darmo, who 'rejected our eagerness to commiserate and share' in her memories; Thomson worries about upsetting the 'safe' memories of war veterans; and Shopes writes that 'although oral history provides outstanding opportunities to democratize the practice of history – to "share authority" in Michael Frisch's resonant phrase – as interviewer and interviewee, scholar and community work together to understand the past, in practice the process requires negotiation, give-and-take, and considerable goodwill'. As Valerie Yow explains in Part I, the interpretative relationship between researcher and interviewee has been the subject of extensive discussion in recent years, and two articles in Part III examine that interpretative relationship in more depth.[21]

Folklorist Katherine Borland considers a situation in which an interviewee disputes the researcher's interpretation of her memories. Borland had interviewed her grandmother Beatrice Hanson, and produced a feminist interpretation of a story about the young Beatrice and her father at a horse race meeting in 1944.[22] Grandmother Hanson 'expressed strong disagreement' with Borland's interpretation of 'a female struggle for autonomy within a hostile male environment'. Borland asserts the value of researchers' interpretations (in this case based upon the 'symbolic construction' of the story) which are not simply 'a recuperation of original authorial intention', yet she also notes the dangers of attacking 'collaborators' carefully constructed sense of self' and outlines a more negotiated interpretative process, an exchange of understandings which might benefit both parties.[23] Borland's postscript reports a happy ending in the interpretative relationship with her grandmother, though readers might consider Sherna Gluck's question, posed in the email exchange reproduced in Part I: 'What if Katherine Borland's grandmother hadn't finally agreed with Borland's feminist interpretation of her narrative?'

By contrast, Kathleen Blee describes a research scenario in which such an interpretative exchange was virtually impossible, an oral history of women in the Ku Klux Klan. Blee shows how the testimony of her interviewees was affected by their political agendas, by retrospective censure of the Klan, and by the desire 'to appear respectable to an oral historian'. Yet she also argues that such interviews are revelatory about motivations and ideologies – 'how and why ordinary people might become attracted to the politics of racial hatred' – and enable historians 'to scrutinize the accounts of political actors, and to probe those experiences, beliefs and narratives that do not fit conventional historical interpretations'.[24] Blee questions the recommended practice of an empathetic interview relationship, and struggles with an ethical concern that she may have empowered her interviewees by helping them 'to construct a narrative that "makes sense" of the Klan and its actions'. This study pinpoints a central tension in the interpretative role of the oral historian, between responsibility to the interviewee and responsibility to society and history.[25]

Notes

1   On critics of memory as a historical source, and initial responses by oral historians, see notes 12–14 in the Introduction to Part I, 'Critical developments'.
2   Portelli, 'What makes oral history different', in Part I (Chapter 3). Recent memory studies that support Portelli's model include: D. Draaisma, *Why Life Speeds Up as You Get Older: How Memory Shapes Our Past*, trans. by A. Pomerans and E. Pomerans, Cambridge: Cambridge University Press, 2004; D.B. Pillemer, *Momentous Events, Vivid Memories*, Cambridge, Mass.: Harvard University Press, 1998; D.L. Schacter, *Memory Distortion: How Minds, Brains and Societies Reconstruct the Past*, Cambridge, Mass.: Harvard University Press, 1995. For an excellent oral historian's review of the memory literature, see V.R. Yow, *Recording Oral History: A Guide for the Humanities and Social Sciences*, Walnut Creek: AltaMira Press, 2nd edition 2005, pp. 35–67.
3   For overviews about oral history interpretation, see Yow, *Recording Oral History*, pp. 282–310; D.A. Ritchie, *Doing Oral History: A Practical Guide*, New York: Oxford University Press, 2nd edition 2003, pp. 110–133; B. Roberts, *Biographical Research*, Buckingham: Open University Press, 2001, pp. 93–133; P. Thompson, *The Voice of the Past: Oral History*, Oxford: Oxford University Press, 3rd edition 2000, pp. 173–189 and 265–308; J. Jeffrey and G. Edwall (eds), *Memory and History: Essays on Recalling and Interpreting Experience*, Lanham, Md.: University Press of America, 1994; A. Portelli, *The Death of Luigi Trastulli and Other Stories: Form and Meaning in Oral History*, Albany: State University of New York Press, 1991.
4   C. Linde, *The Creation of Coherence*, Oxford: Oxford University Press, 2003. For other references on the narrative construction of identity see note 27 in the Introduction to Part I, 'Critical developments'. On the significance of forgetting for personal identity, see N. Norquay, 'Identity and forgetting', *Oral History Review*, 1999, vol. 26, no. 1, pp. 1–21. A logical corollary of the notion that remembering is 'an active process of creation of meanings' is the argument that oral testimony is not just a source for researcher interpretation but is itself already a sophisticated interpretation by the narrator of his or her experience. See also Chapter 39 in this volume by Rosanne Kennedy.
5   On Vietnam veteran memory, see P. Budra and M. Zeitlin (eds), *Soldier Talk: The Vietnam War in Oral Narrative*, Bloomington: Indiana University Press, 2004; P. Hagopian, 'Voices from Vietnam: veterans' oral histories in the classroom', *Journal of American History*, 2000, vol. 87, no. 2, pp. 593–601. On war and memory, see T.G. Ashplant, G. Dawson and M. Roper, *Commemorating War: The Politics of Memory*, New Brunswick, N.J., Transaction Publishers, 2004; M. Evans and K. Lunn, *War and Memory in the Twentieth Century*, New York: Berg, 1997; A. Portelli, *The Order Has been Carried Out: History, Memory, and Meaning of a Nazi Massacre in Rome*, New York: Palgrave Macmillan, 2003; *Oral History*, 1997, vol. 25, no. 2, special issue on 'War and Peace'.
6   Rob Perks estimates that about 2,500 individual British-based Holocaust survivors and child refugees have been recorded and archived. Tony Kushner estimates that 'over 100,000' Jewish Holocaust testimonies have been collected world-wide (Rob Perks, 'Holocaust oral testimonies and sound archives in Britain', paper presented at Yale University Library conference, 'The Contribution of Oral Testimony to Holocaust and Genocide Studies', October 2002). Mark Roseman cites Lawrence Langer and other writers about Holocaust survivor testimony. See also H. Greenspan, *On Listening to Holocaust Survivors: Recounting and Life History*, Westport, Conn.: Praeger, 1998. In this volume, see Chapter 16 by Mark Klempner; Chapter 35 by Joanna Bornat;

Chapter 39 by Rosanne Kennedy; Chapter 40 by Irina Sherbakova. For a more general study of traumatic memory and life stories, see K.L. Rogers, S. Leydesdorff and G. Dawson (eds), *Trauma and Life Stories*: *International Perspectives*, London: Routledge, 1999.

7   For the biography of Marianne Ellenbogen, see M. Roseman, *The Past in Hiding*, Harmondsworth, Penguin, 2000. In recent years several oral historians have, like Roseman, usefully contrasted oral testimony with other forms of life-story narratives, contemporary and retrospective, oral and written: R.W. Cherny, 'Constructing a radical identity: history, memory and the seafaring stories of Harry Bridges', *Pacific Historical Review*, 2001, vol. 70, no. 4, pp. 571–599; S.F. Miescher, 'The life histories of Boakye Yiadom: exploring the subjectivity and "voice" of a teacher-catechist in colonial Ghana', in L. White, S.F. Miescher and D.W. Cohen (eds), *African Words, African Voices*: *Critical Practices in Oral History*, Bloomington: Indiana University Press, 2001, pp. 162–193; M.R. Kamp, 'Three lives of Saodat: communist, Uzbek, survivor', *Oral History Review*, 2001, vol. 28, no. 2, pp. 21–58.

8   Oral history studies that have used psychological or psychoanalytic approaches to interpret memory include M. Roper, 'Analysing the analysed: transference and counter-transference in the oral history encounter', *Oral History*, 2003, vol. 31, no. 2, pp. 20–32; M. Roper, 'Re-remembering the soldier heroes: the psychic and social construction of memory in personal narratives of the Great War', *History Workshop Journal*, 2000, issue 50, pp. 181–204; W. Hollway and T. Jefferson, 'Narrative discourse and the unconscious: the case of Tommy', in M. Andrews, S.D. Sclater, C. Squire and A. Treacher (eds), *The Uses of Narrative*: *Explorations in Sociology, Psychology and Cultural Studies*, New Brunswick, N.J.: Transaction Publishers, 2004, pp. 136–149. See also note 27 in the Introduction to Part I, 'Critical developments'.

9   For the origins and use of the notions of 'composure' and 'social recognition', see A. Thomson, *Anzac Memories*: *Living with the Legend*, Melbourne: Oxford University Press, 1994; G. Dawson, *Soldier Heroes*: *British Adventure, Empire and the Imagining of Masculinities*, London: Routledge, 1994; P. Summerfield, *Reconstructing Women's Wartime Lives*, Manchester: Manchester University Press, 1998; P. Summerfield, 'Dis/composing the subject: intersubjectivities in oral history', in T. Cosslett, C. Lurie and P. Summerfield (eds), *Feminism and Autobiography*: *Texts, Theories, Methods*, London: Routledge, 2000, pp. 91–106; Roper, 'Re-remembering the soldier heroes'; R. Horowitz and R. Halpern, 'Work, race, and identity: self-representation in the narratives of black packinghouse workers', *Oral History Review*, 1999, vol. 26, no. 1, pp. 23–43 (though note that footnote 2 on p. 25 of this latter article wrongly attributes the idea of 'composure' to Luisa Passerini).

10   On memory and life review in older age see Chapter 35 in this volume by Joanna Bornat; and S. Chandler, 'Oral history across generations: age, generational identity and oral testimony', *Oral History*, 2005, vol. 33, no. 2, pp. 48–56.

11   See note 36 in the Introduction to Part I, 'Critical developments' for references on history and modern memory. Contributions to recent debates about collective memory include P. Nora, 'Between memory and history: Les Lieux de Mémoire', *Representations*, Spring 1989, vol. 26, pp. 7–25; D. Glassberg, 'Public history and the study of memory', *Public Historian*, Spring 1996, vol. 18, no. 2, pp. 7–23 (see also responses by Frisch, Lowenthal, Kammen and Shopes in Spring 1997, vol. 19, no. 2, pp. 31–56); A. Confino, 'Collective memory and cultural history: problems of method', *The American Historical Review*, 1997, vol. 102, no. 5, pp. 1386–1403; S.A. Crane, 'Writing the individual back into collective memory', *The American Historical Review*, 1997, vol. 102, no. 5, pp. 1377–1385; P. Frizsche, 'The case of modern memory', *Journal of Modern History*, 2001, vol. 73, no. 1, pp. 87–117; W. Kansteiner, 'Finding meaning in memory: a methodological critique of collective memory studies', *History and Theory*, 2002, vol. 41, no. 2, pp. 179–197.

12   A. Green, 'Individual remembering and "collective memory": theoretical propositions and contemporary debates', *Oral History*, 2004, vol. 32, no. 2, pp. 35–44. Susannah Radstone argues that cultural memory studies often wrongly assume that models of personal memory are replicable in studies of cultural memory: S. Radstone, 'Reconceiving binaries: the limits of memory', *History Workshop Journal*, 2005, issue 59, pp. 134–150.

13   For oral history studies which explore the relationships between personal and cultural memory, see the references in note 9, above, and the following chapters in this volume: Chapter 23 by Ann Laura Stoler, with Karen Strassler; and Chapter 39 by Rosanne Kennedy. See also L. Passerini, 'Work ideology and consensus under Italian fascism', *History Workshop*, 1979, issue 8, pp. 82–108; R. Grele, 'Listen to their voices: two case studies in the interpretation of oral history interviews', *Oral History*, 1979, vol. 7, no. 1, pp. 33–42; J. Bodner, 'Power and memory in oral history: workers and managers at Studebaker', *Journal of American History*, 1989, vol. 75, no. 4, pp. 1201–1221; R. Samuel and P. Thompson (eds), *The Myths We Live By*, London: Routledge, 1990; V. Yans-McLaughlin, 'Metaphors of self in history: subjectivity, oral narrative and immigration studies', in V. Yans-McLaughlin (ed.), *Immigration Reconsidered: History, Sociology and Politics*, New York: Oxford University Press, 1990; and A. Portelli, 'The death of Luigi Trastulli: memory and the event', and 'Uchronic dreams: working-class memory and possible worlds', in Portelli, *The Death of Luigi Trastulli and Other Stories*, pp. 1–26 and pp. 99–116; S. Amin, *Event, Metaphor, Memory: Chauri Chaura, 1922–1992*, Berkeley, University of California Press, 1995; A. Heimo and U. Peltonen, 'Memories and histories, public and private: after the Finnish Civil War', in S. Radstone and K. Hodgkin (eds), *Contested Pasts: The Politics of Memory*, London: Routledge, 2003, pp. 42–56. On the relationship between oral history and 'public history', see note 1 in the Introduction to Part IV in this volume.

14   S.H. Armitage and S.B. Gluck: 'Reflections on women's oral history: an exchange' (see Chapter 6).

15   See also T. Lummis, *Listening to History: The Authenticity of Oral Evidence*, London, Hutchinson, 1987. Other oral historians who write about thematic analysis of sets of interviews include: Daniel Kerr, Chapter 37 in this volume; Thompson, *The Voice of the Past*, pp. 247–251; R. Jensen, 'Oral history, quantification and the new social history', *Oral History Review*, 1981, vol. 9, pp. 13–25; R. Sharpless, 'The numbers game: oral history compared with quantitative methodology', *International Journal of Oral History*, 1986, vol. 7, no. 2, pp. 93–108; P.S. Li, 'Constructing immigrants' work worlds from oral testimony', *Canadian Oral History Association Journal*, 1989, no. 9, pp. 9–12; J. Rose, 'Willingly to school: the working-class response to elementary education in Britain, 1875–1918', *Journal of British Studies*, April 1993, vol. 32, pp. 114–138; R.E. Doel, 'Oral history of American science: a forty-year review', *History of Science*, 2003, vol. xli, pp. 349–378. For debates about secondary analysis of archived interviews see the Introduction to Part IV of this volume; also J. Bornat, 'A second take: revisiting interviews with a different purpose', *Oral History*, 2003, vol. 31, no. 1, pp. 47–53; B. Godfrey, '"Dear reader I killed him": ethical and emotional issues in researching convicted murderers through the analysis of interview transcripts', *Oral History*, 2003, vol. 31, no. 1, pp 54–64; J.C. Richardson and B.S. Godfrey, 'Towards ethical practice in the use of archived transcripted interviews', *International Journal of Social Research Methodology*, 2003, vol. 6, no. 4, pp. 347–355 (and in the same issue, 'A response' by P. Thompson, pp. 356–60); N. Mauthner, O. Parry and K. Milburn, 'The data are out there, or are they? Implications for archiving qualitative data', *Sociology*, 1998, vol. 32, no. 4, pp. 733–745; O. Parry and N. Mauthner, '"Whose data are they anyway"? Practical, legal and ethical issues in archiving qualitative data', *Sociology*, 2005, vol. 38, no. 1, pp. 139–152; L. Bishop, 'Protecting respondents and enabling data sharing: Reply to Parry and Mauthner', *Sociology*, 2005, vol. 39, no. 2, pp. 333–336; O. Parry and N. Mauthner, 'Back to

basics: Who re-uses qualitative data and why?', *Sociology*, 2005, vol. 39, no. 2, pp. 337–342.

16   For an exemplary community oral history, see Bill Nasson, 'Oral history and the reconstruction of District Six', in S. Jeppie and C. Soudien (eds), *The Struggle for District Six*: *Past and Present*, Cape Town: Buchu Books, 1990, pp. 44–66. See also in this volume: Chapter 37 by Daniel Kerr; Chapter 41 by Patricia Lundy and Mark McGovern.

17   See notes 8 and 29 in the Introduction to Part I, 'Critical developments' for general references on, respectively, oral tradition and the narrative study of lives. Oral history writings about narrative include I. Hofmeyer, '*We spend our years as a tale that is told*': *Oral Historical Narrative in a South African Chiefdom*, London, James Currey, 1993; A. Portelli, *The Battle of Valle Giulia*: *Oral History and the Art of Dialogue*, Madison, University of Wisconsin Press, 1997; M. Chamberlain and P. Thompson (eds), *Narrative and Genre*, New Brunswick, N.J.: Transaction Publishers, 2004; S.G. Davies, 'Review essay: storytelling rights', *Oral History Review*, 1988, vol. 16, no. 2, pp. 109–115; S. Featherstone, 'Jack Hill's horse: narrative form and oral history', *Oral History*, 1991, vol. 19, no. 2, pp. 59–62; R.C. Smith, 'Review essay: storytelling as experience', *Oral History Review*, 1995, vol. 22, pp. 87–91; M.F. Chanfrault-Duchet, 'Narrative structures, social models, and symbolic representation in the life story', in S.B. Gluck and D. Patai (eds), *Women's Words*: *The Feminist Practice of Oral History*, London: Routledge, 1991, pp. 77–92; S. Schrager, 'What is social in oral history?', *International Journal of Oral History*, 1983, vol. 4, no. 2, pp. 76–98; R.H. Williams, '"I'm a keeper of information": history-telling and voice', *Oral History Review*, 2001, vol. 28, no. 1, pp. 41–64. For (African) historians' criticisms of 'postmodern' narrative approaches see Chapter 39 by Kennedy in this volume, and the discussion in C. Hamilton, '"Living by fluidity": oral histories, material custodies and the politics of archiving', in C. Hamilton, V. Harris, J. Taylor, M. Pickover, G. Reid and R. Saleh (eds), *Refiguring the Archive*, Dordrecht: Kluwer Academic Publishers, 2002, pp. 209–227. For references on narrative and 'testimonio', see Chapter 38 by William Westerman in this volume, and note 15 in the Introduction to Part V, 'Advocacy and Empowerment'.

18   On gay and lesbian history, see note 11 in the Introduction to Part V of this volume.

19   Oral historians who consider how different cultural groups understand the world and narrate life stories in different ways include E. Tonkin, *Narrating Our Pasts*: *The Social Construction of Oral History*, Cambridge: Cambridge University Press, 1992; J. Cruikshank, *The Social Life of Stories*: *Narrative and Knowledge in the Yukon Territory*, Lincoln, University of Nebraska Press, 1998; B. Attwood and F. Magowan (eds), *Telling Stories*: *Indigenous History and Memory in Australia and New Zealand*, Crows Nest, New South Wales: Allen & Unwin, 2001; W. Schneider, *So They Understand*: *Cultural Issues in Oral History*, Logan: Utah State University Press, 2002; S. Burton, 'Issues in cross-cultural interviewing: Japanese women in England' (see Chapter 13, this volume); Y. J. Kopijn, 'The oral history interview in a cross-cultural setting', in M. Chamberlain and P. Thompson (eds), *Narrative and Genre*: *Contexts and Types of Communication*, New Brunswick, N.J.: Transaction Publishers, 2004, pp. 142–159; T. Giles-Vernick, 'Lives, histories and sites of recollection', in White, Miescher and Cohen (eds), *African Words, African Voices*, pp. 194–213; L. Campbell, 'Walking a different road: recording oral history with Darby Jampijinpa Ross', *Oral History Association of Australia Journal*, 2004, vol. 26, pp. 1–9.

20   For aural and visual clues in oral testimony see, respectively, Hardy (Chapter 30) and Sipe (Chapter 31) in Part IV, 'Making histories'. On sensory memory, see also M. Langfield and P. Maclean, '"But pineapple I'm still a bit wary of": sensory memories of Jewish women who migrated to Australia as children, 1938–1939', in A.J. Hammerton and E. Richards (eds), *Speaking to Immigrants*: *Oral Testimony and the History of Australian Migration*, Canberra: Research School of Social Sciences, Australian National University, 2002, pp. 83–110.

21   On the oral history interpretative relationship see, in this volume, Chapter 5 by Valerie Yow; Chapter 35 by Joanna Bornat; and Chapter 37 by Daniel Kerr. See also P. Friedlander, *The Emergence of a UAW Local: 1936–39: A Study in Class and Culture*, Pittsburgh, Pa.: University of Pittsburgh Press, 1975; A. Portelli, 'Research as an experiment in equality', in Portelli, *The Death of Luigi Trastulli*, pp. 29–44; M. Frisch, *A Shared Authority: Essays on the Craft and Meaning of Oral and Public History*, Albany: State University of New York Press, 1990; and *Oral History Review*, 2003, vol. 30, no. 1, special issue on 'Shared Authority'.

22   For feminist approaches to interpreting oral history, see note 33 in Part I, 'Critical developments'. On the gendered differences between men and women remembering see, in this volume Chapter 40 by Irina Sherbakova and Chapter 42 by Nigel Cross and Rhiannon Barker. See also I. Bertaux-Wiame, 'The life history approach to the study of internal migration', *Oral History*, 1979, vol. 7, no. 1, pp. 26–32; C. Daley, '"He would know, but I just have a feeling": gender and oral history', *Women's History Review*, 1998, vol. 7, no. 3, pp. 343–359.

23   Two other examples of interpretative conflict and collaboration within family oral histories are A. Kikumura, 'Family life histories: a collaborative venture', *Oral History Review*, 1986, vol. 14, pp. 1–7; and A. Thomson, 'Memory as a battlefield; personal and political investments in the national military past', *Oral History Review*, 1995, vol. 22, no. 2, pp. 55–74.

24   On oral history with political activists, see *Oral History*, 1996, vol. 21, no. 1, special issue on 'Political Lives'.

25   On this tension in interpretative responsibility, see K.L. Rogers, 'Critical choices in interviews', *Oral History Review*, 1987, vol. 15, no. 2, pp. 165–184; E. Luchterhand, 'Knowing and not knowing: involvement in Nazi genocide', in P. Thompson and N. Burchardt (eds), *Our Common History: The Transformation of Europe*, London: Pluto, 1982, pp. 251–272; R.J. Grele, 'History and the languages of history in the oral history interview: who answers whose questions and why?', in E. McMahan and K.L. Rogers (eds), *Interactive Oral History Interviewing*, Hillsdale, N.J.: Lawrence Erlbaum, 1994, pp. 1–18 and 163–164.

Chapter 17

Fred H. Allison

REMEMBERING A VIETNAM WAR FIREFIGHT
Changing perspectives over time

This chapter contrasts two accounts about a brutal firefight by a US Vietnam War veteran – one recorded during the war in 1968 and the other in an oral history interview in 2002. Fred Allison explores how remembering is shaped by context, viewpoint and audience, and how narrative is used to make coherent and meaningful sense of significant and traumatic events. Allison is a retired marine and an oral historian with the History and Museums Division of the US Marine Corps University, Quantico, Virginia. Reprinted from *Oral History Review*, 2004, vol. 31, no. 2, pp. 69–83. © 2004, Oral History Association. All rights reserved. Used by permission.

THE MILITARY TRUCK ground to a dusty stop. The marine driver, acting like something was wrong, got out and kicked the tyres. Out the back slipped an eight-man Marine Corps Reconnaissance (Recon) patrol and shadow-like disappeared into the brush of the Charlie 2 area, I Corps, South Vietnam. The driver got back in and roared off down the road. The Recon team, code named 'Box Score', headed into bad guy country. It was February 1968.

PFC Michael Nation, twenty years old, from Southern California, 'in-country' for four months, was rear security on the patrol. He had been on several such patrols; they were almost routine, almost comfortable. The team lived and worked together, they were professionals and they were close.

The second day into the mission, the Recon patrol, call sign 'Box Score', encountered the enemy. The marines did not know it but they had walked into the midst of two companies, about 200 North Vietnamese (NVA) troops. First, they only heard them – light-hearted voices, laughing, maybe having lunch. Then they spotted six or seven NVA troops coming down a trail opposite from the direction they heard the voices. The lieutenant leading the Box Score patrol, Terry Graves, determined to 'snare' one of the trail walkers as a prisoner. The marines hid themselves along the trail, waiting for an opportune moment. As they lay concealed, one of the NVA troops discovered Mike Nation. For self-preservation, Nation opened fire; the other marines did likewise, and wiped-out the small group on the trail. The ambush brought a desultory smattering of small-arms fire from the enemy. One of the marines received a slight thigh wound. The patrol summoned a medevac helicopter. As the first medevac helicopter hovered and bounced down intense enemy fire erupted, damaged it, and drove it off. In the meantime intensified enemy fire wounded three other patrol members, two seriously. The marines were now in the snare and the enemy was not about to let them off easily.

Another helicopter swooped in. Despite heavy enemy fire, it managed to land. The marines got two seriously wounded marines on board, then others boarded, including Mike Nation, the U.S. navy hospital corpsman, Steve 'Doc' Thompson, and Adrian 'Trini' Lopex. In the seconds that it was on the ground enemy machine gun fire viciously raked the helicopter. One round hit Lopez as he climbed aboard. Observing the effect the enemy fire had on the helicopter, the lieutenant knew it had to leave immediately. Refusing to climb aboard, he instead shouted to the pilot, 'Get out, get out!' It immediately took off leaving him and two other marines still on the ground. Moments later another helicopter dropped in and picked up these last three marines. It got just a few feet above the ground, however, when enemy fire ripped into it causing it to crash into a small streambed. Enemy troops swarmed over the site and killed those who survived the crash, except one. Somehow, Danny Slocum, of the Box Score patrol, evaded detection and death. He made it back to friendly positions the following day, wounded and shaken, but alive. He, Mike Nation, and 'Doc' Thompson were the only survivors of the patrol. The two marines who had been seriously wounded earlier (Steven E. Emrick and Robert B. Thomson), died of their wounds. The bullet that hit Lopez's thigh found a major artery and his life-blood spilled out on the deck of the helicopter that carried the marines to safety.

The unit's intelligence officer conducted interviews with the three survivors of the Box Score patrol two days after the firefight, a routine occurrence. The interviewer eventually donated copies of these interviews to the Marine Corps Oral History Collection.[1] These interviews, like most of the 10,000 or so interviews done with the marines during the Vietnam War, took place chronologically and geographically close to the event that is itself the focus of the interview.

If the same individual is re-interviewed later about the same events, the availability of these contemporaneous interviews provides an opportunity to investigate how combat veterans remember their experiences, both immediately and over the long term. One of the marines of the Box Score patrol, Mike Nation, was selected to be re-interviewed and thus provides a case study of veterans' memory of combat. Serving as rear security on this patrol, Nation had been on several patrols, but he had seen little combat. His previous patrols had little contact with the enemy, certainly nothing approaching the intense combat experienced on 16 February. Junior and inexperienced, he did not know, or really care, why or how decisions were made. As he said, 'I was still tail-end Charlie so a lot of what happened as far as what proceeded to happen I have nothing to do with, no knowledge of except, "let's go"'.[2]

The 1968 interviews with Nation and the other survivors are eerily compelling. The background sounds on the recording impart the ambiance of the Marine Corps base camp at Dong Ha, South Vietnam. One hears men talking and jesting. There is hammering, an aircraft flies overhead, and an occasional 1960s rock song provides a barely audible backdrop that takes the listener back to the 1960s and Vietnam. Mundane and everyday life, sure, yet, the marines interviewed were talking about intense, deadly combat. They killed the enemy, saw their bodies blown apart as they fired into them, and they saw their buddies die bloody gruesome deaths. Yet they spoke of those events with an unemotional, mundane candor that imparted an everyday quality to their stories. This characterizes Nation's 1968 interview, in which he is unemotional and business-like. One would not think the battle was that unusual or terrible.

But it was – no doubt the worst any of them had been in. Five of the eight patrol members were killed. All of the patrol members received medals for heroism and valor; indeed, patrol leader Second Lieutenant Terry Graves received the Medal of Honor, posthumously. For the short period that it lasted, the combat these men endured was as intense as that at Omaha Beach in 1944 or Gettysburg in 1863 and when one considers the odds, it assumes 'Custer's Last Stand' characteristics.

In 2002, Nation was willing to speak of the events of 16 February 1968. He was friendly, cooperative, and open. He remarked that that day's events 'probably go through my brain at least once a week'. His memory of the events had also been enhanced by recently listening to his 1968 interview; he had attained it through the same Marine Intelligence Officer who had interviewed him in 1968, although Nation had had only limited contact with fellow marines from Vietnam. Although privy to his 1968 story, there were remarkable differences between the two interviews that do indeed give us insight into memory and how it is shaped over time. The comparison also provides a window into the world of the combat soldier/marine.

One of the most apparent differences is that in the 2002 interview there is cohesion to his account that did not exist in the original interview. In the 1968 interview, Nation's description of events is disjointed, narrow and excruciatingly detailed, a reflection of the confusion and fog that surrounded the firefight. In the 2002 interview however, he has bound up his account into an understandable story, with a beginning, middle, and end.

His personal and narrow view of the battle is evident in this excerpt from the 1968 interview:

> One round I saw landed about I guess maybe three feet away from the Doc. Me and him had been trying to get Slocum up on his feet. At first he didn't want anyone to help him, because he said he was ok to do it, you know, he didn't need any help. But, apparently he said, I remember him saying his knee, no his leg, didn't want to bend, you know, he said it was too tight. I guess it hurt too much to bend it to get up. So we started helping him up and the round came in and hit right close to the Doc and we let Slocum down again.

Nation does not even address this episode in the later interview. At the time however, it was apparently significant. This finely detailed account is replaced with testimony that paints a clearer and broader picture. Here is how he describes helping the wounded in 2002:

> So we're dragging them, giving them artificial respiration, trying to stay down, and still getting fired on. We're getting fired on all the time,

continuously. And you move, they fire at you, you move, they fire at you, we're dragging and dragging and dragging these guys, getting them going.

Another important distinction between the two interviews is that Nation adds much more color and description to the later interview. Unlike in the earlier interview, events now seem to take on significance and drama. He is not only telling a story, but he makes it interesting to the listener, in effect painting a word picture. Compare his account of the events surrounding Lopez's wounding. In 1968 he describes it in a mundane fashion:

That's when I noticed that Lopez got hit in the leg but when I first got in the chopper we got hit pretty hard from the side, there. The whole side of the chopper seemed to be coming in at us. Some of the stuff hit me in the face, but I didn't think I got hit. So, I turned around and I looked and saw Lopez's leg was bleeding. So the gunner told me that behind me was a first aid pack for the chopper. Well, I turned around and I got that and I handed it to the gunner and he opened it up. And then I asked for the Doc to give me his K-Bar [a marine combat knife] because I had lost mine somewhere. I didn't know where it was. I think I had used it first when Emrick got hit, cutting off his shirt, I'm not sure. The Doc gave me his K-Bar and I cut his pants leg open and started pressing on this thing with a bandage on his wound. It was bleeding real bad, it was all over the bottom of the chopper and everything.

The passage contains significant detail but again, a narrow focus. Nation seems at least as concerned about his Marine Corps-issue fighting knife as he is of Lopez's wound. This is perhaps explainable in that his combat training had taught him that a marine keeps up with his gear, especially a weapon. In combat a knife was an essential tool of his trade. Compare Nation's 2002 description of the same events:

Lopez starts to get in and I'm turning around and he's yelling at me, he says, 'Dang it man, I'm hit!' And I look down, his leg, his inside thigh, he'd been hit in the artery and blood's just gushing. So, I dropped Emrick and grabbed Lopez and put a tourniquet, grabbed a tourniquet from somewhere, one of us still had one on us and I'm pushing on that leg, on that wound, trying to get that blood to stop and its just gushing like a sieve. The gunner is firing helping pull people in. Honeycutt [James Earl] starts to get on, and the shit hit the fan, this chopper starts taking rounds like you wouldn't believe . . . ding, ta ding, ta ding.

Here, Nation arranges the story to focus on what is most important: Lopez and his wound, not the knife. There is more drama, color, and expression, even sound effects.

This characteristic of the later interview is most striking in that part of the interview in which Nation describes how he initiated the ambush. In the 1968 interview Nation again sees very little of significance in this part of the fight, although five close buddies died in the following struggle:

They were on the trail, on this ridgeline [which] apparently ran over on this ridgeline where I had seen them, because they came on down the trail. Well, one guy got about 15 or 20 feet away from me and he kinda looked over my way a little bit and there was another one that just seemed to kinda pop right out of the ground. Apparently from my position I didn't see him coming up or walking up there. But he stood up high, but the other one I think had possibly seen me, so I had to open fire there.

Then with incredible understatement, Nation notes why he had to fire at them: 'They were getting a little too close for comfort.' Note the difference in his 2002 interview:

We peeled off, everybody peeled off getting the hasty ambush set up, and when it came my turn and I guess it was either Doc Thompson or Lopez, I don't know which it was that was with me at the very tail end, by the time we got down to the far end where we peeled off at, there was no place to peel off to. But there was a crater, a bomb crater. Well we went into a bomb crater. We were as useless as can be there because you couldn't see, you couldn't hear, you're down inside this thing, you move up a bit, you slide back down, you move up a bit, you slide back down. The thing is eight, ten feet deep, it had been a pretty hefty bomb that hit that thing. So assumingly these NVA are continuing down the road, well, they did, down this trail, and all I could do was look up and see slope and sky. And all of the sudden one of them was standing right there, right above me on the edge of the crater and it looked like he was going to try to take a leak on me [laughs]. So, I guess he figured that was a pretty safe place to pee at, right inside of a bomb crater. Well, that was the last place he ever saw. And I set off the ambush I guess, I shot him straight with the M-14, and took the top of his head off, along with the hat he was wearing, his bush hat, it flew forty, fifty feet in the air.

In the later interview we have it all, color, drama, gore, even humor. And something else is added: justification. Nation justifies shooting the enemy soldier in the 2002 interview. Instead of he was a 'little too close for comfort,' he explains more fully: 'It was a situation that you couldn't . . . hopefully we could have let them get by, you know, that would have been the best bet. But when the guy is standing there looking at me there is no choice, there is no concealment, I'm in the bottom of this bomb crater and had no choice but to blow him away.'

Are we to assume that Nation has exaggerated, fabricated, or overly dramatized events in his later testimony? Possibly, but not necessarily; after all, most of the basics facts jibe with the original. Could those things that are added have been part of the actual event and just not expressed in the original? Absolutely, and this tells us much about the combat experience and how combat veterans recall it and tell it to outsiders.

In the early interview, Nation's business-like, officious, and succinct description is explainable in that although it was the most intense combat Nation had experienced, such an event was not beyond the realm of possibility for a combat marine in Vietnam in 1968. It fit the environment, what he had been trained to expect and possibly heard about from more experienced veterans. He was thus mentally, psychologically, and physically prepared for such an event.

This perhaps explains why in describing boarding the helicopter that Nation dwells on the loss of his knife. This was not supposed to happen. What if he would have needed it later, for combat, the reason he was there and why he had a knife in the first place? Therefore in the first interview, done by a marine officer from his unit and thus a fellow member of the combat environment, he stuck to the pertinent details. There was no need to make the event comprehensible to the interviewer, because the interviewer himself already understood the culture of Vietnam combat. Just as one experiencing the Depression has no need to relate the bleakness of life to someone who is also experiencing that bleakness.

In the later interview however, Nation has to interpret the events for me since we were not in the Vietnam combat culture. But he has had to make the events understandable to himself too in order to provide an interpretation of them to an outsider. In his mind over the years, he has made the events of that day understandable by placing them in context and creating a logical story of them, something that did not yet exist when the original interview occurred. All he could state at that time was what he saw from his personal, narrow frame of reference.

This characteristic of recounting life events is what Charlotte Linde describes in her book *Life Stories*, and defines as the 'creation of coherence'. Linde writes that 'life stories involve large-scale systems of social understandings and of knowledge that are grounded in a long history of practice; indeed, these stories rely on presuppositions about what can be taken as expected, what the norms are, and what common or special belief systems are necessary to establish coherence'.[3] Although this is not Nation's life story, the same principle applies.

Belief systems have associated behaviors, rituals, morals, and actions that are considered appropriate and good. Linde writes that 'life stories express our sense of self . . . we use these stories to claim or negotiate group membership and to demonstrate that we are worthy members of these groups'.[4] In both interviews Nation reflects his loyalty to his fellow Recon marines. These relationships, forged in combat, are popularly described as the 'band of brothers'. The highest attribute, in this relationship is taking care of one's buddies, to sustain the group, the small unit; to create and nourish those bonds that create this band of brothers. This is required for success against the enemy, personal survival, and possibly mental stability. Nation reveals the strong bond between himself and his fellow marines. This is the underlying theme in both interviews. There is more focus on his fellow marines, supporting, affirming, and caring for them, than on dealing with the enemy, a perfectly natural state for combat marines.

Nation allots considerable time in each interview to describing how the wounded were cared for. In the 1968 interview, Nation defends the reputation of his fellow marines. He assures the interviewer that everyone was doing their job, and doing it well. 'Honeycutt was to my left, he was shooting all the time. He was doing a real good job out there, all of them were.' Describing the wounded Slocum's action he asserts, 'We then got up there and formed a 369 [an all-round defensive position], and all the time Danny Slocum, he was real good, and he held tight, no problems at all. He still had complete control, you know, he was staying calm.' In another passage: 'Meanwhile, Thompson with his 79 [an M-79 grenade launcher] was doing real good. He came up behind me and he wanted to see the area was where the VC were at I was shooting. So I put tracers and he would fire the 79 right where the tracers were. It was perfect, he never missed.'

The only indication that anything was awry was Nation's comment: 'Meanwhile Lopez had been right next to Emrick, and Lopez was pretty shook up, I guess we all were.' This final phrase is in defense of Lopez, it assures us that Lopez although having troubles, was still performing as well as any of them. He assures us that, even in dying, they did so as appropriate for combat marines:

> And I remember Emrick saying get the radio off. That's what he was talking about. He wasn't worried about himself because he kept saying get the radio off of him, best we could. Me and Lopez finally got the radio off by snapping it off the bottom of the pack and everything. Then I flipped him over and he said, 'Oh my God,' you know. That's the last thing he said.

Although the band-of-brothers attribute is one characteristic that spans both belief systems, it is expressed differently in the later interview. He translates this loyalty so that it makes sense in a larger context: again the whole story is given to include value judgments, explanations, and drama. In the later interview, out of Vietnam and the combat culture, he knows now indeed how horrible the experience was and explains why they were not more afraid. In 2002 he says, 'None of us were really scared, we were pretty damned concerned. This was not a good spot to be in, but you know at this point, you got to do what you got to do, and there ain't no sense in sitting here crying about it, let's fire and let's do what we can and let's get the hell out of this situation if we can, with whatever we can.' Nation equates combat with an act of nature, there is no blame attached and to give up would be worse than continuing. He attests, 'You know, its funny as hell to get stuck in a situation like that, I mean it had never happened to any of us, obviously, so what the shit do you do? You got to keep going at it.' Such explanations are not in the original because, again, these attitudes were already understood.

Also, in the later interview, Nation reveals the moral support laced with humor that enhanced the band-of-brothers bond and thus enabled them to cope: 'But all through this time you know we tried to keep ourselves joking and this and that. Somebody would say something and everybody would crack up [laughing] all the sudden, so we had a good attitude, or the best you could with the situation.' He provides an example of their joking around: 'I had a picture one of my buddies had sent me of LBJ and he was laughing, he was getting on an airplane, just a big smile on his face, laughing, and on the bottom it said, "Who do you think he's laughing at?" This buddy of mine in the states was a draft dodger, had sent it to me. So I passed that over to the lieutenant and he cracked up over that one.'

In conclusion these two interviews with Mike Nation indicate that he has taken his narrow, fragmented and personal view of a combat experience and made it into a comprehensive and understandable account of what not only happened to him but also the entire Box Score patrol. He has added context and justification to it to create a well-rounded story of much greater significance than it had when initially interviewed, and which did not exist in his mind two days after the battle.

Early, immediate accounts of combat, however, give us an audio window to view combat as the participants saw it. The interviewee is still part of it, and the interview reflects it, in detailed but disjointed testimonies that expose a narrow frame of reference. Interviews reveal what the individual saw from his perspective and depict the confusion associated with combat. Only later, when a veteran considers and rehashes his experiences out of the combat/military environment, does he begin to evaluate the events, attach significance to them, and paint a word picture that an outsider may understand. This could become especially significant when the event is of considerable historical value, where information from outside sources, other participants, books, TV, or movies is available and could be used to enhance an individual's memory to move beyond what he witnessed.

This does not seem to be the case in Nation's interviews. The basic facts and sequence of the later interview matches that of the first. This was aided no doubt by his having listened to his 1968 interview. The distinct difference remains in how he has interpreted the basic information over the years. There is an elaboration, explanation, and cohesion to make it an understandable and interesting, if not dramatic, story.

This case study of before-and-after interviews with Mike Nation suggests that contemporary combat interviews, done within hours of the event, although disjointed and narrowly detailed, are an accurate portrayal of what an individual experienced in combat. They give the most immediate view of the event before the memory has worked to organize and interpret the event that initially might not have been orderly or understandable.

Later interviews with veterans are valuable, certainly, and perhaps more under-standable to those who are not ensconced in the context of the event. The weakness of later interviews is that one's memory naturally works to either forget the horrific experience or make sense of it. Making sense of it means providing explanations, context, drama, value, significance, and justification. All of these could be enhanced by information gained by other means other than personal experience, thus possibly weakening the value of the interview as a primary source. An analogy would be comparing a photograph of an event with a painting done later of the same event. They both portray the event; one is stark, and bland, while the latter is appealing to the eye, evocative, and interpretative. When we have both, interviews done immediately after the event and one done later, we have the best of both worlds, the raw, stark facts enhanced by explanations, context, and interpretation. Unfortunately these opportunities are few and far between.

The matter-of-fact tone of Nation's 1968 interview indicates also that he was ensconced in a belief system that characterized marine combat units in Vietnam. This belief system operated in a culture where brutal combat was a likelihood and mutual support and belief in one's associates was a fundamental element of faith to endure in this culture. Nation's interviews reveal the overriding value combat soldiers and marines place on their fellows.

This loyalty lasts a lifetime. At the conclusion of his 2002 interview Nation remarked, 'I just wish the hell they were still alive.'

Notes

1   Captain George W.T. O'Dell, intelligence officer for 3rd Force Recon, interviewed the three survivors of the Box Score patrol two days after the battle. In 2002 O'Dell

forwarded copies of these interviews to the Marine Corps' Oral History office, in Washington, D.C. He had kept the originals after the war and had them converted to CD. The recordings were remarkably clear.

2   Michael P. Nation, telephone interview by author, 23 February 2002, tape recording and transcript, Marine Corps Oral History Collection, Marine Corps Historical Center, Washington Navy Yard, D.C.

3   Charlotte Linde, *Life Stories: The Creation of Coherence*, New York: Oxford University Press, 1993, p. 219.

4   Ibid.

Chapter 18

Mark Roseman

SURVIVING MEMORY
Truth and inaccuracy in Holocaust testimony

In exploring patterns of discrepancy in the memory of German-born Jewish Holocaust survivor Marianne Ellenbogen, Mark Roseman argues here that a 'concern with accuracy' shows no disrespect to survivors, and that, 'on the contrary, it helps to illuminate the very processes of memory which we are seeking to understand'. Roseman's study conveys the psychic difficulty of remembering 'unbearable reality' and the need to 'impose *control* on memory and on the moments that caused such pain'. Mark Roseman is Professor in History and Jewish Studies at Indiana University, and has published a biography of Marianne Ellenbogen: *The Past in Hiding*, Harmondsworth, Penguin, 2000. Reprinted from *The Journal of Holocaust Education*, 1999, vol. 8, no. 1, pp. 1–20, with permission from Vallentine Mitchell & Co. Ltd.

Introduction

WHENEVER WE LISTEN to or read the testimony of a Holocaust survivor there is an understandable reluctance to challenge the testimony's accuracy or veracity. It seems an unwarranted imposition on individuals who have already suffered so much to subject their memories to further interrogation. One does not wish to give the Holocaust denier ammunition by drawing attention to flaws in survivor testimony. In any case, it is one of the distinguishing characteristics of the Holocaust that the survivor's testimony is often *all* there is: friends and relatives have been murdered; the family property, family letters, everything that belonged to the survivor's past life has been destroyed. In such cases, there is very little left to compare or cross check and we simply have to accept the testimony as it is.

The starting point for the present article is a biography of a Holocaust survivor, during the research for which I was forced to confront issues of accuracy in oral testimony.[1] The subject of this biography is a German-born woman, Mrs Marianne Ellenbogen, née Strauss. I was made aware of her experiences by Dr Mathilde Jamin of the Ruhrland museum in Essen, who, in the 1980s, had come across a short report written by Marianne Ellenbogen, published in an obscure Essen journal, *Münster am Hellweg*.[2] Before Marianne died, I was able to conduct a number of lengthy interviews with her. One of the most unexpected and striking aspects of the subsequent research into Marianne's life has been the discovery of many different kinds of written records that could he juxtaposed with Marianne's own oral testimony. Perhaps one should rather refer to the juxtaposition of sources of differing levels of contemporaneity, since what is revealing is often not the contrast between the *written* and the *spoken* but rather that between perceptions and memories 'fixed' or recorded at different points of distance from the events which they describe, that is, in reports and letters *then*, in interviews and conversations *now*. In any case, when the content of Marianne's interviews was compared with sources from the Nazi and post-war periods, a number of important differences and discrepancies emerged. So much so, that the process by which Marianne's past life regained shape in the present sometimes felt like a detective story (albeit a harrowing and tragic one) as a chain of clues and witnesses forced consecutive reappraisals of the events of more than fifty years ago.

The discrepancies between records and testimony took a number of different forms. Quite often Marianne's or other witnesses' testimony showed that the contemporary records were misleading, either because they were deliberately designed to mislead – as, for instance, in Gestapo files – or because the writer lacked some information. Sometimes the discrepancies had nothing to do with inaccuracy and reflected rather the different perceptions of the contemporary and the retrospective observer. The particular focus of the present article is a third form of discrepancy, namely, where the contemporary records revealed that Marianne's (and other survivors') memories were inaccurate and had changed over time.

These kinds of inaccuracies seemed to be important and revealing, yet when we turn to the relevant literature and, specifically, to recent analyses of Holocaust survivor testimony, we find that scholars have given them little attention.[3] Indeed, many studies explicitly cast doubt on the appropriateness of referring to the reliability of memory. This is very clearly and explicitly stated by Lawrence Langer, one of the least pretentious and most impressive scholars of Holocaust testimony:

> One preliminary issue remains, and that is the reliability of the memory on which these testimonies must draw for the accuracy and intensity of their details. How credible can a reawakened memory be that tries to revive events so many decades after they occurred? I think the terminology itself is at fault here. There is no need to revive what has never died. Moreover, though slumbering memories may crave reawakening, nothing is clearer in these narratives than that Holocaust memory is an insomniac faculty, whose mental eyes have never slept. In addition, since testimonies are human documents rather than merely historical ones, the troubled interaction between past and present achieves a gravity that surpasses the concern with accuracy. Factual errors do occur from time to time, as do simple lapses; but they seem trivial in comparison to the complex layers of memory that give birth to the versions of the self that we shall be studying in this volume.[4]

The aim here is not to criticise Langer's work. Clearly, there are many questions concerning memory and identity that can be approached and answered without taking on the issue of the accuracy of those memories. Nevertheless, my experience – forming the heart of this paper – is that the 'concern with accuracy', which Langer dismisses, is actually helpful to understanding those very 'complex layers of memory' which he seeks to uncover.

Marianne's story

Let me briefly introduce the individual, Marianne Ellenbogen, whose biography I have undertaken to write. Marianne was born in 1923 into a prosperous Jewish family in Essen where she grew up the older of two children. Her parents were extremely patriotic German Jews – her father was decorated in the First World War – and did not seek to leave Nazi Germany until it was too late. As a result the whole family became trapped. Marianne survived the war, only leaving the country in December 1946, when she arrived in Britain. She lived the next fifty years in Liverpool, in the north-west of England until her death in 1996.

Though there are many remarkable aspects to her story, for our purposes two should be highlighted at the outset. The first is that, unlike most members of her family and many of her closest friends, she was never in a Nazi camp. She spent the first part of the war living, very unusually, with her family under the official protection of the *Abwehr*, the Wehrmacht's counter-intelligence organisation;[5] after 1943, when the family was deported to Theresienstadt and then to Auschwitz, Marianne went on the run, assisted by a little known left-wing group called the *Bund*.[6] She spent two years on the move, travelling backwards and forwards across Germany, staying for a few days at a time with different members of this group. During these years Marianne's life was directed by incredible energy and courage, and not with the passivity or inactivity that we might associate with someone in hiding.

It may well be, therefore, that Marianne's experience lacked some of the defining characteristics of the 'archetypal' Holocaust survivor. Yet a great many of the characteristic traumatic experiences – of being defined, singled-out and pursued by the state, of living in a condition of permanent threat and anxiety, of experiencing loss and uncertainty in relation to loved ones, of having to deal with traumatic memories and the guilt of surviving where so many did not – dominated her subsequent life and testimony as much as those of other Holocaust survivors.

Like many other survivors, Marianne never talked about her experiences until shortly before the end of her life – and even then her extreme reluctance to talk was only just outweighed by the conviction that the record had to be kept. So complete had her silence been until her conversations with me that after she died I found that not even her son and grandchildren had any but the vaguest idea about her life before arriving in Britain.

The second striking feature of Marianne's experience is the range of sources which survive to document it. The starting point for my research was, of course, Marianne's testimony, offered in a series of interviews in 1989 and 1996.[7] It proved possible, however, to augment this eyewitness account with other oral sources, including personal or expert testimony gathered in interviews, telephone conversations and correspondence, from in the region of a hundred respondents in Britain, Germany, Israel, USA, Sweden, France and Argentina. The equally extensive written sources came in many different forms.[8] There are official documents, including the unusually extensive Gestapo records on the family, as well as municipal records of the expropriation of their property. Marianne's personal papers are among the most dramatic of the sources, including two rich wartime diaries, one of them documenting her period underground, and extensive correspondence, including a unique extended correspondence from 1942 between herself and her fiancé, then incarcerated by the Nazis in Izbica.[9] Some wartime correspondence between Marianne and members of the *Bund*, the group which protected her, also survives, as does the personal diary of Dr Artur Jacobs, the figure behind the *Bund*. The restitution papers are voluminous, providing a great deal of information about family life before the war and there are also many family letters, including cards sent to Sweden from Theresienstadt and even one from Auschwitz-Birkenau.

Examining the records

The first thing to emerge when Marianne's memories were compared with contemporary records was that, in a number of cases, a kind of polarisation had taken place in her testimony. On the one hand, there were small exaggerations or magnifications of experience. Particularly where there had been some traumatic event the circumstances surrounding that event had often taken on slightly larger dimensions in Marianne's memory. Periods of time were doubled or trebled. The duration of her father's internment in Dachau after *Kristalnacht* in 1938 became, in her memory, six weeks when in reality it was 'only' three. Similarly, after her flight in 1943, her family was held in prison in Essen during which time the Gestapo hoped that Marianne would turn up. This period of temporary internment prior to deportation to Theresienstadt lasted just over a week, whereas Marianne remembered it as being three weeks. As is common in the accounts of other Jewish witnesses, in Marianne's testimony, uniform wearers of very different provenance were metamorphosed in memory to 'SS men'. *Wehrmacht* soldiers, railway officials, ordinary police on the trains and other figures became fused with the archetypal threat figure: the SS man. More subtly, Marianne's account of her school days, I think, retrospectively exaggerated the degree of persecution. However, other witness statements are contradictory on this period. And here, where the issue is one of impressions rather than specific incidents, it may be that Marianne's memory accurately reflects her own subjective perception at the time.

On the other hand, elsewhere, memory had served rather to diminish or underplay events of the war. For example, Marianne's oral recollections of those who had helped her, above all the various members of the *Bund* who had housed her for a couple of weeks at a time (and sometimes on a number of different occasions), contained no hint of the tensions and conflicts that then emerged from a reading of her underground diary and the correspondence contained within it. What emerged from the diary was that Marianne continually struggled to forget herself and to think of others; to rise above her subjective misery and pain. In doing so, she threw herself into acting as advisor and confidante to her hosts, leading to some rather sad results; the bold and beautiful girl was so keen to help her *Bund* friends with their various relationship problems that she more than once caused something of a ruckus. On other occasions, disputes of a more philosophical nature are alluded to. Yet all these issues had disappeared from memory, not least out of a desire to leave untarnished the image of those who had assisted her and to whom she owed her life.

More interesting than these tendencies to polarise the good and the bad, however, were the various points in her personal narrative where the chain of events, as described by her, did not match with the events as described by other sources. For example, in April 1942, while Marianne's own family were still living under official protection, her fiancé, Ernst Krombach, and his parents were designated for deportation to the East. Their eventual destination was to be Izbica, a little known ghetto in Poland to which many thousands of German, Austrian and Czech Jews were deported as a holding place *en route* to the death camps.[10] According to Marianne, the night before their deportation the Krombachs were taken to the Holbeckshof barracks where many Essen Jews were interned, and from there, the following day, to the railway station. Marianne said she went to the barracks with them and spent the night there with Ernst, pleading with him to make a run for it. Accompanying the family to the barracks seemed an incredible act of courage, since there was the considerable risk that if found there she would simply have been deported along with the Krombachs.

I was a little unsettled when, after this particular interview session, it occurred to me to wonder what possibilities for escape she had actually been thinking of. Since, as she had already told me, she met Artur Jacobs from the *Bund* for the first time on the Kronbachs' last evening in Essen, she could not yet have talked to him about the possibility of escape. When I asked Marianne about this she said that she had known that the *Bund* had offered Ernst assistance already, prior to her meeting Jacobs.

Subsequently, other worrying details emerged. We know that the Essen Jews designated for the Izbica transport were deported on 21 April 1942. A moving diary entry from Jacobs confirmed that this was true for the Krombachs:[11]

20 April

A final word from Dr Krombach (as, drained and overtired, he bade me farewell. Tomorrow they start on their journey):

'We have had to shoulder many burdens. Often we thought we would go under. But we have also experienced much that gave us hope. Egotistical feelings faded away – one was ashamed of them. We pulled together and learned something of the power of the whole'.

'It may be', he added after a pause, 'that later, when we've got through this, we'll look back on this as the most important time of our lives and won't regret having gone through it, brutal though it was'.

Then, amongst Marianne's papers, I found Ernst Krombach's last letter from Essen to her. The date was written on the letter as '20/21.4.1942' and it was clear that he had written it during the night:

Jeanne![12]

The last night in the apartment and therefore for a last time a bit of
'peace'. An unusually hard fate is ours to carry. There is no doubt about
that. It will certainly be difficult for us, suddenly to cope with a difficult situation on our own, particularly as recently we were together
every day and lived almost like a married couple. What else could satisfy
us! How valuable it was to experience being together in a time of the
most awful conditions and what will it be like when we can live together
as free human beings! There are no words for the enriching feeling of
belonging together, a togetherness that is not bound to any time, or
place or anything else . . .

It is clear from Marianne's diary that she received the letter only once Ernst's transport was already under way. There is, therefore, no doubt that the Krombachs spent
their last night in Essen in their apartment and that Marianne was *not* with them the
whole time. She visited them in the evening at the flat – that was where she met
Jacobs but later she must have gone home.

Later, I found in the published reminiscences of former Essen Jews an account
by Hanna Aron of the deportation of her boyfriend, also to Izbica, on a subsequent
transport from Essen to the ghetto in June 1942.[13] Aron described how *she* had
spent the night in the Steele barracks with *her* partner, Richard Fuchs, the night
before *his* departure. Aron's account was substantially the same as the one Marianne
had told me and, in this case, there is documentary evidence to confirm, at least,
that Richard and Rosalie Fuchs (his mother) *were* deported from the Holbeckshof
barracks to Izbica. Yet I had no reason to believe that Marianne had ever read Aron's
reminiscences. The published collection from Essen was not on her book shelf.

Having learned that Hannah Aron's maiden name was Drucker, however, and
knowing that Marianne had worked closely with her mother in an office of the rump
Jewish community, I investigated further. I learned, through a mutual acquaintance,
that Marianne and Hanna Aron had known each other well and from Hanna Aron,
whom I interviewed in Connecticut, I learned that she and her mother had in fact
gone to live with Marianne's family in March 1943, nine months after this incident.
They had spent six months with the Strauss family before Marianne's parent's deportation.[14] Since I also learned that Marianne's family had known Richard Fuchs well
– he had been a private tutor for Marianne's brother – it seems extremely likely
that Hanna Aron told Marianne the story of her farewell from her lover and that at
some point she must have adopted the account as her own.

Here is a second example. In July 1943, the protection from the *Abwehr*
collapsed. On 6 August 1943, a letter arrived with the Düsseldorf Gestapo to the
effect that the *Wehrmacht* had no longer any interest in the Strauss family. The family
were now vulnerable to deportation to the East. On 31 August, two Gestapo officials arrived at the house and gave the family two hours to pack ready for departure
from Germany. The destination was to be Theresienstadt. These two hours of preparation, and Marianne's escape from the house, were in Marianne's memory
undoubtedly the most intense two hours of her life. She often returned to them in
her conversations with me. In the one short written account of her life, which she
prepared in the 1980s, the most vibrant, dramatic passages dealt with this period.[15]

My impression on hearing them was that every single detail was engraved in her memory and certainly what she told me in the 1990s matched what she had written in the 1980s.

Marianne told me that her parents knew of her plans. Before leaving, she quietly asked her father if she could take her brother with her. He agreed and slipped her a thick wad of money he was keeping illegally in the house. Marianne said that her brother Richard, aged 17 and a homely boy, did not want to leave his parents. So, when the two Nazi officials went down to the cellar to inspect the loot the family had in their packing cases, Marianne saw her chance. She gave a brief wave to her mother in the kitchen, slipped down the steps and ran, at any moment waiting for a pistol shot. It did not come.

On a research trip to Düsseldorf after Marianne's death I went through the voluminous Gestapo files and found that on 3 September one of those two Gestapo officials, *Kriminalsekretär* Kosthorst, had been obliged to submit a detailed report on her disappearance.[16] His account was different from Marianne's. According to the report, he was on the first floor supervising the family of Siegfried Strauss, whilst *Kriminal oberassistent* Hahn was on the second floor with the family of Alfred Strauss, Marianne's uncle. Marianne had asked if she could go downstairs to get food for the journey, they had agreed, and she had then disappeared. It seemed that the Gestapo men wished to cover up their own dereliction. Rather than rummaging through the family possessions in the cellar they were upstairs and had 'generously' allowed Marianne to get food; their trust had then been abused. It struck me as I looked at the report that I was probably the first and last reader to know that the Gestapo account was a lie.

Some time after I had seen the Gestapo records, however, I met up with another witness who told me that she had met briefly with Marianne after the war.[17] Without any prompting from me, she offered her own vivid memory of Marianne's account of her own escape – how the Gestapo had been with the family, how she had asked if she could go and get bread, and had then disappeared. This suggested that in the immediate aftermath of the war Marianne's own account of her flight had matched that of the Gestapo and only changed later.

Controlling the unbearable past

Obviously, my aim here is not to challenge the fundamental veracity of Holocaust survivor testimony. Compared with the fundamentals of persecution and loss, the kinds of discrepancies I have detailed here are trivial. On the fundamentals, Marianne's memories were almost entirely borne out by other sources. Many things she said appeared, at first, very unlikely but were then corroborated. For example, her claims about the role of the *Abwehr* in protecting the family seemed implausible even to herself, yet the Gestapo records prove them to have been true. It seemed unlikely that she could, as she claimed, have graduated from the Jewish Seminar for *Kindergarden* teachers in February 1942 with an official German *Staatsexamen*; the discovery of the official certificate complete with Swastika proved that indeed she had. Perhaps most hard to believe was her recollection that in 1944 she was able to obtain very precise information via the BBC about the fate of her parents in Auschwitz. Yet this, too, has been born out by other evidence.[18] The discrepancies, then, have to be viewed against the background of this underlying veracity. On this point, my limited experience of closely examining survivor testimony very much backs up the position of Lawrence Langer.

Another important qualification needs to be made. As intimated above in the introduction, it is not the case that, in piecing this story together, the process of elucidation and corroboration is a one-way process. The written records cannot be taken as 'gospel', against which the 'flawed' spoken testimony can be found wanting. On the contrary, many of the Gestapo records and other materials are designed to mislead. When we read from the report of *Kriminalsekretär* Kosthorst that he gave the Strauss family 'a fixed deadline (*befristele Auflage*) by which to pack the items they would need',[19] it is only Marianne's account of how Kosthorst took her mother's only flat walking shoes away from her, thereby preventing a half-way decent preparation, that conveys the true nature of the event. And, even where the record keepers did not dress up their barbarity in official language, there are huge gaps in the reports and letters which can only be filled by Marianne's own testimony.

The fact remains, though, that there *are* these interesting inaccuracies in her memory. The kinds of discrepancy that have been examined above – and there are others – do not seem to be attributable to the random deterioration or fluctuation of memory in an older person. There *were* such slips of course; but in the examples under consideration here, there seemed to be too much of a pattern, and they seemed to occur in relation to situations about which Marianne's memory was otherwise as vivid as though the events had happened yesterday.

So, what did the discrepancies mean? It seems clear that the changes were related to moments of great trauma. For Marianne, traumatic memory was not linked to direct personal suffering – she had, after all, been spared the worst, and her ability to cope with the ever-present threat to her safety was absolutely remarkable. Instead, Marianne's trauma was related to guilt, above all the guilt inspired by having left her family, and having allowed others to leave her. It was, for Marianne, insupportable that she had allowed her fiancé to be taken. In her underground diary from 1944, two years after Ernst's departure, she wrote:

> How much my thoughts are with you today! More than for many a long while. Two years lie like a chasm between the past and today – two years with all the events and experiences they have brought, with their many challenges, burdens, horrors and so few happy times. How I carry you today in my feelings, in my blood, in my heart! Everything is again so close – your presence, your love, your understanding. Oh, love, if you were only always so close to me. My flight and restless seeking would not be necessary. How evenly everything would flow! Often I think with Angst and guilt how, how it is possible that I could lose you like this.

Even during the war, on the run with her own fate unsure, Marianne felt guilt at letting her loved ones go. The enormous burden of having survived herself under such circumstances was something she explicitly and implicitly came back to many times in our conversations. 'I put my parents at risk, I put my whole family at most dreadful risk. They [the Gestapo] could have done anything they wanted', was a typical expression of such feelings.

The small changes in her testimony show, I would argue, how Marianne had struggled to cope with these feelings of loss and guilt. Thus, in her testimony, she borrowed Hanna Aron's story (and sincerely believed it to be her own memory, I am sure) of accompanying her fiancé into the barracks before departure. In her account she went a little further distance with him than she had actually gone in reality. Incidentally, this was no one-off telling of the story. Interestingly, her son *had* heard *this* part of her testimony from her, and was understandably angry with me that I doubted its veracity.

Regarding the story of how she got out of the house, I wondered for a while what the significance of the change might be. Did Marianne wish to deny the fact that her escape depended on a kind of 'abuse' of trust; that is, that she had tricked the Gestapo? This is unlikely; she was often very aware of the nuances in goodness and badness in those around her. Instead, I came to the conclusion that what she had done was invent a route that her brother might have accompanied her on. Both could have slipped down the stairs while the Gestapo men were in the cellar. But asking to get bread from the kitchen was a ruse which could hardly legitimate *both* youngsters going down the stairs – it allowed the escape of only one. In summation, the discrepancies suggested that where her experience had been most traumatic, the trauma resulted in an inability to cope with memory as it was, a pressure that led, on the one hand, to an unwillingness to communicate about it to the outside world, and, on the other, to the process of subtle modification.

Although we can understand the process by which such changes in memory took place, we may well feel that even if these alternative versions had been true, they would not have made her any less 'guilty'. From our perspective as outsiders, she was not guilty anyway. On the other hand, in Marianne's own perception, even if she *had* slipped out of the house on a route Richard had the opportunity to take, even if she *had* spent the night with Ernst, it is probable she would have felt no less guilt after the war. She might well have felt the need to make other changes, other adjustments, to cope with the past. The details are thus not in themselves crucial and do not make a material difference to her position. The important thing, I believe, was for Marianne to put some psychological distance between herself and the unbearable reality – to impose *control* on memory and on the moments that caused such pain.

This analysis, that Marianne was trying to impose some control on a memory which could not otherwise be borne, is further suggested by another aspect of her testimony and that of others, namely, the emergence of legends about the fate of her loved ones. Consider, for example, the fate of her fiancé, Ernst. As mentioned above, Marianne managed, through various routes, to sustain a correspondence with Ernst in Izbica. In late 1942, a contact in the Wehrmacht visited the ghetto, bringing back post from Ernst in August and news of Ernst and his family in November and December. In December 1942, Marianne told me, she learned that Ernst had been blinded by medical experiments: 'Ernst, he [the German soldier] said, had been used for some medical experiments and lost his sight. And whether that was permanent or not he didn't know'. That was the last news from the ghetto about Ernst.

Although this information was so clear in her memory that it seemed hardly open to doubt, nevertheless, it did surprise me that in this small town medical experiments were carried out that are not known to historical research. I corresponded with Thomas Blatt, a well-informed Izbica survivor and one of the handful of survivors from the Sobibor revolt, now living in the USA. He was adamant that there was no such facility. I then managed to make contact with Ernst's brother Heinz (later Enriqué) Krombach, who had emigrated to Argentina in the 1930s. His story was that Ernst had been blinded by the SS during a break-out attempt.[20] Indeed, this version of events has appeared in published form, in an account of his father's life, part of a memorial volume about Jewish lawyers in Essen.[21] Thomas Blatt said there had been no breakout attempt by German Jews.

At an early stage in my research, I found the draft of a letter sent by Marianne in January 1943 to family friends of the Krombachs. In this letter Marianne wrote that Ernst's father died of an infection and that Ernst had been blinded by an accident. I was not sure whether relatively 'neutral' causes were being cited here to confuse a censor or whether this was what she really believed at the time. I found a later draft letter, dated May 1943, sent to Julie Koppel, a former Essen nurse, who was then working as a Red Cross nurse in Sweden. This letter contained exactly the same information.

The diary of Dr Jacobs shed further light on the incident. On 31 December 1942 he made probably the most depressed entry of the whole war:

> Marianne has just gone. I feel numbed. I keep thinking it isn't true. You're dreaming, it can't be true, and I try to push it away. Dr. Krombach dead, his wife gone, the boy blinded . . .

> The other fates similar. Only just 1/10th of the Essen Jews there, the others dead or transported further – Frau Krombach two days after the death of her husband. That is how it works. If the man dies, the wife is sent on.

> The boy worked in an explosives' factory and lost his sight in an explosion. Where he is, what he is doing, how he is living, if anyone is helping him when it takes maximum effort just to look after yourself – nobody knows.

> The Jewish fate is brutally captured before you in all its naked horror and hopelessness.[22]

This suggested that the language of the letters was not a code – and that an accident really had been the cause, at least as reported to Marianne. I then found another interesting document, a letter in the archive of the old synagogue in Essen written by Liesel Sternberg, a former employee and friend of David Krombach.[23] Liesel – who, it transpired, was living just two miles from my house in Britain and granted me an interview[24] – was trying in 1945 to find out the whereabouts of the Krombachs. In this letter Miss Sternberg referred to a letter which Ernst's brother Heinz had written to her in September 1943. In that letter, Heinz had said that he had learned from Julie Koppel that Ernst had been blinded in an accident at work.

Apart from the awful details of the Krombach's fate, what is striking here, is that both Marianne and Heinz shared the same information and subscribed to the same version. As Heinz said to me, when I interviewed him in Buenos Aires, he had had no new information since then. Yet independently of each other, Marianne and Heinz had given the tragic end to Ernst's life an extra persecutory twist – each providing a different senario.

Another example of the creation of a family legend concerns Marianne's aunt, Lore Strauss, nee Dahl, with whom Marianne had been extremely close and shared a house in 1941–1943. Marianne told me that she received a letter in 1946 from the wife of the Essen cantor, Frau Ogutsch, who, Marianne said, had been with her aunt to the last:

> She [Frau Ogutsch] wrote to me say that she was a witness to how my aunt was shot by the SS on the retreat . . . When the few people who were still alive, when the Russians were marching forward, they [the SS] emptied these concentration camps of the ones who were still there and drove them wherever away from the following Russians. And whoever sat down by the wayside or just gave up or even wanted just to rest, for a few minutes it would have been, would just be shot. And by that time that it was completely, I mean they were completely, they were more dead than alive, they were completely emaciated, they had dysentery, they had anything you can think of, they were completely worn out. And apparently she just couldn't make it and she just sat down and they shot her. And I think a few miles later the people who were still alive, within a matter of probably hours they were rescued, they were liberated. So she really could have, just for a matter of a few hours, have survived the war. That is the only story I have of all these near relations where I know what happened . . . up to the end.

Long after Marianne's death, in the very last pile of documents in her house, I came across the two letters she had received from Frau Ogutsch in 1946. Though they were very informative about her parents' experiences in Theresienstadt – Ogutsch had worked with Lore in a children's home – they contained nothing about Lore's later fate. But next to these letters was one received almost at the same time from some distant relatives, the Ansbachers from Frankfurt, who had also been in Theresienstadt with Marianne's parents. Their daughter Sigrid had survived the war and was now in Sweden. Selma Ansbacher wrote:

> Dear Marianne, when we were liberated by the Russians and the war was over, we knew that something awful had taken place in Auschwitz. We came back to Frankfrut on 22 June 1945 and none of our dear children here. But let me say straight away that Sigrid is alive and has been in Sweden since last July. But our dear Heinz did not come back. I know that you are on your own in life. How often we spoke about you in Theresienstadt. Your parcels all arrived and you brought your dear ones much happiness. We were together every day. Perhaps you can come here and I will tell you more about your dear ones.

And continued:

> Now I have to tell you something very, very sad. We have been in contact with our Sigrid since October last year. We discovered via Julius, my husband's brother, who is in America, that Sigrid is alive and Sigrid discovered through America that we had been saved. Sigrid wrote

and told us her awful story, all the places she was taken. She was with aunt Lore until 24 January 1945 in Kursbad b/Trachenburg über Breslau.[25] Then the Russians came and they had to flee. Aunt Lore had typhus and lay in the sick bay and here comes the terrible thing, Marianne; Aunt Lore was shot. Sigrid wrote, it was terrible. Tante Lore said to her, she should tell everything to Onkel Alfred. Our Sigrid suffered terrible things, she was in the KZ Gross Rosen, Mauthausen and finally in Bergen-Belsen. There she got typhus and arrived in Sweden July with a weight 32 kg, a girl of 17.[26]

Here too, then, the underlying story was correct but the sad details had been slightly changed in Marianne's account. In contrast to the story about Ernst, Lore's fate had not been rendered more brutal. Rather, here, the impression of a senseless waste had been intensified by the fact that Marianne recalled Lore's death as taking place not in the hospital but on the death march, just a few hours before liberation.

I found these sources only after Marianne's death and was therefore not able to ask her what she made of the discrepancies. But when I visited Enriqué (Heinz) in Buenos Aires I was able to ask him. I approached the matter very gingerly, since he had already burst into tears as I took photos of Ernst out of my photo wallet. I had not expected that he would have none left of his brother at all. In the interview, however, Enriqué admitted that he found it rather surprising that he had invented a slightly different fate for his brother (through a process that he could now no longer reconstruct). As he said, it was hardly the case that his own version was any more acceptable or endurable than the one of which he had originally been informed. On the contrary, the story of the SS punishment was even more unbearable than that of the accident. Instead, it seemed to me that there were two processes at work. First, both little exaggerations in Marianne's and Ernst's accounts had reinforced the meaning of their loved one's fates. The brutality with which the Krombach's had been treated and the senseless waste of Lore's life were reinforced by these modified accounts. Moreover, what both individuals were trying to do was bring the past under control in some small way. The details were not so important. What was important was not to be exposed quite so powerlessly and passively to an unbearable past.

Conclusion

What added poignancy to my juxtaposition of Marianne's testimony and the documents, and also confirmed the impression that she was unable to confront the past as it was, was the fact that at the time of her death she had not revealed to me the existence of most of the papers in her possession. During my conversations with her she had known, as I did not, that her house was heaving with records and momentos. Evidently, she could not bring herself to confront them. Marianne's son told me that his mother was normally so orderly, filing everything in its proper place. Yet those papers relating to the Holocaust period were stuffed into envelopes and folders, nothing thrown away but nothing catalogued, in nooks and crannies all over the house. The house itself was suffering badly from subsidence and there were big cracks in the back room walls. There could be no more eloquent symbol of the burden she was carrying than the way this whole structure seemed gradually to be sinking under the weight of her unmasterable past.

For many Holocaust survivors it is simply not possible to make the kind of comparison of records I have briefly ventured in this article. The range of surviving documents that shed light on Marianne's experience in Nazi Germany is rarely found. Usually, therefore, we have to be satisfied with the lonely testimony of the survivor and to put the question of accuracy to one side. My argument, however, is that where it *is* possible to compare survivor testimony with other sources, it is no disrespect to the survivors to do so. Such an exercise does not imply a wish to or an expectation of challenging the fundamental veracity of their testimony. On the contrary, it helps illuminate the very processes of memory which we are seeking to understand.

Notes

1   This is the modified version of a paper originally delivered at the Xth International Oral History Congress, Rio de Janeiro, June 1998. I would like to thank the Nuffield foundation for financing my attendance at the conference and part of the research work on which this paper is based. Thanks are also due to Keele University for research support and to Vivian Ellenbogen for making family papers available.

2   Marianne Ellenbogen, 'Flucht und illegales Leben wahrend der Nazi-Verfolgungsjahre 1943–1954' in *Das Münster am Hellweg* No. 37, (1984), pp. 135–42.

3   See Lawrence L. Langer, *Holocaust Testimonies. The ruins of memory*, Yale University Press, 1991. Other influential works on survivor testimony consulted include: Bruno Bettelheim, *Surviving the Holocaust*, London: Fontana, 1986; Cathy Caruth (ed.), *Trauma: Explorations in Memory*, Basil: John Hopkins University Press, 1995; Geoffrey R. Hartman (ed.), *Holocaust remembrance. The shapes of memory*, Oxford: Blackwell, 1994; Kenneth Jacobson, *Embattled selves. An Investigation Into the Nature of Identity, Through Oral Histories of Holocaust Survivors*, Atlantic Monthly Press. 1994.

4   Langer, *Holocaust Testimonies*. p. xv.

5   The family were among the estimated several hundred Jews who enjoyed protection from the *Abwehr*. The full story of that protection, which derived above all from the anti-Nazi convictions of Oster and Dohnanyi, has not yet been told. The best account available is Winfried Meyer, *Unternehmen Sieben. Eine Rettungsaktion für vom Holocaust Bedrohte aus dem Amt Ausland/Abwehr im Oberkommando der Wehrmacht*, Frankfurt/M, 1993. The Jews were protected under the cover of using them as agents abroad and, indeed, some were spirited across the border into Switzerland and elsewhere. In the summer of 1943, however, the *Abwehr* lost whatever independence from the SS it had enjoyed and was forced to drop its remaining Jewish 'agents'.

6   The full name of this Essen-based group was '*Bund. Gemeinschaft für sozialistisches Leben*'. It was not formally connected to the more famous Jewish *Bund* in Poland.

7   In this article, I do not provide detailed references to the interviews with Marianne and to the papers within her family's possession, but only to externally held material. Full references are included in my biography of Marianne, *The Past in Hiding*, London: Penguin, 2000.

8   Many of these were in Marianne's own possession. In addition, archives consulted include the Alte Synagoge, Essen, the Stadtarchiv Essen, the Hauptstaatsarchiv Düsseldorf, the Federal German Archive, Berlin, the Zentrum für Anti-

semitismusforschung, Berlin, Yad Vashem, Jerusalem, the Leo Baeck Institute, New York and the Wiener Library, London.

9   See note 10 below.

10   The best sources on Izbica in the English language are: Andrzej Trzcinski, *A Guide to Jewish Lublin and Surroundings*, Lublin, Warsaw, 1991; Yitzhak Arad, *Belzec, Sobibor; Treblinka. The Operation Reinhard Death Camps*, Bloomington and Indianapolis, 1987; Thomas Blatt, *From the Ashes of Sobibor. A Story of Survival*, Evanston, Illinois, 1997.

11   Stadtarchiv Essen (StAE), Nachlass Jacobs, Artur Jacobs, Diary, entry 20 April 1942.

12   His nickname for Marianne (after Joan of Arc).

13   In Edna Brocke, Barbara Vögeler, Michael Zimmermann *et al.*, *Stationen jüdischen Lebens: von der Emanzipation bis zur Gegenwart. Katalogbuch zur Ausstellung 'Stationen jüdischen Lebens' in der Alten Synagoge Essen*, Bonn,1990.

14   Information from Mrs Hannah Aron, West Hartford, Connecticut.

15   Ellenbogen, 'Flucht und illegales Leben während der Nazi-Verfolgungsjahre 1943–1954'.

16   HauptStaatsarchiv Düsseldorf (HStaD) RW58, 74234, Sheet headed 'Betrifft: Flucht der Jüdin Marianne Sara Strauß . . .' Essen, 3 September 1943.

17   Interview with Lilli Arras, Geldern, 10 January 1997.

18   BBC Written Archive Centre, German Service, Sonderbericht scripts January 1943–April 1945, confirm that in 1944 the BBC did send very detailed information about the fate of the occupants of specific transports from Theresienstadt to Auschwitz. Through other sources, Marianne knew her parents were on these transports. I am very grateful to Gabriel Milland for the BBC reference. Danuta Czech also notes the BBC reports, which were monitored in Auschwitz itself, see Danuta Czech, *Kalendarium der Ereignisse im Konzentrationslager Auschwitz Birkenau 1939–1945*, Hamburg, 1989, pp. 800–1.

19   HStaD RW58 74234. My translation.

20   Enriqué's informant was a red cross nurse in Sweden, Judith Koppel, originally from Essen. From Marianne's own correspondence it is clear that Koppel was dependent on information from Marianne herself.

21   Bernd Schmalhausen, *Schicksale jüdischer Juristen aus Essen 1933–1945*, Essen, 1994, pp. 81–82.

22   StAE, Nachlass Jacobs, Artur Jacobs, diary, 31 December 1942.

23   Alte Synagoge, Essen AR 4434, Liesel Sernberg to Dr Alexander, 20 August 1945.

24   Sadly he has since died.

25   Research into the probable location of the two women suggests that Kursbad is a misreading of Kurzbach, one of the sub-camps of Gross-Rosen, situated north east of Breslau. Other details, for example, the fact that Sigrid was sent on to Bergen-Belsen, the dates they arrived and the camp was closed, support this conclusion. See Isabell Sprenger, *Gross-Rosen. Ein Konzentrationslager in Schlesien*, Cologne: Böhlau Verlag, 1996, pp. 260ff; Gudrun Schwarz, *Die nationalsozialistischen Lager*, revised ed. Frankfurt/M: Fischer, 1996, p. 198; Israel Gutman (ed.) *Encyclopaedia of the Holocaust*, London: Macmillan, 1990, p. 625.

26   Ellenbogen, Nachlaß, Ludwig and Selma Ansbacher, Frankfurt, to Marianne, 1 May 1946.

Chapter 19

Alistair Thomson

ANZAC MEMORIES
Putting popular memory theory into practice in Australia

In 'Anzac memories' Alistair Thomson offers the notion of memory 'composure' as one model for understanding the psychological and social processes of remembering, and suggests a 'popular memory' approach to interviewing that might unravel the complex strands of memory. Thomson shows how the identity of Australian First World War veteran Fred Farrall was shaped by his war memories and, in turn, how changes in cultural memory and in Fred's subsequent life experience affected how he was able to remember the war. Alistair Thomson is Reader in Continuing Education and History at the University of Sussex. Reprinted with permission from *Oral History*, 1990, vol. 18, no. 2, pp. 25–31.

[. . .]

ACCORDING TO THE 'ANZAC LEGEND', during the Great War of 1914–18 Australian soldiers proved to themselves and to the rest of the world that the new breed of Anglo-Celtic men from the south was worthy to rank with the nations of the world.[1] Gallipoli, where the Australians first went into battle on April 25 1915, was regarded as the baptism of fire of the new Australian Commonwealth, and the commemoration of Anzac Day on April 25 each year became the Australian equivalent of American Independence Day or Bastille Day in France (without the revolutionary overtones). [. . .]

This essay focusses on the life and memories of Fred Farrall, one of about twenty Melbourne working class veterans of the Great War whom I've interviewed [. . .].[2] I don't pretend that Fred Farrall was a typical 'digger' [another nickname of the Australian soldiers], far from it. The search for national character has been one of the obsessive dead ends of Australian history-writing, and in this essay I won't be analysing the extent to which the Anzac legend is an accurate representation of the 'typical' Australian soldier.[3] I'm more interested in the interactions between Anzac legend stereotypes and individual soldiers' identities, in the experience of difference as well as conformity, and in the ways that 'typical' can be oppressive. I want to assess the relationship between Fred Farrall's memory of the war and the national mythology which publicly defines his experience as a soldier, and to use his case study to make sense of the general relationship between individual memory and collective myth.

The theory of memory (and national myth) which informs this essay was developed by the Popular Memory Group at the Centre for Contemporary Cultural Studies in Birmingham. The group focussed on the interactions between 'private' and 'public' memories, and used the following approach to individual memory. We compose our memories to make sense of our past and present lives. 'Composure' is the aptly ambiguous term used by the Popular Memory Group to describe the process of memory making. In one sense we 'compose' or construct memories using the public language and meanings of our culture. In another sense we 'compose' memories which help us to feel relatively comfortable with our lives, which gives us a feeling of composure. We remake or repress memories of experiences which are still painful and 'unsafe' because they do not easily accord with our present identity, or because their inherent traumas or tensions have never been resolved. We seek composure, an alignment of our past, present and future lives. One key theoretical connection, and the link between the two senses of composure, is that the apparently private process of composing safe memories is in fact very public. Our memories are risky and painful if they do not conform with the public norms or versions of the past. We compose our memories so that they will fit with what is publicly acceptable, or, if we have been excluded from general public acceptance, we seek out particular publics which affirm our identities and the way we want to remember our lives.[1]

Some critics of oral history have claimed that the fact that we compose our memories invalidates the use of memory by historians. That might be true for oral historians who have sought to use memory as a literal source of what happened in the past. But if we are also interested, as we must be, in the ways in which the past is resonant in our lives today, then oral testimony is essential evidence for analysis of the interactions between past and present, and between memory and mythology.

This approach to memory requires a review of interviewing technique. In my initial interviews with Melbourne war veterans I wanted to see how the experiences of working-class soldiers contrasted with the Anzac legend, and used a chronological life story approach as the basis for questions. The interviews did reveal many differences between their lives and the legend, but I was also struck by the extent to which memories were entangled with the myth; for example, some men related scenes from the film *Gallipoli* as if they were their own. Therefore, guided by the ideas of the Popular Memory Group, I devised a new approach for a second set of interviews with some of the same men. In the new interviews I wanted to focus on how each man composed and told his memories by exploring four key interactions: between public and private, past and present, memory and identity, and interviewer and interviewee. The personal information which I had already gained in the first interviews made it possible for me to tailor my questions specifically for each man in terms of his particular memories and identities. If I had not done the original interviews I would have needed to integrate the life story approach with the new approach.

To investigate the relationship between public and private memories I made the public myth a starting point for questions: what was your response to various war books and films, past and present, and to Anzac Day and war memorials? How well did they represent your own experiences; how did they make you feel? We also focussed on specific features of the legend: was there a distinctive Anzac character; how true was it for your own nature and experience? Were you so very different from the soldiers of other armies? I asked each man to define certain keywords in his own words – 'digger', 'mateship', 'the spirit of Anzac' – and discovered that some of the men who seemed to be uncritical of the legend had contrary and even contradictory understanding of its key terms.

Another section of discussion focussed on experience and personal identity: how did you feel about yourself and your actions at key moments (enlistment, battle, return)? What were your anxieties and uncertainties? How did you make sense of your experiences and how did other people define you? How were you included or excluded, what was acceptable and unacceptable behaviour (what was not 'manly'), and how and why were some men ostracised? Of course these memories, and the relative composure of memory, had shifted over time (the past/present interaction), so we discussed how postwar events – such as homecoming, the Depression and World War Two, domestic change and old age, and the revival of Anzac remembrance in the 1980s – affected identity and memory. The new interview approach showed me that how we remember and articulate will change over time, and how this can be related to shifts in public perception.

Another related and difficult focus of the new interviews was upon the ways memories are affected by strategies of containment, by ways of handling frustration, failure, loss or pain. This required a sensitive balance between potentially painful probing and reading between the lines of memory. What is possible or impossible to remember, or even to say aloud? What are the hidden meanings of silences and sudden subject changes? What is being contained by a 'fixed' story? Deeply repressed experiences or feelings may be discharged in less conscious forms of expression, in past and present dreams, errors and Freudian slips, body language and even humour, which is often used to overcome or conceal embarrassment and pain. Discussion of the symbolic content and feelings expressed by war-related dreams suggested new understandings of the personal impact of the war, and of what could not be publicly expressed. And my interview notes about facial expression, body movements and the mode of talking were revealing about emotive meanings of memories which would not be apparent in interview transcripts.

This approach raised ethical dilemmas for me as an oral historian. Interviewing which approached a therapeutic relationship could be damaging for the interviewee as well as rewarding for the interviewer. It required great care and sensitivity, and a cardinal rule that the well-being of the interviewee always came before the interests of my research. At times I had to stop a line of questioning in an interview, or was asked to stop, because it was too painful. Unlike the therapist, as an oral historian I would not be around to help put together the pieces of memories which were no longer safe.

One partial response was to make the interview, and the interview relationship, a more open process. I tried to discuss how my questions affected remembering, and what was difficult to say to *me*. To encourage dialogue instead of monologue I talked about my own interests and role. In some ways this change in my role (limited by the fact that I never gave up my role as interviewer) affected the remembering. Sometimes it encouraged a man to open up to me and reconsider aspects of his life, although others resisted that opportunity. The explicit introduction of my attitudes into the interviews may have encouraged men to tell stories for my approval, though I usually felt that it facilitated discussion and provoked dissent as much as agreement. In Fred Farrall's case that was not such an issue, as by the time we met his memory of the war was relatively fixed. Although over the years we developed a close and trusting relationship, in which Fred's remembering was actively encouraged by my interest, he seemed to tell the same stories in the same ways to his various audiences, including me. Fred's war story had not always been so fixed, and I gradually realised that his memory of the war, and his identity as a soldier and ex-serviceman, had passed through three distinct phases, shaped by the shifting relationship between Anzac meanings and his own subjective identity.

Born in 1897, Fred Farrall grew up on a small farm in outback New South Wales. He didn't like farm work and, inspired by the patriotic fervour which swept the country after the Gallipoli landing, was glad to join a 'Kangaroo March' of rural recruits for the Australian Imperial Force (AIF). He enlisted in an infantry battalion and was sent to France and the Somme in 1916. By his own admission Fred was not much of a soldier. He was young, naive and under-confident, and wasn't very good at fighting and killing. Like many soldiers of all nationalities, he was terrified in battle and miserable in the trenches, and began to doubt his own worth and that of the war itself. His best mates were killed and mutilated at his side, and though Fred survived the war in one piece, he was a physical and emotional wreck:

> When I came home I was admitted to Randwick Hospital for six months to see what they could do with the trench feet condition, and the rheumatism and a nasal complaint that I contracted on the Somme . . . I didn't realise this at the time, but I long since realised it. But I had neurosis, that was not recognised in those days, and so we just had it. You put up with it. And that developed an inferiority complex, plus, really, I mean extremely bad . . . Well, I had reached a stage with it, where, when I wanted to speak I'd get that way that I couldn't talk. I would stammer and stutter and it seemed that inside me everything had got into a knot, and that went on for years and years and years.

From the fortunate, retrospective stance of a survivor who overcame his neurosis, Fred attributes his shell-shocked condition to the effect of constant bombardment on the Somme. He admits that he was unable to express his fear during and after the battle, and was discouraged from doing so: it was not manly or Australian. Many of Fred's stories contrast his own inadequacy with the supposed bravery of other Australians. The legend of the Australian soldier – the best fighter in the war – caused many diggers to repress their feelings, and worsened the psychological trauma of the war.[5]

Fred's condition, and his sense of personal inadequacy, was worsened by his return to Australia.

> I was something like pet dogs and cats that are turned out in the Dandenongs [a mountain range near Melbourne] . . . If anyone was to ask me now what I was like at that time, I would say that in some respects, it could truthfully be said, and I suppose this applied to many

others, many others, that we wouldn't be the full quid. In other words, we weren't what we were like when we went away. I don't know whether you've heard Eric Bogle's songs. Well he mentioned that in something he said about Vietnam . . . And then when I got into civilian life, well this was something new, and to some extent it was, it was terrifying. You're out in the cold, hard world. Nobody to look after you now. You've got to get your own accommodation, your own meals. In short, you've got to fend for yourself.

For men like Fred who were teenagers when they enlisted, the social experience of repatriation was especially traumatic. Fred was lucky. Because of his ill-health he couldn't go back to work on the family farm, but a cousin and her digger husband gave him a room in their home in Sydney, and got him back on his feet. He enrolled in a government vocational training scheme to become an upholsterer, but the scheme was badly organised, and though the government subsidised trainees' wages, employers were not interested when the subsidy ended. Fred searched for work for almost two years before he got a job in a motor car factory. I asked him whether his war service badge helped him to get a job. It didn't, and he wouldn't wear it for many years:

> Well, we didn't value it.

> *Why?*

> Well, it'd be hard to explain other than that first of all, we, of course, had been disillusioned. What we'd been told that the war was all about, didn't work out that way. What we'd been told that the government would do when the war was over, for what we'd done, didn't work out either.

> *In what ways?*

> Well, you see, the pensions in the 1920s, unless you had an arm off or a leg off or a hand off or something like that, it was almost as hard to get a pension as it would be to win Tatts [an Australian lottery]. There was no recognition of neurosis and other disabilities . . . And anyway, the doctors that they had in those days, I suppose they were schooled in what, how they were to behave and so they treated the diggers as they interviewed them and examined them as though they were tenth-rate citizens. Something like we look upon the aboriginals. There was great hostility between the diggers on one hand and the Repatriation officials on the other.

Fred felt that ex-servicemen were regarded as 'malingerers', and refused to use the Repat. until 1926, when he had a breakdown and had no choice.

Despite this hostility, the war remained a haunting memory for Fred. He chose to marry on the anniversary of his war wound, he named his house after the places where his two best mates were buried, he remembered (and still recites) in exact detail the places and dates where many friends were killed. These private forms of commemoration, which transformed grotesque experience into relatively safe lists and rituals, were Fred's way of coping with the past. Experiences and feelings which he could not cope with were unconsciously expressed in his dreams:

> Oh well, the dreams I had were dreams of being shelled, you know, lying in a trench, being in a trench or lying in a shellhole, and being shot at with shells. And being frightened, scared stiff. Here, to now, I didn't know there were so many others like me until I read this book on Pozieres.[6] That most of them had this fear, and when you come to think of it, well how could they be otherwise . . . You don't know when the next shell that is coming is going to blow you to pieces or leave you crippled in such a way that it'd be better if you had been blown to pieces . . . [In the dream] you'd be going through this experience and you'd be scared stiff, you'd be frightened. You'd be frightened, and wakened up, probably, by the experience.

One reason why Fred could not come to terms with his wartime fears and feelings of inadequacy was because he could find no appropriate public affirmation of his experience as a soldier. He found that he could not talk about his war:

> Well, well it was a different atmosphere in the 1920s for instance, and the early 1930s. First of all those that were at the war were reluctant to talk about it, and those that were not at the war, didn't go to the war and the women and that, didn't seem to want to hear about it. So the war slipped into the background as far as the average person was concerned . . . I never talked about it. Never. For years and years and years. Now just why that was I don't know. But, the soldiers, generally speaking, were not very enthusiastic about army life and were ever so pleased to get into civilian clothes again . . . When we got back, there was a sort of hostility toward anything to do with the war, by a lot . . . All they wanted to do was distance themselves as far as they could from anything to do with the army, with the Repat., or the war.

Fred shut away his beautifully embossed discharge certificate in a dusty drawer, and he declined to wear his medals or to attend Anzac Day parades or battalion reunions. The nature of Anzac Day and of other public forms of commemoration, and the perceived neglect by the government, was partly to blame for Fred's inability to express or resolve his ambivalence about his war experience. This was not true for all diggers. Many of the men I interviewed describe how they enjoyed the celebration of their digger identity on Anzac Day, and the humorous reminiscence of veterans' reunions. Public remembrance and affirmation helped these men to cope with their past, filtering out memories which were personally painful or which contradicted the legend. The nascent Anzac legend worked because many veterans wanted and needed to identify with it.

Fred's initial interview explanation of his non-participation is that Anzac Day was a drunken binge, and that he wasn't a drinker. He stresses his own sobriety and complains that the popular 'larrikin' image of the digger – boozer, gambler and womaniser – has not accurately depicted his own experience and view of the AIF. I hadn't expected this response, but it shows how another aspect of the digger stereotype – larrikin as well as fighter – could misrepresent an individual's experience, exclude him from public affirmation rituals, and make him feel uncomfortable about his own identity. Several other old diggers expressed the same unease about the larrikin image which has featured prominently in recent Anzac films, and remembered that even during the war they were made to feel uncomfortable by this behaviour and reputation. Others revelled in the stereotype, which conjured up exciting memories of their own wild youth.

Fred also avoided Anzac Day because its patriotic rhetoric did not match his wartime doubts about the worth of Australian involvement, or the bitterness he felt about the postwar treatment of the soldiers. But the main reason for his non-participation in Anzac ritual was the extreme confusion and distress he felt about the war. The public celebration of Anzac heroes was a painful reminder of his own perceived inadequacy as a soldier and as a man, and Fred was unable to enjoy the solace and affirmation it offered to other returned servicemen.

Although Fred Farrall was traumatised by his memories and identity as an Anzac throughout the 1920s, he gradually found another life and identity in the labour movement, which in turn helped him to compose a sense of his war which he could live with more easily. Fred recalls that he was politically confused after the war, but that a work-mate persuaded him to join the Coachmaker's Union in 1923: 'that was the beginning of my active part in politics . . . [and] sowed the seeds of my socialism that I developed a few years after and have had all my life'. He became active in the union, joined the Labour Party in 1926 and then, unemployed and disillusioned with the Labour government of 1930, he joined the Communist Party. In the labour movement Fred found supportive comrades and gradually regained his self-confidence. The new and empathetic peer group – many of them were ex-servicemen – and eager reading of radical tracts about the war, helped him to articulate and define his wartime and postwar disillusionment. He believes that was true for many other diggers, and cites the example of his friend Sid Norris:

> In that respect, the making of a big change politically speaking, Sid was but one of thousands of diggers who abandoned their prewar opinions of God, King and Empire being worthy of any sacrifice. The bitter experience of what wars were all about, the making of big profits for some people, was a lesson that changed the diggers' political ideas from conservatism to radicalism. And, Alistair, this is one part, or side, of the Anzac legend that has never been dealt with by the writers of the Great War. Maybe you can give it some thought.

Although Fred had not himself made that recognition during the war, in the late 1920s his new political understanding helped him to emphasise particular senses of his experience as a soldier. Thus Fred now ironically stressed the story of an Irish labourer on his father's farm who had warned him not to go and fight in the rich men's war, and he represented himself as an unwitting victim of an imperialist war. He also stressed that the relationship between officers and men in the AIF was not so very different to that between employers and workers in peacetime Australia, and that the diggers were often rebellious towards authority (he recalled one incident in which he and two mates planned, unsuccessfully, to kill an unpopular officer). These understandings of the war were part of a more radical Anzac tradition championed by some activists in the labour movement.[7] As a proponent of this tradition Fred articulated his disillusionment about repatriation, and deducted that Anzac Day was 'a clever manoeuvre' intended to bring the soldiers back together again and stifle their anger about pensions and unemployment. [. . .]

Fred also became sceptical of the returned servicemen's organisations which controlled Anzac Day. He recalls that the soldiers in the trenches talked about the need to organise for decent conditions after the war, and that he joined the Returned Sailors' and Soldiers' Imperial League of Australia (RSSILA – now the powerful RSL) on the day he was demobbed. But the RSSILA had been created and controlled by an alliance of citizen and ex-servicemen conservatives, and was granted government recognition as the official representative of returned servicemen 'in return for defending the powers that be' (who were frightened by the violence of dissatisfied diggers and the presence of more radical veterans' pressure groups).[8] In the early 1920s Fred's inner turmoil and physical handicaps had probably kept him away from RSSILA meetings, but this alienation was now confirmed by political suspicion:

> In other words it was the officers in somewhat the same position in civilian life as they were in the army . . . It was not an organisation in the best interests of the ordinary digger . . . It was a political organisation of the extreme right wing and there was no place in it for anyone that had any democratic principles.

By the end of the 1920s Fred Farrall had aligned himself against the RSSILA and was fighting with members of the communist-led Unemployed Workers' Movement in street battles against RSSILA club men and the proto-fascist New Guard movement. By 1937 he was a confident opponent of the official legend and its RSSILA organisers, and was arrested for distributing pacifist leaflets at an Anzac Day parade.

Ironically, by the time Fred had consolidated his radical view of the war, the RSSILA's more conservative Anzac legend, which celebrated the triumph of Australian manhood and the baptism of the nation, was well entrenched. Radicals did contest that version of the war – in Melbourne, for example, some ex-servicemen protested that the proposed Shrine of Remembrance would glorify war, and campaigned for the more utilitarian memorial of a veteran's hospital – but by 1930 radicals had lost the battle for the Anzac legend and the label 'radical digger' was a contradiction in terms. Fred Farrall gradually shed his identity as a returned serviceman and settled into the role of 'a soldier of the labour movement'.

Although the labour movement's version of the war did help Fred to feel relatively secure with an analysis of the war as imperial and business rivalry, and his sense of himself as a naive and then begrudging victim, it did not (maybe could not?) help him to express or resolve his traumatic personal feelings about the war. Theories about arms profiteers made him angry, but didn't help him to cope with memories of terror, guilt or inadequacy. Nor could he enjoy the wider public affirmation of Anzac Day, which helped other ex-servicemen feel proud of their war service. Thus, for many years Fred usually ignored his military past and tried to forget his painful memories.

There's a third phase in Fred Farrall's war story. Some time in the 1960s or early 1970s he started to read and talk outside of the labour movement about his war. He attended the annual Anzac Day ceremony and reunion of his old battalion. He pinned his war service badge back in his lapel, and retrieved his discharge certificate from its dusty hideaway and stuck it up on his living room wall (above a more recent photo of himself as the Mayor of the Melbourne municipality of Prahran). After years of silence he now talks eagerly and at length about the war to students, film makers and oral history interviewers. Why?

Fred explains the change in a number of ways. It's partly the renewed interest of an old man about his youth: 'I suppose as you get older you have some sort of feeling for what happened long ago'. He's also enjoying the respect, even veneration, which the few remaining Great War diggers receive, from people in the street who notice an AIF badge, and from Veterans' Affairs officials who tell them it is a 'badge of honour' and pay their increasing medical costs:

> Well, there was a time when it just didn't fit into that picture at all . . .
> Well, we've never had much over the years of value from that sort of
> thing so if there is anything now, even to the extent of getting some
> respect, well I think it's worth doing.

Those comments hint at more general processes. In the resurgence of interest in the Anzacs, the specific and often contradictory experiences of individual veterans are being clouded by a generalised, almost nostalgic version of the diggers and their war. Furthermore, in this modern reworking of the legend aspects of their war experience which were once taboo are now publicly acceptable. The Vietnam War and the influence of the peace and anti-war movement have altered public perceptions of war so that the soldier as victim is a more acceptable character – though he still takes second place to the Anzac hero. Fred can now talk more easily about his experience of 'the war as hell', and of his own feeling of inadequacy as a soldier, because those aspects of the war are portrayed in the history books and films of the 1980s. He marvels at how well some recent Anzac historians and television directors depict the horror and degradation of trench warfare. The personal pleasure of having his experience as a soldier recognised and affirmed after years of alienation was vividly expressed when I asked Fred about his visit to the Australian War Memorial in Canberra (second only to the Sydney Opera House as a national tourist attraction):

> Nearly got a job there. I was there about eighteen months ago, you know,
> and oh gee, look here, I got the surprise of my life . . . I was treated like
> a long lost cousin [and was asked to talk about the western front to other
> visitors]. 'Well', I said, 'I wouldn't mind doing that, but', I said, 'I'm a
> worker for peace and not for war'. 'Oh', the bloke said, 'you know this
> place was built as a Peace Memorial and so you're at liberty to express
> your opinions along those lines as you see fit'. . . . So up I went. Well I
> was there for two or three days really. It looked as though I was going
> to have, at eighty odd, as though I was going to get a permanent job.

No doubt Fred brought the galleries to life with his stories of the misery of trench warfare – the rain, mud, rats, lice, shellfire, explosions, fear – and felt satisfied that at last his story of the war was being told. And he believed that he was making a message of peace.

Yet in this profoundly important reconciliation with his wartime past, and between his own memory and the public story of the Anzacs, Fred's political critique has been displaced. The War Memorial and war films admit that for the poor bloody infantry 'war is hell', yet they still promote the digger hero and the Anzac legend. Fred is so pleased with the new recognition that he doesn't see how other aspects of his experience are still ignored. He doesn't consider the absence of any depiction of tensions between officers and other ranks in the AIF, or the postwar disillusionment of many diggers, or of the analysis of the war as a business, all important themes in his discussion with me. Fred assumes that any museum depicting the horror of the western front must be a 'peace memorial', but doesn't recognise the political ambiguity of a museum in which little boys clamber over tanks and want to grow up to be soldiers.

Fred's memory still has a radical cutting edge. He still condemns the artificial patriotism of Anzac Day and carries his war medals on Palm Sunday peace rallies, using the new interest in the Anzacs to make his own criticism of war and Australian society. But he doesn't direct that critique at the Anzac writers and film makers who are the post powerful myth-makers of our time. The effectiveness of the 1980s Anzac legend is that it convinces even radical diggers like Fred that their story is being told, while subtly reworking the conservative sense of the war, national character and Australian history into an appropriate form for the 1980s. The 'hegemonic' process seems similar to that undergone by the diggers who did join the RSSILA and Anzac Day back in the 1920s. On each occasion individuals are included and their memories selectively affirmed by the public rituals and meanings of remembrance. That affirmation may be essential for individual peace of mind, but in the process contradictory and challenging memories are displaced or repressed.

Fred Farrall's case study highlights the dynamic relationship between individual memory and national myth, and suggests ways in which oral history can be more than just the 'voice of the past'. Oral history can help us to understand how and why national mythologies work (and don't work) for individuals, and in our society generally. It can also reveal the possibilities, and difficulties, of developing and sustaining oppositional memories. These understandings can enable us to participate more effectively as historians and in collective struggle for more democratic and radical versions of our past and of what we can become.

Notes

1   'Anzac' stands for Australian and New Zealand Army Corps, though the New Zealanders are usually left out of the Australian legend.

2   The interviews with Fred were recorded in July of 1983 and April of 1987, and the tapes and transcripts of the interviews, together with others from the project, are available in the collection of the library of the Australian War Memorial.

3   For such a critique see my chapter, 'Passing Shots at the Anzac Legend', in V. Burgmann and J. Lee (eds), *A Most Valuable Acquisition*: *A People's History of Australia since 1788*, Melbourne: McPhee Gribble/Penguin, 1988.

4   See 'Popular memory: theory politics, method', in R. Johnson, *et al.* (eds), *Making Histories*: *Studies in History Writing and Politics*, London: Hutchinson, 1982.

5   For an analysis in these terms of the nature and effects of shell shock, see E. Showalter, 'Rivers and Sassoon: the inscription of male gender anxiety', in M.R. Higonnet, *et al.* (eds), *Behind the Lines: Gender and the Two World Wars*, New Haven: Yale University Press, 1987, pp. 61–69.

6   P. Chariton, *Pozieres: Australians on the Somme 1916*, North Ryde: Methuen Haynes, 1980.

7   L.F. Fox, *The Truth about Anzac*, Melbourne: Victorian Council Against War and Fascism, 1936.

8   See M. Lake, 'The power of Anzac', in M. McKernan and M. Browne (eds), *Australia: Two Centuries of War and Peace*, Canberra: Australian War Memorial/Allen & Unwin, 1988.

Chapter 20

Trevor Lummis

STRUCTURE AND VALIDITY
IN ORAL EVIDENCE

Trevor Lummis argues that 'the problem at the heart of using the interview method in history still remains that of moving from the individual account to a social interpretation'. Here he shows how aggregation and tabulation of data within interviews from British fishing communities can be used to create generalizations about historical behaviour and attitude. Trevor Lummis was formerly Senior Research Officer at the Department of Sociology, University of Essex, and is now a freelance historian and author. Reprinted from *International Journal of Oral History*, 1983, vol. 2, no. 2, pp. 109–120. Reproduced with permission of Greenwood Publishing Group Inc., Westport, Conn., USA.

T HE VALIDATION OF ORAL EVIDENCE can be divided into two main areas: the degree to which any individual interview yields reliable information on the historical experience, and the degree to which that individual experience is typical of its time and place. The major concern of this paper is to suggest ways in which simple aggregation can be used to assess validity, for as the data in oral history archives lacks the random quality required for formal statistical validity, some acceptable method of generalising from a number of interviews has to be developed. This need not be merely an exercise in positivistic methodology, but the process of structuring data should be part of the interpretative process and might be used to elucidate some of the wider problems of omission and distortion in oral evidence as they relate to the life-cycle and/or wider cultural events.

[. . .]

As this procedure has been criticised for being 'positivistic', it should be stated that the method is not tied to any specific epistemology. Whether retrospective interviewing is capable of establishing 'factual' data, or whether it can only record an 'interpretation' of previous facts, structuring the evidence is equally valuable. If oral evidence is to move from a form of biography to an historical account, it must proceed from an individual to a social experience. Even if interviews are 'interpretations', it is still necessary to try to establish how interpretations change through time, their distribution in social groups, and the reality which formed them. If they cannot be used to contribute to historical understanding, there is no reason for historians to interview people. Before turning to the method of establishing the validity of a group of interviews, however, I would argue that structuring a number of interviews can contribute to understanding memory – even in the shape of structured silences.

The notion of 'silences' comes from Luisa Passerini's work which, although using a large number of interviews with ordinary workers, has consciousness firmly at the centre of its concerns.[1] Here just two of the dimensions she uses will be mentioned – the 'silences' on the years under Fascism and 'inconsistent' answers, which are accounts which make no reference to major historical event and processes. In commenting on her article, a *History Workshop* editorial notes that the idea of a collective silence is supported by work from Germany and that, in the British context, there is little beyond the anecdotal to be found in oral accounts covering the period of the General Strike of 1926. The editorial speculates as to whether that could be the result of a similar silence, or whether it is 'simply that the "political" impinges on individual lives in very different ways from the personal'.[2] There are three aspects here, all part of the structure of memory – the degree to which memories are censored, the reference points for chronology, and the related issue of how the public and private spheres cohere in the individual consciousness.

That a number of people who experienced Fascism and Nazism should avoid spontaneous mention of those years is a reasonable proposition. Those ideologies were in overt political control for only a brief period, and suffered an overwhelming military and political defeat. I do not believe, however, that the scant references to the General Strike in Britain can be explained along these lines. The trade union movement may have been defeated, but it was not total, and within twenty years trade unions were enjoying greater power than they had previously experienced. Trade unionism is not a creed or activity rejected by all progressive opinion, and there is no reason to assume any self-censorship. Nevertheless, the omission is an interesting one, and the answer to this phenomenon probably lies in the distinction between public and private – that is, the link between memory, experience, and how this is structured in the mind. The example cited by Passerini of a narrative which recounted life up to and including World War I and then the period of the early 1920s before moving to World War II reminded me of my interviews with informants from that age cohort. They too relate their early years, their introduction to work, service in World War I, and their return to work. Then, unless there is some dramatic personal event, they jump to World War II. This leads me to speculate on whether the silences noted are due to censorship or, as was suggested above, simply that public events do not impinge on personal narrative and chronology.

Structuring a number of interviews should be one method of determining to what degree silences and omissions of this general nature are due to 'censorship' or because political events pass largely unregarded. Structuring their chronology would be a start, for it seems that most interviews are a mixture of public and private chronology, but that on the whole the public is used only where it impinges on the private. For example, narratives tend to be separated into periods on the basis of personal and familial events births and deaths, leaving school, changing occupations, moving house, and so on. Public time intrudes mainly where events force a change in private experience, as when war forces changes in occupation, family separation, and geographical movement. A comparison between the chronology of different cohorts should reveal whether this is the case. The date of the private life-cycle events of each cohort will fall into a different period of public historical events. Therefore, a comparison of the silences and omissions of different cohorts should reveal whether public events do impose silences on particular cohorts. Given the required international cooperation, this comparison might be further tested through comparison with cohorts in other countries. The different cultures, stages of industrial development, and political regimes might even reveal which aspect of the public dimension seems to shape consciousness and ideology.

Ultimately, the question of how memory functions may be a problem for medical rather than historical research, but the structuring and analysis of the way in which people do organise their chronology and relate their life to the public domain would provide some guidance for the use of oral evidence.

The possibility of understanding the structure and consciousness of individual interviews through their comparative structure is, however, only one of two dimensions of validity. The other is the degree to which an interview, or group of interviews, might be representative of a wider social group.

The problems of using interviews as if they were a representative sample is an issue which needs to be discussed. At present, historians simply assume that their informants' experiences are in some sense typical of whichever group they come from, the parameters of that group affinity being set by the historian. This may not be an unrealistic process of historical analysis where the evidence is related to a specific piece of research. But the problem of the valid use of oral evidence is going to increase as the number and range of interviews in archives grows. The problem of interpreting oral evidence and its validity becomes linked to the problems of archiving and of selective retrieval. Paul Thompson's project 'Family Life and Work Experience before 1918' took a quota sample of 444 informants based on the census categories of 1911, in order to ensure that the research was broadly representative of the social structure of the period.[3] However, most oral history projects (including the two main additions to the Essex University Archive) are focussed on a particular group or area, and the interviews do not fill a quota but trace and interview those who participated in the particular circumstance. Although each project by itself may have proceeded quite reasonably on the basis of historical common sense, subsequent researchers wishing to use interviews from more than one project need some means of assessing whether the interviews are in any way typical of the group they are studying.

This is essentially a mundane but necessary task, for to make generalisations based on oral evidence is to claim, at least implicitly, that the interviews used are representative. Quantification and generalisation – 'a few', 'the unskilled', 'some', and similar terms – appear constantly in historical narrative and almost as frequently do not indicate at all what evidence affords a basis for such statements. Attempting to categorise and quantify qualitative evidence presents enormous problems. Still, tabulation can provide a means of assessing how representative are a group of interviews, by revealing the level of internal consistency and by demonstrating the degree of conformity to the broader historical picture known from other sources.

Some data are readily tabulated: age, marital status, number of siblings, religion, and political preference can be coded without any great qualitative loss. This allows for an initial comparison with distributions known from other historical sources. The demographic details, for example, can be structured to provide a comparison with what is known about family size and the facts affecting mortality. The tables which follow are taken from data given by informants about the number of siblings and deaths in their family.[4] It should be noted that 'Reported Number of Sibling Deaths' cannot be compared directly with official statistics on births and losses in the family of children up to the age of twelve or thirteen. Table I(A) gives the figures for the whole sample, providing a general baseline. Given the known effect for the period, one should expect a higher mortality rate among those living in urban areas than those in rural areas. Table I(B) shows that the sample conforms to this trend. Table I(C) divides the group into cohorts by decade of birth; the change in sibling mortality is what would be anticipated from a valid sample. The increase in family size was by then falling, although it could represent a local trend since it was a prosperous decade for the local fishermen. Because no figures for the occupation are available, the point remains speculative.

If a sample is conformable to known trends, one can have some confidence that the internal distinctions will reflect real distinctions. This assumption is enhanced by Table I(D). High mortality is associated with poverty and class. So, given that there is a structured differential in income between the status groups, this should be reflected in similar variations in the mortality rate in the sample. And this trend appears much more strongly in fact, than the qualitative material would lead one to expect. Once one is confident that the tables have some significance,[5] they can be used to aid interpretation. Table I(E) is an example. This shows that the families of men engaged in trawling and drifting share similar mortality rates, whereas the inshore fishermen and non-fishermen share similar but remarkably lower rates. As it is known from the interviews that this is not due to income differences, one is obliged to consider other aspects, and the most plausible one is the pattern of work. In the two groups with high mortality, the man is away from home and the woman is left to cope with the family on her own. The other two groups are at home regularly. This focusses attention on the structure of family life and behaviour. Once again, the simple structuring of the data has given insights which were not evident from the qualitative material. For example, the use of corporal punishment in the home to socialise children reveals the same pattern as the mortality figures, and the absence of the male from the home changes the woman's use of punishment rather than that of the man. Thus, one is forced to consider the interaction between work patterns, family life, and the effect that this has on individual behaviour, rather than, a simple relationship between poverty and mortality.

Oral evidence is sometimes criticised on grounds that people cannot, or do not, distinguish with sufficient care between their current ideas and those that they held at an earlier period. This is an issue to which there are no simple answers. Once again, however, there is some value in structuring interviews in order to assess the care with which information has been given.

Table II shows the political allegiance of the informants and their fathers. The information is as unexceptional as it need be in order to show its authenticity. If, on the other hand, the few Labour supporters to be found in the occupation and area had been reported in the earlier cohorts, there would have been good reason to suspect careless reporting. In fact, many of the informants report changing to Labour in 1945. The interesting factor here is that this takes place not as a simple shift along a continuum, but has Liberal moving to Conservative and Conservative moving to Labour. This accuracy is important for political history, because it has been claimed since the Ballot Act of 1872 that 'we cannot make precise correlations between electoral behaviour of small localities and the appropriate statistics of personal income, occupation, religious affiliation and so on'. The advantage of oral history is that it does allow for these patterns to be established in great detail. The internal consistency of this very small group is impressive: it shows (in tables not given here) the drifter-men, mainly Liberal, and the trawler-men, Conservative, as suggested in contemporary sources, although the sample also shows that this is modified by status. It even demonstrates the commonly asserted link between the Church of England and the Conservatives, and the Liberals and Nonconformity.

The structuring of data from one fairly homogeneous group of views is instructive on two levels. It shows that this small accidental sample of elderly informants (mean average date of birth 1897, one-third born in the 1880s) displays an impressive congruence with wider historical trends, even when the interviews are divided into numerous cells. Second, even though the occupation had an unusually high level of cultural identity between the working fishermen and small owners, the structured evidence reveals stratified distinctions in behaviour and attitudes which were not apparent from perusing the qualitative evidence of individual interviews. Thus, structuring the evidence not only provided some grounds for generalising the evidence in the interviews, but actually contributed to a more accurate appreciation of its meaning and to a reshaping of the interpretation drawn from it. The value of such restructuring will, to a large extent, depend on the research problems.

Table I Reported family size and mortality

	Average no. of siblings per respondent	Reported number of sibling deaths	Percentage of sibling mortality	Number of respondents
A All respondents	8.0 (482)	1.0(58)	12	60
B Urban	8.0	1.2	15	32
Rural	8.0	0.7	9	28
Respondent born				
C To 1889	9.6	1.3	14	18
1890–1899	7.0	1.0	14	27
1900–1909	8.0	0.5	7	15
Respondent's father				
D Trawling and drifting				
Owners	8.2	0.8	11	9
Skippers	8.3	1.3	16	13
Crew	9.5	2.3	25	6
E Drifting	8.0	1.3	16	16
Trawling	9.4	1.6	17	12
Inshore	6.7	0.5	7	20
Non-fishermen	8.9	0.8	8	12

Table II Political pattern by decade of birth: respondents and their fathers *

	Conservative	Liberal	Labour	Apolitical	Don't know	Total
To 1870	38% (11)	21% (6)	–	14% (4)	24% (7)	29
1871–1880	53% (16)	30% (9)	–	3% (1)	17% (5)	30
1881–1890	14% (3)	32% (7)	5% (1)	18% (4)	32% (7)	22
1891–1900	35% (9)	15% (4)	8% (2)	15% (4)	27% (7)	26
1901–1910	46% (6)	–	8% (1)	–	46% (6)	13
Totals	38% (45)	22% (26)	3% (4)	11% (13)	27% (32)	120

Note: * The date of birth of the father has been arbitrarily placed twenty-five years earlier than that of the respondent

In my own case, a great deal of basic historical reconstruction was necessary because of lack of satisfactory documentary evidence on even such basic information as earnings. It was essential to reconstruct in detail the working practices – control of recruitment, crew autonomy, and so on in order to understand how the occupational values affected industrial and social attitudes and perceptions.

Oral accounts from those who experienced the specific situation provide unsurpassed and irreplaceable evidence for actual behaviour. I am also convinced that there are enormous advantages to be gained if these accounts are as fully biographical as is practicable. For instance, an understanding of the socio-industrial values of the fishermen was greatly enhanced by access to their earlier lives. Many were recruited from the rural hinterland of the fishing ports, and their experience of the material and social conditions of the countryside helps to explain their response to new circumstances. Nevertheless, the problem at the heart of using the interview method in history still remains that of moving from the individual account to a social interpretation.

Notes

1   L. Passerini, 'Work, ideology and consensus under Italian fascism', *History Workshop*, 1979, no. 8.
2   'Editorial', *History Workshop*, 1979, no. 8.
3   For a fuller account of this project see P. Thompson, *The Voice of the Past: Oral History*, Oxford: Oxford University Press, 1978.
4   These tables and many others can be found in Social Science Research Council Final Report, HR 2656/1 by T. Lummis and P. Thompson. Those used here are largely self-explanatory. In Table I(E) the categories refer to three separate types of fishing which imposed distinct work routines, and therefore affected the level of contact with family and community. Non-fishermen were largely manual workers. Table I(D) refers to the status groups in only two of the categories since the distinctions were not present in the other two.
5   Note that this is not statistical significance. Because of the unknown bias of mortality and so forth, no oral history sample can be a random sample. What is attempted here is the customary process of historical analysis based on the available evidence.

Chapter 21

Linda Shopes

ORAL HISTORY AND THE STUDY OF COMMUNITIES
Problems, paradoxes, and possibilities

There are now vast sets of oral history interviews available in archives throughout the world and researchers increasingly recognize the value of such collections for 'secondary analysis'. Here Linda Shopes discusses how to find and use interview collections relevant to the study of communities. She urges researchers to immerse themselves in the interviews – and to heed the aural recordings as well as the written transcript – so that they can begin to uncover patterns and develop social or historical generalizations. Linda Shopes is a historian at the Pennsylvania Historical and Museum Commission. Reprinted with permission from *The Journal of American History*, 2002, vol. 89, no. 2, pp. 588–598. Copyright © Organization of American Historians (www.oah.org/).

Definitions and delimitations

'COMMUNITY ORAL HISTORY' is a protean term, invoked by scholars and grass-roots historians alike to describe a variety of practices developed for a variety of purposes. The term 'community' itself is vague and conceptually limited, with generally positive associations and not entirely deliberate implications of commonality and comity. A community oral history project typically refers to one defined by locale, to a group of interviews with people who live in some geographically bounded place, whether an urban ethnic neighborhood, a southern mill village, or a region of midwestern farms. Yet 'community' also refers to a shared social identity, and so we speak of interviews with members of the gay community, the black community, the medical community. In fact, many community oral history projects combine the two meanings of the term, focusing on a particular group's experience in a particular place – steelworkers in Buffalo, Chicanos in El Paso, jazz musicians in Los Angeles.

Distinctions exist among broad genres of oral history. One axis of difference is defined by the provenance of interviews: at one end, there are interviewing projects developed by grass-roots groups to document their own experience; at the other, interviews conducted by scholars to inform their own research or to create a permanent archival collection for future scholarly work. In practice, most oral history projects fall somewhere between the two poles: historical society volunteers develop a project to document some aspect of local life in collaboration with the local college; a scholar, working on his own research project, makes contact with the retirees' group of a union local as a means of entrée for interviews he wishes to conduct about the union's history and along the way agrees to participate in a union educational program.

The second axis is defined by voice, that is, the extent to which the narrator's voice or the historian/interpreter's voice dominates the final product of the interviews. At one end are archival collections of interviews that are almost entirely in the narrators' voices; at the other are scholarly monographs in which the historian incorporates interviews along with other sources into his interpretation of the past. In fact, most oral history projects fall somewhere along this spectrum of possibilities.[1] Thus a filmmaker can produce a film about a community's experience using testimony from participants, contemporary accounts, and scholarly 'talking heads' in various proportions; an author can organize evidence from interviews in multiple ways to construct a historical argument; a museum exhibition about a neighborhood can use short quotations from interviews as label text or play extended excerpts from the actual audio- or videotapes.

The multiple ways voice gets rendered in community oral history projects open up a range of interpretive questions. The intersection of voice and provenance further complicates matters – my point here is simply to map the terrain over which this essay roams. In the following discussion, I will address both practical and interpretive issues involved in using oral history to study communities, considering first the use of extant interviews and second the conduct of one's own interviews.

Using extant interview collections

No comprehensive survey of extant oral history collections exists – the enormous number of collections, their diverse points of origin, and the rapidity with which new projects develop render this a futile exercise. While more specialized finding aids exist, the best tool for identifying interview collections relevant to a particular community study is the World Wide Web. A broadly defined search can easily turn up thousands of references: a quick review of those will generally identify the largest, most important collections; a more systematic review can often turn up more localized or idiosyncratic groups of interviews.[2]

What a Web search will *not* identify are interviews done by a scholar for his own research and retained in his possession or interviews done by local groups that may not have the resources or the know-how to develop even modest electronic finding aids – or even the awareness that the interviews may interest anyone outside their own communities. The former can sometimes be identified in the footnotes and bibliographies of published work on the topic at hand. The latter are more difficult to locate, but as essentially virgin sources of local knowledge, they may be well worth the effort to do so. One may find such collections through personal contact: local librarians, archivists at local historical societies, oral history specialists at state and regional historical organizations, and project directors of major topical collections frequently know of oral history collections that, having never been properly archived or cataloged, have never been used by scholars. Another means of locating collections is a query to H-Oralhist, the H-Net-affiliated listserv maintained by the Oral History Association; its more than thirteen hundred subscribers constitute a collective storehouse of useful leads and contacts. H-Oralhist's Web site is also a useful gateway to numerous collections.[3]

Having identified a cache of community interviews, how might the historian approach them, with what sorts of questions in mind? What might one expect to find? What strengths and weaknesses are typical of such interviews? To understand it is important to understand their provenance. Who conducted them, when, for what purpose, under what circumstances? What broad assumptions and specific questions informed the inquiry? Answers to those questions may lie in a project's administrative records, including the schedule of questions developed for the interviews, biographical data amassed for both interviewers and interviewees, and the interviewers' research and interview notes. They can also be teased out of descriptive, promotional, and published materials issuing from the project. Placing extant interviews in the intellectual and social context of their generation allows the researcher to read them more astutely, to understand how the context unavoidably shaped the inquiry.

For example, some twenty years ago I was involved in a community documentation project in Baltimore, Maryland, that attempted to assert the viability of blue-collar urban neighborhoods against a host of contemporary threats. The goal was worthy, but in our eagerness to identify the social networks and institutional ties that held the communities we were documenting together, we interviewed few former residents, and when we did, we shied away from questions about why they moved away, about what they found unsatisfactory about the neighborhood. Nor did we interview those whose actions directly or indirectly threatened neighborhoods' viability: business people and employers who had relocated, directors of lending institutions, developers. Not surprisingly, our inquiry proved our point; it was also intellectually impoverished by our failures of historical imagination.[4]

In fact, locally generated oral history interviews frequently rest on naïve assumptions about what properly constitutes history and how to approach it. Interviews are typically structured around the life histories of individual narrators, rather than around critical questions about broad themes of social life that cut across individuals' experience. Questions probe the details of everyday life and the peculiarities of place; answers are replete with stories about ritual events and local characters and endless information about 'what was where when'. In such projects there is often little understanding of how the details might add up, little obvious coherence within a group of interviews, little understanding, in the end, of history as anything more than an accumulation of facts. A celebratory impulse also inflects many community interviews, both those that fall within what might be termed the 'genteel tradition,' which views the past as a benign refuge from the unsettling present, and those akin to interviews conducted for the Baltimore project, motivated by the activist, history-from-the-bottom-up impulse of 1970s social history. The causes of this are manifold and reflect the deeply social nature of oral historical inquiry: a community insider, interviewing a peer, does not want to risk disturbing an ongoing, comfortable social relationship by asking difficult or challenging questions; a community-based history project is part of an initiative to encourage economic development, and interviews become a means of putting the community's best face forward; a project seeking to affirm a group that has been socially marginalized decides that it would be disrespectful to air problematic or unsavory aspects of the community's history that reinforce stereotypes. Even when interviews probe difficult aspects of personal or social history, the impulse is to celebrate the interviewee's ability to prevail over or survive difficult circumstances, not an especially surprising tendency, given how deeply this trope is embedded in our national culture.[5]

Interviews conducted for scholarly projects, though less likely to succumb to the celebratory and ahistorical tendencies of community-driven projects, are not without their limitations. Typically, interviews with a scholarly provenance are narrowly focused inquiries, shaped by the investigator's very specific research questions. Unrelated areas of inquiry about which the narrator could nonetheless speak in an informed way are not pursued; hints of a more interesting story underneath the story are ignored.[6] More subtly, scholarly interviewers, interested in details and anecdotes that support or illustrate their understanding of the subject at hand, at times fail to perceive that their own frames of reference may be incongruent with the narrators' and so ignore lines of inquiry that could get at the insider's view. Thus interviews conducted by scholars for their own work are frequently of limited value to other researchers with other research agendas. Nonetheless, prior knowledge of the intellectual agenda driving the interviews can help subsequent users assess their strengths and weaknesses.

Given the limits of both community-based oral history collections and interviews conducted by scholars for their own work, the most useful extant interviews for historians researching a community are likely to be those conducted under the auspices of ongoing oral history research programs as archival projects for the use of future researchers or by professionally run historical organizations as documentation projects. While it is important to assess such interviews in light of their provenance, their strengths are often considerable: typically they are framed around questions drawn from contemporary historiography and include multiple narrators, variously positioned within the community; they tend to range widely over individual narrators' life experiences so as to be of value to users with varying interests; they are generally the work of skilled interviewers who are knowledgeable about the subject at hand and unconstrained by the rules of polite conversation from asking hard questions about it.[7]

Whatever the provenance of the interviews one has identified and whatever their limits, the next step for the historian who wants to draw upon the evidence of oral history is to immerse herself or himself in the interviews themselves. It is a mistake to rely solely on visually skimming or electronically searching transcripts for a sense of what interviews contain or for specific information and useful quotes. Regrettably, transcripts are all too often inaccurate: some omit sections of an interview, others add material that is not there, yet others include significant errors. Moreover, information conveyed orally by tone, pacing, and inflection is lost when spoken words are translated into writing. So although researchers will understandably continue to rely heavily on transcriptions, it is important periodically to listen to the original tapes. A body of community interviews yields its riches only to a researcher with the patience for extensive, careful engagement with both transcripts and tapes. Because narrators generally speak about typicalities and common lifeways, the insights gleaned from interviews are cumulative, obvious only after one has absorbed hours of talk. They also often lie below the surface of the words, and it takes time to get at them. Any given interview can offer specific details and colorful anecdotes for a community study; a body of interviews, thoughtfully considered, can open up an understanding of the local culture, those underlying beliefs and habits of mind, those artifacts of memory that propel individual lives, give coherence to individual stories, and perhaps extend outward to a larger significance.

Let me give a couple of examples, based on my review of dozens of interviews conducted as local history projects throughout Pennsylvania, some generated by grassroots groups, others with more scholarly origins. Working my way through a stack of tapes and transcripts, I began to realize how consistently narrators formulated their stories of the past in relation to specific places. Memories, it seemed, were rooted in places; interviews were replete with references to streams, hills, homes, streets, stores, churches, theaters, farms. In some interviews, local history was defined almost entirely by specific places, quite independently of interviewers' questions. One narrator, for example, when asked at the end of the interview to identify 'three of your most memorable experiences in Hershey' (the community under discussion), responded by linking memories to specific places: marrying her husband at the First United Methodist Church, attending the ground breaking for the Hershey Medical Center, and attending events at the Hershey Theater. Recollections of specific places often led to a chain of human associations, again suggesting narrators' need to locate memories someplace. 'When we moved back home up the hill from the Bard farm, I was eight years old,' one narrator began. He continued:

> My mother raised turkeys. We used to carry them all the way from that hill, down across the old covered bridge to East Middletown and she sold them for eight cents a pound. . . . We'd cut back by Sam Seiders's farm and then we'd cut across old Ev Booser's farm in back of where Detweilers lived to the dam. . . . The Sam Demy farm later became Sam Seiders's farm and is now Simon Grubb's, Seiders's grandson's farm. Mrs Seiders had a retarded brother. When [Sam] Hess [her father] sold to old man Bard, there was a $2000 dowry set aside for this boy and the interest used for his keep. Sam Hess, before he died, had the stone house where Mart Seiders lived built for this boy. This was his home and the old mother's after the father died. When the mother died and he got worse, the relatives took turns with him and Matt bought his house.

Here information about a woman's contribution to the family economy, the transmission of property, and the care of the disabled in a turn-of-the-century community is embedded in a chain of associations about a specific piece of property.[8]

While the profound attachment to place revealed in these interviews is hardly unique to Pennsylvania, it is suggestive of broader themes in regional culture – the deep strand of conservatism, tending in some toward parochialism; the localism evidenced by the division of the state into more than five thousand separate jurisdictions; the difficulties bedeviling efforts at regional planning. Although the place consciousness of these interviews may simply be the artifact of their creation as local history projects – local history is de facto about some place – I submit that the nearly automatic equation of local history with locale suggests how deeply place matters in individual consciousness and that a shared sense of identity, a sense of community, often includes a shared set of spatial referents. More to my point here, only by working through many interviews did I come to this insight.

The same exercise alerted me to yet another dimension of local culture, one that gives hints of how memories of the past give meaning in the present. Not surprisingly, given the dominance of industry in Pennsylvania's economy in the past two centuries, many oral history projects in the state, though ostensibly about specific places – Homestead, Nanticoke, Pittsburgh – really are collections of life-history interviews with (predominantly white and male) industrial laborers in those communities. If there is a single theme running through the interviews, it is the importance of 'hard work' in the shaping of a person's life and identity. 'Our people . . . they're the ones who built the steel mills to what they are today!' the union activist Adam Janowski stated proudly and emphatically in a 1976 interview with the historian James Barrett for the Homestead Album Oral History Project. 'They took everything in stride, I'll tell you,' he continued. 'I seen them myself. I was a young man and I seen how hard those fellows used to work.' This observation is repeated in one way or another in interview after interview, and narrators' consciousness of 'our people,' in Janowski's words, as hardworking undoubtedly reflects the material conditions of their lives.[9]

Most of these interviews are utterly silent on issues of race, itself evidence of the way community has been conceived and talked about. Here Janowski is unusual, for he revealed an explicitly racial dimension to his understanding of 'our people,' whom he defined this way:

> After the [1919 steel] strike they wanted to lay [black strikebreakers] all off. At least they laid off ninety percent because the men was experienced in their jobs and the foremen could call the white man a goddamn hunky and tell him to get that goddamn thing moving! But they couldn't say that to a black man. He would pick up a bar and hit him over the head, you know? Our people took that all the time. They're the ones who built the steel mills.

Perhaps still bitter about black strikebreakers more than a half century later, undoubtedly mindful of the way 'his people' indeed 'took that all the time,' perhaps reading the black militance of the 1970s back a half century, Janowski suggested how white workers' sense of themselves as 'hardworking' is deeply racialized.[10]

Almost twenty years later, Theresa Pavlocak, an elderly resident of the anthracite coal region of eastern Pennsylvania, implied a similar connection between hard work and racial identity in an interview for the historian Thomas Dublin's study of deindustrialization in the region. She remembered the Great Depression this way: 'If you didn't have job in the colliery, the men had no work. So they had WPA [Works Progress Administration]. They worked on the roads. You didn't get welfare. We never got the welfare. We did it the hard way.' Further into the interview, she reflected on her generation's lifetime of labor: 'People were proud; they didn't want no welfare. Not like now; people look for it. In those days, people were proud; they didn't want it.' And toward the conclusion she commented on the success of her own and her friends' children and contrasted it with the situation of some newcomers, often a euphemistic way of referring to recent black and Latino migrants to the region:

> It seems like [our] children are all [moved] away from here and it's just a new generation coming in here – different people. We have quite a bit of welfare. There's a lot of new people moving in on welfare – in order to help them, for them to pay the rent. They get their rent and a few dollars, whatever they get. If they're happy on welfare, I guess they stay there. Most of them don't want to, though. No. Like all my friends' children, they're all educated or they're away, they all have good jobs. My son, he has a good job.[11]

Like Janowski, Pavlocak reveals an identity grounded in a generation of people who indeed worked hard and in a sense of difference from newcomers, who are sometimes not white and who presumably do not work as hard as they themselves did. For her, as Dublin has observed, the Works Progress Administration projects of the 1930s, as well as the Social Security and black lung compensation benefits (for coal miners disabled by years of inhaling coal dust) that have more recently sustained many older people in the region, are not forms of 'welfare'; nor is the difficulty of obtaining work in an era of deindustrialization understood as an explanation for newcomers' apparent lack of ambition.[12] If we take Janowski's and Pavlocak's ways of viewing the past as fairly typical of their race, generation, and class, their interviews suggest how identity and memory are implicated in contemporary racial politics. Perhaps to overstate my point: such insights, however modest, do not come from quickly scanning interview transcripts. Only slowly do underlying strands of a community's culture reveal themselves, as interview after interview sounds the same themes; only occasionally does an interview provide a flash of insight that enables us to read the culture outward and make connections with broader historical concerns.

Conducting one's own interviews

Perhaps, however, a search has turned up no interviews on the community under study or extant interviews do not adequately address the questions driving the inquiry. Perhaps the notion of engaging with people who have lived the history one is researching is intriguing; perhaps the broad theoretical questions about historical memory, narrative construction, and popular notions of history that underlie oral historical inquiry seem relevant to one's work. Perhaps too getting students involved in an oral history project seems to be a creative way of linking scholarship to teaching. For any of those reasons, a historian may want to undertake a community oral history project. My comments here are necessarily briefer than those in previous sections. There are numerous credible how-to guides to oral history, and anyone beginning an interviewing project should consult them.[13] Here, I wish to address two points: ways of structuring community interviews to avoid common problems and oral history as an occasion for public history.

Having noted the problematics of community as an organizing principle for an oral history project and the limitations of many interviews that adopt it as a frame

of reference, I offer the following suggestions for avoiding pitfalls. First, concep-
tualize a community history project around a historical problem or issue rather than
a series of life-history interviews. A community is formed around the intersections
of individual lives: what are the points of connection, tension, or alienation? What
historical problem defines the community, and how can this problem be explored
through questions to individual narrators? I find the latter question especially challenging, for how does one address an abstract concept or issue through the medium
of lived experience? Suppose, for example, the problem is suburbanization, the
development of a distinctly suburban community on top of what had previously
been farmland and woods. What questions can the interviewer ask that connect an
individual's experiences to the broad theme of suburbanization in ways the narrator
can understand and address meaningfully? How is an individual's experience part of
something bigger, and what sorts of questions make that connection, if not for the
interviewee, then for the researcher?

Second, define the universe of narrators broadly. Historians are generally sensitive to racial, ethnic, and gender diversity, and one would expect a group of
interviewees to reflect this sensitivity. But who else may have a meaningful connection to the problem at hand? We tend to interview insiders and people with
a long-term relationship with a community. But what about outsiders and newcomers? What about people external to the community whose actions impinge on
it? Ask: whom am I missing? Using the example of suburbanization, it might be
appropriate to interview different cohorts of residents, that is, people who moved
in at different times; those who moved away from the area as well as those who
lived there before it became a suburb, those whose decisions led to the develop
ment of the suburb, including local officials, developers, and bankers. Including a
range of narrators simultaneously deepens the inquiry and extends it outward,
helping us understand both the internal complexity of the community under study
and its relationship to a broader historical process.

Third, approach interviews in a spirit of critical inquiry. In part this means
asking the hard questions that may cause discomfort, that address difficult or controversial topics that may reveal ruptures in the community. More generally, it means
defining an interview as a mutual exploration of the problem at hand, an opportunity for an informed interviewer to talk in depth with a knowledgeable participant
about a subject of mutual interest. In an investigation of suburbanization, it may
mean asking questions about money, mortgages, and taxes; expectations and values;
achievements and disappointments; racial segregation or exclusion; gender dynamics;
social divisions within the community. The conversation may not be easy, but the
result may well be to foster a more nuanced and humane understanding of the way
individuals live in history – which is what oral history does best.[14]

Finally, an oral history-based community study can quite logically become an
occasion for public history, understood broadly as doing serious history for and with
nonspecialists outside an academic setting. Insofar as an oral history interview
requires formal engagement with a person who typically lies outside the scholarly
world about matters that are nonetheless historical, oral history is de facto a kind
of public history. And insofar as an oral history research project involves more
than one narrator, there are built-in opportunities to expand the conversation
outward, into a public discussion about history. This can take the form of a modest
public program or history workshop, in which several narrators talk with scholar-

interviewers about broad interpretive questions, or more extensive projects such as museum exhibitions, radio and film documentaries, and community publications in which those interpretations are presented to others. Two strong caveats, however. First, oral history is long-haul work. Making contact with community representatives, gaining entrée, cultivating trust, and then doing, analyzing, and presenting a body of interviews cannot be accomplished in one or even two semesters. It requires a commitment of years. Second, working with a community group to develop a public history project or program is complicated and at times contentious. Although oral history provides outstanding opportunities to democratize the practice of history – to 'share authority,' in Michael Frisch's resonant phrase – as interviewer and interviewee, scholar and community work together to understand the past, in practice the process requires negotiation, give-and-take, and considerable goodwill.[15] Scholars do not get to exercise critical judgment quite so forcefully or conform to current historiographic thinking quite so deftly; laypeople do not get to romanticize the past quite so easily. Scholars can learn that local people often have thoughtful if haltingly articulated understandings of how change happens; laypeople can learn how what is local has links to national and international developments. While there are fine examples of the process working well, at times negotiated history can be unsatisfactory to all parties – too critical and de-localized for community members, too uncritical and narrow for scholars. The tension points to a deeper issue: the essential disjunction between professional history and history as it is popularly understood. While it may at times be necessary to decline participation in a community project on principled grounds, it is precisely the opportunity such projects provide for opening up dialogue with the public about the nature of historical inquiry that, to my way of thinking, makes them eminently worth doing.[16]

Notes

1   On ways oral history has been presented in written form, see Alessandro Portelli, *The Battle of Valle Giulia*: *Oral History and the Art of Dialogue*, Madison, 1997, 3–23.

2   It is important to distinguish between online finding aids for oral history collections and online transcripts of interviews. Many oral history collections are listed and described online, but the number of complete interview transcripts online remains small.

3   It is important to remind colleagues of their professional obligation 'to deposit their interviews in an archival repository that is capable of both preserving the interviews and making them available for general research'. See 'Statement on interviewing for Historical Documentation,' *American Historical Association*, www.theaha.org/pubs/standard.htm#Statement on Interviewing (June 10, 2002). To post a query or view the listing of oral history collections and projects, go to H-Oralhist, www2.h-ncz.msu.edu/-oralhist/ (June 10, 2002).

4   See Linda Shopes, 'Oral History and Community Involvement – The Baltimore Neighborhood Heritage Project', in *Presenting the Past*: *Essays on History and the Public*, (eds) Susan Porter Benson, Stephen Brier, and Roy Rosenzweig, Philadelphia, 1986, pp. 249–263.

5   On the limits of local oral history, see Linda Shopes, 'Oral History', in *Pennsylvania*: *A History of the Commonwealth*, (eds) Randall M. Miller and William Pencak, University Park and Harrisburg, 2002, pp. 549–570.

6   On the limits of interviews conducted for individual research projects, see Ronald J. Grele, 'Why Call It Oral History? Some Ruminations from the Field', *Pennsylvania History*, 60, October 1993, pp. 506–509.

7   Major repositories of community oral history collections include the Southern Oral History Program, University of North Carolina, Chapel Hill; Institute for Oral History, Baylor University, Waco, Tex.; Center for Documentary Studies, Duke University, Durham, N.C.; Center for the Study of History and Memory, Indiana University, Bloomington; T. Harry Williams Center for Oral History, Louisiana State University, Baton Rouge; Minnesota Historical Society, St Paul; Chicago Historical Society; Northeast Archives of Folklore and Oral History, University of Maine, Orono; Oral History Program, University of Alaska, Fairbanks; and South Dakota Oral History Center/Institute of American Indian Studies, University of South Dakota, Vermillion.

8   For the Hershey story, see Betty H. Baum interview by Monica Spiese, May 1, 1991, transcript, pp. 26–28, Hershey Community Archives Oral History Program (Hershey Community Archives, Hershey, Pa.). For the Seiders's farm story, see Clayton Heisey interview by Mrs Herbert Schaeffer, February 1, 1972, transcript, p. 6, Middletown Oral History Project (Middletown Public Library, Middletown, Pa.). There is a growing number of studies on the relationship between place consciousness and local identity. See Joseph A. Amato, *Rethinking Home: A Case for Writing Local History*, Berkeley, 2002; David Glassberg, *Sense of History: The Place of the Past in American Life*, Amherst, 2001; and Dolores Hayden, *The Power of Place: Urban Landscapes as Public History*, Cambridge, Mass., 1995.

9   Adam Janowski interview by James Barrett, June 14, 1976, transcript, p. 12, Homestead Album Oral History Project, Archives of Industrial Society, University of Pittsburgh, Pittsburgh, Pa.

10   Ibid.

11   Thomas Dublin, *When the Mines Closed: Stories of Struggles in Hard Times*, Ithaca, 1998, p. 208, p. 214, pp. 216–217.

12   For Dublin's commentary on the Pavlocak interview, see ibid., pp. 30–31.

13   Two of the best guides are Donald A. Ritchie, *Doing Oral History*, New York, 1994; and Valerie Raleigh Yow, *Recording Oral History: A Practical Guide for Social Scientists*, Thousand Oaks, 1994. See also Laurie Mercier and Madeline Buckindorf, *Using Oral History in Community History Projects*, Los Angeles, 1992; and Rose T. Diaz and Andrew B. Russell, 'Oral Historians: Community Oral History and the Cooperative Ideal', in *Public History. Essays from the Field*, (eds) James B. Gardner and Peter S. LaPaglia, Malabar, 1999, pp. 203–216.

14   For a thoughtful essay on the difficulties of doing local history, see Kathleen Norris, *Dakota: A Spiritual Geography*, New York, 1993, 79–88.

15   See Michael Frisch, *A Shared Authority: Essays on the Craft and Meaning of Oral and Public History*, Albany,1990.

16   On the development of community history in dialogue with communities, see Barbara Franco, 'Doing History in Public: Balancing Historical Fact with Public Meaning', *Perspectives*, 33, May 1995, pp. 5–8; and John Kuo Wei Tchen, 'Creating a Dialogic Museum: The Chinatown History Museum Experiment', in *Museums and Communities: The Politics of Public Culture*, (eds) Ivan Karp, Christine Mullen Kreamer, and Steven D. Lavine, Washington, 1992, pp. 285–326.

Chapter 22

Elizabeth Lapovsky Kennedy

TELLING TALES
Oral history and the construction of pre-Stonewall lesbian history

In recent years narrative studies has emerged as a buoyant field of inter-disciplinary research with particular relevance to oral history. Here Elizabeth Lapovsky Kennedy analyses the exquisite style and structure of storytelling by working-class lesbians in New York State and argues that 'there is a tremendous amount to be learned by fully exploring the subjective and oral nature of oral histories'. Elizabeth Lapovsky Kennedy is the Head of Women's Studies at the University of Arizona. Reprinted from *Radical History Review*, 1995, no. 62, pp. 58–79. © 1995 MARHO: The Radical Historians' Organization, Inc. All rights reserved. Used by permission of the publisher.

O RAL HISTORY HAS BEEN CENTRAL in creating knowledge about lesbian and gay male life before Stonewall. This is particularly true for working-class lesbians whose oppression as women and as lesbians, combined with race and class oppression, has made it unlikely that they leave many written records. However, even upper-class women, unless they were inclined to the literary world, were not likely to leave documents about their lesbianism.[1] Despite the prominence of oral testimony in lesbian and gay history, there has been surprisingly little discussion of the problems and possibilities of the method. Most theoreticians of oral history have come to see the practice as revealing two different but complementary kinds of 'truth'. First, oral history adds new social facts to the historical record. Second, being based in memory, it explores subjectivity – an individual's interpretation of the past.[2] In my own work I have tried to embrace and pursue both kinds of 'truth'. But I have been hampered by the fact that the tradition of gay and lesbian oral history has thought much more about the former, what I will call for want of a better term the 'empirical', than the latter, and has not fully considered the interconnections between the two.

The 'empirical' concerns of lesbian and gay oral history emerged from the desire to document and legitimize lesbian and gay history at a time when most people thought no such thing existed. The spirit of the early gay and lesbian history projects, such as the Lesbian Herstory Archives in New York City, the Buffalo Women's History Project, and the San Francisco Lesbian and Gay History Project, was to grab a tape recorder and go out and record the memories of our elders before they were lost. The urgency with which lesbians and gays went in search of their history, first in grass roots community projects and later in the academy, to reclaim a history before its bearers died, encouraged a focus on dates, places, names, and events. Furthermore, the fervent desire to legitimize their findings, and therefore gay and lesbian history, encouraged a downplaying of the oral and subjective nature of the life stories that were collected. At that time, 'serious' history emphasized object-ivity and viewed first-person narratives with suspicion. But this kind of defensiveness is no longer necessary. Most social historians have transcended the polarization between the reliability of social facts derived from written sources – letters, news-paper accounts, court records – and those from oral sources. They have come to understand that many newspaper accounts are based on interviews and recollec-tions, and that letters and diaries are first-person accounts. Furthermore, postmodern thinking has questioned the objectivity of historical accounts, revealing the partiality of all sources. In fact, today in gay and lesbian studies it is 'empirical' work that is on the defensive.

In the past fifteen years the most forward-looking oral historians have come to understand the subjectivity and orality of their sources as a strength rather than a weakness.[3] They have explored how oral testimony – the actual storytelling – conveys unique information and how the subjective – what the past means to a particular individual – adds new dimensions to history. They have also emphasized the interactive process between the historian and interviewee in constructing the interpretation, and have considered the political uses of their work. These kinds of exploration are very appropriate for gay and lesbian history. Not being born and raised in a public lesbian and gay culture, each gay and lesbian person has to construct his or her own life in oppressive contexts, a process that oral history is uniquely suited to reveal. Furthermore, the celebration of the twenty-fifth anniver-sary of Stonewall, which occasioned the writing of this article, has accelerated the formation of powerful cultural myths about the place of Stonewall in gay life. Self-consciousness about how research methodologies contribute to this process is very timely.

This article argues that while gay and lesbian historians need to continue the 'empirical' uses of oral history – of adding social facts to the historical record, and of analyzing how social institutions change – we also need to expand our under-standing of what can be learned from oral sources. First, I will consider how close examination of storytelling styles can reveal information about cultural and class differences among lesbians. Second, I will explore how we can learn more about the meaning of lesbian identity by embracing the subjective. Third, I will discuss the cultural uses of memory in interpreting the gay and lesbian past. And finally, I will examine the constructed nature of oral histories, focusing in particular on how the myths of Stonewall both expand and limit historical research. Together these considerations add new dimensions to the writing of gay and lesbian history and help to clarify the meaning of Stonewall.

Letting the style of storytelling be evidence in its own right

My own experience working with the oral histories for *Boots of Leather, Slippers of Gold* was that black and white working-class lesbians were exquisite storytellers. The life stories we collected for the most part were breathtakingly beautiful documents of survival and resistance in very difficult situations. At first my proletarian bias led me to assume that this was because most of the interviews were with working-class lesbians. As active agents in shaping a public lesbian community and identity, working-class lesbians were conscious about their place in history and therefore highly articulate. But as more and more oral histories of middle- and/or upper-class lesbians have been published, as in *Inventing Ourselves*: *Lesbian Life Stories* or *Cherry Grove, Fire Island*, I have had to revise this perspective.[4] Despite their commitment to a life of discretion and privacy, many upper-class women also tell compelling stories. It seems that a significant number of lesbians are good storytellers, no matter their class or cultural group.

Audre Lorde's *Zami*: *A New Spelling of My Name*, which the author describes as a biomythography, provides some clue as to why this should be.[5] Although Lorde is writing about a black working-class experience, her insights seem applicable to many lesbians. Because the majority of lesbians grow up in a heterosexual culture, they have no guidelines and no patterns for creating a homosexual life.[6] They, therefore, are constantly creating their lives, developing a biomythography, so to speak. Lesbians who are completely private are no exceptions; they cannot passively accept the traditional structure of a woman's life; they must create their own guidelines for living, and therefore actively engage the process of storytelling.

Because storytelling plays a prominent role in lesbian life, we can scrutinize the style of lesbian stories for what it tells us about the culture of the narrator. Do styles differ significantly and can they provide a new window into class, racial-ethnic, and regional variations in lesbian oppression and resistance? In *Boots of Leather, Slippers of Gold* we marshal all kinds of evidence to make our points, but we never use this sort of analysis of the structure and style of storytelling. To my knowledge I cannot think of any other lesbian and gay oral historians that do so. It seems an appropriate time to open up this new direction of analysis.

Buffalo working-class lesbians who were 'out' in the 1940s and 1950s tell the story of their finding, building, and enjoying lesbian community with excitement and humor. The structure of their stories conveys their connection to audience and community. For example, Arlette, a black fem, remembers how she was intrigued by mannish-looking women the first time she saw them on the street:

> The first time I saw really gay women, mannish-looking women was here in Buffalo, New York. And I didn't know what they were. I really thought that they were men. . . . The first gay lady I saw here . . . to me she was fascinating. I kept looking at her, and I said, 'That's a good-looking guy, but it's a funny-looking guy . . . .' I couldn't never tell if she was a man or a woman 'cause I never got close enough to her, but there was one strange thing, she would have on lipstick. I said, 'This woman's different.' She's got on men's clothes, her hair was very nice, cut short. She treated a lady like a gentleman would with a lady out, but I said, 'Is that a man or a woman?' So I made it a point to get close

enough to hear her voice, 'cause I knew if I could hear her talking I could tell. Then I found out, this is a woman. And I said, 'Golly, got on men's clothes and everything, what kind of women are these?' Then I started seeing more women here dressed in men's attire. I said, 'Well, golly, these are funny women.' Then they kind of fascinated me. What could they possibly do? Everybody wants to know what can you do. I got curious and I said, 'I'm going to find out.'

This small fragment is like a dance of anticipation and curiosity. It captures many of the significant ingredients of black working-class lesbian life: the drive toward and excitement of finding lesbians, the importance of the appearance of studs for creating lesbian visibility, the daring of fems who sought out studs. Most importantly for this analysis, the storyteller makes herself an active participant in the process of discovery of community, telling us explicitly what she said and thought. It also conveys a connection to a wider audience, 'everybody', and the humor is based on the public's curiosity about lesbians. [. . .]

As we listened to and worked with these oral narratives, we realized that these stories were not told for the first time to us, the oral historians, but that they had been shared before with friends at parties and in bars. Sometimes we inadvertently repeated questions to a narrator after several years had elapsed, and we would hear remarkably similar stories, embellished with similar details. This made sense to us because working-class lesbians spent a lot of time socializing together in explicitly lesbian space. Their lives were defined by finding and supporting other lesbians in a hostile environment and by developing strategies to live with some dignity and pride. What better way to accomplish this than by sharing stories about these successes and defeats. Essentially we were tapping into an oral tradition that supported lesbians, allowing them to survive in a hostile environment, very much like the oral tradition of African Americans in the South or industrial workers in Italy.

The content and style of these stories are radically different from those of middle-class lesbians of an earlier time period, who not only did not announce their lesbianism to the world, but also never talked about being lesbians with each other. They therefore never shared stories about lesbian life and community. This tendency can be seen in the life story of Julia Reinstein, an eighty-eight-year-old woman, who lived as a lesbian from 1928 to 1942 in South Dakota and rural western New York. During this time Julia's status as a successful teacher – not her lesbianism – defined her public identity. Nevertheless, she had an active lesbian sexual life, and once she settled down with a partner, she developed a small intimate circle of lesbian friends. The recurrent refrain throughout her story is 'It just wasn't talked about.' [. . .] The silence about lesbianism didn't diminish Julia's ability to construct an interesting and compelling life story, but her stories lack the dramatic flair characteristic of working-class lesbian stories. They have not been fine-tuned over a lifetime or used to engage an interested audience in the comedy and tragedy of being lesbian. Julia's stories were not told at the time the events took place; they have only come to be told recently as the contemporary lesbian community began to seek out the stories of its elders and also as Julia prepared to tell these stories to her daughter. They were not part of bringing lesbianism into the public world, but rather reflect the crafting of a private world where lesbianism could flourish.

The contrast between Julia's storytelling style and that of Arlette [. . .] illuminates the nature of class relations in pre-Stonewall lesbian communities. It provides yet a different kind of evidence for the argument that working-class lesbians took leadership in developing a public community in ways that middle-class lesbians did not. The humor, agency, and community that are part of the fabric of working-class lesbian stories help to confirm the analysis that working-class lesbians were key in laying the groundwork for the Stonewall rebellion and for the gay liberation movement. Furthermore, by looking at the style of storytelling, the reader comes to see precisely how working-class lesbians took leadership: not merely 'what they did', but how, through the sharing of stories, they created a unique community and culture.[7]

Taking advantage of first-person narratives to gain new insights about lesbian identity: being out or being discrete

In her work on Italian fascism, Luisa Passerini argues that oral history adds a critical dimension to the study of fascism.[8] Because of the uniquely subjective nature of life stories, she contends, oral histories provide a way to learn about an individual's struggle with the authority of fascism. What makes some individuals conform to the arbitrary power of the state while others resist it? How do individuals construct strategies of resistance? Passerini views these as some of the most important questions in history. Her questions about fascism strike me as parallel to questions in lesbian and gay history about how individuals cope with and resist heterosexism and homophobia. How do individuals decide to construct and express their identities?

In the mythology of gay and lesbian history, before Stonewall gays lived furtive, closeted, miserable lives, while after Stonewall gays could be free and open. Stonewall is quintessentially about being out of the closet, about fighting back, about refusing to be mistreated any more. However, the rich subjectivity expressed in personal narratives of lesbians and gay men expands our understanding of the construction of identity, problematizing the concepts of 'hidden' and 'out' and making the division between them less rigid.

In Buffalo, black and white working-class lesbians during the 1940s and 1950s – and I hesitate to extend this generalization to gay men – took leadership in being out. One of the central tensions in lesbian bar life was between those who were more out, more public, and those who were more discrete. Being out was expressed through butch-fem roles, or by appearing in public as a butch or as part of a butch-fem couple. In *Boots of Leather, Slippers of Gold* we were able to document that between the 1930s and 1950s working-class butches and fems became bolder, took more risks, and actively developed a sense of community and consciousness of kind. Lesbians of the 1940s gathered together on weekends and built a public social life; rough-and-tough lesbians of the 1950s pushed this assertiveness and openness to the point where they wore their men's clothes as much as possible, went out to socialize every day of the week, and fought back when needed. This visibility, however, was not in and of itself liberating because, in the anti-gay climate of the times, it entailed embracing the terrible stigma of being 'queer', of being a 'dyke'. Before the 1970s, lesbian and gay life was based on an insoluble paradox. For most lesbians and gay men, to be out to the public entailed being engulfed by stigma and, therefore, isolated from sustained and meaningful relationships with other than a small group of similarly stigmatized people.

Life stories of the working-class women who were leaders in creating and defending lesbian community express this contradiction: the freedom that comes from socializing with your own kind and pursuing your romantic attractions is always shaped by the pain of being a complete social outcast. The life story of Sandy, whose leadership was undisputed in the 1950s, is riddled with bitterness as a legacy of her struggle to build a lesbian life. The other side of the fun of being with her lovers and friends [. . .] is a feeling that her life has amounted to nothing because of who she is.

> You know it pisses you off, because like today, everything is so open and accepted and equal. Women, everyone goes to where they wear slacks, and I could just kick myself in the ass, because all the opportunities I had that I had to let go because of my way. That if I was able to dress the way I wanted and everything like that I, Christ, I'd have it made, really. Makes you sick. And you look at the young people today that are gay and they're financially well-off, they got tremendous jobs, something that we couldn't take advantage of, couldn't have it. It leaves you with a lot of bitterness too. I don't go around to the gay bars much any more. It's not jealousy, it's bitterness. And I see these young people, doesn't matter which way they go, whatever the mood suits them, got tremendous jobs, and you just look at them, you know, they're happy kids, no problems. You say 'God damn it, why couldn't I have that?' And you actually get bitter, you don't even want to know them. I don't anyway. 'Cause I don't want to hear about it, don't tell me about your success. Like we were talking about archives, you know where mine is, scratched on a shit-house wall, that's where it is. And all the dives in Buffalo that are still standing with my name. That's all, that's all I got to show.

The oral histories from working-class lesbians who were much more cautious than Sandy in the 1940s and the 1950s – that is, they did not always wear men's clothes and were not always willing to physically fight men who insulted them – convey less self-hate and bitterness. Also, those women whose families accepted their gayness did not seem to have as much self-hate and bitterness. Sandy's parents had been divorced when she was young, and she had no relationship with her father and a very difficult relationship with her step-father. Her relationship with her mother was also tense, with little communication and understanding. In contrast, Marty, who came out explicitly to her parents and involved them in her life, seems to have internalized no stigma about being gay. She was unambivalently ebullient about gay life, despite the fact that she has been the subject of many insults and fights due to her appearance and her work as a bartender in a gay bar. Her lovers and friends regularly came to her parents' house for Sunday dinner, and she discussed aspects of her life with her mother, including her relationships. The only time Marty was concerned about discretion was in relation to her family. She avoided activity that would cause her parents unnecessary trouble with their neighbors or their extended families. This evidence suggests that the connection we, the children of Stonewall, make between happiness, freedom, and being out is much too simplistic. [. . .]

These life stories from lesbians in western New York challenge the simple equations of discretion and secrecy with furtiveness, despair, and self-hate, and of openness with liberation and happiness. They suggest that class relations and social position played a very important role in shaping whether discretion was restricting and painful for lesbians in the mid-twentieth century. At least for some upper-class women, being discrete allowed them to live multifaceted lives as teachers and respected citizens and as lesbians. Their families continued to protect their reputations as upstanding members of the community. The severe restrictions on the behavior of all upper-class women made the requirements of discretion unremarkable. In contrast, once working-class women gave up the protection of a marriage, they had little promise of reward – financial stability or community respect – for accepting the social restrictions of discretion. Coming out gave them the excitement of associating with others of their own kind, the ability to find partners when a relationship broke up, and pride in who they were. But the virulently antigay climate of the 1940s, 1950s and 1960s meant that for many their lives could not be multifaceted, but had to be marked first and foremost by the stigma of being 'queer', 'butch', or 'gay'.

These life stories also suggest that the distinction between open and secret needs to be refined to indicate the context in which it occurred – that is, to clarify to whom one was open or hidden – and to specify relationships between parents and children. Although Julia [Reinstein] defines herself as completely discrete, her parents were, in fact, fully aware of her relationships with women and were part of a system of discretion that protected her. Although Marty sees herself as completely open and proud of her life during the 1950s, even with her parents, she felt compelled to be discrete in aspects of her life that would affect her family. She was careful not to do things that would embarrass them with their neighbors or other members of the extended family. Although Sandy was completely open in her daily life, never backing down from an occasion to defend herself as a lesbian, she never fully shared her lesbianism with her family, who she felt would not accept it. These life stories suggest the chillingly simple proposition that when daughters were accepted by their families, as in the case of Marty and Julia, their lives were whole and productive, no matter whether they were discrete or open. [. . .]

Understanding memory as a cultural phenomenon

Recent theorists of oral history analyze memory as a part of culture in ways that might be extremely useful for gay and lesbian historians. For example Alessandro Portelli's analysis of oral histories of workers in Terni, an industrial town in northern Italy, vividly shows that oral histories can contribute much more than new information about dates, places, and events.[9] The workers' stories about the murder of Luigi Trastulli – a twenty-one-year-old steel worker – by police varied as to the date; some dated it in 1949, which in fact is the correct date, while many others dated it 1953, at the same time as a mass strike. This inconsistency could be taken to show the unreliability of oral history and the faultiness of memory. Portelli suggests otherwise. Although the stories in this case do not help in ascertaining dates, which can be obtained from other sources, they do relay information about how workers think about their lives and the value they give to dignity and pride. Portelli argues that many people had moved the date to 1953 because in their minds the mass strikes of that time avenged the death of Trastulli. It was too painful to consider that a fellow worker did not die for a major cause, and that his death had not been revenged. Thus oral histories, if sensitively used, can provide a window into how individuals understand and interpret their lives.

This kind of interpretation is essential for gay and lesbian oral history. In writing *Boots of Leather, Slippers of Gold*, which is based on oral histories with forty-five narrators, we came upon many cases where narrators' memories were internally contradictory or conflicted with one another. An example that was significant for the development of our analysis involved disagreement about the quality of bar life. For some narrators, time in the bar was the best of fun, for some it was depressing, and for others it was both. We came to understand that these contradictory memories conveyed precisely the freedom and joy and the pain and limitation that characterized bar life in the mid-twentieth century.

Lesbian and gay history provides fertile ground for the scrutiny and interpretation of memory. For instance, in his book *Stonewall*, Martin Duberman questions whether a dyke started the Stonewall riots by swinging at the police when they ushered her into the paddy wagon, as reported in the *Village Voice*.[10] Some of Duberman's narrators are sure it was a dyke while others are adamantly sure it was not. An appeal to the validity of the written sources does not have much utility in this case because gays and lesbians know how frequently the press can be wrong. In trying to reconcile these different views, Duberman says, there were many things going on at once, and it was hard to know what actually started things off. In fact, Duberman records a variety of views as to what started the riot.

Another way to use the information of the disputed nature of the Stonewall story is to consider what this disagreement tells us about the contested relationship between men and women in the gay community. The assignment of agency to women by participants in Stonewall is completely in keeping with women's role in the bar community. Lesbians were always known as 'trouble' and respected as good fighters. In the gay imagination, based on the experience of the 1950s and 1960s, it is highly likely that a woman would start swinging. Yet, at the same time, the denial of women as leaders in fighting back reverberates the dominant view of women in heterosexual society as passive with little skill in fighting. It also encapsulates the male-dominated atmosphere in the Stonewall Inn. Women, when there, were made invisible. One Buffalo lesbian who went sporadically to the Stonewall Inn and was in fact there on the night of the riots, but left to meet a blind date shortly before 11 p.m., remembers always being mistaken for a drag queen.[11] The conflicting memories about how the Stonewall riots started concisely express the ambiguous position of women in gay culture and capture the cultural process of making lesbians and women invisible in history.

Given that social constructionists have analyzed the formation of both gay and lesbian identities, there is surprisingly little research on the relationships of gay men and lesbians at any point in history.[12] What struck Davis and me in our research was how many women insisted that men and women got along perfectly in the past unlike today. As our research proceeded, we gathered evidence that suggested that these statements were ideological. Women and men socialized together on some occasions but not on others, and there was always an underlying tension between the men and women in public life, if not in personal relationships. In *Boots of Leather, Slippers of Gold*, we suggest that the narrators emphasized this harmony to highlight how different the situation was in the past, when there was no ideological commitment to differences between gay men and lesbians as there is today. But as I think more about memory and the constructed nature of lesbian and gay identity, I wonder if the narrators aren't affirming the unity of women and men that they saw as important for survival.

Constructing the interview and interpretation: the biases of the Stonewall metanarrative

Researching the Stonewall riot, like studying any major historical event, reveals both the possibilities and limitations of oral history. To do so we need oral histories to correct the historical record of life before and at the time of Stonewall; we also need to be fully aware of how the myth of Stonewall, as the central event of twentieth-century gay and lesbian history, constructs the nature of the oral histories we collect and the interpretations we derive from them.

Unquestionably, Stonewall is a key moment for lesbian and gay history. It did transform the lives of many gays and lesbians, and it also became the turning point for the rapid spread of a new kind of gay and lesbian politics and movement. But the history is more complicated than that, and oral history has begun to indicate this. Oral histories show that working-class women, who were rendered invisible by the politics of Stonewall, made an active contribution to developing the sense of solidarity and pride that made Stonewall possible. And although Stonewall is quintessentially about being out, many working-class lesbian and gay men were out before Stonewall.

Such correctives to the historical record are extremely important and are unquestionably the strengths of oral history. But at the same time, oral histories have been shaped by the myths of Stonewall. Many scholars in empirical fields have come to question abstract standards of objectivity and to understand the constructed nature of interviews and their interpretation. The general orientation of contemporary anthropologists, feminists, and oral historians is to encourage reflexivity – that is, the conscious identification of the social position of the interviewer and interviewee – and to recognize that knowledge is the result of a dialogue between the two. In most situations, this involves an awareness of the power differentials, due to class and race privilege associated with most researchers. The implications of such an approach are immense, easily a subject for an entire article or book.[13] Here I will narrow my focus and suggest some of the ways in which the centrality of Stonewall in the iconography of most lesbian and gay researchers shapes or biases oral-history research.

By periodizing twentieth-century lesbian and gay life as pre- and post-Stonewall, we are creating a metanarrative, an overarching story, of lesbian and gay history, where we understand bar communities, resort communities and homophile organizations as laying the groundwork for the development of gay liberation politics. By definition, seeing Stonewall as a major turning point in gay and lesbian life commits researchers to a certain vision of gay and lesbian history, one that makes central the creation of a fixed, monolithic gay and lesbian identity, most often understood as white and male. A pernicious effect of this metanarrative of Stonewall is that it tends to camouflage women's voices and make racial/ethnic groups and cultures invisible.

To do an adequate job in revealing lesbian participation in pre-Stonewall life we need to combine homosexual and women's history.[14] Davis and I attempt this in *Boots of Leather, Slippers of Gold*, and although we were successful in placing lesbians at the center of the study, we were not able to escape telling lesbian history from the perspective of the development of a fixed lesbian identity. Rather we explicitly embraced this bias. We were interested in understanding the ways in which lesbian bar communities were predecessors to gay liberation. This beginning perspective was very useful because it allowed us to reveal the ways in which working-class lesbians built solidarity, developed a consciousness of kind, and expressed pride in being lesbian in the 1940s and 1950s. From this, we were able to argue that bar communities provided a tradition of being public to gay liberation and were also a fertile ground in which gay liberation could grow. For a lesbian to swing at the police, as was possibly done at Stonewall, was a mode of being in the world that Buffalo lesbians had already perfected. As important as this perspective was and is to our work, it also limited the work, skewing it towards the necessity of building a stable lesbian and gay identity. I am not so much concerned that work like ours is partial because all research is; rather I am interested in bringing to the fore the people whom the Stonewall myth excludes. A perfect example of the repercussion of our perspective was our unwillingness at the beginning of the research process to interview women who were no longer living as lesbians. We felt that people had to be gay 'through and through'. As a result we missed interviewing many woman who had been fems in the community of the 1940s and 1950s. Who else did our perspective exclude? *Boots of Leather, Slippers of Gold* is a history of survivors: those who were bold and brazen and could survive the stigma and the ugliness of oppression. Some women were no longer able to tell their stories, having been wasted by alcohol or sickness. Others never felt comfortable in the bar community due to the prominence of roles and/or working-class culture and wanted to forget it. When we located potential narrators and asked them to share their memories of lesbian community during the 1940s and 1950s, several people turned us down, expressing some variation of 'what [lesbian] community?' In their minds, the divisiveness outweighed the solidarity and had not allowed them to thrive.

The writings of lesbians of color in the last fifteen years have made amply clear that lesbians of color do not have one single identity, but rather multiple identities.[15] In the case of the African-American lesbians in Buffalo, they were part of the larger bar community, but they also maintained their own African-American house parties and bars. They cannot be considered, nor did they consider themselves, lesbians first and African-Americans or Native American second, or vice versa. Therefore a metanarrative that focuses on the formation of a unitary lesbian identity and politics might include African-American and Native American women, as *Boots of Leather, Slippers of Gold* did, but by definition communities of color cannot be the central focus. We need therefore to orient the interviews and open our interpretive frameworks to multiple centers of lesbian life and to ask fundamental questions about how these varied points interact rather than assume that they fit together in a linear history of Stonewall.

In arguing, as I have done throughout this article, that there is a tremendous amount to be learned by fully exploring the subjective and oral nature of oral histories, I have also suggested that the 'empirical' and 'subjective' should not be falsely polarized. They are fully complementary to one another. I am convinced that gay and lesbian oral history is at a point where, to grow, it needs to fully embrace the subjective and oral nature of its documents. By doing so its 'empirical' goals are not compromised but expanded.

Notes

1   [See] E. Newton, *Cherry Grove, Fire Island: Sixty Years in America's First Gay and Lesbian Town*, Boston: Beacon Press, 1993; E. Lapovsky Kennedy and M. Davis, *Boots of Leather, Slippers of Gold: The History of a Lesbian Community*, New York: Routledge, 1993.

2   For an eloquent statement of these two truths, see A. Portelli, 'Introduction', in *The Death of Luigi Trastulli and Other Stories: Form and Meaning in Oral History*, Albany: State University of New York Press, 1991, pp. vii–x.

3   See, for instance, L. Passerini, 'Italian working class culture between the wars', *International Journal of Oral History*, 1980, vol. 1, pp. 4–27; P. Thompson, *The Voice of the Past: Oral History*, 2nd edition, Oxford: Oxford University Press, 1988; M. Frisch, *A Shared Authority*, Albany: State University of New York Press, 1990; S. Berger Gluck and D. Patai (eds), *Women's Words: The Feminist Practice of Oral History*, New York: Routledge, 1991; and Portelli, *The Death of Luigi Trastulli*.

4   Hall Carpenter Archives, Lesbian Oral History Group, *Inventing Ourselves: Lesbian Life Stories*, New York: Routledge, 1989; Newton, *Cherry Grove, Fire Island*.

5   A. Lorde, *Zami, A New Spelling of My Name*, Trumansburg, N.Y.: The Crossing Press, 1982.

6   I am grateful to my colleague, Masani Alexis DeVeaux, for illuminating this point in one of her lectures to my gay and lesbian community seminar.

7   I am grateful to Molly McGarry's reader's report for emphasizing this point, and offering this sentence as a way of highlighting it.

8   Passerini, 'Italian working class culture between the wars'.

9   Portelli, *The Death of Luigi Trastulli*.

10 M. Duberman, *Stonewall*, New York: Penguin Dutton, 1993, pp. 197–198.

11 This information comes from a personal communication with Madeline Davis who has spoken directly with the lesbian who frequented the Stonewall Inn.

12 To my knowledge Marc Stein is the only person who has written on this topic. M. Stein, 'Sex politics in the city of sisterly and brotherly love', *Radical History Review*, Spring 1994, vol. 59, pp. 60–93. Esther Newton is also addressing this issue in her most recent work, as evidenced by her paper, 'Baking ziti at the coronation: homophobia, sexism and the subordinate status of lesbians in Cherry Grove', given at the 93rd Annual Meeting of the American Anthropological Association, 2 December 1994, Atlanta, Georgia.

13 And in fact there will be a new book on the subject. E. Lewin and W. Leap (eds), *Doing Lesbian and Gay Field Work, Writing Lesbian and Gay Ethnography*, Champaign/Urbana: University of Illinois Press, forthcoming, in which I have a paper.

14 [See] M. Cruickshank, *The Gay and Lesbian Liberation Movement*, New York: Routledge, Chapman and Hall, 1992; Newton, *Cherry Grove, Fire Island*.

15   See, for instance, C. Moraga and G. Anzaldua (eds), *This Bridge Called My Back*: *Writings by Radical Women of Color*, Watertown, Mass., Persephone Press, 1981; B. Smith (ed.), *Home Girls*: *A Black Feminist Anthology*, New York, Kitchen Table: Women of Color Press, 1983; A. Lorde, *Sister Outsider*: *Essays and Speeches*, Trumansberg, N.Y.: Crossing Press, 1984; and G. Anzaldua, *Borderlands*, *La Frontera*: *The New Mestiza*, San Francisco: Spinster's/Aunt Lute, 1987.

Chapter 23

Ann Laura Stoler, with Karen Strassler

MEMORY-WORK IN JAVA
A cautionary tale

Ann Laura Stoler and Karen Strassler consider issues in post-colonial memory through analysis of interviews with Javanese former servants of Dutch colonialists. By listening to 'the content of the form' in what appeared at first hearing to be rather 'flat', muted accounts, Stoler and Strassler realised that 'concrete and sensory memories' – articulated through gestural and aural clues and distinctive word use and repetition – can evoke 'sensibilities that other ways of telling do not'. Ann Laura Stoler is Professor of Anthropology and Historical Studies at the New School for Social Research, New York. Karen Strassler worked as a member of the research team whilst completing her Ph.D. at the University of Michigan, and is now an Asssistant Professor of Anthropology at City University of New York. Extracted with permission from A.L. Stoler, *Carnal Knowledge and Imperial Power: Race and the Intimate in Colonial Rule*, Berkeley: University of California Press, 2002, pp. 162–203 and 270–281. © 2002 The Regents of the University of California.

THROUGHOUT [THIS BOOK] I have worked off and with a specific set of colonial perceptions and practices: how concubinage was seen by Dutch authorities, how servants were viewed by their employers, how Dutch women were made ready for their tasks as good modern housewives – and why all of these mattered so much to colonial authorities. But this chapter does something different. It attempts an about-face. It turns to the ways in which Javanese women and men who worked as servants in late colonial Indonesia saw their Dutch employers. The about-face then is directed at colonial inscriptions of the quality of those domestic relations.[1]

But this chapter is also an about-face of another kind, for it situates memories of domestic service by those who served against the density of the archives about them. Its tenor and tentativeness responds to Doris Sommer's injunction that scholars should 'proceed with caution' in their treatment of colonial narratives, temper their interpretive license, and not imagine that all encounters can be unpacked with hermeneutic finesse. As Michel-Rolph Trouillot put it in his book cover comments, Sommer upsets the 'false intimacy of the liberal embrace.' This chapter speaks to these issues and asks what such a cautionary reflection may say about what we think we know about colonial memories.

At no time has there been more fascination with the contrast that memories of colonialism afford between the 'elegance' of domination and the brutality of its effects.[2] While images of empire surface and resurface in the public domain, colonial studies has materialized over the last decade as a force of cultural critique and political commentary and, not least, as a domain of new expert knowledge. One could argue that the entire field has positioned itself as a counterweight to the waves of colonial nostalgia that have emerged in the post-World War II period in personal memoirs, coffee table picture books, tropical chic couture, and a film industry that encourages 'even politically progressive [North American] audiences' to enjoy 'the elegance of manners governing relations of dominance and subordination between the races.'[3] Still, Nietzsche's warning against 'idle cultivation of the garden of history' resonates today when it is not always clear whether some engagements with the colonial are raking up colonial ground or vicariously luxuriating in it.[4]

From the vantage point of the postcolonial, the notion of a history of the present has strong resonance and appeal. Colonial architecture, memorials, and archives and the scientific disciplines that flourished under the guidance of colonial institutions are dissected as technologies of rule whose 'legacies' and 'influences' are embodied in our comportments and leisures, lodged in our everyday accoutrements, and embedded in the habitus of the present. Remembering – and reminders of – past colonial relations of power has emerged as fundamental to a range of postcolonial intellectual and political agendas that make the recording, rewriting, and eliciting of colonial memories so pertinent and charged.

Yet what remains surprisingly muted in ethnographic histories written 'from the bottom up' and elite histories viewed upside down is an explicit engagement with the nature of colonial memories – not only with what is remembered and why but also with how the specifically 'colonial' is situated in popular memory at all. This chapter rests on a relatively simple but disconcerting observation: 'the colonial' is invoked with such certitude of its effects by those studying it and 'colonial memory' with such assuredness of its ever presence that both are treated as known and knowable quantities rather than as problematic sites of inquiry in themselves.

But this was not where this project began. It was initiated as a response to that specific archive on the colonial domestic order, documented and celebrated in personal memoirs and public records of Europeans, particularly the Dutch, who lived and worked in late colonial Indonesia. We have seen how enduring these images of family life were and how centrally servants figured in them. Thus this memory project addressed the two most tenacious forms in which servants were cast in Dutch renderings: the threatening image offered in housekeeping guides, child-rearing manuals, and medical handbooks warning against the contaminating influence of servants on European children; and, in stark contrast, the favored image (recurrent in colonial memoirs devoted to fond reminiscences of affections shared) of the servants in whose company childhoods were spent.[5] Our questions worked around these images: What resonances did these castings have in people's lives?

What was remembered by those whose touch, smell, and gestures were the very objects of such aroused recollections?[6] Over a period of nearly two years, we talked with Indonesian women and men who had worked between the 1920s and 1950s as gardeners, gofers, kitchen helpers, nursemaids, cooks, housekeepers, and watchmen in Dutch colonial homes.

The memories they chose to recall present a challenge to two prevailing postcolonial stories. One is the popular romance of the beloved and nurturing servant that dominates Dutch memoirs. The other is the story of subaltern memory as the truth of the colonial past. This project adheres to neither. Instead it pushes the accounts of former servants against these Dutch renderings to explore how the dissonance in their perceptions of intimacy and affect may unsettle our certainties about what constituted the colonial and how it figures in people's memories today.

As an opening question, we ask why colonial studies, despite its obvious commitment to questions of memory, has dealt in such circumscribed ways with the nature of remembering and the particular forms that memories of the colonial take. We then turn to the specific recollections of former servants to question how their colonial memories were framed, how concrete and sensory memories of cooking, cleaning, and child care evoke sensibilities that other ways of telling do not. Two concerns grew out of this project: a longer reflection on the politics of interpretive license and what might be gained by making memory-work the subject rather than a given of colonial analysis.

Colonial sentiments and tactile memories

> My recollections of events of this time escape me but there is one thing that will always stick in my mind: how [she] would carry me in a *slendang*[7] at dusk and would rock me to sleep by humming the 'Nina Boho' lullaby. I still remember how heavenly I found that, so entirely 'imprisoned' in her *slendang*, in the curve of her arm, flat against her body, rolling with her slow rocking gait, with the veil-like material of her *kebaja* [blouse] gently grazing my cheek and her humming resonating in her breast so that I could feel it with the rise and fall of her voice. It was as if she flowed through me.[8]

> She would . . . take me in her lap. The fragrance of her body and her clothes, of her *sarung* especially, I must have intensively inhaled, a sort of preerotic! She caressed me by nestling me against her . . . Now still I recollect this fragrance, because smells can remind me of it! . . . [S]uch was my relationship to her.[9]

> It was like this with the Dutch. . . . I was told to take care of the child. At ten at night I'd go back in and give it something to drink, some milk, then a change of clothes, whatever clothes were wet, you know, . . . then I'd return to the back [servants' quarters] again, like that.[10]

The quotations above, two from Dutch memoirs and one from a Javanese woman who worked as a nursemaid (babu), recall colonial intimacies in distinctive ways. Both Dutch accounts are marked by lush sentimentality, by sensuous evocations of bodily intimacy. The nursemaid's comment also gestures to everyday rhythms, to bodies and substances, smells and spaces. Hers too is strikingly tactile. But it is spare. Emphasizing routines, tasks, and commands, she evokes a place of work, not the coziness of home. If for the remembered Dutch child 'home' is the body of the servant, for the nursemaid the place of belonging is out 'back.'

Our interest was to explore the 'structure of feeling' of these 'intimate' relations so differently remembered, the emotional economy and the sensory regimes in which those relations were rendered possible, then retold and remade.[11] Students of the colonial know so much more about how European colonials saw their servants than how their servants saw them. On this premise we questioned how Indonesian women and men today remembered 'the Dutch' they knew at once up close and only from afar, what language they used to describe those daily exchanges, and how they remembered what struck them at the time as distinctly European. We sought out neither the richest storytellers nor those locally celebrated for their vivid recollections. We were as interested in those who were reluctant to speak as in those who eagerly proffered their stories; as drawn to those who could muster no easy frame, whose recollections would not distill into a storied and ready counter-narrative. In most cases, we were struck by an unease in recounting 'the colonial,' by the singularly uncozy and 'charmless' accounts people offered about their jobs and the sensibilities that pervaded Dutch colonial homes. The play of repetitions that seemed so innocuous – that the Dutch were all 'so good,' that Dutch employers were 'so very clean' – drew us to plumb less for the deep grit of their accounts than to follow their surface grain.

It would have been a straightforward task to take 'speaking back to the archives' to mean contrasting the sentimentalism of Dutch nostalgia with the distinctly unsentimental remembrances of those who served them. Sentimentalism so underwrites colonial nostalgia that scholars' attempts to write against it have tended either to avoid the subject of sentiment or to limit their focus to affective extremes, that is, to conditions of palpable duress, dislocation, and diaspora.[12] In doing so, they have called attention to a variety of technologies of memory: place-names, ritual enactments of subjugation, commemorative events, and the violence of conflicts indelibly inscribed in bodies and minds.

Here instead we address the emotional economy of the everyday: when, where, and with whom sentiments were withheld, demanded, and 'freely' displayed. We attend to a more prosaic genre of *aides de memoire*, tied to the non-eventful and the senses.[13] Colonial domestic relations were invoked through recollections of the color and texture of clothes, the taste and smell of unfamiliar foods, the sound of partially understood conversations and commands, and reference to sweat, soaps, chamber pots, and fragrance.[14] Sentiments lay not outside of – or behind – tactile memories but embedded in them.

We asked what these acts of remembering and retelling might signal about the duties and dispositions that went with domestic work and what it meant to be in the service of those who were often inept at 'being colonials': provincial brides on their first trip to the Indies, recently transferred government bureaucrats, plantation supervisors climbing the corporate ladder, young doctors on philanthropic missions, and crusty old colonial hands who might just be learning what it meant to be self-consciously European.

Memory in colonial studies: storage and the hydraulic model

Concern with the politics and techomnemonic strategies of remembering permeates a range of disciplines, public debates, and epistemic fields. It might be claimed that only in an extremely narrow, even parochial definition of what constitutes memory could one argue that memory-work is not on the colonial studies agenda. Surely the scholarly study of colonialisms is itself a memory project, as has been that of postcolonial subjectivity.[15] Issues of 'memory' have played an increasingly prominent role in how students of colonialism understand the relationship between the facts of the colonial archive and ethnographically elicited historical knowledge, between archival production and the politics of its consumption,[16] between a particular set of memory aids – manuscripts, metaphors, bodies, and objects – and how this stored knowledge may be refashioned by postcolonial populations for their needs today.[17]

Still, the treatment of memory in colonial studies has developed in relation to specific political concerns and thus in particular ways. Some of these bypass important insight about the 'fragile power' of memory noted by those who study it more specifically.[18] The storage model, captured in Locke's metaphor of memory as a 'storehouse of ideas,' has long been discredited.[19] Yet students of the colonial often unwittingly hold to a variant of it: memory as a repository of alternative histories and subaltern truths. This 'hydraulic model' rests on the premise that memories are housed as discrete stories awaiting an audience, as repressed or unrecognized sources poised to be tapped.[20]

In colonial studies, memory has been the medium, not the message, the access point to untold stories of the colonized. In efforts to restore a more complete memory of the colonial and struggles against it, oral histories are often invoked to counter official versions and the sovereign status they implicitly give to European epistemologies.[21] Subaltern acts of remembering have not been in question, because it is official memory that is on the line; the process of remembering and the fashioning of personal memories are often beside the political points being made – and may in fact be seen to work against them.[22] Oral histories, designed to extract counternarratives of important anticolonial events, document unheralded and heroic popular participation in them. By Ranajit Guha's account, these 'small voices' may counter the weight of official discourse because they remain undomesticated and unsullied by 'state-managed historiography' and 'the monopolizing force of official knowledge.'[23] Students of colonial history seem to want to have it both ways, a story of a hegemonic colonial state, saturating both the cultural frame and the cracks in which the colonized live, *and* a story in which deft evasion leaves the memories of these same actors unscathed by state intrusion.[24]

A crucial premise underwrites this hydraulic model: subaltern accounts already possess hidden circuits of movement. Silenced or unsanctioned by the state, these camouflaged 'hidden scripts' await decoding. The job of ethnography is then to identify them in their secreted form, whether it be folktale, shaman ritual, scatological humor, midnight gossip, or charivari song.[25] But the very search for those concealed inscriptions of colonial violence and resistance often assumes the production of narrative and the prevalence of telling. Those with whom we talked in Java put that notion of 'subaltern circuits' in question again and again.[26] For it was not clear that these circuits were devoted to the historical or specifically clogged with the colonial. Nor was it clear when, where, and whether colonial memories circulated at all.

A commitment to writing counterhistories of the nation has privileged some memories over others. Because it is often restoration of the collective and archived memory of the making of the postcolonial nation that has been at stake, the critical historian's task has been to help remember what the colonial state – and often the nationalist bourgeoisie – once chose to forget.[27] The assumption is that subaltern narratives contain trenchant political critiques of the colonial order and its postcolonial effects. But this commitment may generate analytic frames less useful for understanding memories that are unadorned with adversaries and heroes, that are not about nationally salient events with compelling plots or violent struggles. This focus on event-centered history may in fact block precisely those enduring sentiments and sensibilities that cast a much longer shadow over people's lives and what they choose to remember and tell about them.

It might be argued that this is all beside the point. Everyone knows that memories are not stored truths but constructions of and for the present. Whether applied to the personal or the social, in this 'identity' model memory is that through which people interpret their lives and redesign the conditions of possibility that account for what they once were, what they have since become, and what they still hope to be.[28] Treating memory as a self-fashioning act of the person or the nation places more emphasis on what remembering does for the present than on what can be known about the past.

Yet we are wary of starting from the premise that acts of remembering can and should be reduced to transparencies about the making of the self. Both the identity and the hydraulic models limit what can be learned about how the colonial is remembered. They either reduce acts of memory to constructions of the present or uphold memory as privileged access to a real past. We chose rather to highlight some of the interpretive problems that these models often elide. By treating memory as interpretive labor, the focus is on not only *what* is remembered but *how*. Marking off a colonial, then, from a postcolonial now flattens out a set of intervening and crosscutting points of reference. Instead we emphasize an ongoing and uneven production process. While recoding is obviously a repeated act, it is less obvious how idioms of the past are reworked with a differently inflected but equally active voice in the present. Recursive play occurs in the very terms in which memories are stated, in the possibilities of using a single phrase to 'play different games.'[29]

Domestic sub/versions

> Manang, our gardener, smelled of different kinds of smoke. He never hurried and I liked being near him: it was restful. My father and the other men used to return from the tea gardens in shirts dark with sweat, their faces wet. Not Manang. He never looked hot. Manang wore faded khaki shorts that used to be my father's, no shirt, and a straw hat that hid his eyes. His large flat feet had spaces between the toes because he didn't have to wear shoes. . . . I wanted feet like that, and his shiny brown skin, and I tried to walk bow-legged like him.[30]

R: Dutch children weren't allowed to be held, [because] later they'd smell of [our] sweat. Holding them wasn't allowed. . . . [T]hey [the Dutch] were afraid [of their children] being soaked in sweat, the sweat of Javanese. . . . [T]he sweat of Javanese is different you know.

D: Why?

R: Javanese people's sweat smells, right.

D: What about Dutch people's sweat?

R: Yeah, Dutch sweat smells worse, 'cause they eat butter, milk, cheese.[31]

These recollections – from a Dutch man's memoir of his Indies boyhood and from Ibu Rubi, a former house servant – allude to the banal intimacies of everyday life, where 'sweat' and scent could mark the lines of difference between kinds of people. They could also distill the dangers and pleasures of contact across those lines. In contrast to nation-centered narratives, the domestic occupies a space that is neither heroic nor particularly eventful nor marked by the brash violences in which colonial relationships are more often thought to be located.[32] As significantly, there is no site where Dutch colonial memoirs linger more knowingly, where more nostalgic energy has been placed.[33] It is a familiar story: the feminized, depoliticized home as the locus for a kinder, gentler colonialism.

Dutch stories of former servants are filled with tender anecdotes and demonstrations of affection, loyalty, and mutual recognition. Thus Annie Salomons could write in 1932, with only a touch of irony, '[T]hat washer boy, despite the fact that I could not yet distinguish him from his fellow men, was my dearest friend.'[34] Childhood memories of Indies servants are central even when the nostalgia is critical, as in Rudy Kousbroek's sober recollections serialized in the Dutch press and recently made into a much praised film, where he refers to the 'entire repertoire [of stories] of [his] loving *babu*' that remained so vividly in his mind.[35] In colonial fiction, memoirs, and children's literature, servants serve as the supporting cast and scenic backdrop and often as the main (and only) source of local knowledge.[36] Sometimes they mark the real and experienced; elsewhere, the imagined and the feared.[37] Dutch accounts of former servants who smuggled food to their imprisoned employers inside Japanese internment camps provide testimony to good treatment repaid and loyal service given long after employers could no longer afford their salaries.[38]

If those who write memoirs and belles lettres subscribe to this imagined vision of domestic bonds, scholars have been taken with another. For the latter, domestic service typifies the Hegelian dilemma and the subaltern condition.[39] In this site of intimate humiliation, contempt, and disdain, subaltern power accrues from the knowledge that those they served were deeply dependent on them.[40]

But both representations are in sharp contrast to the picture of Dutch colonial households conjured by Indonesian women and men who worked as servants. They avoided such expressions of affect, both in how those relations are remembered and in what sorts of emotions are made visible in the telling. Our attempts to elicit 'feelings' often fell flat. In response to 'How did you feel about working for the Dutch?' Ibu Kilah, a former cook, answered with a blunt, mocking response that emphasized the material rather than the emotional economy of those relations: 'My feeling? I was happy because I was paid five and a half silver coins.' Later, when asked about her relationship with her employer, she responded: 'My relationship? Well, she was my employer, my boss, so I had to do whatever, you know. I had to be obedient, for example, if I was asked to help with this, help with that. . . . [S]o I was cared for, so my relationship was good with my boss.'[41]

Ibu Kilah's unsentimental recollections suggest no easy interpretation. Were relations between servants and those they served utterly bereft of tenderness, or were care and nurturing factored into the sale of emotional labor, cherished and valued only by those Dutch who were recipients of it? Students of Javanese culture might argue that this apparent lack of sentiment reflected a more general cultural aversion to emotional display.[42] Or were we deaf to sentiments expressed in unfamiliar ways? We imagine that if this were a more sustained ethnographic project, our elicitations would have been muted and the answers very different.[43] Nevertheless, a focus on memory-work itself opened avenues we had not imagined. As the rest of this chapter suggests, it pointed us repeatedly to 'the content of the form'[44] to how and why former servants talk without sentimentality about sentiment and recollect the colonial past without telling scripted, storied narratives.[45]

Memories outside the comfort zone

That the accounts of former house servants often speak past rather than back to the colonial archive and the nostalgic memoirs of their Dutch employers should not be surprising. People's memories were clearly shaped by dominant historical narratives, by popular literary representations of domestic service, and by contemporary concerns. But if the different orientations of these accounts are predictable, their uneven densities were not. Rather than tap into well-honed, circulating stories, most people seemed unaccustomed to and uneasy relating their colonial experiences. Certainly what people chose to say to *us* was textured by what we inadvertently solicited and by what they thought we wanted to hear. Still, reticence about the colonial seemed to signal a discomfort that extended beyond the interview dynamics. Subtle shifts, evasions, and formulaic responses located the fault lines of memory, the places of discomfort and disinterest as well as those of safety and concern.

Inevitably this reticence was in part the product of a political climate of fear and repression. The research was conducted in the final years of the New Order regime, before the onset of the devastating economic crisis that would bring an end to Suharto's rule in May 1998. Despite growing concern about succession and the 1996 riots over his maneuvers to neutralize an opposition leader, there was little doubt at the time of these interviews that Suharto and his regime were firmly entrenched. So too were certain authorized versions of Indonesian history, within which daily life under the Dutch was marginally placed. When we explained to one former servant's adult granddaughter that we were interviewing people about the Dutch period, she immediately took it to mean that we were looking for revolutionary fighters (*pejuang*).[46]

Questions about servant life in the 1930s and early 1940s more often provoked a swift change of subject than an unleashing of hoarded narratives. People frequently redirected the interviews to other periods, especially the Japanese occupation. In fact, 'the colonial' was rarely a discrete domain of retelling. Again and again we heard that the Dutch were 'good' and the Japanese were the ones who were truly 'bad.' In popular memory and official history, the Dutch and Japanese periods are discursively paired, mnemonically fused, almost inaccessible independently. It is a fusing that upsets one tacit assumption of those who study the colonial – that the key opposition organizing contemporary memories is that between a colonial past and a postcolonial present, as if there was a direct line binding them and little of significance in between.

This fixation on the Japanese occupation was not particular to our interviews. In a country that has celebrated its independence from 'three hundred fifty years of Dutch rule' with annual flourish, life under the Dutch regime has been consistently marginal to New Order stories about national beginnings.[47] Instead the brief Japanese occupation stands as the dark period before liberation, with Dutch colonialism typically invoked as a *zaman normal* (a time of normalcy, a term frequently used for the prewar years) and as a benign contrast.

The Japanese occupation was a safe topic of public discourse – as long as it remained circumscribed by a script of sacrificial suffering that was widely known. People vividly recalled eating corn and other foods considered fit for animals and wrapping themselves in palm fibers and banana leaves when cloth was scarce. Detailed descriptions of Japanese soldiers who forced people to bow before them, of arbitrary beatings, abuse, and brutal deaths, were readily offered. Such stories attest to the extremity of those times but also to the sanctioning of certain kinds of memories of violence. Accounts of having gone hungry during the Japanese period were enough to mark one's heroic participation in the nationalist experience. These highly personalized accounts are almost dissonant in Indonesian, a language in which self-reference is avoided. By contrast, in hushed accounts of the 1965 coup and its bloody aftermath – a decidedly dangerous topic – that 'I' quickly disappeared, replaced by a discourse of silences and vague allusion.

People seemed less sure what to do with the 'I' when it came to memories of the more ambiguous and normalized violences of the Dutch. Narrations of the nation emphasizing exemplary sacrifice and (male) heroism may have made memories of domestic service seem inappropriate to tell. But the hesitancy, thinness, and discomfort when it came to remembering Dutch colonialism was all the more striking because it has not always been so in Indonesia and certainly is not the case elsewhere. The recollection of colonial injustices may express shared nationalist sentiments in other postcolonial contexts, but to Indonesia's New Order government, anti-imperialist sentiments smacked of the 'extreme' and demonized leftism of the Sukarno era. Such sentiments were deemed bad for the burgeoning tourist industry and for foreign investments. Capitalizing on the pleasures and pathos of a lost colonial era (*tempo doeloe*) had become a lucrative national industry in the Netherlands and Indonesia, with international appeal. More important in shaping reticence about the Dutch colonial regime, however, may have been the New Order state's own eerie resemblance to it.[48]

If the reasons that popular representations of the nation's history did not dwell on the colonial are complex, the effects are clear. To tell of one's experiences during the Dutch period conferred neither glory nor legitimacy nor 'recognition.'[49] Those with whom we spoke often assumed our interest in the heroic and actively worked to pull discussion in that direction.

The frequent return to the Japanese occupation as a comparative referent was only partly an effect of official nationalist narratives. As important, the occupation cast a different light on both the quotidian and the extraordinary violences of Dutch rule. For many former servants, the ravages of World War II and the volatility of the revolution years (and subsequent periods) prompted reworked recollections of the *zaman Belanda* (the Dutch period) as one of relative *personal* security.

Witnessing Dutch internment did not erase memories of Dutch control but it was often a pivotal moment. The experience of having watched their employers taken away and never heard from again, having seen their well-furnished homes emptied of belongings, having watched fathers separated from wives and children, and having seen life behind barbwired internment camps recast many former servants' recollections of their employers. Ibu Kilah, for example, who recalled bringing food in to the camp for her 'Nyonya,' remembered feeling 'pity' that she was living in crowded conditions and growing thiner by the day. Yet in contrast to nostalgic Dutch recollections that dwell more on the loyalty and generosity of Javanese servants during these hard times, she said flatly that she stopped working when her Nyonya's money began to run out and the demands of other Dutch women in the camp became too onerous.[50]

Others called on their experiences during the occupation and the revolution to frame their accounts of working in Dutch homes, thereby both steering the interview to a 'safer' moment and emphasizing how radically colonial relations had altered. Before the occupation, Pak Mulyo had worked for seven years as a gardener for the top administrator of a sugar factory outside Yogyakarta. He responded to our opening question about his job by recounting instead his experience on the cusp of independence. First describing how Sukarno provided for the starving and destitute Dutch released from camps after the Japanese surrendered, he linked himself to the nationalist leader by recounting his parallel generosity toward a desperately hungry Dutch man in a refugee camp to whom he brought an egg because he 'felt sorry for him.' Pak Mulyo remembered refusing the Dutch man's offer to give him something in return and concluded the anecdote, 'Yeah, so that was it, working with a Dutch man.'[51]

Pak Mulyo took an opening question about working for the Dutch as an invitation to tell how he worked *with* one. The context became one in which he could turn the tables and feel the pleasure of pity if not power per se. Noting that 'this Dutch man was a good one,' he stressed his exercise of choice while justifying his sympathy for a former colonizer. Beginning with this anecdote, his retelling of domestic service moved outside our frame. Instead his story was one of reversed fates and nationalist liberation. Only then did he talk about tending a Dutch man's garden.

There seemed to be no comfortably correct stance to take in relation to the colonial past. But what was unsafe? Recounting work for a Dutch person because one's previous service rendered one's patriotism suspect? Disparaging a colonial European (often, though not always) to a white interviewer? Or merely having an opinion at all?[52] The submerged anxiety that ran through some interviews at times surfaced with clarity, as with Pak Purwo, a man in his eighties from a village outside

Yogyakarta. He had worked only briefly and part time as a gardener for a Dutch administrator in a sugar factory, in addition to working on the plantation and in the factory itself. The interview took place in the yard of his home, just several hundred yards from the former site of the factory, which had been burned down during the revolution.

P: Am I going to be tried, Mas?[53]

D: Oh no, we want to gather stories, Mbah. About the past. For history, not for being tried.

P: Oh, if that's the case, I'll tell a long story.

D: Yeah, Mbah, for history, in the old days how Javanese people worked in the homes of Dutch people. Because there hasn't been a book about it yet.

P: Later I'll tell, OK. Up to the era of Independence, Mas?

D: Oh, just the Dutch period, Mbah.

P: Up to the Japanese period?

D: Yes, the Japanese period.

P: Later I can.

D: You're not going to be tried, Mbah. I'm from UGM [the University of Gadjah Mada, in Yogyakarta], Mbah.

P: Oh, Gadjah Mada.

D: Gathering stories of when Javanese people worked as gardeners.

P: So, nothing's going to happen to me, right?

D: Oh nothing, Mbah. It's for school.

P: Later will I be brought to court?

D: No, Mbah. Only for history, for a book.

P: Don't later say, 'That man used to work for the Dutch [*ikut Belanda*].'[54]

D: Oh no, no, it's just for history.

P: Oh, yeah, yeah.

D: So we're just asking for stories.[55]

Uneasy focusing on the Dutch period, Pak Purwo preferred to talk about the Japanese occupation and the Independence period. He was keenly aware that telling the past has political stakes. In New Order Indonesia's 'elaborately tended heritage' of fear, one could not be sure what actions and motivations might be attributed to one fifty (or thirty) years later.[56] But his fear may also reference silenced memory of nationalist violence in which former male servants of the Dutch were often suspected of – and sometimes murdered for – treason against the Republic.[57] Clearly, 'history' and 'stories' provided neither reassuring nor safe frames for colonial memories.

Unscripted memories and refused scripts

A common assumption about collecting oral histories is that despite their variations, a good listener can discern a shared (if contested) narrative frame, a cultural schema that underlies how people make sense of their unique histories. But what emerged here was an unhomogenized body of accounts built around the minimal scaffolding of sanctioned formulas. People's recollections moved between con-crete detail and pat statement, between rich commentary and terse responses and awkward silences. Their memories could neither call on familiar plots nor be contained in packaged narratives. Many people undermined their own neat encap-sulations as soon as they were offered. Ibu Kilah made the sweeping statement that under the Dutch 'all Javanese were servants,' only to describe in the next breath a highly stratified Javanese society in which elite Javanese could exploit their servants more than did Dutch employers. People seemed unused to talking about and perhaps even recollecting these experiences. In contrast to the elaborated, often-repeated stories of the Japanese occupation that rolled off the tongue, these accounts seemed uncrafted, rough hewn, and apparently unrehearsed.

If this was subjugated knowledge circulating in subaltern spheres, their children and grandchildren seemed to care and know little about it. One woman, who had worked as a housemaid, said that her children were uninterested in her memories and considered her opinions old-fashioned.[58] Here it was both she and the history she had lived that were irrelevant. Another who had worked as a *genduk* (a young girl who cared for and played with Dutch children) said her children never asked about working for the Dutch. Youthful impatience with stories of the old days is no surprise, but this insistent disregard raised a familiar question: what happens to marginalized memories, excluded from the valued, 'usable past'?[59] Was there no common script in part because there was no audience and no forum for their telling? Tapping into subaltern narratives was not the direction to go. Instead that very absence led us to explore the availability and amenability of narrative forms to encompass these recollections.

But the unscripted nature of people's accounts could only partly be attributed to the lack of an appreciative audience. The accounts also took shape in a negative space around the one widely circulated and gendered local script for colonial service: the tale of the sexually exploited and morally debased female domestic. Through evasions and silences people worked to keep their accounts from fitting into this ready mold, even as they alluded to it in whispers. If in Dutch literature colonial servants are either nurturing or threatening, in Indonesian literature they appear as figures of calculating opportunism or pathetic victims of power. It is not the care-giving babu but the seductive nyai, the housemaid-concubine, who dominates portrayals of colonial domestic roles.[60] Merely to state that one had worked in a Dutch home was to invoke such plots, to stir suspicion, to suggest a hidden story. Even to acknowledge having known women who were 'kept' or sexually assaulted was to risk being tainted oneself.

Stories of women forced to sexually service Dutch men and their sons emerged only rarely. Must women were reluctant to speak of this subject, and most denied that their employers had ever made sexual advances. Ibu Soekati had been nearly raped by her employer when she was still a teen. In our first interview, she merely mentioned with a chuckle that he had been *nakal*, a word that can suggest inappropriate sexual behavior but is also often used to describe the innocuous antics of a mischievous child. It was only at a later meeting that she recounted how he had chased her around the house when no one else was there. Yet she cast his assaults as the acts of a crazy man, muting both the seriousness of his abuse and the severity of her condemnation.[61] Many others who similarly acknowledged their employers' improprieties emphasized how exceptional their experiences were. These stories were not part of family lore, nor were they topics for humor or moral instruction. Few of the children or grandchildren appeared to know anything of them.

Most people couched the subject of sexual relationships and illegitimate pregnancies in the removed language of rumor. Nearly everyone knew of someone 'distant' or had heard 'stories' of such things happening in 'other places.' In the first interview, Ibu Kilah only whispered that 'Dutch men liked Javanese women' but in later meetings told of Javanese servants made pregnant by their employers, vague rumors she claimed to have heard from a neighbor rather than from her mother (who had worked as a babu) or from her own experience (although she had worked as a servant all her adult life). She suggested that women who had sex with their employers were just after money, echoing the disdain for concubines so prevalent in Indonesian popular representations. Overly eager to elicit more, we later pushed her to remember again. She acknowledged that Javanese servants might be 'forced' to have sex with their employers while insisting on her own immunity to such advances. When we asked if her employer had ever propositioned her, she responded curtly that she was already married (and thus protected) and that before her marriage she had been far too young to have been an object of such desires.[62]

Others, rather than resist the available script, drew on it in ways that reinforced their distance from it. Pak Hardjo, for example, denied knowing anyone sexually involved with a Dutch employer but demonstrated his knowledge of such scenarios by staging an impromptu skit, in which he placed us (the three interviewers) in the roles of 'Babu,' 'Tuan,' and 'Nyonya.'

> H: I don't really know, but I sort of know. For example there is a servant, . . . for example, Karen is the servant of Ann and Ann is the wife of Dias. Then by chance Ann's husband likes Karen.
>
> A: Yes, but I don't like that.
>
> H: You don't know about it.
>
> A: Oh, OK, I don't know.
>
> H: Ann doesn't know, but Karen, well eventually she has relations with Ann's husband. And the Nyonya [Ann] instead of just . . .
>
> A: Later we divorce? Or not?
>
> H: No, she [he points to Karen] is asked to leave. Sent away.

> K: And what happens to my child? . . . I take the child with me, or I leave it?

> H: It stays with you. The child stays with you.

> A: So where are all of those children now? Where are those children now?

> H: I don't know.[63]

As frequently happened, Pak Hardjo stopped the conversation short with his disavowal. He said that he heard of this scenario from the babu of the household where he worked, who in turn had heard it from a friend. Did his 'drama' reflect a personal memory rather than the wide currency of the script and its familiar cast? Or was the point rather his delight in placing us in these fitting colonial roles?

There are obviously many ways to read the silences, evasions, and careful crafting of recollections of sexual encounters. How far should we take our interpretive license? The accounts could be interpreted as people's refusals to place themselves in plots that readily cast them as pawn or victim. They could also be read more simply as a 'strategic refusal' (as Doris Sommer calls it) to entertain our questions.[64] Why share these disturbing memories and why tell a *londo* (a white or Dutch person) about a londo at all? Are such silences, as David Cohen warns, 'not a consequence of a forgetting, a loss of knowledge, but rather of powerful and continuous acts of control in both public and private places'?[65]

There were exceptions. Some accounts sliced through the roles accorded servants in local narratives. Ibu Sastro spoke bluntly about being propositioned by an elderly employer as her daughter-in-law and adult granddaughter nodded with recognition, having obviously heard these stories before.[66] She recounted her Tuan's crude manner and rude questions ('Are you married? Marry me, okay?'[67] and laughed to remember that such an old Dutch man could have imagined she would comply. With humor undercutting the pathos of a recollection searing enough to be recalled in minute detail, she evoked acute feelings of both vulnerability and self-possession:

> So he wanted that, but I didn't want it. 'I'll give you money later, if you want' [he said]. I didn't say anything. I didn't say I didn't want it, I didn't say anything, I just took my clothes and went home. I didn't say anything, I was afraid. . . . I didn't say anything to anyone, not to the Nyonya, not the cook, not the gardener, I said nothing to anyone. I took my slendang and I went home, afraid.

Her fluid telling now contrasting with her younger self's terrorized silence, she assigns the trauma of the encounter to the past and positions herself as one for whom the event now makes a good story.

> [He said,] 'What do you want coming here, asking for money?' . . . He called me a bitch [*bajingan*]. 'If you don't want me to have you then you're just a bitch.' 'Just pay me now!' [I said]. He gave me four rupiah, four and a half rupiah. 'Here's your money, now get out of here! I don't

want to see you!' So if he didn't want to see me, fine. . . . He threw
that money at me [laughs], I wasn't even allowed to enter the house.[68]

[. . .]

Reverberating refrains: on the judgments of excess

The difficulty lies in learning to conceive of history in such a way that
the concept no longer excludes repetition but registers its vitality.[69]

Not surprisingly, Javanese servants' accounts were littered with bits of stories that
Dutch colonials liked to tell about their charity and civilities. More interesting was
how and when these were invoked, the different work they could do, and where
they seemed to fall short. What at first appeared to be easy formulas designed to
deflect unwelcome questions arrested us, over time, by the range of critique and
comment they conveyed.

The label 'good,' so flat and empty that we first took it as an obstruction,
became an unexpected point of entry. The power of 'good' rested in the space left
open by its descriptive thinness and blandly approving sense. [. . .] Calling a Dutch
employer 'good' clearly could place a dangerous story within a safe frame, as when
Ibu Soekati recalled, 'In my experience, I mean, all [of the Dutch I worked for]
were good,' and then immediately described how she had been practically raped by
her employer while his wife and children were on vacation.[70]

Calling the Dutch 'good' could serve to set them off from the 'cruel' Japanese
but might also register the finely shaded social (and racial) distinctions among
Europeans. The 'good' Dutch often meant the totok, or full-blooded Dutch, as
opposed to mixed-blood [. . .] Operating as a class term, it could distinguish doctors, teachers, clergymen and high-ranking government officials from 'factory
Dutch' ('Belanda fabrik'), 'poor Dutch' ('Belanda miskin'), and 'retired Dutch'
('Belanda pensionan') who were perceived as stingy and crude. One woman recalled
that it was only the 'factory Dutch' who had sex with Javanese women servants,
never doctors and teachers. Another suggested that only 'black Dutch' (Ambonese
in the Dutch military) kept Javanese concubines. Those former servants who were
Christian might use 'good' to distinguish 'Christian Dutch' from their less
respectable compatriots. Some categories (such as 'factory Dutch' and 'red Dutch')
differed from those found in Dutch colonial writings. But others seemed to rein-
scribe colonial distinctions, placing 'full-blooded' bourgeois Dutch at the top of the
colonial social scale.

Besides referencing stratifications in Dutch society, 'the good Dutch' also
suggested the tenor of specific relations within domestic space. 'Good' was more
often an assessment of how well an employer adhered to the tacit rules that both
obeyed than an endorsement of Dutch character, more often appraisal of specific
comportments than a moral judgment. It could signal that an employer provided
one with sufficient money to live and food to eat. For some, it marked those who
said 'please' before a command, or who called a person by name and not by the
job he or she performed. For others, it distinguished those who trusted their servants
enough not to bolt their cupboards and closets or inspect for hoarded change when

a servant returned from the market. Some people used it to describe those who spoke in Javanese instead of barking commands in Dutch, while others reserved it as a stamp of approval on those Dutch who learned to maneuver the intricacies of high and low Javanese.

Used most often in the sense of 'proper,' 'good' in no way muted the gestures of subordination built into colonial relations. Ibu Sastro, for example, described her colonial employers as 'good' and then contrasted them with 'today's Dutch,' who are more respectful because they recognize that 'Java belongs to the Javanese.'[71] Even when the rules of 'proper' domestic relations were followed, they were hardly fair. A 'good' Dutch might get angry only if you had done something wrong. But Ibu Kilah recalled that even if she repeatedly scrubbed a dirty garment, if the stain remained she was 'wrong.'[72] People expressed anger most directly when speaking of employers who transgressed these tacit rules. Ibu Darmo recalled crying in rage when she was wrongly accused of stealing soap.[73] Ibu Kasan said she quit one evening because after being told no guests were coming for dinner, they did come, and she was berated by the adult daughter for not preparing enough food and accused of 'having no brain.' The young woman later came to her home and begged her to return, but she refused, saying, 'I guess I can't work if I don't have a brain.'[74]

Other attributes of the Dutch, their 'cleanliness' and their 'discipline,' were called on in ways that could similarly convey multiple meanings. People's memories often seemed to gel around these catchwords. Ibu Rubi, for example, made Dutch 'cleanliness' the leitmotiv of her account. She had worked in the 1930s and early 1940s for both Dutch and Indo employers, for Ambonese soldiers in the Dutch army, and, both before and after Independence, for Chinese-Indonesians. [. . .] She said of working in a Dutch home, 'Everything was clean and healthy, [one had] a strong body. I lucked out.'[75] But this apparent endorsement became less self-evident as her repeated statement that the Dutch were 'clean' accumulated weight through her interviews. Repetition transformed a seemingly straightforward assessment into something else.

> R: I liked working for the Dutch, it was so perfectly clean. . . . The Dutch were, well, clean, healthy, the food was healthy. If you ate fish, what is it, you know, leftover fish that had been sitting around, they didn't like it. When you cooked, all kinds of things still had to be bloody when you cut into them. I didn't like it, but I was forced, made to eat it, to be healthy.
>
> D: Eventually did you like it?
>
> R: Yeah, I put it in my mouth, later I spit it out.

Ibu Rubi seems to approve concern for her health even as she rejects the attempt to impose that concern on her body. [. . .] She goes on to talk of clothes that had to be washed three times before they were acceptable to her employers, floors that had to be mopped several times a day, and kitchen utensils subject to daily spot checks. Repetition turns her words from the virtue of cleanliness to the effects of its excess. The more she underlines Dutch cleanliness, the more she seems to mock it. With her words of praise punctuated with anecdotes about servants forced to eat things against their will, the ground shifts to a Dutch obsession borne by those who worked for them. The fastidious concern shown by one of her employers for the cleanliness and health of a wet nurse, she emphasized, was not for the benefit of the servant but for the health of the Dutch infant she nursed. She was given clean food and medicine, 'told to sleep there, forbidden to go home, because if she went home she'd be dirty. Her breast milk would be dirty.'[76]

Yet if praise turned to critique in Ibu Rubi's account, it folded in on itself again when she recalled so absorbing these Dutch notions of cleanliness that she became estranged from her own 'dirty' neighborhood (an experience also recounted by others). She told of returning to the village and furiously attempting to clean everything, even trying to mop dirt floors, to the surprise of her neighbors. When asked if they minded she says: 'No, it was OK, it was for cleanliness, good health.' Ibu Rubi condensed judgments in familiar tropes that could be turned to different ends. Her constant shuttling between praise and criticism unsettles any comfortable interpretation of 'cleanliness' in her account.

'Cleanliness' was also ambiguous in Ibu Rubi's account, because the term is as charged in the present as it was in the past. Like 'discipline,' which also frequently punctuated people's accounts, 'cleanliness' was both part of the repertoire of concepts that Dutch household manuals used to prescribe domestic relations and a catchword of the New Order. Government-sponsored billboards urged discipline and 'a culture of cleanliness' as requisite virtues for a 'developed' Indonesia.[77] Such historically dense vocabularies raise basic problems of interpretive license. To what degree were people's descriptions of the colonial past to be read as commentaries on the postcolonial present? And given that they must be to some extent 'about' both, how to calibrate the relative weighting of the two? Ibu Rubi's account evokes a relation to Dutch sensibilities that shifts over time, that swings between rejection and attraction – both in the colonial past and in looking back from her vantage point of the present.

On sense and sensibility: memories of the concrete

Our interviews tended to stay close to the mundane rhythms and concrete physicality of everyday life – not only because our questions were directed precisely to the intimacies of domestic work but also because people so resolutely held us there. Those memories recounted with the most energy and engagement were rooted firmly in the senses – in Dutch disciplines imposed on their bodies, in the repugnant or delicious tastes of Dutch foods, or in the clashes over child-rearing styles that so often produced friction between Dutch employers and the women they hired for child care. If telling eventful stories is one way of relating experience, telling the routine and the habitual is another.

That Javanese servants remembered tastes, smells, textures, and sounds so differently from their Dutch employers is unsurprising. This domestic space was, after all, 'home' to the Dutch and 'workplace' to their servants. Nor is it surprising that recollections of these clashes of sensibility were affectively charged. But the fact that affective memories are called up through the senses is perhaps more widely accepted than the fact that moral and political judgments are as well.[78] Feelings of being imposed on, of being bored, and of being judged and chided were not framed as personal testimonials of political injustice but were embedded in the sensory recall of the unremarkable, in the often minute emotional accommodations of the everyday.

People remembered detailed menus of meals eaten more than fifty years ago and would recite with energy and care each ingredient and each stage of preparation. This clustering of memories around practices of cooking and eating was obviously linked to food's symbolic power and daily importance. At times lists of foods cooked and prepared seemed assertions of specialized knowledge, displays of privileged familiarity, or recitals of sheer tedium, as when Ibu Kilah recalled, 'Then, the only food [the Dutch] ate was potatoes, potatoes, always potatoes, potatoes with this, potatoes with that. . . . [P]otatoes, potatoes, potatoes nonstop, . . . with steak.'[79] Food talk was a shared idiom, a shorthand to conjure up adaptations and differences muted and sharpened by what one swallowed. To say that a Dutch family 'ate rice' was to identify them approvingly as acclimatized to the Indies (or as having some Javanese blood). Genduk Ginem recalled that one of her totok Nyonyas had 'become Javanese,' as evinced by the fact that she 'rarely ate potatoes.'[80] For Ibu Rubi to recount that the Ambonese soldiers ('black Dutch') for whom she had once worked slaughtered chickens by crushing their necks under their feet was to offer proof of their uncultured ways.[81]

Our questions about what the Dutch were like were frequently answered with discussions of the foods Dutch people ate. Initially, we took this turn to the concrete as a retreat from judgment, as a way of moving carefully onto neutral ground. What could be less risky than to respond that the Dutch were people who lived on potatoes? But when Ibu Adi said, 'Everywhere the white Dutch are all the same. The food is the same,'[82] was she deflecting the question or commenting on the standardized 'European' milieu that many totok Dutch so carefully tended and that she – through a different lens – observed?

Memories of eating Javanese food in the back quarters while employers ate Dutch food in the dining room were, for many, signature scenes of a cultural divide in the home. The sharing of food, by contrast, could be invoked to signal that those very differences were overcome or transgressed. Ibu Patmi had worked in her early teens for a Dutch widow and her adult daughter whom she remembered with great affection. She offered a recollection of eating with them at their dining room table as evidence of not being treated like a servant: 'I was treated the same.' This memory seemed to carry more weights than that of sleeping every night on the floor beside her Nyonya's bed.[83]

Food was remembered as a principal arena in which Dutch fears about contact and contamination were played out but also as a site where the seductive pull of Javanese ways often proved too powerful to resist. Several people recalled that Dutch children were not allowed to eat Javanese food sold on the street or slipped to them by servants in the back of the house. Ibu Sastro imitated her Tuan's warning not to buy his child *gudeg* (a sweet, spicy central Javanese stew) from streetside stands: 'Don't give him rice and gudeg, later he'll know how good it is and won't want to eat potatoes.'[84] But the child continued secretly to buy it and, she told us with delight, no longer wanted potatoes. Ibu Adi, with similar pleasure, recalled her employers' children sneaking into the kitchen to steal the *tempe* she was preparing for the servants' meal.[85]

Several men drew a comparison between the food they ate and that given to the beloved family dog. A mini-parable of colonial relations, this was one of the rare times that people called on a rehearsed and available narrative. Told almost identically by three of the six men, it detailed daily subordinations with humor and poignancy. [. . .] Pak Mulyo recalled that the pet dog had its own babu who prepared its special meals:

> Even its plate gleamed. Its food, waah, when I saw it, . . . the food, it was just like the boss's. There was meat, there was egg. Stew. Wow, that's what I thought. . . . [S]ometimes I even said to the dog's babu, 'Wah, just give it to me, Bu.' 'Yeah,' she replied, 'go ahead and help yourself. Later the boss will yank your ear.'[86]

But if the subject of food often elicited vivid anecdotes, other questions evoked memories tied to the senses that emerged in less storied forms. Chronological ordering and narrated sequences of events did not dominate these recollections.[87] Storied segments were often overwhelmed by a jumble of lists, names, fragments of dialogue, foreign words, and gestures seemingly unmoored from narrative threads.[88] Litanies of seemingly obscure details contained muted affective strains. Long lists of tasks performed, foods cooked, and schedules imposed were not indifferent recollections. They registered, in ways no story could, the repetitive and often deadening regularity of domestic work.[89] When Genduk Ginem recited her daily routine of sixty years ago by the precise hour, she evoked the rigid and imposed rhythms of Dutch households and habits.[90]

If memories are forged into stories in uneven and incomplete ways, what is missed by focusing so resolutely on their narrative structure? As those who call attention to the sensory nature of memory remind us, oral historians too often focus on the disembodied 'voice,' a move that edits out inarticulate forms of remembering. In our interviews, gestures often evoked what language could not, as when Ibu Kilah suddenly cringed, her body unmistakably adopting the curled posture of a scared child, as she described witnessing her mother yelled at by an abusive employer. Pak Hardjo demonstrated how, as a young errand boy, he rocked the children in his arms and carried them on his back. When we asked how he felt when his employers left Indonesia, he was silent but used his hands to show how the tears ran down his face. Ibu Patmi frequently patted herself firmly on her head to show how her Nyonya showed approval and affection, saying 'goed, goed' as she performed the gesture.

Interrupted with Dutch sounds and physical gestures, people's accounts blurred incomplete and intimate knowledge, invoking both the understood and the foreign. Recitations of remembered Dutch words – 'eten, slepen, koken, wassen' – punctuated their accounts as if these words were emblems of the foreign codes they had to learn to work in Dutch homes. Their always partial mastery was expressed in the common assertion that one could understand Dutch but not speak it: the words 'wouldn't come out.' Ibu Sastro noted that one had to be 'gutsy' (berani) to work in a Dutch home precisely because one had to confront a language only partially understood. [. . .] Ibu Darmo too remembered overhearing her employers talking about which servants were trustworthy but understanding only the gist of their words.[91]

The partial nature of translation was evident in how Dutch curses were trans-formed into Javanese verbs: for doing something wrong one could be *di-godverdom* or *di-kerdom* or *di-verdoma* (with the Dutch curse 'God damn you' here given a Javanese-Indonesian prefix indicating the passive voice). When asked to translate 'Godverdom, zeg!' Ibu Ruhi glossed it as 'Ah, not like this!'[92] More often, people offered no translations when they imitated Dutch commands like 'kom hier,' conveying meaning instead through harsh tone and imperious gesture.

These concrete and sensory recollections of the everyday called up an intimate landscape of affective ties and asymmetric relations. Neither dramatic tales with sweeping moral judgments nor wrenching testimonials, they registered an uncom-fortable space where servants' sensibilities jostled uneasily against those of their employers.

Beyond the stories we want to tell

> Ibu Darmo tells us she's eighty-one. With delight I say that my mother is too. She looks at me straight for the first time since we sat down and simply says: 'I thought whites [*londo*] were all dead by that age. I didn't know they could live that long.'
>
> Ann's fieldnotes, July 12, 1997

Ibu Darmo receives us in a small sitting room behind her grocery store that opens onto the road. We are uncomfortable that there are five of us, and Dias waits outside. Nita and Didi have met with her before and are not as ill at ease as we are. Ibu Darmo is not ill at ease at all. She sits back with her legs crossed, looking us over. She neither satisfies us with redemptive rage and juicy tales nor offers a study of resigned accommodation. She merely tolerates our presence. She is as the French say *correct*, that is, minimally polite. No one makes us feel quite so stopped short. Reading through the transcripts of a previous interview, all five of us are struck by this elderly woman with her blunt phrases and keen memory for details and dialogued scenes. This is someone, we imagine, who might speak back to the archive in interesting ways that we could still hear.

But we imagined Ibu Darmo could speak back to the archives, perversely perhaps, because she more than anyone else with whom we spoke would not speak directly to us.[93] She addressed herself solely to Nita and Didi, as if we were not there. While others politely attended to our questions, she did not bother to listen or appeared to find them incomprehensible. She had little interest in our venture. She offered no refreshment, by Javanese etiquette an obligatory part of this encounter. We were made to know not only that we were an intrusion, but that there was little point in apologizing for our presence or effusing our appreciation here. In response to Ann's misplaced effort to find some common ground in noting that her mother and Ibu Darmo are the same age, Ibu Darmo halts us with her blunt response: 'I didn't know *londos* lived so long.' Beginning and end of discussion. Recalling for us that both Dutch adults and children called her 'Babu' and not by her own name, she has little interest in making connections with our kin. Ann's mother was an aged white, an unusual category of persons in colonial Java, as she noted, but a 'londo' nonetheless.

Unlike others whose recollections were more haltingly told, Ibu Darmo could fluently recount how she first began working for her Tuan, the names of his children, and her many time-consuming tasks. But the spareness of her account stood out more than the acuity of her recall. These were not warm recollections. When we asked if she had since heard from one of the daughters who had left Java at nineteen, she said indifferently, 'I have no idea about her now, I don't know if she's alive or not, I don't know.' She imitated acrimonious dialogues between the two grown daughters but offered no anecdotes of affection, no grumbling endearments, no kind words. Instead she conveyed how tedious and burdensome the work had been. She was supposed to be a washerwoman but was called on to sweep, dust paintings, and do ironing that had to be finished long after she was supposed to go home for the day. She described conflicts between the servants, like the time she advised the cook and the houseboy not to steal and they gave her the silent treatment for weeks.[94]

Her recollections were neither scripted nor soothing. She was dismissive rather than degraded, disdainful rather than defiant. We left after a short visit, disquieted by her willingness to share her memories even as she rejected our eagerness to commiserate and share in them. But to celebrate Ibu Darmo's refusal to engage us may be to be charmed all over again.

In the past decade, students of colonial studies have turned their attention to representations of colonial pasts and the subaltern voices submerged within them. That work has sought to resituate popular experience and subjugated knowledge at the center of nationalist histories rather than as marginalized addenda to them. Whether colonial history is conceived as a 'scarce resource' or a marker of the modern, the work of remembering other colonial pasts in the form of counter-histories carries a sense of urgency as contemporary political demands are fueled by indictments of colonial categories and claims.[95]

We had intended to speak back to the colonial archive and to Dutch nostalgia, to pierce the dense weave of public documents and family archives in which those memories were secured, to counter the literary and archival caricatures that swung between servant as icon of danger and as metonym of the loyal colonized. Yet in talking with people who had worked sporadically as youths, at intervals as married couples, and even as longtime retainers in Dutch colonial homes, it was not 'colonial memories' per se that were poised for extracting a different historical rendering. Our attention was instead arrested by the ways in which people moved between formulaic refrains and concrete detail, between Javanese politesse and blunt Dutch curse, from recipe ingredients and dry shopping lists to dramatic reenactments of pointed dialogues. Their recollections of touch, taste, and smell were not shaped into tidy plots, much less congealed as anti-Dutch resistance narratives. Moving fluidly between the 1930s and the Japanese occupation, between the present and the 1950s – between dense layerings of other aspects of people's lives – these accounts refused the colonial as a discrete domain of social relations and politics, of experience and memory.

Attending to memory-work does not mean abandoning entirely the project of speaking back to colonialist histories and nostalgia. It does mean letting go of some received wisdoms and cherished assumptions – that the colonial is ever present in postcolonial lives; that postcolonial subjectivity by definition pivots on the transition from the colonial to the postcolonial; that there are subaltern circuits in which colonial critiques are lodged; that there is resistance in the smallest of gestures and the very lack of gesture at all; and that telling of the colonial past is a therapeutic act. Opening these up as questions to be asked, instead of treating them as foregone conclusions, makes it less easy to take interpretive license, less easy to be sure of what we know about the colonial, and less comfortable with some postcolonial claims. It invites more work on colonial memory itself while making 'the colonial' a subject rather than an assumed category of analysis.

Notes

1   In collaboration with Karen Strassler, a Ph.D. candidate in anthropology at the University of Michigan, I carried out interviews in 1996 and 1997. We were assisted by two Indonesian researchers, Nita Kariani Purwanti, an anthropologist, and Didi Kwartanada, a historian, as well as Dias Pradadimara, a Ph.D. candidate in history at the University of Michigan.
     The research was focused in Yogyakarta, a city best known as the seat of Javanese culture and for its crucial role in the nationalist revolution. In the 1930s it was a provincial capital surrounded by sugar plantations. There was a clearly marked European area, surrounded by the dense urban *kampung* neighborhoods where many of the people we interviewed were still living. A few people we interviewed lived outside of the city, having worked as house servants for employees of the sugar estates.
     Discussions among the five of us yielded inevitable differences of opinion that appear here principally in our effort to keep a wide range of interpretive possibilities in play. Nevertheless, my and Strassler's interests shaped the chapter's argument and final form, and we alone are responsible for its shortcomings.
2   Renato Rosaldo, *Culture and Truth: The Remaking of Social Analysis*, Stanford, Calif.: Stanford University Press, 1985, p. 68.
3   Ibid.
4   Friedrich Nietzsche, 'The Uses and Advantages of History', in *Untimely Meditations*, trans. R.J. Hollingdale, Cambridge: Cambridge University Press, (1876) 1996, p. 68.
5   As E.M. Beekman has noted in his introduction to E. Breton de Nijs' fictionalized memoir, *Faded Portraits*, some of the most powerful Dutch colonial memoirs and novels are marked by 'an evocation of a place with its tactile and factory peculiarities' (3). Also see Ernest Hillen, *The Way of a Boy: A Memoir of Java*, London: Penguin, 1993.
6   We know of no autobiographies written by Indonesian men and women who worked in domestic service. Most of the Indonesian memoirs of life in the colonical period [. . .] are accounts of people who, though sometimes of humble origins, were well educated – often in Dutch schools.
7   A *slendang* is a cloth worn across the chest over one shoulder so that an infant can lie across the front of the body [. . .]
8   Lin Scholte, *Bibi Koetis voor Altijd*, Amsterdam: E. Querido, 1974, pp. 43–44.
9   Robert Nieuwenhuys, *De Schim van Nenek Tidjah*, Amsterdam: Huis Clos, 1995, p. 56 [. . .].
10 Ibu Tinem, 24 March 1997, interview with Didi Kwartanada and Nita Kariani Purwanti.
11 Raymond Williams, *Marxism and Literature*, London: Oxford University Press, 1977, p. 134.

12 See my chapter, 'States of Sentiment, Reasons of State', in *Along the Archival Grain*: *Colonial Cultures and Their Affective States*, Princeton: Princeton University Press, forthcoming.

13 See Paul Stoller, *Embodying Colonial Memories*: *Spirit Possession, Power, and the Hauka in West Africa*, New York: Routledge, 1995; on the sensory experience of history, see C. Nadia Seremetakis, ed., *The Senses Still*: *Perception and Memory as Material Culture in Modernity*, Boulder, Colo.: Westview Press, 1994.

14 We were inspired here by Carolyn Steedman's *Landscape for a Good Woman*: *A Story of Two Lives*, New Brunswick, N.J.: Rutgers University Press, 1987.

15 Although many postcolonial intellectuals do not discuss memory per se, analysis of postcolonial subject formation can be considered an investigation of remembering and the enduring effects of colonialism. Here we are looking at something different: explicit articulations of past experience (rather than subject-effects) among a population of largely uneducated, nonelites (rather than postcolonial intellectuals). See, among others, Frantz Fanon, *Black Skin, White Masks*, trans. Charles Lam Markmann, New York: Grove Press, [1952] 1967; Homi K. Bhabha, *The Location of Culture*, New York: Routledge, 1994; and Gayatri Chakravorty Spivak, *In Other Worlds*: *Essays in Cultural Politics*, New York: Metheun, 1987.

16 See, among others, Michel-Rolph Trouillot, *Silencing the Past*: *Power and the Production of History*, Boston: Beacon Press, 1995; and Joanne Rappaport, *Cumbe Reborn*: *An Andean Ethnography of History*, Chicago: University of Chicago Press, 1994. On how colonial archives 'remember' see Ann Laura Stoler, 'In Cold Blood: Hierarchies of Credibility and the Politics of Colonial Narratives', *Representations* 37 (Winter 1992), pp. 151–89.

17 See Stoller, *Embodying Colonial Memories*, Shahid Amin, *Event Metaphor, Memory. Chari Chaura, 1922–1992*, Berkeley: University of California Press, 1995; Gyanendra Pandey, *Memory, History and the Question of Violence*: *Reflections on the Reconstruction of Partition*, Calcutta: K.P. Bagchi, 1999 and 'Violence Out There: Memories of Partition', paper presented at the conference, Religion and Nationalism in Europe and Asia, Amsterdam, November 1995. For work on how the colonial is 'remembered' in contemporary cultural discourse, see Michael T. Taussig, 'Culture of Terror – Space of Death: Roger Casement's Putamaya Report and the Explanation of Terror', *Comparative Studies in Society and History*, 26 (July 1994), pp. 467–497; John Pemberton, *On the Subject of 'Java'*, Ithaca: Cornell University Press, 1994; Fernando Coronil and Julie Skurski, 'Dismembering and Remembering the Nation: The Semantics of Political Violence in Venezuela', *Comparative Studies in Society and History*, 33, no. 2, 1991, pp. 288–377; E. Valentine Daniel, *Charred Lullabies*: *Chapters in an Anthropography of Violence*, Princeton: Princeton University Press, 1996. Jennifer Cole's 'The Work of Memory in Madagascar', *American Ethnologist*, 25, no. 4, 1998, pp. 610–633, critiques the assumption that the experience of the colonial pervades postcolonial subjectivities and cultural discourse. While we are concerned here with present-day memories of the mundane routines of colonial life, Cole raises important questions about how colonial memories figure in everyday contemporary life.

18 The neurocognitive psychologist Daniel L. Schacter uses this term to refer to the simultaneous durability and malleability of personal memory in *Searching for Memory*: *The Brain, the Mind, and the Past*, New York: Basic Books, 1996.

19 For a critique of the retrieval model in psychology, see Asher Koriat and Morris Goldsmith, 'Memory, Metaphores and the Laboratory/Real-Life Controversy: Correspondence versus Storehouse Conceptions of Memory', *Behavioural and Brain*

Sciences, 19, no. 2, 1996, pp. 166–228; in historical anthropology, See Trouillot, *Silencing the Past*.

20   On the notion of the archives as a source waiting to be tapped, see my 'Colonial Archives and the Arts of Governance: On the Content in the Form', in *Refiguring the Archive*, Carolyn Hamilton (ed.), Cape Town: David Philip, 2002. Obviously this hydraulic model of memory is indebted to a Freudian tradition in which memory-work involves releasing repressed memories in a redemptive exercise.

21   Or as Luise White, Stephan Miescher, and David William Cohen put it so well: 'The African voice – cradled, massaged, and authenticated within the expert approaches of the African historian – comes to represent (or at least presents the opportunity to reach for) truth while it provisions scholarly claims to objectivitiy.' *African Words, African Voices: Critical Practices in Oral History*, Bloomington: Indiana University Press, 2001.

22   See, for example, Amin's *Event, Metaphor, Memory* [. . .].

23   Ranajit Guha, 'The Small Voice of History', in *Subaltern Studies X: Writings on South Asian History and Society*, eds Guatam Bhadra, Gyan Prakash, and Susie Tharu, Delhi: Oxford University Press, 1996, pp. 1–12.

24   See, Lila Abu-Lughod, 'The Romance of Resistance: Tracing Transformations of Power through Bedouin Women', *American Ethnologist*, 17, no. 1, 1990, pp. 41–55.

25   See, James C. Scott, *Weapons of the Weak: Everyday Forms of Peasant Resistance*, New Haven: Yale University Press, 1985, and *Domination and the Arts of Resistance: Hidden Transcripts*, New Haven: Yale University Press, 1990; Michael T. Taussig, *Shamanism, Colonialism, and the Wild Man: A Study in Terror and Healing*, Chicago: University of Chicago Press, 1987.

26   Ted Swedenburg's compelling study of Palestinian nationalism and selective forgetting takes as its explicit subject the nature of acts of memory. Nevertheless, the frame is still the event-centered history of nationalist narratives and alternative versions in 'subaltern circuits'. *Memories of Revolt: The 1936–1939 Rebellion and the Palestinian National Post*, Minneapolis: University of Minnesota Press, 1995. In a noncolonial context, Luisa Passerini begins from the premise that popular memory contains 'stories handed down and kept alive and adapted for the interview': *Fascism in Popular Memory: The Cultural Experience of the Turin Working Class*, trans. Robert Lumley and Jude Bloomfield, Cambridge: Cambridge University Press, 1987, p. 19.

27   See, Gyan Prakash, 'Writing Post-Orientalist Histories', *Comparative Studies in Society and History*, 32, no. 2, 1990, pp. 383–408; Dipesh Chakrabarty, 'Postcoloniality and the Artifice of History: Who Speaks for "Indian" Pasts?', *Representations*, 37, Winter 1992, pp. 1–26.

28   Thus Boyarin argues that 'identity and memory are virtually the same concept', Jonathan Boyarin, ed., *Remapping Memory: The Politics of Timespace*, Minneapolis: University of Minnesota Press, 1994, p. 23.

29   It is Michel Foucault's notion of 'polyvalent mobility' that we think of here. See *The Archaeology of Knowledge*, trans. A.M. Sheridan Smith, New York: Pantheon, 1972, pp. 36–37.

30   Hillen, *Way of a Boy*, p. 3.

31   Ibu Rubi, 27 February 1997, interview with Kwartanada.

32   On the polarity between sensational, narratable, and thus memorable events and the sensory structure of the everyday as a zone of inattention and forgetfulness, see Seremetakis, *Senses Still*, pp. 19–20.

33   Emphasis on domestic memories may reflect discomfort in Holland with memories of the war against the emergent Indonesian republic as well as other violent aspects

of Dutch rule. See Vincent Houben, 'A Torn Soul: The Dutch Public Discussion of the Colonial Past in 1995', *Indonesia*, 63, 1997, pp. 67–90.

34 Annie Salomons, *Het Huis in de Hitte*: *Drie Jaar Deli*, Amsterdam: Nederlandsche Keurboejerij, 1932, p. 5. See also Hein Buitenweg, *Op Java Staat en Huis*, The Hague: Servire, 1960; Maria Dermoût, *Nog Pas Gisteren*, Amsterdam: E. Querido, 1964.

35 See Rudy Kousbroek, *Terug naar Negri Pan Erkoms*, Amsterdam: Meulenhoff, 1995, p. 243; and the film *Het Meer der Herinnering*. [. . .]

36 Dorothée Buur's annotated bibliography on Indische children's literature lists more than eighty-six stories in which 'servants' appear and sixty eight with babus (*Indische Jeugdliteratuur*: *Geannoteerde Bibliografie van Jeugdboeken over Nederlands-Indië en Indonesië*, *1825–1991* (Leiden: KITLV), 1992. [. . .]

37 As in de Nijs's *Faded Portraits* and in Louis Couperus's *The Hidden Force*, trans. Alexander Teixeira de Mattos, Amherst: University of Massachusetts Press, (1900) 1985. [. . .]

38 See, for example, Hillen, *Way of a Boy*, p. 24.

39 Elsbeth Locher-Scholten [. . .] 'Orientalism and the Rhetoric of the Family: Javanese Servants in European Household Manuals and Children's Fiction', *Indonesia*, 58, October 1994, p. 19.

40 See, Anne McClinton, *Imperial Leather*: *Race, Gender and Sexuality in the Colonial Contest*, New York: Routledge, 1995, for a nuanced reading of servant-employer dependencies in imperial Britain and the colonies.

41 Ibu Kilah, 13 June 1996, interview with Karen Strassler.

42 See, Hildred Geertz's classic, *The Javanese Family*: *A Study of Kinship and Socialization*, New York: Free Press of Glencoe, 1961; [. . .] Ward Keeler, *Javanese Shadow Plays*, *Javanese Selves*, Princeton: Princeton University Press, 1987.

43 See, Greta Uehling's Ph.D. dissertation on memory and sentiment among Crimean Tatars: 'Building Memories: Recalling the Deportation, Exile and Repatriation of Crimean Tatars to Their Historic Homeland', University of Michigan, 2000.

44 Hayden V. White, *The Content of the Form*: *Narrative Discourse and Historical Representation*, Baltimore: Johns Hopkins University Press, 1987.

45 On the important distinction that psychology draws between 'retelling' and 'remembering', see Maurice Bloch, *How We Think They Think*: *Anthropological Approaches to Cognition, Memory, and Literacy*, Boulder, Colo.: Westview Press, 1998.

46 From fieldnotes of 9 July 1997.

47 See Gouda, *Dutch Culture Overseas*, pp. 36–37. [. . .]

48 See Pemberton, *On the Subject of 'Java'*.

49 James T. Siegel, *Fetish, Recognition, Revolution*, Princeton: Princeton University Press, 1997.

50 Ibu Kilah, 13 June and 7 July 1996, interviews with Strassler; and 28 September 1996, interview with Stoler and Strassler. It was not until the third interview that she explicitly stated this was why she had left.

51 Pak Mulyo, 18 March 1997, interview with Purwanti and Kwartanada.

52 Among many Javanese it is considered impolite – as well as impolitic – to assert an opinion too directly. See Clifford Geertz, *The Religion of Java*, Glencoe, Ill.: Free Press, 1960; Laine Berman, *Speaking through the Silence*: *Narratives, Social Conventions, and Power in Java*, New York: Oxford University Press, 1998.

53 'Mas' is a polite Javanese term of address for a young man; 'Mbah' is a polite term for an elder.

54 The idiom typically used to mean 'to work for' (*ikut*) literally means 'to follow, or go along with', connoting loyalty as well as employment. [. . .]

55   Pak Purwo, 22 March 1997, interview with Kwartanada and Purwanti. Interestingly, it was only when Nita momentarily left the room soon after the interview had begun that Pak Purwo began his anxious questioning of Didi.

56   Mary Steedly, *Hanging without a Rope*: *Narrative Experience in Colonial and Postcolonial Karoland*, Princeton: Princeton University Press, 1993, p. 225.

57   Rudolph Mrazek, 9 December 1997, pers. com. [. . .]

58   Ibu Tinem, 9 July 1997, interview with Stoler, Strassler, and Kwartanada.

59   Renato Rosaldo, *Ilongot Headhunting*, *1883–1974*: *A Study in Society and History*, Stanford, Calif.: Stanford University Press, 1980, p. 231.

60   See, Pramoedya Ananta Toer's 'Djongos + Babu', originally published in *Tjerita Dari Djakarta*: *Sekumpulan Karikatur Keadaan dan Manusianya*, Djakarta: Grafica, 1957 [. . .]; Toer, *This Earth of Mankind*: *A Novel* [*Bumi Manusia*], trans. Max Lane, New York: Penguin, (1975) 1990; Jean Taylor, 'Nyai Dasima: Portrait of a Mistress in Literature and Film', in *Fantasizing, the Feminine*, ed. Laurie Sears, Durham, N.C.: Duke University Press, 1996, pp. 225–248.

61   Ibu Soekati, 17 June 1996, interview with Strassler; and 3 October 1996, interview with Strassler, Stoler, and Dias Pradadimara.

62   Ibu Kilah, 13 June and 7 July 1996, interviews with Strassler; 28 September 1996, interview with Stoler and Strassler.

63   Pak Hardjo, 30 September 1996, interview with Stoler, Strassler, and Pradadimara.

64   Doris Sommer, *Proceed with Caution, When Engaged by Minority Writing in the Americas*, Cambridge, Mass.: Harvard University Press, 1999.

65   David William Cohen, *The Combing of History*, Chicago: University of Chicago Press, 1994, p. 18.

66   In the first interview, Ibu Sastro avoided the topic of sex. But in two subsequent interviews (4 April 1997, with Purwanti and Kwartanada; 10 July 1997, with Purwanti, Strassler, and Stoler) she told the same account, almost verbatim.

67   The word used for 'marry' here is *kawin*, which can be used to mean formal marriage or simply being engaged in a (usually long-term) sexual relationship. In our 10 July 1997, interview, she clarified that in this context *kawin* meant 'play around' (*main-main saja*) sexually only, not marriage.

68   Ibu Sastro, 4 April 1997, interview with Purwanti and Kwartanada.

69   Bruce Robbins, *The Servant's Hand*: *English Fiction from Below*, New York: Columbia University Press, 1993, p. 33.

70   Ibu Soekati, 17 June 1996, interview with Strassler. [. . .]

71   Ibu Sastro, 10 July 1997, interview with Stoler, Strassler, and Purwanti. [. . .]

72   Ibu Kilah, 28 September 1996, interview with Stoler and Strassler.

73   Ibu Darmo, 12 July 1997, interview with Kwartanada, Purwanti, Stoler, and Strassler.

74   Ibu Kasan, 3 October 1996, interview with Strassler, Stoler, and Pradadimara.

75   Ibu Rubi, 27 February 1997, interview with Kwartanada.

76   Ibid.

77   Here we cannot know to what extent the apparent 'salience' of Dutch cleanliness indicates how important this quality seemed then and how much it reflects the term's contemporary currency. On salience as a 'treacherous concept', see Marigold Linton, 'Ways of Searching and the Contents of Memory', in *Autobiographical Memory*, ed. David C. Rubin, Cambridge: Cambridge University Press, 1986, pp. 50–67.

78   On emotion as part of the vocabulary of appraisal and criticism, see Francis Dunlop, *The Education of Feeling and Emotion*, London: Allen & Unwin, 1984; and my discus-

sion of the sentiments as expressions of feeling and of judgment in 'States of Sentiment, Reasons of State', in *Along the Archival Grain*.

79 Ibu Kilah, 28 September 1996, interview with Stoler and Strassler.

80 Genduk Ginem, 1 March 1997, interview with Kwartanada and Purwanti.

81 Ibu Rubi, 27 February 1997, interview with Kwartanada.

82 Ibu Adi, 12 November 1996, interview with Kwartanada.

83 Ibu Patmi, 18 June 1996, interview with Strassler.

84 Ibu Sastro, 4 April 1997, interview with Kwartanada and Purwanti.

85 Ibu Adi, 12 November 1996, interview with Kwartanada.

86 Pak Mulyo, 18 March 1997, interview with Kwartanada and Purwanti.

87 See, Berman's *Speaking through Silence*, for an analysis of Javanese women's narrative styles (conducted in Yogyakarta). She argues that in lower-class Javanese women's narratives, repetition and the relating of mundane details are crucial ways in which speakers invite group participation.

88 See Barbara Hernstein Smith, 'Narrative Versions, Narrative Theories', in *On Narrative*, W.J.T. Mitchell (ed.), Chicago: University of Chicago Press, 1981, p. 225.

89 But see also Marilyn R. Waldman, 'The Otherwise Unnoteworthy Year 711: A Reply to Hayden White', in Mitchell, *On Narrative*, p. 242, for a discussion of the 'implicit stories' embedded in lists.

90 Genduk Ginem, 1 March 1997, interview with Purwanti and Kwartanada.

91 Ibu Darmo, 12 July 1997, interview with Kwartanada, Purwanti, Stoler, and Strassler; and 31 March 1997, interview with Purwanti and Kwartanada.

92 Ibu Rubi, 27 February 1997, interview with Kwartanada.

93 On refusal to become an ethnographic subject, see Kamala Visweswaran, *Fictions of Feminist Ethnography*, Minneapolis: University of Minnesota Press, 1994.

94 Ibu Darmo, 12 July 1997, interview with Kwartanada, Purwanti, Stoler, and Strassler.

95 Arjun Appardurai, 'The Past as a Scarce Resource', *Man*, no. 2, 1981, pp. 201–219; Nicholas B. Dinks, *Colonialism and Culture*, Ann Arbor: University of Michigan Press, 1992, introd.

Chapter 24

Katherine Borland

'THAT'S NOT WHAT I SAID'
Interpretative conflict in oral
narrative research

Here folklorist Katherine Borland considers a situation in which an interviewee –
her own grandmother – disputes the researcher's interpretation of her memories.
Borland asserts the value of researchers' interpretations (in this case based upon
the symbolic construction of the story) which are not simply 'a recuperation of original authorial intention', yet she also notes the dangers of attacking 'collaborators'
carefully constructed sense of 'self' and outlines a more negotiated interpretative
process which benefits both parties. Katherine Borland is an Associate Professor
of Comparative Studies in the Humanities at Indiana University. Reprinted from
S. Berger Gluck and D. Patai (eds) *Women's Words*: *The Feminist Practice of Oral
History*, New York: Routledge, 1991, pp. 63–75, with permission.

I N THE SUMMER OF 1944, my grandmother Beatrice Hanson, put on
a pale, eggshell-colored gabardine dress with big gold buttons down the side, a
huge pancake-black hat, and elbow-length gloves – for in *those* days ladies dressed
up to go to the fair – and off she went with her father to see the sulky (harness)
races at the Bangor, Maine, fairgrounds. The events that ensued provided for a lively
wrangle between father and daughter as they vied to pick the winner. Forty-two
years later Beatrice remembered vividly the events of that afternoon and, in a highly
structured and thoroughly entertaining narrative, recounted them to me, her folk-
lorist-granddaughter, who recorded her words on tape for later transcription and
analysis. What took place that day, why it proved so memorable, and what happened
to the narrative during the process of intergenerational transmission provide a case
study in the variability of meaning in personal narrative performances. This story,
or, better said, these stories, stimulate reflexivity about our scholarly practice.

Let me begin with the question of meaning and its variability. We can view
the performance of a personal narrative as a meaning-constructing activity on
two levels simultaneously. It constitutes both a dynamic interaction between the
thinking subject and the narrated event (her own life experience) and between

the thinking subject and the narrative event (her 'assumption of responsibility to an audience for a display of communicative competence'[1]). As performance contexts change, as we discover new audiences, and as we renegotiate our sense of self, our narratives will also change.

What do folklorists do with the narratives performed for/before us? Like other audience members, we enjoy a skillfully told tale. But some of us also collect records of the performance in order to study them. Oral personal narratives occur naturally within a conversational context, in which various people take turns at talk, and thus are rooted most immediately in a web of expressive social activity. *We* identify chunks of artful talk within this flow of conversation, give them physical existence (most often through writing), and embed them in a new context of expressive or at least communicative activity (usually the scholarly article aimed toward an audience of professional peers). Thus, we construct a second-level narrative based upon, but at the same time reshaping, the first.

Like the original narrator, we simultaneously look inward towards our own experience of the performance (our interpretive shaping of it as listeners) and outward to our audience (to whom we must display a degree of scholarly competence). Presumably, the patterns upon which we base our interpretations can be shown to inhere in the 'original' narrative, but our aims in pointing out certain features, or in making connections between the narrative and larger cultural formations, may at times differ from the original narrator's intentions. This is where issues of our responsibility to our living sources become most acute.

Years ago, scholars who recorded the traditions, arts, and history of a particular culture group gave little thought to the possibility that their representations might legitimately be challenged by those for and about whom they wrote. After all, they had 'been in the field', listening, taking notes, and witnessing the culture first-hand. Educated in the literate, intellectual tradition of the Western academy, these scholars brought with them an objective, scientific perspective that allowed them, they felt, to perceive underlying structures of meaning in their material that the 'natives', enmeshed in a smaller, more limited world, could not see. Therefore, it is not surprising that general ethnographic practice excluded the ethnographic subject from the process of post-fieldwork interpretation, nor that folklorists and anthropologists rarely considered their field collaborators to be potential audiences for their publications. More recently, some researchers sensitive to the relationships of power in the fieldwork exchange have questioned this model of the scholar as interpretive authority for the culture groups he/she studies.[2]

For feminists, the issue of interpretive authority is particularly problematic, for our work often involves a contradiction. On the one hand, we seek to empower the women we work with by revaluing their perspectives, their lives, and their art in a world that has systematically ignored or trivialized women's culture.[3] On the other, we hold an explicitly political vision of the structural conditions that lead to particular social behaviors, a vision that our field collaborators, many of whom do not consider themselves feminists, may not recognize as valid. My own work with my grandmother's racetrack narrative provides a vivid example of how conflicts of interpretation may, perhaps inevitably do, arise during the folklore transmission process. What should we do when we women disagree?

To refrain from interpretation by letting the subjects speak for themselves seems to me an unsatisfactory if not illusory solution. For the very fact that we constitute the initial audience for the narratives we collect influences the way in which our collaborators will construct their stories, and our later presentation of these stories – in particular publications under particular titles – will influence the way in which prospective readers will interpret the texts. Moreover, feminist theory provides a powerful critique of our society, and, as feminists, we presumably are dedicated to making that critique as forceful and direct as possible. How, then, might we present our work in a way that grants the speaking woman interpretive respect without relinquishing our responsibility to provide our own interpretation of her experience?

Although I have no easy answer to this question, I believe that by reflecting on our practice we can move toward a more sensitive research methodology. In the spirit of reflexivity I offer here a record of the dispute that arose between my grandmother and myself when I ventured an interpretation of her narrative. First, I will summarize the narrative, since the taped version runs a full twenty-five minutes. Then I will present her framing of the narrative in performance and my reframing during the interpretive process. Finally, I will present her response to my interpretation. While I have already 'stacked the deck' in my favor by summarizing the story, reducing it through my subjective lens, my grandmother's comments powerfully challenge my assumption of exegetical authority over the text.[4]

Beatrice began her story with a brief setting of the scene: in the grandstand, she finds herself seated directly behind Hod Buzzel, 'who', she states, 'had gotten me my divorce and whom I *hated* with a passion'. Hod is accompanied by his son, the county attorney (who, Beatrice says, 'was just as bad as his father in another way – he was a snob'). Beatrice's father knows them both very well.

Beatrice, the narrator, then explains the established system for selecting a horse. Observers typically purchase a 'score card' that lists the past records of horses and drivers, and they evaluate the horses as they pace before the grandstand. Beatrice's personal system for choosing a horse depends most heavily on her judgement of the observable merits of both horse and driver. She explains:

> And if I could find a *horse* that right pleased me, and a driver that pleased me that were together . . . *there* would be my choice, you see? So, this particular afternoon . . . I *found* that. Now that didn't happen all the time, by any means, but I found . . . perfection, as far as I was concerned, and I was absolutely *convinced* that *that* horse was going to win.

Beatrice decides to bet on Lyn Star, an unknown horse driven by a young man. She knows that this young man's father is driving another horse in the race. Her father and the Buzzels select Black Lash, a horse with an established reputation for speed.

The subsequent action exhibits an inherent potential for narrative patterning. Sulky races, in which a driver sits behind the horse in a two-wheeled single-seat carriage, are presented in a series of three heats. In other words, the same group of horses races against each other three times during the afternoon, alternating with three groups of horses who race against one another in the same fashion. Normally, drivers act on their own, competing individually against their opponents, but the appearance of a father and son in the same race suggests to Bea the possibility that these two may collaborate with one another in some way. Each heat, from the perspective of the audience, involves three stages: selecting a horse and placing a bet, observing the race proper, and collecting on one's winning tickets. With regard to the particular race narrated, an additional structural element is provided by the repetitive strategy employed by the father and son upon whom Bea has placed her hopes.

In each heat, the father quickly takes the lead and sets a fast pace for the other horses while the son lopes along behind. As the horses turn into the second lap and start their drive, the father moves over to let his son through on the rail (the inside lane of the track) thereby forcing Black Lash, the next-to-front runner, to go out and around him. Dramatic tension is produced by the variable way in which this strategy is played out on the course. In the first heat, Lyn Star wins by a nose. In the second, he ties in a photo finish with Black Lash. In the third, the father's horse, worn out by his previous two performances, drops back behind the others, leaving Lyn Star and Black Lash to really race. But because of the way the races have been run, Lyn Star's driver had never really had to push his horse. He does so this time and leaves Black Lash half a length behind.

As a superlative narrator, Beatrice recognizes and exploits the parallels between the observed contest and the contest between observers who have aligned themselves with different horses. She structures her narrative by alternating the focus between a dramatic reenactment of events in the grandstand and a description of the actual race as it unfolds before the observers. Within this structure, the cooperation between the father and son on the racecourse provides a contrast to the conflict between father and daughter in the grandstand.

Before the first heat, Bea's father asks her, 'D'you pick a horse?' And she responds that, yes, she has chosen Lyn Star. At this, her father loudly denounces her choice, claiming that the horse will never win, she'll lose her money, and she should not bet. Beatrice puts two dollars on the horse. When Lyn Star wins, Bea turns triumphantly to her father. Undaunted, he insists that the race was a fluke and that Bea's favorite horse will not win again. Nevertheless, Beatrice places six dollars on Lyn Star in the next heat. By now, though, her father is irate and attempts first to trade horses with her so that she won't lose her money, and then, when she declines this offer, he refuses altogether to place her bet. Young Buzzel, who has become an amused audience of one to the father–daughter contest in the grandstand, offers to take her money down to the betting office. Since Bea has never placed her own bets, she accepts.

With the third heat Beatrice's father catapults their private argument into the public arena, as he asks his daughter, 'What are you going to do this time?' Beatrice is adamant, 'I am *betting on my horse* and I am betting *ten bucks* on that horse. It's gonna win!' At this, Beatrice, the narrator, explains, 'Father had a fit. *He* had a fit. And he tells everybody three miles around in the grandstand what a fool I am too. . . . *He* wasn't gonna take my money down!' So Beatrice commandeers young Buzzel to place her bet for her again. When Lyn Star wins by a long shot, Bea's father is effectively silenced:

> And *I* threw my pocketbook in one direction, and I threw my gloves in another direction, and my score book went in another direction, and I jumped up and I hollered, to everyone, 'You see what know-it-all said! *That's* my father!' And finally one man said to me . . . no, he said to my father, 'You know, she *really* enjoys horse racing, doesn't she?'

To understand how Bea frames her narrative, we must return to a consideration of her initial description of how a horse is chosen. This prefatory material orients the audience to a particular point of view, emphasizing that the race should be understood as an opportunity for racegoers to exercise their evaluative skills in order to predict an eventual outcome. Indeed, the length and detail of this portion of the narrative emphasizes the seriousness, for Beatrice, of this preliminary evaluative activity. This framing of the story gains significance if one considers that Bea's knowledge of horses was unusual for women in her community. Emphasizing the exceptionality of her knowledge, she explained to me that her father owned and raced horses when Bea was a child and 'though I could not go *fishing* with my father on Sundays, or *hunting* with him on any day of the week, for some strange reason, he took me with him, mornings' to watch his horses being exercised.

Additionally, in her framing of the narrative, Beatrice identifies the significance of the event narrated, its memorability, as the unique coming together of a perfect horse and driver that produced an absolute conviction on her part as to who would win the contest. Since this conviction was proved correct the narrative functions to support or illustrate Bea's sense of self as a competent judge of horses within both the narrative and the narrated event. In effect, her narrative constitutes a verbal re-performance of an actual evaluative performance at the track.

What do I as a listener make of this story? A feminist, I am particularly sensitive to identifying gender dynamics in verbal art, and, therefore, what makes the story significant for me is the way in which this self-performance within the narrated event takes on the dimension of a female struggle for autonomy within a hostile male environment. Literally and symbolically, the horse race constitutes a masculine sphere. Consider, racing contestants, owners, and trainers were male (although female *horses* were permitted to compete). Also, while women obviously attended the races, indeed, 'ladies dressed up' to go to the races, they were granted only partial participant status. While they were allowed to sit in the grandstand as observers (and, having dressed up, one assumes, as persons to be observed), they were not expected to engage as active evaluators in the essential first stage of the racing event. Notice that even at the very beginning of the story Bea's father did not want her to bet. Betting is inherently a risk-taking activity. Men take risks; women do not. This dimension of meaning is underscored in the second heat when Beatrice, the narrator, ironically recounts that her father was going to be 'decent' to her, in other words, was going to behave according to the model of gentlemanly conduct, by offering to bear his daughter's risk and bet on her horse for her.

Significantly, as the verbal contest develops, Beatrice displays greater and greater assertiveness as a gambler. Not only does she refuse to align herself with the men's judgement, she also raises the ante by placing more and more serious bets on her choice. From an insignificant bet in the first heat – and here it bears recalling that in racing parlance a two-dollar bet is still called a 'lady's bet' – she proceeds in the second and third heats to bet six and ten dollars, respectively.

In portraying the intensification of the contest, Beatrice, the narrator, endows Beatrice, the gambler, with an increasingly emphatic voice. Her tone in addressing her father moves from one of calm resolution before the first and second heats – 'That's the horse I'm betting on', and 'No, I'm gonna stay with that horse' – to heated insistence before the third heat – 'I am *betting on my horse!*' (each word accentuated in performance by the narrator's pounding her fist on the dining-room table).

Finally, if one looks at Beatrice's post-heat comments, one can detect a move from simple self-vindication in the first heat to a retaliatory calumniation of her father's reputation delivered in a loud disparaging voice – 'You see what know-it-all said! *That's* my father!' Thus, at the story's end, Beatrice has moved herself from a peripheral feminine position with respect to the larger male sphere of betting *and* talk, to a central position where her words and deeds proclaim her equal and indeed superior to her male antagonist. Symbolically underscoring this repudiation of a limiting feminine identity, Bea flings away the accessories of her feminine costume – her gloves and her pocketbook.

If on one level the story operates as a presentation of self as a competent judge of horses, on another it functions to assert a sense of female autonomy and equality within a sphere dominated by men. From yet another perspective, the verbal contest between father and daughter results in a realignment of allegiances based on the thematic contrasts between age and youth, reputation and intrinsic merit, observable in the contest between the horses Black Lash and Lyn Star. When her father (tacitly) refuses to place her bet before the second heat, young Buzzell, whom Bea has previously described as an antagonist, and who has been betting with the older men, offers to place her bet for her. In effect, he bets on Beatrice in the contest developing on the sidelines.

Furthermore, with regard to the narrator's life experience, one can view the narrative as a metaphor for a larger contest between Beatrice and her social milieu. For in the early 1930s Beatrice shocked her community by divorcing her first husband. This action and her attempt to become economically independent by getting an education were greeted with a certain amount of social and familial censure. For instance, Beatrice recalls, when her mother entered the date of the divorce in the family bible, she included the note: 'Recorded, but not approved'. It also forced Beatrice to leave her two young daughters in the care of their paternal grandparents for the five years she attended college, a necessity that still saddens and troubles her today.

My grandparents agree that, in the ideology of marriage at that time, 'you weren't supposed to be happy'. My grandfather relates that his grandmother suffered severe psychological strain during menopause, was committed to a psychiatric hospital, and, while there, crossed her name off her marriage certificate. In a slightly more active form of resistance, Beatrice's grandmother, after injuring herself while doing heavy farm work, took to her bed for several years. However, as soon as her son married, she got up, moved in with him, and led a normal, active life, becoming the strong maternal figure of Bea's own childhood. Bea's mother separated herself psychologically from both her husband and her family by retreating into a strict, moralistic, and, in Bea's view, hypocritical religiosity. For Bea's predecessors, then, a woman's socially acceptable response to an unhappy marriage was to remove herself from the marriage without actually effecting a formal, public separation. Although Bea's first husband was tacitly recognized by the community as an unfit husband – irresponsible, alcoholic, a spendthrift and a philanderer – Beatrice was expected to bear with the situation in order to protect her own reputation and that of her family.

By divorcing her first husband Beatrice transgressed middle-class social decorum and was branded 'disreputable'. The appearance in the present narrative of the divorce lawyer and Bea's negative reaction to him leads me to link Beatrice's performance and status at the races to her previous loss of reputation in the larger village society. In both instances Beatrice had to prove in the face of strong opposition the rightness of not playing by the rules, of relying on her own judgment, of acting as an autonomous individual. I would suggest, then, that the latent associations of this narrative to circumstances critical to the narrator's life, even if not consciously highlighted in the narrative, may reinforce its memorability.

What is essential to emphasize, however, is that this is *my* framing of the race-track narrative informed by contemporary feminist conceptions of patriarchal structures, which my grandmother does not share. Moreover, after reading an initial version of this interpretation, Beatrice expressed strong disagreement with my conclusions. I quote a portion of the fourteen-page letter she wrote to me concerning the story:

> Not being, myself, a feminist, the 'female struggle' as such never bothered me in my life. It never occurred to me. I never thought of my *position* at all in this sense. I've always felt that I had a fine childhood. It seems, now, that I must have had a remarkable one. To begin with, I had a very strong father figure. Surrounded by the deep and abiding love of my Grandmother Austin (whom I adored); the clear, unfaltering knowledge of my father's love and his openly expressed pride in me, and the definite disciplines set by my grandmother which provided the staunch and unchallengeable framework in which I moved, I knew absolute security. (The disciplines were unchallengeable because I never had the least desire to challenge them. I would have done anything not to disappoint Grandma or make her feel bad, and I was so very happy and secure that only an idiot would have tried to upset the situation.)
>
> In consequence of all this, as I grew older, the inner strength which that sense of security had built in me, served always to make me feel equal to anyone, male or female, and very often superior. Feminism, as such, was of no moment to me – none at all. Privately, it has always seemed ridiculous, but that's neither here nor there. It makes no difference to me what anybody else thinks about it.
>
> So your interpretation of the story as a female struggle for autonomy within a hostile male environment is entirely YOUR interpretation. You've read into the story what you wished to – what pleases YOU. That it was never – by any widest stretch of the imagination – the concern of the originator of the story makes such an interpretation a definite and complete distortion, and in this respect I question its authenticity. The story is no longer MY story at all. The skeleton remains, but it has become your story. Right? How far is it permissible to go, in the name of folklore, and still be honest in respect to the original narrative?

Beatrice brings up a crucial issue in oral narrative scholarship – who controls the text? If I had not sent my grandmother a copy of my work, asking for her response, I could perhaps have avoided the question of my intrusion into the texts I collect. Discussions with our field collaborators about the products of our research are often overlooked or unreported by folklore scholars. Luckily, my grandmother is quite capable of reading, responding to, and resisting my presentation of her narrative. For my own and my grandmother's versions provide a radical example of how each of us has created a story from her own experience. While I agree that the story has indeed become *my* story in the present context, I cannot agree that my reading betrays the original narrative.

Beatrice embraces an idealist model of textual meaning that privileges authorial intentions. It makes sense for my grandmother to read the story in this way. From my own perspective, however, the story does not really become a story until it is actualized in the mind of a receptive listener/reader. As my consciousness has been formed within a different social and historical reality, I cannot restrict my reading to a recuperation of original authorial intentions. I offer instead a different reading, one that values her story as an example to feminists of one woman's strategy for combating a limiting patriarchal ideology. That Bea's performance constitutes a direct opposition to established authorities reveals for me how gender ideologies are not wholly determinative or always determinative of female identity.[5]

Nevertheless, despite my confidence in the validity of my reading as a feminist scholar, personally I continue to be concerned about the potential emotional effect alternative readings of personal narratives may have on our living subjects. The performance of a personal narrative is a fundamental means by which people comprehend their own lives and present a 'self' to their audience.[6] Our scholarly representations of those performances, if not sensitively presented, may constitute an attack on our collaborators' carefully constructed sense of self. While Bea and I have discussed our differences at length and come to an amicable agreement about how to present them (i.e., the inclusion of her response to my initial reading in the final text), I might have avoided eliciting such a violent initial response from her if I had proceeded differently from the outset.[7]

I could have tried to elicit my grandmother's comments on the story's meaning before I began the process of interpretation. During the taping session itself, however, this would have proved problematic. As I stated earlier, oral personal narratives occur naturally within a conversational context, and often the performance of one narrative leads to other related performances. These displays of verbal art provide an important context for understanding how the narrative in question is to be viewed, and from my perspective it would not be productive to break the narrative flow in order to move to the very different rhetorical task of interpretation and analysis.

Furthermore, during a narrative performance of this type, both narrator and listener are caught up in the storytelling event. Although associative commentary about the stories is common, at this stage in the fieldwork exchange neither narrator nor listener is prepared to reflect analytically on the material being presented. Indeed, the conscious division of a storytelling session into discreet story units or thematic constellations of stories occurs at the later stage of review and study.

Nevertheless, the narrator's commentary on and interpretation of a story can contribute greatly to the researcher's understanding of it. I now feel I ought to have arranged a second session with my grandmother in which I played her the taped version and asked her for her view of its function and meaning. Time constraints prevented me from doing so. I did solicit an interpretation from Bea with not much success after I had written and she had read my initial version of this article. At that time Beatrice insisted that the story was simply an amusing anecdote with no deep or hidden meanings. Although it may be that some narrators are not prepared to interpret their own stories analytically, Bea's reaction may have been due to her sharply felt loss of authorial control.

With the benefit of hindsight, let me review two points that proved especially sensitive for my grandmother. First, Bea reacted very strongly to the feminist identity my interpretation implied she had. Though some might quibble that this problem is simply a matter of labels, the word 'feminist' often has negative, threatening connotations for women who have not participated in the feminist movement. More important, Bea's objection points to an important oversight in my own research process.

When I began the task of interpretation, I assumed a likeness of mind where there was in fact difference: I was confident that my grandmother would accept my view of the story's meaning. After all, she had been very excited about working with me when I told her I wanted to study older women's life experience narratives. She sent me a great deal of material and commentary on the difficult conditions of women's lives in nineteenth- and early twentieth-century Maine, material and commentary that seemed on the surface to convey a feminist perspective. Moreover, she offered her own accounts and stories, some of which dealt with very sensitive matters, assuring me that I should feel perfectly free to use whatever proved helpful to me in my research. How, then, did we, who had a close, confidential, long-standing relationship, manage to misunderstand each other so completely?

The fieldwork exchange fosters a tendency to downplay differences, as both investigator and source seek to establish a footing with one another and find a common ground from which to proceed to the work of collecting and recording oral materials. Additionally, as we are forever constructing our own identities through social interactions, we similarly construct our notion of others. My grandmother has always appeared to me a remarkably strong, independent woman, and thus, even though she has never called herself a feminist, it was an easy step for me to cast her in that role. Although she knew that I considered myself an activist feminist, to her I have always been, first and foremost, a granddaughter. She was, therefore, unprepared for the kind of analysis performed on her narrative. The feminist movement has been criticized before for overgeneralizing about women's experience in its initial enthusiasms of sisterly identification. Yet it bears repeating that important commonalities among women often mask equally important differences.[8]

For Beatrice, another troubling feature of my interpretation is the portrait it presents of her father. Here the problem arises from our different understandings of what the narrative actually is. I approach the story as a symbolic construction and the people within it are, for me, dramatic characters. Thus, Beatrice's father, the antagonistic figure of the story, becomes a symbol of repressive male authority in my interpretation. For Beatrice, however, the story remains an account of a real experience, embedded in the larger context of her life. She brings to her reading of the 'characters' a complex of associations built up over a shared lifetime. From this perspective my interpretation of her father is absolutely false. Whether or not it 'works' for the father figure in the story, it does not define the man. In fact, Beatrice's father was one of the few people who encouraged and supported her during the difficult period after her disastrous first marriage. She remembers her father with a great deal of love and admiration and speaks often of the special relationship they had with one another. Indeed, if anyone was the villain of Beatrice's youth, it would have been her mother, a cold, judgmental woman. Nevertheless, in a written account of the racetrack story composed shortly after the event took place, Beatrice herself remarks that at the track, 'Father and the Buzzels were acting very male', quarreling over the results of the races.[9]

When I sent Beatrice a copy of my essay in which *her* narrative had suffered a sea change, she naturally felt misrepresented. To complicate matters, my original essay contained a great deal of theory that was unfamiliar and at times incomprehensible to her. Embedded in the context of my own scholarly environment, I had not bothered to provide any accompanying explanation of that theory. Thus, if I had 'misread' her text, I also gave her every opportunity to misread mine. I now feel that had I talked to Bea about my ideas *before* I committed them to writing, presented her with drafts, or even arranged to have her read the paper with me so that we might discuss misunderstandings and differences as they arose, her sense of having been robbed of textual authority might not have been as strong as it was.

I am not suggesting that all differences of perspective between folklorist and narrator, feminist scholar and speaking woman, should or can be worked out before the final research product is composed. Nor am I suggesting that our interpretations must be validated by our research collaborators. For when we do interpretations, we bring our own knowledge, experience, and concerns to our material, and the result, we hope, is a richer, more textured understanding of its meaning.

I am suggesting that we might open up the exchange of ideas so that we do not simply gather data on others to fit into our own paradigms once we are safely ensconced in our university libraries ready to do interpretation. By extending the conversation we initiate while collecting oral narratives to the later stage of interpretation, we might more sensitively negotiate issues of interpretive authority in our research.

Quite possibly, this modification of standard practice would reveal new ways of understanding our materials to both research partners. At the very least, it would allow us to discern more clearly when we speak in unison and when we disagree. Finally, it would restructure the traditionally unidirectional flow of information out from source to scholar to academic audience by identifying our field collaborators as an important first audience for our work. Lest we, as feminist scholars, unreflectively appropriate the words of our mothers for our own uses, we must attend to the multiple and sometimes conflicting meanings generated by our framing or contextualizing of their oral narratives in new ways.

Postscript

On July 8, 1989, after a ten-month absence, I visited Beatrice and gave her a copy of the present version of this paper for her final comments. She took it to her study, read it, and then the two of us went through it together, paragraph by paragraph. At this juncture she allowed that much of what I had said was 'very true', though she had not thought about the events of her life in this way before. After a long and fruitful discussion, we approached the central issue of feminism. She explained, once again, that feminism was not a movement that she had identified with or even heard of in her youth. Nevertheless, she declared that if I meant by feminist a person who believed that a woman has the right to live her life the way she wants to regardless of what society has to say about it, then she guessed she was a feminist.

Thus, the fieldwork exchange had become, in the end, a true exchange. I had learned a great deal from Beatrice, and she had also learned something from me. Yet I would emphasize that Bea's understanding and acceptance of feminism was not something that I could bestow upon her, as I had initially and somewhat naively attempted to do. It was achieved through the process of interpretive conflict and discussion, emerging as each of us granted the other interpretive space and stretched to understand the other's perspective. While Bea's identification with feminism is not crucial to my argument, it stands as a testament to the new possibilities for understanding that arise when we re-envision the fieldwork exchange.

Notes

1   R. Bauman, *Verbal Art as Performance*, Prospect Heights, Ill., Waveland, 1977, p. 11. For a discussion of the differences between narrated and narrative events, see R. Bauman's introduction in his *Story, Performance, and Events*, New York: Cambridge University Press, 1986. [Editor's note: a number of discursive footnotes have been deleted from the original.]

2   For a discussion of new experiments in ethnographic texts, see J. Clifford and G.E. Marcus (eds), *Writing Culture: The Poetics and Politics of Ethnography*, Berkeley, Calif.: University of California Press, 1986, and G.E. Marcus and M.M.J. Fischer, *Anthropology as Cultural Critique: An Experimental Moment in the Human Sciences*, Chicago: University of Chicago Press, 1986.

3   For a discussion of the sexist bias in folklore scholarship generally, see M. Weigle, 'Women as verbal artists: reclaiming the daughters of Enheduanna', *Frontiers*, 1978, vol. 3, no. 3, pp. 1–9.

4   The racetrack narrative I present here forms part of an extended taping session I conducted with my grandmother during a three-day visit to her home in December 1986. A transcription of the full version of Beatrice's narrative appears in my article 'Horsing around with the frame: the negotiation of meaning in women's verbal performance', *Praxis*, Spring 1990, pp. 83–107.

5   Beverly Stoeltje discusses the dialectic between individual behavior, changing environments, and ideals of womanhood in '"A helpmate for man indeed": the image of the frontier woman', in C. R. Farrer (ed.), *Women and Folklore: Images and Genres*, Prospect Heights, Ill.: Waveland Press, 1975, pp. 25–41.

6   Victor Turner views performances as reflexive occasions set aside for the collective or individual presentation of the self to the self in 'Images and reflections: ritual drama, carnival, film and spectacle in cultural performance', in his *The Anthropology of Performance*, New York: The Performing Arts Journal Publications, 1987, pp. 121–132. For a discussion of how personal narratives are tools for making sense of our lives, see B. Myerhoff, 'Life history among the elderly: performance, visibility and remembering', in J. Ruby (ed.), *A Crack in the Mirror: Reflexive Perspectives in Anthropology*, Philadelphia: University of Pennsylvannia Press, 1982, pp. 99–117.

7   In several lengthy post-essay discussions, Beatrice, my grandfather Frank, and I discussed both the story and what happened to it during the process of transmission.

After hearing the revised version (in which my grandmother's comments were included), Frank stated that he had learned to see features of the society in which he grew up that he had never really been aware of before. Beatrice was less enthusiastic about my alternative reading, but agreed that my perspective was thought-provoking. For her, the more general issue of how stories are transformed with each new telling was the most interesting point of the essay, and she expressed a desire to continue working on projects of the same type.

8   Equally serious is the tendency to discount as vestiges of false consciousness attitudes or behaviors that do not fit into our own vision of feminist practice. In a cogent critique of this tendency in feminist research, Rachelle Saltzman demonstrates how women who use sexist-male jokes within their own gender group see this activity as an expropriation for use rather than an acceptance of a belittled female identity, in 'Folklore, feminism and the folk: whose lore is it?', *Journal of American Folklore*, 1987, no. 100, pp. 548–567.

9   Quotation from a letter written to Beatrice's second husband, Frank Hanson, 6 August, 1944.

Chapter 25

Kathleen Blee

EVIDENCE, EMPATHY
AND ETHICS
Lessons from oral histories of the Klan

Kathleen Blee describes a scenario in which it was virtually impossible for a researcher to reach mutual agreement with her interviewees about the interpretation of their memories, an oral history of women in the Ku Klux Klan. She pinpoints a central tension in the role of the oral historian, between responsibility to the interviewee and responsibility to society and history. Kathleen Blee is Professor of Sociology at the University of Pittsburgh. Reprinted with permission from the *Journal of American History*, 1993, vol. 80, no. 2, pp. 596–606. Copyright © Organization of American Historians (www.oah.org/).

MANY CONTEMPORARY oral histories are rooted in principles of progressive and feminist politics, particularly in a respect for the truth of each informant's life experiences and a quest to preserve the memory of ordinary people's lives. Feminist scholars have been in the forefront of efforts to elaborate these ideals as methodological principles, seeking ways to dissolve the traditional distinction between historian-as-authority and informant-as-subject and to create what the sociologist Judith Stacey calls 'an egalitarian research process character-ized by authenticity, reciprocity, and intersubjectivity between the researcher and her "subjects"'.[1]

Such oral history practices have been designed primarily to study and record the lives of 'people who, historically speaking, would otherwise remain inarticu-late'.[2] From this tradition of history from the bottom up has come a rich and sensitive body of interviews with union organizers, feminist activists, civil rights workers, and others whose experience progressive and feminist scholars share and whose life stories and world views they often find laudable.

Historians have paid less attention to the life stories of ordinary people whose political agendas they find unsavory, dangerous, or deliberately deceptive.[3] Oral history is a particularly valuable source of rectifying this scholarly lacuna since right-wing, reactionary, and racial hate groups tend to be secretive and highly transient, limiting the availability and usefulness of traditional documentary sources. But there are few guidelines for using oral history to study the non-elite Right. Traditionally, oral historians have emphasized caution, distance, and objectivity in interviews with members of elites and egalitarianism, reciprocity, and authenticity in interviews with people outside elites. However, this epistemological dichotomy reflects implicit romantic assumptions about the subjects of history from the bottom up – assumptions that are difficult to defend when studying ordinary people who are active in the politics of intolerance, bigotry, or hatred.

The use of oral history to study the far Right also raises more general issues of historical interpretation. The ability of oral history to provide new and accurate insights into the lives and understandings of ordinary people in the past depends on a critical approach to oral evidence and to the process of interviewing. Thus, efforts to formulate an approach to oral history that recognizes the range and complexities of narratives garnered from people outside elites and helps us judge these sources critically can assist historians working with other sources and methods.

In the mid-1980s I interviewed former members of the 1920s Ku Klux Klan (KKK) and Women of the Ku Klux Klan in Indiana. These Klan organizations recruited several million men, women, and children across the United States into a political crusade for white, Protestant supremacy. Although the Klan's anti-Semitic, anti-Catholic, and racist politics ultimately had little effect on a national level, the intense concentration of Klan members in some communities and states allowed the Klan to dictate the outcome of elections, the policies of law enforcement, and the nature of community life in these areas. In Indiana, as many as half a million women and men are estimated to have joined the Klan during the 1920s. In parts of southern and central Indiana where the majority of white, native-born Protestants were Klan members, the Klan controlled nearly every local electoral office, police agency, and school board. In these communities, the Klan terrorized African-Americans, Catholics, Jews, and immigrants with sporadic incidents of physical violence and with unrelenting intimidation, boycotts, and efforts to terminate from employment, evict from housing, and expel from the community all those it deemed to be an obstacle to an agenda of white Protestant supremacy. In this article, I use interviews with former Klan women and Klansmen from the heavily Klan-dominated communities in Indiana to examine issues of historical interpretation, which I label as evidence, empathy, and ethics.[4]

Interpreting evidence from oral histories

Oral history can open new vistas of historical understanding, but it can also mislead and confuse. Accounts by those who have participated in campaigns for racial and religious supremacy, for example, often are laced with deceptive information, disingenuous denials of culpability, and dubious assertions about their political motivation. But with careful scrutiny and critical interpretation, even these interviews can yield surprisingly informative and complex historical information.

One issue that plagues studies of right-wing extremists is the desire of informants to distort their own political pasts. The evidence that such informants present to the oral historian is at once revelatory and unreliable. It is revelatory because, as Paul Thompson recognized, 'what the informant believes is indeed a fact (that is, the fact that he or she believes it) just as much as what "really happened"'. But it is also unreliable, as Claudia Salazar notes, because 'to debate matters of politics inevitably forces us to look back from the text to the world . . . This move is fundamental if we want to avoid the entrapments of a purely discursivist stance'.[5]

Historical interpretation always requires attention to the partiality, bias, and distortions of any individual's particular historical account when garnering evidence from narratives of direct experience.[6] But reliance upon narrated accounts and memory for historical understanding of right-wing extremists is problematic on another level. In an important discussion of oral history methodology, Alessandro Portelli notes that 'memory is not a passive depository of facts, but an active creation of meanings'. Meanings are created in social and political contexts; memory is not a solitary act.[7] Thus, it is not simply that narratives constructed by former Klan members to explain their role in one of history's most vicious campaigns of intolerance and hatred are biased by their own political agendas and their desire to appear acceptable to an oral historian but also that informants' memories have been shaped by subsequent public censure of this and later Klans.

The former Klan members that I interviewed all related tales of 'clannish' Catholics and Jews, or offensive African-Americans, or troublesome immigrants. The tales were recounted as direct experience but were often indistinguishable from the stories manufactured and disseminated by the Klan to justify its crusade for white supremacy. Related in interviews, however, such tales suggest motivations and a self-consciousness about Klan membership that did not exist for most members when they were members. In the Klan's heyday, few members would have felt called upon to put forth reasons – however distorted – for their desire to ensure white Protestant supremacy. In the homogeneous, overwhelmingly white, Protestant, and native-born communities in which the Klan took deepest root, Catholics, African-Americans, Jews, and immigrants were simply 'others' – so far removed from the social and political life of white Protestants that rationalizations were unnecessary. The inferiority and ominous character of nonwhites and non-Protestants were simply assumed in the receptive population in which the Klan sought recruits. Only later, with the Klan under attack, did stories meant to exonerate its participants appear.[8]

But if interviews of extremists can elicit such distorted accounts, the recovery of narrated experience also, paradoxically, offers the possibility of constructing more accurate explanations of how and why people become attracted to political movements of hatred and bigotry. Oral histories can tap into the complexity of political experiences and beliefs more directly than can documentary sources. They allow us to scrutinize the accounts of political actors, and to probe those experiences, beliefs, and narratives that do not fit conventional historical interpretations, in addition to revealing 'the tangible "atmosphere" of events'.[9]

The history of histories of the Klan is a case in point. The voluminous historiography of the 1920s Ku Klux Klan has virtually ignored the role of women in this movement. Standard documentary sources, assembled by contemporaries and historians who assumed that women were politically insignificant, focused entirely on the male Klan. By thus overlooking women's actions in the Klan, historical accounts seemed to confirm that Klan women were minor, incidental players, offering mere window dressing behind which men carried out the real politics of hatred and bigotry.[10]

Oral histories of former Klan women, however, tell us otherwise. Women played a significant role in the second Klan's vicious campaigns of rumor, boycotts, and intimidation of African-Americans, Catholics, Jews, and other minorities. Certain stores, according to my informants, were patronized by Klan women because they were 'known to be owned by Ku Klux Klan members'. In contrast, one former Klanswoman recalls, businesses owned by Catholics, Jews, and African-Americans 'were hurt terribly because people wouldn't go in there because the Klan would tell you not to'. Informants discussed these boycotts as informal, almost unspoken community norms that governed majority-white, Protestant, and Klan-dominated communities in the 1920s, as did a man who related growing up with just 'an understanding that if you rented your farm, you better not rent it to a Catholic'.[11]

Moreover, oral histories of Klan women reveal that many held complicated attitudes toward gender, race, economics, and nationalism, attitudes that did not fit traditional political categories, such as reactionary or progressive. Ideologies of Klan women in the 1920s were complicated, blending occasional thoughtful, some-times progressive, views with rigid adherence to dogmas of nationalism, racial hierarchies, or Christian supremacy. Although they slavishly followed the male Klan's politics of white Protestant supremacy, for example, they charted a different political course on issues of gender and women's rights (the rights of white, native-born, and Protestant women, that is).

While the men's Ku Klux Klan promoted traditional views of gender roles, a separate female organization – the Women of the Ku Klux Klan – praised women's rights organizations, the participation of women in the temperance movement, and the extension of the right to vote to women. It promoted the National Woman's Party, supported the Equal Rights Amendment (ERA), which was first introduced in the 1920s, and celebrated women who 'made it' in traditionally male work-places.[12]

By manipulating the issue of women's rights in this fashion, the women's Klan attempted to link the interests of white, native-born Protestant women to those of the Klan. Its leaders sought to broaden the Klan's appeal to women while obscuring the Klan's agenda of racial and religious hatred. In documentary sources such revealing ambiguities in the ideology of the Klan are erased. It is through oral historical accounts, subject to critical interpretation, that these contradictions can be recovered and explored.

Moreover, the evidence of oral history is embedded not only in narrative accounts but also in the process of interviewing. An informant's mode of presen-tation can be scrutinized for clues to the meanings that historical actors gave to their experiences when they occurred; this was the case when informants rushed to assure me that the Klan was 'uplifting', 'just a celebration', 'a fantastic thing', a group that 'gave people a feeling they were doing the right thing'. Modes of presentation can be deceptive – oral history approaches can lead unwary scholars to underesti-mate the devastating effects of far-right and hate-based politics. Claudia Koonz, in her excellent study of women in Nazi Germany, *Mothers in the Fatherland*, for example, argues that in Germany 'history recorded the "bad things"; memory preserved a benign face of fascism'. Indeed, the muting of past atrocities may be endemic to the epistemology of oral history. As Cynthia Hay notes, 'Oral history has often been criticized on the grounds that it is confined to a cosy view of the past . . . [which can] at best obtain banalities about experiences which were anything but banal.'[13]

The benign memories of which Koonz warns arose in many of my interviews with female and male members of the 1920s Ku Klux Klan. But unlike Luisa Passerini, who found the pro-Fascist sentiments of Turin workers disguised within 'declarations expressing dissociation or distance from the regime', I found that my Klan informants, unless pressed, felt little need to obscure their political beliefs. Although many informants recounted being involved in economic boycotts and threats against Catholic, Jewish, and African-American families and their property, none expressed any consciousness of having done wrong; few seemed even to appreciate why they might be viewed as intolerant or bigoted. Except when defending against the historical condemnation of subsequent generations, they felt no need to explain why they found the Klan appealing. To them, life in the Klan was normal, a given, needing no explanation. The only puzzle was why later generations regarded 'their Klan' so negatively.[14]

Such mundane reactions are not without value. They can reveal, as well as conceal, the force and terror of this Klan. In areas of the United States in the 1920s the Ku Klux Klan so dominated communities in which white Protestants were the majority that Klan life became inseparable from non-Klan life. With the myriad of Klan weddings, baby christenings, teenaged auxiliaries, family picnics, athletic contests, parades, spelling bees, beauty contests, rodeos, and circuses, it is perhaps little wonder that the 1920s Klan is recalled by former members as an ordinary, normal, taken-for-granted part of the life of the white Protestant majority. For members, the Klan defined the fabric of everyday life, at once reinforcing and dictating relations of kinship and friendship and practices of celebration and sorrow. In the minds of its members, the Klan became understood as little more than 'just another club'.[15]

The political culture and activities of the Klan so closely paralleled the daily lives of my informants that they could assert, without irony, that 'everybody was in the Klan' or that 'it was a fun organization . . . like a Halloween parade. You'd mask up, wear sheets and be entertained'. This led also to eerily abstracted and contradictory statements by informants, like a woman who insisted that 'the one Jew in town, he became part of the community. I don't think anybody ever thought about doing anything to him . . . [but] people didn't go to his store'. That a political movement could urge that Americans 'put all the Catholics, Jews and Negroes on a raft in the middle of the ocean and then sink the raft' and be remembered by its adherents as an ordinary, unremarkable social club is staggering. Hannah Arendt's 'banality of evil' is found here – in the millions of people who joined a crusade of violent hatred so easily, so unreflectively. Oral histories are exceptionally sensitive sources for recording the lack of self-consciousness in historical subjects, the sensation of normality and conventionality that fueled the Klan of the 1920s.[16]

But if oral histories can reveal the depth of such unspoken, unacknowledged, everyday hatred and bigotry, such interviews can also be puzzling. Decades after this wave of Klan activity subsided, its former members struggle in interviews to justify their involvement against history's condemnation, to construct – retrospectively and consciously – a narrative of life in the Klan that will exonerate them in the eyes of their children and grandchildren.

Over and over, I heard implausible and internally contradictory stories of forced enlistment into the Klan. One informant initially claimed that he had no idea what brought him into the Klan, that it was just something that happened to everybody. When I later pressed him to describe his activities in the Klan, he changed stories, declaring that he had been helpless in the face of exceptional pressure to join, and that 'there were so many people leaning on me, I had little choice'.[17]

Narratives of self-justification nearly always included claims that the Klan was necessary, that it remedied civil ills, and that it was provoked by its very victims. Gabriele Rosenthal found that Germans who witnessed World War II but did not face persecution constructed stories that asserted they were victims. A similar pattern is evident among former Klan members who declared, for instance, that devastating boycotts organized in Klan-dominated communities were necessitated by the financial power of 'naturally clannish' Catholics and Jews. Or, that 'the colored people were hard to get along with. The white people got along with everybody'. The lack of reflectivity and the stress on self-justification in these interviews are outgrowths both of the acceptability of these white supremacist beliefs in certain populations at a specific time and of a more conscious effort by partisans to deny the consequences of their political efforts. That denial allowed informants to see their role in the Klan as 'great theater' or 'entertaining, more exciting than Chatauqua'.[18]

Empathy and ethics

Oral histories of the far Right also raise questions about empathy and ethics. Daphne Patai, a women's studies scholar and oral historian, notes than many feminist scholars have replaced the 'model of a distanced, controlled, and ostensibly neutral interviewer' with that of 'an engaged and sympathetic interaction between two individuals'. Further, feminist principles of oral history can foster a 'fear of forcing or manipulating individuals into discussing topics they did not want to talk about.'[19] While such concerns are often overlooked in interviews with elites, where the relationship between interviewer and informant is assumed to be unequal and possibly adversarial, empathy can also be problematic in oral histories of ordinary people. Here again, principles that serve well for studying sympathetic informants can prove immobilizing with members of hate groups. Would it be possible, or even desirable, to create an empathic environment when interviewing Klan members?

Some argue that the researcher should strive for rapport with any informant to maximize the information that can be garnered from the interview, even at the expense of downplaying or forgoing sensitive topics. Based on his experience interviewing Gerald L.K. Smith, for example, Glen Jeansonne cautions that the oral historian 'should not place himself or herself in an adversary relationship unless it is unavoidable' and that 'it is best to leave the subject a graceful exit and not ask tough questions back to back'.[20]

In my interviews with former Klan members, however, I made few efforts to establish such rapport or to shy away from controversial topics. Indeed, I was prepared to hate and fear my informants, to find them repellant and, more important, strange. I expected no rapport, no shared assumptions, no common-ality of thought or experience. Moreover, I expected them to be wary of me and reluctant to express their true attitudes. But this was not the case. Instead of partici-pating reluctantly in the interviews, these former Klan members seemed quite at ease. (This openness was due in part to the fact that I found informants through advertisements in local publications and contacts with local historians and civic leaders. As self-identified former Klan members willing to talk with me about their experiences, they are not necessarily representative of all who participated in the 1920s Klan.)

The apparent ease of rapport in these interviews stemmed largely from the informants' own racial stereotypes. These elderly informants found it impossible to imagine that I – a native of Indiana and a white person – would not agree, at least secretly, with their racist and bigoted world views. Even challenging their beliefs had no effect on their willingness to talk. They simply discounted my spoken objec-tions as 'public talk' and carried on the 'private talk' they assumed was universal among whites.[21]

Moreover, even my assumptions about how I would experience the interviews were incorrect. Far from being the stock characters of popular portrayals of Klan members – uniformly reactionary, red-neck, mean, ignorant, operating by an irrational and incomprehensible logic – many of the people I interviewed were inter-esting, intelligent, and well informed.

Although it might be comforting if we could find no commonality of thought or experience with those who are drawn into far-Right politics, my interviews suggest a more complicated and a more disturbing reality. It was fairly ordinary people – people with considered opinions, people who loved their families and could be generous to neighbors and friends – who were the mainstay of the 1920s Klan. Ordinary women and men sustained this deadly outburst against those they saw as different and threatening.

Oral historians are acutely sensitive to the meaning of silences in the narrative and to barriers to communication between us and our informants.[22] Yet, in my interviews with Klan members it was the *lack* of silence and the *ease* of communi-cation that revealed their world views. Such seeming empathy was fraudulent – supported by my informants' inability to understand that racial politics could differ among those who shared a common racial heritage and by my unwillingness to violate the tenuous empathy that propelled the interviews along. Nonetheless, rapport with politically abhorrent informants can be surprisingly, and disturbingly, easy to achieve in oral history interviews.

Closely related to the dilemma of empathy are ethical issues about the know-ledge generated in oral histories of those on the far Right. Rarely do researchers question the value of historical scholarship. Indeed, historical research, far more than work in the social, natural, or physical sciences, is often viewed as at least harmless, more often liberating. This is particularly true of the social histories and oral histories that seek to empower contemporary groups with authentic accounts of the lives and struggles of their forefathers and foremothers.

Oral historians agree that people try to make sense of events by placing them in narratives, in story lines.[23] Is it not possible that oral histories may help infor-mants construct a narrative that 'makes sense' of the Klan and its actions? After interviewing a female Nazi leader, Koonz reflected:

I realized that I had come to get information and she intended to give me a sanitized version of Nazism that would normalize the Hitler state in the minds of contemporaries. She saw the chance to share her views with an American as a way of taking her message to not only a younger generation, but a new audience.[24]

Feminist scholars insist that a researcher cannot be content merely to record another's life story for scholarly publication but must 'return the research' to the subject as a means of empowering the informant and his or her community and thereby leveling the inherent inequality between researcher and subject.[25] But is this ethical principle, too, based on romantic assumptions about the consequences of fortifying the political agendas of ordinary people? Does this principle serve any purpose in an oral history of the Klan?

For this issue, there is no easy solution. It seems obvious that a researcher should not actively seek to empower the Klan.[26] But perhaps the nature of oral history research – here eliciting and conducting interviews with former Klan members – itself empowers informants, by suggesting to them, and to their political descendants, the importance of the Klan in American history. An oral historian of civil rights activists in New Orleans wrote of her informants, 'Their interview narratives became monuments to the personal acts of making history. They defined and understood their personal experience as history itself.' The hazards of similarly empowering a political vision of racial and religious hatred are all too clear.[27]

Moreover, interviews and oral histories should not be used uncritically in the study of contemporary racism and political extremism. Here, the case of David Duke – repackaged former leader of the Ku Klux Klan and the National Association for the Advancement of White People – is instructive. Massive media attention to Duke's electoral efforts in the 1980s and early 1990s in Louisiana netted hundreds of interviews with Duke supporters. Yet, taken together, these interviews were dangerously misleading. Those who consented or who even sought to be interviewed were almost uniformly lower middle-class, poorly educated, and inarticulate.

But the near election of a former Klansman to statewide office was not fueled by these people, nor necessarily by forces of ignorance or economic marginality. The structure of institutionalized racism into which Duke tapped, and even the votes that nearly gave him the keys to Louisiana's gubernatorial mansion, lay deep within educated, middle-class, mainstream white Louisiana. Interviews with those unsavvy or unrestrained enough to utter racists sentiments on camera or before a tape recorder are of limited value – and indeed can create a distorted image of racial hatred – unless they are placed in the context of institutionalized racism.

Similarly, the mainstay of the 1920s Klan was not the pathological individual; rather the Klan effectively tapped a pathological vein of racism, intolerance, and bigotry deep within the white Protestant population. My interviews with former Klan members shed light on how and why ordinary people might become attracted to the politics of racial hatred. However, they do not reveal much about racism itself – how it is generated and how it becomes embedded in the institutions of modern society. An accurate and politically effective understanding of the politics of hatred and right-wing extremism must be developed on two levels – as the racial, class, or national prejudices held by individuals and as the institutionalized practices and structures whereby these attitudes are empowered and reproduced over time.[28] In this effort, oral history accounts, used with caution and attention to their limitations, can play a significant role.

Notes

1   J. Stacey, 'Can there be a feminist ethnography?', in S. Berger Gluck and D. Patai (eds), *Women's Words: The Feminist Practice of Oral History*, New York, 1991, p. 112.

2   R. Fraser, *Blood of Spain: An Oral History of the Spanish Civil War*, New York, 1979, p. 31.

3   Exceptions to historians' inattention to people whose politics they abhor include interviews with Spanish Falange militants and fascists and with Boston antibusing activists. See S.M. Etwood, 'Not so much a programme, more a way of life: oral history and Spanish fascism', *Oral History*, 1988, vol. 16, no. 2, pp. 57–66; Fraser, *Blood of Spain*; and R.P. Formisano, *Boston against Busing: Race, Class, and Ethnicity in the 1960s and 1970s*, Chapel Hill, 1991. The persistence, even increase, in radical Right and racial hate groups around the world today underscores the need to understand the historical attraction of ordinary people to such politics.

4   K.M. Blee, *Women of the Klan: Racism and Gender in the 1920s*, Berkeley, 1991, pp. 4–7, 145–153.

5   P. Thompson, *The Voice of the Past: Oral History*, New York, 1978, p. 138; C. Salazar, 'A Third World woman's text: between the politics of criticism and cultural politics', in Gluck and Patai, *Women's Words*, p. 102.

6   Some recent feminist scholarship, however, argues that the greatest possibility for distortion lies in privileging interpretation over direct experience, resulting in an explanatory circle in which experience confirms interpretation and interpretation describes experience. See D.E. Smith, *The Conceptual Practices of Power: A Feminist Sociology of Knowledge*, Boston, 1990; and P.H. Collins, *Black Feminist Thought: Knowledge, Consciousness, and the Politics of Empowerment*, Boston, 1990. On the advantages of working to 'listen in a new way', bracketing theories that structure 'what to hear and how to interpret', see K. Anderson and D.C. Jack, 'Learning to listen: interview technique and analysis', in Gluck and Patai, *Women's Words*, p. 18.

7   A. Portelli, *The Death of Luigi Trastulli, and Other Stories: Form and Meaning in Oral History*, Albany, 1991, p. 52; J. Bodnar, 'Power and memory in oral history: workers and managers at Studebaker', *Journal of American History*, 1989, vol. 75, p. 1202. See also J.A. Neuenschwander, 'Remembrance of things past: oral historians and long-term memory', *Oral History Review*, 1978, vol. 6, pp. 45–53.

8   Blee, *Women of the Klan*, pp. 84–91, 154–157, 171–173.

9   Fraser, *Blood of Spain*, p. 1.

10   For treatments that give little notice to women in the Klan, see W.C. Wade, *The Fiery Cross*, New York, 1987; and L.J. Moore, *Citizen Klansmen: The Ku Klux Klan in Indiana, 1921–1928*, Chapel Hill, 1991. For descriptions of some women's Klans, see D.H. Bennett, *The Party of Fear: From Nativist Movements to the New Right in American History*, Chapel Hill, 1981; and D. Chalmers, *Hooded Americanism: The History of the Ku Klux Klan*, Durham, 1987.

11   Blee, *Women of the Klan*, pp. 147–153. Anonymous informants in central Indiana, interviews by Kathleen M. Blee, August 26, 1987, August 25, 1987, audiotapes (in Kathleen M. Blee's possession).

12   On the views of the Women of the Ku Klux Klan toward women's rights, see Blee, *Women of the Klan*, pp. 49–57. Some publications by the women's and men's Klans in which these views are evident are *Fiery Cross*, December 14, 1923, p. 9; ibid., August 15, 1924; *The KKK Katechism: Pertinent Questions, Pointed Answers*, Washington, 1924; and *Imperial Night-Hawk*, September 3, 1924.

13   Anonymous informants in central and southern Indiana, interviews by Blee, August 8, 1987, May 13, 1987, August 26, 1987, audiotapes (in Blee's possession); C. Koonz, *Mothers in the Fatherland: Women, the Family, and Nazi Politics*, New York, 1987, p. xix; G.C. Wright, 'Oral history and the search for the black past in Kentucky', *Oral History Review*, 1982, vol. 10, p. 86; C. Hay, 'The pangs of the past', *Oral History*, 1981, vol. 9, no. 1, p. 41.

14   L. Passerini, *Fascism in Popular Memory: The Cultural Experience of the Turin Working Class* (trans. A. Lumley and J. Bloomfield), New York, 1987, p. 129.

15   Anonymous informant in southern Indiana, interview by Blee, August 21, 1987, audiotape (in Blee's possession); Blee, *Women of the Klan*, pp. 1, 163–171.

16   Blee, *Women of the Klan*, p. 150; E. Willadene, 'Whitley County survives the Ku Klux Klan', *Bulletin of the Whitley County* [Indiana] *Historical Society*, October 1987, pp. 3–17; H. Arendt, *Eichmann in Jerusalem: A Report on the Banality of Evil*, New York, 1963.

17   Anonymous informant in central Indiana, interview by Blee, May 13, 1987, audio-tape (in Blee's possession).

18   G. Rosenthal, 'German war memories: narrability and the biographical and social functions of remembering', *Oral History*, 1991, vol. 19, no. 2, pp. 39–40; Blee, *Women of the Klan*, pp. 150, 156; anonymous informants in southern Indiana, inter-views by Blee, May 24, 1987, August 27, 1987, audiotapes (in Blee's possession).

19   D. Patai, 'U.S. academics and third world women: is ethical research possible?', in Gluck and Patai, *Women's Words*, p. 143; Anderson and Jack, 'Learning to listen', p. 13.

20   G. Jeansonne, 'Oral history, biography, and political demagoguery: The case of Gerald L.K. Smith', *Oral History Review*, 1983, vol. 11, p. 93.

21   Claudia Koonz makes a similar point about her interview with Gertrud Sholtz-Klink, chief of the German Nazi women's bureau: 'I wondered that people would be so open in their defense of the Nazi state'. See Koonz, *Mothers in the Fatherland*, p. xviii.

22   Cf. D. Janiewski, '"Sisters under their skin?": the effects of race upon the efforts of women tobacco workers to organize in Durham, North Carolina', *Oral History*, 1979, vol. 7, no. 2, p. 31. See also Portelli, *Death of Luigi Trastulli*, p. 53.

23   Portelli, *Death of Luigi Trastulli*, p. 52.

24   Koonz, *Mothers in the Fatherland*, p. xxii.

25   For a cognent discussion and critique of this position, see Patai, 'U.S. academics and third world women', p. 147.

26   Even this principle is not always followed. Glen Jeansonne secured an interview with the famous anti-Semitic demagogue Gerald L.K. Smith in part through correspond-ence that 'consistently stressed to him the importance of his career'. Jeansonne, 'Oral history, biography, and political demagoguery', p. 92.

27   Cf. Salazar, 'A Third World woman's text', p. 96; K. Lacy Rogers, 'Memory, struggle, and power: on interviewing political activists', *Oral History Review*, Spring 1987, vol. 15, p. 182.

28   See S. Harding, *Whose Science? Whose Knowledge? Thinking from Women's Lives*, Ithaca, 1991, p. 214.

PART IV

Making histories: introduction

OVER THE PAST DECADE popular interest in history, memory and personal testimony has grown, stimulated by reflections about the passing of a millennium and by commemorations of the defining events of the twentieth century, particularly the world wars. Individual memory and experience is now explored and presented in a wide variety of 'public history' settings: from archives and libraries to books and local history reminiscence groups, from theatres and schools to radio and television, from museums and galleries to the new arts-based multimedia and the World Wide Web.[1] 'Oral history' is no longer a phrase understood only by specialists and academics: it has become a familiar strap-line on popular history publications and people's history television programmes, denoting accessibility and intimacy. It is in the vanguard of the latest innovations in information technology and actively engaged with debates about the relationship between text, image and sound, and the virtual environment of the internet. This section examines how oral testimony might be preserved and presented to a wider audience: the decisions involved, the degree to which the process is collaborative, what impact selection and editing have on the evidence itself, and how such notions as 'documentary' and 'linear representation' of the past are being challenged by new technology.

Whilst the process of collecting testimony can be an end in itself, for many oral historians the long-term preservation of their recordings remains a central objective. As pioneering oral historian Raphael Samuel argued as long ago as 1971, the role of the 'collector of the spoken word . . . is that of archivist, as well as historian, retrieving and storing priceless information which would otherwise be lost . . . his greatest contribution may well be in the collecting and safe preservation of his material rather than in the use he can immediately find for it'.[2] Yet, as Ellen Swain notes in her survey of the shifting encounter between archivists, librarians and oral historians over the past fifty years, it has been an uncomfortable relationship. Some collectors have been rather cavalier in preserving, documenting and depositing their data. And some information professionals, whilst recognizing the potential that oral history has for what Jim Fogerty refers to as 'filling the gaps' in collections, or for providing researchers with 'road maps', have voiced concerns about their own role.[3] Can they be – should they be – both passive curators and active creators?[4] Doesn't postmodernism question 'the notion that archivists are or can be objective caretakers of documents as their bias, interests, and backgrounds shape the ways in which they collect and maintain archival holdings'?[5] Steeped in largely paper-based documentary sources, traditional archivists and librarians in the North (particularly in Europe) have been slower to recognize the value of oral and audio-visual sources than their colleagues in the developing countries of the South, where archivists have more readily embraced oral testimony as a substitute for the lack of written archives.[6] In the former communist countries of Eastern Europe and the former dictatorships of Latin America, oral history has emerged as a corrective to state-manipulated archives, taking a key public role in rescuing and preserving memories of repression and state terrorism which would otherwise be lost.[7] Else-where new testimony-led archives have featured prominently in reconciliation processes and land rights cases, as we see in Part V.

They may differ in emphasis, but publicly funded archives, libraries and museums world-wide agree that, although significant progress has been made in developing shared data and catalogue standards, [8] many still lack the prioritized resources required to initiate interviewing projects. And these resourcing issues are even more acute in developing countries, where shelving, environmental controls and automated catalogues are sometimes lacking.[9] The primary challenge of oral history for all curators remains access: of bringing their holdings to public attention; of finding the means to make recordings and transcripts searchable by users (increas-ingly remotely); and of disseminating their collections to new audiences, a process that is still frequently hampered, not only by inadequate resources and entrenched attitudes but also by poor documentation and absence of legal consent.[10] At the same time, though, some are also becoming aware of the thorny ethical debate raised by the reuse and reanalysis of archived data for purposes at variance with the creators' own.[11]

In fact, as Francis Good outlines in Chapter 27, the debate continues amongst oral historians about the role and status of text-based versions of oral accounts. For years many oral historians tended to view a transcript as the equivalent of the original source, and in the past even destroyed tapes once a typescript had been prepared, though this seems to have been banished by the availability of cheaper technology and by the growing interest in orality, linguistics and discourse analysis which require the recording to be retained.[12] Good explores the time-consuming and exacting process that is at work in rendering speech into grammatical text, high-lighting concerns about 'the loss of "information" by selective editing of language used by interviewees, and the fear that the distinction between primary and secondary sources is muddied or simply ignored' in a quest for readability.[13] He also reflects on some more creative transcription methods involving verse forms.[14]

Moving from the oral to the 'written' raises additional challenges when the editing involves a group or is part of a creative process where the aim is to produce a publication of some kind. Jane Mace ran community reminiscence and adult literacy and writing groups in London for many years, working at the cusp of 'talking and writing'.[15] Here, she details the process of collaborative negotiation that leads to publication, believing ultimately that the final product 'should be one that satisfies the authors, whether I have regrets about some of their choices or not'.[16] This highlights the tension that always exists between the process of gathering on the one hand, and the 'public' outcome on the other, which Bornat explores in Part V in relation to reminiscence 'therapy' (or life review) and collaborative memory-based theatre.[17] In fact a different kind of collaboration emerges from Marjorie Shostak's retrospective piece about her pioneering book *Nisa – The Life and Words of a !Kung Woman*, in which the conversion of the oral to the written was, perhaps more typically, firmly in the hands of the researcher. Nisa liked the idea of her words being made permanent (those that 'the wind won't take away'), but had little involvement in the editing of the final book. One reason for this more unequal relationship was the lengthy translation and editing process, marked by the challenge of representing the constant repetition typical of Nisa's form of expression.[18]

Both Mace and Shostak raise the issue of the wider 'audience'. Who do the interviewees think they are talking to and who do they think will be reading or listening to their story? Apart from the interviewer, are they addressing family members, peer group or posterity? Is the audience they have in mind the same one as the interviewer/writer has in mind? Don Ritchie has pointed out that the authors of some of the best-known 'oral history' books have handled oral evidence 'rather loosely'. Tapes are absent or bear little resemblance to the published text. One of Studs Terkel's interviewees is quoted as claiming that his words had been rearranged 'in such a way that I can't make sense of them'.[19] Does this comment make us read Terkel's books with a new eye, and are we content for him as editor/writer to have license to interpret and rearrange as he sees fit? As readers we cannot readily compare the written text with the original interview, and in the case of British writer and oral historian Tony Parker such comparison is impossible because he destroyed his interview tapes.[20]

Terkel is as well known as a radio presenter as he is a writer, and the broadcast and digital revolution, described here by Charles Hardy, is transforming the way in which oral history is being collected and presented. As Michael Frisch argues in Part I, direct online computer access to audio-visual records in a non-linear way, and with less recourse to text-based search tools, challenges the way in which we can engage with personal testimonies. They can be copied, reassembled and interpreted in infinitely different ways by non-professionals in new environments that allow the material to be shared with people world-wide through the internet, or in more intimate family settings. And as the new digital media converge, so the benefits of each discrete format of personal testimony (oral, visual, written, artefact-based) can be juxtaposed, compared and thought about together and separately, as Peter Read foresaw over ten years ago with the advent of CD-ROM but for which we now look to the World Wide Web.[21] Making history in this way encourages historians to 'reflect on and anticipate our audiences' desires, intentions and questions, as well as to consider the context in which the people we have interviewed and recorded were themselves responding to their real or intended audience'.[22] In the new web-based environment, access is not necessarily dependent on literacy. People can become involved in a way they never could in the creation and use of a book.

Yet the Web also poses entirely new challenges, and debate amongst archivists and oral historians about web-based access to interview data is getting underway. As has been pointed out: 'The electronic archive offers new possibilities for speed, mobility and completeness of access to cultures which have become digitalized, which raise fundamental questions about ownership, intellectual property rights, censorship and democratic access'.[23] Mary Larson and Karen Brewster have surveyed mainly US-based websites using oral sources, noting that very few provide access to entire audio interviews and that most are 'finding aid sites', in some cases offering only short excerpts of interview material to avoid copyright and permission issues.[24] They also remarked on the lack of a consensus about online rights statements and site-user agreements, and debated whether or not existing copyright and clearance forms provide for Web use. Hardly any of their surveyed sites had provided what they regarded as appropriate contextualizing information for oral history material. As a result, Brewster's own institution, the University of Alaska Fairbanks, has added a site-user agreement which visitors are required to read and agree to before access to original oral history data is permitted.[25] This has become a model for best practice for sites mounting large quantities of unedited oral history audio online.[26]

As Hardy points out, the entire multi-media production process is being democratized: high quality digital audio recorders have become ever-cheaper, and for the first time a new breed of easy-to-use digital video recorders has fallen within the budgets of individual and community-based oral historians. Video is likely to be a feature of the next decade of oral history fieldwork in a way it has not been over the past decade, but as yet there remains a remarkable paucity of writings on the subject, particularly outside the United States. In part this relative silence is because videographers and broadcast programme-makers seem notoriously reluctant to expose their methodology to public gaze and debate, whilst the pressures of the television industry provide few opportunities to be reflective and self-critical in print.[27] In part it is because some oral historians harbour concerns about the intruding presence of a camera. In Chapter 31 Dan Sipe surveys the field of film and video, stressing the extra layers of historical meaning that can emerge from the visual, and arguing that historians are in danger of relinquishing their role in shaping public history to television producers and film-makers.

Interestingly, Hardy argues that in the new digital age, radio will persist as people learn to 'think in sound' rather than text,[28] and in Part V Daniel Kerr writes about the collaborative use of radio with homeless people in America. Hardy also notes how developing technologies – such as solid-state and three-dimensional audio – are transforming the use of sound in public spaces like museums and galleries. In fact, museums, like archives, are no longer impartial and passive recipients of artefacts but are now dynamic participants in creating and presenting public histories. Museums throughout the world have been particularly active in collecting oral testimony in recent years. For some, oral history has been merely a means of gathering information about material culture; for others it has underpinned community 'outreach' work in which the museum ventures outside its hallowed building.[29] For a few major museums oral history has been central to exhibition design: for example, at the Museum of London, Ellis Island Museum in New York, the Holocaust Memorial Museum in Washington, and the District Six Museum and Robben Island, both in Cape Town, South Africa.[30] In each case oral history has been used not merely as text but also as sound, explicitly seeking an empathetic response from visitors and encouraging interactivity between objects and experiences. The People's Story in Edinburgh was largely created by local people: they decided what they wanted to see in their museum and set about collecting objects and setting up reminiscence groups to achieve it.[31] Robben Island's *Cell Stories* was drawn from former prisoner reminiscences. Occasionally the voices of tradition in the museum world have argued that the function of museums is to preserve and interpret artefacts, that oral history is technically difficult to include in a gallery space, and that it is an expensive luxury. However, as Anna Green's chapter here shows, from the experience of constructing an oral history exhibition in New Zealand, technical problems can be overcome and oral history displays can greatly increase attendance and popular involvement in museums.

A notable feature of the 1990s was the growth in audio artists utilizing recorded memories in a variety of highly innovative ways, such as buried soundtracks in public parks and public sound works in disused shopping malls: the Hayward Gallery in London recently mounted a major exhibition of sound art.[32] There is enormous scope for collaborative work with oral historians, as illustrated here by academic Toby Butler who worked with artist and composer Graeme Miller on *Linked*, an oral history-based public art installation in East London, in which testimonies from people who once lived in an area flattened to make way for a new motorway are transmitted to headphones worn by visitors to this 'outdoor exhibition'. In a challenging subversion of the 'acoustiguide', the oral testimonies are 'cut up, mixed, diced; excerpts are repeated; bells, chords and sounds are added. For the most part stories are coherent; some touching and funny anecdotes survive intact; but periods of the broadcast initially seem anarchic and even unfathomable'. No single engagement with the piece is the same and the listener is both sensitized to the place and reflective of the memories in it.[33]

Part IV concludes with Rina Benmayor's article about the use of new technology in transforming the teaching of oral history. For many years it has been recognized that oral history can encourage children to acquire new skills and 'become historians'. In Part V we hear from a group of teachers representative of a growing world-wide trend in the teaching of history in schools which emphasizes a multi-disciplinary and eclectic approach embracing oral history, both as source material and project work.[34] Working with undergraduates, Benmayor found that using email and web-based techniques fostered a more interactive collaborative learning environment in which students worked in a team, utilized a range of skills, carried our original research, and disseminated the results.

Whilst oral history can play a major role in telling us more about our past and in democratizing the study of history, it also encourages us to consider our own motives as collectors and curators, and reflect on the way our presence can shape the evidence as it is interpreted, selected, shaped, presented and 'consumed'. As

Michael Frisch has remarked, it involves us all 'in exploring what it means to remember, and what to do with memories to make them active and alive, as opposed to mere objects of collection'.[35]

Notes

1   The concept of 'public history' and its interplay with oral history is overviewed by J. Liddington, 'What is public history? Publics and their pasts, meanings and practices', *Oral History*, 2002, vol. 30, no. 1, pp. 83–93. Also C.T. Morrissey, 'Public historians and oral history: problems of concept and methods', *The Public Historian*, 1980, no. 2.

2   R. Samuel, 'Perils of the transcript', *Oral History*, 1971, vol. 1, no. 2, pp. 19–22.

3   J.E. Fogerty, 'Filling the gap: the role of the archivist', *American Archivist*, 1983, vol. 46, no. 2, pp. 148–157; and D.A. Ritchie, 'Preserving oral history in archives and libraries' in *Doing Oral History*: *A Practical Guide*, New York: Oxford University Press, 2nd edition, 2003, pp. 155–187. The *Journal of the Society of Archivists* in Britain has almost totally ignored oral history. Elsewhere see W. MacDonald, 'Origins: oral history programmes in Canada, Britain and the United States', *Canadian Oral History Association Journal*, 1991, vol. 10, pp. 12–24; R. Lochead, 'Oral history: the role of the archivist', *Phonographic Bulletin*, 1983, no. 37, pp. 3–7; D. Lance, *An Archive Approach to Oral History*, London: Imperial War Museum/IASA, 1978; F.J. Stielow, *The Management of Oral History Sound Archives*, New York: Greenwood, 1986; D. Treleven, 'Oral history and the archival community: common concerns about documenting twentieth-century life', *International Journal of Oral History*, 1989, vol. 10, no. 1; A. Ward, *Manual of Sound Archive Administration*, London: Gower, 1990. For oral history in libraries in the British context, see C. Cochrane, 'Public libraries and the changing nature of oral history', *Audiovisual Librarian*, 1985, vol. 11, no. 4, pp. 201–207. For the US context see Willa Baum's writings, especially 'The expanding role of the librarian in oral history', in D.K. Dunaway and W.K. Baum (eds), *Oral History*: *An Interdisciplinary Anthology*, London: AltaMira Press, 2nd edition, 1996. For Australasia see M.P. Chou, 'Small windows on the Pacific: oral history and libraries in Australia, New Zealand and Papua New Guinea', *International Journal of Oral History*, 1985, vol. 6, no. 3, pp. 163–178; J. Downs, 'Oral history in New Zealand public and national libraries: how useful is it?', *Oral History in New Zealand*, 1998, vol. 10, pp. 24–29.

4   J.-P. Wallot and N. Fortier, 'Archival science and oral sources', in R. Perks and A. Thomson (eds), *The Oral History Reader*, London: Routledge, 1st edition, 1998.

5   Quoted in Swain Chapter 26, this volume.

6   W.W. Moss and P.C. Mazikana, *Archives, Oral History and Oral Tradition*: *A RAMP Study*, Paris, UNESCO, 1986, provides a good overview. See also C. Hamilton, '"Living by fluidity": oral histories, material custodies and the politics of archiving', in C. Hamilton, V. Harris, J. Taylor, M. Pickover, G. Reid and R. Saleh (eds), *Refiguring the Archive*, Dordrecht: Kluwer Academic Publishers, 2002, pp. 209–227; S. Peet and K. Manungo, '"We have a tradition of story-telling": oral history in Zimbabwe', *Oral History*, 1988, vol. 16, no. 2, pp. 67–72.

7   See, for example, M. de Moraes Ferreira and J. Amado (eds), *Usos & Abusos da História Oral*, Rio de Janeiro: Fundação Getulio Vargas, 1996; Introduction, in M. Loskoutova, *Oral History Reader*, St Petersburg: European University at St Petersburg, 2003; G. Kozák, Z. Kőrösi and A. Molnár (eds), *Oral History Archive, Budapest*, Budapest: Institute of the History of the 1956 Hungarian Revolution, 1996; R. Perks, 'Ukraine's forbidden history: memory and nationalism', *Oral History*, 1993, vol. 21, no. 1, pp. 43–53.

8   M. Matters (comp.), *Oral History Cataloguing Manual*, Chicago, Ill., Society of American Archivists, 1995. See also C. Clark, 'The National Sound Archive IT Project: documentation of sound recordings using the Unicorn collections management system', *IASA Journal*, 1995, no. 5, pp. 7–25; and B.H. Bruemmer, 'Access to oral history: a national agenda', *American Archivist*, 1991, vol. 54, no. 4, pp. 494–501.

9   C.A. Paton, 'Whispers in the stacks: the problem of sound recordings in archives', *The American Archivist*, 1990, vol. 53, pp. 274–280; Moss and Mazikana, *Archives*, pp. 43–45.

10 B. Robertson, 'Keeping the faith: a discussion of the practical and ethical issues involved in donated oral history collections', *Oral History Association of Australia Journal*, 1989, vol. 11, pp. 18–29. For discussion of oral history, copyright, ethics and legal consent see the excellent chapter on 'Legalities and ethics' in V.R. Yow, *Recording Oral History*, Walnut Creek, Calif.: AltaMira Press, 2nd edition, 2005; also J. Neuenschwander, *Oral History and the Law*, Carlisle, Pa., Oral History Association, 2002; A. Ward, 'Is your oral history legal and ethical?' (http://ohs.org.uk/ethics/).

11 For the lively debate about the reuse of data see, J. Bornat, 'A second take: revisiting interviews with a different purpose', *Oral History*, 2003, vol. 31, no. 1, pp. 47–53; N. Mauthner, O. Parry and K. Milburn, 'The data are out there, or are they? Implications for archiving qualitative data', *Sociology*, 1998, vol. 32, no. 4, pp. 733–745; O. Parry and N. Mauthner, 'Whose data are they anyway? Practical, legal and ethical issues in archiving qualitative data', *Sociology*, 2004, vol. 38, no. 1, pp. 139–152; L. Bishop, 'Protecting respondents and enabling data sharing: reply to Parry and Mauthner', *Sociology*, 2005, vol. 39, no. 2, pp. 333–336; O. Parry and N. Mauthner, 'Back to basics: who re-uses qualitative data and why?', *Sociology*, 2005, vol. 39, no. 2, pp. 337–342.

12 This was a policy, now abandoned, pursued by the Oral History Office at Columbia University. At Essex University in Britain, a survey of academics in 1994 by the Economic and Social Research Council's Qualidata found that 'at least 80% of qualitative datasets . . . were either already lost or at risk, and even of those archived, half had gone to totally unsuitable archives, some without cataloguing or public access . . . material lost or at risk would, at present costs, have taken £20 million to create' (internal report, 1997).

13 Amongst the huge literature about transcription, see Ritchie, *Doing Oral History*, pp. 64–75; Yow, *Recording Oral History*, pp. 227–236; D.K. Dunaway, 'Transcription: shadow of reality', *Oral History Review*, 1984, vol. 12, pp. 113–117; W.K. Baum, *Transcribing and Editing Oral History*, Nashville, Tenn.: American Association for State and Local History, 1977; K. Moore, 'Perversion of the word: the role of transcripts in oral history', in *Words and Silences*, *Bulletin of the International Oral History Association*, 1997, vol. 1, no. 1, pp. 14–25, and the commentaries from Frisch and Block in the same volume (pp. 26–31, 32–35); B. Godfrey and J. Richardson, 'In deep water: the ethical use of transcripted oral material', *Oral History Association of Australia Journal*, 2001, no. 23, pp. 74–79; M. Hutching, 'The distance between voice and transcript', in A. Green and M. Hutching (eds), *Remembering*: *Writing Oral History*, Auckland: Auckland University Press, 2004. On editing transcripts for publication, see M. Frisch, 'Preparing interview transcripts for documentary publication', in his *Shared Authority*: *Essays on the Craft and Meaning of Oral and Public History*, Albany, N.Y.: SUNY Press, 1990, pp. 81–146; S.A. Allen, 'Resisting the editorial ego: editing oral history', *Oral History Review*, 1982, vol. 10, pp. 33–45.

14 K. Woodley, 'Let the data sing: representing discourse in poetic form', *Oral History*, 2004, vol. 32, no. 1, pp. 35–48; S.B. Gluck, 'Pitch, pace, performance – and even poetry: returning to orality. The CSULB virtual oral/aural history archive model', paper presented to the XIIIth International Oral History Conference, Rome, June 2004; B. York, 'Between poetry and prose. Oral history as a new kind of literature', *National Library of Australia News*, August 1999, vol. IX, no. 11.

15   J. Mace, *Literacy, Language and Community Publishing: Essays in Adult Education*, Clevedon: Multilingual Matters, 1995; *Playing with Time: Mothers and the Meaning of Literacy*, London: UCL Press, 1999.

16   See also R. Jones, '*Blended Voices*: crafting a narrative from oral history interviews', *Oral History Review*, 2004, vol. 31, no. 1, pp. 23–42; C. Wilmsen, 'For the record: editing and the production of meaning in oral history', *Oral History Review*, 2001, vol. 28, no. 1, pp. 65–85; L. Sitzia, 'Catching stories: 2. Making a community history book', *Oral History*, 1998, vol. 26, no. 1, pp. 38–45; G. Jordan, 'Voices from below: doing people's history in Cardiff docklands', in S. Berger, H. Feldner and K. Passmore (eds), *Writing History: Theory and Practice*, London: Hodder Arnold, 2003; P. Duffin, 'Turning talking into writing', in J. Bornat (ed.), *Reminiscence Reviewed*, Buckingham: Open University Press, 1994, pp. 116–125; J. Bornat, 'The communities of community publishing', *Oral History*, 1992, vol. 20, no. 2, pp. 23–31; A. Progler, 'Choices in editing oral history: the distillation of Dr Hiller', *Oral History Review*, 1991, vol. 19, pp. 1–16; and Chapter 41 in Part V this volume, on making a community history book in Northern Ireland.

17   A. Rouverol, 'Collaborative oral history in a correctional setting: promise and pitfalls', *Oral History Review*, 2003, vol. 30, no. 1, pp. 61–85; and '"I was content and not content": Oral history and the collaborative process', *Oral History*, 2000, vol. 28, no. 2, pp. 66–78. More generally on reminiscence theatre, see G. Langley and B. Kershaw, 'Reminiscence theatre', *Theatre Papers*, 1981–2, no. 6; E. Dodgson, 'From oral history to drama', *Oral History*, 1984, vol. 12, no. 2, pp. 47–53; P. Schweitzer, 'Dramatizing reminiscences', in Bornat (ed.), *Reminiscence Reviewed*, pp. 105–115; M. Harcourt, 'A walk in someone else's shoes', *Oral History in New Zealand*, 1994, no. 6, pp. 14–20; *Oral History Review*, 1990, vol. 18, no. 2, was a special issue devoted to theatre and performance in the US.

18   On the problems of translation, see Susan Burton in Part II; also M. Andrews, 'A monoglot abroad: working through problems of translation', *Oral History*, 1995, vol. 23, no. 2, pp. 47–50; L. Abu-Luhog, Introduction, in *Writing Women's Worlds*, Oxford: University of California Press, 1993.

19   Quoted in Ritchie, *Doing Oral History*, p. 128.

20   Tony Parker discusses his approach to editing and writing with Paul Thompson, 'Tony Parker: writer and oral historian', *Oral History*, 1994, vol. 22, no. 2, pp. 64–73.

21   P. Read, 'What oral history can't tell us: the role of the CD-Rom', *Oral History Association of Australia Journal*, 1994, no. 16, pp. 87–90. For a recent overview see S.B. Gluck, D.A. Ritchie and B. Eynon, 'Reflections on oral history in the new millennium: roundtable comments', *Oral History Review*, 1999, vol. 26, no. 2, pp. 1–27; also W. Schneider and D. Grahek, *Project Jukebox: Where Oral History and Technology Come Together*, Anchorage, Centre for Information Technology, University of Alaska at Anchorage, 1992; R. Rosenzweig, '"So, what's next for Clio?" CD-ROM and historians', *The Journal of American History*, 1995, vol. 81, no. 4, pp. 1621–1640.

22   K. Flick and H. Goodall, 'Angledool stories: Aboriginal history in hypermedia', in R. Perks and A. Thomson (eds), *The Oral History Reader*, 1998, pp. 421–431.

23   M. Featherstone, 'Archiving cultures', *British Journal of Sociology*, 2000, vol. 51, no. 1, pp. 161–184.

24   M.A. Larson, 'Potential, potential, potential: the marriage of oral history and the World Wide Web', *The Journal of American History*, September 2001, pp. 596–603; K. Brewster, 'Internet access to oral recordings: finding the issues', Alaska, University of Fairbanks, 2000, at www.uaf.edu/library/oralhistory/brewster1/. See also Katy Barber, 'Oral history & the World Wide Web', seminar at Oral History Association annual meeting, Portland, Oregon, 27 September 2004, at www.ccrh.org/barber/oah/benefits.htm; Ritchie, *Doing Oral History*, pp. 176–179, 245–251.

25 (http://uaf-db.uaf.edu/Jukebox/PJWeb/proguseaa.htm).

26 R. Perks and J. Robinson, '"The way we speak": web-based representations of changing communities in England', *Oral History*, 2005, vol. 33, no. 2, pp. 89–100.

27 J. Blatti, 'Public history and oral history', *The Journal of American History*, 1990, vol. 77, pp. 615–625; P.M. Henson and T.A. Shorzman, 'Videohistory: focusing on the American past', *The Journal of American History*, 1991, vol. 78, pp. 618–627; P. Thompson and J. Bornat, 'Interview with Stephen Peet', *Oral History*, 1982, vol. 10, no. 1, pp. 47–55; G. Lanning, 'Television History Workshop Project No 1: The Brixton Tapes', *History Workshop*, 1981, no. 12, pp. 183–188; S. Humphries, 'Unseen stories: video history in museums', *Oral History*, 2003, vol. 31, no. 2, pp. 75–84; M. Hastings, 'Hacks and scholars: allies of a kind', in D. Cannadine (ed.), *History and the Media*, Basingstoke: Palgrave Macmillan, 2004, pp. 103–117; Connie Broughton, 'Filming Nana: some dilemmas of oral history on film', in Susan H. Armitage with Patricia Hart and Karen Weatherman (eds), *Women's Oral History: The* Frontiers *Reader*, Lincoln: University of Nebraska Press, 2002, pp. 173–182; J. Lembke, 'From oral history to movie script: the Vietnam veteran interviews for *Coming Home*', *Oral History Review*, 1999, vol. 26, no. 2, pp. 65–86; G.H. Hartman, *Preserving Living Memory: The Challenge and Power of Videotestimony*, Washington DC: United States Holocaust Memorial Museum, 1995.

28 Again, little has been written about oral history and radio, but see C. Hardy, 'Prodigal sons, trap doors, and painted women: some reflections on urban folklore, life stories, and aural history', *Oral History*, 2001, vol. 29, no. 1, pp. 98–105; D.K. Dunaway, 'Radio and the public use of oral history', in Dunaway and Baum, *Oral History*, pp. 306–320; C. Fox, 'Oral history on public radio: "a match made in heaven"', *Oral History Association of Australia Journal*, 1990, vol. 12, pp. 38–46; H. Molnar, 'Women's oral history on radio: a creative way to recover our past', *Oral History Association of Australia Journal*, 1990, vol. 12, pp. 47–56.

29 R. Perks *et al.*, 'Working knowledge: oral history', *Museum Practice*, 2004, issue 25, pp. 44–61; S. Davies, 'Falling on deaf ears? Oral history and strategy in museums', *Oral History*, 1994, vol. 22, no. 2, pp. 74–84; S. Jones and C. Major, 'Reaching the public: oral history as a survival strategy for museums', *Oral History*, 1986, vol. 14, no. 2, pp. 31–38; D. Hyslop, 'From oral historians to community historians: some ways forward for the use and development of oral testimony in public institutions', *Oral History Association of Australia Journal*, 1995, vol. 17, pp. 1–8; J.K.W. Tchen, 'Creating a dialogic museum: the Chinatown History Museum experiment', in I. Karp, C.M. Kreamer and S.D. Lavine (eds), *Museums and Communities: The Politics of Public Culture*, Washington, Smithsonian Institution Press, 1992, pp. 285–326; B. Factor, 'Making an exhibition of yourself: museums and oral history', *Oral History Association of Australia Journal*, 1991, vol. 13, pp. 44–48; J. Cassidy, 'Migration memories on multi-media at a museum', *Oral History Association of Australia Journal*, 2003, no. 25, pp. 90–95; S.A. Crane (ed.), *Museums and Memory*, Stanford, Calif.: Stanford University Press, 2000.

30 A. Day, 'Listening galleries: oral history on display', *Oral History*, 1999, vol. 27, no. 1, pp. 91–96; R. Perks, 'Ellis Island Immigration Museum, New York', *Oral History*, 1991, vol. 19, no. 1, pp. 79–80; P. Davison, 'Museums and the reshaping of memory', and H. Deacon, 'Remembering tragedy, constructing modernity: Robben Island as a national monument', both in S. Nuttall and C. Coetzee (eds), *Negotiating the Past: The Making of Memory in South Africa*, Cape Town and Oxford: Oxford University Press, 1998; C. McEachern, 'Working with memory: the District Six Museum in the new South Africa', *Social Analysis*, 1998, vol. 42, no. 2, pp. 48–72; B. Nasson, 'Oral history and the reconstruction of District Six', in S. Jeppie and C. Soudien (eds), *The Struggle for District Six: Past and Present*, Cape Town: Buchu Books, 1990, pp. 44–66; T. Kushner, 'Oral history at the extremes of human experience: Holocaust testimony in a museum setting', *Oral History*, 2001, vol. 29, no. 2, pp. 83–94;

L. Taksa, 'Globalization, memory and industrial heritage – remembering and forget-ting the noise, jobs, skills, conflicts and camaraderie of a forgotten era', paper presented to the XIIIth International Oral History Conference, Rome, June 2004.

31   H. Clark and S. Marwick, 'The People's Story – moving on', *Social History in Museums*, 1992, vol. 19, pp. 54–65.

32   T. Oakes, 'Showing your workings: artists in the sound archive', *IASA Journal*, 2000, no. 15, pp. 5–11; Al Johnson, 'Land of laundries: an oral history installation', *Oral History*, 1998, vol. 26, no. 2, pp. 82–85; W. Furlong, *Audio Arts*: *Discourse and Practice in Contemporary Art*, London, Academy Editions, 1994. Anthony Roland's *Talking Trees* zoned audio installation in London's Regent's Park ran during August and September 2000 using cordless headsets. *Sonic Boom*: *The Art of Sound*, London: Hayward Gallery, 2000 (CD/book).

33   See also Butler's 2005 project, *Soundscape*: *Voices From the Hidden History of the Thames* at www.memoryscape.org.uk/index.htm.

34   For a selection of the huge literature, see note 4 in the Introduction to Part V.

35   Frisch, *Shared Authority*, p. 27.

Chapter 26

Ellen D. Swain

ORAL HISTORY IN THE ARCHIVES
Its documentary role in the
twenty-first century

The developing relationship between archivists, librarians and oral historians has not always been a comfortable one. This chapter argues that oral history is a vital component of collection development because it provides some historical context, then explores the role of the archivist as curator-creator-collector, the need for collaboration, and the challenges that the new digital environment poses to issues of access and dissemination. Ellen Swain is archivist at the University Archives, University of Illinois at Urbana-Champaign, and chair of the Society of American Archivists' Reference, Access and Outreach Section. From *The American Archivist*, Spring/Summer 2003, vol. 66, pp. 139–158, reprinted by permission of the Society of American Archivists (www.archivists.org).

F OR NEARLY A HALF-CENTURY, archivists and librarians have debated the theoretical and practical applications of oral history for archives and research libraries. Libraries first utilized oral sources to 'fill in' the historical record in the early 1950s, and by the late 1960s, a handful of articles in the library and archival literature proclaimed its documentary value. In 1968, shortly after the founding of the Oral History Association (OHA), library science professor Martha Jane K. Zachert published her *College and Research Libraries* article 'The Implications of Oral History for Librarians,' to underline the new responsibilities and opportunities facing librarians.[1] Although it was not an in-depth or 'landmark' study, Zachert's article was one of the first attempts to outline the ways in which oral history would impact libraries and archives in the coming decades. As such, it provides a useful framework for analyzing and evaluating archival, library, and oral history scholarship on the subject. Zachert's article also offers a basis for understanding how the role of oral history in archives and libraries was constructed in the past and how it can be viewed today.

Significantly, this investigation reveals that over the past ten years, oral history literature has continued to examine the archivist's role in oral history while archival and library scholarship has abandoned this crucial discussion for other topics. Oral history continues to be an important research methodology and tapes and transcripts need to be effectively integrated into academic library collections. Archivists and librarians must assume an active role in oral history discourse, collaborate with each other and colleagues in other fields, and be attuned to current scholarship needs if archives and special collections departments are to be viable, utilized research sources in the future.

Historical background

To understand oral history's role in the archives and library, it is important to first place it in historical context. Significantly, the origins of oral history in the United States are rooted firmly in archives and libraries. The Columbia University Oral History Research Office, founded in 1948, was one of the first and most notable programs. Dedicated to documenting the 'movers and shakers' in society, Columbia and other early programs found little support from skeptical history departments or from archivists who were critical of oral history's reliance on faulty memory.[2] Beginning in the mid-1950s, oral historians promoted oral history's value for library collections to library and archival audiences with some success.[3] Not until the social history movement in the late 1960s and 1970s did oral history become a widespread means to recover 'history from the bottom up.' Its earliest use, instead, was as an archival documentation strategy to supplement records of prominent historical figures.[4]

This archival emphasis – the practical use of oral history to supplement or explain information in existing archival collections – dominated the oral history field in the late 1960s and early 1970s. The OHA, founded in 1967, focused on the archival use of oral history to 'build' collections rather than as a historical practice of 'reflection upon those documents or speculation on how they might be used to develop new ways to view and do history.'[5] Archivists and librarians played a crucial role in the new organization by insisting that oral history interviews were public documents that should be open and accessible to all. Archivists such as Lila Goff, James Fogerty, James Mink, and William Moss were instrumental in providing leadership in OHA and in the Society of American Archivists (SAA) and in 'bridging the gap' between the two organizations.

In 1969, SAA established an oral history committee mandated to clarify 'points of common interest in archives work and oral history such as oral history as manuscripts; accessibility of oral history tapes and manuscripts; loan of transcripts; oral history and libel; and the training of oral historians.'[6] By 1973, archivists began to view oral history more favorably, as evidenced by an SAA membership survey which found that '73% of responding SAA members believed that oral history should be viewed as a regular archival activity (i.e. those who engaged in oral history should consider themselves professional archivists).'[7] That same year, OHA identified over three hundred U.S. oral history centers or projects and by the end of the decade the number had reached over one thousand.[8]

From 1975 to 1985, a series of external events changed the focus of American oral history and the OHA. The publication of Paul Thompson's *The Voice of the Past* accentuated the 'nature of the historical enterprise,' by focusing on how the practice provided new ways of doing history and capturing history from the 'bottom up.' International activities and National Endowment for the Humanities (NEH) funding inspired more historians to turn to oral history to uncover the forgotten or unacknowledged history of women, minorities, and 'ordinary' life. As oral history began to take root within the history profession, OHA began to emphasize historical analysis of the ways in which the field provided new means to study memory and history.[9] Archivists who used oral history to supplement existing documentation were joined by historians who capitalized on oral sources to understand those members of society with little or no documentary record.

Archivists responded positively to the growing popularity of oral history. In 1978, SAA's oral history committee printed a revised and amended version of OHA's interview guidelines in the SAA newsletter. The new version addressed the role of the archivist, in addition to those of the interviewee, interviewer, and sponsoring institution. In 1981, the SAA oral history committee became a professional affinity group, and in 1983 it organized as a section devoted to the study of 'provenance, evaluation, appraisal, arrangement, access, legal agreements, and ethical guidelines as they pertain to the oral history interview as an original document.'[10] Despite SAA's active response, many archivists remained skeptical of the value of oral history. A 1982 survey found that only 31% of 110 randomly selected college and university archivists were responsible for oral history.[11] SAA continued its involvement with the practice by sponsoring oral history workshops for its membership and in 1989 by collaborating with the American Historical Association (AHA) and OHA on AHA's 'Statement of Interviewing for Historical Documentation.'[12] No doubt the archival presence was responsible for the statement's stipulation that historians deposit their interviews with a library or archives.

Articles on oral history appeared in the library and archival literature in the 1960s, the 1970s, and in even greater numbers in the 1980s. Authors debated the value of the oral history interview, the appropriateness of creation of oral history interviews by archivists, as well as procedure and use issues. They also analyzed the implications of the new social history movement of the 1970s for archival documentation strategies, emphasizing the need for oral history to 'fill in' scholarship gaps.[13]

Since the early 1990s, however, few archival and library publications in the United States have addressed the role and use of oral history in research institutions. Instead, archivists and sound librarians have discussed oral history in terms of digital management, in the larger context of sound archives. With few exceptions, articles have reported on specific projects in the U.S. and in other countries or at nonacademic institutions. On the other hand, oral history readers and anthologies have continued to address the role of archives in the field.[14]

The absence of archival publications on oral history since the early 1990s is curious as oral history was at the height of its popularity among historians during this period.[15] The SAA Oral History Section's slowly growing membership statistics underline its popularity, and acceptance among archivists.[16] Another indication of broad acceptance is the findings of a 2001 University of Nevada survey that a third of the oral history programs responding had been founded after 1990.[17]

Why then have archival and library publications not addressed more fully the role of oral history in archives and libraries in recent years? Furthermore, what are oral history's implications for twenty-first-century archives and libraries?

The following section uses the five points of Zachert's article as a framework to examine more than three decades of oral history discussion and practice both to illustrate how archivists and librarians have engaged the subject over time and to draw conclusions about oral history's role in and demands for archives and libraries today.

Create rather than simply acquire materials

Writing at the advent of the oral history movement, Zachert argued that oral history provides a unique opportunity for academic librarians to draw on their research expertise, public relations skills, and knowledge of collection gaps to make a 'creative, intellectual contribution.'[18] This argument is part of a larger debate over archivists' role as curator of materials or as creator of documentation that has taken on new meaning for postmodern theorists in recent years. Over the last decades, one of strongest deterrents to oral history's acceptance among archivists and special collection librarians has been the idea that they, as neutral, impartial curators of collections, can or should not 'create' records. Of course, this neutrality or object-ivity is a noble but unattainable goal. The origins of this aversion to 'creating' records are grounded in traditional, twentieth-century archival theory.

Theorists proclaimed that the responsibility to safeguard and uphold the authen-ticity of 'the record' was central to an archivist's duties. Theory dictated that archivists must maintain 'documents as nearly as possible in the state in which [they] received them, without adding or taking away, physically or morally, anything.'[19] In addition, they must not allow personal biases or interests to determine what materials they acquire for the archives. As William Moss explained in 1988, when archivists *conducted* oral history interviews, they participated in and to some extent determined the nature and content of the record produced.[20] Many archivists felt they jeopardized their preferred status of neutrality concerning record content.

In the context of these admonitions, archivists debated the appropriateness of their active participation in oral history, both as collector and creator. Ronald Filippelli, expressing 'bewilderment over the intensity of [this] debate', asserted in 1976 that subject expertise is the key, not whether the interviewer is an archivist or historian.[21] In 1981, archivists at the Canadian Oral History Association took up the issue most forcefully. Derek Reimer urged his colleagues to 'call yourselves "historical researchers" or "cultural conservators" but don't lose the opportunity of recording vanishing resources because of some arbitrary linear subdivision of the world of knowledge which says that archivists do not participate in the creation of records.' Reimer insisted that archivists will be known in the future by their collec-tions, not 'by the purity of archival theory or the niceness with which we can distinguish between the true work of an archivist as opposed to a collector of oral documents.' Archivists are the most knowledgeable about collection deficiencies and can best fill in gaps.[22]

Arguing against archival participation, Jean Dryden responded to Reimer's address by insisting that active involvement in oral history is a dangerous departure from the traditional role of archivist. Archivists can identify 'gaps' in their collection, but they do not have the expertise, the funding, or the time needed to conduct extensive research or anticipate questions of future researchers. Dryden believed that other archival activities such as reducing backlogs and establishing active acquisition programs are far more important than 'creating records of marginal value.'[23] Two years later, the role of the archivist in oral history was the focus of debate at an International Association of Sound Archives (IASA) conference. Participants emphasized the need for documenting gaps in the archives, promoting deposit of interviews therein, and employing trained historians in archival work.[24] More to the point, participant Ronald Grele suggested that the question was not whether archivists could or should conduct interviews. They already were doing so with promising results.[25]

By the mid- to late-1990s, new scholarship turned the archival impartiality argument on its ear. In a selection for *The Oral History Reader* (1998), Canadian archivists Jean-Pierre Wallot and Normand Fortier suggested that archivists are not neutral gatherers; they appraise records. Based on their biases and abilities, they choose which records and subject matter to collect and which to discard. In a sense, archival collections reflect their collectors. For Wallot and Fortier, involvement in oral history, then, was not a matter of 'abdicating archival principles.' Instead, it meant 'influencing the creators of oral history and following procedures themselves if creating oral history.'[26] This argument is tied to an early strand of scholarship that focused on collection development in light of social history scholarship interests.

The social history movement of the 1970s called archival neutrality into question by bringing to the forefront issues concerning collection development and appraisal and legitimizing the use of oral history. Historians in the movement turned their attention from studying prominent political leaders and organizations to focusing on understanding society through the experiences of groups underdocumented by 'mainstream' repositories, such as women, minorities, civil rights and peace activists, and laborers. To do so, historians needed materials about these subjects that the archives did not contain.

As early as 1975, SAA president Gerald Ham called for a more active and creative role for archivists in documenting history, as their 'soundness of . . . judgment and keenness of . . . perceptions about scholarly inquiry' will determine the 'scope, quality and direction of research in an open-ended future.' One component in the making of an activist archivist was using oral history to 'fill in' gaps and address the less-documented social aspect of history.[27]

In 1981, Frederic Miller addressed this issue by arguing that the new historical movement required archivists to 'adapt' their practices to address current historical research needs. Miller argued that archival principles and practices were not immutable but were instead the 'product of the understanding of the historical research at the time they were formulated.' Since this understanding mirrors societal and technological changes, archivists needed to re-evaluate conventional archival wisdom by 'discarding what has become outmoded, reordering priorities, and retaining what remains useful.'[28] Dale Mayer pointed out that oral history could be an excellent means for documenting social history. In 1985, he emphasized that new research interests required archivists to 'discover new ways of thinking about their most basic responsibilities.'[29]

By the late 1990s, the social history movement created new implications for archivists. As Reimer and Wallot had suggested, archivists *were* judged by the collections they had or had not acquired. In 1999, Francis Blouin described a new line of scholarship that focused on 'archives' as the *object* of study. Historians and others seeking to examine the underrepresented social aspects of history found little documentation of relevance in the archives. Blouin illustrated how these gaps in documentation affirmed certain historical realities and reflected archivists' biases as well as the constitutive role that status quo institutions played in defining both the historical record and history itself. He implored archivists to think more carefully about appraisal practices and their role as mediators of information. He argued, furthermore, that archivists needed to know how to respond to new questions being asked of the profession.[30]

Most recently, Mark Greene, Thomas Nesmith, and others have evaluated the role of archives, and indirectly the role of oral history and other memory-based documentation, within a postmodernist framework. At the heart of these discussions is the old debate concerning archivists' role as creator of materials or as objective curator of documents. Greene argues for the adoption of an 'archives paradigm' which embraces Bruce Dearstyne's definition of records as 'any type of recorded information, regardless of physical form or characteristics, created, received, or maintained by a person, institution or organization' and embraces the idea that all records – including those of transactional and institutional nature – are subject to archival mediation and subjective evaluation. Those who propose a 'record-keeping paradigm' do not approve of memory-based documentation as oral history is not a transactional record of evidential value and does not satisfy legal requirements of evidence. Greene applauds Adrian Cunningham's assessment that the 'elevation of the transactional record above all other sources of memory, evidence and storytelling impoverishes us all and makes us look plain silly in the eyes of the wider community.' Oral history matters in piecing together history.[31]

Torn Nesmith also focuses on postmodern theory to understand the role of archivists in 'mediating and thus shaping, the knowledge available in archives.' Postmodernism shatters the notion that archivists are or can be objective caretakers of documents as their bias, interests, and backgrounds shape the ways in which they collect and maintain archival holdings. Nesmith asserts that archivists 'help author records by the very act of determining what authoring them means and involves, or what the provenance of the records is.'[32] Oral history is no longer the only type of documentation under scrutiny. Postmodernists have placed archival practice under the microscope and concluded that both the individuals who use the archives and those who provide access its holdings construct and author the meanings and 'truths' of documents. Whether or not these arguments are valid, as Nesmith suggests, they offer a new lens through which to consider the archivist's role as collector or as creator.

Another component of the criticism of archivists' involvement in oral history is the argument that it adds to the mountain of paper documentation created by twentieth-century recordkeeping practices. In 1972, historian Barbara Tuchman took archivists and others to task for adding to the 'explosion of modern paperwork' with questionable oral history documentation. For her and others, a large number of oral history projects provided unreliable documentation based on faulty memory and addressed insignificant subject material.[33] James Fogerty answered this criticism by pointing to the poor quality of existing documentation. Oral history, blended 'with archival research,' may be 'crucial to complete understanding of information in the papers and is the only way to add information that the papers do not contain.' Fogerty and Tuchman agreed on the necessity of undertaking oral history with an 'eye to making a genuine contribution to the historical record.'[34]

Almost a decade after the publication of Fogerty's 1983 article, Bruce Bruemmer reiterated that the 'nature of modern documentation demands oral history as a component of historical research' since it can fill in gaps and is a good hook to primary resources.[35] These sentiments were reaffirmed by Jean-Pierre Wallot who pointed out that researchers needed documents in all types of media to create a 'total archives.'[36] Donald Richie, in his 1995 oral history manual, characterized oral history as filling in gaps that paper documents do not address and providing 'road maps' for researchers.[37]

It is clear that outside societal forces – historical research movements, social events, and technological advances – have required archivists and librarians to re-evaluate and, in some cases, change their perceptions of their roles and activities. The research demands of the social history movement of the 1970s brought to light the need for new resources that addressed underdocumented groups. Archivists, tentatively and slowly began to embrace or at least tolerate the idea that their role might involve active documentation strategies, such as oral history, to provide a more inclusive societal history.

These technological advances – the tape recorder, fax machine, e-mail, and the Internet – have pushed archivists and librarians to redefine their responsibilities in broader terms. In 1967, Arthur Schlesinger observed that in 'three-quarters of a century, the rise of the typewriter has vastly increased the flow of paper, while the rise of the telephone has vastly reduced its importance.' Helen Samuels amended this statement to include the impact of the copy machine, e-mail, and database systems on the ways in which we communicate.[38] When the twentieth-century proliferation of paper resulted in a loss of information, archivists, traditionally tied to paper-based documentation, used oral history to capture missing pieces in the correspondence. Oral history will have an important documentary role in the twenty-first century as more and more information, crucial to historical understanding, is disseminated over electronic media. For instance, college students at the turn of the twentieth century maintained elaborate scrapbooks and diaries, and corresponded with friends and family on mailed stationery. Their counterparts in 2003 maintain elaborate Web pages, record their thoughts and activities on blogs (Web-logs), and correspond through e-mail. Oral history, as well as Web-based documentation strategies, will be critical for understanding student experience in the coming decades.

Furthermore, as electronic records stored in different outdated formats continue to be lost, archivists again must step into the active role of 'creating' new documentation by migrating old formats to new, capturing Web pages to print or disk, and providing primary resources on the Internet. Nesmith emphasizes this point by arguing that archivists' mediating role will increase in the computer age as electronic records 'are said to need transformation into a settled landscape or orderly records making and keeping and archival control.'[39]

New responsibilities/skills

In 1968, Zachert insisted that oral history required librarians to develop new skills and expand their knowledge, particularly in regard to copyright and legal issues. Writing before the enactment of the Fair Use provisions in the 1976 Copyright Act, she implored librarians and archivists to become knowledgeable about copyright restrictions and liabilities. Willa Baum in her 1978 Louisiana State University Library School lecture, 'The Expanding Role of the Librarian in Oral History,' advised librarians to secure release forms for all oral history tapes and offered practical guidance on protecting interviewees' privacy through restriction agreements.[40] However, it was not until the 1985 publication of John Neuenschwander's work, *Oral History and the Law*, that archivists' and oral historians' awareness and understanding of legal issues was enriched. Urging his readers to secure release forms with all oral histories created by or deposited in the archives, Neuenschwander emphasized the importance of keeping abreast of legal developments. His biennial reports at OHA meetings continue to update the membership on outcomes of new cases, legal stipulations, and other developments concerning oral history litigation.[41]

With Internet and Web capabilities, archivists and librarians entered a new realm of legal problems and issues in the mid-1990s. Reflecting in a special *Oral History Review* issue on oral history at the millennium, Bret Eynon argued that the spread of digital technology is 'forcing archives to rethink their roles, and function, and to confront difficult questions of security, protection and accessibility.'[42] At OHA in 1998, archivists discussed the implications of placing oral history interviews on the Web. Discussion included the need to protect interviewee's privacy, the danger of misuse and manipulation of sound recordings and transcripts, and the 'unmonitored access' of the Internet that would result in a loss of archival control over the interviews. Other questions concerned whether 'deeds of gift that had not anticipated electronic reproduction and distribution would permit the posting of interviews on the Internet without the express permission of the interviewees or their next of kin.'[43]

Karen Brewster's 2000 study of Internet access to oral histories illustrates how libraries with oral history collections dealt with them on the Web. Her analysis of sixty-four Web sites found that, overall, mainstream institutions had done 'the hard and expensive work of researching copyright and going back to speakers from old interviews to seek permission for Internet access to their recordings.' Much was lacking, however. While some sites had clear copyright protection statements, others did not mention the issue at all. In addition, interpretation of copyright regulations varied from institution to institution.[44]

Archivists and librarians, in recent years, have discussed oral history in the context of digitizing sound archives. Most encouraging are collaborative efforts that draw on expertise across disciplines to address rights management, preservation, and use of sound collections. The Council on Library and Information Resources' *Folk Heritage Collections in Crisis* report, the product of a symposium of archivists, librarians, preservationists, faculty, and folklorists who consulted on preservation and access to American folk heritage sound collections, indicated that rights in the digital realm are highly ambiguous and require collaborative guidelines and study.[45]

Although sound and digitization archivists and librarians are working admirably with other disciplines in addressing access, copyright, and preservation issues, collaboration is essential in all aspects of archival and library practice. Ronald Grele emphasized this point by arguing that oral historians needed the skills of both historian and archivist.[46] Archivists must step outside the archival box and engage oral historians by showing interest in their scholarship and interview tapes; providing leadership in access, legal, and preservation issues within OHA; promoting the importance of depositing oral histories in the archives; and making contacts to help develop archival holdings.

Integration into library collections

Zachert pointed out in 1968 that oral history introduced new media – namely audio-tapes and reels – into paper-based collections. Two decades later, Graham Eeles and Jill Kinnear strongly argued that oral history belonged in libraries where it would be widely accessible and utilized in the context of other library resources. They stressed, however, that preservation of these recordings and transcripts had not received enough attention.[47] In 1991, Dale Treleven also asserted that archivists had not met the preservation challenge but instead were tied to 'professional and organizational traditionalism at a time when products of new technology require change.' Treleven argued that archivists, 'secure in daily routines tied to paper documents, have been reluctant to explore the new technologies and master details about the special care required for the products generated by those technical processes.'[48]

Treleven also pointed out that Frederick Stielow's *Management of Oral History Sound Archives* (1986), published nearly *forty years* after the advent of electromagnetic tape recordings, was the first major attempt in the U.S. to suggest a comprehensive archival strategy for oral history tapes and sound and visual recordings of other kinds. Sound archives, including speeches, music productions, and radio programs, and oral history interview recordings presented similar technical problems for the archivist. Trevelen suggested that archivists had been remiss in not acquainting themselves with the foreign sources and manuals available by the 1980s and that most had 'lagged in shifting human and financial resources to processing, preserving, cataloging, and disseminating information about oral history tapes.'[49]

Zachert could not foresee how the advent of virtual sound archives projects, such as the National Gallery of the Spoken Word (NGSW) at Michigan State University (MSU), would transform the issue of oral histories' and sound archives' integration into library collections. Funded by the National Science Foundation, MSU's revolutionary project has brought together digitized audio from several repositories' collections into a single searchable online database. Clearly, as magnetic tape and paper documents are digitized, integration of different types of media becomes less of an issue for the 'virtual' archives. Of course, not insignificant barriers to this process include funding and staffing. Despite this expense, the CLIR's *Folk Heritage Collections in Crisis Report* asserted that archivists' and preservation experts' reluctance to move forward with the technology, even as it changes, will result in the loss of analog media.[50] Although no one group had the solutions to preserving these media, the CLIR report emphasized that 'it was clear that each sector that was represented, from archives to the law, holds part of the solution, and only collaboration will achieve lasting progress.'[51]

As archivist Frank Burke pointed out in the 1976 reader *Archive-Library Relations*, archives and libraries hold much of the same materials and formats, including audio-visual materials. The difference in their operation lies in how these materials are cataloged or processed. Like archives, libraries faced difficulties in integrating these formats into their collections.[52] It is crucial for librarians and archivists to collaborate with one another to better understand how to care for audiovisual materials and explore opportunities for cooperative projects, the sharing of temperature-controlled audio-visual facilities, and the pooling of financial resources.

Bibliographic control and access

Zachert's fourth implication focused on the need to promote oral history collections through description in national resources such as the National Union Catalog for Manuscript Collections (NUCMC). Others, too, suggested interlibrary loan as a dissemination method.[53] By 1985, Clive Cochrane insisted that oral historians had concentrated too much on recording practices and not enough on access.[54] Six years later, Bruce Bruemmer argued that archivists 'are at fault for the lack of access – uniform or otherwise – to oral history collections.' At the cutting edge of Internet development, he wrote that archivists needed to increase access to oral history through new databases, MARC records, and interlibrary loan.[55] He also provided a national agenda for improved access to oral history. Goals for greater access, Bruemmer argued, could be attained only with a change in attitude toward access on the part of archivists and oral historians.[56]

Bruemmer's article, written in an effort to raise awareness of the need for enhanced access to oral history sources, led to SAA's successful application to the National Historical Publications and Records Commission (NHPRC) to fund a much-needed oral history cataloging manual. Marion Matters' SAA publication *Oral History Cataloging Manual* was published in 1995 and has become the 'most widely used oral history cataloging tool developed to standardize library and archival cataloging of oral history transcripts and tapes.'[57]

Since the publication of Bruemmer's article and the SAA's manual, library technological publications and conferences frequently have focused on access of sound collections through digitization and Web installation. Projects such as the NGSW, the Library of Congress' American Memory, and the University of Alaska-Fairbanks's Jukebox provide examples of how sound has been transferred to digital formats. A great advantage, Bret Enyon explained in 1999, was that transcripts and tape contents on the Web were not only available to remote users but could be accessed by keyword searches and supplemented with digitized written documents, photographs, and graphs. However, he pointed out that archivists who placed oral history interviews on the Web risked losing control of the use of collections.[58]

Preservation of analog and digital sound recordings also took center stage in discussion. The *Report on the Task Force on the Library Artifact* (2001) indicated that preservation of sound was difficult because of the fragility of recording media. Projecting access needs of future researchers is important, although archivists could determine these needs only by the present generation of users.[59] One of the key findings of a survey of collections undertaken by the American Folklore Society, the

Society for Ethnomusicology, and the American Folklife Center in 2000 was that much of what has been recorded is poorly controlled, badly labeled, and lacking critical documentation about rights to use. This was the case largely because in the past, professions such as anthropology, ethnomusicology, and folklore failed to secure releases from their informants.[60]

The University of Alaska-Fairbanks, a leader in oral history management and creation, presents a good example of archives-library collaboration. Since the establishment of its Project Jukebox program in the early 1990s, Alaska-Fairbanks has made substantial strides in enhancing access to its oral history collection through the inclusion of oral history catalog records in the university library database, the creation of MARC records for the collection, and providing oral history transcripts and tapes to distant users through the library's interlibrary loan program. Circulation statistics for the oral history collection increased significantly. The program is working to integrate more completely the archival and library collections through an online digital media database.[61]

The University of Alaska-Fairbanks's work to integrate archival and oral history material into a common library database stands as a model for how librarians and archivists can work together to provide greater access to oral history and to their other collections. Although archives and libraries hold many of the same types of records, they catalog or process them differently. While libraries create catalog records for individual books, archives create catalog records for individual collections, most of which contain numerous documents and formats. Many archival institutions do not create MARC records for their collection holdings but instead rely on 'in-house' archives databases, which can be searched from the archives Web site but not the library catalog. Therefore, the possibility for collaboration and integrated special collection and library database systems is exciting and necessary. Not only will library-archives collaboration provide greater access to collections, the process will foster greater understanding between the two professions.

Further study

Zachert's fifth and final implication of oral history for librarians centered on the need for additional study of bibliographic control problems. Zachert implored librarians in 1968 to embrace the opportunity to study information retrieval from new storage media, namely audiotapes and reels. As discussed earlier in regard to integration issues, librarians and archivists have dealt with sound materials haphazardly in the past. Importantly, the publication of Matters's oral history cataloging manual has enhanced access in recent years. Oral history cataloging records now appear in a standardized format in national and international databases such as OCLC and RLIN, as well as those of local and regional libraries and repositories. This format allows users to conduct more useful and productive searches of library and archives holdings.

Technological advances have revolutionized access capabilities in exciting ways, and sound librarians and archivists are collaborating with lawyers, computer technicians, and others to study preservation and access issues. National online databases for sound archives, integration of archival and oral history material with library catalogs, full-text searching capabilities for oral history transcripts, and complete audio of interviews on the Web are ensuring greater use of materials.

Of course, more study of and collaboration on these issues is necessary. As oral history recordings are provided to the public through digital sound databases, new issues arise. Archivists and librarians must find ways to ensure that oral history transcripts and audio are utilized by researchers in complete adherence to the wishes and legal restraints outlined by their creators. And, as with all audio-visual material, they must continually work to preserve these tapes in or transfer them to stable formats so that they remain available for future researchers. Certainly, collaboration with experts in audio and digital technology and with members of the legal profession is *the* vital component in this process.

In addition to the need for further study of bibliographic access issues, other important issues, not addressed by Zachert's article, require investigation. Archivists and librarians need to examine and consider cost and funding implications involved with oral history. Ronald Filippelli in 1976 argued that because of the high financial cost of oral history, archives should undertake a project with the expectation that it will become a major element of the program, with designated staff and support services. Anything 'less will result in a slipshod program – the money might better be used for putting [one's] existing backlog in shape.' Filippelli emphasized that archives should actively seek outside money to support such endeavors and that institutions should cooperate on projects to pool resources and provide experience.[62] In 1988, archivists at an SAA annual meeting session discussed the importance of conducting studies that compared costs of oral history and traditional records processing. Unfortunately, such studies have not received appropriate attention in subsequent years.[63]

Furthermore, archivists and librarians need to embrace opportunities to educate 'would-be' oral historians-students, historians, and the public – concerning proper interview techniques and equipment, the crucial importance of conducting background research on the subject of investigation, legal considerations, and the value of making oral histories available through deposit in libraries and archives. Archivists and librarians are in a position to influence and educate these interviewers to increase the likelihood that oral history will be done properly and will be shared, through libraries and archives, with future researchers.

Finally, the Web's impact on the role of oral history in archives is substantial and deserves careful attention. Robert Perks, Curator of the Oral History at the British Library National Sound Archive in London, argues that oral history on the Web will be in the forefront of democratizing and popularizing archives for the next generations. As archives are available 'not only remotely but interactively,' they will be opened to users who 'are not naturally inclined to visit archives and libraries, or who are more comfortable with oral and visual, rather than written, forms of memory and narrative.' The twenty-first-century archives will provide access to its holdings through multimedia approaches involving 'audio-visual recordings with maps, photographs, documents, transcripts and commentary.'[64] Not only will these approaches require new relationships with sound archivists, computer specialists, law experts, and others, they also will pull the archives out of the basement and into the public light by creating more awareness of the archives' holdings and expanding its user base.

Concluson

Three themes emerge from this review of scholarship. First, a general lack of scholarship by archivists and librarians in the last ten years concerning oral history's implications for information professionals reflects a move away from publication on documentation strategy toward greater emphasis on electronic access issues. Secondly, the need for archivists and librarians to collaborate with each other and with other professionals to discuss oral history issues and to build partnerships that enhance historical knowledge is paramount to the archival and library mission and collection development. Finally, archivists and librarians must become more attuned to historical research trends to serve an increasingly diversified clientele with changing needs. Oral history can play an important part in this process.

Providing information to meet the needs of researchers is central to the mission of the academic archives and library. Certainly, the early oral history programs in the U.S. introduced a means for providing a more complete historical picture for future users. And, it was by no mistake that these early programs were connected with academic institutions mandated to preserve and make accessible these oral sources. Why aren't archivists and librarians, early leaders in the profession, more prominent and visible in oral history circles today? Why hasn't the role of oral history in the library been a topic of discussion in recent scholarship?

One possible answer is that archivists and librarians over the past decade have tended to align themselves with the technological sciences rather than the history profession. They are 'information specialists' who have expertise in Web page development, digital access tools, and database design. While archivists in the past most often held doctoral degrees in history, they now have dual degrees in library and history, and their focus is on providing access tools and legal knowledge to their materials rather than in-depth subject expertise. Clearly, the oral history literature published over the last ten years and reviewed here reflects this trend in that it deals primarily with access to sound resources through digitization and Web development.

In addition, oral history practices and procedures are well established. OHA and SAA guidelines and policies outline the procedures of oral history interviewing and collecting, and SAA's cataloging manual is a recognized and widely used resource among librarians and archivists. Oral history isn't as 'cutting edge' as it was in the 1970s and 1980s. Perhaps the lack of scholarship on the subject does not reflect a lack of interest, but rather a greater acceptance. Even if this assertion is correct, there are substantial reasons to insist that information professionals focus more attention on this area. The unlimited potential for collaboration among disciplines; library outreach to faculty, students, and the community; classroom education; and research through oral history practice demand active and innovative discourse.

Only a few archivists have chosen to write about oral history topics in the oral history literature, rather than in archival or library journals.[65] However, oral historians, reaching beyond the confines of their own disciplines, continue to highlight archival topics in anthologies, oral history readers, and some journals. The less interdisciplinary approach of archivists and librarians matches their stereotyped image as introverts who delight in caring for papers and books rather than mingling with people.[66] In contrast, oral historians come from many fields and interact easily with colleagues from many disciplines. As James Fogerty pointed out, oral historians are more outward looking and collaborative in nature than their colleagues in archival and library science.[67] As such, they are inclined to seek, embrace, and explore the viewpoints of other fields.

Collaboration with and understanding of other disciplines, although not always practiced or embraced, is essential to all aspects of library and archival practice. Lila Goff, James Fogerty, James Mink, and William Moss have bridged the archival and oral history professional gap and others from throughout the field must work to keep the bridge open in the years to come. One important way to 'bridge the gap' is to invite oral historians to participate in archival and library conferences. Bruce Bruemmer called for a 'proactive advocacy' in which archivists construct relationships between the oral history and library and archives fields not only by attending oral history conferences and meetings but also by inviting oral historians to participate in archival forums.[68] This holds true for other professions as well. Museum professionals, historians, anthropologists, computer technicians, public librarians, and others can provide invaluable insight into historical research and recordkeeping needs and practices.

Finally, archivists and librarians must be knowledgeable about research trends and needs of their users. As indicated in previous discussions, oral history is an important component in this collection development endeavor. Of course, collaboration is essential in this process as well. Archivists and librarians must be aware of collection gaps, become familiar with their user groups, keep tabs on what questions are being asked, develop relationships with faculty on campus, and enhance their knowledge of their collection subject area or identify and connect with those who are experts in the subject. If archives and libraries are to be relevant and responsive to the research interests of their users, they must seek out and identify the resources these users need through oral history, active collection development, and appraisal. If they do not hold the resources needed by current scholars, scholars will go elsewhere. In light of recent trends to study 'archives' and their societal and institutional biases, archivists and librarians need to examine their role as historical mediators of history. As urged by Francis Blouin, informational professionals should evaluate archival processes continually and be attuned to changing patterns in the methods and materials of historical research.

What is the role of the archivist and librarian in oral history? In 1983, an oral historian offered this: 'collaborator, critic, colleague, teacher, friend.'[69] Archivists and librarians must acknowledge the importance of oral history to historical documentation, and at whatever level – creator, collector, appraiser – familiarize and engage themselves in its practice. The profession is being judged by the collections archives and libraries hold and the access they provide.

Notes

1   Martha Jane K. Zachert, 'The Implications of Oral History for Librarians', *College and Research Libraries*, 29, March 1968, pp. 101–103. Zachert's work is the *only* article to appear in *C&RL* that deals specifically with oral history.
2   Ronald J. Grele, 'Directions for Oral History in the United States', in *Oral History: An Interdisciplinary Anthology*, 2nd edn, ed. David K. Dunaway and Willa Baum,

Walnut Creek, Calif.; London and New Delhi: AltaMira Press, 1966, pp. 64–65.

3   For example, Vaughn Bornet wrote in 1955 that 'a handful of the members of the historical and archival professions are convinced of the value of oral history. If the remainder – the doubters – are to be won over, the reminiscence-manufacturing industry must set and maintain high and uniform standards for its final product', Vaughn D. Bornet, 'Oral History Can Be Worthwhile', *American Archivist*, 18, July 1955, p. 253.

4   Grele, op.cit., pp. 65–66.

5   Grele, op.cit.

6   Records, 1936–[ongoing], Society of American Archivists, UWM Manuscript Collection 172, Golda Meir Library, University Manuscript Collections, University of Wisconsin-Milwaukee.

7   Committee on Oral History of the Society of American Archivists, 'Oral History and Archivists: Some Questions to Ask', *American Archivist*, 36, July 1973, p. 363.

8   William W. Moss and Peter C. Mazikana, *Archives, Oral History and Oral Tradition: A RAMP Study*, Paris: UNESCO, 1986, p. 16.

9   Grele, op.cit., pp. 65–70.

10 Records, 1936–[ongoing], op.cit.

11 Nicholas C. Burckel and J. Frank Cook, 'A Profile of College and University Archives in the United States,' *American Archivist*, 45, Fall 1982, p. 420. These survey results provide an interesting contrast to SAA's 1973 membership survey in which 73% believed oral history should be considered a regular archival activity. College and university archivists may have deemed oral history acceptable, but nine years later, most had not integrated oral history into their archival activities.

12 'Statement on Interviewing for Historical Documentation', *Journal of American History*, 77, September 1990, pp. 613–614. This statement is an appendum to the American Historical Association's 'Statement on Standards of Professional Conduct.' It was approved May 1989 by the AHA Council.

13 For oral history articles in the 1960s, see, for example, three essays by Donald Swain, 'Problems to Practitioners of Oral History', pp. 63–69; Saul Benison, 'Reflections on Oral History', pp. 71–77; and Gould Colman, 'Oral History – An Appeal for More Systematic Procedures', pp. 79–83, in *American Archivist*, 28, January 1965. For articles published in the 1970s, see, for example, Ronald Filippelli, 'Oral History and the Archives', *American Archivist*, 39, October 1976, pp. 479–483; and William Moss, 'Oral History: An Appreciation', *American Archivist*, 40, October 1977, pp. 429–439. For articles published in the 1980s, see, for example, David Lance, 'Oral History Archives: Perceptions and Practices', *Oral History*, 8, no. 2, Autumn 1980, pp. 59–63; James Fogerty, 'Filling the Gap: Oral History in the Archives', *American Archivist*, 46, Spring 1983, pp. 148–157; Thomas Carleton, 'Videotaped Oral Histories: Problems and Prospects, *American Archivist*, 47, Summer 1984, pp. 228–236; William W. Moss and Peter C. Mazikana, *Archives, Oral History and Oral Tradition: A RAMP Study*; Graham Eeles and Jill Kinnear, 'Archivists and Oral Historians: Friends, Strangers, or Enemies?', *Journal of the Society of Archivists*, 9, no. 4, October 1988, pp. 188–189; and Dale Treleven, 'Oral History and the Archival Community: Common Concerns about Documenting Twentieth-Century Life', *International Journal of Oral History*, 10, February 1989, pp. 50–58.

14 Oral history articles published in library and archival literature in the 1990s include: Bruce H. Bruemmer, 'Access to Oral History: A National Agenda', *American Archivist*, 54, Fall 1991, pp. 494–501; Charles T. Morrissey, 'Beyond Oral Evidence: Speaking (Con)strictly About Oral History,' *Archival Issues*, 17, no. 2, 1992, pp. 89–94; David

Gerard, 'The Word Made Flesh: Some Reflections on Oral History', *Library History*, 9, nos. 3 & 4, 1992, pp. 122–126. Jean-Pierre Wallot and Normand Fortier's article, 'Archival Science and Oral Sources', in *Janus*, no. 2, 1996, was reprinted in Robert Perks and Alistair Thomson (eds), *The Oral History Reader*, London and New York: Routledge Press, 1998, pp. 365–378. An article that addresses the subjective and unreliable nature of memory is Walter Menninger, 'Memory and History: What Can You Believe?', *Archival Issues*, 21, no. 2, 1996, pp. 9–106. Articles concerning oral history's archival role in specific countries include: Robert B. Perks, 'Bringing New Life to Archives: Oral History, Sound Archives and Accessibility', *International Association of Sound Archives Journal*, 12, July 1999; and Lisa Klopfer, 'Oral History and Archives in the New South Africa: Methodological Issues', *Archivaria*, 52, 2001, pp. 100–125.

15   Grele, op.cit. p. 74.

16   In 1985, the Oral History Section membership totaled eighty-five people. In 1994, the Section's membership was 140 or 4% of SAA's total individual membership, and in 2001 it totaled 163 or 5%. Records, 1936–[ongoing], Society of American Archivists, UWM Manuscript Collection 172, Golda Meir Library, University Manuscript Collections, University of Wisconsin-Milwaukee.

17   Mary Larson, internal report at the University of Nevada Oral History Program. E-mail correspondence from Mary Larson to Ellen Swain, 18 September 2001 and 14 February 2002, in possession of the author.

18   Zachert, 'The Implications of Oral History for Librarians', p. 102

19   Hilary Jenkinson, 'Reflections of an Archivist', in *Modern Archives Reader: Basic Readings on Archival Theory and Practice*, Maygene F. Daniels and Timothy Walch (eds), Washington, D.C.: National Archives and Records Services, 1984, p. 20.

20   William W. Moss, 'Oral History', in *Managing Archives and Archival Institutions*, James Gregory Bradsher (ed.), London: Mansell Publishing Limited, 1988, p. 149.

21   Ronald L. Filippelli, 'Oral History and the Archives', p. 180. For a negative view of oral history see Hugh Taylor, 'Oral History and Archives: Keynote Speech to the 1976 Canadian Oral History Conference', *Canadian Oral History Association Journal*, 1, 1975–76, p. 3.

22   Derek Reimer, 'Oral History and Archives: The Case in Favor', *Canadian Oral History Association Journal*, 5, 1981–82, pp. 30–33.

23   Jean Dryden, 'Oral History and Archives: The Case Against', *Canadian Oral History Association Journal*, 5, 1981–82, pp. 34–37.

24   Richard Lochead, 'Oral History: The Role of the Archivist', Rolf Schuursma, 'Oral History: The Role of the Archivist'; and Ronald Grele, 'Oral History in Archives', *Phonographic Bulletin*, 37, July 1983, pp. 3–15.

25   Grele, ibid. p. 13.

26   Jean-Pierre Wallot and Normand Fortier, 'Archival Science and Oral Sources', in *The Oral History Reader*, Robert Perks and Alistair Thomson (eds), London and New York: Routledge, 1998, p. 375.

27   F. Gerald Ham, 'The Archival Edge', *American Archivist*, 38, January 1975, pp. 9, 13.

28   Fredric M. Miller, 'Social History and Archival Practice', *American Archivist*, 44, Spring 1981, pp. 119, 124.

29   Dale C. Mayer, 'The New Social History: Implications for Archivists', *American Archivist*, 48, Fall 1985, p. 399.

30   Francis X. Blouin, Jr, 'Archivists, Mediation, and Constructs of Social Memory', *Archival Issues*, 24, 1999, pp. 101–111. A year-long study, 2000–2001, on 'Archives, Documentation, and the Institutions of Social Memory' at the University of Michigan

(UM) investigated the changing relationship between the role of archivist and historical pursuits. At the 2001 SAA Annual Meeting, Blouin and colleagues reported results of the conference in a session on the UM seminar.

31 Mark A. Greene, 'The Power of Meaning: The Archival Mission in the Postmodern Age', *American Archivist*, 65, Spring/Summer 2002, pp. 44–48.

32 Tom Nesmith, 'Seeing Archives: Postmodernism and the Changing Intellectual Place of Archives', *American Archivist*, 65, Spring/Summer 2002, p. 24, p. 35.

33 Donald Ritchie, *Doing Oral History*, New York: Twayne, 1995, p. 132.

34 James E. Fogerty, 'Filling the Gap: Oral History in the Archives', pp. 49–50. James Fogerty comments on Tuchman's approval of oral history in e-mail correspondence to Ellen Swain, 25 February 2002, in possession of the author.

35 Bruce Bruemmer, 'Access to Oral History: A National Agenda', *American Archivist*, 54, Fall 1991, p. 496.

36 Jean-Pierre Wallot, 'Building a Living Memory for the History of Our Present: New Perspectives on Archival Appraisal', *Journal of the Canadian Historical Association*, 2, 1991, p. 265.

37 Ritchie, op.cit. p. 33.

38 Helen Willa Samuels, *Varsity Letters: Documenting Modern Colleges and Universities*, Lanham, Md. and London: SAA and Scarecrow Press, 1998, p. 9.

39 Nesmith, *op.cit.* p. 39.

40 Willa K. Baum, 'The Expanding Role of the Librarian in Oral History' in *Oral History: An Interdisciplinary Anthology*, pp. 321–40, eds Dunaway and Baum. Originally published in *Library Lectures*, 6, 1978, pp. 33–43.

41 John Neuenschwander, *Oral History and the Law*, Carlisle, Pa: Oral History Association, 2002.

42 Bret Eynon, 'Oral History and the New Century', *Oral History Review*, 26, Summer/ Fall 1999, p. 24.

43 Donald Ritchie, 'Oral History and the New Century', *Oral History Review*, 26, Summer/Fall 1999, p. 13.

44 Karen Brewster, 'Internet Access to Oral Recordings: Finding the Issues', Oral History Program, Elmer E. Rasmuson Library, University of Alaska Fairbanks, 25 October 2000 (www.uaf.edu/library/oralhistory/brewster1/), 1 March 2003.

45 Council on Library and Information Resources (CLIR), *Folk Heritage Collections in Crisis*, May 2001. The 'Survey of Folk Heritage Collections', Appendix 2, found that 25% of organizations responding reported having release forms for the greater bulk (76 to 100%) of their collections. An alarming 39% of all individuals responding did not have release forms for their material.

46 Grele, op.cit. p. 15.

47 Graham Eeles and Jill Kinnear, 'Archivists and Oral Historians: Friends, Strangers, or Enemies?', pp. 188–189.

48 Dale Treleven, 'Oral History and the Archival Community: Common Concerns about Documenting Twentieth-Century Life', pp. 54–55.

49 Treleven, ibid. Bruce Bruemmer also discusses this lack of scholarship in 'Access to Oral History', p. 495.

50 CLIR, *Folk Heritage Collections in Crisis*, p. 9.

51 Ibid. p. 16. Other collaborative conferences include the Best Practices for Digital Sound Meeting, held at the Library of Congress, 16 January 2001. A cross-disciplinary endeavor to discuss reformatting, metadata, data management, and intellectual property, the conference grew out of an ALA preconference on sound in the digital age that addressed the lack of accepted standards to use in voice-digitization projects.

From that meeting, participants began to hold informal dinner meetings at ALA with other library colleagues with similar interests, including those from CLIR, Research Libraries Group, the National Agriculture Library, and a number of universities. In December 2000, some of these same people attended the Folk Heritage Collections in Crisis conference. Michael Seadle, 'Sound Practice: A Report of the Best Practice for Digital Sound Meeting, 16 January 2001 at the Library of Congress', *RLG DigiNews*, 5, 15 April 2001, pp. 20–24.

52   Frank G. Burke, 'Similarities and Differences', in *Archive-Library Relations*, ed. Robert L. Clark, Jr, New York: Bowker, 1976, p. 31.

53   See Filippelli, op.cit. p. 482.

54   Clive Cochrane, 'Public Libraries and the Changing Nature of Oral History', *Audiovisual Librarian*, 11, Autumn 1985, p. 205.

55   Bruemmer, 'Access to Oral History', p. 495. Bruemmer cited the University of Alaska-Fairbank's 'Project Jukebox', the first hypermedia application of sound recording, graphics, and pictures in the early 1990s, as an excellent access project example; SAA did address the need for oral history cataloging methods when it published Marion Matters' *Oral History Cataloging Manual*, Chicago: Society of American Archivists, 1995.

56   Bruemmer, ibid., p. 497.

57   Matters, *Oral History Cataloging Manual*, e-mail correspondence from James Fogerty to Ellen Swain, 25 February 2002, in possession of the author.

58   Eynon, op.cit., pp. 23–24.

59   *The Evidence at Hand: Report of the Task Force on the Artifact in Library Collections*, Washington, D.C.: Council on Library and Information Resources, November 2001, (www.clir.org/pubs/reports/pub103/contents.html), 1 March 2003.

60   Of the 297 responses from organizations and individuals involved in folklore and ethnomusicology, 90% of all respondents do not have any of their collections available through the Web. CLIR, 'Folk Heritage Collections in Crisis', Appendix 2.

61   E-mail correspondence from Robyn Russell, Collection Manager, Oral History Program, Alaska and Polar Regions Department, Rasmuson Library, University of Alaska-Fairbanks, to Ellen Swain, 1 March 2002, in possession of the author.

62   Filippelli, op.cit., p. 483.

63   William J. Mather's remarks as session chair, 'What is the Bottom Line?: The Real Costs of Oral History', Society of American Archivists Annual Meeting, Atlanta, Georgia, 30 September 1988, in possession of William Maher. Dale Trevelen also calls for cost comparison in 1991 in 'Oral History and the Archival Community', p. 53.

64   Robert B. Perks, 'Bringing New Life to Archives', p. 24.

65   Oral history readers and anthologies that include sections on the role of the archives/library include: Dunaway and Baum (eds), *Oral History: An Interdisciplinary Anthology*; and Perks and Thomson (eds), *The Oral History Reader*. A manual that includes information about the role of archives and libraries is Donald Ritchie, *Doing Oral History*. Jean-Pierre Wallot and Normand Fortier, authors of chapter 30, 'Archival science and oral sources' in *The Oral History Reader* are prominent Canadian archivists. It is important to note that Wallot and Fortier's article is reprinted from *Janus*, 1996.

66   Sidney J. Levy and Albert J. Robels, *The Image of Archivists: Resource Allocators' Perceptions*, Chicago: Society of American Archivists, 1985, p. iv.

67   E-mail correspondence from James Fogerty to Ellen Swain, 21 December 2001, in possession of the author. This is an obvious truth when one compares the OHA inter-

disciplinary membership directory to that of SAA. According to David K. Dunaway, oral history of the 1990s is characterized by a 'rising interdisciplinary.' Dunaway and Baum (eds), *Oral History: An Interdisciplinary Anthology*, p. 9.

68   Bruemmer, ibid.
69   Grele, op.cit., p. 15.

Chapter 27

Francis Good

VOICE, EAR AND TEXT
Words, meaning, and transcription

Transcription – moving from voice to text – continues to be debated by oral historians: strategy, practice and technique vary considerably world-wide. This chapter assesses the debate, glancing at such issues as notation, mediation, poetic forms, editing policy, new technology, ethics, and representation. Since 1985 Francis Good has been managing the Oral History Unit at the Northern Territory Archives Service in Darwin, Australia, which currently holds over 2,200 hours of recordings, mostly transcribed. Reprinted, with some minor amendments, from the *Oral History Association of Australia Journal*, 2000, no. 22, pp. 102–109, with permission.

ALTHOUGH NOT UNIVERSALLY practised, transcription of oral history interviews is a key element of the enterprise more often than not. Manuals and handbooks invariably provide advice on the issues, problems and strategies involved, but practice and comment show considerable divergence at times. While not wishing to overview the substantial literature on the subject, I thought it might be a useful exercise at the turn of the century to attempt an overview of some of the issues which show interesting variations in approaches to transcription, and to offer some of my own perspective.

The differences can be fundamental pointers on how we perceive our roles as oral historians and what we believe we are trying to achieve. Opinions vary, not only on how it should be done but also on its worth and significance, and even if it should be attempted at all. The context is one of concern, sometimes dissatisfaction, that the process distracts attention from its source, the spoken word. The dangers are real. Few can now accept a purely documentary and text-oriented approach to oral material at face value, and the distance between a transcript and the voice is usually well appreciated – but to what extent is another matter.

In dealing with ideas about transcription, two principal concerns are the loss of 'information' by selective editing of language used by interviewees, and fear that the distinction between primary and secondary sources is muddied or simply ignored.

On the first issue, Kate Moore[1] recently criticized the way editors of transcription change or delete material in the belief that it is necessary to curb excessive 'redundancy' of raw oral communication, the 'readability' imperative. Approaches vary with individual objectives and values. Manuals such as Willa Baum's[2] will provide much detail on elements that can come in for the editor's attention, and strategies for dealing with them. Changes can range from thinning out 'crutch' words and phrases ('like', 'you know', 'of course'), to substantive matters such as giving names for unidentified pronouns, or correcting grammar. Baum, while recognizing that her approach may not suit others, advocates even further distancing from the oral:

> Produce a useable research manuscript. This will involve cutting out unnecessary impediments to the flow of the story, possibly reordering the material so that the researcher can follow it.[3]

Immediately one can see that there are different motivations for differing kinds of intervention, and that with more intervention the greater is the distance that opens up between the primary oral and the research users' text. Readability is one thing, and the archivist historian's concern with making sense of detail is another.

However, Moore has no time for attempts to make the text 'readable' and would have us include detailed representations of every single utterance that can be captured in print in the so-called 'verbatim' transcript. For her, pauses, hesitations, part- and whole-word repetitions, frequent exclamations such as 'all right', 'really', etc. are all fertile ground for analysis and potentially valuable inference of meaning, and she is able to give some cogent examples. Value is also seen in retaining verbal encouragement of interviewers in 'back-channelling' expressions such as 'mm', 'uh-huh', etc., since these facilitate examination of interactive processes; for her this is worthy of study in itself, and can help explain the role such processes play in actually shaping the information elicited. Moore believes we should heed findings of related disciplines such as speech research and conversational analysis (yet another example of oral historians crossing borders).

Changing the choice of words and their variations, syntax, etc. is another worrying interpretive activity for Moore, who challenges notions of 'respectability' which often motivate this kind of interference. This is not a new notion, of course. In the 1970s, Baum also cautioned against the notion of going too far down this road into 'vanity biography'.[4] In fairness, though, there can be legitimate concern about the difficulties in gaining acceptance of a transcript by subjects who may be uncomfortable with their speech when confronted with a printed version of it 'in the raw'. My own experience indicates that some of this difficulty can be alleviated by careful negotiation and explanation in the early stages of interviewee contact. How successful this can be, of course, is a moot point since it involves an element of second-guessing respondents' expectations and preconceptions about the nature and usage of transcripts. Also, disentangling the respondent's perceptions from behind-the-scenes pressure of relatives who feel they have a stake in presenting their family in a 'respectable' light can be a minefield too. As Ronda Jamieson reported on the experience of the California State Archives at Sacramento, this can lead to the abandonment of interviews,[5] and the Imperial War Museum at one time found the process of gaining respondents' approval so pesky it was discontinued.[6] Overall, there is an ethical dilemma here: whose history is it anyway, and does the respondent not have a right to decide how they wish to be represented in the record? Are the rights of interviewees here secondary to the needs of institutions to finalize a record that was expensive to compile?

Another difficulty for Moore is that punctuation is the only tool at hand for indicating oral prosody, and 'the nuances of intonation, rhythm, expression of emotion', etc. Punctuation has purely literate origins. It is sometimes required to avoid misinterpretation that the eye on the page can make, but is easily ignored, strangely enough, by the ear listening for meaning in the flow of speech heard. In transcription, one can easily be fooled into thinking it indicates the 'way' something is said when its use is purely an indication of the editor's idea of correct grammar. Some will use commas to indicate small pauses that we use to emphasize a following word, while others will avoid them where they have no 'correct' function in separating clauses etc. This presents a conundrum for readers. I am reminded of the advice I heard somewhere recently for young actors seeking different ways to say a line: 'Never read the punctuation'; and who could forget comedian Victor Borge's classic mocking rendition of audible punctuation.

In the matter of print conventions and presentation, Barry York[7] is one who argues that sensitivity to the lyric aspects of speech can be a basis for presenting phrases or sentences in the manner of '*verse libre* (free verse) poetry' which may bring us closer to aspects of the oral source. He has a laudable concern for the loss of some of the more elusive 'charm' of speech in transcript, which most of us would share. He makes it clear that he has an open mind on the subject, but is the expressiveness of the interesting example he quotes a product of the speaker, or the mind of the reader or the transcriber? There is a risk of beguiling readers to 'hear' inflection and cadence that is a product more of their own imagination than what may in reality be apprehended in the original sound.

But elsewhere I have found this strategy quite valid, particularly where it more closely matches an oral rhetorical style involving consistently short and succinct phrasing. Loreen Brehaut cites a good example involving Australian Aboriginal English,[8] which is often very amenable to this approach. A re-presentation of a published text of Tommy Thompson Kngwarreye, a Kaytetye man I recorded in central Australia, is another example:

> About the limestones.
> They find the good lime
> on that big reef,
> and they went out.
>
> They get a load,
> ton and ton,
> and bringem to Barrow Creeks.
> And they get a load of woods.
>
> Our fathers
> —fathers, grandfathers, my grandfather—
> they told-me-bout this story
> before they passed away.[9]

The book in which this passage was published uses a more conventional layout of sentences, but presents the above 'verbatim' version and a standard English transliteration of it in adjacent columns. Rather than distracting attention from it, this strategy can encourage readers to examine the original for better understanding of how it conveys verbal meaning.

Unfortunately, Moore goes on from her analysis to advocate development of better systems of notation to reduce interpretations by transcribers. In a commentary on her paper, Michael Frisch concurs with Moore's wish 'to bring as much orality as possible into our transcribing and editing'. But he characterizes her call for new notation systems as a descent on a 'slippery slope'.[10] In the end, those wishing to move over the border into disciplines involving such elements as conversational analysis would be wise to go back to the sound record. It is simply unrealistic to believe it is possible to capture much of the important information conveyed in speech mannerisms that is missing in conventional print transcript, which York so rightly laments; although, among aspects identified, he includes the 'individual's personality, social class, regional and ethnic origins', and good questions can do much to balance such losses.

Nevertheless, even though I am an advocate of (properly skilled) transcription, I can also sympathize with Moore's frustration at the paucity of transcripts in conveying so much of the humanity of the spoken word. Ironically, people who are dedicated to spending a lot of time wrestling speech into printed text are probably the most keenly aware of the distance between the two. With print only, one cannot adequately capture the music of speech, what York calls its 'special charm'. The voice contains so much subliminal information that we can usually recognize a familiar one instantly from hearing only a few words, as easily as we can identify a face at a glance. But if we are to look to the discipline of linguistics for assistance, we should heed David Crystal's advice that 'no-one has yet described all the nuances of meaning which can be conveyed by the intonation system' of language use.[11] Some of the difficulty can be easily demonstrated by looking at a table he provides of symbols used in notations, which charts how the pitch of the voice moves in nine different ways of saying 'Yes', a table by no means completely definitive – visual information such as facial expression would often be required too. Anyone doubting the degree of variation that can occur in punctuating printed text of the spoken word should attempt a sobering exercise furnished by Crystal,[12] in which readers are invited to consider some unpunctuated text, then compare their punctuation decisions to his, which are bound to differ.

In the end, we must learn to live with the fact that transcription of the spoken word is more of an art than an exact science; techniques attempting to convey its orality in print vary widely. There is a world of difference between the grammar rules we follow in spoken and written language, and trying to fashion the former into the latter will always be an individually subjective reflection of the transcriber's thought processes. The best we can do is to carefully consider the options, which may be suitable for any given set of objectives, and then follow this up with a systematic and consistent editing style.

At this point, one is tempted to buy into the argument that, given the variance and problems, why transcribe at all? There are genuine concerns, which require answers. Enthusiastic 'no transcription' advocates often point out that there is much value in the alternative approach of compiling a tape log, which provides guidance on content to users of the record, rather than literal representation. This gives users no option but to use the audio record. Any oral historians with a feeling for orality and experience of the way researchers will rarely access a sound recording where a transcript is available must sympathize with this view. In any collection of oral records, such logs can be a valuable research tool, as they are amenable to text search and retrieval software. Such a system, using ISYS[13] software, has enabled researchers at the Northern Territory Archives Service for some years now regularly to plunder about 1,000 summaries with content listings, comprising approximately 530,000 words; and the application can also be developed for web use by the world at large. Where appropriately compiled, such text can capture concepts as well as proper names. Made available in this way it doubles as a kind of page-referenced index without the effort of compiling one separately.

On the other hand, it is well to remember that there is still a strong element of mediation in such material, involving, as it must, many subjective and evaluative post-interview decisions about what elements to include. There is also considerable disquiet that the absence of a transcript cleared by the interviewee puts the onus on users to ensure a professional and ethical approach to quotations they idiosyncratically transcribe for themselves. Many collecting agencies believe they have a responsibility to clear interpretations of language use with narrators. These are not pedantic issues when you consider how long the material (we hope) will be around as language and convention change over time, or when compared with the lack of respect for source veracity found in sensational journalism (to take just one example).

Not all information change that happens in transcripts is linguistic, of course: information content about events, people and places, dates, and so on can also come in for the editor's attention. Here the conceptual territory can swing between two extremes. In contrast to a complete 'hands off', inclusive and non-interventionist approach, particularly for the purely archival document, some approaches, such as that of Baum mentioned above, ensure that the presenter's notion of complete and accurate historical data dominates the final form of text representation of an interview. This may vary from seemingly common-sense corrections of the odd date or name, to whole sections amplifying, clarifying and sometimes replacing what was originally said.

Often, this happens (in varying degrees) as a result of the process of clearing transcripts with informants. Proponents argue that it is a commonly accepted notion in the world of oral history, in contrast to journalism, that ethical behaviour demands this step. Clearance with interviewees has a long and honourable history, which was recently sketched on the email discussion list H-Oralhist (affiliated with the USA-based Oral History Association). At Columbia University it started with the notion that narrators had a right to see what was going into print. Ron Grele[14] reports that they still see this step as a way of respecting the rights of interviewees to review and agree to sentence structure that will represent them over archival time, and freezing the transcript against subjective and variable approaches to quotation by users.

If it matters that we are going beyond the primary source by changing the transcript in this way, there are adequate ways of indicating to the reader that material has been added or changed (such as use of square brackets for additions, for example). Indeed, these changes make the transcript, in part, a second primary source, and if the information is what respondents want to put on the record, then it is just as important as their first thoughts. We must consider their right to do so if they wish.

The accumulation of additions to transcript by informants, such as the following, justify the process of transcription and clearance even if they only happened occasionally, whereas in practice they are not uncommon. Often very useful nuggets of information for researchers crop up:

> [In 1969, in consultation with Dr Alan Walker (Paediatrician, Darwin Hospital) I prepared a set of notes for duplication to assist rural health staff in the assessment and management of frequently encountered health problems of Aboriginal children – such as anaemia, failure to thrive, chronic suppurative otitis media, hookworm control etc. It was a guide to facilitate and standardise assessment of severity, local management and guidelines for referral for more specialised care. My mind went back to those brief notes when I saw the comprehensive manual now available to the N.T. rural health workers as a reference text.][15]

Over time, the stream of corrections of mistakes, completion of sentences, clarifications and expansions, etc., contributed by post-recording interviewees has augmented the research value of the Northern Territory Archives' collection quite significantly.

It is also worth mentioning that, in some work, sensitive material that respondents want to place on restricted or time-embargoed access can often be identified in the process of gaining initial clearance of a transcript. In my own experience, merely the knowledge that interviewees will have the opportunity to restrict access selectively has resulted in interviews that might not have happened otherwise; or after consideration of the transcript it can turn out that narrators feel comfortable without placing the restrictions on elements they were concerned about originally. (With computer-based word-processing one can easily offer to arrange for sections to be placed under restrictions without holding up the entire record.)

By the way, processors anxious about the inordinate time it can take some respondents to send back a transcript – a very real problem, often lamented – should note Dale E. Treleven's message[16] that UCLA gets a signed form at the outset which allows that if it has not been returned in 30 days it can be assumed to be correct! It could be argued that this is a different take on interviewees' rights, although I find it perfectly reasonable.

Even more divergence from the oral source can arise in the re-presentation and compilation of text for documentary and historical analysis. Much material in the wider published domain is highly compiled, where we can expect only portions of the original material that fit prevailing editorial priorities. Maximum permissible word count is a very real consideration; sections can be rearranged, language can be massaged to add effect – the list could go on. This is a process that David Neufeld describes as 'the transition from raw material to finished historical narrative,' and 'the professional mediation of sources that professional historians are supposed to do'.[17]

The substantial differences possible in fashioning published 'oral' text are quite clear when comparing the end results in publications which provide good explanations of methodology in prefaces. To demonstrate this in workshops, I use contrasting examples, including the following two from the Australian Aboriginal context.[18] In *The Lost Children*, personal accounts in some sixty hours of tape recordings were presented:

> As editors, we made as few changes as possible to the text, preserving the original manner of speaking. Some of the transcriptions had to be shortened, and the use of individuals' names in contexts likely to cause offence had also to be omitted. Then the texts were returned to the speakers for their own correction. Some chose to leave the edited version as it was; others preferred to substitute their original speaking style for a written style. This decision was left entirely up to the contributors.[19]

For his book *Dreamtime Nightmares*, Bill Rosser's recorded stories often read as though crafted from imagination into a smooth-flowing written narrative:

> 'What do you remember about your childhood? Did you go to school?' 'Hey?' He looked at me in disbelief. I repeated the question. 'No,' he answered laconically, 'no school'. He began to laugh at what was, to him, an absurd question. 'Nah,' he continued after a while, 'In those days no Aboriginal kid went to school.'[20]

Rosser kept notes about what was happening while he recorded,[21] and the published stories often include details such as a pause to light a smoke and gaze reflectively out of a window while remembering long-past times. As a reader, one feels the ebb and flow of feelings and ideas, and the interpersonal flavour of the occasion, aspects which are often unapparent in purely verbatim, unadorned transcription. But practically all the book's content is directly quoted speech, and for nearly all of it the words are presented strictly as they were recorded:

> As a historian, I have transcribed those experiences verbatim. Nothing is added, nothing is suppressed, but for the sake of clarity, it has been necessary to rearrange some of the material either chronologically or with regard to subject matter.[22]

Perhaps works such as these explain methods more often because of the more apparent difference between the oral English usage and 'standard' modes, especially where English is not the speaker's first language. Newcomers to oral history practice need to appreciate from the outset the differences between the archival record and the material that they are most familiar with in published sources – the public face of the enterprise that is actually only a subset of the world of oral history. Such factors are still significant, yet less often apparent, where the original oral was closer to 'standard' language use expected in published text.

A particularly detailed and eloquent example of the complex decision-making process followed by one editor reworking orally-based text for publication is afforded by Michael Frisch.[23] In no way claiming his approach is exemplary, he provides detailed insight on how he approached the problems in terms of his particular aims. He emphasizes that there is significant difference between the primary level of the sound recording, which goes through one level of interpretation in 'verbatim' transcription, and further refinement in reworked material of historical documentary. Understanding how far this process goes for any of the various stages in re-presentation of oral records is fundamental for our appreciation of its layers of meaning. The problem is that we need to know, and may not, just how much mediation has gone on. I wonder at the level of undetectable massaging that has gone into published oral history in text form over the years.

I would be more comfortable with some of the debate about aspects of transcript if arguments were based on more careful distinctions between kinds of text and was related to different purposes for different levels of distance from the original. Frisch makes the point that where compilation is the business of dealing with documents *from* the past, 'interview materials are unique in themselves being documents *about* the past'.[24] In both published, reworked material and what often passes for 'verbatim' archival records the level of information that is given to readers about the mediation process is probably the most wanting area in production of orally-based text. There is a real concern and a sad pretence if the secondary element of text is misrepresented by default as the mirror of the original speech.

We are all familiar with the notion that the oral history enterprise is more than just production output from discrete inputs, and that it actually arises out of a complex interactive social process. But even at the more tertiary level of seeking to make material more accessible for wider audiences there can be layers of mediation. In Australia we find complex considerations where transcriber/editors are preparing book material from the spoken word in community projects with Aboriginal people who use different forms of English. Loreen Brehaut[25] provides insights on some of the really difficult process issues needed to rationalize cross-cultural preconceptions, with which I can sympathize from my own experience. What editors may have thought were enhancements can baffle the original informant. Heather Goodall, working with communities in north-western New South Wales, in the process of making material from oral contexts more accessible through compilation for presentation in CD formats, comments on the contrasts between conversational and speaking styles which reflect both the internal 'within community' modes, and 'public modes' of speaking which arise where indigenous people publicly intervene in political processes. She contends with an uneasy dialectic between 'people's history and public history' in a 'continuing situation of tense political conflict'.[26]

Clearly, we should consider Alistair Thomson's point that we are talking about more than just a research methodology, and must think about matters of advocacy and empowerment.[27] Marlene R. Atleo points out that 'we need to be more respectful of "lived lives". We need to be able to see through their integrity and appreciate them in their fallibilities whether old age or infirmity because they are [their] stories'.[28] Such considerations in the context of 'veracity' issues in transcription lead to contrasting positions. For Sally Wilde, so much expressive language that many want to tidy out of text is what she believes makes 'the informant come alive in print'.[29] But Warren Nishimoto of the University of Hawaii advocates encouraging interviewees to make any changes they need, not just for the sake of accuracy or readability but even 'to make them feel good about their transcript so that they would release it for public use'.[30] In her 1992 study, Ronda Jamieson reported that Nishimoto 'considered transcripts the primary source and not tapes', because they could be better reviewed by informants.[31] (Importantly, though, they discourage minor grammatical changes.) This is in stark contrast to the response she reported from Donald Hyslop of the Southampton City Museums, who 'considered the tape to be the primary source and felt that transcripts pandered to academic researchers who could not be bothered to listen'.[32]

My view is that editorial intervention, at any level, only becomes problematic when the reader is not given information that explains the process and the source of changes. As a user, I would want to be able to judge for myself if the intervention goes too far for my purposes. We all draw our own line in different places in the sand: there can be legitimate concern about factual accuracy and completeness of the record, but care is needed not to fall into linguistic imperialism or historical policing. It is a process that attracts highly loaded and subjective descriptions like 'appropriate' and 'sensitive', which do little to invalidate disquiet about the level of intervention and loss of other kinds of meaning from the oral original.

Clearly the issue is more critical the greater the level and kind of intervention. I acknowledge the right of presenters to make their own way through the ethical landscape, but users have a right to as much information as may be feasible in order to be able to appreciate, even if they may not fully understand, what the process entailed. And this holds not just for published material, whether intensely or only marginally editorialized, but also for material that is purely archival in purpose, since the methods here can vary widely from mere 'tidying' to substantial 'expert' mediation. Reference numbers, date and place of interview, who recorded it and so on, are common elements of data provided. But what was the context of the recording? What kind of process did the transcript go through? Is it a first draft, who checked it and what did they do to it? Is there enough information for readers with an interest in language aspects to detect how far they can rely on what they see? What is the system, if any, employed to indicate outright changes in the text from what is heard on tape? Can users identify what was added by compilers?

In the end, all readers of transcription, indeed users of any kind of record of human action, need to comprehend the extent to which we are consuming a constructed artefact. As we seek to understand the human experience through the records of other lives, we should constantly remind ourselves that it is necessary to interpret and contextualize a bit more actively than we usually want to, and this is so with all forms of record, not just mass news media. In the oral history context, the original sound recording is also secondary to real-life experience, so there is an obligation to provide users with information on how this too was fashioned. All the processes involved in how the medium has massaged the message need to be better understood. Given the array of strategies available, and the values they reflect in the elements of transcript, editors should be pinning their colours to the page.

Although new technologies such as interactive digital media bring the symbiosis between audio and text into a new ball-park, there is still a long time ahead in which vast amounts of transcription will take place, and will be the principal source for users of oral records. Rather than making it harder for editorial change of text to mask the precious original voice, it is now very easy to edit audio for similar purposes, and we are all aware that the same pressures to do so will apply – as they have always done for print. My plea for proper information on provenance and process simply becomes more critical.

Digital media have the potential to enhance user access to audio. Digital sound comes with time codes, whether recorded on mini-disk or DAT, yet another level of information we should provide to users of transcripts. While some digital media are not particularly good for public usage in repositories, time-coded CD copies are very user-friendly, and can also be made of analog tapes that have no time codes. Transcription is now also possible using digital copies of recordings. Software from the court reporting environment allows simultaneous operation of computer word-processing and playing of 'clean' digital sound off hard disk, using a foot-pedal that controls playback and backspacing the way cassette systems are supposed to but often do not do very well or consistently. But until they can plug the sound directly into our brains it will remain easier and far quicker to read large volumes of text than to listen to audio, and the use of transcript is likely to burgeon with techno-logical advancements rather than diminish. For those concerned with the confusion of authority and conflict of rights and responsibilities that become critical in reliance on transcript, the use of CDs, relatively cheap for even small repositories and getting cheaper, allied with the time-code and index marker point information placed in transcripts, can encourage time-strapped researchers away from intense dependence on text only.

On another technological note, I believe optimistic assessments of how soon a computer will be able to transcribe the human noises we call communication, by means of 'speech recognition' software, have yet to appreciate the real difficulties in any way that is practical for the task of coming to grips with large volumes of casual speech from many different individuals, which is the reality of the world of oral history. I do not see it as a technical problem of data processing: we are not entirely sure of what exactly is being processed, and human practice shows that results are highly dependent on subjective variables.

The variance in transcription strategies, and their relationship to meaning, underscores the degree of skill required. Projects do well to bear this in mind when making rational decisions about whether to transcribe or not. There should be recognition, not least in setting remuneration levels, of the kind of skills needed. Keyboard operators should have appropriate experience. Copy-typists might transcribe well, but it takes a maturity of ideas about language and some insight on the divergence between spoken and written approaches to grammar. Another processing issue is that no matter how good initial drafting might be, subsequent checking to the tape is always necessary. Within projects, while options will be selected that suit project objectives and values, and the perceived roles and rights of stakeholders, it is just as essential in archival transcript work that consistent overall editorial control is applied as it is in publication work in general.

Making the process more transparent for users will benefit the discipline in general, as we can all learn from others. It is fascinating to observe that among the many programs reviewed by Jamieson,[33] while many had internally consistent editorial approaches, in-house sets of rules and rationalized procedures, there was considerable variance in editing policy, kinds of clearance, and so on. To my mind this emphasizes the need for policy and provenance statements. I concur with Frisch:

> I do believe that becoming more self-conscious about the issues implicit
> in editing can help each practitioner engage and resolve these challenges
> in ways that are appropriate to his or her own interests and needs.[34]

Notes

1   K. Moore, 'Perversion of the word: the role of transcripts in oral history', in *Words and Silences, Bulletin of the International Oral History Association*, 1997, vol. 1, no. 1, p. 14.

2   W. Baum, *Transcribing and Editing Oral History*, Nashville, Tenn.: American Association for State and Local History, 1977.

3   Ibid., p. 40.

4   Ibid., p. 39.

5   R. Jamieson, *Some Aspects of Oral History in New Zealand the United States of America and the United Kingdom. Report for the Winston Churchill Memorial Trust of Australia*, Perth: Oral History Association of Australia (WA), 1992, p. 18.

6   Ibid., p. 75.

7   B. York, 'Between poetry and prose. Oral history as a new kind of literature', in *National Library of Australia News*, August 1999, vol. IX, no. 11, p. 12.

8   L. Brehaut, 'A terrible responsibility: Editing the spoken word for print', in M. Hamilton (ed.), *Tales of the Century: Oral History Association of Australia (OHAA) Journal*, 1999, no. 21, p. 30.

9   Tommy Thompson Kngwarreye, interviewed by Francis Good in 'Cutting limestone', in G. Koch (ed.), *Kaytetye Country. An Aboriginal History of the Barrow Creek Area*, Alice Springs: Institute for Aboriginal Development, 1993, p. 51.

10   M. Frisch, 'Of slippery slopes and misplaced hopes: a comment on Kate Moore, "Perversion of the word: the role of transcripts in oral history"', *Words and Silences, Bulletin of the International Oral History Association*, June 1997, vol. 1, no. 1, p. 26.

11   D. Crystal, *The Cambridge Encyclopedia of the English Language*, Cambridge: Cambridge University Press, 1995, p. 248.

12   Ibid., p. 214.

13   ISYS software from Odyssey Development Pty Ltd, Crows Nest, New South Wales, see www.isys-search.com.au.

14   R. Grele, 'Re: Editing by interviewee', 7 April 1998, in H-NET/OHA Discussion List on Oral History, h-oralhist@h-net.msu.edu, archived at www2.msu.edu/logs.

15   Dr John Tibbs, interviewed by Francis Good, June 1996, Northern Territory Archives Service, NTRS 226, TS 911.

16   Dale E. Treleven, 2 March 1999, 'Transcript return', in H-NET/OHA (see note 14 for web address).

17   David Neufeld, 'Re: Critique requested on oral history methodology – transcribing and editing', 2 February 1998, in H-NET/OHA (see note 14).

18   And for another contrast, see B. Shaw (ed.), *The Life Histories of Four Aboriginal Men: Countrymen*, Canberra: Australian Institute of Aboriginal Studies, 1986, p. 2.

19   C. Edwards, 'The text', in C. Edwards and P. Read (eds), *The Lost Children: Thirteen Australians Taken from their Aboriginal Families Tell of the Struggle to Find their Natural Parents*, Sydney: Doubleday, 1992, p. xxv.

20   Bruce Bismark, quoted in B. Rosser, *Dreamtime Nightmares*, Canberra, Australian Institute of Aboriginal Studies, 1985; also Penguin, 1987, p. 93.

21   B. Rosser, *Dreamtime Nightmares*.

22   Ibid, p. xv.

23   M. Frisch, 'Preparing interview transcripts for documentary publication: a line-by-line illustration of the editing process', in *A Shared Authority. Essays on the Craft and Meaning of Oral and Public History*, Buffalo: State University of New York Press, 1990, p. 81.

24   Ibid., p. 83.
25   Brehaut, 'A terrible responsibility', p. 27.
26   H. Goodall, 'Re: Editing by interviewee', 8 April 1998, and 'Re: public/people's history', 13 April 1998, in H-NET/OHA (see note 14).
27   A. Thomson, 'Fifty years on: an international perspective on oral history', in M. Hamilton (ed.), *Tales of the Century: Oral History Association of Australia (OHAA) Journal*, 1999, no. 21, p. 86.
28   M.R. Atleo, 'Re: Critique requested on oral history methodology – transcribing and editing', 3 February 1998, in H-NET/OHA (see note 14).
29   S. Wilde, 'Oral history methodology', 4 February 1998, in H-NET/OHA (see note 14).
30   W.S. Nishimoto, 'Re: Editing transcripts', 17 February 1999, in H-NET/OHA (see note 14).
31   Jamieson, *Some Aspects of Oral History*, p. 9.
32   Ibid., p. 73.
33   Ibid.
34   Frisch, 'Preparing interview transcripts for documentary publication', p. 82.

Chapter 28

Jane Mace

REMINISCENCE AS LITERACY
Intersections and creative moments

This chapter examines the collaborative, and sometimes contested, process of selecting and shaping oral testimony for publication, drawing on experience working with reminiscence and adult literacy groups in London. Jane Mace is an author, trainer and consultant in adult literacy education. Extracted from Jane Mace (ed.), *Literacy, Language and Community Publishing*: *Essays in Adult Education*, Clevedon, Avon: Multilingual Matters, 1995, pp. 97–117, by permission of the author (www.janemace.co.uk) and the publisher.

A REMINISCENCE GROUP is a group, usually of older, or elderly people who have come together in order to share recollections of their past experience. [. . .] In my experience of setting up and convening six reminiscence groups since 1980, the people who agree to join them do so because they see an opportunity to reflect aloud, with others, on their life experience. They do not, in the first instance, see their role as writers, nor, for that matter, as listeners: but as tellers; and when I and others invite them to take part, we are inviting them to see themselves primarily as oral historians. The work of facilitating such groups means, certainly, encouraging participants to be attentive listeners, as well as narrators; but, in addition, we also invite them to see themselves as potential or actual writers. [. . .]

Reminiscence work, approached as a process which is about literate as well as oral narrative, entails a series of moves between talking, listening, writing and reading. Ever since, as a literacy educator, I first began doing reminiscence work, I have become increasingly fascinated with the meaning of these moves. Neither writing nor speech are as much about *communication* as they are about *creation*: we use language, whether spoken or written, not merely to transmit something ready-made from our experience or thinking, but in order to *create* new meaning and new worlds.

The work of reminiscence, taking this view, is primarily a creative activity. I am interested in how oral accounts may become written texts, through a process in which participants have time to reflect on and develop the first version of a story – and, if they choose to do so, to be able to edit, amend and elaborate on it as a piece of writing. The published version of this process is, by definition, selective (just as any of the earlier interviews, group discussion or written drafts were). For those who make the choice to have their texts appear in print, the process entails, first, reading back a transcribed version of their talk on the page and then deciding how far that written version accords with the version of themselves that they feel willing for others (unknown) to read – rather than for a group or individual (known) to hear.

In this chapter, I want to analyse some of these issues as they occur during the course of a specific approach to reminiscence work with elderly people which I call 'lines and intersections', in order to explore in what ways a move to *writing* changes what was originally an *oral* reflection on experience. [. . .]

Over the period of a reminiscence project's life, I see a series of intersections between what seem to be lines of speech and text, creating and re-creating. At the point where these lines intersect there is a new kind of creative moment. One line, for instance, is that of an individual speaking while others are listening. Another is a group following a text while one person reads it aloud. When such reading causes one of the group to look up and offer their own comment or begin a narrative of their own, I see an intersection, exactly the kind of moment that this kind of reminiscence work is intended to encourage, with the aim of enabling a mutual enrichment between the oral and the written work.

Other examples of what I mean by such intersections are:

*   when one person's account of an event (re-read as transcript) is echoed and re-told by another;
*   when one member's text is brought in for others to read, following it on a copy as they listen to it being read aloud; and this reading causes another to look up and add her own anecdote or reflection to that of the author.

Two other intersections which interest me are the delayed effects of oral work in a group or an interview, as when

*   recollections expressed in speech (in interview or group) stimulate either speaker or listener later to seek out documentary sources (diaries, old reports, letters) to bring back for sharing in a later discussion; and
*   when the recollection of the voices and thoughts prompted by talking with others leads an individual, later and alone, to contemplate writing as they have not done before.

[. . .] All the intersections I have described depend on a central interconnection: that between the individual interview and the group meeting. Individuals agree to be interviewed; some, but not all of them, subsequently agree to join a group which meets several times; during the group meetings, individuals are given the attention of the whole group. At each stage, the job of the adult educator coordinating the project is to set up these lines and encourage these intersections.

From our observations of our own practice and that of others, Jane Lawrence and I suggested[1] that reminiscence work in an adult education setting tends to follow a series of phases over a period of eighteen months to two years, from outreach and interviewing to an open meeting, after which a group forms and meets regularly, to exchange recollections and prepare some of these recollections to share with others in the form of a display, publication, or performance. This pattern was true for my own work with three such projects: the 'S.E.1 People's History Group' (1979–90), the 'Now and Then Group' (1981–84) and the 'Cottage Homes Making History Project' (1992–93). [. . .]

Publications from reminiscence work, as I have already said, can only provide a very selective account of the authors' recollections. But their function is not only to provide a slice of social history: in an important sense, the publication from reminiscence activity is the creation of and a souvenir from the reminiscence work itself. Reminiscence work, if it is to convey something of its making, needs to include something in its published work from the interchange which preceded the individual narratives. This both makes the creative moments more visible to other readers, and brings them back to mind to those who were originally part of the group itself. It was for this reason, in one published autobiography, *A Sense of Adventure* by Dolly Davey, that I proposed interleaving Dolly's first-person narrative with extracts from group discussion between Dolly and other group members.

There was a sequence of events (and creative moments) by which Dolly's text evolved between June and December 1979:

1   First, Dolly came to a meeting of the group as companion to an older neighbour, and talked (on tape) to three people.
2   I sent Dolly the transcript, went to see her at her home, and we talked again, on tape.
3   I transcribed this, too, and sent it to Dolly.
4   She read the transcript and wrote some additional pieces.
5   I copied parts of the transcripts and Dolly's writing, and other members of the S.E.1 group read these.
6   At further meetings of the group, Dolly talked some more and her husband, Fred, joined the discussions. Again, I transcribed the tape and returned the transcripts for participants to read.
7   Finally, Dolly and I separately read the whole, I wrote an introduction, and she and I agreed the completed text.

The book which resulted consists largely of Dolly's narrative. In brief, this relates how she left her home in Yorkshire in 1930 to come to London. After four years working as a domestic and lady's maid, she met and married Fred. This is an extract from the text as it appeared in the finished book, when she relates a historic day soon after that:

> It was 18 months after we got married that he was invited to come up to my home, and he did. He rode from London to Yorkshire, on a push-bike. I left on Sunday morning at 10 o'clock on the twelve-and-sixpenny excursion, and he left on the Friday and arrived at my home the same time as I did – just in time for dinner! It was really an achievement, because he had never been up there before, and he didn't know the

route. It was one great north road then. There wasn't an Ml or anything like that.[2]

On the same page, immediately after this, we included the following extract from the discussion in which Fred, with Dolly, recalled this event for three others of us (Jenny, Gladys and me) in one of the S.E.1 People's History group meetings:

Fred: Her mother said that if we could get there, she might be able to get me a job. We had Eva then, our eldest. The labour money was twenty-eight shillings a week, and the train fare to Stockton was twelve and six. I said, 'We can't afford that. You can go on the train, I'll borrow a bike, and we'll save twelve and sixpence'. Twelve and sixpence was terrific, what you could get for it; and I didn't think no more of it. Borrowed a bike off a boy across the road called Freddie Kippick.

Dolly: You left on the Friday night, I left on the Sunday morning, and we practically met at the door.

Fred: I was about five minutes after.

Jane: Do you remember the journey?

Fred.   Yes.

Jane: Was it raining?

Fred: No.

Jenny: You were lucky.

Fred.   When would it be, in August? Must have been, because I remember picking Victoria plums by the roadside. The first night I slept somewhere in St Albans, I think it was; and the next night I spent in Doncaster racecourse. Just went off the road, like, and you were on the course. Just put a ground-sheet down, and a blanket. I bought fish and chips for threepence, and a bottle of Tizer. And I started off with half a crown.

Dolly: I got there at lunchtime, and my mother was just dishing the lunch up, 4 o'clock.

Fred: I had a terrific ride.

Gladys: All that way on a bike?

Fred: Yes, Dick Turpin had nothing on me, love, by the time I got there.

The combination of Dolly's account with this interchange between her, Fred and their listeners conveys a different sense of the reminiscence process (the intersections and creative moments) than would have been possible with the first-person narrative of Dolly alone. It was that mix of telling and retelling, which was the work of her autobiography [. . .]

Part of my original question remains to be answered? What is the difference (and dilemmas) between oral and written narratives? Who makes the changes to oral transcripts, in order to transform them into written texts? What kind of changes are seen to be necessary? The editorial work is sometimes shadowy; a combination of reminiscence worker/educator and interviewee/author. Both need to see the transcript – or at least that amount of the tape which the transcriber has managed to translate to paper. A next move made by many reminiscence workers (including me) is to offer a draft of what the text might look like if some of the repetitions and (usually all) the interviewer's questions are removed. The interviewee/author then offers their own editorial changes. Some (but in my experience, a minority) reading the transcript of their speech on paper, engage in writing new material, to be added to it; fewer still choose to rewrite the whole thing. (Of the sixteen authors in this position in the Cottage Homes Making History Project, for instance, two women sat down at long-unused typewriters and rewrote much of their texts; a third wrote an additional three pages about earlier work experiences which she felt were crucial to add to the narrative; the rest expressed satisfaction with the text as it stood, apart from minor amendments.)

The exercise of editorial control, however, while it entails apparently small decisions of detail, can make significant alterations to an author's meaning and purpose, in any publishing enterprise, and in community publishing it is often the most shadowy stage of the process. It is, therefore, this minority of participants who choose to rewrite their draft texts which interests me; and in this last section we shall look at a set of moves made by one woman and me from our original interview to the transcript of the interview tape, and the 'public' written text of her narrative. I am giving her the pseudonym 'Nora' because, although her final published text, as a stencilled booklet, was public and therefore quotable, I have not had her permission to quote, as I will be here, from the transcript of her interview with me.

Nora was the third of the seventeen people I visited in their homes in Lambeth between January and March 1979. Her completed text was one of four that I typed, duplicated and printed, and of which we circulated and sold a total of 120 copies (including twenty sets lodged with Lambeth libraries). What follows is an account of what she first told me, how I then edited it and how she, in turn, added to it and altered it before it became published. The very first words recorded on the tape of her interview with me were these:

> We used to live up in the top flat till 1940. Then we moved down here.
> I've sort of grown up here. What was I? Thirteen, when I came here.

In the next forty minutes of our interview, Nora went on to tell me of the other places where she lived, and how she had gone on to work for over forty years as an office worker with the General Nursing Council. She then introduced almost immediately what was to be one of the two main stories in our conversation: the night of the Zeppelin raid (in 1915). There followed, in the interview and transcript, some regret for the changes in the local neighbourhood and shops; some more reference to the Zeppelin raid, and then the account of an incident (her second story) which took place nearly twenty-five years later in the Second World War, when she and her brother were caught in an air raid. She talked then of an unexploded bomb which landed in her street, how everyone had had to be evacuated, and how she had defied the air raid warden and had walked down the street when she came home to get groceries. Finally, we talked about the 1951 Festival of Britain, a reiteration of Nora's feeling of regret at the loss of neighbourliness and shops, and a brief summary of her childhood years.

The first moments of Nora's life, then, actually only came up in the last moments of our interview; and in the transcript, this narrative of her childhood appears on the last page. What she said is in Quote A:

> *Quote A*
> Going back to my childhood, we lived at Clapham, and of course there was five of us in the family. My father died a fortnight before I was born. And my mother had the boarding house then, so kept us all. Well, there was a gap – there was the two girls and a boy, then a baby boy died, so there was a gap. And my younger brother and I were the two kids then. And of course the others being older, they had all their friends in and out. And we had quite a happy, oh, I had a happy home. We were never short of anything: I'm not going to say there weren't things we would have liked, but you couldn't get, you saved up for them because my mother wouldn't have anything on hire purchase.

I sent Nora a copy of the transcript of our dialogue, and went to meet her a week later. She had read it, and wanted to add several things for precision. She also made other comments, as we talked, which I noted down. I undertook to do my own editing on the transcript, ensuring that these additions and comments were included, and later sent her the edited version to read. In my editing, I did two things which until recently I found myself doing consistently in reminiscence work since:

(a) deleted my questions to her; and
(b) changed the sequence of her recollections into a chronology of life history.

When we met again a few weeks later, she had been busy. She had got out her old typewriter, obtained a new ribbon, and had re-typed her own version of the text.

Nora and I, then, both made changes to her original talk with me to a written text for others. Through my editing, the last thing Nora had told me in the interview had become the first paragraph I put in her edited text (namely her summary of early family life, quote A). This replaced what had actually been the first thing she had told me about in the interview – a reference to the flat in which we were both sitting ('What was I? Thirteen, when I came here'). The text, I reasoned then, would be read by others not sitting as I was with her, and would need a different introduction to the author and what she had to say. Now, fifteen years after that interview, I am not so sure. As I suggested at the beginning of this chapter, reminiscence is always a present activity; and autobiographical writing, no less so. Why not begin the narrative with the author's present context?

Nora, in any case, accepted this re-ordering: but chose to amend the wording. I now want to compare what she wrote (and we published) with the paragraph transcribed from her original words. What she wrote is Quote B:

> *Quote B*
> **I was born in June 1902. My father had died in May** *leaving my mother with five children – the four older still at school.* Mother then took in boarders in order **to keep the home going and us all together. We were always encouraged to bring our friends home,**

and therefore had a happy home life. We were never short of **essential** things: I cannot say there were not other things we would have liked, but you had to save up for them, because my mother would not have anything on hire purchase. *She was a wonderful mother, and taught us the value of things.*

The key changes Nora made amounted to:

• the *rewording* of four statements (bold type);
• the *addition* of two pieces of information (italic type);
• and the *deletion* of her original version of the number of brothers and sisters in the family: 'there was a gap – there was the two girls and a boy, then a baby boy died, so there was a gap. And my younger brother and I were the two kids then. And of course the others being older, they had . . .'

Nora was working to produce a text for a public readership; she was consciously thinking about the effect of the writing on others. So, for example, to give historical information for the reader, she added the date of her birth. The *change* in this first sentence, however; also had the effect of changing the relationship between her birth and her father's death – which, in the earlier version, was very direct ('a fortnight before I was born'). The *omission* of detail about her as a child, in relation to her brothers and sisters, removes another personal dimension – resonant, perhaps, with old emotions which Nora would rather keep private. She then altered the identity of the children who brought friends home from 'they' to 'we'. This alteration, the change to a passive voice, and the formal connective 'therefore', effectively hid her child self still further from the reader. The change is from 'they had all their friends in and out' to: 'we were always encouraged to bring our friends home'.

Did Nora feel she had portrayed herself as too vulnerable, excluded from her mother's greater freedom with the older children, or from their games? Had she decided she wanted to convey a longer time span than her very early years, to a time when perhaps she too *was* encouraged to have 'all her friends in and out'? Or did she simply want to write what she felt was a more elegant and formal sentence, with less interruption? Perhaps she wanted all three. I do not know: for, at the time, these were not the questions I was asking her.

Tags like 'Of course' and 'as I say', are common features of oral discourse, designed to include the listener in the speaker's knowledge and carry her along in the story's flow; as in: 'And *of course* the others being older, they had all their friends in and out'. In a written text when reader and writer are at a greater distance from each other than speaker and listener, it makes sense to leave it out, as Nora decided to do. But what of the change from 'and we had quite a happy, oh, I had a happy home' to 'and therefore [we] had a happy home life'? Is that hesitant 'oh' in her original voice a sigh of pleasure at recalled happiness? Is it a hesitation, as she remembers sorrow or other feelings which were also there? Or is it an adult's sympathy for her seven-month pregnant mother, suddenly widowed with five children, she herself not yet born? (The intonation of her voice on the tape, which I have listened to again recently, could be interpreted in any of these ways.) In any case, in removing the 'we had quite a happy, oh, I had a happy home' Nora also erased past and present emotion, favouring instead a more impersonal and unequivocal assertion for her reading public: an authorised version that she preferred to her original, more ambiguous one.

Nora's final change, from 'any' to 'essential' ('we were never short of anything/essential things') I see as a change to precision. It was a happy home life with everything 'essential' provided for them; but as children, they were short of things they wanted. This time the text gives a glimpse of something that was less vivid in the original interview: the recalled longing of a child for 'inessentials'.

Some of the changes which Nora made to other parts of my edit of her transcript meant, as some of these did, the removal of her own presence in the text. They also took away some of the rhythm and buoyancy which had been in her original spoken version. Here, for example, is what she told me, first, about a cafe breakfast which she and others had enjoyed the morning after they had been turned out of their flats following the fall of an unexploded bomb, when the 'all clear' sirens had sounded. Her original words had been:

> We all went in there, and had breakfast, of bacon and egg, and rolls.
> I've never tasted bacon so good since. It was marvellous!

In her re-typed version, Nora changed this to:

> We went into the cafe and had breakfast: tea, bacon and egg, and bread
> and butter. It was a really grand meal and much appreciated by us all.

Her personal pleasure, voiced with enthusiasm, is gone: instead, Nora has chosen the more banal voice of a formal thank-you letter.

While there were losses, however, there was also gains in the transpositions and additions which Nora made to her transcript. In re-reading it, she had seen things she wanted to add, to explain things more fully to a readership she was now holding in her imagination. An important example, from the paragraph she wrote out, is the sentence she added as a tribute to her mother: 'She was a wonderful mother, and taught us the value of things'.

Nora and I both worked on her text: each in a different way, but both taking an active part in its shape, style and tone. Over the years since then, I have changed both my own editorial habits. Sometimes, as with Dolly's book, I have left in some of my own questions in preparing texts for publication; and sometimes I have suggested that texts begin in the middle rather than in the supposed beginning of a life. The important idea that I still work with is that the final text should be one that satisfies the authors, whether I have regrets about some of their choices or not. [. . .]

Notes

1   J. Lawrence and J. Mace, *Remembering in Groups: Ideas from Literacy and Reminiscence Work*, London: Oral History Society, 1992.

2   D. Davey, *A Sense of Adventure*, London: S.E.1 People's History Project, 1980, p. 22.

Chapter 29

Marjorie Shostak

'WHAT THE WIND WON'T TAKE AWAY'
The genesis of *Nisa – The Life and Words of a !Kung Woman*

Marjorie Shostak, who died in 1996, was an anthropologist and photographer at Emory University, Atlanta, Georgia. Her groundbreaking book, the life history of a woman from the hunting-gathering people of the Kalahari Desert, was first published in 1981 and explored the question of whether there can be true under-standing between people of profoundly different cultures. This retrospective piece about how she and Nisa worked together and how the book was written, contrasts with Chapter 28 by offering a different model of collaboration. Shostak returned to Botswana in 1989 after being diagnosed with breast cancer, and *Return to Nisa* was published posthumously. Reprinted from Personal Narratives Group (ed.), *Interpreting Women's Lives: Feminist Theory and Personal Narratives*, Bloomington: Indiana University Press, 1989, pp. 228–240, by permission of the editors, author and publisher.

THIS ESSAY ABOUT personal narratives is something of a personal narrative in its own right. It explores questions I have asked myself for eighteen years, since I first collected life histories in the field – questions I have never formally addressed in print, or perhaps even fully answered for myself. How best to handle the material, how to present it fairly, and how to find forms suitable for publica-tion – these are some of the problems, both practical and ethical, that I have grappled with. My solutions have been compromises, at best, idiosyncratic constructions bound by the material and by my individual experience. Nevertheless, I offer them here in the hope that they may help clarify these problems for others working in similar ways.

First some background about me and my research. Armed with the life histories of Cora Dubois (*The People of Alor*, 1944) and Oscar Lewis (*The Children of Sanchez*, 1961), I went, in 1969, to the northern fringe of Africa's Kalahari Desert in northwestern Botswana to begin a twenty-month stay with the !Kung San (Bushmen). My goal was to collect life histories, a vehicle through which I hoped the people's experiences, thoughts, and feelings might be expressed. I returned again five years later and stayed five months, continuing this line of research along with others.

What fascinated me about the !Kung was that, although their ways had begun to change, people still maintained much of their hunting and gathering tradition: wild plant foods composed about 65 percent of the diet, and wild game meat the rest. People were seminomadic and lived in groups that fluctuated in composition, usually numbering between fifteen and thirty. Social life was essentially egalitarian, with minimal differentials in wealth, and with no formal status hierarchies or social classes. Work was hard, but there was plenty of time for leisure: women gathered about two to three days a week, and men hunted about three to four days a week. Food was usually more than adequate, sometimes abundant, and only rarely scarce. Children, adolescents, and the elderly were not regularly enlisted in the food quest.

This way of life is similar in many ways to that of our remote ancestors living tens of thousands of years ago, long before the advent of agriculture. This was the context in which our humanity formed and flourished, nourishing the remarkable breadth of human abilities as we know them today. How reasonable or difficult this way of life was is lost in the past, its shadows sketched in archeological sites, on the walls of caves, and in the very presence and persistence of humans on earth today.

The !Kung are one of a very few human groups who have lived in recent times as hunters and gatherers. They are fully modern people, in no sense remnants or leftovers from the past – physiologically, psychologically, or intellectually. All have also had some degree of contact with outside cultures, some for hundreds of years. Nevertheless, even in the most marginal areas – the only ones in which hunters and gatherers now remain – a pattern of life prevails that is likely to be similar, in many ways, to ones followed by hunters and gatherers of the past. Even modern hunters and gatherers living in diverse locales – Australia, central and southern Africa, South America, and the Arctic – share many organizational features.

I was fortunate not to be one of the first anthropologists to study the !Kung San – fortunate because by the time my first field stay was completed, a large body of data collected by other anthropologists and medical scientists was available. Without this work, my own ability to interpret, make sense of, and relate personal narratives – singular voices within a highly varied range – to a more generalized whole would have been compromised.

The life-history interviews were extensive and intimate and were conducted without interpreters. The first hurdle, of course, was learning the language – replete with clicks and tones and bearing no relationship to anything I had ever heard before. I launched my first 'interviews' after about six months. I asked pregnant women which sex child they preferred, polygynously married women what it was like to share a husband, and a handful of women and men – those most likely to tolerate my intrusive questions – their thoughts about marriage.

The results? At this distance it does not seem surprising, but at the time it felt quite devastating: my ambitious questions coupled with still-too-rudimentary language skills led to failures dismal enough that, had I had the inclination to pursue other lines of research, I might have adopted a new stratagem with embarrassing speed. But I didn't (of course), and by the end of the next six months, things had begun to look brighter: my interviewing skills and language ability had improved to the point that a 'research protocol' was developed, one that lasted until the end of my stay.

That protocol was the interview itself. My initial approach was to include anyone willing to talk to me about his or her life. After conducting a number of what turned out to be fairly tense interviews with men, I realized that they felt uncomfortable talking with me about intimate subjects – much as I did with them. Subsequently, I turned my attention solely to women.

By the end, I had invited eight women to work with me. Each set of interviews was introduced in the same way: I explained that I wanted to learn what it meant to be a woman in the !Kung culture so that I could better understand what it meant to be one in my own. I previewed the topics I hoped to discuss: earliest memories, feelings about parents, siblings, relatives, and friends, childhood play, marriage, relationships with husbands and/or lovers, childbirth, parenting, feelings about growing older, and thoughts about death. The women were encouraged to discuss anything else that they felt touched the core of their lives. An interview lasted about an hour, was conducted exclusively in the !Kung language, never included other people, and was tape-recorded. Each woman was interviewed eight or more times.

I tried to elicit specific incidents rather than generalized statements. Discreet memories were more likely to capture the texture of the women's experiences and to highlight the variations among the different women in their life stories and in their interpretations of these stories. The tape recorder was used not only for detail but to enable the reconstruction of how memories followed one another and how words were used; the goal of the final translation was to reflect a sense of the !Kung language, to preserve its nuances, beauty, and subtlety of expression.

There was considerable variation in the women's willingness to be drawn into this process, but overall the interviews were successful: each woman opened a piece of her life to me, and each piece reflected on and deepened my understanding of the experiences of the others. Of the eight, one woman stood out: Nisa.

Perhaps because she was emotionally vulnerable at the time of the interviews, or just because she took pleasure in the process of reviewing her life, Nisa put more effort into our work than did any other woman. She also had exceptional verbal gifts and articulated her story by reaching more deeply into herself and by choosing her words more deliberately than did the others. While I ordinarily was directive with them, Nisa quickly grasped the requirements and took charge; the momentum was often hers. We completed fifteen interviews during my first field trip, and six more during my second. Her story is the one I ultimately translated, edited, and published.

The result is Nisa: *The Life and Words of a !Kung Woman*. A short outline of its structure reflects the way I resolved the questions raised by the material. As I saw it, three distinct 'voices' – or points of view – needed to be incorporated. The first was Nisa's. Presented as first-person narrative, her voice was translated and edited from the taped interviews and chronologically ordered into fifteen chapters, from 'Earliest Memories' to 'Growing Older'.

The second voice was the 'official' anthropologist's, putting Nisa's story into cultural perspective: the ethnographic background to topics Nisa discussed was reviewed in headnotes preceding each chapter of her story. The third voice was my own, not primarily as anthropologist but as a young American woman experiencing another world. This voice was sandwiched on either side of the fifteen chapters of narrative and ethnographic notes. A personal introduction set up the overall framework of Nisa's story, and an epilogue summarized my second field trip, including my final encounter with Nisa and my closing thoughts.

Finding an acceptable balance for these three voices was problematic: it took many drafts before that balance was arrived at. Along the way, I confronted and tried to resolve a number of methodological and ethical questions, which can more generally, perhaps, be understood as questions about the uses of personal narrative, especially those conducted in cross-cultural settings. Five of these questions follow.

1. Can personal narrative be used as ethnography? Since no person is ever truly representative of a culture as a whole, how should an informant's personal biases and distance from statistical norms be handled?
One of the first issues I struggled with was how to deal with Nisa's representativeness, or lack of it. Nisa's life experiences were different in many ways from those of most other women: she had no living children, she had been married five times, and she was unusually uninhibited, if not an outright extrovert. I wanted her individual voice to be presented clearly, but other women's experiences were needed to balance it.

The interviews conducted in an identical manner with seven other women provided the broad base I needed: Nisa's experiences were compared to theirs. The base became even broader when material collected by other fieldworkers was included. My position, ultimately, was quite favorable: when Nisa said she first married at age nine, I looked up the age curve of first marriage for girls in one publication, the marriage ceremony in another, and the economic and political considerations involved in a third.[1] I found out, for example, that although on average girls first marry around age sixteen, some, especially in Nisa's generation, married as early as age nine. The headnotes summarized this perspective, enabling the reader to place in context Nisa's sometimes unusual experiences in her own unencumbered narrative.

2. Can a personal narrative be used even as a true account of the person who is relating it? How dependent is a personal narrative on a particular interviewing relationship?
Here, a class that I audited, taught by Vincent Crapanzano at Harvard University in the late 1970s, provided guidance. He noted that personal narratives do not exist independently of the collaborative process involved in their collection. People's stories are not in final form, shape, and content, waiting patiently for a glorified mechanic (i.e., biographer, anthropologist, or the like) to open their 'verbal tap', allowing the preformed story to escape. Instead, an interview is an interaction between two people: one, with unique personality traits and interests at a particular time of life, answers a specific set of questions asked by another person with unique personality traits and interests at a particular time of life.

In presenting Nisa's story, I therefore took care to describe our relationship as best I could: an essentially practical one which we both thoroughly enjoyed but which did not involve significantly more time than when we actually were working together. There was no doubt that Nisa, aged fifty and experiencing a difficult adjustment to menopause, filtered her life story through her then-current perspective; there was also no doubt that Marjorie Shostak, aged twenty-four, recently married, a product of the American 1960s, asked questions relevant to a specific phase of her life. I asked Nisa to tell me what it meant to be a woman; her answer was her narrative: selected memories retained through time – real, embellished, imagined, or a combination of all three – which best served her current definition of self. Her narrative thus reflected a finite contract between fifty-year-old Nisa and twenty-four-year-old Shostak; any other combination, no doubt, would have produced a different result.

3. *Can personal narratives be used freely in our own work for our own purposes? Is the collection and publication of personal narratives a boon for researchers while being a thinly disguised 'rip-off' of informants? Where does our ultimate responsibility lie?*
It was less clear for me, not working toward an academic degree, than for most graduate students and faculty what I had to gain by working on Nisa's narrative. Indeed, had I not been personally 'hooked', feeling almost a sense of responsibility for publishing it, the course of my life during the past eighteen years would have been very different. But I *was* hooked, although never without ambivalence.

The first time its value was impressed upon me was soon after I returned from the field and passed around some preliminary translations; they were met with tremendous enthusiasm and encouragement. An article I subsequently published was followed by a call from the Harvard University Press, inquiring about my future plans for writing a book.

It took ten years before *Nisa* was finally published. Work on the book was only one of the reasons it took so long; I was also intensely involved in other projects. By the time I made a firm commitment to completing *Nisa*, I had translated her twenty-one interviews twice: once after my first field trip, and again after my second. Having become more proficient in the !Kung language, I felt I could render more subtle and accurate translations from the original tapes.

However smoothly or roughly my life might otherwise have gone, I have nevertheless clearly profited by having published the book. But what did Nisa gain? The actual interview process seemed a positive one for her, and, in some small way, it may even have helped her. Our initial work took place during an emotionally stressful time: the recent onset of menopause was bringing home the finality of her childlessness; by that time, all of her four children had died.

Talking about her life, reviewing the births, the deaths, the marriages, the many additional loves, the highs and the lows – all while 'teaching' me about life and womanhood – Nisa also took pride in her skillful handling of the situation. She reveled in the knowledge that she was teaching me the 'truth' about life, while others, she would explain, often taught me 'lies'. She benefitted in other ways (as did the other women), with presents and with an agreed-upon payment. Status also accrued to her among the !Kung for being involved with 'anthropologists' work'.

But there was more. Nisa responded to our talk as though she appreciated the chance to contribute to something 'bigger' than what was typically asked for by the anthropologists. She was well aware that I planned to bring the verbatim material I collected back to the people with whom I lived. They, I had explained, would be interested in learning about !Kung women's lives. She approached the tape recorder as an ally, one with tentacles reaching out to worlds beyond her own. She jokingly referred to it as an 'old man' – a symbol, perhaps, of a wise, experienced presence that could receive the full import of all she hoped to say. During the very first interview, she expressed this concern directly: 'Fix my voice on the machine so that my words come out clear. I am an old person who has experienced many things, and I have much to talk about'.

She was also aware of the fragility of talk – and of experience. Reflecting on the interview process itself, she once said, 'I'll break open the story and tell you what is there. Then, like the others that have fallen out onto the sand, I will finish with it, and the wind will take it away.' Perhaps she recognized that with me there was a chance that the wind *might* not take *all* of it away.

Indeed, during the last interview of my first visit, she spoke about my taking 'our talk' with me when I left. She said she would collect more talk and 'save it for me'. When I returned four years later, she reminded me of this: she said she hadn't forgotten her promise and collected things to talk to me about. This and other responses to the challenge of our work suggested that the interviews were a welcome outlet for her, a satisfying and otherwise unavailable avenue for self-expression.

What about more material rewards? When I returned to the field, I spoke to Nisa about my desire to publish her account – something that would not, in fact, happen for another six years. I likened the final book to products for sale in stores, a parallel with which she was already familiar. If it sold, I told her, she would get something out of it. If it didn't, she might not.

Her initial response was, 'If this is what you want to do, that's good. But you're the one who has to do it, not me.' I explained that, indeed, it would be years of my work, but that it was her story. Concerned about her privacy, we agreed that I would use pseudonyms. Together we settled on 'Nisa' and other names. Giving her consent, she said that if the book sold, she would like some cows. I reviewed with her the most problematic stories – those involving violence, and others that might be seen as personally compromising – and asked if she wanted any of the material excluded. She answered without hesitation, 'all our talk, all that this "old man" [the tape recorder] has heard, wants to enter the talks'.

Nisa has received her cows and continues to receive gifts from me. As a result, she has become one of the people with wealth and stature in the changing world of the !Kung. I have contributed additional time and money helping the community she lives with. But where my ultimate responsibility lies in relation to her is still somewhat unsettled. L.L. Langness and Gelya Frank discuss some of the subtleties of the interview relationship.[2] They point out that informants sometimes harbor 'unexpressed expectations' of anthropologists. In the process of receiving attention from outsiders, usually from those with higher status than their own, informants may become vulnerable. They cite the claim of cross-cultural psychologist David Guttman that '[informants] too often experience our transient gestures toward equality as massive seductions', and recommend close supervision of anthropologists not only by experts in their particular field but by – and here they may overestimate the wisdom of these practitioners – clinical psychologists or psychiatrists as well.

These concerns are legitimate, but they can also be exaggerated and even patronizing to informants. In Nisa's case, I think the seduction worked both ways. I didn't enter Nisa's life until she was about age fifty, and when I did, it was for a very short period of time. When I returned four years later, her life in the interim had clearly been fully lived, although she had not forgotten to 'collect' stories for my return. Even if my impact on her was larger than I recognize, my belief now, as then, is that – except for the later financial rewards – I have played an essentially minor and positive role in her life.

That does not justify my shirking from what I see as a continuing responsibility toward her and her community or underestimating what she gave. She offered weeks of her time, telling her story with gusto, courage, imagination, and humor, along with thoughtfulness, occasional sadness, anger, and longing. For me, 'talking her talk with me' and trying to make sense of it involved many years of my life. The ultimate gain for either of us can hardly be considered to be financial. Nisa gave her talk; I tried to keep the wind from taking its beauty away.

4. *How does the editing and translation process affect how personal narratives are used? What factors must be considered when translating, editing, and presenting a personal narrative once it has been collected?*

Shaping Nisa's narrative required considerable discipline and attention to detail. A total of twenty-one interviews – representing between twenty-five and thirty hours of tape, all recorded under less than ideal conditions – were translated twice, a process that was tedious and time-consuming. The initial translations were literal, word-for-word transcriptions written in English, but with unusual expressions noted in !Kung. Following a second field trip, I translated and transcribed the initial fifteen interviews again, along with six additional interviews conducted during this subsequent stay.

These translations were broken into segments, usually the length of a story, and were roughly edited. These segments were then grouped, usually by topic, sequenced into loose chronological order, and more finely edited. Details and embellishments from incidents discussed more than once were combined into one account. To clarify the flow from one story to the next, missing or unclear time markers were inserted (for example: 'Not long after', or 'Some time passed'). All questions of clarification, all diversionary comments, and all directive suggestions on my part were eliminated from the final narrative.

In addition to this editing, an overriding structure needed to be created, a 'literary' one that would grab the attention and maintain the interest of American readers. To that end, I experimented with a number of formats. My first approach treated each interview as its own chapter and followed it with ethnographic and personal commentary. This didn't work: the interviews lacked consistent dramatic and emotional integrity; they didn't stand up well on their own. Comments and asides as well as occasional interruptions from the outside frequently disrupted the flow of talk. Or, the conversation jumped around, restlessly, from topic to topic, settling on a clear direction only halfway through. Or, I would introduce a string of interruptions to clarify the flow of details, or merely to have an unfamiliar word or expression defined. The overall progression of interviews did have an interesting character, but ultimately it was not enough to be the most effective form in which to present Nisa's story.

The main alternative was the chronological presentation – the one I chose because it made sense, not just to me but even in terms of !Kung narrative form. Although they had no prior experience with my specific life-review format, Nisa and the other women had no trouble adopting the chronological approach. In Nisa's first interview, we did a 'once-over', quickly reviewing the grand scope of her life from her earliest memories to the interview-present. The second interview started at the beginning again. Throughout that one, and the next thirteen, we proceeded again through her life story, this time much more slowly, stopping often, touching events in depth, carefully moving forward in time until we reached the interview-present. At the end of each interview, we would discuss where we might pick up the next day. The next day sometimes began with a review of the end of the previous day's interview. More typically, it would start with a recent dream, or Nisa would tell me that she had prepared her thoughts in a certain direction for our talks that day.

The six interviews conducted with Nisa during my second field trip, four years later, clarified material collected during the first trip: we reviewed stories I hadn't previously understood, went over unclear time sequences, added material in areas that had been underrepresented, and reviewed events in Nisa's life during my four-year absence. For both sets of interviews, no constraints on time or on the total number of interviews existed; we determined the end of each one, and the series as a whole, at the point both of us felt her story had been told.

Nisa had her own sense of narrative style. Most of her stories were told with a beginning, a middle, and an end; some were short, others lengthy. Usually, the chronological, or linear, mode I encouraged prevailed, although sometimes she, or I, would jump to a related topic. If I interrupted to ask a question, she might reprimand me, 'Wait, I'm getting to that. Now listen.' At times, the process of narration itself became her focus, as when she described the dissolution of one of her marriages and ended her story with, 'That's all, and we lived and we lived.' An unusually long silence followed. Then she added, thoughtfully, and slowly, 'No, there is something in my heart about this that isn't finished. My heart is still shaking. The story hasn't come completely out. I'm going to talk more about it until it does. Then, I'll go on to another. Then, my heart will be fine.'

The chronological approach also found support in !Kung traditional storytelling. The !Kung exercise sophisticated narrative pacing and sequencing skills in a rich body of oral myths, those describing the time 'in the beginning' – when God walked upon the earth and animals were still evolving from people – as well as in their animal tales, stories of character and intrigue, dependent on chronology and an orderly succession of events. Similarly, frequent recountings of hunts and experiences while gathering require subtle verbal cues and accurate time sequencing. It is possible that had I been less directive, a fairly comparable indigenous narrative form would have emerged.

But with few conventions to guide me, each editing decision was guided by my ultimate goal: to present Nisa's unique experience of life – as expressed in her interviews – as a distinct voice within the context of !Kung culture as I, and other researchers, saw it at that time. Because, as 'objective' as each researcher tried to be, our collection and interpretation of data were inevitably influenced by the intellectual 'umbrella' we shared. (For example, since then, the !Kung's long history of contact with other cultures, which we were aware of but did not emphasize, and the 'myth' of their isolation have come much more to the fore.) My headnotes reflect a view generally shared by anthropologists in 1981, and, in some ways, the narrative material chosen does as well.

As described above, questions of clarification were eliminated, duplicate accounts were collapsed, extraneous story fragments were excluded, and a chronological sequence was imposed. In addition, a small number of stories I didn't understand, and anecdotes and minor incidents about people not central to the themes of the narrative (such as customs of or gossip about the neighboring Bantu-speaking people) were also eliminated. Stories that covered duplicate ground, and that would have impeded the general flow of the narrative, were also left out (for example, dreams that were similar to ones included, or secondary stories about lovers – none important or containing details not already in the narrative; even in its published form, many readers find the narrative too heavily weighted in that direction and find some of Nisa's numerous amorous encounters tedious). There is no doubt that I also held subtle and not-so-subtle biases toward the material.

Nowhere were the editing choices more delicate than in the translation process itself. I would not be honest without admitting that there were times when I was tempted to 'adjust' the narrative beyond what could be considered justifiable. Nisa, as those familiar with the book know, is a strong, earthy, sexual, highly self-contained but not always exemplary character. I was sorely tempted to leave out some of her less appealing traits to highlight those that ennobled her. A slight shift in the translation, so subtle that no one but I would know, could also have achieved this end. How much grander Nisa might have appeared had I translated everyday idiomatic speech into literal, poetic utterances! 'The sun rose' is prosaic; 'The dawn broke open the darkness' is poetry. But if every !Kung child and adult, dull or witty, described the sunrise in the same standard way, then, when Nisa used those words, my responsibility was to translate it into standard English – which I tried very carefully to do as I went along.

Another translation problem was the use of repetition. In a culture with strong oral traditions, repetition often becomes part of the ritual form. For example, as one memory ended, Nisa often said, 'and we lived and we lived and we lived'. (The phrase might actually be repeated several more times.) Although a more 'literary' expression could have been employed, such as 'a few moons (or rainy seasons, etc.) passed', Nisa used repetition: it symbolized the passage of ordinary time, bridged two stories or parts together, and acted as a dramatic device around which to organize her thoughts – a technique used widely by other storytellers. In translating her words, such strong strings of repetitions did not work in English, and I often substituted 'and time passed', or 'and we just continued to live'. In a sense, this epitomizes the problem of translation: the !Kung expression conveys a different sense of time than do the English ones – a sense of the past that is more immediate and continuing. Instead of losing that completely, I left some of it in, trying to retain its flavor, but substituted words or reduced the repetitions drastically to make it work on the printed page.

My editor at the Harvard University Press once asked in jest, but with telltale nervousness in his laugh, 'You do have interviews with Nisa on tape . . . don't you?' Ultimately, Nisa's narrative and the assumption of my having edited our work responsibly and professionally have been accepted on faith. Not that this faith has been misplaced; it has not. Nevertheless, the handful of people who could have checked my translations never have. I suppose they never felt the need; most of them had worked with me in the field, had evidence of my language abilities, had heard many similar stories themselves, and had heard enough gossip about the personal nature of my work from the !Kung themselves that they trusted that I did what I claim to have done. Above all, they knew enough about the !Kung to know that Nisa's narrative, even when it surprised them, rang true.

5. *Can personal narratives be used as a mirror or guide to our own lives?*
If they could not, most of us would probably be much less keen on doing them. After all, they are difficult to obtain (especially in foreign contexts), laborious to work with, and tricky to present. Methodological obstacles are vast: becoming proficient in another language, developing rapport, learning interview techniques, insuring reliability of data, adopting appropriate sample size, maintaining objectivity, and recognizing one's own biases. Ethical issues are no less complex: protecting an informant's privacy (within the community as well as without), educating informants about the collaboration so that they truly can give informed consent, recognizing the informant's sensitivity toward us and ours toward her or him, and translating, editing, and presenting the informant's 'true' voice in such a way that the idiosyncratic and the generalizable can be distinguished.

The impetus for surmounting these obstacles came, for me, from the realization that if I didn't do it, no one else was likely to. After all, fewer and fewer !Kung remained connected to their fast-disappearing hunting and gathering traditions, and the other anthropologists who worked with them had different research interests. While a well-told story of any person's life is of value, one that came from a culture which reflected a most ancient form of human organization – a form in which all our human potential originally became manifest – seemed potentially to be of great significance. When I devised my project, I hoped I would learn from the !Kung what it meant to be human.

The impetus for collecting personal narratives, however, came from an overlapping but distinct set of issues: recently married, living in the field with no other outsiders, I found fieldwork much more isolating than life as I had known it before. I learned much about the !Kung language, their !Kung way of life, and who they were as people. Setting aside, as best I could, involvement in my own world, I nevertheless remained an outsider, there to interpret and bring back pieces of another way of life. In truth, I was drawn to interviewing people because I felt lonely; I hoped, perhaps, that 'structured friendships' would allow me to share in people's lives and feel part of the community. After initial difficulties, they did just that.

A few years before *Nisa* was published, my literary agent sent part of the manuscript to numerous publishers. At one house it was rejected because, it was claimed, Nisa's voice wasn't interesting enough; she sounded as if she could be 'the woman next door'. Despite the rejection, I was elated. That was, after all, what I had been hoping for. Nisa – at home, in the Kalahari Desert, part of a society with no chiefs, no status hierarchies, and minimal inequities of wealth, semi-nomadic, small-scale, and minimally materialistic (each person's possessions weigh about twenty-five pounds) – was being mistaken for 'the woman next door'! Her experiences must reflect something universal, after all.

My desire to find a guide, someone to mirror my own life, had been realized. Nisa's voice reverberated not only within me but within others. Considering her story, perhaps it is not so surprising: a woman living in one of the most remote areas of the world, facing life with courage, humor, spirit, and dignity, who, despite repeated tragedy, carried on with a sense of entitlement to enjoy what was yet to come. She had told this story with care and generosity, a story with echoes of an ancient time, reflecting themes tens of thousands of years old.

Conclusion

One of the people Barbara Myerhoff interviewed for her study of a community of aging Jewish immigrants in California was Shmuel. He had come to the United States from Eastern Europe early in this century, at a time when pogroms against Jews were rampant. Speaking about life in Poland before it was all 'wiped out like you would erase a line of writing', he said about death: 'It is not the worst thing that can happen for a man to grow old and die.' He continued, 'But if my life goes, with my memories, and all that [the knowledge of a way of life destroyed by Hitler] is lost, that is something else to bear.'[3]

It is Shmuel, Nisa, and the silent others they represent, as well as for ourselves, that we should continue to record these lives and memories. The ethical and methodological problems may be formidable, but they are small compared to the goal. Indeed, the most important ethical message regarding life histories is not a restriction but an obligation: we should make every effort to overcome obstacles, to go out and record the memories of people whose ways of life often are preserved only in those memories. And we should do it urgently, before they disappear.

No more elegant tool exists to describe the human condition than the personal narrative. Ordinary people living ordinary and not-so-ordinary lives weave from their memories and experiences the meaning life has for them. These stories are complex, telling of worlds sometimes foreign to us, worlds that sometimes no longer exist. They express modes of thought and culture often different from our own, a challenge to easy understanding. Yet, these stories are also familiar. It is just this tension – the identifiable in endless transformation – that is the currency of personal narratives, as they reveal the complexities and paradoxes of human life. As we cast our net wider, searching for those close as well as those far away, the spectrum of voices from otherwise obscure individuals helps us learn tolerance for differences as well as for similarities. What better place to begin our dialogue about human nature and the nature of human possibilities?

Notes

1   R. Lee and I. DeVore, *Kalahari Hunter-Gatherers*, Cambridge, Mass.: Harvard University Press, 1976; L. Marshall, *The !Kung of Nyae Nyae*, Cambridge, Mass.: Harvard University Press, 1976; R. Lee, *The !Kung San*, Cambridge: Cambridge University Press, 1979; N. Howell, *Demography of the Dobe Area !Kung*, New York: Academic Press, 1979.

2   L.L. Langness and G. Fran, *Lives: An Anthropological Approach to Biography*, California: Chandler & Sharp, 1981.

3   B. Myerhoff, *Number Our Days*, New York: Dutton, 1978, pp. 73–74.

Chapter 30

Charles Hardy III

AUTHORING IN SOUND
Aural history, radio and the digital revolution

This chapter examines the impact on oral and 'aural' history of new developing digital technologies, in particular the democratization of multi-media collection and production, the increasing use of recorded sound in public spaces, and radio's persistence as a primary factor in encouraging people to 'think in sound' rather than text. Charles Hardy is Professor of History at West Chester University, Pennsylvania, and co-author with Sandro Portelli of *I Can Almost See the Lights of Home*, an essay in sound that won the 1999 Oral History Association non-print award. This chapter is an updated excerpt from 'Authoring in sound: an eccentric essay on aural history, radio, and media convergence' (1999) available online at www.albany.edu/faculty/gz580/documentaryproduction.

I N THE TWENTIETH CENTURY the technological triumph of motion pictures, recorded sound, radio, and television brought about monumental changes in the nature of human communications. Today we are in the midst of a second, digital revolution that is laying the groundwork for an international and interactive information infrastructure in which once separate media are already converging; a celestial jukebox in which information will be recorded, stored, transmitted, and received digitally. What this means is that more and more people will be generating documents about themselves and receiving information about the world, past and present, in multiple-media formats. From the 1920s through the 1980s radio was the dominant electronic medium of spoken-word communication, but in the 1990s it lost its monopoly. Today, radio is but one outlet for spoken-word programming that can be distributed in a growing variety of media and formats: CDs and cassettes, the internet, DVDs, solid-state digital players that permit ever-expanding levels of interactivity, and a host of multi- and multiple-media combinations.[1]

To author the history of the twentieth and now the twenty-first century, scholars working in digital media need usable records – documents that accurately reproduce the sound and visual events that they captured and froze in time. Increasingly affordable technologies today permit sound gatherers to record high-fidelity interviews and other sound and moving image documents, and to convert those materials into sound and multimedia 'articles', 'documentaries', 'constructions', 'essays', 'movements', 'compositions', 'exhibits', and still emerging forms of scholarly and popular discourse that can be released in a variety of stand-alone and multiple media formats. Targeting car drivers who wanted alternatives to the fare offered them by both commercial and non-commercial radio, the books-on-tape industry exploded in size – and for a short time prolonged the life of the analogue audio cassette – during the 1990s. At first most books-on-tape were like old wine poured into new bottles; written words read aloud. But the industry has slowly begun to develop an ear. More and more publications are paying attention to production values, utilizing actualities, sound effects, and ambiences. Today one can find autobiographies read by their authors, dramatic recreations, and publications that include archival recordings. Warner Books, for example, released *The Autobiography of Martin Luther King Jr.*, edited by Claybourne Carson, first as a book, in 1998, and then as a book on tape (Warner Books, 1999) composed of King's recorded speeches and interviews.[2]

Print/CD publications permit authors to use print and sound in a complementary fashion, playing to the strengths of each medium. Ambitious, collaborative projects, *Remembering Slavery: African Americans Talk About Their Personal Experiences of Slavery and Emancipation*, and *Remembering Jim Crow: African Americans Tell About Life in the Segregated South*, both packaged oral history-based radio documentaries that aired on National Public Radio (NPR) with annotated collections of oral testimonies. While the former used actors to bring to life transcriptions of Works Progress Administration interviews with former slaves, the latter drew upon interviews conducted by graduate students in the early 1990s that were among the 1,300 oral history interviews in the Behind the Veil collection at Duke University. Here radio broadcast also served as marketing and promotion for the New Press book-and-audiotape/CD publications. Both, now, also have their own websites.[3]

The 1990s witnessed a growing number of similarly ambitious multiple-media publications. A collaboration between the Smithsonian Institution and NPR, *Wade in the Waters: African-American Sacred Music Traditions*, included a 26-hour radio series, travelling museum exhibit, four-cassette music anthology packaged with a 115-page Educator's Guide (Washington, DC, NPR, 1994), and musical recordings released on cassette and CD by Smithsonian/Folkways. To tell the story of the exciting literary movement of the American Southwest, University of Arizona English professor David Dunaway produced *Writing the Southwest*, a complementary book (New York, Plume/Penguin, 1995) and radio series that included thirteen, half-hour radio documentaries.

Television broadcasters and video documentarians also use oral histories and other sound recordings. The explosion of new broadcast and non-broadcast outlets has created a voracious demand for spoken-word documents. In the 1990s the communications and entertainment industries recognized that the nation's libraries and archives are a major, under-utilized source of inexpensive 'software' – raw material to help fill the ever-expanding universe of electronic and digital space. Swamped by requests from broadcast journalists and documentary producers, and then website content providers, growing numbers of sound archives are setting up fee-charging schedules and retooling their reading rooms to accommodate the growing number of researchers.[4]

Joining the soaring numbers of high-quality video and sound documentaries are multi-media textbooks that team text, documents, still and moving images and audio recordings. A superb example is The American Social History Project's two *Who Built America?* CD-ROMs. Volume 1, which won the 1994 American Historical Association James Harvey Robinson Prize, incorporated several thousand pages of text, hundreds of high resolution photographs, sixty graphs and charts, four hours of audio – including oral histories – and forty-five minutes of film. That a reviewer in *The Wall Street Journal* found the oral histories with ordinary people 'some of the most fascinating entries' indicates the ability of oral histories to hold their own against other visual and audio-visual materials. This came to life for me while listening to a segment on composer Eubie Blake, who while talking about his early musical education plays a song as his music teacher taught it to him, and as he 'ragged' it on his own.[5]

A growing number of oral history projects are finding their way onto CD and the internet. One of the first significant oral history projects committed to the digital domain was undertaken by the Rasmusson Library Oral History Program at the University of Alaska Fairbanks. In the mid-1990s the Program created a series of innovative, interactive computer workstations that teamed interviews with native elders with pictures, maps, text, and short video clips that highlighted local history. Historians working on this Jukebox Program quickly experienced how authoring in multimedia alters the way one thinks about history; how it led them to, in William Schneider's words, 'think beyond individual interviews to the corpus of comparative perspectives which we are assembling . . . In a sense we resemble orchestra conductors encouraging many voices and variation and sometimes are able to leave our listeners with lasting impressions of what went on, what it was like, and what we think it means.'[6]

Ongoing improvements continue to transform the internet. The arrival of CD-quality, high-fidelity sound streaming to the World Wide Web, and now moving images, may prove to be the most revolutionary developments of all. Opportunities for journalists and academics abound. One of the first websites to pioneer the use of the web for the archiving and distribution of aural history programming was *Talking History* at University of Albany State University of New York. Under the direction of historian Gerald Zahavi, since 1996, *Talking History* has grown into an impressive online library of interviews and aural history documentaries, 'Contributing Producers' pages, and audio documents drawn from sound archives across the United States.

Zahavi was also the guiding spirit behind the creation the *Journal for MultiMedia History* (JMMH), 'the first peer-reviewed electronic journal that presents, evaluates, and disseminates multimedia historical scholarship'. The pioneering journal includes two feature articles that demonstrate its mission 'to utilize the promise of digital technologies to expand history's boundaries, merge its forms, and promote and legitimate innovations in teaching and research that we saw emerging all around us'.[7]

The second volume of the JMMH (1999) featured 'I Can Almost See the Lights of Home: A Field Trip to Harlan County, Kentucky', an experimental aural history 'essay in sound' created specifically for web publication rather than radio broadcast.

A collaborative work that Alessandro Portelli and I scripted while participating in the Columbia University Oral History Research Office's 1997 Summer Institute, 'Lights of Home', includes articles by Portelli on his fieldwork in Harlan County, Kentucky and by me on the 'authoring' of the 'essay in sound'; a full transcription of the sound essay; and an index organized by 'chapter' and 'movement' which enables browsers to move their way through the heart of the publication: a 2.5 hour stereo audio essay. My essay also includes excerpts from early radio documentaries and rejected mixes for 'Lights of Home', then enables browsers to hear discarded mixes discussed in the written essay. Winner of the 1999 Oral History Association Nonprint Media Award, 'I Can Almost See the Lights of Home', offered, according to the editors' Introduction:

> a new mode of thinking about and presenting oral history. . . . it is an attempt by two oral historians, one from Pennsylvania, USA, and the other from Rome, Italy to create a new aural history genre that counterpoises the voices of subject and scholar in dialogue – not merely the dialogue that takes place in the real time of an oral interview, but the one that occurs as interpretations are created and scholarship is generated. . . . It challenges oral historians to truly explore the full dimension of the sources they create and utilize in scholarship – to engage the 'orality' of oral sources. It challenges all historians to consider alternative modes of presenting interpretations, modes that render the very act of interpretation more visible while preserving and respecting the integrity of primary sources.

How well it does so is, of course, open to debate.[8]

Museums that experimented with sound installations in the 1970s and 1980s often experienced nagging problems with the cart machines and other analogue tape technologies then available. These were expensive, high-maintenance, low-fidelity technologies that broke down with great regularity and that required periodic replacement of tapes. Walking tours were limited by the lock-step, linear character of the programming and the requirement that each user carry a cassette recorder, tape, and headphones. Today, a growing variety of portable, solid state audio play-back units have the potential to revolutionize the use of sound in museums, exhibits, battlefields, towns, and other locations. Information can be presented in multiple languages and at different levels of expertise – such as for children or adults. Multiple pathways through the programming (i.e. 'interactivity') enable 'browsers' to customize their tours and listen to as much or as little as desired.

The replacement of audio cassette players, with their fixed, linear programmes, by MP3 players, for example, can revolutionize audio walking tours. Audio walking and driving tours have tremendous potential for historic parks and districts, and the sites of important historical events. Imagine, when visiting the City of Birmingham, Alabama, for example, being able to walk through a historic site such as the Schloss Industrial Furnace, your tour narrated by former workers who describe the steel-making process, labour relations, life stories, and significant events, or listening to an audio walking or driving tour composed of oral histories, news reports, music, and sounds of the crucial moments of the Civil Rights during the spring and summer of 1963.[9]

The only way to really experience the potential for the use of oral histories in audio tours is to listen to one. An excellent early example is *Alcatraz: Cellhouse Tour*, a half-hour, self-guided, audio walking tour used at the National Park Service's Alcatraz prison museum in San Francisco. Here, former corrections officer Tom Donohue serves as the guide, leading the visitor through the prison and introducing the voices of prisoners and guards, all residents of Alcatraz between 1934 and 1963, who describe their daily routines and recall the most bloody prison break and only successful escape. The producers made excellent, spare use of the sound of cell doors shutting, footsteps on hard pavement, and other effects to punctuate recollections and stories about individual cells, the library, mess hall, and solitary confinement. The Alcatraz tour also made effective use of complementary media, including an accompanying booklet, and panels of historical photos and portraits of the narrators and other residents.[10]

Stereo is only a poor analogue of the way we actually hear. Binaural and new three-dimensional sound systems, already being marketed for use with computer games, may also revolutionize the whole world of sound reproduction, enabling authors to work in multi-channel, three-dimensional soundscapes that enable the sophisticated positioning and movement that brings sound to life. Sooner than we might expect, multi-channel sound, driven by the four- and five-channel sound systems already common with DVD home entertainment systems, may emerge as a very viable and attractive medium for aural historians. A quick search on the World Wide Web can provide an excellent introduction to some of the pioneering work already taking place in multi-channel radio and elsewhere.

The ongoing innovations in sound technology that enable authors to present their work in three-dimensional sound are tremendously important. We have all experienced the opening of sonic space that takes place when one shifts from monaural and stereo sound. A single, monaural sound source offers information about distance, but little about position. Stereo creates a limited two-dimensional field, enabling limited linear movement, some information about position, and separation between direct and background sounds. It still, however, presents a listener with only a facsimile of the three-dimensional soundscapes we hear in real life. A closer analogue to human hearing, binaural sound, captures a much fuller range of movement. A number of sound ecologists have already embraced binaural recording to document endangered natural soundscapes. Ongoing innovations in multi-channel sound processors, advanced sound systems, and speaker design will soon replace stereo with 'three-dimensional' sound. We are standing on the edge of a revolution in audio technology that will quite literally add another dimension to aural history.[11]

Three-dimensional sound has tremendous potential for museums. High fidelity, multi-channel sound installations and sound environments presented through multiple speakers bring a space sonically to life, moving sounds through and around the listener. To date, zoos have shown the greatest interest in multi-channel sound installations, using them to recreate the sounds of tropical rainforests and other natural environments. The potential is as great for historical museums. Through the use of four or more independent channels and the new generation of extraordinary speakers now appearing on the market, one can create sound movement within and through a gallery space. A horse-drawn trolley, for example, could pass diagonally across a room as a conversing couple crosses on the opposite diagonal. A steamship could move slowly from left to right along one wall, while one hears a team of black longshoremen singing work songs in the distance, a hushed conversation from two speakers occupies a more restricted audio field, and a flow of aural reminiscences describing the place and time emanates from different exhibit cases in the room. Discovery and control are created here not by a button or switch but by a visitor's physical movement. (This is much the same as what one does when listening to or moving among conversations at a party.) And again, such a sound environment could be experienced differently each time the visitor returned to the space. A constant barrage of sound can be both confusing and exhausting. But thoughtfully used in combination with silence, well-designed three-dimensional sound environments can be a crowd-pleasing and effective tool for exhibit inter- pretation. (Remember, too, that higher fidelity permits greater intelligibility at lower volume.)[12]

The use of three-dimensional sound and multi-channel installations leads to the question of what true 'aural histories' can sound like. How can aural and audio history publications, exhibits, or essays be best authored and structured? How could the different sound elements be juxtaposed and blended to best effect? What system of cues and markers will give the listener the ability to efficiently scan, locate, and sample?

Traditional historical studies are grounded in written-word communication. Traditional museums are dedicated to the preservation of material artefacts. Aural history, based on spoken words and other sounds that are recorded and stored, is part of electro-acoustical communications. A good museum exhibit, like an arcade or child's room, offers choices, enabling visitors to determine their own course through the exhibition. Using the arcade or museum exhibit as a model, the listener within such a space should be able to move freely among the mix of sound elements that most attracted his or her attention. Such a sonic display would, like a piece of good music, provide the listener with the ability to follow the instrument(s) of choice: to create their own mix. As Glenn Gould's *Solitude Trilogy* has demonstrated, all the voices need not be understood in a single pass, just as all the display copy and exhibition pieces need not be looked at in a strict sequential manner. What could be more tedious? How many of us actually explore an exhibit in a fixed and linear fashion?[13]

The implications for the understanding and presentation of history are also intriguing. Perhaps multi-channel aural histories represent an important tool for the authoring of 'post-modern' histories by providing a means of sharing authority, privileging multiple rather than univocal perspectives, and opening space – using simultaneity and dimension in the presentation of history that is not possible in the printed word, bound as it is to a linear unfolding. One of the constant challenges historians face in the college classroom is to disabuse their students of the notion that history is fixed; that one interpretation is true and others false. Perhaps multi- channel aural histories can assist in loosening this linear world-view. Perhaps they will remain nothing more than a failed experiment or academician's pipe dream. But as historians we do know that motion pictures, television, the phonograph and radio – and other new communication technologies – have all been treated at first as novelties, their power to transform recognized only later.

So aural historians already have an extraordinary range of broadcast and non- broadcast media in which to present their work: radio and television, stand alone

CDs and DVDs, CDs with print supplements, exhibit soundstations, wands, and websites. All these wonderful new digital technologies have one thing in common: they are high-fidelity, multi-channel media. Digital field recording and distribution media are rapidly outmoding the low-fidelity, monaural, audio cassettes favoured by oral historians for the last quarter of a century.

The ongoing digital revolution is rapidly accelerating the democratization of sound recording, production, and distribution. In the era of open-reel analogue tape technology, sound documentary production was an expensive and esoteric craft practised by few competently, and even fewer with skill. Today one can record and edit CD-quality interviews on a laptop computer – one still needs good external microphones – and author sophisticated multi-track, broadcast-quality sound documentaries with digital audio workstation software (DAWs) downloaded free from the World Wide Web. If sound programming is to hold its own against works in print, and against still and moving images, however, authors are going to need to learn how to think and to author in sound.

Oral history, as we know, is a dialogue and joint creation. Biographies and other histories based on oral history interviews falsify the nature of both memory and the oral history interview in certain ways by creating the illusion of sequentiality and a single point of view. To pursue a musical metaphor, traditional historical writing may be analogous to the breaking down of the musical composition of one's life into single instrumental lines that we then examine one voice at a time. This may enable us to hear and understand certain voices, but no matter how many of these separate elements we listen to we will never be able to experience or understand the music – or our lives – until we reassemble them back into the whole. All of the segmentation and division and compartmentalization and dissection necessary for historical analysis is essential to our understanding of the past. But synthesis is also required to bring the history back to life. The articulation of thought and memory are first aural, not visual processes. It would seem logical, then, that at some point aural historians must learn to think and create in sound. To do this we must overcome a lifetime of arduous, formal, typographically based training, and recognize that this education has closed our ears as much as it has opened our eyes.

It has been my experience that young people tend to have less of a problem with this than older scholars and audiences. To more and more of them written communication is the equivalent of a foreign language. Brought up in a world of electrical and digital media, they are quite naturally information scanners. Although this is by now common knowledge, if not cliché, in contemporary academic circles, most of us have not yet figured out what to do about it. Marshall McLuhan, for all of the nonsense that accompanied many of his insights, was one of the first to recognize the profound perceptual and cognitive shifts brought about by the electronic mass media. Pioneer audio documentarian Tony Schwartz understood McLuhan's insights not as theoretical abstractions but experientially, coming to them from years spent working in sound. Speaking about the lack of understanding of sound among educators, in 1981 Schwartz wrote:

> Where we would expect to find the most imaginative use of the new tape technology, we find the most stodgy and dated approach. Schools use tape and cassette programs that are not creatively constructed originals, but merely a copy of another environment. Tapes and cassettes

are misused as containers for older media: print and lectures. These
programs make little use of the temporal and spatial potential of tape.[14]

Those who would author in sound must learn to 'think' in sound; to free
themselves from the perceptual prisms that cut them off from aural history, from
many of their less well-educated interviewees, from their students, from general
audiences, and from some of the worlds that they devote their lifetimes to collecting
and interpreting.

The ongoing digital revolution has witnessed and contributed to the birth of a
growing number of superb radio programmes using aural reminiscences that have
made creative use of sound media, and that have explored the construction of
memory, the relationship between interviewer and interviewee, gender, class, and
race, other issues at the heart of recent oral history scholarship. An excellent
example is independent radio producer Dmae Roberts's 1990 Peabody award-
winning 'docuplay,' *Mei Mei: A Daughter's Story*. This is the story of Roberts's
attempt to understand herself by learning about her mother and making peace with
her, told through a sophisticated and engaging use of recurring motifs and storytelling techniques, including oral history, interior monologues, and *mise-en-scène*
actualities.

Theirs was a love-hate relationship common to many parents and children, but
exacerbated by the fact that the two were products of different cultures. (Roberts's
father was an American.) The story was fraught with dramatic possibilities: a
daughter ashamed of her old-world mother and mother disappointed in her
American daughter, each carrying the psychological scars and burdens of a lifetime.
In addition, Roberts's mother had grown up in war-torn China during the 1930s
and 1940s and had twice, as a child, been sold by her parents. So here were the
makings of a fascinating story, both deeply personal and of epic historical sweep,
that could touch upon family history, modern Chinese history, the American immigrant experience, the conflict between old-world parents and their Americanized
children, and the universal story of the relationship between a mother and a
daughter.

Oral history was Roberts's primary source of information about her mother's
past, but she was working with a reluctant informant. When interviewed, her
mother spoke without feeling of her own early life, giving information only reluctantly and in small bits and pieces. In addition, Roberts's effort was inhibited by a
language barrier: her mother's limited grasp of English and her own weak grasp of
Chinese. What this meant for the documentary was that she could not rely on oral
history actualities to carry the programme. These problems, then, forced Roberts
to be creative in presenting her mother's story. She chose to use only brief oral
history segments with her mother as referents and starting points; a spare use that
makes those segments that she does present all the more powerful and meaningful.
Roberts then used her own first-person narration to fill in the biographical details,
contextualize and frame her mother's story, and to explain the significance of these
autobiographical fragments to her own search for an understanding of her mother
and herself. The challenge of how to present her mother's voice, however, still
remained. Roberts solved this problem by having a young Chinese-American woman
voice her mother's words. At times Roberts draws listeners into the past by letting
them hear a dramatization of a critical moment in her mother's life. At other times

we hear her mother's own halting recollections. This mixed voicing is a very effective documentary technique. Moving the story back and forth in time also shifts it from the historical to the universal.

The spoken word is only one element in effective sound communication. The dynamic tension between intimacy and distance is furthered by Roberts's artful creation of a dream-like atmosphere through the use of ethereal Chinese music, reverb, and the hypnotic repetition of key words and phrases that explain the source of her mother's world-view and states of mind, and that drive home their significance. The thickness of her mother's Chinese accent serves as a metaphor of the wall between mother and daughter. Through revoicing and dramatizing her mother's account, Roberts was able to overcome the difficulty she had in relating to her mother. The dramatization also draws the listener into her mother's story as both participant and observer. All these techniques, then, help to overcome the distance of time and race and culture – the differences of appearances.

Rather than present her listeners with a full novelistic – or historical – recapitulation, Roberts presented her mother's story in a fashion that mimicked and recreated how she had learned about it herself: in tantalizing, veiled, and disconnected fragments that she had to piece together. The barrier of language is exacerbated by her mother's reluctance to free ghosts from the cemetery of her own memories, ghosts that might yet come back to harm her. From small bits and pieces, however, we learn what we need to know to make sense of her mother's life and hear enough biography to ground her life story historically. Roberts's dual focus, as she states at the beginning of the programme, is both about her mother and 'growing up with her'. Through the course of her mother's fragmentary recollections, Roberts recognizes what she believes to be the pivotal moments of her life. Sold as a child by her parents and forced to work as a servant in the midst of the Japanese occupation and then the Second World War, her mother attempted three times at the age of thirteen or fourteen to commit suicide. Each time the Buddha came to her and told her that it was not yet her time.

Rather than just narrate these pivotal events, Dmae presents the interview segments in which her mother actually speaks about her attempted suicides, and then dramatizes them by telescoping the three attempts into a single episode, creating an audio dreamscape that represents what was taking place in her mother's mind during her near-death experience: her interior dialogue with the female Buddha, Kuan Nim Posa:

> [Actuality] Kuan Nim Posa that's her whole name. We talk to Taiwanese. You don't understand. We talk to Chinese. You don't understand . . . I was hanging and Buddha stopped me. Buddha gave me power. She said, 'It's not your time yet'. I was thirteen and fourteen. I tried suicide three times.
> *How?*
> Through hanging.
> *You tried to hang yourself?*
> Yeah.
> *Three times?*
> Yeah.
> *How come?*

Because I didn't want to live, that's how come. Don't think of it as
happy to live for, no?
No. That's terrible. That's a terrible thing to do to yourself.
And Buddha has to come stop me. So Buddha gave me power.
How did she stop you?
I don't know how to explain it. She come down here.
But did you actually tie a rope up?
Yeah. But Buddha come down and turned me loose.
You were hanging?
Yeah.
And she turned you loose?
And come down and stopped me.
Did she say anything or do anything?
Yeah.
What did she say?
[???] Going be a long way to go. That's why I got power from Buddha,
Kuan Nim Posa.

[Recreation] 'The first time I tried to kill myself I was thirteen years
old. I tied a sheet to the ceiling in a circle I put my head in a circle. I
was hanging and Buddha stopped me. I was hanging and Buddha stopped
me. Buddha gave me power. She said "It's not your time yet." Though
my life was terrible. I tried to hang myself three times and each time
Buddha stopped me. Then I would fall asleep and dream of her. Kuan
Nim Posa.'

[Reverb. English translation over actuality spoken in Chinese] 'So
beautiful. She took me to heaven I flew up and up. My feet never
touched the ground. Her feet never touched the ground. And I saw
heaven. So beautiful. So beautiful. All different colors of people. No
houses, no trees. Just beautiful clouds. I didn't want to go back. I didn't
want to go back. But she said I had to. I didn't want to go back. But
she said it wasn't my time yet'.

Roberts returns to this scene two or three times during the course of the programme, for here she finds the pivotal symbolic event that explains her mother's
existence. In this use of incremental repetition and the condensation of multiple
events into a single story, the documentary again mirrors the nature of the oral
history interview and autobiographical reminiscence. Because audio, like speech
itself, is an oral medium, repetition is a natural and valuable technique for the
presentation of information.

Roberts's split focus on her mother and growing up with her mother also makes
explicit the dual focus and relationship between interviewer and interviewee.
Clearly, Roberts's relationship to her mother is much more intimate than that of
the typical oral historian or journalist and interviewee. But by foregrounding the
double focus she achieves the self-reflexivity so valued by many contemporary
scholars: not just to acknowledge the interviewer's role in the process but to incorporate oneself into the interpretation as a co-subject, if not of the history, then of
the creation of the historical document. Again, Roberts's motives are clear and

compelling. Her objective is to find out who she is, and why her mother is the way she is. And as shared traits appear in the course of the story, she notes for us those inheritances from her mother.

Roberts's open acknowledgement of purpose may be unappealing to scholars and journalists whose training in the 'objective' method has taught them to conceal their motives – not just from others but in some instances from themselves as well. But Roberts's dual focus is methodologically sound, historically rich, deeply personal, aesthetically engaging . . . and not at all pedantic or boring.

The second pivotal episode in *Mei Mei* – and final resolution to the story – comes in the form of a transformative moment shared by mother and daughter on a trip to Taiwan. Early in the piece Roberts tells how the time they were spending together in order for her to produce the piece had led to a renewal of the vicious bickering of her childhood. Indeed, it had reached the point that they stopped speaking to each other. Nonetheless, mother and daughter embarked on a trip back to Taiwan, for her mother to renew old ties and Roberts to meet unknown family members and better understand herself. Being the good documentary producer, Roberts kept her field recorder running. In an exchange recorded on their trip, we hear her mother burst into laughter at Roberts's attempt to speak in broken Chinese. 'The laughter', Roberts tells us, 'lasts longer than any memory I had held onto.' And so the programme, and Roberts's exercise in family oral history, reaches its resolution. The anger and separation of a Chinese mother and her Chinese-American daughter is replaced, however briefly, by a moment of sharing. The voyage did not, however, heal all the wounds between mother and daughter. Their struggles would continue. But Roberts's account of her own transformation does help make real the therapeutic capacities of family/oral history.[15]

Mei Mei: A Daughter's Story is but one example of how sound documentary producers have been attempting to think, and to author in sound. As new media and the ongoing digital revolution give rise to new forms of scholarly discourse, aural historians can, and should – indeed must – reconceive the established scholarly forms of written discourse in order to communicate effectively in sound, and in the emerging world of digital media.

Notes

1   The literature on the cognitive revolution brought about by the mass media is, of course, quite large. Neil Postman's, *Amusing Ourselves to Death*, New York: Penguin Books, 1985, is a very accessible and thought provoking, if highly biased, introduction. Broader early studies include H. Innis, *Empire and Communications*, originally published 1950, 1986 edition edited by D. Godfrey, Victoria, B.C.: Press Porcepic; and *The Bias of Communication*, Toronto: University of Toronto Press, 1964; M. McLuhan, *The Gutenberg Galaxy: The Making of Typographic Man*, Toronto: University of Toronto Press, 1962, and *Understanding Media: The Extensions of Man*, New York: McGraw-Hill, 1964; also W. Ong, *Orality and Literacy: The Technologizing of the Word*, New York: Methuen, 1982.

2   The Books on Tape industry – and aural historians – could learn much from radio drama producers. Outstanding among these is Tom Lopez of ZBS MEDIA, who weaves recordings gathered from all over the world into his beautifully produced and

imaginative audio dramas in a process he calls 'writing in sound'. For a good
introduction to Lopez see his 2002 interview with Roger Gregg at www.audio
theater.com/profiles/lopez.html.

3   I. Berlin, M. Favreau and S. Miller (eds), *Remembering Slavery: African Americans Talk
About Their Personal Experiences of Slavery and Emancipation*, New York: Free Press, 1998;
W.H. Chafe, R. Gavins and R. Korstad (eds), *Remembering Jim Crow: African Americans
Tell About Life in the Segregated South*, New York: Free Press, 2001. The *Remembering
Slavery* radio documentaries were produced by Smithsonian Productions, and the
Remembering Jim Crow programmes by Stephen Smith at American Radio Works.
See http://rememberingslavery.si.edu/audio.html and http://americanradioworks.
publicradio.org/features/remembering/.

4   Those who would author the history of the twentieth century in sound and multimedia
must sooner or later find their way to recorded sound collections. The Association
of Recorded Sound Collectors (ARSC) has since 1966 served as the organizational
umbrella for a national network of private record and tape collectors who hold an
encyclopaedic knowledge of the nation's sonic history. ARCS's mission is 'to promote
the preservation and study of historic recordings in all fields of music and speech'.
Sound archives also came of age in the 1990s. The Society of American Archivists
now has a well-organized and active sound archivists subgroup, which organizes
sessions and roundtables at annual meetings. The Museum of Radio and Television
in New York actively collected radio dramas and documentaries from both commercial and non-commercial networks and stations. An annotated listing of sound
collections can be found in the ARSC membership directory, which is published every
two years.

5   R. Rosenzweig, S. Brier and J. Brown, *Who Built America? From the Centennial
Celebration of 1876 to the Great War of 1914*, New York: American Social History
Productions Inc., The Voyager Company, 1993; *The Wall Street Journal* (9 September
1993), B1. Volume 2 of Rosenzweig *et al.*'s *Who Built America? From the Great War of
1914 to the Dawn of the Atomic Age in 1946* (American Social History Project in collaboration with the Center for History and New Media), included 45 minutes of
videotape and more than 7 hours of archival audio. To learn more see The American
Social History Project, Center for Media and Learning: www.ashp.cuny.edu/
index04.html.

6   W.S. Schneider, 'Blazing an interactive trail to record and preserve Alaska
history', *AHA Newsletter*, 1994, vol. 22, no. 2, pp. 3–5. For more examples of digital
media's potential to reshape historical scholarship, see P. Read, 'Presenting voices in
different media: print, radio and CD-ROM', in R. Perks and A. Thomson (eds),
The Oral History Reader, London: Routledge, 1998, pp. 414–420; M. O'Malley and
R. Rosenzweig, 'Brave New World or blind alley? American history on the world
wide web', *Journal of American History*, 1997, pp. 132–155; and S. Chodorow, 'The
medieval future of intellectual culture: scholars and librarians in the age of the
electron,' *ARL: A Bimonthly Newsletter of Research Library Issues and Actions*, December
1996.

7   See www.talkinghistory.org/. Zahavi also began to teach a radio documentary
production course, the syllabus for which he has placed online. This syllabus, updated
on a regular basis, is a unique and outstanding resource for anyone interested in aural
history. See 'Producing Historical Documentaries and Features for Radio', course
syllabus and online resource: www.albany.edu/faculty/gz580/documentaryproduc-
tion/index.html. *The Journal for MultiMedia History* is online at www.albany.edu/
jmmh/.

8   Editors' Introduction, 'I can almost see the lights of home: a field trip to Harlan County Kentucky', *Journal for MultiMedia History*, 1999, vol. 2, (www.albany.edu/jmmh/). 'I can almost see the lights of home' was also broadcast by WMMT, Mountain Community Radio, in Whitesboro, Kentucky. Volume 3 of the JMMH includes an oral history interview with Kitchen Sisters, the producers of *Lost and Found Sound*, the extraordinary radio documentary series on the history of recorded sound. The interview may be either read or listened to in its entirety. It also includes video excerpts of the interview, photographs, and weblinks.

9   Using parabolic speakers that isolate sound, and new digital technologies, museums in the 1990s began to make innovative use of sound progamming. At Ellis Island, for example, one may now dial up and listen to excerpts from hundreds of oral interviews conducted with men and women who entered the Unites States through the nation's most important port of entry.

10   Alcatraz Cellhouse Tour (cassette and booklet), ISBN 0962520632, may be obtained through the Golden Gates National Park Conservancy website at www.parks conservancy.org/detail.aspx?ID=127.

11   To learn more about acoustic ecology, see The Acoustic Ecology Institute www.acousticecology.org/; and the World Forum for Acoustic Ecology, http://interact.uoregon.edu/MediaLit/WFAE/home/index.html. For an introduction to the pioneering work done by R. Murray Schafer and the research group he organized at Simon Fraser University in the late 1960s, see The World Soundscape Project website, www.sfu.ca/~truax/wsp.html.

12   In the 1990s museums began to make innovative use of sound in their exhibits. The Civil Rights Museum in Birmingham, Alabama, for example, made very effective use of sound stations. Visitors could listen through a cracked door and shuttered window to a dramatic recreation of black families in 1963 talking in hushed tones about the turmoil taking place outside. A gallery early in the exhibit contained a series of figures outlined in glass suspended from the ceiling, whose voices fill the gallery from different locations, representing the wide variety of opinions about race relations held by Alabamans during the early years of the Civil Rights movement.

13   Essential reading for anyone interested in the structures and history of sound communication is R. Murray Schafer's *The Tuning of the World*, New York, Random House, 1977. For an analysis of Glenn Gould's pioneering work in radio documentary see Pamela Dean and Charles Hardy III, 'Oral history in sound and moving image documentaries', in L.E. Myers, R. Sharpless and T.L. Charlton (eds), *Research Handbook for Oral History*, Lanham, Md.: Rowman & Littlefield, 2006.

14   Tony Schwartz, *Media: The Second God*, New York: Random House, 1981, p. 170.

15   See D. Roberts, 'Working with success, struggle and doubt', *Current*, 12 December 1994, available at www.current.org/people/peop423r.html; and 'An interview with Dmae Roberts', www.thirdcoastfestival.org/pages/extras/interviews/2002/roberts.html.

Chapter 31

Dan Sipe

THE FUTURE OF ORAL HISTORY AND MOVING IMAGES

Oral historians continue to favour audio over video as their recording equipment of preference, partly through habit and concerns about the intruding presence of a camera (and camera operator), but also because of cost and skills deficit. This chapter surveys the field of film and video and argues that visual recording can yield additional meanings. Dan Sipe is a historian and film-maker who teaches at Moore College of Art and Design in Philadelphia. Reprinted from *Oral History Review*, Spring/Fall 1991, vol. 19, nos 1/2, pp. 75–87. © 1991, Oral History Association. All rights reserved. Used by permission.

A N EPOCH IN THE PRACTICE of history is coming to a close. For hundreds of years the printed word has been the dominant mode of communication for the historical profession, in the process shaping its basic assumptions and structures. Today, the printed word is being superseded by a diversity of communication forms with the greatest impetus coming from moving images. As a methodology rooted in multiple modes of communication, oral history can play a pivotal role in accelerating the historical profession's comprehension of this radical shift in the nature of communication. In return, moving images can more fully express oral history's reflexive dimension, which makes more explicit the human role in the creation of history. The relationship between moving images and oral history, always reciprocal, holds particular promise amidst the present revolution in communications.

A challenging manifestation of this change in communication is the rapidly growing disjunction between the practice of professionals based in academia and the practice of history in society. On the one hand we find history professionals who remain deeply wedded to writing, as they examine more areas and fields with more numerous and sophisticated methodologies than ever before. On the other hand, film and video, especially as broadcast on television, have spawned a staggering array of historical works which arguably are the major influence on the public's historical consciousness. Closer to home, consider the number of people creating family and local histories with moving pictures; better yet, note the number of video year-books for schools being produced. The glaring contradiction is that these two major trends have intersected very little: professional historians have had limited effect on the history presented through moving images; the changes in communication wrought by moving images have wielded even less influence on the historical profession.

The core of the conundrum lies in the role of communication in the history of history. The historical profession has always been structured around the medium of the written word. Writing and history have been synonymous, as evidenced by the word 'historiography'. Writing is an essential part of the 'deep structure' of the practice of history; it is the form of our content, but in Hayden White's words, we have not questioned 'the content of our form'.[1]

The practice of history as we conceive of it today began with the transition from orality to literacy, which led to written records and the earliest works we recognize as history.[2] The next great shift came with the advent of the printed word, which transformed society and the practice of history. As the era dominated by the printed word winds down, historians are faced with complicated questions about the use of a variety of mixed and changing forms of communication, ranging from simple audiotape to the promising complexities of videodiscs linked with computers.

The technologies of moving images are changing at a bewildering pace, yet history using moving images does not even have a rubric, a commonly agreed upon title. It is not that moving images have been rejected by historians. The majority of historians seem to find the concept of history using moving images at least somewhat intriguing and a goodly number are enthusiastic; historians seem to be accepting the idea of a relationship between moving images and history. The *Journal of American History* and the *American Historical Review* now print film reviews and articles on the subject, while the major historical associations have film committees, give awards to films, and even schedule sessions at their conventions. Valuable work has been done on the history of film and on analysis of films as evidence for social and intellectual history in journals such as *Film and History*. A very few historians such as Robert Rosenstone, Natalie Zemon Davis, Robert Brent Toplin, Daniel Walkowitz, and John O'Connor have invested time and energy considering the possibilities of film or video for serious, original historical work.[3] New York University, to take one encouraging example, now trains historians in the use of film and video as part of its public history program.

Yet this good will and interest add up to very few historians doing history through moving images. The barrier seems to be that the historical profession is structured around the medium of the written word and is somewhat insulated in its academic setting. And in fact, doing history with moving images presents a substantial challenge to this setting and its assumptions. As Robert Rosenstone notes, history on film and video 'is not history in the sense that academics think of it. It is history with different rules of representation, analysis, and modes of reading and comprehension that we do not yet fully understand.'[4] Moving images contradict the deep structures of the historical profession, and as a result historians do not yet have the training, the institutions, the motivations, the professional structures, or the categories to effectively use moving images. To do this, in truth, would require learning complicated new skills and undergoing a different type of socialization.

Why should historians make this change? Robert Rosenstone has offered an eloquent case for the sheer intellectual and artistic challenge of history using moving images. He suggests that film can offer an alternative that dramatically expands the possibilities of history. While acknowledging recent transformations of the practice of history, he points out that:

> We have changed the nature of history radically, but not the nature of
> the consciousness and hence the form that expresses that history. . . .
> The opportunity now [exists] for a new way of Seeing the Past. More
> radical because it breaks with form and not just with content.[5]

When discussing such issues, it is very easy to focus on film only as it affects the presentation or communication of history. But it may be just as important to consider its impact on historical evidence as such. The dominance of writing has been based on its power as a form of evidence – writing has been so central to history precisely because it nearly always creates a document. One writes on a surface which then constitutes a document, a piece of evidence. Moving images also automatically document themselves, and they offer extraordinary evidence. The experiments of Edward Muybridge photographing a running horse with multiple cameras remind us that the medium has its roots in the quest for superior evidence. The videotape of the police assault on Rodney King only reaffirms the potency of moving images as evidence.

However, for most historians motion pictures are irrelevant as direct evidence because none exist for their period. And for a substantial minority of historians of more recent times, film evidence exists as part of a stunning flood of data. Except for historians of film or those social and intellectual historians who use feature films as evidence of the spirit of a period, filmic evidence was also extremely limited until television generated an increased flow. Given the complexities of working with moving images discussed above and the lack of training, support, or rewards from the profession, understandably few historians who could use moving pictures as evidence have taken up the challenge. Historians are thus effectively cut off from utilizing the most powerful communication and evidentiary form of our time. The traditions and structures of the profession seem to militate against any major change. The one powerful exception is the rising field of oral history.

Oral history and moving images have considerable potential synergy. They intersect in two crucial and related ways. First, filmed or videotaped oral history demonstrates the possibilities of moving images as substantive evidence, linked to an interview's explicit articulation but carrying information and documentation in its own right. By encouraging such a focus on image as part of integral historical evidence, visual oral history can help lead historians away from the limited conception of moving images as merely an alternative form for evoking, communicating, or translating written history. Oral history can demonstrate the power of film and video as evidence while moving images provide a new level of evidence for oral history.

Secondly, moving images combined with oral history have a special power to encourage and support a comparative, reflexive approach to history itself. Historians have generally become more familiar with the notion of understanding a work of history as a construction, and of considering the variant ways in which historical works have been and might be constructed. But, ironically, writing has been so central in this that its centrality as a shaper of the construction process itself has been largely assumed and hence unexamined. Other modes of evidence and communication, in combination with or in juxtaposition to written texts, may help to encourage a much-needed examination of the assumptions and deep structures of history as a whole. Film and video can support the emerging reflexivity of oral history practice, and a more consciously developed relationship between oral history and moving images may thus enhance the quality and credibility of both and suggest new directions for historical practice as a whole.

Let us first consider evidence. Moving images with recorded sound constitute not merely supplemental, but definitively superior evidence for oral history, as well as the best example of the potential of film and video as evidence. For most of human history, an interview would be 'recorded' in another memory, or perhaps preserved as an oral tradition in a formalized tale with a memory aid such as a poetic form. Retelling was an indispensable component of such oral history. The written word came to provide a better documentary record, but audiotape has given modern oral history the capacity to revive the oral dimension, in the form of easily generated, mechanically accurate evidence that writing could not match. Oral history has, in effect, reintroduced orality as a mode of research and communication for doing history. Although oral history usually involves secondary orality, that is the orality stemming from recorded sound in a literate culture, it has begun to challenge the monopoly of the written word.[6]

The power of moving images extends this challenge in a number of significant ways that begin with the paradoxical realization that orality, at its core, is not purely a concept grounded in sound. The spoken word is embedded in a setting, a situation, a context. People speak with body language, expression, and tone. They respond to and refer to their setting and to objects. Many people learn to communicate not with the precision or brilliance of their words but with energy and effect – as interviewers often learn when they discover a vibrant interview reduced, in the transcript, to a series of leaden, banal sentences. And in historical research the loss is not randomly distributed: those most diminished by translation from speech to writing tend to be the less educated, the less formally articulate – those who are usually socially and politically the less powerful, the less heard.

The visual dimension of moving images counteracts this tendency, adding layers of expression and evidence as it captures human interaction and settings. In this sense film and video emerge as the most effective ways to record evidence for most oral historical purposes. This is not to say that all or even most interviews must be videotaped, but when the quality of the evidence is crucial and the interview is significant, moving images should be the first choice.

The word 'choice' suggests reflexivity, the second dimension noted above. It has become more widely recognized that what is so unusual about oral history as a historical field is that most of its evidence is not found but generated. Oral historians do more than document memory; they elicit it. In essence, oral history is the collaborative creation of evidence in narrative form between interviewer and narrator, between living human beings. To be fully descriptive historically, oral history should thus document not only the interview's explicit information, but the process itself. The dialogic relationship between interviewer and narrator, the role of memory, and the function of narrativity – all are central to how interviews illustrate the construction of history as a process. And all these aspects are more clearly revealed when moving images are used.

The interaction between the interviewer and the narrator is a crucial dimension of oral history, a point made most compellingly by Eva McMahan.[7] However, such interview relationships are difficult to decipher from a transcript, especially if not specifically discussed. Subtle cues of voice, posture, gesture, and eye contact, all the non-verbal indicators of affect, indicate the quality of a relationship, but few of those cues are generally transcribed. These aspects of an interview that are outside words – the 'unworded' dimensions – are crucial evidence if we take the dialogic aspect seriously. If videotaping is done purely for evidentiary research purposes, the interviewer should probably be included in the image unless there is some clear reason not to. When videotaped, the interviewer yields some control, becoming less of an interpreter while the viewer becomes more of one. Consequently, the viewer is empowered while the narrator's story is less mediated; he or she is in more direct communication with the audience. Interviewers could move to an even more reflexive style by inviting the narrator to reflect on the interview and the interviewer, perhaps at the end of the session.

The richer detail of videotaped interviews also records more fully the expression and process of memory generation. One can watch the external signs of the processes of memory and see whether the interviewer encourages, probes, or challenges the memory of the narrator – stances often communicated non-verbally. Oral historians always face the problematic of memory for history and cannot evade its deepest challenges by dealing with safely distanced memories recorded long ago.[8] The plastic nature of memory requires the fullest documentation of its presentation and for this no other medium can match moving images.

Moving images can also capture the creation and presentation of oral narrative. Oral historians are more likely to recognize narrativity as a mode of discourse because they help create it, and videotaped oral narrative offers particular opportunities for insight into this process. Hayden White, who has done more than any other historian to raise the question of narrativity, sees film as offering an opportunity to find an alternative mode of discourse.[9] In this respect, filmed oral history invokes three far from identical forms of narrativity – the written word, the spoken word, and the filmed word – that can be compared and contrasted for their historical implications. If moving images are used only to document interviews, the spoken word will inevitably have primacy. But when images are edited into constructed presentations, historians must also engage the logic of the filmed word, a primarily visual dimension with its own codes for how evidence can constitute and communicate historical statements.

The concern of oral historians with the dialogic role of the interviewer, memory, and narrativity thus all can be advanced by moving images as an additional mode of communication. Moving images also have more immediate, even prosaic advantages for oral historians. Film or videotape documentation can simplify the work of the interviewer. Instead of trying to conduct an interview while simultaneously grasping the setting, the relationships, and all the other unworded data, the oral historian can concentrate on the interview and study the footage later. The many benefits of using moving images for evidence easily outweigh apprehensions about cost, technical skills, or the effect of a camera on a narrator. More complicated aspects of filming or videotaping usually arise only when shooting for broadcast.

Why, then, have oral historians not become more actively engaged with moving images, even at the primary level of evidence gathering? The *Oral History Review* remains exceptional among the major oral history journals in systematically reviewing films and tapes and in following video developments. The *International Journal of Oral History* gave very intermittent coverage and *Oral History* rarely even mentions moving images. Disappointingly, the 1991 Oral History Association convention offered no sessions devoted to moving images, even though the OHA newsletter regularly reports the availability of tapes and films.

Some oral historians are videotaping interviews and even producing tapes, although they seem to have received relatively little recognition.[10] Some archives now use videotape regularly and accept videotapes as archival material. There is, then, a group of oral historians of undetermined size that recognizes the utility of video. Still, video seems to inhabit some sort of twilight zone: many oral historians at least tacitly accept its value and some even use it, but few deal with it or comment on it systematically. Eva McMahan has a short but thoughtful section in her recent book *Elite Oral History Discourse*, but even the revised version of Paul Thompson's fine overview *The Voice of the Past* fails to deal with film or video in a meaningful way. Since Thompson does give substantial attention to radio and even theater, it is clear that this represents a specific choice not to engage the potential role of moving images in oral history.[11]

More revealing is another significant book, Michael Frisch's *A Shared Authority*, which does deal perceptively with film and oral history. In several essays on films, Frisch adroitly discusses memory, the relationship between an audience and a work of oral history, and the American sense of history. Moreover, he understands film and television as media in subtle ways and assumes the importance and relevance of film and video to oral history. Frisch does not, however, discuss the role of the moving image in and of itself.[12] I suspect that a sizable group of sophisticated oral historians assume and accept a profound affinity between moving images and oral history just as Frisch does. They embrace it so thoroughly that they do not develop it. While their assumption is correct, all the dimensions of the affinity between oral history and film and video need to be examined.

My own awareness of the power of moving images for oral history springs from my work on a major filmed oral history research project documenting the recent history of a village in China.[13] Years of conceptualizing and editing documentary films from powerful interviews in a language I do not speak made me acutely aware of the visual dimension of oral history. The enthusiasm of leading scholars of modern Chinese history for the filmed interviews made me recognize the power of filmed oral history as evidence. Moreover, because everyone involved recognized that the material was singular, our work revolved around shaping the films to represent the interviews rather than using the interviews to illustrate a script. As a historian, I experienced the capacity of filmed oral history to add extra dimensions to interviews and to more fully communicate a narrator's story.

Most of the people interviewed for these films were Chinese peasants, uneducated or little educated, and every word they uttered had to be translated. Yet the films literally let them speak. The dramatic highpoint of *Small Happiness*, the documentary on women in the village, occurs when an old woman confesses to smothering her infant son years before because she had no food for him. But her words are just the bare outline. Her story is just as much told in her anguished expression, her tone, her pauses, her breathing, the way she holds her body.

Transcripts alone could not have communicated, as the combination of words and images can do, the pace, rhythm, or overlapping of interview dialogue. Three older women sitting in a row with bound feet are asked if as girls in pre-revolutionary China they had wanted their feet to be bound. Simultaneously, they erupt that of course they had wanted to. But it is the rapidity and simultaneity of their response, as well as their affect and tone, that tell us most about their feelings. For these peasants, the quintessential 'unheard' people, the visual dimension is absolutely crucial to their stories, and moving images lessen the mediating role of the interviewer.

It is similarly easy to find examples, in recent films, of how images can help document and unfold complex evidence, rendering transparent the relationship between interviewer and narrator and thus opening to audiences the process of historical construction. *Twenty Years Later* is a Brazilian film made in 1985 by Eduardo Coutinho.[14] The film had its genesis in a radical docudrama that began shooting in 1964 and recreated the murder of a peasant organizer. Many radical peasants including Elizabeth, the organizer's wife, played themselves, with Coutinho serving as director. The coup of 1964 ended the filming, the footage was seized by military, and the participants fled the area. Twenty years later, the footage was returned to Coutinho, now a successful filmmaker. He set out to find the participants and discover what had happened to them, all the while documenting the process of the search. The film pivots on tracking down the widow who had to give up most of her children and had lived anonymously in a tiny village for years. The cost to this family of their parents' courageous politics is palpable. The wife now eschews politics, with one of her sons leading her through a litany of apolitical views. Silences, pacing, and affect are once again key. The cost to the woman shows on her face. Her banal words are telling precisely because of the lifeless way she presents them, especially when juxtaposed with footage of her earlier incarnation as a firebrand.

In the film Coutinho shows the old footage of the dreary, romanticized docudrama to its erstwhile stars; we see them, and we see them seeing themselves. Moreover, we witness a transformation of the filmmaking style from a heavily directed work to a much more reflexive one. The peasants in the new film are unscripted and undirected. The film crew, and Coutinho as director and inter-viewer, play their roles openly in front of the camera. Moreover, the wife who lost her husband, her children and her very name is now at the center rather than her martyred husband. Inescapable to viewers is the chasm of privilege between her and Coutinho, between two classes, between artist and subject. Coutinho may restore her name and reunite a tattered family, but these things are gifts that he has the power to bestow. Even though he opposes those with real power in Brazil, Coutinho has prospered and has much more control, much more power than his interview subject. Elizabeth controls only the expression of her memory. If she seems wary and cautious, if she sounds bowed and almost broken, that is her decision. Publicly expressed memory can be perilous; her memory is situational not out of politeness but out of an experience of danger and vulnerability. Any interviewer working from the bottom up has a privileged position, but Coutinho's privilege has a history – to his credit he does nothing to soften or conceal it. No matter how great his desire to empower, to listen, to help, there is a grotesque imbalance between them that film can express clearly and straightforwardly.

This power of the interviewer-historian-filmmaker is expressed in the last scene when the film crew is finally leaving and the woman who has suffered so much, who has been silenced for years and has only cautiously spoken, sees the car pull away. Finally, Elizabeth bursts out with an affirmation of her radicalism. Coutinho, the man with the car, with the camera, pulls away from this old woman; and the positioning, the objects, the affect are central as she finally speaks her mind and redefines herself and the film. It is an extraordinary moment, which even a very capable writer would find difficult to evoke and a transcript could not imaginably convey – but even a mediocre cameraperson would be able to capture it. This scene is emblematic of the power of moving images as evidence and reflexivity, for its ability to capture a density of evidence beyond any other form.

A similarly fine example of how filmed oral history can engage the problem of memory and subjectivity, so central to oral history, is Lise Yasui's *Family Gathering*, a documentary of the internment of her Japanese-American father's family during World War II.[15] Yasui opens the film with what turns out to be her mistaken memory of meeting her Japanese grandfather as a small child; we see him as she did in numerous home movies. Then she tells us of learning that he died before she could meet him, but that she still feels that in some sense the meeting took place; we ponder the ways in which we 'know' the past: home movies, useful or satisfying memories, our memories of other people's memories. Clearly, memory has a constructed and plastic aspect: we wonder what is the purpose and meaning of Yasui's faulty memory of her grandfather.

She then goes on to tell a tale of the family's internment, with a particular focus on her grandfather's imprisonment without trial as a dangerous person. What sets the film apart is that Yasui documents the process of trying to get information from her family, of pushing to expose their memory of experiences and issues they had never talked about. Finally, late one night, her father reveals to her that the grandfather had committed suicide years after the war, never having recovered from the humiliation of an unjustified imprisonment. So history is about inquiry, and memory is the pivot – both Yasui's naive, constructed memory of her grandfather and the edited, controlled, repressed memory of her family. Throughout, the visual images she offers are central to the tension and paradoxes of these relationships, as she and the family lived them over time and express them in the moment of the film's examination. In this way, the film succeeds powerfully in capturing the complexity of memory as we really live with it.

Filmmakers such as Coutinho and Yasui have almost instinctively used oral history as evidence; their presentations have begun to explore some of the key questions for oral history as a whole. Yet the discussion of the relationship between oral history and moving images is only beginning. As historians come to give increasingly serious consideration to the potential of film and video both as evidence and as a mode for communicating historical narrative and interpretation, oral history has a pivotal role to play: it offers perhaps the clearest route to appreciating the power of filmed and videotaped historical evidence. And it is the historical methodology most open to multiple modes of communication, most able to reveal the reflexive dimensions of the historical process.

The goal is not the overthrow or displacement of the printed word, but rather to have the moving images of film and video recognized as generating discrete modes of discourse with their own ways to encode information, express concepts, and embody ambiguity and certainty. Developed in this way, moving images provide a counterpoint to writing that can reveal the underlying assumptions of much of our historical practice and make transparent some of history's basic methods. Ultimately, this approach is consonant with a conception of history based on multiple methodologies, varied forms of evidence, and diverse modes of discourse. No single approach or form would dominate, but forms could be used fluidly depending on the goals of the historical inquiry, spurring the development of a variety of hybrid forms.

With film and video recognized as a means of actually 'doing' history, the ongoing transformation of the practice of history can continue to advance in some intriguing new ways. Oral history already has nudged the historical profession in new directions; increasing recognition and use of moving images can help it push both inquiry and historical communication even farther. To this end, the time has come for sustained, systematic description, discussion, and analysis of how moving images can work as an integral dimension of oral historical practice.

Notes

1   H. White, *The Content of the Form*, Baltimore: Johns Hopkins University Press, 1987.

2   W.J. Ong, *Orality and Literacy*, London: Methuen, 1982.

3   For representative pieces by Rosenstone, Toplin, and O'Connor, see the 'AHR Forum' in *American Historical Review*, 1988, vol. 93, pp. 1173–1227. Also, see N. Zemon Davis, 'Any resemblance to persons living or dead: film and the challenge of authenticity', *Yale Review*, Summer 1987, vol. 76, pp. 457–482. Toplin and Walkowitz are among the few historians who are also filmmakers.

4   R.A. Rosenstone, 'Revisioning history: contemporary filmmakers and the construction of the past', *Comparative Studies in Society and History*, 1990, vol. 32, p. 837.

5   R.A. Rosenstone, 'What you think about when you think about writing a book on history and film', *Public Culture*, 1990, vol. 3, p. 64.

6   W.J. Ong, *Interfaces of the Word*, Ithaca: Cornell University Press, 1977, pp. 53–81.

7   E.M. McMahan, *Elite Oral History Discourse*, Tuscaloosa: University of Alabama Press, 1989.

8   D. Thelen, 'Memory and American history', *Journal of American History*, 1989, vol. 75, pp. 1117–1129.

9   H. White, *Metahistory*, Baltimore, Johns Hopkins University Press, 1973, *Tropics of Discourse: Essays in Cultural Criticisms*, Baltimore: Johns Hopkins University Press, 1978, and *The Content of the Form*, Baltimore: Johns Hopkins University Press, 1987, and 'Historiography and historiophoty', *American Historical Review*, vol. 93, pp. 1193–1199.

10 P.M. Henson and T.A. Schorzman, 'Videohistory: focusing on the American past', *Journal of American History*, 1991, vol. 78, pp. 618–627.

11 McMahan, *Elite Oral History Discourse*, pp. 108, 113–117, and Paul Thompson, *The Voice of the Past*, Oxford: Oxford University Press, 1988.

12   M. Frisch, *A Shared Authority*: *Essays on the Craft and Meaning of Oral and Public History*, Albany: State University of New York Press, 1990.

13   R. Gordon and C. Hinton, *One Village in China* [The Long Bow Trilogy: *Small Happiness*, *All Under Heaven*, *To Taste a Hundred Herbs*], New Day Films, 1985–1988. See *OHR* Media Forum discussing this project, Fall 1988, vol. 15, no. 2.

14   E. Coutinho, *Twenty Years Later*, Cinema Guild, 1984.

15   L. Yasui, *Family Gathering*, New Day Films, 1988.

Chapter 32

Anna Green

THE EXHIBITION THAT SPEAKS FOR ITSELF
Oral history and museums

Museums have taken a major role in collecting and presenting personal testimonies over the past twenty years, and some have rooted their whole collecting policy and exhibition strategy in oral history, particularly where artefacts are absent or as a corrective to a public history warped by state-based terrorism and repression. Yet oral history continues to struggle for prioritized resources. This chapter about a community-based exhibition succinctly demonstrates the impact of oral history. Anna Green is Head of the School of Social Sciences at Auckland University of Technology, New Zealand. This chapter was first presented as a paper at the US Oral History Association conference in October 1996 and a version appeared in *Oral History Review*, Winter 1997, vol. 24, no. 2, pp. 53–72.

I S IT POSSIBLE TO construct a museum exhibition structured around sound and storytelling? This is the question we faced early in 1995, following the completion of a large oral history project on the community of Frankton Junction, New Zealand. Over the previous eighteen months my graduate oral history class recorded about two hundred life histories with men and women who had lived and worked in this railway community, once the largest railway junction in New Zealand. In addition to the interviews, we had sought permission to borrow and copy photographs of everyday life from family photograph albums. Despite the gradual dispersion of the railway workforce over previous decades, the response was overwhelming, and the oral testimonies and photographs combined to create a rich account of life in a working-class railway community from the 1920s to 1970s. A grant from the Environment and Heritage Fund of the New Zealand Lottery Board then made it possible to return the history to the community in the form of an exhibition.

Determined to make the oral history the central focus for the exhibition, but having no previous experience in museums, I began research with a small team of graduate students, exploring the journals and handbooks on social history in museums. Was it possible to construct an exhibition around oral testimonies presented in audio, not transcript, form? There was virtually nothing to be found on this subject. Stuart Davies's comment in 1994 that 'oral history occupies an ambivalent, uncomfortable and vulnerable position in museums' seemed to be an understatement.[1] For example, a handbook for museum professionals, frequently cited in the British and New Zealand literature, contains one short chapter on oral history. Two-thirds of this chapter is devoted to the inherent unreliability and flawed nature of memory, and the author finally concludes that oral history has limited value and may best be presented, heavily contextualised, in a separate 'library' space.[2]

The journal articles indicated that most social history museum curators continue to perceive oral history as, at best, a useful adjunct to the material object collections. 'History provision without objects would be and usually is something else . . . objects make museums', wrote one museum curator in 1993.[3] The role of objects in stimulating reminiscence among visitors has received favourable comment.[4] But when oral history was incorporated into exhibitions, the spoken word was usually transformed into text on walls, and consequently lost the multi-layered complexities and entrancing vigour of oral narration. On those occasions when oral history remained in its original form, it frequently accompanied a recreation of social or working life and as a consequence sound was defeated by the busy visual panorama and became little more than background noise. None of this does justice to oral history, nor the importance of memory as a living, active engagement between past and present. Memories should not be regarded like shards of pots, inert fragments from a long-dead past. As Michael Frisch has suggested, we need to 'involve people in exploring what it means to remember, and what to do with memories to make them active and alive, as opposed to mere objects of collection'.[5]

To achieve this, the memories must become the central focus of an exhibition or display. The Frankton exhibition team decided to try and construct a museum exhibition using oral testimonies as an oral source: in other words sound and listening would take precedence over sight and looking. We shared the conviction that creating a highly detailed stage-setting can distract visitors from listening to the oral testimonies. Furthermore, we did not wish to allow surviving material objects, or photographs, to determine the direction and content of the exhibition. The oral testimonies focussed upon human relationships at home and at work, drawing upon the whole range of human experience. The photographs, in contrast, primarily recorded special and happy family occasions, or masculine work or sporting culture. Only one set of photographs, taken by a professional photographer of his wife, recorded the experience of married women engaged in household work, in contrast to the strength of these memories in the oral histories. While there were many photographs of children at play, there were none, of course, of corporal punishment, or the ritual exchange of insults on the way to school between Catholics and Protestants. Consequently the themes for the exhibition were derived from the oral histories, and the lack of correspondence between the audio and visual aspects of the exhibition, apparent in nearly every section, was briefly discussed in the accompanying written guide.

The oral history exhibition

The exhibition was a co-operative venture with the staff at the Waikato Museum of Art and History, whose design, photographic and technical expertise were invaluable.[6] A special graduate class also worked with me on the exhibition, and their individual and collective contribution to the project is gratefully acknowledged.[7]

The shape of the gallery space, and the desire to create five separate sections to the exhibition, determined the final plan, which is shown in Figure 1.

Technical problems

The principal technical problem we had to overcome was that of making the oral history accessible and audible, while minimising sound bleeding in a relatively open-plan exhibition. We did not want any barrier, such as the requirement to use earphones, to stand between the visitor and the oral history. Furthermore, it was essential that the visitor was comfortable while listening, and this indicated the need to use seating. We were fortunate to be loaned old red railway seats, temporarily

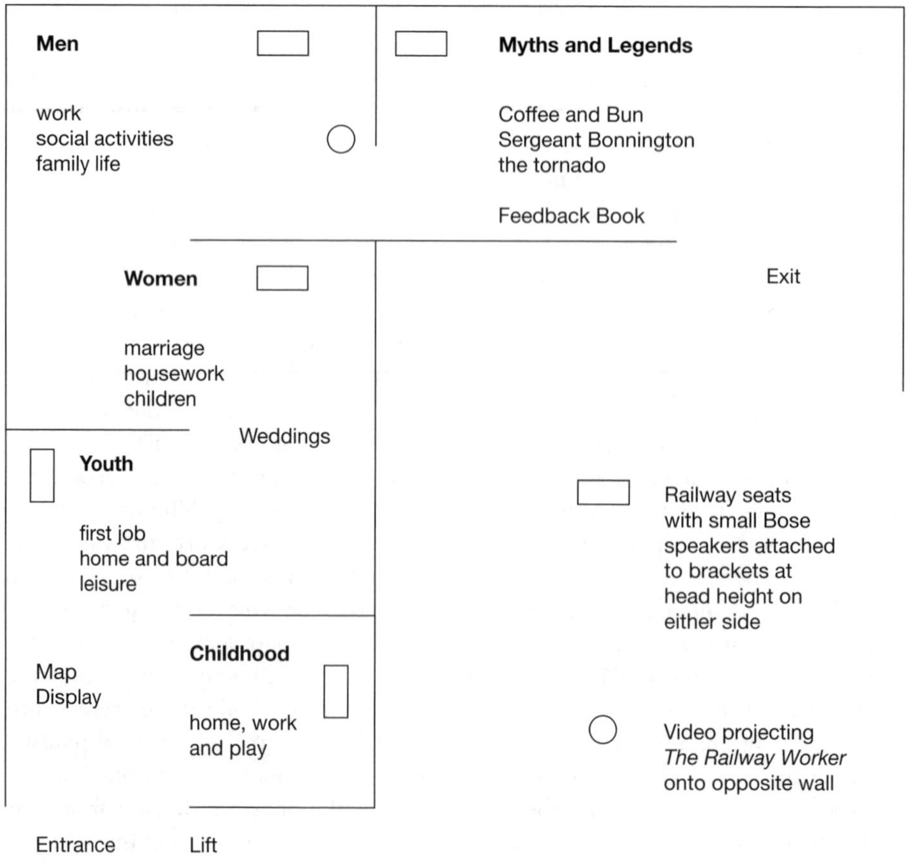

Figure 1 Final plan of the exhibition

removed from carriages undergoing renovation, by the Waikato Branch of the New Zealand Railway and Locomotive Society. Each seat became an independent sound unit, with the CD player hidden underneath. The oral histories were transmitted through robust bookshelf-sized speakers, with internal amplifiers, attached to brackets at ear-level on either side of the seat. Placing the speakers in this way reduced the volume necessary for comfortable listening, and sound bleeding between sections was negligible. To further emphasise the oral history, the lighting was deliberately subdued. The walls were painted a dark green, and both the railway seats and the surrounding photographs were illuminated by spotlights.

Exhibition goals

We began with three goals for the oral history exhibition:

- to represent as fully as possible the diverse range of oral testimony;
- to encourage visitors to reflect upon their own memories;
- to enable visitors to contribute their own responses and memories.

The extent to which we were able to achieve these goals was dependent upon a number of factors, including the principles of selection, editing and sequencing developed as we worked our way through the tapes. Following advice from the curatorial staff we agreed that the whole exhibition should only be approximately one hour in length, therefore each of the five sections could only use ten minutes of recordings. This entailed selecting, in total, under sixty minutes of oral history from the three hundred hours or more recorded! For the first four sections on children, youth, men and women, we decided to include material on the three broad themes of family life, work and leisure. With ten minutes' playing time, only two or three quotations could be included on each particular topic. The childhood section, for example, finally consisted of twenty oral history extracts, roughly half a minute each in length.

Selection

To represent the diverse range of experience within the oral testimonies with an oral history cohort of this size was going to be an immense problem from the start. Our first decision was to include only firsthand experience as far as possible. This reduced the pool of information on any one theme to more manageable proportions. Sound quality also eliminated some recordings, and played a far greater role in the selection process than we would have liked. We found that it took very little extraneous noise to render a recording unusable for exhibition purposes. A panting fox terrier, chiming clock and intrusive interviewer rendered some oral histories unusable.

But we were still left with many more stories than we could include. Two criteria in particular became central to the choices we subsequently made. The first related to the context – an exhibition – and the need to interest a wide range of people. We tried to choose topics within the themes that would have most appeal to a contemporary audience. Although we agreed that the broad themes of work, family life, and play/community activities should form the internal skeleton for the first four sections, there were of course many different aspects to these themes from which we could have chosen. Stories which appeared to offer the most interesting options for engaging with the present-day audience through lively narration, humour or emotion tended to survive the radical selection process in which we were constantly engaged.

The second criterion was based upon the weight of evidence within the oral testimonies themselves. We decided to make representativeness the major criterion for inclusion. Subjects and perspectives dominant within the testimonies were selected (linked by a minimalist narrative smoothing the transition from one subject to another). This may seem, on the face of it, rather indefensible, particularly in a postmodern world. There were, however, positive aspects to this approach. The choice of representative stories did enable us to strengthen the focus of the exhibition. An example of this is evident in the childhood section. Nearly every interview described incidents of severe corporal punishment, either at school or at home. These accounts are profoundly moving, indicating that experiences of physical violence can remain a source of mental anguish throughout life:

> People always hammered their kids in those days, I mean, God, my mother used to take to me with the bloody stock whip actually and she used to beat the living hell out of me, I mean, . . . just because I bloody well annoyed her, you know. But it was the thing that was done.[8]

> I was the one who always got the hidings, I think, only because I used to answer him back . . . I can remember one occasion when I was up the road where I used to play at the end of Lake Road, which was only just up round the corner, and I was coming home, it was dark, my father yelled out to me, 'hurry up', I said, 'I'm coming', when I got to the back door he was waiting behind the back door and let me have it. I was bruised all over.[9]

The disadvantage of selecting representative stories lay in the risk of stereotyping experience. This was most problematic in the section on women, where housework and motherhood dominated the accounts almost to the exclusion of all else. Gaby Porter has rightly warned us about the risks of representing women's lives with a narrow domestic focus.[10] We had no desire to reinforce a conservative popular belief that a married woman's place is in the home. But it was important that we remained faithful to the experiences repeatedly described in the oral testimonies. These were dominated by descriptions of the hard physical work involved in looking after a house and family of five or six children, prior to the widespread ownership of refrigerators, gas or electric ovens and washing machines. Such accounts make the indispensable contribution of working-class women to the household economy transparently obvious. Heating the copper and washing everything by hand, scrubbing the floors and cooking meals on a wood- or coal-fired stove at irregular times for family members on shiftwork showed that household labour was time-consuming and physically arduous in the middle decades of the century.[11] The contrast with housework in contemporary society is implicit within the testimonies, and challenges facile comparisons with the present.

Editing

Editing the tapes for inclusion within the exhibition involved both technical and ethical considerations. We were fortunate in having access to the Pro-Tools computer software on which to edit the tapes, but the process took far longer, and was far more expensive, than had been anticipated. To transfer the recordings from analogue to digital audiotape, and edit every oral history extract, took approximately five days. I had budgeted for five hours. The interviews were conducted in the homes of the interviewees, and consequently while the quality of sound was generally quite good, individual voice levels fluctuated enormously. We tried to make the sound levels more consistent, so that listeners would not have difficulty adjusting between loud and quiet voices, but this was only possible to a limited extent. However, we were able to remove interjections, irritating laughter and extraneous noises, when they did not overlap with the voice of the interviewee. While students recording the interviews had been asked to confine themselves to non-verbal responses (smiling, nodding), many did not. Yet those students who engaged actively with the interviewee, through humour and shared interests, created a rapport and environment that appeared to elicit much more lively and extended storytelling. Although these stories required more extensive editing, they became the backbone of the exhibition.

While constructing the exhibition tapes, we were also aware of the need to protect the personal authenticity of people's memories. It is important not to distort the intentions of the interviewee, or alter the tenor of their testimony. Editing the extracts for inclusion on the exhibition tape became a matter of balancing the desire for short, dramatic or effective extracts with the narrator's provision of an explanatory or ambivalent conclusion to these stories. The following example of this dilemma is taken from the section on men, where Matt Andrew discovered that while some celebrated the male work culture, others were less sure:

> – but, again, it was wrapped up with the job you were doing, and as an indication of how you became isolated from your family, I was working in the lounge one night on some papers and an argument developed at the kitchen sink with the son and the daughter and my wife, and I could hear it of course. I thought, now, the next thing that's going to happen is that we'll get Dad. The discussion and the argument went on and it was resolved, and I was still sitting there. I suddenly realized that I had become an extension of the family, and that I was no longer involved in the decision-making process. I was no longer involved in the discipline of it.

The first version of the tape extract ended at this point, and the focus of the story is sharp and clear. However, the interviewee goes on to say:

> And whilst that may be comforting to some people, it was disturbing to the extent that I resolved that I would resign, I would not stand at the next election for national counsellor.[12]

The inclusion of the final statement may have detracted slightly from the impact of the story. But it helps to explain why the narrator chose to retell this particular experience, for it was the catalyst that made him resolve to give up his position within the railway union. In so doing, the attention of the listener is drawn to the narrative purpose which often underlies our stories about the past.

Sequencing

The sequencing of the recordings may also enable the curator to illustrate other aspects of storytelling in oral history. This was of particular relevance in the final exhibition section – on Frankton myths and legends – which drew upon the imaginative and collective dimensions of memory. One of the legends concerned the 1948 tornado, which caused considerable damage, and was responsible for the deaths of three people. It was remembered by virtually everyone, and the stories were a combination of direct experience, hearsay and imagination. Jane Moodie wished to illustrate the evolution of community myth, through which accounts of the tornado acquired the patina of repeated narration and were characterised by humour and exaggeration. From the wide range of possible stories, she chose examples which gradually moved from the prosaic to the much more imaginative:

> When the tornado struck we were right in the middle of it and of course the whole roof went off the house, but the ceiling was left and it was just full of about four or five inches of this greasy railway soot. And of course then there was a really heavy rain came after the passing of the tornado, and it just washed all this sticky, dirty, greasy soot just came down the walls and on to everything in the house. It was unbelievable.[13]

> But Mrs Hill down the road actually, they had a rotary clothesline, and her husband was a guard on the railway, and she heard this terrible roaring, you see, and she went outside to see what it was. And here was the clothesline about fifty feet up in the air, going round and round, and round and round, and round, and she had Johnny's railway overalls pinned to the line – and it was going round and round and round, and the overalls were standing straight out.[14]

> Yeah, I was there, right in it. We were playing up in Seddon Park and we went down to Frankton and watched the house where the railway line crossing Lake Road is, my sister and me, and we actually saw the house get picked up and taken across the railway, and the people sitting at the table having their tea.[15]

Interaction

Finally, we hoped that the exhibition as a whole would encourage visitors to reflect upon their own lives and memories, and make comparisons with their experiences in the present. In particular, we wondered whether a younger generation would compare the memories of the earlier generation with their own experience and current orthodoxies about family and working life. The recollections of shift-work, and the havoc it played upon the ability of men to play an active role in family life, have as much relevance now as in the past. Questions such as these were raised within the printed exhibition guide. This provided a brief summary of each section, concluding with a couple of questions intended to elicit comparisons with visitors' own experiences. The section on men, for example, read:

> Shiftwork dominated the daily experience of those men who worked for New Zealand Railways. The long, irregular hours adversely affected their family lives. Jobs on the railways were keenly sought after, however, for these offered both security of employment and opportunities for advancement. A hierarchy based upon skill divided the workforce, while a powerful camaraderie existed among workmates.
> * How would you define the roles of the husband and father today? Do they differ from the roles apparent in the memories recounted here?
> * Do irregular working hours have an impact upon your family?

We thought that questions such as these might encourage people to contribute their ideas to the exhibition. Limited resources meant that we could not record oral histories in the museum, and so we opted for a book with written comments at the end of the exhibition.

The book contains pages and pages of comments and memories, from both older and younger visitors. Virtually none directly address the questions posed in the exhibition guide, a lesson perhaps for the didactic curator! Many entries begin, 'I remember', which suggests that the exhibition did encourage the audience to reflect on their own memories or those of their parents or grandparents. Some visitors described encounters they observed within the exhibition space: men and women sharing memories, or sitting on the railway seats and engaging in one-sided arguments with the oral history! Others found the exhibition profoundly moving, with one visitor writing simply, 'I cried, memories of feelings.' Very few entries indicate discomfort with the absence of objects, while many expressed satisfaction with the focus of the exhibition along the lines of the following entires: 'Real history – good to hear people giving their own version of what happened', and 'Wonderfully interesting exhibition, more should be made of oral histories.'

Conclusion

Is it possible to construct an exhibition around oral history in an audio form? The Franklin Junction exhibition suggests that the answer is a resounding yes. The oral testimonies communicated directly with each visitor, and conveyed a richness of experience and imagination which was sufficient to capture their interest. The subjects, family life, childhood and work, have resonance for us all. People will sit and listen, if the stories interest them and the environment is comfortable and inviting. There is no need to banish oral history to the walls, listening posts, booths, earphones or, worse still, libraries!

For the museum itself, the exhibition significantly increased attendance and attracted many who had never visited before. However, the human resource devoted to this exhibition far exceeded those normally available to museum staff. Combining the project with my graduate teaching programme, and acquiring external funding, made it possible to record large numbers of people, work our way through the tapes, and construct the exhibition within the space of two and a half years. Returning the history to the community has to be done within a reasonably short time-frame, if most of the contributors are to live to hear it. 'Love, Labour and Legend' was the result of a rewarding collaboration between academic historians and museum staff in the sphere of public history. I hope that there will be many more exhibitions that speak for themselves in the future.

Notes

1   S. Davies, 'Falling on deaf ears? Oral history and strategy in museums', *Oral History*, Autumn 1994, vol. 22, no. 2, p. 74.

2   G. Griffiths, 'Oral history', in D. Fleming, C. Paine and J. Rhodes (eds), *Social History in Museums: A Handbook for Professionals*, London: HMSO, 1993, pp. 111–116.

3   G. Cavanagh, 'The future of museum social history collecting', *Social History in Museums*, 1993, vol. 20, p. 61.

4   J. Urry, 'How societies remember the past', in S. Macdonald and G. Fyfe (eds), *Theorizing Museums*, Oxford: Blackwell/The Sociological Review, 1996, p. 50.

5   M. Frisch, *A Shared Authority: Essays on the Craft and Meaning of Oral and Public History*, New York: State University of New York Press, 1990, p. 27.

6   In particular, Sally Parker (Senior Curator), Michele Orgad (Exhibitions Manager), Max Riksen (Designer), Stephanie Leeves (Photographer), Kent Eriksen (Exhibition Preparator).

7   The members of the exhibition graduate class were Matt Andrew, Chanel Clarke, Sue Garmonsway and Jane Moodie.

8   Frankton Oral History Project (FOHP), interview 172, tape 1, side B, 39.4 m.

9   FOHP, interview 157, tape 1, side B, 18.6 m.

10   G. Porter, 'Putting your house in order: representations of women and domestic life', in R. Lumley (ed.), *The Museum Time Machine*, London: Routledge, 1988, pp. 102–127.

11   See S. Garmonsway, 'Just a wife and mother: the domestic experiences of Frankton women, 1940–1960', unpublished MA thesis, University of Waikato, 1996.

12   FOHP, interview 022, tape 1, side B, 7.1 m.

13   FOHP, interview 014, tape 1, side B, 17.6 m.

14   FOHP, interview 172, tape 1, side B, 28.2 m.

15   FOHP, interview 187, tape 1, side B, 6.0 m.

Chapter 33

Toby Butler and
Graeme Miller

LINKED: A LANDMARK IN SOUND,
A PUBLIC WALK OF ART

Collaborations between audio artists and oral historians are becoming more common and new technology is enabling recorded memories to be presented in innovative ways in a variety of public spaces, encouraging a shifting and dynamic reflection of memory and place that embraces new audiences. As part of postgraduate research in cultural geography at Royal Holloway, University of London, Toby Butler worked with Graeme Miller, a well-known theatre-maker, artist and composer. Reprinted from *Cultural Geographics*, 2005, vol. 12, pp. 77–88. © Edward Arnold (Publishers) Ltd (www.hodderarnoldjournals.com).

IN 2003 A NEW PERMANENT public art installation, *Linked*, by Graeme Miller, was established along a four-mile motorway in East London.[1] This is a discussion of *Linked* by Toby Butler, followed by Graeme Miller's account of his work in their conversation about the project.

I am getting off the tube at Leyton. It is nearly four o'clock on a cold autumn day. Soon the narrow platform will be filling with schoolchildren. I hurry up the steps to the exit. I put the battery that I took out of the smoke alarm this morning into the tiny radio receiver. I put the spongy headphones on. No sound, but the sponge helps warm up my ears. I walk through the ticket office, and out on to the street. Mostly I can see traffic – cars, buses, taxis. I take a few steps along the pavement. Suddenly I hear music, a voice in my head. I am startled – of course, the headphones. They are working already! A violin is softly playing two notes repetitively. A male voice is talking about a plan for a supermarket – he says it will obliterate the local economy. He says his house will be made into a motorway. I am looking down on an enormous Asda. It looks like it has just opened. I realise I am standing on a big road bridge. It passes over the Central line and a busy motorway. The traffic is barely moving on one side of the carriageway.

I walk back to the tube station, which is on the highest point of the bridge, to get better reception. The violin is still playing, and a brass hand bell rings occasionally, gentle, powerful music. A Cockney voice asks: 'Where's London? Where's London?' He goes on to say: 'The only time my dad ever got somewhat emotional was when he thought of the war. And he was a fire warden. He went and stood on the bridge at Leyton tube station. And the whole of London was on fire.'

I look over to the tower blocks and skyscrapers on the horizon. It is a view of London I haven't seen before. The sun is ready to start its descent behind the city. The voice says: 'And it was burning from stem to stern. And you could smell the burning flesh. And you could feel the heat.'

I start to feel slightly choked up. A strange wave of emotion passes through my body. '"Where's London? Where's London?" These people were from Blackpool and then the fire engine had come down from Glasgow. And this bloke said to him, "Where is London mate?" And my dad said to him. "There it is mate. There it is mate." I look. There it is.'

The voice continues: 'We are finished. No, we are not finished. We are not finished. And my dad said no. They can bomb us, they can burn us, but they will never break us. And that was my dad's attitude. And my mum's attitude. My old mum said they will never break us. No. We will pick ourselves up and sort ourselves out.'[2]

I pace up and down the bridge. It is cold: I dig my hands into my coat pockets. Listen, I look. I stare in at the people slowly driving their cars. They don't know what is going on, what I am experiencing. They haven't got a clue. They don't realise that they are walk-on parts in the play today. They are driving over the ruins of a community. A part of London that was flattened. Not by bombs – the 350 homes were predominantly Victorian terrace houses that survived the Blitz. They were flattened slowly by earth movers, cherry-pickers, bulldozers. The homes were flattened for a road-building scheme designed to provide a faster route for traffic to get into London and remove traffic from local roads. I am standing above the M11 link road which, by the time it opened on 6 October 1999, had displaced a thousand people.[3]

As I stare at the new road four years later, another voice speaks to me from my earphones. 'I know that if my house was still there, it would be hanging in space above the inside northbound lane. I can still feel myself in that place, that bit of air, the place where I lay down to go to bed, the place where I had showers, I feel a bit naked suspended in the air there.'[4]

Linked, by Graeme Miller, is subtitled 'a landmark in sound, an invisible artwork, a walk.'[5] It is also an outdoor exhibition, a journey into the past and present and an extraordinary use of oral history recordings. It consists of 20 transmitters, mounted on lampposts along the borders of a six-lane motorway in east London. The transmitters continuously broadcast recorded testimonies from people who once lived and worked where the motorway now runs. The broadcasts can be heard with the aid of a small receiver which is available free of charge from local libraries. The range of the transmitters varies according to the terrain, but can generally be heard within 50 metres of the lampposts. A map of the walking trail is handed out with the receivers; it follows neighbouring roads along the route, frequently passing next to or over bridges across the motorway which give dramatic views of the road and the surrounding landscape.

Linked is funded by, amongst others, the Heritage Lottery Fund and the Museum of London. The involvement of bodies devoted principally to history in a contemporary arts project might be surprising to some. But several aspects of the project were extremely attractive to the Museum. First, *Linked* involved the gathering of 120 hours of in-depth oral history interviews that will be added to the Museum's important collection of recorded interviews with Londoners. The museum had already been given a large collection of photographs and documents by the 'No M11 Link' campaign in 1999. Secondly, the installation, which spans nearly four miles of Leyton, Leytonstone and Wanstead in east London, provided the opportunity to display history away from the museum, and a series of related exhibitions were prepared by the museum for display in four libraries along the route. Finally, *Linked* was not the first site-specific artwork to enter the museum's collection – for around 15 years the museum has actively collected works of urban art.[6]

Linked also fitted in nicely with the Museum's 'Voices' programme of lottery funded activities designed to reach new audiences and experiment with the presentation of oral history. Yet there are also interesting differences between the cultures of museum display and contemporary art. Miller was keen not to have the transmitters marked on the map that walkers will follow. He wanted the public to happen upon the recordings, like an Easter egg hunt. The museum staff, perhaps more used to making things as accessible as possible, were keen to make the route easier and more user-friendly. Miller interestingly identifies this as a cultural difference in approach:

> [We are] torn between my desire to allow people to get a bit lost, because I think it is good to get a bit lost, and the consumer's desire to have everything cut and dried and expecting to hear continuous sound from one end to the other without any interference or problems isn't necessarily the point. So there is a slight difference of culture between the slickness of a modern exhibit in a museum that is all very cut and dried and crisp and well tailored, and my desire, my elements are more kind of interventionist, about say enticing people to get lost in a Tesco's car park in Leyton but to discover something wonderful en route; to drift; but that involves making that investment of their own time.

I became involved in the *Linked* project through my involvement with the Museum as co-sponsor of my research. My minor (but interesting) role was to attend a series of meetings held throughout the process of gathering testimony from people who had once lived or worked at the road site. Bi-weekly meetings were attended by the five-strong interviewing team, the artist Graeme Miller and Mark Godber from Arts Admin (the organisation administering the project). My role was to liaise between the Linked team and the museum, and come up with some guidelines for collecting and documenting interviews that would make sure that the resulting recordings could be successfully (and legally) archived by the museum.

Some sound alternatives

Linked is an adventurous experiment in mounting an exhibition outdoors. Of course, museums are no strangers to self-guided walks and history trails; for example, the

Museum of London has previously worked on a 'wall walk' along the site of the old walls of London. Walkers can follow a circular trail following the wall foundations and signs have been placed at points of interest around the city with historical information. Using earphones to hear narration of an outside area is also a well-established technique; for example, English Heritage principally narrate the history of Stonehenge using audio guides which visitors carry with them on their walk around the stones. Companies such as Acoustiguide are developing ever more advanced headsets. In exhibition halls all over the country visitors can tap numbers into compact disc players – or even palm-sized computers – to instantly hear information about an artwork or an exhibit.

Six years ago, when *Linked* was first planned, the use of transmitters to play recordings was very unusual; now it is becoming more widespread in exhibitions. So it is fair to say that the technology that *Linked* uses is not particularly remarkable, or at least not as remarkable as it once was. However, in some respects the use of the *Linked* technology does push the boundaries of public oral history. With the cooperation of the local authority, transmitters have been mounted high on lampposts over a large area, making the urban street a long Tarmac stage for exhibiting oral history. This has some very exciting possibilities for presenting and interpreting urban landscape, city culture and architecture.

The transmitters, which were custom made and cost £1,000 each, are built to last: the recordings are broadcast from particularly stable, non-volatile computer chips and the transmitters are solid-state – they have no moving parts to wear out. The company that constructed them, Integrated Circles, have even guaranteed them to work for 100 years. All they need to keep going is electricity, so it seems entirely possible that *Linked* could run for many years, even decades – an unusual span of time for an exhibition, particularly for the art world, which is more used to exhibitions running for weeks or months rather than years. The changing landscape of Leyton, Leytonstone and Wanstead will also play a big, unchartable role in the future artwork which spans several miles and many years. Miller says that *Linked* has been designed with this in mind:

> The context will change beyond what was intended, in a sense what was intended was to embrace that change; I don't have any particular expectations. [The broadcasts are] not memories that you can write in stone anyway, they are almost deliberately sabotaged not to be a version of the truth because they are too incomplete to tell any coherent version, but they can arouse a lot of curiosity . . . [in the future] people will come and have another look at it, people change generation, outlook, landscapes change, it will be interesting how audio hieroglyphs stand up to test of time.

I have already noticed this change in context at work, just three months after the launch. Leyton's landscape is mutating already; next to the new Asda, the route passes by the new plate glass of a Fitness First gym. Walking through the acres of cars in the supermarket car park, where I have learnt from the transmitter there were once cows grazing, I can now ponder the link between driving to a shop instead of walking, and the soon-to-open mirrored room of treadmills next door. This, I now realise, is a linked moment; I have been linked.

The consciousness of listening

Miller's approach to editing memories from oral history interviews might shock those purists amongst us who like their oral history straight, and preferably with a transcript to hand. At times it is as though all meaning has been pulled out completely; interviews are cut up, mixed and sliced; excerpts are repeated; bells, chords and sounds are added. For the most part stories are coherent; some touching and funny anecdotes survive intact, but periods of the broadcast initially seem anarchic and even unfathomable.

The opaqueness of *Linked* has much in common with Janet Cardiff's *The missing voice*, a Walkman-guided walk around the streets of Whitechapel, which presents a series of observations, unanswered questions, bursts of music and elusive frag-mentary stories.[7] As David Pinder notes, the overall effect is to heighten your senses. The stories mix with your own thoughts and memories as you wander the streets; ambiences are created, affecting the senses of self through what Pinder terms urban space-times. He notes that the 'melding' between the artwork and the conscious-ness of the participant also means that the walk is a highly specific experience that will differ according to the mood and circumstances of each listener on a particular day; 'it will clearly not be experienced by people in the same way.'[8]

Miller uses several methods to encourage the listener to become sensitive to their present, unique surroundings and thus develop a unique experience: musicality (including rhythm and repetition); building in space for thought, both in the broad-casts themselves and between the receivers; and finally the occasional use of the present tense by the broadcast voices.

The overwhelming effect of the musicality and repetition in the broadcast is to slow listening down. Verging on hypnotism, they encourage the listener to concen-trate and really pay attention to what is being said. Miller describes these background musical textures such as tolling bells and violin strings as an 'audio Oxo cube' which thickens the atmosphere and creates a sense of suspension. He also allows room in his compositions for the listener to think for themselves, as there are frequent periods of time without words, or word repetitions that are musical rather than meaningful. He deliberately leaves musical spaces, 'a lulling moment', between fragments of stories to allow the listener time to participate with their own thoughts; 'a kind of mutual surface for where your voice meets other peoples . . . for that reason slowing things down is very desirable, because it filters out, it creates a kind of architecture of space that is the equivalent of silence actually, it is like a little church, you are creating a little church on a street corner that filters out the background.'

I found that these textures had a large part to play in an effect that I would describe as a hyper-aware meditative state. It is hyper-aware because, through the words and emotions of the speakers, you are receiving vivid experiences from the past. Meanwhile you are visually and, next to busy roads, aurally confronted by the present.

Miller actively uses the present in his work in several interesting ways. The streets of Hackney deliver new details that might seem unrelated to the *Linked* experience but, in a state of creative awareness of your surroundings, can soon be integrated into the journey in some meaningful way; a piece of graffiti perhaps, a new building or a poster that you would usually pass by and ignore. Making connections between the past and the listening present can become playful, surprising and rewarding. Conversely, at its most disorientating and at times frustrating, *Linked* offers no visual clues or reference points to what you are hearing. You might as well close your eyes. I did exactly that when I heard deeply personal descriptions of homes that have been replaced by the motorway trench before me. There just seemed to be no point of reference to hang the descriptions onto – just acres of Tarmac. The houses have to be entirely constructed in the imagination and it isn't easy.

Yet it is the geographical present that can give an audio story immense power. I began with the description of London in the Blitz from Leyton bridge. Looking at London's skyscrapers and tower blocks, built on the bomb craters and ashes of a burning city which I could sense once again, gave me a new awareness of urban space-time, a lurching feeling of time travel. At times this effect was heightened considerably by the way interviewees speak. The interviewing team were asked to encourage people to talk in the present tense, viewing the past in their mind's eye as if it is happening in front of them. Being interviewed in this way can feel like a session with a psychiatrist, and many participants found it difficult or impossible to keep up for long, drifting back to the comfort zone of the past tense. Yet some interviewees clearly enjoyed the challenge, and Miller used several of these accounts in *Linked*. The effect can be quite startling, because the interviewee sounds strangely present in an almost ghostlike way. The idea is that the voice is present alongside the listener in a temporal as well as a geographical sense, so two people's present tenses are meeting in the same place.

Although Miller's own voice barely features on the walk, it is not difficult to appreciate that *Linked* is also a deeply personal work. The artist lived for ten years in Grove Green Road and for several years he brought up his handicapped son there. He lived, along with many other artists, in houses that were condemned for the road building programme. He never considered his neighbourhood as material for an art project; he just lived there, finding that he was making closer links with his local community as he connected to support networks in bringing up his son. He also lived through the biggest road protest that Britain had ever encountered. Experiencing the trauma of watching his neighbourhood, and finally his own house, get torn down by the Highways Agency led to a desire to somehow rebuild what had been destroyed. To get a better idea of the artist's thinking and feeling behind the project, I asked Graeme to explain in his own words how he came to create *Linked*, his extraordinary sonic artwork.

In the last year [of living in the house] I was working on the only other transmitter piece that I have done, in Salisbury, and became very involved in the meaning of the land and what it is to walk there and what the memories of that place were. But even then I wasn't particularly thinking about where I was. But it was beginning to disturb me and more and more to the point that it caused me to make an extremely dark bit of theatre called *The desire path*, which was about walking, about being in a city and that city swallowing you up.

And the experience of blight, of watching houses disappear when you are there . . . one day you would walk past a house the next day there would be a gap. And the sense of a power that was bigger than you that could just wipe away buildings. The paranoia of familiar things being removed – it is like someone sneaking into your house and removing the fireplace overnight. You develop those bonds with the exterior. I didn't have a lot of time to think about what it meant at the time other than that I didn't like it. It causes a sense of deep disturbance in me and sense of foreboding. Almost a sense of what was to happen.

One morning after the protest had finished by a day, everything seemed to be settled, finally out of this place in two months' time and rehoused. At 8.30 am the front door smashed down and police and bailiffs stormed into our house in riot gear, Robocop style, kept us all separated, completely freaked my son out, went through all our files, all our folders, just did a full sort of military police job on us, then told us that we had a few minutes to get all our stuff out. We finally negotiated for 24 hours and people came from all over London to get our stuff out. And the moment we brought the last box of stuff out, this huge bulldozer came down and tore the house down behind us. You could physically see, it was like closing the latch and having the keys in my hand, I had the keys in my hand but the whole house was gone, the front door was left standing. It led to nothing. It was very, very, very traumatic.

It probably took me about two years for the noise to stop really, I was so unprepared for that, although people go through things like that in Palestine on a routine basis – but I am sure it takes them that long for them to recover as well, and worse.

But it was strange – again hard to explain to people who lived only a mile away what it was to be in this war zone or to have been an accidental victim of some-thing . . . one of the protestors who was our friend, Paul Morazo, who was a sort of eco-activist, asked if he could spend the night with us and I think that may have been [the reason for the raid]. So in a sense we experienced what collaborators may have done sheltering people from the Resistance, and then the state coming down on you like a ton of bricks. But it didn't make any sense – there were two things, one that I had for myself to find some kind of revenge. Revenge was the first word that came to me – but I thought I can't make his into a revenge piece, but an answer, a response, I have to respond to this and I didn't have the strength to respond to it, but I kept thinking well, what I have got is my voice – don't muck around with a writer or an artist, you are able to bite back in some way.

Also what I later thought about was this idea that there is memory within the landscape. That had been with me a long time and I was working with that idea. And then my direct experience of what was wrong, what was happening during the blight years was that memory was being erased, there was a sterilization process going on, both I think for accidental reasons, that would happen through any major reconstruction of an area, so it becomes unrecognizable, but also through the political desire to expunge the places of resistance if you like. I can really see that happening now – the Israeli army, for example, seem to be using the bulldozer as a political mop, as if that will get rid of the actual political opposition that lies behind. I'm sure it won't succeed, but time and again people use it; like areas of London like the Jago, which became such a problem of poverty and crime they just obliterated it and rebuilt in a 'let's start again', way.

The denial of history seems to be something that I feel I need to respond to as an artist. Years before, I did a workshop in Denmark, where I was told a story about a road that was built in Bratislava. A military highway was built by the Soviet authority right the way through the city and it went across the front door of the cathedral. It couldn't open against the rail of the highway and you had to go in through the side door. The road also demolished what was then one of the oldest synagogues in Europe and the whole Jewish quarter around it; it was an act of political road-building. But the brilliant bit about the story, in the space underneath this elevated section of road, people started chalking the ground plan of the synagogue on the ground. And then people would come and scrub it away. And the next morning it would get re-drawn, not by any one person but by a group of people. Then they started extending it to include the baker shop next door to the synagogue and eventually this whole Jewish quarter would reappear in chalk. They said that when you talked to people, it was as if the road didn't exist and as if the synagogue did exist, and I thought, that's it, that is more or less what I can do, just as an intervention – I became interested. Not all art you do will necessarily have that aim, but I think every now and again there might be an opportunity, uncool as it is, to make a difference. I felt there was this possibility of really intervening in a real area and to sort of do something that would make those houses reappear.

The fourth element that triggered *Linked* is going back not long after to where my house was, this building site, and I couldn't put my ten years back. That compounded that thought about a sort of, I would now call it, an ecology of human memory and landscape that you both read and write into the landscape, and you can even sense narratives. You may not know what they are, but you know that they are there, you sense them inhabiting, they seem to like nooks and crannies, they seem to have certain requirements. They don't like big, flat uninhabited spaces and in the same way birds won't nest – they will hunt on the edge of the motorway, but they won't nest within a certain distance of big highways.

I think stories, history are instances of it. If you stop on the hard shoulder, you have broken down – you are stuck with some shredded tyres and bits of cassette tape in the bushes – and there is no sense of time whatsoever, even though real, horrible major events happen there, people lose their lives and you can't get a grip on what those might have been. It is just forgetting – I don't know why, it is the traffic, the concrete – it feels timeless, time doesn't seem to flow there.

So at the simplest level and motivation I was going to put the houses back, I was going to put them back and do them in a way that would just project them back literally with radio waves, radio waves would fill up that space, so literally, that volume . . . because the road is a trench as well, it is going to be even more clear that it is an empty space rather than a flat plane, because it is carved down – it seems to occupy a certain volume, and that seems like the empty volume that you can pump full of radio waves and rebuild those houses.

And so the trick was – and still is – to get as many people to experience that as possible – to somehow reach that same critical mass you might reach, say, in the Bratislava instance, where somehow you could argue that the houses exist at least as much as the road does – they just exist at a different level – but it tips the balance. So this idea that you put something in place that would tip the balance came out of living there, having already had that sort of distanced view of landscape and space and memory as an artist, but then fuelled by this direct experience about what it is to have your own memory-scape removed by external forces – not just by your own forgetting.

Notes

1   Linked receivers and a map of the route can be borrowed free from public libraries at Leyton, Harrow Green, Leytonstone and Wanstead (on the Central Line). See www.LINKEDM11.net.

2   Track 2, Graeme Miller, *Linked*, London 2003.

3   Leyton MP Harry Cohen gave these figures in a speech to Parliament. House of Commons debate, 11 March 1994, London: Hansard, 1994. col. 593.

4   Track 5, Graeme Miller, *Linked*.

5   Graeme Miller, *Linked* (catalogue), London: Arts Admin and the Museum of London, 2003.

6   Cathy Ross (Head of Later London History Department, Museum of London), 'Forward', in *Linked*, 2003, p. 3.

7   Janet Cardiff, *The missing voice (case study B)*, London, 1999.

8   David Pinder, 'Ghostly footsteps: voices, memories and walks in the city', *Ecumene* 8, 2001, p. 15.

Chapter 34

Rina Benmayor

CYBER-TEACHING IN THE ORAL HISTORY CLASSROOM

Teachers at every level of education have embraced oral history as a learning methodology which allows cross-generational engagement and the acquisition of research and interpersonal skills, whilst encouraging an empathetic personalization of history. This article details how the use of web-based technology can foster a collaborative learning environment. Rina Benmayor is Professor and Chair of the Institute for Human Communication at California State University Monterey Bay, and President of the International Oral History Association 2004–6. Reprinted with permission from *Oral History*, Spring 2000, vol. 28, no. 1, pp. 83–91.

I TEACH AT CALIFORNIA State University Monterey Bay (CSUMB), a new campus in a large state university system. CSUMB was established to serve the working-class, ethnically diverse, and immigrant populations of California and particularly of the tri-county region, communities which have been traditionally under-represented and under-served in higher education.[1] Ours is a largely working-class student body, thirty per cent of which is of Mexican heritage – self-identified as either Chicana/o, Mexican American, or Mexicana/o. Many are the children of migrant farm workers who settled in the surrounding Salinas Valley and Watsonville. Most of our 1800 plus students combine school with full- or part-time work. Many are raising families, and many are re-entry students. Sixty per cent of our students are transfers from community colleges in the region, and six of every ten students are female.

As one might expect of a new university, many of the student support structures are yet to be established.[2] Mandated to be a multicultural, pedagogically innovative campus 'for the 21st century', institutional programmes need to ensure access, retention, graduation, and quality opportunity for working class and under-served students. What are the effects of these programmes, or lack of them, on the lives of students – particularly those for whom the public university is a new experience?[3] Here was an opportunity for oral history to play an action-research and community service role.

When I began designing the course, I decided to structure the entire class around a theme that I hoped students would find personally engaging and rewarding. The central question became: What is the experience of first generation college students on our campus, and what does the campus need to do to ensure their success? Students would conduct life histories of other students (on and off campus), and through their research, provide University administrators with culturally specific insights into the needs of our first-generation students. These insights could have direct impact on the design, structure, philosophy, and quality of services to support their retention, success, and graduation.

I hoped that the students would be able to approach this topic with passion and personal investment. Although they did not take part in defining this topic, they felt connected to it from the start. Some in the class were first-generation, some were Chicana/o, Mexican American or Mexicana/o, some were from migrant farm-worker families, some were re-entry women students, most were working class, and all had friends and classmates who fit the category. Moreover, all the students had an acute understanding of the need for more and better student support services on campus.

It was a happy choice. By the end of the course students demonstrated a passion not only for the topic but for the collaborative learning process as well.

Integrating technology

From the outset, let me say that while I am exploring the use of new media for teaching oral history, I remain critical about where and when new technologies should be used and about what value they can add to the learning process. I continue to believe that the real (versus virtual) classroom is the primary and best space for interactive learning. However, new media (multimedia, CD-Roms, web-based archives, hypertext authoring, email, electronic discussion lists and chat rooms) have interesting implications for pedagogy in the broad sense, and for the teaching of oral history in particular. The digital world provides exciting new possibilities for representing, interpreting, archiving, and teaching ethnographic and field-based research. But the key verbs are 'enable, help, enhance, facilitate, promote', empha-sising the role of technology as a tool. Even in the most utilitarian sense, electronic media can make a difference in the architecture of the classroom. Rather than a space to 'deliver' information, technology can help to turn the oral history classroom into a project-based, collaboration workshop.

In *Engines of Inquiry*, a pathbreaking 'cyber-book', Randy Bass, argues that:

> there are three things that drive the learning of experts: the *questions* that we want to ask, the *cultural record* and materials that we have to work with, and the *methods* and theories that govern our practice . . . The question confronting us as teachers . . . is how can information tech-nologies play a role in the engines of inquiry that drive learning?[4]

Bass offers a useful synthesis of how 'information technologies can serve to enhance six kinds of quality learning' – distributive learning, authentic tasks and complex inquiry, dialogic learning, constructive learning, public accountability, and reflective and critical thinking.[5] I refer to many of these categories throughout this essay, to suggest ways in which my experiment with oral history and new digital media embodied many of these quality learning goals. I found that even very simple electronic applications facilitated the learning process, enhancing communication, building teamwork and collaborative construction, facilitating reflection and interpretation, and enabling socially responsible research and almost instant archive-building. Some of these moments of good learning are worth capturing here.

Initial strategies

One of the advantages of beginning an oral history class with a pre-selected topic is that students do not have to begin secondary research from scratch. Having a bibliographic point of departure (secondary readings already on reserve) students were able to advance swiftly to discussing issues and theoretical approaches and preparation for fieldwork.

Identifying subjects for interview creates tension and takes time. My pre-planning included establishing connections with college-bound programmes at local middle, high school, and on our own campus.[6] In addition, students were able to draw upon their own friends and peers on campus for some interviews. The eighteen students in the class conducted a total of thirty-six interviews, on and off campus, with Chicana/o, Mexicana/o, African American, Asian American, and European American students. Interviews were conducted in the traditional one-on-one fashion, and each student was asked to transcribe and critically annotate their best interview. Other than this, all other stages of the process involved group work, culminating in a collaboratively constructed newspaper feature, a webpage, a public presentation, and a new section of the Oral History Archive (all detailed further ahead). The availability of electronic communication and centralisation was a critical ingredient to our ability to work collaboratively.

Digital tools

Before moving into the more substantive discussion of teaching and learning, let me diverge briefly to detail some of the technological strategies that facilitated the learning process – the design of digital tools, email communication, electronic assessment and archiving. First, I set up a class folder on email, where course materials, assignments, original documents (transcripts), and student work could be easily accessed and exchanged. This became our 'class central'. Then I designed templates to facilitate field journaling and interview transcription. And finally I developed a comfortable process of electronic commentary, assessment, and an instant electronic archive.

1. Interview journal template

Students were asked to write field journals for each interview, attending to three main areas: the interview process, interview content and new knowledge gained, and interview environment. Journals became field records for consultation during the analytical process. In order to habituate students to keeping journals, I designed a three-page Interview Journal Template.[7]

The template specified the questions and issues to be addressed in the student's reflection. The template was posted to the Class Folder so that students could download it to their desktops and enter their field notes and comments. Having the questions and form readily available helped students complete this assignment within hours after the interview. Once completed, students posted their journals to the Class Folder for me to retrieve, read, insert comments, assess, and return via email. The entire process was electronic.

2. Transcription template

One of the most difficult and time-consuming steps in the oral history process is transcription. Therefore, I asked the head of our technology support office to design a template to make transcription easier on the students. He used the 'Style' function in MSWord to construct a template whereby students could focus on typing what they were hearing, rather than worrying about format. Striking the 'Enter' key automatically switched the format from Question to Answer, and back to Question (from Non-Bold to Bold and back). Students could then transcribe tapes without stopping to format manually each voice shift. Once transcribed, they went back to revise spelling, punctuation, and format errors. Format revisions encouraged re-listening to the tape for accuracy of content transcription.

3. Email communication

Our campus email network – *First Class* – provided a centralised communication space, a Class Folder. I used the Class Folder to facilitate information exchange, teamwork, assessment, and archival development. The Class Folder provided a virtual 'workshop' space that complemented and supported in-class group work. It also provided an automatic electronic file for document exchange of field journals, transcripts, logs, critical annotations, and other student work.

The Class Folder provided twenty-four-hour access, enabling students to access class materials and templates, retrieve and post assignments and exchange interview excerpts and drafts of their critical commentaries. I posted all the digitised tools, such as the Journal Templates, Transcription Template, Release Forms, the Interview Guide, and Guidelines for Sound Recording. Students downloaded the materials when they needed to. They returned completed assignments and documents by email to the Class Folder, where I or other students could retrieve them. One of the advantages of electronic centralising is that students are more able to access and learn from each other's work. I set strict deadlines for submissions, and deducted points for late postings, so that stragglers would not have the advantage of reading others' work before submitting their own. Although the danger of plagiarism exists, I found the pedagogical advantages more compelling. Most students agree that learning improves dramatically when, in retrospect, they can see how others approached the assignment or when an advanced model is provided.

4. Assessment, class management and grading

One of the more significant impacts of these experiments with technology is that it changed the way I organised and managed record keeping. I kept electronic folders for each student in which originals and graded versions of their work were archived.

Electronic exchange also changed my assessment practices. Email and MSWord enabled me to download, assess, grade, and return assignments to students with surprising ease. While student work was posted on the open Class Folder, I returned graded work to each student individually, protecting the confidentiality of grades. Using the 'Revision' or 'Track Changes' function (under Tools), I entered comments directly in the students' electronic documents. Revisions appear in another colour and underlined, and can be inserted anywhere in a text. I would insert my comments as I read the text, and then review and often revise them for clarity and precision. I found that the screen focussed my attention. This strategy is less useful, perhaps, in assessing very long papers, as it is more difficult to retain a sense of the whole when working on the screen. However, I found electronic commentary very useful in helping students acquire better oral history field research and archival skills. Because commentaries and revisions appear in another colour, attention can be drawn to detail. For example, I could signal exact sites of format errors in transcripts or subject indexes, and, of course, call attention to spelling errors or incomplete citations. More importantly, I could signal sites of effective or ineffective interview techniques, of good or poor listening, thus attending to the dynamics of the oral process.

I did not find any significant time difference between electronic and hand grading. In fact, I found that for journals and transcripts, the screen helped me focus my attention on the dynamics of interview process and the detail of good transcription and archival techniques. And the comments were always neat and legible. Nonetheless, I also asked students to maintain course portfolios with the hard copy of every assignment handed in, and a print-out of the graded version they received back.

5. Electronic archive development

Electronic delivery of documents automatically created a virtual archive of all transcripts, subject indices (tape logs), and other materials (field journals) pertinent to a particular interview.

Distributive and constructive learning

As Bass points out, new technologies give 'direct access to the growing distribution of cultural knowledge across diverse resources'.[8] It also provides the means to 'distribute the responsibility for making knowledge . . . and to construct and share their ideas . . . in a whole range of public learning contexts'. The experience of our oral history classroom confirmed that, indeed, technology enabled and enhanced sharing particular cultural knowledge gained by each student in the field. It also facilitated students' ability to share responsibility for building a collective analysis that took multiple public forms.

Building an interview guide

Technology significantly facilitated collective construction of a framework for fieldwork and interpretation. The computer enabled us to turn the classroom into a hands-on workshop, and to expose everyone to a critical design and selection process. Based on team assessments of secondary research, students determined which issues needed to be explored through oral history. Then we came together in our 'smart classroom', and with professor at the keyboard, digitally built an Interview Guide. The various topics for exploration (transition from high school to college, expectations of college, financial support, cultural support, campus support, culture/race/gender issues, and future goals) formed categories for interview questions. Subsequently, these same categories provided a framework for analysis, interpretation, and writing.

Each student was asked to bring to class ten questions they thought important to ask his/her interviewees. In class, students met in small groups to put forward five best questions from the group. Each group entered their selections into the computer. We projected all the entries on the large screen, and while I sat at the keyboard, students guided the revision process. They determined the categories, clustered the questions by category, and analysed the efficacy of each question (identifying whether it was an open- or closed-ended, leading or non-leading, double barrelled, loaded question, and so on). They made collective choices – to keep, revise, or dump a question. They identified repetitions, natural clusters, sequences, and closed gaps. All eyes were focussed on the screen and voices freely called out, 'That's a loaded question', 'That's a good one', 'That goes together with . . .', 'That's a good follow-up'.

By the end of the session, students not only had a comprehensive interview guide, but they also understood how to construct open-ended questions, follow up questions, questions asking for feelings as well as facts, questions that would elicit longer or shorter narratives, and so on. Their guide had been constructed collaboratively, reflecting critical thinking, collective deliberation, and a new understanding of interview methods and strategies. Coupling digital technology with group work enabled the class to address the dialogic nature of oral history, understand how teamwork can produce best thinking, and practice shared responsibility. And, although blackboards can serve the same didactic function of recording group thought, digital technology in the classroom enabled us to produce a needed document on the spot (we did the same for our Release Forms), that could be emailed immediately to everyone for use in the field.

Cross talk: weaving a collaborative analysis

To construct their analysis and build a collectively authored article, students worked in groups. They broke into small teams of two or three. Each team had the responsibility to develop and write that section of the analysis (for example, the transition from high school to college, financial aid, family supports and mentoring, institutional support structures, culture, race, and gender issues). This way, the topical categories of the Interview Guide structured the outline of the article and the division of labour in the classroom. Based on extensive classroom discussions of interview findings, each team outlined the points it wanted to make, drew on transcripts and secondary readings to develop its critical analysis, negotiated a point of view and conclusions, integrated specific life history excerpts, and wrote drafts of each section. Drafts were then circulated, reviewed and revised by the entire class until we had a polished and integrated piece.

How did technology support this process? Email facilitated a sustained dialogic environment outside the classroom. It enabled immediate access to and circulation of primary documents (transcripts, excerpts) and drafts for collaborative review. The digital medium enabled students to 'pull out' the texts they wanted to use, assemble drafts, and print them out for review the next day in class. The classroom then became a workshop space, where teams brainstormed, outlined arguments, identified materials, discussed perspectives, built collaborative interpretations, defined next steps, assigned homework tasks, edited texts, arranged for the next stages of document sharing, revised and polished drafts. Technology enabled a 'weaving' process, where electronic exchange from home facilitated group process in class and built each successive stage of production.[9] Electronic communication helped build the momentum of the project and significantly streamlined production of various collectively authored pieces (newspaper feature, oral presentation, and webpage).

In the end, technology stimulated a student-constructed process and product. Technology also enhanced the decentralisation of the learning. Students worked autonomously within their teams, and I became a resource and facilitator rather than a singular authority in the classroom.

Complex inquiry and critical thinking

There are several ways in which new media helped model the complexity of interpretation. To begin with, we produced a digital working archive of primary interview documents. I asked each student to transcribe their best interview. Once the transcripts existed in digital form, the entire corpus or select pieces were immediately accessible to other members of the class. In essence, we created our own primary database which the student teams could retrieve, examine, and use with great ease. They could now place pieces of transcript side by side, compare texts, compare perspectives, and construct interpretations. The interpretation process, however, was guided.

In order to engage students in collaborative analysis, I devised inquiry assignments. The objectives were to engage students in analysis from more than one perspective, to stimulate 'cross talk', and to help weave different pieces of narrative into a collaborative interpretation.

Multiple perspectives

At the beginning of this class I had hoped to find a way to merge the multiple interpretations of a single piece of text into one document. This way, many students could comment on the same piece of text, and examine each other's interpretations. Such an exercise might help train students to consider varying interpretations and to engage in more complex analysis. However, I was not aware of any programme that would allow me to do this easily. I wanted to keep my use of technology simple, requiring a minimal learning curve for all.

Instead, in order to illustrate multiple levels and perspectives in critical interpretation and the dialogic interaction between the text and the interviewer's analysis, each student developed a multi-layered *explication de texte*. Each successively annotated the same piece of interview transcript, as described below.[10] Each student selected a substantial segment of transcript addressing one of the interview topics. Criteria for selection include:

- Does the segment give insight into the topic?
- Does it reinforce/contradict secondary readings and research?
- Does the emotion and tone influence meaning?
- Does it convey something about memory?

Each segment of transcript was annotated four different times, each time attending to a different dimension of analysis:

1   Subject content: What issues related to first-generation students stand out in this excerpt and why? Does your material reinforce/contradict secondary research or present new insights into our subject?
2   Oral v. Written: How does the meaning you derive from reading the written transcript stack up against your impression from listening to the oral delivery on tape? How do tone and emotion add meaning to the topic?
3   Memory: What can you say about the strategic role of memory in this excerpt? Is memory here nostalgia? Is it breaking or reinforcing silences? Is it playing a role of historical affirmation?
4   Self-reflection: What is your own personal experience with regard to the issues and experiences narrated by your interviewees?

Annotations were posted to the Class Folder, so students would be able to read each other's interpretations prior to class discussions and group work.

Although we were not able to merge and juxtapose the various annotations into one document, students learned how to build analysis in stages, using different criteria and different perspectives. From a pedagogical standpoint, the ability to easily confront texts in their original and edited versions, in their visual, spoken, and written representations, provides a richer palette for illustrating the constructed nature of interpretation itself. Clustering also has the potential to promote a more dialogic critical practice. The single authoritative control of a body of material and its interpretation can be reshaped into a more polysemic, dialogic model, where multiple and competing interpretations of, and debates around, a single text are linked.

Real research and public accountability

Oral history involves producing primary research materials. At teaching institutions, where funds for research are often limited, deficits can be turned into opportunities for what Bass terms 'authentic inquiry'.[11] Our Oral History and Community Memory Archive is being built through student coursework and independent projects. The interviews, transcripts, logs, and research papers are accessible to other students, faculty, and the public. In this way, students are engaged in real research that exists beyond the life of a class. Oral history is not a make-believe exercise. The policy outcome of this particular class project also made the work all the more purposeful.

When I designed the class, I expected that students would present the results of their research in a public forum. The tapes and transcripts would also comprise a new section of the oral history archive. It was the students' idea to publish a special insert in the school newspaper and to make a webpage. Understanding that they were engaged in real research, they pointed out that newspaper and web publication would extend the life of the project beyond the class experience and provide lobbying tools for planning student services. The products emerged in succession, each building on the one before it: Newspaper Article > Public Presentation > Webpage.

Newspaper article

In an extensive four-page feature article, titled 'First In My Family To Go To College', students synthesised their research and presented their findings to the campus community. The article was read widely by students and administrators, and students felt a strong sense of individual and collective accomplishment – that despite the labour-intensive nature of oral history research, the end result made an impact. The newspaper article provided the narrative framework for the more extensive webpage.

Public presentation

Once the newspaper article had been assembled, students then had to grapple with how to best take this material to the 'stage', and adapt it for public presentation. Not surprisingly, the face-to-face human context in which eighteen students spoke directly to an audience composed of the people they had interviewed, other students, and campus administrators and planners, was moving. It was a bonding experience that concluded three months of teamwork. Students were challenged to produce a synthesis that was didactic, critical, dramatic, and attentive to ethical oral history practice. Again in teams, they scripted out a presentation that combined dramatic readings of selected oral histories, paraphrasing of narratives, and analytical interpretations.[12] Many students also wove in their own personal stories, as many were first-generation college students themselves.

The process of developing the script followed a similar working pattern to that of the newspaper article. Students used the classroom to work in teams to script and rehearse the presentation. They used email exchange at home to produce drafts. The entire event (ninety minutes) was video-taped, and a clip of this material, along with audiotape, was integrated into the webpage.

Class webpage

The web provided an important forum for presentation of our research, one that increased the after-life and purposefulness of the project far beyond a grade. The class webpage (http://classes.monterey.edu/HCOM/HCOM314SL-01/world/index.html) now forms part of the permanent electronic archive of the University. It stands as an example of the relationship of oral history research to the life of the students and the campus itself.

Structurally, the webpage permitted us to link a kaleidoscopic set of materials for multiple (different) readings by multiple (distinct) audiences. These materials include:

- primary texts – narrative excerpts
- research tools and templates
- interpretive analysis
- critical commentaries and references
- multimedia integration of audio and video
- still photographs and graphics
- links to the Archive
- links to related documents – the class syllabus, the Interview Guide
- an email box inviting commentaries and questions from website visitors.

The website also serves as a permanent archive for all the class materials and assignments. In time, I hope to be able to add readings and make the webpage the digital reserve reading site as well. Since the subject of first generation college students lends itself to longitudinal study, I will teach the class in Spring 2000, focusing on the same topic. Students will be able to re-interview many of those who participated as interviewees in Spring 1998. In this case, the webpage provides an already structured resource for comparative study.

Archive

As with all my other oral history classes, the interviews and final work are archived in our campus Oral History and Community Memory Archive. From the beginning, students were aware that they were producing primary documents to be archived for future research. Thus, the importance of care, accuracy, appropriate transcription and formatting. Students also felt that their work had a lasting value and tried to produce the best primary documents they could.

Currently, the interview tapes, transcripts, and subject logs are physically archived with appropriate releases. Except for the tapes and releases, all other materials also exist in electronic form. Building a fully functional *virtual* archive will be a long and complex process, involving the establishment of ethical protocols of permissions, access, and so on. Even the process of digitising audio and video documents involves complicated technical questions for experts. In the meantime, students in other classes may access the materials by coming to the physical archive.

Digital technology enables the construction of rich virtual archival sites that cluster primary documents, original and translated texts, complete and edited versions, secondary resources, visuals, sound, competing critical analyses, and lengthy bibliographies.

Next steps

Since Spring 1998, the work of the oral history class has been presented to various planning committees concerned with student success and retention. The research has been recognised as a model of how our own curriculum can effectively tie student learning to institution building. I look forward to the follow-up longitudinal study. In terms of technology, I will be enhancing the webpage to include an electronic reserve reading room, more voice and video, student field journals, and I will continue to design and refine exercises for critical inquiry. In these ways, my course will become 'web-based' but it will remain a course delivered in the real classroom. I am anxious to find appropriate software tools for modelling the polysemic and dialogic nature of oral history process and interpretation. We will also be experimenting with mounting a virtual archive, with streamed audio and video.

The comfort which successive generations of students will have with information technologies suggests that creative adaptation of oral history teaching methods must include electronic strategies. If there is one image in my mind that represents this class, it is the day we built our interview guide, when I was able to completely step out of my role as professor, to become the 'inputter', the person at the keyboard who merely executed instructions. The screen had everyone's rapt attention, and students became the directors, empowered through new media to become constructors of their own learning.

Notes

1   California State University at Monterey Bay opened in Fall 1995, with very little advanced planning. Consequently, the infrastructure, the curriculum, the student support services and policies are still being designed and planned with the University in full swing.

2   Students who are first in their families to go to college are a growing college population. Campuses recognise their responsibility in providing targeted, culturally informed supports to ensure college success. This often involves programmes and support mechanisms that are sensitive to the combined emotional, practical, academic, financial, social and cultural pressures felt by students who do not have this experience in their family memory and history. Support services include advising, academic and emotional counselling, career counselling, mentoring, tutoring, and the provision of social spaces, cultural clubs and organisations.

3   Our student body reflects larger state demographics: increased immigration, and a general explosion in numbers of college-age youth. It also feels the effects of right-wing California politics: increased xenophobia reflected in the passing of Propositions 187 (denying social services to undocumented immigrants), 209 (rolling back Affirmative Action, which has had dramatic immediate effects in the public university systems), and 227 (abolishing bilingual education). In this right-wing political climate, increased pressure is placed on the public university to remove what conservatives call 'special interest' programmes and courses of study – those that serve the interests of women, immigrants, and students of colour in general.

4   Randy Bass, *Engines of Inquiry: A Practical Guide for Using Technology to Teach American Culture*, Georgetown: American Studies Crossroads Project, 2nd edn, 1997, pp. 1–14.

5   Ibid.

6   A group of Chicano/Mexicano freshmen agreed to participate in the research. They were recruited to our campus by Educational Talent Search, a programme that works with middle schools and high schools to bring first generation students to

college. We also worked with local middle and high school programmes that give skills training and support to students who will be first in their families to go to college.

7   To design the Interview Journal templates, I used the Header and Footer function in Word.

8   Bass, op. cit.

9   Most students have personal computers at home. The emphasis given to technology on our campus encourages students to acquire home computers. Low-income students are often able to acquire economic assistance for purchase of a personal computer, and email, word-processing, and internet software is provided to all at no cost. In addition, the campus has computer laboratories accessible throughout the day and evening for students to complete assignments on campus.

10   For a discussion of text annotations in oral history, see Ronald J. Grele, 'Personal narratives: what and how', *Acoma, Rivista Internazionale di Studi Nordamericani*, vol. 10, Spring 1997, pp. 4–6. The entire volume serves as an excellent model of this process, as each essay is built around extensive annotations.

11   Bass, op. cit.

12   The webpage integrates an audio clip of an interview, and video clips of the public presentation.

PART V

Advocacy and empowerment: introduction

K NOWLEDGE AND UNDERSTANDING of the past has a profound impact upon contemporary social and political life. Though the use of recorded interviews is not necessarily a radical historical intervention in itself, many oral historians aim to transform history and society through their work.[1] Oral testimony is frequently used alongside other sources to recover neglected or silenced accounts of past experience, and as a way of challenging dominant histories which underpin repressive attitudes and policy. Some oral historians involve interviewees in the process of interpreting their lives and developing strategies for personal and social change. And oral historians have been engaged in the truth and justice processes of societies that are coming to terms with histories of conflict and oppression. The chapters in Part V consider a range of ways in which oral history has been empowering for individuals and has been used for advocacy by social groups and political movements, and explore the issues posed by advocacy oral history.

Oral history and reminiscence work are two sides of the same coin: though both deal with memory, oral history is primarily concerned with historical understanding whilst reminiscence work is primarily concerned with the value of remembering for the narrator. In the 1960s, developments in the psychology of old age began to challenge an orthodoxy that reminiscence or 'life review' was 'an abnormal or pathological activity, something to be discouraged', and suggested instead that guided remembering could have therapeutic benefits for older adults and might inform a more respectful and informed approach to people in care.[2] In the opening chapter Joanna Bornat notes the development of reminiscence work in British residential homes and hospitals, in social welfare fieldwork, and through adult education and self-help groups. She discusses how the separate but parallel fields of oral history and reminiscence work might learn from each other: about the nature of memory and remembering in later life; about dealing with traumatic memories of the past and the challenging present circumstances of old age; about reminiscence groups and other social contexts for remembering; and about the value of interpreting and presenting memories (including through theatre) in partnership with narrators. In short, 'the more holistic approach to remembering in the life of older people is one which might benefit oral history, introducing more interpretative layers once "the person who is" comes to be valued as much as "the person who was"'.[3]

Schools are an important context for intergenerational oral history projects in many countries. In 'Voices of experience: oral history in the classroom', Cliff Kuhn and Marjorie McLellan bring together a 'roundtable' of North American secondary school teachers to talk about the processes, benefits and challenges of oral history in schools. On the one hand, intergenerational work can be enormously affirming for local, often elderly, people who enjoy a new, positive relationship with young people and relish the interest in their memories. As Susan Moon says of an interview by her black students with 92-year-old Miss Bertha, whose grandmother was an ex-slave, 'that was a shining moment in my teaching career, to hear those children and that woman; she was animated, because somebody cared enough to ask about her history. You know what I'm talking about? It made her whole life viable, and I think that was important.' On the other hand, students gain enhanced respect and understanding about their elders, and often about their own family and community history; they develop confidence and self-esteem and a wide range of transferable skills – independent study and group work, listening and interviewing, editing and technical production, fund-raising and public presentation – and their notion of history can be transformed, as Tony Daspit concludes: 'I hope that the students saw then that what has been silenced is sort of the commoners' experience in history, and that those stories are important. So I hope that it just gives a chance to recognize that they can be producers, they are producers of history. It's a question of realizing it and focusing it. And they also learn how difficult this is.'[4]

Chapters in other sections of this *Reader* show how oral history can be a significant resource for political groups and emergent social movements:[5] in the women's movement (Armitage and Gluck, Anderson and Jack, and Bozzoli),[6] for trade unionists and working-class communities (James, Green, and Butler and Miller, who also explore how oral history can be used to foster collective understandings and commitment within geographic communities which have suffered economic or social dislocation),[7] for indigenous peoples (Good and Shostak)[8] and in colonial and post-colonial societies (Stoler and Strassler),[9] for refugees and immigrant and ethnic communities (Haley, Burton, and Benmayor),[10] in gay and lesbian politics (Kennedy)[11] and for people with disabilities (Walmsley).[12] Here Daniel Kerr shows how oral history promoted 'dialogue in the streets among the homeless' of the US city of Cleveland, and how 'a democratically organized project built on the framework of what Michael Frisch terms "shared authority" can play a significant role in movement building'.[13] Kerr's project started with life-history interviews but then shifted away from a victim model and refocused on homeless people's own analysis of homelessness. He brought homeless people into a structured dialogue by presenting their video interviews in public, producing a radio programme focusing each week on one person's account of homelessness, and convening workshops at a drop-in centre in which participants analysed their experiences and drew out common themes about the history and causes of homelessness. Perhaps most importantly, the project built upon and linked existing discussions among homeless people, 'identified avenues of resistance', and 'emboldened people' to campaign for social change. Kerr notes tensions between scholarship and advocacy and argues, perhaps controversially, that research can be *more* objective if it is more inclusive. Elsewhere in this *Reader* the Popular Memory Group (Chapter 4), Katherine Borland (Chapter 24), Kathleen Blee (Chapter 25), and Patricia Lundy and Mark McGovern (Chapter 41) offer a cautionary note about the dilemmas and difficulties of advocacy oral history, asking if and how it is possible to create a shared interpretative authority between researchers and narrators.[14]

William Westerman's chapter provides another example of the direct use of oral history in a particular political struggle, that of the Central American refugees who use their own life-story testimonials to educate North Americans about the situation in their countries, and to gain financial and political support. Westerman shows how these testimonials are constructed for maximum political effect and presented through a range of narrative forms: as performance, in writing, and etched into the bodies of victims of torture.[15] Apart from gaining support for their cause, the narrators attain therapeutic benefits and public affirmation through telling their stories. The process of 'bearing witness' – by refugees and other victims of social and political oppression – can thus be empowering for individual narrators, and can generate public recognition of collective experiences which have been ignored or silenced. It can also have direct social and political outcomes, as evidenced in the struggles of indigenous peoples over land rights and compensation.[16]

In 'Stolen generations testimony: trauma, historiography, and the question of "truth"', Rosanne Kennedy considers the contested memory of Australian Aborigines who were taken from their families and placed in foster families or state institutions.[17] Kennedy notes how this memory is produced and treated differently in diverse contexts: oral history recordings compared with autobiographical writing; in law courts and national inquiries or 'memory commissions'; by historians and in self-help advocacy groups such as Link-Up. Drawing upon theoretical approaches to Holocaust and abuse survivor testimony, she argues against the criticism that personal accounts have been unduly influenced by the collective memory of a 'stolen generation', and asserts that these accounts should be regarded as sophisticated interpretative narratives that incorporate sharp social and historical insights, and not simply as evidence for interpretation (or rejection) by historical 'experts'. Yet Kennedy also notes that some Aboriginal witnesses 'may not have had the cultural resources available to them that would enable them to interpret their own experience', and thus highlights the important though problematic supporting role of oral historians and other memory workers.

In totalitarian regimes power is maintained in part through the control of memory.[18] In her study of 'The Gulag in memory', Irina Sherbakova explains how the past was continually reinvented by the Soviet regime and describes the fitful process of liberalization which made it possible to challenge those fabrications. Using interviews she has conducted since the 1970s with survivors of the Soviet prison and labour camps, Sherbakova evokes the impact of fear and distortion upon individual remembering, and how survivors have been torn between the urge to speak out and the danger of talk. Remembering is a process of struggle for survivors, and in the social and political life of a nation. Organized movements of survivors and the families of victims – such as the Memorial organization in the former Soviet Union – have (like Link-Up with Aboriginal Australians) helped individuals and societies to remember and make better sense of traumatic pasts. Throughout Central and Eastern Europe (and, more recently, in the states of the former Yugoslavia or in Rwanda), oral history has been used as one resource for the identification and excavation of mass graves, as a way of 'rehabilitating' the reputations and rights of victims of persecution, and as evidence in court actions against the perpetrators of injustice.[19]

Patricia Lundy and Mark McGovern introduce their article about a northern Irish commemorative project by explaining that 'in the last three decades truth-telling has come to be seen as a key element of post-conflict transition in societies throughout the world', and they identify at least twenty-four national 'truth commissions', of which the most famous was the Truth and Reconciliation Commission in South Africa. Despite good intentions and many positive outcomes, the political compromises required by official truth-telling sometimes marginalize memories that do not fit their conciliatory aims, and they can reinforce the trauma of silence or misrecognition.[20] Ironically, Northern Ireland has not had a truth commission because '*not* confronting the causes and competing explanations' of the northern Irish conflict 'was part of a deliberate State strategy to obtain a *realpolitik* consensus' following the Good Friday Agreement that more or less ended armed conflict in 1998. In the absence of official truth-telling, Lundy and McGovern consider 'the contribution of community-based truth-telling to achieving truth and justice' in Northern Ireland. They review their work with the Ardoyne Commemoration Project in a working-class Belfast enclave, and detail the significant practical challenges of participatory oral history and the personal and political benefits of a 'victim-centred approach to truth-telling that can be transferred not only to other communities in the north but to other parts of the world'.[21]

The two final chapters in this section demonstrate how oral history can serve a functional role which empowers individuals and communities. In a number of countries in the South oral history is used alongside development projects to ensure that foreign aid interventions – for example new agricultural technologies – draw upon local knowledge and complement traditional land use (in fact, these aims and approaches are not dissimilar to those of urban redevelopment projects in the industrialized North such as that described by Butler and Miller in Chapter 33).[22] Nigel Cross and Rhiannon Barker introduce the SOS Sahel Oral History Project, which recorded stories from men and women in sub-Saharan Africa about their changing environment and ways of life: 'We did not set out to accumulate facts, but rather to find the stories, to improve the techniques for their collection and, most important of all, to demonstrate their value and utility'. In effect, through oral history young, local aid workers develop a more mutually respectful relationship with their elders, and memories of effective social relations and land use are used as a resource for community and environmental survival.

Sanjiv Kakar also demonstrates the utility of life stories in his account of the uses of oral history in leprosy projects in India. Interviews with villagers provide essential information about the local conditions and attitudes which shape the experience of leprosy, and ensure that eradication strategies are appropriate for particular communities. Indeed, oral history projects have helped to break down the silence and stigma which surrounds leprosy, and interviewees have become activists in community health and education schemes. Kakar also shows how the oral testimony of leprosy patients can 'enable a more sensitive reading of colonial records' and 'help to fill in the gaps within colonial histories' which denied the experience of leprosy patients in the community. This two-way use of both oral and written life histories – to improve historical understanding *and* contemporary care strategies – is a significant recent development in health and welfare practice in many countries.[23] Though such professional uses for oral history seem far removed from its origins in community, academic and archival projects, respect for the life stories of people who might otherwise have been ignored – by history, by society, in professional practice – is a powerful common thread.

Notes

1   On the radical aims of oral history, see M. Riordan, *An Unauthorized Biography of the World: Oral History on the Front Line*, Toronto, Canada: BTL Books, 2005; and the following chapters in Part I: Thompson (Chapter 2), Popular Memory Group (Chapter 4) and Armitage and Gluck (Chapter 6).
2   See R. Butler, 'The life review: an interpretation of reminiscence in the aged', *Psychiatry*, February 1963, vol. 26, pp. 67–76, quoted in J. Bornat, 'Oral history as a social movement: reminiscence and older people', *Oral History*, 1989, vol. 17, no. 2, p. 17.
3   A number of anthologies explore the theory and practice of reminiscence work in different settings, including but not only with older adults, and outline debates about therapeutic and other outcomes: J. Bornat, P. Chamberlayne and L. Chat (eds), *Reminiscence: Practice, Skills and Settings*, London: Centre for Biography in Social Policy, University of East London, 1999; J. Bornat (ed.), *Reminiscence Reviewed: Perspectives, Evaluations, Achievements*, Buckingham: Open University Press, 1994; B.K. Haight and J.D. Webster (eds), *The Art and Science of Reminiscing: Theory, Research, Methods and Applications*, Washington, DC: Taylor & Francis, 1995; see also M. Kaminsky, *The Uses of Reminiscence: New Ways of Working With Older Adults*, New York: Haworth Press, 1984; H.R. Moody, 'Twenty–five years of the life review: Where did we come from? Where are we going?', in *Journal of Gerontological Studies*, 1988, vol. 12, pp. 7–21; *Oral History*, 1989, vol. 17, no. 2, special issue on 'Reminiscence'; *Oral History Association of Australia Journal*, 1990, no. 12, special issue on 'Oral history and social welfare'. In an article on 'Reminiscence as literacy', reproduced in Part IV of this *Reader* (Chapter 28), Jane Mace considers related issues in a community education project with older adults. Other practitioners have explored the role of oral history in community education and literacy projects for adults of all ages, in which the writing and telling of life stories has been used to develop skills and strengthen personal and collective identities. See, for example, J. Lawrence and J. Mace, *Remembering in Groups: Ideas From Reminiscence and Literacy Groups*, London: Oral History Society, 1980; R. Benmayor, 'Testimony, action research, and empowerment: Puerto Rican women and popular education', in S. Berger Gluck and D. Patai (eds), *Women's Words: The Feminist Practice of Oral History*, New York

and London: Routledge, 1991, pp. 159–174; M. Breen and D. Sobel, *Popular Oral History and Literacy*, Toronto: Storylinks, 1991.

4   On oral history in schools, see B.A. Lanman and L. Wendling (eds), *Preparing the Next Generation of Oral Historians*: *An Anthology of Oral History Education*, Walnut Creek: AltaMira Publishers, forthcoming 2006; D.A. Ritchie, *Doing Oral History*: *A Practical Guide*, 2nd edition, New York: Oxford University Press, 2003, pp. 188–221; G. Whitman, *Dialogue with the Past*: *Engaging Students and Meeting Standards Through Oral History*, Walnut Creek: AltaMira Press, 2004; D. Schwarzstein, *Una Introducción al Uso de la História Oral en el Aula*, Buenos Aires: Fondo de Cultura Económica, 2001; A. Redfern, *Talking in Class*: *Oral History and the National Curriculum*, Colchester: Oral History Society, 1996; B. Lanman and G. Mahaffy, *Oral History in the Secondary School*, Los Angeles: Oral History Association, 1988; E. Wigginton, *Sometimes a Shining Moment*: *The Foxfire Experience*, Garden City, N.Y.: Doubleday, 1985; C.R. Lee and K.L. Nasstrom (eds), 'Practice and pedagogy: oral history in the classroom', Special issue, *Oral History Review*, 1998, vol. 25, nos 1–2; *Oral History*, special issue on 'Oral history and the national curriculum', 1992, vol. 20, no. 1; *Oral History Association of Australia Journal*, 1986, no. 8, special issue on 'Oral history, children and schools'; Maura Cronin, 'Experiences of supervising undergraduate oral history research', *Women's Studies Review* [Galway], 2000, vol. 7: *Oral History and Biography*, pp. 1–11; P. Hagopian, 'Voices from Vietnam: veterans' oral histories in the classroom', *Journal of American History*, 2000, vol. 87, no. 2, pp. 593–601; A. Ross, 'Children becoming historians: an oral history project in a primary school', *Oral History*, 1984, vol. 12, no. 2, pp. 21–31. On college projects, see the article by Rina Benmayor (Chapter 34, this volume); A. Thomson, 'Teaching oral history to undergraduate researchers', in A. Booth and P. Hyland (eds), *The Handbook of University History Teaching*, Manchester: Manchester University Press, 2000, pp. 154–165.

5   Note that oral history has also been used to understand the power and ideology of elites. See, for example, C. Courtney and P. Thompson (eds), *City Lives*: *The Changing Face of British Finance*, London: Methuen, 1997; M. Roper, *Masculinity and the British Organisation Man Since 1945*, Oxford: Oxford University Press, 1994; R. Perks, '"Corporations are only there because people allow them to be": the growth of corporate oral history in Britain', paper presented at the Oral History Association annual meeting, Oregon, 2004.

6   See also Gluck and Patai, *Women's Words* (especially Part IV, 'Community and advocacy'); note 33 in the Introduction to part I, 'Critical developments'; and references in Ritchie, *Doing Oral History*: pp. 297–298.

7   See also J. Green, 'Engaging in people's history: the Massachusetts History Workshop', in S.P. Benson, *et al.* (eds), *Presenting the Past*: *Essays on History and the Public*, Philadelphia, Pa.: Temple University Press, 1986, pp. 337–359; L. Niethammer, 'Oral history as a channel of communication between workers and historians', in P. Thompson (ed.), *Our Common History*: *The Transformation of Europe*, London: Pluto, 1982, pp. 23–37; S. Linqvist, 'Dig where you stand', *Oral History*, 1979, vol. 7, no. 2, pp. 26–30. On oral history with geographical communities, see also G. Jordan, 'Voices from below: doing people's history in Cardiff Docklands', in S. Berger, H. Feldner and K. Passmore (eds), *Writing History*: *Theory and Practice*, London: Hodder Arnold, 2003, pp. 299–320; L. Shopes, 'Oral history and community involvement: the Baltimore Neighbourhood Heritage Project', in Benson, *et al.*, *Presenting the Past*, pp. 249–262; J. Bornat, 'The communities of community publishing', *Oral History*, 1992, vol. 20, no. 2, pp. 23–31; J. Modell and C. Brodsky, 'Envisioning Homestead: using photographs in interviewing', in E. McMahan and K.L. Rogers (eds), *Interactive Oral History Interviewing*, Hillsdale, N.J., Lawrence Erlbaum, 1994, pp. 141–161; R. Samuel, 'Oral history and local history', *History Workshop*, 1976, no. 1, pp. 191–208. See also references in Ritchie, *Doing Oral History*, pp. 298–299.

8   See also B. Attwood and F. Magowan (eds), *Telling Stories: Indigenous History and Memory in Australia and New Zealand*, Crows Nest, New South Wales: Allen & Unwin, 2001; J. Cruikshank, *The Social Life of Stories: Narrative and Knowledge in the Yukon Territory*, Lincoln: University of Nebraska Press, 1998; J.S.H. Brown and E. Vibert (eds), *Reading Beyond Words: Contexts for Native History*, Orchard Park, N.J.: Broadview, 1996; H. Goodall, 'Colonialism and catastrophe: contested memories of nuclear testing and measles epidemics at Ernabella', in K. Darian-Smith and P. Hamilton (eds), *Memory and History in Twentieth Century Australia*, Melbourne: Oxford University Press, 1994, pp. 55–76; P. Taylor, *Telling It Like It Was: A Guide to Aboriginal and Torres Strait Islander History*, Canberra: Institute of Aboriginal and Torres Strait Islander Studies, 1996, pp. 33–89; M. King, 'New Zealand oral history: some cultural and methodological considerations', *New Zealand Journal of History*, 1978, vol. 12, no. 2, pp. 104–123.

9   See also A.G. Gold and B.R. Gujar, *In the Time of Trees and Sorrow: Nature, Power and Memory in Rajasthan*, Durham, N.C.: Duke University Press, 2002; L. White, S.F. Miescher and D.W. Cohen (eds), *African Words, African Voices: Critical Practices in Oral History*, Bloomington: Indiana University Press, 2001.

10 See also A.J. Hammerton and A. Thomson, *Ten Pound Poms: Australia's Invisible Migrants*, Manchester: Manchester University Press, 2005, pp. 15–25; A.J. Hammerton and E. Richards, *Speaking to Immigrants: Oral Testimony and the History of Australian Migration*, Canberra: Research School of Social Sciences, Australian National University, 2002; R. Benmayor and A. Skotnes (eds), *International Yearbook of Oral History and Life Stories. Vol. III, Migration and Identity*, Oxford: Oxford University Press, 1994; G.Y. Okihiro, 'Oral history and the writing of ethnic history', in D.K. Dunaway and W.K. Baum, *Oral History: An Interdisciplinary Anthology*, second edition, Walnut Creek: AltaMira Press, 1996, pp. 199–214; D. Allen, 'Mythologising Al Nakba: narratives, collective identity and cultural practice among Palestinian refugees in Lebanon', *Oral History*, 2005, vol. 33, no. 1, pp. 47–56; L. Serikaku, 'Oral history in ethnic communities: widening the focus', *Oral History Review*, 1989, vol. 17; C.H. Bailey, 'Precious blood: encountering inter–ethnic issues in oral history research, reconstruction, and representation', *Oral History Review*, 1990, vol. 18, pp. 61–108; A. Thomson, 'Oral history and migration studies' *Oral History*, 1999, vol. 27, no. 1, pp. 24–37 (in a special issue on 'Migration'); *Oral History Association of Australia Journal*, 1984, no. 6, special issue on 'Migrant oral histories'; *Oral History*, 1980, vol. 8, no. 1, special issue on 'Black oral history'; *Oral History*, 1993, vol. 21, no. 1, special issue on 'Ethnicity and oral history'; *Canadian Oral History Association Journal*, 1989, no. 9, special issue on 'Oral history and ethnicity'; and references in Ritchie, *Doing Oral History*, pp. 294–296.

11 See also Hall Carpenter Archives, *Inventing Ourselves: Lesbian Life Stories*, and *Walking After Midnight: Gay Men's Life Stories*, both London: Routledge, 1989; T. Nightingale, 'Hidden histories: oral research on gay and bisexual men', *Oral History in New Zealand*, 1994, no. 6, pp. 11–13; G. Wotherspoon, *City of the Plain: History of a Gay Sub-Culture*, Sydney: Hale & Iremonger, 1991; E. Lapovsky Kennedy and M. Davis, *Boots of Leather, Slippers of Gold: The History of a Lesbian Community*, New York: Routledge, 1993.

12 See also D. Gittens, *Madness in its Place: Narratives of Severalls Hospital, 1913–1997*, London: Routledge, 1998; D. Atkinson, M. Jackson and J. Walmsley (eds), *Forgotten Lives: Exploring the History of Learning Disability*, London: Bild, 1997; S. Rolph. 'Ethical dilemmas: oral history work with people with learning difficulties', *Oral History*, 1998, vol. 26, no. 2, pp. 65–72; K. Hirsch, 'Culture and disability: the role of oral history', *Oral History Review*, 1995, vol. 22, no. 1, pp. 1–27; R. Fido and M. Potts, '"It's not true what was written down": experience of life in a mental hospital', *Oral History*, 1989, vol. 17, no. 2, pp. 31–34; D. Atkinson, '"I got put away": group-based reminiscence with people with learning difficulties', in Bornat, *Reminiscence Reviewed*, pp. 96–104.

13   M. Frisch, *A Shared Authority*: *Essays on the Craft and Meaning of Oral and Public History*, Albany: State University of New York Press, 1990.

14   See also note 21 in the Introduction to Part III, 'Interpreting memories'.

15   On Latin American 'testimonio' and activist anthropology, see L. Stephen, *¡Zapata Lives! History and Cultural Politics in Southern Mexico*, Berkeley and Los Angeles: University of California Press, 2002; A. Arias, *The Rigoberta Menchu Controversy*, Minneapolis: University of Minnesota Press, 2001; S. Stoll, *Rigoberta Menchu and the Story of All Poor Guatemalans*, Boulder, Colo.: Westview Press, 1999; J. Maloof, *Voices of Resistance*: *Testimonies of Cuban and Chilean Women*, Lexington: University Press of Kentucky, 1999; J. Beverley. 'The margin at the centre: on *testimonio* (testimonial narrative)', in G.M. Gugelberger (ed.), *The Real Thing. Testimonial Discourse and Latin America*, Durham, N.C.: Duke University Press, 1996, pp. 23–41.

16   C. Choo and S. Hollback, *History and Native Title, Contemporary Theoretical, Historiographical and Political Perspectives*, Perth: University of Western Australia Press, 2004; J.A. Neuenschwander, 'Native American oral tradition/history as evidence in American Federal courts', *Words and Silences*: *Journal of the International Oral History Association*, 2004, new series, vol. 2, no. 2, pp. 11–17; A. Parsonson, 'Stories for land: oral narratives in the Maori land court', in Attwood and Magowan, *Telling Stories*, pp. 21–40; A. McGrath, '"Stories for country": oral history and Aboriginal land claims', *Oral History Association of Australia Journal*, 1987, no. 9, pp. 34–46; J. Cruikshank, 'Oral tradition and oral history: reviewing some issues', *Canadian Historical Review*, 1994, vol. 75, no. 3, pp. 403–418.

17   See also B. Attwood, '"Learning about the truth": The stolen generations narrative', in Attwood and Magowan, *Telling Stories*, pp. 183–212; A. Haebich, *Broken Circles*: *Fragmenting Indigenous Families 1800–2000*, Fremantle: Fremantle Arts Centre Press, 2000.

18   On memory and totalitarianism, see also A. Applebaum, *Gulag*: *A History of the Soviet Camps*, London: Allen Lane, 2003; E. Jelen, *State Repression and the Labors of Memory*, Minneapolis: University of Minnesota Press, 2003; C. Merridale, *Night of Stone*: *Death and Memory in Russia*, London: Granta, 2000; V. Skultans, *The Testimony of Lives*: *Narrative and Memory in Post-Soviet Latvia*, London: Routledge, 1998; T. Smith, R. Perks and G. Smith, *Ukraine's Forbidden History*, Stockport: Dewi Lewis Publishing, 1998; L. Passerini (ed.), *International Yearbook of Oral History and Life Stories. Vol. I, Memory and Totalitarianism*, Oxford: Oxford University Press, 1992; E.F. Xavier Ferreira, 'Oral history and the social identity of Brazilian women under military rule', *Oral History Review*, 1997, vol. 24, no. 2, pp. 1–33; R. Perks, 'Ukraine's forbidden history: memory and nationalism', *Oral History*, 1993, vol. 21, no. 1, pp. 43–52.

19   On the use of personal testimony in quasi-legal contexts, see M. Dembour and E. Haslam, 'Silenced hearings? Victim-witnesses at war crimes tribunals', *European Journal of International Law*, 2004, vol. 15, no. 1, pp. 151–177; A. Portelli, 'The oral shape of the law: the "April 7 case"', in A. Portelli, *The Death of Luigi Trastulli and Other Stories*: *Form and Meaning in Oral History*, Albany: State University of New York Press, 1991, pp. 241–269.

20   On truth commissions, see D. Levenson, 'The past can be an open question: oral history, memory and violence in Guatemala', *Words and Silences*: *Journal of the International Oral History Association*, 2004, new series, vol. 2, no. 2, pp. 23–29; K. Christie, *The South Africa Truth Commission*, London: Macmillan Press, 2000; G. Minkley and C. Rassool, 'Orality, memory and social history in South Africa', in S. Nuttall and C. Coetzee (eds), *Negotiating the Past*: *The Making of Memory in South Africa*, Oxford: Oxford University Press, 1998, pp. 89–99; A. Krog, *Country of My Skull*, London: Jonathan Cape, 1998. On the 'witnessing fever' of recent decades, see note 21 in the Introduction to Part I, 'Critical developments'.

21 G. Dawson, 'Trauma, place and the politics of memory: Bloody Sunday, Derry, 1972–2004', *History Workshop Journal*, 2005, issue 59, pp. 151–178; G. Dawson, *Making Peace with the Past? Cultural Memory, the Irish Troubles and the Peace Process*, Manchester: Manchester University Press, forthcoming 2006.

22 See H. Slim and P. Thompson (eds), *Listening For a Change: Oral History and Development*, London: Panos, 1993 (and, by the same authors, Chapter 11 in this volume); O. Bennett, 'Review article: oral testimony as a tool for overseas development', *Oral History*, 1995, vol. 23, no. 1, pp. 89–92. For a comparable project in the UK, see *People, History and Change in Birmingham's Heartlands*, Birmingham: Birmingham Museums and Art Gallery/Birmingham Heartlands Development Corporation, 1993; M. Riley, '"Ask the fellows who cut the hay": Farm practices, oral history and nature conservation', *Oral History*, 2004, vol. 32, no. 2, pp. 45–53. For Australia see C. Landorf, 'A sense of identity and a sense of place: oral history and preserving the past in the mining community of Broken Hill', *Oral History*, 2000, vol. 28, no. 1, pp. 91–102.

23 See J. Bornat, R. Perks, P. Thompson and J. Walmsley (eds), *Oral History, Health and Welfare*, London: Routledge, 2000; Bornat, *Reminiscence Reviewed*; R.P. Martin, *Oral History in Social Work*, Newbury Park, Calif.: Sage, 1995; *Oral History*, 1995, vol. 23, no. 1, special issue on 'Health and welfare'.

Chapter 35

Joanna Bornat

REMINISCENCE AND ORAL HISTORY
Parallel universes or shared endeavour?

Oral history and reminiscence work are two sides of the same coin: though both deal with memory, oral history is primarily concerned with historical understanding whilst reminiscence work is primarily concerned with the value of remembering for the narrator. In this chapter Joanna Bornat, Professor of Oral History at the Open University in England, discusses how the parallel fields of oral history and reminiscence work might learn from each other: about the nature of memory and remembering in later life; about dealing with traumatic memories of the past and the challenging present circumstances of old age; about reminiscence groups and other social contexts for remembering; and about the value of interpreting and presenting memories in partnership with narrators. Reprinted with permission from *Ageing and Society*, 2001, vol. 21, pp. 219–241. © Cambridge University Press.

Introduction

FOR THE LAST 20 YEARS OR MORE I have occupied a position which, as far as I am aware, has not been shared by anyone else. I am an oral historian who also writes and researches on issues relating to reminiscence and life review. It is paradoxical that many of the debates and discussions developed in oral history and reminiscence and life review research are so similar, while conducted in two quite separate universes, often with a singular lack of awareness of the other's existence and concerns or expertise. Issues such as contexts for remembering, the effect of trauma on remembering, storytelling, the interview relationship, ethics, the nature of memory, the role of remembering in establishing identities and finally, outputs and dissemination are all typical of debates in each domain.

An outsider might find it difficult to distinguish the two areas. Each is concerned with recall of the past and, in the main, this involves communication with older people. However, things feel quite different when viewed from the inside, and it is this difference which I explore here. In part the differences are rooted in differing disciplinary origins and in part in the distinctive aims and objectives of the two approaches. In the UK context, this article offers some comments on the key distinguishing characteristics of oral history and reminiscence and life review while pointing out what is shared. In covering two areas, each with rich and active populations of researchers and students, I have made some selections and some necessary omissions. I may also be guilty of misrepresentation in my attempt to portray similarity and difference. For these decisions I apologize in advance. The chapter is structured around three key areas of work:

*   method, the interrogative nature of oral history and reminiscence;
*   context, partnerships in the interpretation of memories; and
*   presentation, the ownership and control of personal memory.

I illustrate each with examples from both universes.

Defining difference

In order to establish similarities and differences, some definitions are required. Beginning with discipline origins, it is clear that there are some quite obvious boundaries to be drawn. Yet, as I will go on to show, these boundaries have shifted over the years, and in some areas have almost disappeared. Defining difference at once becomes complex.

Oral history

Oral history in the UK and elsewhere draws on the disciplines of history and sociology for its origins. However, as Thompson argues, the origins of oral history lie in a particular understanding of what history is. His argument that 'All history depends ultimately upon its social purpose' points to an instrumental role, for history and its making. The social purpose of history may, in some cases, be the maintenance of the status quo or to support divisions within and between societies. History, however, can take a quite alternative stance, challenging and revising what is accepted. It is within this tradition that oral history developed in the late 1960s. History as a critical endeavour, undertaken as an activity with a view to bringing about change, features strongly in the writings of many oral historians though, as Thompson also points out, the extent to which change is invoked 'depends upon the spirit in which it is used'.[1]

Frisch, writing in a US context, offers a way of pinpointing the particular social role of oral history in distinguishing between what he calls the two poles of 'more history' and 'anti-history'.[2] What he means by the 'more history' approach is the contribution which oral history makes to revealing aspects of the past which are not available through more conventional documentary sources. By means of the interview, oral historians are able to access personal experience, eye witness accounts and the memories of people whose perspectives might otherwise be ignored or neglected. In this way we are able to add information to the historical record. So, for example, histories of major industries are altered by accounts from the workshop floor, from women and migrant workers, in relation to unemployment or struggles over hours and wages.[3] The history of health and welfare is extended beyond administrative and organizational structures to include accounts from recipients of welfare, experiences of disability, histories of illness and of the development of professional expertise.[4] [. . .]

The 'anti-history' approach, Frisch argues, takes a stronger line, challenging orthodoxy by identifying the unique quality of the oral history process. Talking about the past with those who participated in it, even created it, is a means of by-passing the control of academic scholarship, and being able to 'touch the "real" history . . . by communicating with it directly'.[5] Portelli, a leading oral historian from Italy, describes how, even within families, the sensation of history becoming alive shifts behaviour:

> I remember sitting in Santino Cappanera's parlor in Terni, Italy, taping an interview about his life as a steel worker and political activist. His teenage daughter was in the next room, doing her homework. After about twenty minutes, she had moved her chair to the hall, outside the parlor; a little while later, she was standing by the door; about one hour into the interview, she came and sat next to us, listening.[6]

The search for 'anti-history' was very much at the heart of oral history's origins in the UK. As a challenge to orthodoxy, both in terms of sources and methods, it offered a clear social role to those historians who, since the 1960s, have been seeking to give voices to the hidden histories of women, childhood, working people and those stereotyped as different by virtue of their colour, origins or sexual orientation. This radical agenda of oral history has persisted in subsequent decades, continuing to determine both content and method.

In their analyses, Thompson and Frisch demonstrate how oral history as a research-based activity with a human and social focus, presents evidence of both continuity and challenge in relation to its disciplinary forebears. Oral history, however, has origins which are also interdisciplinary. Plummer, identifying a 'humanistic method' in sociology, shows how letters, diaries, photographs and life histories were typically used as evidence by 19th- and early 20th-century social investigators.[7] The shift towards qualitative rather than quantitative methods in sociology was pioneered by Thomas and Znaniecki in their study *The Polish Peasant*, first published in 1918–20, where they distinguished the importance of 'subjective interpretation' in understanding individual and social action, in contrast with observation of 'objective factors'.[8] A focus on the subjective as a category for understanding and analysis has had a particular influence on the way that oral history has developed in the UK. In part this was due to individual and personal histories. The first major oral history survey, carried out in 1968, was led by a historian based in a sociology department.[9] In part this was also due to a particular point of origin, when history and sociology had grown closer and were seeking common ground.

Bertaux, the French oral historian, made the case when he argued for history as a basic element within the social sciences, pointing out how the past and the present are inextricably linked: 'People are not merely carrying contemporary structures, they are also carrying those parts of earlier structures that have made them what they are.' However, he goes on to emphasize that what people do with the past is also a significant part of the equation: 'People are not mere products . . . potentially they have their own praxis.'[10]

Subjectivity, seen both as a challenge and as a valued asset in research drawing on memory, has provoked debates within oral history since its earliest days. The meanings which people give to their own and public versions of the past, has proved a rich source for more creative developments. The recognition of ambivalence in the remembering of Italy's fascist period, of fabulation and the wishful memories of Italian communists and composure among Anzac veterans have all helped to shift awareness and stretch the oral historian's perspective to a valuing of the personal and reflective in people's responses.[11]

Linked to subjectivity is awareness of the interviewee's own needs and wishes during the interview process. Amongst oral historians there has been a slow realization, one which is scarcely ever recorded as part of the formal process of data collection. Most will, however, have had their own particular awakening, a moment when it became clear that the experience of being interviewed was as helpful to the interviewee as to the interviewer. Thompson briefly summarizes researchers' records of thanks realizing that the interview could be interpreted as a therapeutic 'confessional'.[12] Here is an area where reminiscence and life review have much to contribute.

Reminiscence and life review

Where oral history tends to focus on the content of memory, what is perhaps more characteristic of reminiscence and life review is attention given to process and outcomes for participants. Groups of older people, with or without leaders, whose main concern is the retrieval of past experience and its recording and preservation can be said to be taking part in oral history. When those same group members share and communicate memories with a view to understanding each other or a shared situation, or with the aim of bringing about change in their current lives, they are involved in reminiscence and life review. In the same way, the interviewer who focuses on a life history with a view to finding out about the past and an individual's life in that past, is working as an oral historian. The interviewer who encourages life review, reflecting on those same experiences but with a view to encouraging greater self-awareness and personal reflection by that older person, is engaging in reminiscence.

What care workers identify as reminiscence comes in a wide variety of forms. In a study of reminiscence-based activities in nursing and residential homes in England, five types have been identified, ranging from the formally planned to the informal impromptu.[13] Each type is likely to have a range of possible outcomes including word-of-mouth accounts, life-story books, discussions, displays, outings, contributions to individual care plans, themed days, intergenerational contacts, inputs to the educational curricula of local schools and colleges and, of course, drama. For all parties, older people and those who facilitate the process, the impact of reminiscence and life review is an issue for evaluation and comment.

It is perhaps significant that the turn to more biographical ways of researching the past and to working with older people, happened at around the same point in time and with, in many respects, similar aims. How a paper published in a journal of psychiatry in 1963 came to be the rallying cry for developments in reminiscence and life review over the following decades on both sides of the Atlantic, will have to be another story. The paper in question, [by Robert] Butler,[14] had both clinical and practical significance and was to lead to what I have described elsewhere as a 'social movement' in relation to work with older people.[15] Butler argued that reminiscence and life review are a normal and essential part of ageing. He was contesting the then more prevalent view, that these activities were symptoms of pathological and progressive cognitive deterioration. What is important about his contribution is that he legitimized an intervention which nurses and care workers had previously felt was natural and appropriate, but which they had been discouraged from promoting. Dobrof,[16] for example, tells the story of her own epiphany, and there are others who had similar experiences once they felt free to encourage older people to talk about what they were expert in, their own life stories. Indeed such moments of realization still occur as successive generations of care workers make their own discoveries. Rather like the powerful effect of 'anti-history', the voices of older people, talking about their childhoods, work and life experiences, have a way of cutting through professional practice, revealing the person, the individual behind the case notes, the condition or the diagnosis.

In terms of disciplinary base, reminiscence has deep roots within psychology. While this has determined the pattern of research, it has not had such a strong influence on practice, at least outside those clinical settings where reminiscence is used as the basis for therapeutic intervention.[17] In work with older people, reminiscence and life review tends to draw on an eclectic mix of nursing and social care practice, gerontology, psychology, counselling, the creative therapies and adult education skills. Such a mix leads to a diversity of approaches and a lack of professionalization which is an encouragement to inventiveness and a discouragement to routinization and exclusivity on the part of practitioners. Indeed Bender et al.[18] identify 20 different purposes of reminiscence within what they call the 'three C approach': client/carer/culture.

Reminiscence work is still very much open to experimentation and development, with particular challenges thrown up as the movement has extended to include people who are cognitively impaired through dementia or learning disability.[19] Nevertheless, the research base, with few exceptions, remains firmly within approaches delimited by experimental methods. An evidence base for the efficacy of reminiscence and life review in terms of alleviating depression, raising levels of self-worth or changing behaviour, has long been sought. Reviews of the literature show an overwhelming number of studies reporting positive outcomes for participants.[20] On some measures, however, the evidence still remains inconclusive and the tendency to adopt methods based, for example, on one-off cross-over studies of selected samples of older people has left problems when it comes to replication or the measurement of the effects of change over the longer term.

Perhaps more fruitful are those studies which choose longitudinal or observation-based methods. In these cases it is possible to review changes in attitudes to reminiscence and life review as people age.[21] Opportunities to observe in naturalistic settings have enabled some researchers to identify how reminiscence plays a part in building social relationships amongst care users, and in presenting and maintaining identities for individuals faced with loss and change.[22] Such studies also highlight the significance of context and the contribution which care staff make to interventions, both formally and informally.[23]

In the above review, I have explored the discipline bases and distinctions between oral history and reminiscence and life review. The contrasting disciplinary starting points continue to influence the direction in which each has developed. As I will demonstrate, however, evidence from recent debates suggests that within their separate universes, similar issues are being raised. This suggests that, between them, the two approaches occupy more common ground than might previously have been considered. In what follows I look in more detail at the parallel universes and shared endeavour of these two approaches to memory in late life, drawing on an example of work from each area in relation to method, contexts and presentation.

Method: the interrogative nature of oral history and reminiscence

Elsewhere, I argue that one of the key distinguishing features of oral history is that it is interrogative.[24] A comparison of a tape, its transcription and a written account makes the effect of interrogation quite clear. Where the oral account demonstrates an immediacy and evidence of thought, reflection and individuality, a written version of the same events will be pallid in comparison. Literary conventions iron out the dialect and personal turns of phrase, suppressing its uniqueness. Portelli[25] talks about the role of the interviewer as giving 'a mandate' to the narrator to embark on their account. The initial question prompts responses which may be taken up in unpredictable ways, unpredictable to both sides. This interrogative quality of oral history is, Portelli suggests, an aspect of oral history as genre.

Both oral history and reminiscence play a key role in legitimating the telling of personal stories. A key motive, as suggested earlier, has been to 'give voice', to empower those whose experience of the past has tended to be ignored or overlooked. In settings where individuality is hard to maintain, reminiscence contributes to the presentation of an identity which is not determined by the immediate environment or circumstances. The interviewer or facilitator sets an initial agenda and the interviewee, the narrator, the subject, the group member, responds with an account.

Put this way, the process sounds quite straightforward but, of course, oral historian or reminiscence worker will be able to give any number of examples of experiences where things did not work out in that way. The issue of who has control in an interview or reminiscence discussion is not as clear cut as some commentators might imagine. My own experience has been that interviewees have their own agendas, sometimes developing these in the process of the interview.[26]

Reminiscence in an interview

I have recently been involved in researching family change, using oral history interviews with people of all ages and, in particular, the impact of family break-up and reconstitution – through divorce, death, separation and remarriage/cohabitation – on the lives of older people.[27] Debates about the family life of older people tend to be dominated by concerns over who will care for frail elders.[28]

Our aim was to hear how people talk and make sense of family change. The use of an oral history or life history perspective enabled the people interviewed to reflect on their own lives over time and it was clear, as the interviews accumulated, that for many this was a first opportunity to make sense of past experience.[29]

Ultimately we interviewed 60 people from families in two areas of one medium-sized English town. Looking at the transcripts it soon became clear that people were searching for the right words and language to explain family change and decision-making relating to partnering. The results are narratives which include moral, as much as social and political, explanations for behaviour and which enabled us to see how action recorded in larger data sets is explained and justified at an interpersonal level.

For example, when interviewing Wilma Waldon (a pseudonym), I was keen for her to talk to me about her experience of divorce in three generations of her family, her own, her daughter's and her grand-daughter's. Her account of changing relationships between men and women in marriage was illuminating but framed within a broader narrative which depicted the children from her two marriages as a united group of caring and supportive people. In reflecting on her life, divorces appeared simply as short-term hiatuses, difficult episodes but without long-lasting effects.

I could consider this account in a number of ways. I might decide that she was concealing more difficult and traumatic experiences. However, there is another possible structuring to her account. Her own divorce was acrimonious and the separation which preceded it meant that she was left with three young children and the need to earn a living for them all during World War II. Her daughter's divorce followed years of physical abuse however, whilst her grand-daughter, 'married too young' and 'they no sooner married than they're divorced sort of thing'. Her account mirrors accurately the social history of family change in the UK. As she explains:

> years ago, where the woman was, she hadn't got money and that, to have a divorce. And they were the underdogs, weren't they? Because, I mean, not a lot of them went out to work in them days, did they? Not the women. There was a time when bringing up big families all the while. And I think that they, you know, well – they used to get good hidings and everything else. Well, they were round this way, they was awful. The men just go drinking and coming home, and they'll beat the women up and that. It just used to be awful. And, I mean, if anyone done that, you'll up and leave them straight away, wouldn't you? Say to the children, 'Come on, put your coat on, we're going', you know. But there you are. That's how things were in them days.

Awareness of the historical and social context validates her account. Attitudes towards divorce and separation have changed dramatically over the past 40 years in the UK and her full account of these experiences matches well with what is known from demography and the sociology of the family. But, as well as that, what we hear from her interview is someone who feels that she can give a good account of herself, her decisions and the actions of her children. Our project was indeed interested in how people explained events in their lives, how they reflected on changing attitudes towards divorce and separation but, if I was expecting to hear graphic accounts of tensions, problems and difficulties, she was not going to provide me with any such stories.

As an oral historian with experience of the parallel universe of reminiscence and life review, I am aware of an alternative possible explanation for her rather relaxed and composed account of family change over the last 60 years. I could note the work of Coleman in identifying the four characteristics of 'a successful life story': coherence, assimilation, structure and truth value. Awareness of the psychological tasks facing older people opens the dialogue generated by oral history to an analysis which allows for age-related factors, as well as those which relate to gender and socio-historical structural factors. Indeed, Coleman's analysis fits Wilma Waldon rather well, as he also identifies ways in which older women often report having more control over their lives, as they acquire a sense of greater financial and personal freedom.[30]

It might be reasonable to ask in this case, if such an account is less valid given the salience of life stage factors. How accurate was this picture of the experience of divorce, if the main narrative drive is to promote a sense of reconciliation and harmony in late life? There are two possible responses. First, in its own right, an older person's reflection on family change has significance. In relation to policy and practice, the attitudes and expectations of older family members continue to have significance in determining family obligations and responsibilities. Indeed, our research showed that people continued to carry out parenting roles throughout their lives. Second, an account such as Wilma Waldon's demonstrates how, within one interview, a narrator draws on present and past to explain experiences of family change within the private sphere, while referring out to more public, structural, determinants of opportunity for working-class women over three generations.

Reminiscence on a stage

The Good Companions are a London-based group of older people, nine women and one man, who devised a play *Our Century and Us* with Pam Schweitzer, a well-known producer of reminiscence projects in the theatre, community and institutional settings. The play dramatizes their memories through their words and, in so doing, presents a history of the 20th century which is both personal and public. Some memories are collective, others are quite individual. With songs and stories the play begins at the time of the performers' births in the 1920s and early 1930s, tracks through their growing-up years, their World War II experiences, their working lives and the changing pattern of family life, up to the present day. It is designed for audiences of older people, deliberately making links with audiences through shared experience and reinforcing messages with the help of contemporary songs and music. I was co-organiser of an international conference on 'Biographical Methods and Professional Practice' held in London in October 2000. We invited *The Good Companions* to present this play as part of the programme.

As a member of the audience, I have a first-hand impression of the dynamics of the event. My understanding of the process has been further built up from reports and interviews with those involved. The experience was both moving and enlightening. Although we were confident about the skills of the performers and the relevance of the play to the content of our conference, we were worried that a group of amateur players, older people at that, might not be well received by the delegates. We should have addressed our own prejudices instead. The performance was wildly received by a group of academics, whose emotional responses belied the objectivity and detachment of their own highly professionalized presentations. Clearly something was at work here. The stories narrated by the performers had meanings which communicated across national and international boundaries with people whose backgrounds and ages implied quite different experiences of the 20th century. The performance ended with a standing ovation and lively discussions between the audience and the ten performers.

The Good Companions' play by chance provides an interesting comparison with Wilma Waldon's account. During the play, one of the women takes the stage on her own to describe her experience of divorce in the 1950s. She describes the stigma, the exclusion and rejection which her erstwhile friends and neighbours visited on her. The other performers then joined in with brief exchanges to illustrate this cold and wounding behaviour.

The background to this scene was complex, as we discovered. In devising the play, the performers had discussed at some length how personal the play should be. In particular, in playing out her own real experience of divorce, was this actor in danger of 're-living' her humiliation and pain? In the end the scene was included and, in my view, the play was the better for it. Divorce in the middle years of the 20th century was difficult for many people, men and women. The performers recognized this and, for a while, the balance of the play shifted away from celebration and humour.

The process of arriving at this particular scene involved interrogation, on an individual and group basis. More than that, the scene inevitably interrogates audiences that include people who themselves are divorced or who have to come to terms with their own actions in relation to divorcing neighbours and relatives. The process of reminiscence is also interrogative and, while the individual account stands out as a performative act (whether in a play, a group or in a one-to-one exchange), the extent of that interrogation is set by the individuals taking part. Indeed, the background to the performance illustrates that people arrive at some kind of reconciliation with past life events by taking different paths. *The Good Companions* actor who played out her experience of divorce, had not previously found a way to talk about this painful experience. The process of interrogation from her group members and the shaping of the account for wider audiences, provided her with the means. Working in a reminiscence context enabled her to find a method, in this case a public performance.

In summary, this review of the methods of oral historians and reminiscence workers suggests that there are aspects which can usefully be shared. Awareness of the influence of age and life stage on how a story is narrated can help to broaden oral history, giving it relevance in policy and practice terms. Identifying the dialogic and interrogative nature of oral history helps to remind us that participation involves agency and decision-making, and that the interview is essentially an interactive process involving two parties, each with their own agendas and purposes.

Context: partnerships in the interpretation of memories

By focusing on context I now want to shift the discussion towards a comparative positioning of oral history and reminiscence in relation to their relative contributions to supportive strategies in work with older people. Within oral history circles (in the UK and Australia at least, if not elsewhere), a burning issue persists. This is the question of how a method whose purpose is to *give voice* to people out of the mainstream of history, can ensure that its practice matches this ideal. Is it possible to work in partnership so that the narrator is not alienated from their own story by the analytical skills of the researcher. Early on in oral history little attention was paid to this issue. For some researchers, their own purpose and political stance seemed good enough as a guarantee of shared objectives. People's willingness to be interviewed, to make their story available to others, setting records straight, providing a challenge to the status quo, meant that issues of partnership felt irrelevant. And it is still the case that to hand back a transcript so that someone might alter or change their words is more a feature of archive work than of research or publication. Oral history's origins within the discipline of sociology pull it in the direction of academic research, and the norms of academic life tend not to recognize partnership with subjects as a necessary part of the research process.

The result is that examples of partnership tend to be developed in areas of work which are focused more on practice than research. Certainly, our project studying family change, part of a government-funded programme, included no allowance in terms of budgeting or scheduling for any form of partnership model of research and publication. We soon learned however that, amongst our sample, there were people who had an interest in the outcomes of the project and who were keen that their story might be of use in broadening out debates about family change. One such was a man in his sixties whose wife had left, taking their children with her. She had become a Jehovah's Witness and he was interested to know if others in the sample had had similar experiences of fundamentalist religion coming between couples.

Models of partnership in oral history projects range from handing back transcripts for checking to full-blown collaboration. In some cases, collaboration stems from inequality. So, for example, colleagues at the Open University, working with people with learning disability in the production of oral histories, have developed collaborative strategies which enable people without written communication skills to produce narrative accounts.[31] This more 'bottom-up' model of production has also become commonly practised in community projects, where Michael Frisch's idea of 'shared authority'[32] has been embodied within oral history practice. How this works in practice is detailed in the account of an oral history of the closure of a poultry processing plant in Maine, USA. Here one woman's story was developed in close collaboration with an interviewer and a photographer. At the end of the process, Alicia Rouverol, the interviewer, wrote up her account of what she had learned from the experience:

> If oral history challenges historical generalizations, collaborative oral history . . . challenges our generalizations as historians and folklorists. It complicates our analyses when our interviewees disagree with our interpretations; it forces us to re-think our stance, to consider the critiques and suggestions of our narrators whose stories we seek to tell. We may not agree with their interpretations; and that isn't our obligation. It is our obligation, though, to present multiple and contradictory perspectives when and if they arise within the same body of testimony; to offer in our analyses conflicting interpretations, or what may seem to be paradoxical reflections or assessments.[33]

Rouverol's position challenges the basic conventions of academic writing, in placing the interviewee, the 'subject' on a par with the researcher, and suggesting that the object of research may not necessarily be a tidy categorization or the derivation of comparative constructs.

Feminist oral historians had earlier faced the dilemma of being both subject and researcher, noting the uncomfortable reality that the interview may be both a positive and a negative force, with subsequent analysis driving a wedge between those who should have been experiencing solidarity.[34]

Who exercises interpretive powers is at the nub of this ethical dilemma. Borland, whose grandmother challenged the feminist interpretation she drew from her interview, concludes:

> we might open up the exchange of ideas so that we do not simply gather data on others to fit into our own paradigms once we are safely ensconced in our university libraries ready to do interpretation.[35]

The possibility that interpretation might itself be a dialogic power struggle is suggested by Portelli, when he describes the experience of feeding back his account of a student occupation of 1990 in Rome. Drawing on interviews with students who had taken part, he and his student group presented their interpretation to one of the leaders whom they had interviewed. He rejected their interpretive use of metaphor. As Portelli explains: 'interpretation is always part of a power relationship: to interpret is one thing; to be interpreted is another'. He suggests that the interviewee's 'counter-interpretation' is itself a contribution to an interpretive process which he describes as being part of the 'endless spiral of the search for a necessary and unattainable meaning'.[36]

What Portelli and Frisch are pointing to is the need to find some way to establish partnership in the interpretive process, a partnership which both includes, and controls, academic powers. Indeed Frisch, in a review of Studs Terkel's *Hard Times*, criticises those who take a 'no-history' approach. By this he means the idea that testimony requires no interpretation, that it speaks for itself with 'self-evident and unequivocal significance'. Against this, he argues for the role of 'the historian' in asking the questions and introducing insights which both challenge and situate the 'documents of oral history'.[37]

The search for an interpretive method which is both reliable and recognizable, has led to the development of a method in biographical research which distinguishes the 'lived life' from the 'told story'. This is achieved by undertaking two contrasting analyses drawn from the text of one interview. By this means a 'biographical data analysis' and a 'thematic field analysis' are derived with a view to understanding the interviewee's own theory of action and expressed identity.[38] The biographical interpretive method (BIM) aims to forge conceptual links between the events described in individual life stories and such broader structural issues as class and power. At present such a strategy seems some distance away from partnership or shared authority, given that those who undertake the analysis of the interview data will not necessarily have taken part in the interview. One option to be explored is the possibility of developing the method as a training tool for social care workers. In this way the practice of interpretation is itself opened up to critical review while the words in the interview transcript help to develop understanding and suggest new insights to particular dilemmas in social welfare.

Ethical issues concerning partnership in the process have also exercised reminiscence workers. Concern over the content of sessions, and the question of the extent to which it is representative and therefore equally facilitative of people from different backgrounds persists.[39] Partnership is perhaps most easily guaranteed and sustained where older people are able to take part in the shaping of the process with a view to agreed outcomes. A reminiscence theatre production clearly cannot emerge without the collaboration of the players. People are not likely to want to portray themselves or events in ways that they find unacceptable or unrecognizable. For this reason, producing a play could provide a helpful model in other settings and for other interpretive processes.

Concern has developed in recent years, both in oral history and reminiscence and life review, over how to respond when painful emotions are evoked and how to handle interactions when memories of past trauma are evoked.[40] Such concerns serve as a reminder of the social purpose of oral history and, coupled with ideas of reconciliation and acceptance drawn from clinical work with older people, it seems that both approaches have much to contribute to each other's understanding and practice. These issues are too broad for detailed discussion here; rather I consider evidence from research into reminiscence as an intervention in care settings. In drawing on this I want to suggest that, in responding to expressions of painful emotion, it is important to consider context and circumstances.

Questioning care staff about their experiences of reminiscence work in residential and nursing settings, two separate examples were obtained where, unexpectedly, older people had reacted with extreme emotion.[41] We were told that a man disliked having cot sides on his bed because of his World War II experiences, and that a woman had difficulties about bathing because of her personal history. While not wanting to deny that these people had endured genuinely traumatic and abusive experiences, evoking uncontrollable emotions in their recall, there is a possibility that, by ascribing these episodes solely to past trauma, present abusive or insensitive care practices and interpersonal actions are ignored. So, for example, it might be proper to ask if anyone, whether or not they had been a prisoner of war should be placed in a cot bed against their wishes and that, if someone is expressing fears about bathing, then this might be an outcome of insensitive handling of intimate care. Incidents such as these not only point to a need for care workers and those interacting with older people to have an informed understanding of the history of the last eight or so decades, they also suggest a need to locate reminiscence within the present and to enable this process to highlight the quality of such interactions.[42]

What older people do not require is any kind of denial or censorship resulting from a misplaced search for protective practice.[43]

I have focused on context in order to draw attention to the structures and norms in which oral history and reminiscence and life review operate. Looking at practice in each other's universes, both good and bad, can be instructive and perhaps support the process of learning about issues which are both shared and distinctive.

Presentation: the ownership and control of personal memory

Reminiscence and oral history share a number of different approaches to presenting outcomes, and it is in relation to this stage that the most self-critical debates have taken place, amongst oral historians at least. Phrases such as 'giving back' or 'giving voice' are used to establish the provenance of forms of presentation, and the credentials of promoters. Similarly, where reminiscence and oral history lay claims to contributing to advocacy and empowerment, then who owns the spoken words becomes highly significant.

Debates within oral history centre on separation between subject and the researcher, and on the additional separation where presentation involves the mass media or public settings such as museums and exhibitions. While these boundaries can lead to feelings of loss of control by the person whose story has been told it is worth noting that ownership of the words spoken has a legal basis in some countries. UK law (1988 Copyright Act), for example, now gives separate ownership to the words spoken and to the recording of those words. This means that the owner of the copyright in the words is the speaker, while the copyright in the recording belongs to the person or organization who arranged the recording.

Legally, any further use made of the words means that permission must be sought from the copyright owner, the speaker, although alternatively, copyright can be assigned to the interviewer. At one level this may all appear as an administrative obstacle in the process of presentation, but the law does help to clarify and emphasize the point about ownership in words, stories and narratives which are usually given quite freely. 'Giving back' is thus a redundant concept as, under UK law at least, ownership cannot be alienated in the first place.

How people's words are used and the extent to which they are able to determine their further use, is an issue which has been subjected to much debate within oral history circles. I have already outlined the idea of 'shared authority' in relation to community-based projects and publications.[44] This type of approach is more likely to be followed where questions of witness and authenticity are highly politicized as, for example, in contests over land rights and refugees.[45] Amongst archivists, academics, museum staff, radio and television researchers, community workers and educationalists, different strategies tend to be adopted and much critical attention has been given to ethical practice. Signing off ownership or imposing restrictions as to who may have access to tapes and transcripts and when; adopting a protocol for sharing the production process; abiding by such basic rules as naming interviewees as authors or editors; all these are approaches which have been taken up. Practice is variable, however, and standards can often leave much to be desired. Moreover, as I have already suggested, some contexts are less open to ideals of partnership than others. Academic practice in the UK is only recently, under pressure from recipients of services, changing to include the notion of partnership in areas such as research into health and social care provision.

In other disciplines, the traditional role of the researcher, presenting the product of a research process which may involve a mass of interviewees, is one which is difficult to conceive as developing on a partnership basis. Issues such as confidentiality and sensitivities around categorization and comparability of evidence, might rule out a collective approach to involving interviewees in all stages of writing and presentation. It may be that in these circumstances the safeguarding of subjects' interests is better protected by researcher training in ethical principles and, in particular, in the legal rights of the interviewee.

Oral history practice has produced some useful pointers to how such training might be focused. One possibility (as some feminist oral historians have argued) is to identify topics which have immediate relevance to the wider public. This could be the public which makes up communities local to academics, or the public in the wider world. So, for example, the history of a local industry may have relevance not just for those who work in it, but also as an example of industrial change generally. Another strategy is to create alternative formats so that the published academic article is accompanied by an informal talk, a publication written in a more popular form or a museum display. Of course, such developments are more likely within institutions where there is a commitment to outreach and to developing learning opportunities for members of local communities. Even so, as Olson and Shopes suggest, the role of the interpreter in presenting the experiences of interviewees will still involve intervention and decision-making and the possibility that quotations may be taken out of context.[46]

Within reminiscence and life review, appropriation and control are equally possible, despite the fact that the role of the facilitator is likely to be more personal, ongoing and immediate. Indeed the very informality of some reminiscence exchanges opens up possibilities of misrepresentation, mishandling or inaccurate reporting of personal accounts and the details of private disclosures. Here again, existing protocols relating to client and service user privacy, disclosure and confidentiality, should guard against bad practice. However, given the vulnerability and high dependency of many of those involved in reminiscence activities, there is a certain element of risk involved, particularly where facilitators or group leaders have not had access to basic training in communication skills.

There is an additional problem. Such training is unlikely to include reference to history as a discipline or to the varied social contexts in which people have lived out their lives. Care staff are often forced to rely on popular histories, local experts or whatever resources they have access to in the contexts in which they live and work. The result is that the way reminiscences are communicated and presented may depend on the energy, resources and enthusiasms of those engaged as facilitators. Inevitably this means that the curriculum is likely to be highly idiosyncratic.[47]

To what extent this particular approach is socially, politically and culturally inclusive is debatable and, indeed, awareness of diversity amongst groups of older reminiscers is an issue which reminiscence research has tended to neglect up to now. In this respect it is interesting to reflect on the comments of an older African Caribbean man:

> People cannot reminisce here in Britain which is very important . . .
> by the time I reach 60 I will revert back to talk about family history
> and importance of childhood in the Caribbean, you cannot have those
> reminiscences in old people's home in this country. The people in these
> homes never talk to you. People are not going to listen to you.[48]

In considering the range of possible forms for presenting reminiscence, then it seems likely that drama is the best guarantee of control by participants over any presentation. The members of *The Good Companions* were acting their own words and the process of presentation involved them in discussing and devising both form and content. They are very much a privileged group of reminiscers, and their form of presentation is not one which can easily become universal practice. Even so, the apparent purity of the process is compromised to an extent by the role of the director. Arguably, without the skills of Pam Schweitzer, an experienced theatre director, there would have been no *Our Century and Us*.

Once again, there is evidence of shared endeavour in presenting the outcomes of these two areas of work. The roles of the director, editor, designer, facilitator, academic are basically the same. Across these groups, however, the quality of individual collaborative practice and the commitment to shared ownership in the product is what makes for differences.

Conclusion

I began this article by pointing out the differences between oral history and reminiscence and life review. These were, I argued, mainly in relation to disciplinary origins and attachments and to the urge to legitimate the communication of stories, accounts, memories which challenge historical convention, and which also challenge assumptions about identity in old age. In the subsequent argument, I have touched on a number of areas and have had to leave out many more. In reviewing their parallel universes I have suggested that there is much that is similar. There is the focus on interrogation which is implicit in the methods adopted. There is the influence of context on how accounts are developed and responded to. Finally, when it comes to presentation, the issue of ownership of the product is equally an issue of concern for oral historians and for reminiscence workers.

There may be shared endeavour; there are also differences within the two universes. Oral historians have deliberated issues of ownership and control in relation to their own and participants' contributions to the process, coming up with models of partnership and experimenting with equality in the production and presentation of memories. Reminiscence work has focused more on group processes and the influence of present situation and life stage on remembering. For oral history, the older person has been viewed as the source of evidence; for reminiscence and life review the older person, who they were and who they are now, *is* the evidence. This more holistic approach to remembering in the life of older people is one which might benefit oral history, introducing more interpretive layers once 'the person who is' comes to be valued as much as 'the person who was'. For reminiscence, the bonus to be gained from oral history is recognition of the significance of the told story and its place in the history of a particular life, community and society.

Notes

1   P. Thompson, *The Voice of the Past*, 3rd edition, Oxford: Oxford University Press, 2000, pp. i, 3.

2   M. Frisch, *A Shared Authority. Essays on the Craft and Meaning of Oral and Public History*, Albany, New York: State University of New York Press, 1990, p. 187.

3   P. Friedlander, *The Emergence of a UAW Local, 1936–1939: a Study in Class and Culture*. Pittsburgh: University of Pittsburgh Press, 1975; B. Messenger, *Picking up the Linen Threads: a Study in Industrial Folklore*, Belfast: Blackstaffe, 1980; T. Hareven, *Family*

Time and Industrial Time: the Relationship between the Family and Work in a New England Industrial Community, Cambridge: Cambridge University Press, 1982.

4   J. Bornat, R. Perks, P. Thompson and J. Walmsley, *Oral History: Health and Welfare*, London: Routledge, 2000.

5   Frisch, op. cit.

6   A. Portelli, *The Battle of Valle Giulia: Oral History and the Art of Dialogue*, Madison: The University of Wisconsin Press, 1997, p. 4.

7   K. Plummer, *Documents of Life*, 2nd edition, London: Sage, 2000.

8   W.I. Thomas and F. Znaniecki, *The Polish Peasant in Europe and America*, Dover, New York, 1958, p. 41.

9   P. Thompson and J. Bornat, 'Myths and memories of an English rising: 1968 at Essex', *Oral History*, 22, 2, (1994), pp. 44–54.

10   D. Bertaux, 'The life course approach as a challenge to the social sciences', in T.K. Hareven and K.J. Adams (eds), *Ageing and Life Course Transitions: an Interdisciplinary Perspective*, London: Tavistock, 1982, pp. 27–50.

11   L. Passerini, 'Work ideology and consensus under Italian fascism', *History Workshop*, 8, (1979), pp. 84–92; A. Portelli, 'Uchronic Dreams: working class memory and possible worlds', *Oral History*, 16, 2, (1988), pp. 46–56; and A. Thomson, *Anzac Memories: Living with the Legend*, Melbourne: Oxford University Press, 1994.

12   Thompson, op. cit., pp. 182–183.

13   J. Bornat and P. Chamberlayne, 'Reminiscence in care settings: implications for training', *Adult Education*, 14, 3, (1999), pp. 277–295, pp. 284–286.

14   R. Butler, 'The life review: an interpretation of reminiscence in the aged', *Psychiatry*, 26, (1963), pp. 65–76.

15   J. Bornat, 'Oral history as a social movement: reminiscence and older people', *Oral History*, 17, 2, (1989) pp. 16–24.

16   M. Dobrof, 'Introduction: a time for reclaiming the past', *Journal of Gerontological Social Work*, 7, 1/2, (1984), pp. xvii–xviii.

17   A. Norris, 'Clinic or client? A psychologist's case for reminiscence', *Oral History*, 17, 2, (1989), pp. 26–30; J. Garland, 'What splendour, it all coheres: life review therapy with older people', in J. Bornat (ed), *Reminiscence Reviewed: Perspectives, Evaluations, Achievements*, Buckingham: Open University Press, 1993, pp. 21–31; I. Burnside, 'Reminiscence: an Independent Nursing Intervention for the Elderly', *Issues in Mental Health Nursing*, II, (1990), pp. 33–48; M. Bender, P. Bauckham and A. Norris, *The Therapeutic Purposes of Reminiscene*, London: Sage, 1999; and E. Bruce, S. Hodgson and P. Schweizer, *Reminiscence with People with Dementia: A Handbook for Carers*, London: Age Exchange, 1999.

18   Bender et al., op. cit.

19   F. Gibson, 'What can reminiscence contribute to people with dementia?', in J. Bornat (ed.), *Reminiscence Reviewed: Perspectives, Evaluations, Achievements*, Buckingham: Open University Press, 1993, pp. 46–60; D. Atkinson, *An Auto/Biographical Approach to Learning Disability Research*, Aldershot: Ashgate, 1997.

20   B.K. Haight, 'Reminiscing: the state of the art as a basis for practice', *International Journal of Aging and Human Development*, 33, 1, (1991), pp. 1–32; B.K. Haight and S. Hendrix, 'An integrated review of reminiscence', in B.K. Haight and J.D. Webster (eds), *The Art and Science of Reminiscing: Research and Applications*, Washington: Taylor and Francis, 1995, pp. 3–21.

21   P.G. Coleman, *Ageing and Reminiscence Processes: Social and Clinical Implications*, Chichester: Wiley, 1986. P.G. Coleman, C. Ivani-Chalian and M. Robinson, 'The

story continues: persistence of life themes in old age', *Ageing and Society*, 18, 4, (1998), pp. 389–419

22 D. Boden and D.D.V. Bielby, 'The past as resource: a conversational analysis of elderly talk', *Human Development*, 26, (1983), pp. 308–19; J.B. Wallace, 'Reconsidering the life review: the social construction of talk about the past', *The Gerontologist*, 32, (1992), pp. 120–5; K. Buchanan and D. Middleton, 'Voices of experience: talk, identity and membership in reminiscence groups', *Ageing and Society*, 15, 4, (1995), pp. 457–91.

23 Bornat and Chamberlayne, op. cit.

24 J. Bornat, 'Is oral history auto/biography?', *Auto/Biography*, 3, 1/3, 2, (1994), pp. 17–30.

25 Portelli, op. cit., p. 9.

26 J. Bornat, 'Presenting' in P. Shakespeare, D. Atkinson and S. French (eds), *Reflecting on Research Practice: Issues in Health and Social Welfare*, Buckingham: Open University Press, 1993, pp. 83–94.

27 Project funded by a grant from the Economic and Social Science Research Council (reference number L315253003).

28 J. Bornat, B. Dimmock, D. Jones and S. Peace, 'The impact of family change on older people: the case of stepfamilies', in S. McRae (ed), *Changing Britain: Families and Households in the 1990s*, Oxford: Oxford University Press, 1999, pp. 248–62.

29 A. Portelli, 'The peculiarities of oral history', *History Workshop*, 12, (1981), pp. 96–107; N.K. Denzin, 'Interpretive interactionism and the use of life stories', *Revista Internacional de Sociologia*, 44, 3, (1986), pp. 321–337; G. Rosenthal, 'Reconstruction of life stories', in R. Josselson and A. Lieblich (eds), *The Narrative Study of Lives*, London: Sage, 1993.

30 P.G. Coleman, 'Creating a life story: the task of reconciliation', *The Gerontologist*, 39, 2, (1999), pp. 133–139.

31 Atkinson, op. cit.; J. Walmsley and D. Atkinson, 'Oral history and the history of learning disability', in J. Bornat, R. Perks, P. Thompson and J. Walmsley (eds), *Oral History, Health and Welfare*, London: Routledge, 2000, pp. 180–202.

32 Frisch, op. cit.

33 A.J. Rouverol, '"I was content and not content": oral history and the collaborative process', *Oral History*, 28, 2, (1999), pp. 66–78.

34 S.B. Gluck and D. Patai, *Women's Words: the Feminist Practice of Oral History*, New York and London: Routledge, 1991.

35 K. Borland, '"That's not what I said": interpretive conflict in oral narrative research', in S.B. Gluck and D. Patai (eds), *Women's Words: the Feminist Practice of Oral History*, New York and London: Routledge, 1991, pp. 63–75, p. 73.

36 Portelli, 1997, op. cit., p. 270, p. 272

37 M. Frisch, 'Oral history and *Hard Times*: a review essay', in R. Perks and A.S. Thomson (eds), *The Oral History Reader*, London: Routledge, 1998, pp. 29–37.

38 Rosenthal, op. cit.; T. Wengraf, 'Uncovering the general from within the particular: from contingencies to typologies in the understanding of cases', in P. Chamberlayne, J. Bornat and T. Wengraf (eds), *The Turn to Biographical Method in Social Science: Comparative Issues and Examples*, London: Routledge, 2000, pp. 140–64.

39 J. Harris and T. Hopkins, 'Beyond anti-ageism: reminiscence groups and the development of anti-discriminatory social work education', in J. Bornat (ed.), *Reminiscence Reviewed: Perspectives, Evaluations, Achievements*, Buckingham: Open University Press, 1993, pp. 75–83.

40   L. Hunt, M. Marshall and C. Rowlings, *Past Trauma in Late Life: European Perspectives on Therapeutic Work with Older People*, London: Jessica Kingsley, 1997; K.L. Rogers, S. Leydersdorff and G. Dawson (eds) *Trauma and Life Stories: International Perspectives*, London: Routledge, 1999.

41   Bornat and Chamberlayne, op. cit.

42   J. Adams, J. Bornat and M. Prickett, 'Discussing the present in stories about the past' in A. Brechin, J. Katz, S. Peace and J. Walmsley (eds), *Care Matters: Concepts, Practice and Research*, London: Sage, 1998.

43   An example of this is the website 'Oldfarts', targeted at older people. This includes a discussion list whose moderator describes the 'purpose' in the following way: We want you to enjoy this list . . . (their parenthesis) tell as many friends as you would like about it. Bear in mind, we are trying to reach only the 'OVER 50' crowd. Do not introduce religion (in any form) or politics to the discussions (www.topica.com/lists/oldfarts/).

44   Frisch, 1990, op. cit.; Rouverol, 1999, op. cit.

45   H. Goodall, 'Colonialism and catastrophe: contested memories of nuclear testing and measles epidemics at Ernabella', in K. Darian-Smith and P. Hamilton (eds), *Memory and History in Twentieth Century Australia*, Melbourne: Oxford University Press, 1994; W. Westerman, 'Central American refugee testimonies and performed life histories in the Sanctuary movement', in R. Perks and A.S. Thomson (eds), *The Oral History Reader*, London: Routledge, 1998, pp. 224–34.

46   K. Olsen and L. Shopes, 'Crossing boundaries, building bridges: doing oral history among working-class women and men', in S.B. Gluck and D. Patai (eds), *Women's Words: the Feminist Practice of Oral History*, New York and London: Routledge, 1991, pp. 63–75.

47   A reminiscence worker described a session which included hand-clapping, singing, classical music, a video of the 1953 coronation, the music of Elgar and Wagner, Handel's water music and the Messiah, all with a view to evoking memories of classical music and royalty (personal communication, 19.10.00).

48   D. Plaza, 'Family structure and social change of Caribbeans in Britain: an exploratory study of elderly Caribbean males', paper prepared for the Caribbean Studies Association XXI Annual Conference (1996), p. 16

Chapter 36

Cliff Kuhn and
Marjorie L. McLellan

VOICES OF EXPERIENCE
Oral history in the classroom

Schools are an important context for intergenerational oral history projects in many countries. In this chapter Cliff Kuhn and Marjorie McLellan bring together a 'round-table' of North American secondary school teachers to talk about the processes, benefits and challenges of oral history in schools. Cliff Kuhn is an Associate Professor of History at Georgia State University; Marjorie McLellan is Director of the Public History Program at Wright State University. Reprinted with permission from the Organization of American Historians' Magazine of History, 1997, vol. 11, no. 3, pp. 23–31. Copyright © Organization of American Historians (www.oah.org/).

Introduction

T HE PAST THIRTY YEARS have seen a veritable explosion of student oral history initiatives, in all sections of the country and beyond, from elementary school through college, in a variety of media, and, to be honest, with decidedly uneven results. Pioneering the way was the Foxfire program, originated in 1966 by Eliot Wigginton and his students in Rabun Gap, Georgia. Over the years, Foxfire students have documented through their interviews a rich world of traditional Appalachian practices and folklore, and presented this material in a celebrated series of magazines and books. In turn, Foxfire has spawned a teaching philosophy that has encouraged teachers and their students to build inter-generational bridges and to forge meaningful connections between schools and the wider public that they serve. It has also directly led to numerous other school-based oral history projects across the country, indeed around the world, although, to be sure, not all school-based projects are the offspring of Foxfire. In 1985, Wigginton summarized the Foxfire approach in a book directed toward his fellow teachers entitled *Sometimes a Shining Moment: The Foxfire Experience.*

The shining moments brought about by oral history can occur when students more deeply appreciate their own heritage, as with this student from Toby Daspit's

African American Studies Class at New Iberia Senior High School in Iberia Parish, Louisiana. She describes her interview with her grandmother:

> Growing up back then was a struggle, but a close family kept (my grandmother's family) together. She talked about how they had to grow the majority of their food and long hours working in the field. As the interview went on I found myself getting to know what type of person my grandmother was and what type of people she came from. After the interview I found myself with a feeling of pride to know that my family not only had a strong will to survive but a strong will to love. And I am happy that I am a descendant of (this family).

Shining moments occur when students light up with excitement upon realizing that local voices and familiar places are connected with currents in American history previously only read about in textbooks. And, they occur when students see the pleasure and excitement that their elders take in a magazine article, exhibit, performance, or Web site that they have crafted from their own original oral history research.

Oral history not only energizes teaching, but it also meets curricular mandates in a wide range of subject areas. Through oral history projects, students and teachers engage in an undertaking that reveals what historians do in their own work. Oral history interviews enable students to uncover new information about the past and bring that expertise into class discussions. Students are more committed to a course when they feel a sense of ownership in and competence over the subject matter. As students compare interviews, they engage in critical thinking and learn to contextualize information. Through the assignments, students strengthen social awareness, as well as active listening and questioning skills, while they learn from first-hand experience about historical research and resources.

Students use a variety of technical skills to complete projects: word processing, layout, design, oral communications, budgeting, managing, and record-keeping. Producing oral history interview transcripts and summaries pushes students to solve writing and editing problems. Publishing student work in the form of local history exhibits, a school publication, or a World Wide Web site provides both recognition and a reason for writing; the students' work does contribute to our knowledge of history.

Oral history is inherently interdisciplinary; as students move from planning and field research to public presentation, projects break down the traditional compartmentalization between history, writing, reading, graphic arts, and theater. Student interviews can illuminate course content in potentially any discipline or across disciplines; for example, a history of science project might involve interviews with an industrial chemist, an inventor, or an entomologist at a local university. Oral history similarly breaks down the barriers between the classroom and the community, while forging stronger ties across generations. [. . .]

True to the genre of oral history, we [. . .] present an edited transcript of a teachers' roundtable held at the 1996 spring meeting of the Southern Oral History Organization, one of the [US] Oral History Association's state and regional affiliates. Teachers Toby Daspit, Susan Moon, and Rich Nixon, from Louisiana, Georgia, and North Carolina, respectively, describe some of the challenges and rewards they've experienced doing oral history in the classroom. [. . .]

Voices of experience roundtable

Marjorie McLellan: Tell us about your community, how you came to adopt oral history as a teaching strategy, and the project that you've developed with your students.

Rich Nixon: We are a rural district, and it's a fairly large high school, about 1,300 students, four grades. The county is adjacent to the county that has the capital city of Raleigh, and yet there's quite a difference in the two counties. Our county is very agricultural. Tobacco is still the most important crop. As a result, it doesn't have anything like the type of population that you have in Wake County, where Raleigh is. However, the interstate has come through, and now people can live in the western part of our district and get to Raleigh and the Research Triangle just about as quick as they could if they lived in the northern parts of the city. So we're getting into part of our district a pretty good influx of people who are not natives of the county, and they're bringing in new experiences, new frames of reference. They look outside the county for their jobs, which is changing our makeup.

I teach United States history courses to 11th graders, and over the past four or five years I've become interested in oral history as a way of taking advantage of resources in the community. I frequently do a lot of small types of projects, sometimes nothing more than an assignment to go home and talk to Momma and Daddy about something. Usually I'll have the students write it down and come in and talk about it. Every once in a while I get ambitious, and we go into some major project. I had one we started, and my ambition was more than my capabilities. We got into it, did the interviews, wrote it up, and kind of stalled. The next year I got better organized and found a bit of funding and was able to put together a book on the oral history of the fifties in the local community.

Audience: How did you pick that topic?

Nixon: When I first started teaching, I said to my students, 'Go talk to your grandparents about the Great Depression.' And along the line you realize that your students' grandparents weren't alive during the Depression. They weren't that old. I realized that we're losing resources, people are passing away, and their stories are going with them. So a year before we did this project, I worked with the class on talking to their grandparents about the World War II experience at home. I sent the kids forth, and they came back with all this great stuff. Then I said, 'I'm going to start looking for other people's advice on how to do it,' and came across things like permission forms. That's where I went, 'Uh-oh. Better just put this in the folder. We've had fun, the kids have learned to work with this, and stop there.' Next year I did the ground work, got the permission form and everything. I didn't want to do World War II again, and the fifties is a very fascinating topic for the kids. Plus, we could talk to the parents, most of them, too.

Susan Moon: I'm very rural Georgia and I'm very small town. Our school population is about 650, almost 700, that's grades nine through twelve. My ratio is fifty percent black and forty-nine percent white. And it's a lower socio-economic area. No matter what race you are, you usually eat free lunch. I think the majority of our families are single-parent families. We've had several migrant workers come in, not a lot, I think we have twelve that are in the high school. And we have students who have come over from India whose parents are running the motels. In the summer of 1990 I was looking for the ten hours to renew your certification, and they were offering a course called Foxfire I at North Georgia College. It was the first course I've ever taken in my life that – education courses especially – I took back to my classroom and laid it out on the table, and just whew! You know, it just went on in all different directions. I ended up taking the Level II course, and I went to a Foxfire-sponsored folklore institute at Western Carolina the summer of 1992.

I teach one totally Foxfired class; it's called 'Creative Writing for Publication and Computer,' but the students named it 'Back Roads' because we are a small school located in rural Georgia. We do a lot of different things. We do the school newspaper, and we do the literary magazine, but we also collect oral histories of people in the town. This year we worked on something called 'Elder Tales,' where my students wanted to go out and get stories from their grandparents and bring their grandparents to the classroom.

Toby Daspit: New Iberia is a community of about 30,000 in southwest Louisiana. [There] is only one public high school in the town, about 2,000 students, approximately thirty percent African American, seventy percent white. Most of the students that we have in the course are from the lower socio-economic class – my understanding is students have three options, two options if you're not going to go on to college: to work at the port, Port of Iberia, or join the military.

In the fall of '91, a colleague of mine in the Iberia Parish Special Education Department, Carmelite Blanco, and I took a course in Foundations of Education at the University of Southwestern Louisiana. The goal of the course was to create a project to assist 'at-risk students,' it was the hot term back then. And, it just so happened that Carmelite had contacts with Shadows-on-the-Teche, which is a National Trust plantation home there. Shadows-on-the-Teche is unlike other plantation homes, it's right smack in the middle of downtown New Iberia. I mean, there's a bank next to it, a restaurant across the street, it's right there. You can't avoid it if you live in the community.

Shadows-on-the-Teche was in the process of self-evaluation, and they were moving toward projects aimed at inclusion, including the marginalized African-American experience. And Carmelite created this class called 'Out of the Shadows,' working on this metaphor of pulling out African-American history, especially history that was so important to this plantation. It never went further than the class at this point, and most of us, including myself, were extremely skeptical. She envisioned students spending their spare time after school digging into plantation documents and letters. The next spring, I was approached by Carmelite and some members of the school board with the idea of teaching a course called 'African American Studies: Oral Traditions of the African American Community in Iberia Parish.' What happened in the interim was Carmelite didn't let the idea go. She pushed it, and staff from the Shadows also pushed this idea. I knew nothing about it. I just sort of jumped headlong into it.

We had to go to the state Board of Elementary and Secondary Education to get approval to teach it. So we submitted something that said what the objectives are.

And I hate behavioral objectives, because the world is not that nice and tidy, so they're real nebulous: to 'heighten student awareness of African American history,' to 'develop research skills,' to 'investigate different methods in which history can be studied and presented,' et cetera. Or things like, 'the teacher will evaluate student products according to criteria established.' And they approved it.

The years that I taught the course, along with Jamie Credle and Pat Kahle from the Shadows, there was only one white student that took it, it was just African Americans. At the end of every year, we had a public program where the students would share their interviews and other documents that they produced with the public. The first year we did an oral history of the integration of Iberia Parish schools called 'Crossing the Color Line: An Oral Perspective of the Integration of Iberia Parish Schools'. The next two years, we decided to go back as far as we could with the elderly members of the community. We did 'A Journey Through the Years: An Oral History of the 1930s and 1940s in Iberia Parish,' and 'Somewhere in the Neighborhood: African American Communities in Iberia Parish During the Jim Crow Era'.

McLellan: How do you prepare the students to do oral history? What kinds of work do you do before you send them out to do interviews?

Moon: We do a lot of brainstorming those first two weeks of school, where we sit and talk about what is out there in the community. I usually bring in a touch of humor, too, by reminding them that every town has its local characters. We also get rid of some of the [stereotypes]. Teenagers have a tendency to think that in every small town in America, 'There's nothing to do. What's the first thing I'm going to do: leave.' They start getting interested, and they talk about, 'Well my granddaddy used to do that,' maybe milking cows or whatever. Brainstorming opens up the rapport, too, with the students, because nobody can put a wrong answer on the board when you're doing that. And then we decide which one of these things we want to focus on, and how we're going to do it.

Before I send them out on an interview, we practice interviewing each other. Then we bring in a speaker, and they practice interviewing skills in the classroom. They get so many points every time they ask a good, open-ended question, and they get minus if they ask a question that can be answered 'yes' or 'no.' By the end of six weeks, they are ready to go out and try some of it on their own.

McLellan: Do you set up contacts ahead for them to interview?

Moon: The students themselves have to set up the interview, contact the person, tell them when we're coming, how many people are coming. Foxfire says that everything comes from student involvement, and they're responsible for all of that. Each group sets their own deadline about when they're going to have this done, and when the transcripts are going to be finished. They tell me what they want to do, and that's when it gets engraved in stone. Then it's on the calendar in writing. By the end of the semester, all the work has to be transcribed and in. That portfolio of their work becomes their final exam.

Parents have to sign off on insurance forms at the first of the year. We make sure that insurance form is filled out and parents have signed it, indicating it is all right for those students to go off campus. See, I'm not with them. They go off without a chaperon. Of course, I'm dealing with older students usually, too, eleventh and twelfth graders, and the Back Roads class is nine through twelve. So the little ones go with the older ones, and that makes them grow up. In fact, my ninth graders probably like the class better than any of my other students. They feel big because they're in there with the seniors and the juniors, and they get to do a lot of things that other people [don't].

I also make sure that Back Roads is always the last class of the day, something I look forward to. I used to hate sixth period, but I look forward to sixth period every day. And it comes after lunch, which gives us that other half hour in there if we need [it]. That gives them an hour and a half for interviewing and things like that. A lot of my students do work after school because they have to, and so this gives them a chance to go during the class. They don't miss another class now.

Nixon: I have something of an advantage where I have them for an entire year, so you can ease them into it. Most of the students would much rather come in and sit down and listen to me talk to them all period and tell them what it is I expect of them. It takes a while to try and get them used to how you have them do the work. And I try as much as possible to get out from in front of the classroom. So from the beginning of the year, we work a lot with facsimiles of documents and activities which force them to work with material, which is an unusual process for a lot of them. By the time I'm ready to talk to them about this, they see it as just, 'Well, here comes something else.' It's almost as if they're used to it.

Once they get started, it's almost as if it's a revelation that older people had an existence before the children were born [laughter], and they find out that, 'Hey, guess what my folks used to do,' or, 'Guess what my grandparents used to do.' Going in, it doesn't seem like a lot of fun, but they're always somewhat amused by the responses that they get. And likewise, the people they talk to are always interested in talking, and so it works well once they get into it.

Daspit: When you mention community, I'm interested in pedagogy of place and how place works to sort of destroy this notion that we can universalize history especially and that we can teach United States history to everyone in the country and set these national standards. It's just not that simple. And, like Foxfire, what emerged from the course was a pedagogy from the students. We didn't know what we were doing getting into it, although we knew that we wanted oral history as a central part of it.

Originally our idea was to sort of fill in the gaps, what's missing in history. The first year we identified for them who were the big figures. You know, we definitely want to interview this person, because he was superintendent, we definitely want to hear this person because he was at the school at this time. And what happened the second and third years was what I now see as a real political move from the students, because they resisted this notion of we identifying who they're going to go out [and interview], and they turned more to family members who many of them claim they had never spoken with before, at least not about these issues.

As far as preparing them, practice, doing peer interviews, a mini-interview, which is sort of a mid-term grade. We also have them for a whole year and have the beautiful luxury – I was given $5,000 a year to purchase equipment, to bring in speakers, and that's primarily due to the director of Special Ed. who freed up some money. We would bring in five or six major speakers during the course of the year. That was really nice, to have people who've done oral histories, and hundreds and hundreds of them, sharing their experiences.

McLellan: What kinds of problems or obstacles have you had?

Nixon: The biggest problem I had is the crowding in of so many things I have to do in the course. Both of the major projects that I did, I would sit down and set up a timeline, and we would start pretty much on schedule, but then as we moved through the year, situations developed, and things happened unexpectedly. You get behind here as we need to spend a little bit more time on this than anticipated, and so this deadline gets moved. And then all the minor irritations: you can't get into the computers this day because somebody else is already there, or the copier is broken down. All those kinds of things pile up, so that by the end of the year, if you're not careful, you're sitting there two thirds through, and a week to go.

Daspit: One of the biggest obstacles came from the students themselves, and it was their perception of what history is. They never viewed this as a history class. They always view it as something 'other'. They said, 'This is not history. We're talking about community figures, and then we start talking about parents.' Even with the people you interviewed, that familiar response. Well, my own mother told me, 'I don't have anything to tell you, you should go talk to so and so.' So just disrupting that whole question of what is history, what isn't history.

The major obstacle was transcribing and shifting deadlines because of that. We realized there was a need to provide background information in general African-American history, which took time away from the training and oral history methodology. So our students, basically the last day of school, were turning in transcripts. The last thing they do is turn in an interview. Usually it's handwritten, which we accept, because most of them don't have typewriters at home, or don't know how to type, or we kept trying to get access to computer labs and ran into problems. Students say, 'I have to work today. I couldn't get to the interview.' They don't believe you. How long can it take? That's a big obstacle of them doing it the night before, and trying to pace these things. It's just a long, tedious process.

Nixon: I [. . . turn] it over to the kids as much as I can. As far as the focus of the project, I kind of tossed out the fifties. From there we talked about what do we want to know about it. Then we just threw things up on the board, just ideas we threw out, and tried to come up with a list of questions for interviews that would get at those things. After the students did the interviews and made the transcripts, they came in and as a group arrived at what four or five general areas that they thought the material could be grouped in. Then it was a process of putting them into small committees. The [class] would regroup, and take the material and go to each person's interview and say, 'Well, this part of the interview should be with this committee. This part of the interview should be over here.'

At that point, I'm just the ringmaster to make sure that we can get in labs when we need to get in labs, and make sure they have what they need. It really takes very little work once they get going, because you can see them take ownership of it.

They become interested in making sure that what they've got is what they want. They'll argue about where this passage belongs, whether it's here or should it go in here. Sometimes nobody wants this thing: 'It belongs to you, put it in your section.' So once you set this thing in motion, the best thing to do is just stay out of the way and make sure the logistics are taken care of, and they can run it from there. [. . .]

I was able to get a bit of money from a local organization that supports schools and offers mini grants, which was enough to pay for the binding and the paper that we used. We bought tapes from the educational foundation – the tapes are still stored there at the school for future use. We did all the publishing on the copier at school and used computers at the school to do the printing with the original. When we did the permission form, interviewees knew [their interview] was going to be included in the book, they would be identified by name, we included biographical information, the tapes would be stored and could be used in future classes. The money we got from the organization was enough to cover all the expenses, and the project was done without really much disruption of the normal school day. [. . .]

Moon: We don't have those kinds of funds. There's no budget or anything. I never knew what money was when it came to doing this. To make my money to publish my magazines, we sit outside of a little cafe called the Pastime Grill and rock all night long, begging, 'Please, give us some money!' I do everything I can. We wash cars, we do everything. [. . .]

Kuhn: Who decides what goes in and what doesn't go in there?

Moon: Students. Because that magazine is theirs, they've worked on it, it should be what those students want in that magazine. It has to be their work. But you can see a difference in the type of writing. In other words, there are fewer mistakes in the last magazine than there were in the first one, and it looks a little bit more polished, because they've learned how to use computers, to which we've gotten access.

Nixon: To me at the time – and I still think that – the process was much more important than the product. When we envisioned this, my main goal was having them do some type of authentic research rather than the type of research that we can do in a public school library that has a limited budget. This was something different. They can't go to the encyclopedia or go to a book that has been on the shelf for a very long time and look up something, because they actually have to go out and do real research. So for me, it was an opportunity to give them a chance to do some authentic research and work with some real material to sharpen their skills as historians, look at how to work with it, how to revise it, and at the same time work on their writing and communication skills. All that was really what I wanted to get at. The book was kind of the icing on the cake. The printing of the book was almost a reward for the students and for the participants. When I wrote for a mini grant, the idea was to make sure we had enough money to print a copy for each student and participant, so that we could give something to everyone. Anything extra we would give to libraries, school libraries and local libraries, because it definitely is a community interest type thing. [. . .]

Audience: How do we fit in the fact that a lot of students don't have a very good background in history, or have to take standardized tests?

Moon: I've never had trouble meeting state curriculum [objectives] for anything I do in that Back Roads classroom, because it covers just about everything. They're editing, they're writing, they're speaking, it's public speaking in a way. And it's real world connections and it's real life skills that they get. They read all this world history, and it doesn't mean a thing to them out of the textbook, but when they are living it and seeing it in real life, it makes a big connection for them. As a teacher of writing, I have a tendency to think that students do a lot better writing on things that they're interested in. [. . .]

One thing that concerns me, too, is my grading and my students. Even though I've been doing this for five or six years, I still get so excited about what they're doing, it's hard to be objective. In other words, if I get excited I wonder if I'm being objective enough, because very few people – you have to work hard to fail Back Roads. In other words, you have to really be doing nothing. I worry about that aspect of it, about authentic assessment, and I've tried to address that through going to different workshops.

It's something I think comes with experience, too. I don't think any other teacher can tell you what happens, it just kind of falls into place. You get to the point that if you know your students, you know that you've done the right things and that they're doing the right things. [. . .]

Kuhn: How do you get your students to do better interviews?

Moon: Practice, and also those classroom interviews when we have speakers come in. We do have speakers that deliberately answer those yes/no questions with 'yes' or 'no,' and everybody just sits there. And then an older student will say, 'What has been your most memorable experience?' That gets the conversation going again, and then we all know that we've messed up and had a yes/no question.

Peer pressure has a lot to do with mine, as we go through the process, too. Those that are in that group that are doing that particular project will correct each other. 'Why did you ask that?'

But I do not let mine go with a written set of notes. In other words, they generate that set of questions, but they do not take a piece of paper with them. They have to go from what that person says. And that's the beauty of an interview, too, that these speakers take you in different places that you hadn't even thought about and give you different ideas about the project. [. . .]

Moon: When they come back from those interviews, I'll ask, 'Why didn't you ask about this when she said that?' When they've had a really good interview outside the classroom, they come back, they're very animated and they start talking about what they learned, and that's sometimes a good way to subtly get into – and let them go back maybe. Because sometimes it takes more than one interview to get the stories we're trying to get, so then they'll remember that to ask the next time.

Nixon: One of the things that I try is come up with enough small questions that essentially are coming at the topic from many different ways. When we brainstorm, kids can come up with lots of different ways of essentially asking the same thing.

Maybe this one question didn't lead anywhere, and later they come back with something else that gets at what they wanted from a different angle. It's almost like the shotgun approach, fire and hope you hit something.

Daspit: I found that peer interviews are very useful, because knowing what it's like to sit on the other side of the microphone is really important. And I concur that the sharing of the stories from the interviews really helped a lot, because there was always one brave soul who goes out two or three weeks before they have to go out, comes back and shares. They learn wonderful things like, 'As soon as that tape recorder went off, that's when the real good stories started.'

We did generate questions together. 'Behind the Veil' (A project documenting African-American life in the Jim Crow South, sponsored by Duke University's Center for Documentary Studies) had some sample questions and several other sources, although we urge them, 'Please don't walk in with questions.' I mean, maybe an index card you can peek at. Most students come back and say, 'I asked the first question, and they just talked. Just went from there.'

McLellan: How does this change the students? What do they learn doing it, and how do they come away different from this oral history project?

Moon: One thing that comes out of it, the generation gap in these interviews melts away. My students come back with so much respect for the older people they've talked to, especially the older people. They enjoy the interviews with the older people more than they do the ones who are maybe close to their age or close to my age, which is not ancient yet.

This little lady was almost ninety-two years old that we interviewed. This was the first black lady that we had gotten to interview, and all eight of my black students wanted to go over there at one time, and she's ninety-two years old. She said 'Bring 'em on!' And they were so animated when they got back. They came back bursting back into the classroom. They said, 'You won't believe this. Her grandmother was an ex-slave, and she lived in Pike County, and there's a place over there that you can go and see where she was actually born.' So we took a trip in the next week. We all went over to Pike County where this lady was supposedly born, and Miss Bertha went with us. That was a shining moment in my teaching career, to hear those children and that woman; she was animated, because somebody cared enough to ask about her history. You know what I'm talking about? It made her whole life viable, and I think that was important.

Nixon: I like to think that it changes their perspective of history a bit, because it provides a living link to history. Unfortunately to most of them, history is the stuff in this book, and it's very dry and people act very serious and do very serious things, and it doesn't seem as if it was ever alive. But by talking with people about their past experiences, I think it changes their perception. They start to understand that even though people lived long ago doesn't mean they were a great deal different from the way we are today. I think that's the biggest benefit.

Daspit: I was reminded of a story a second ago. We were on a field trip to a plantation home, and learning absolutely nothing except what Hollywood films have been filmed at that site, and we walked into the old school house, and the bus driver, an elderly African-American gentleman, tagged along with us. One of the students said, 'Well, what's this?' It was a potbelly stove, and the tour guide said, 'I really don't know.' The bus driver said, 'I remember.' And he went on for fifteen or twenty minutes talking about, 'I had to bring the coal in every morning,' and 'You've got this soot all over your clothes.' I hope that the students saw then that what has been silenced is sort of the commoners' experience in history, and that those stories are important. So I hope that it just gives a chance to recognize that they can be producers, they are producers of history. It's a question of realizing it and focusing it. And they also learn how difficult this is. [. . .]

McLellan: What would you warn teachers about before they adopt a project like this, and what reward would you point to that teachers or students could carry away from this?

Moon: Anytime you take on something like this, it is more than the normal eight-hour day. I mean, there's a lot of work involved on your part to keep that momentum going. And sometimes at the end of the day, you're worn slap out, and sometimes your day doesn't end till nine o'clock at night. But the first reward I get from it is seeing students excited about learning and what they're doing. Their enthusiasm is contagious. That's the biggest reward for me, because I'm forty-four years old, but in my mind I'm eighteen, because I stayed there with them. I think this type of project is what keeps me young.

Nixon: My warning would be to make your project much smaller than what you think you can do, because what looks to be very manageable quickly turns into a monster. And she's right, the reward is that something has been done that's worthwhile and it's real, it's authentic, rather than you've gone through this year, and we've talked about the right things, and we've taken the proper tests. But you have something now that's a product of some type of historical inquiry.

Daspit: I think I would warn about some of the ethical issues that come up when we start talking about voice and representation, but that's also a reward, too, because you're digging into those questions as opposed to – it's a lot easier just to sit there and stand up in front of the class and lecture than to turn it over and say, 'We're admitting we don't know what's going to happen.' Money and time become really, really important, too. I mean, if you're talking about thirty-five students at a time, how do you do that? How do you get tape recorders to everyone? How do you share that? And the reward, it's the same from what I'm hearing from all of us. It's a real product for a real audience. Students are actually producing something that other people are going to see or talk about, and it's personally satisfying. I don't know how to phrase it any other way, but it's fun.

Moon: Can I take just one moment? I brought this quote, because it has become part of my philosophy. It's a quote by Aunt Addie Norton in one of the Foxfire books. This to me sums up what I'm doing. It says, 'I tell you one thing, if you learn it by yourself, if you have to get down and dig for it, it never leaves you. It stays there as long as you live, because you had to dig it out of the mud before you learned what it was.' That says a lot about what oral history does for everybody that's involved.

Chapter 37

Daniel Kerr

'WE KNOW WHAT THE
PROBLEM IS'

Using video and radio oral history to develop
collaborative analysis of homelessness

Oral history can be a significant resource for political groups and emergent social movements. Here Daniel Kerr shows how oral history promoted 'dialogue in the streets among the homeless' of the US city of Cleveland, and how 'a democratically organized project built on the framework of what Michael Frisch terms "shared authority" can play a significant role in movement building'. Daniel Kerr has been an activist in squatting and housing movements in New York and Cleveland, and a Ph.D. student at Case Western Reserve University. Extracted from *Oral History Review*, 2003, vol. 30. no. 1, pp. 27–45. © 2003, Oral History Association. All rights reserved. Used by permission.

> It takes the efforts, man, of all of us homeless people to get together and try and come up with solutions. But they don't want to hear our ideas. We go on homeless marches. We go on homeless outings. And we tell them what's the problem. We know what the problem is. But they don't listen to us. You know why? Because there's big dollars involved now.
>
> (John Appling[1])

IN THE FALL OF 1996, after eight months of working with a group I founded that provides food to people living on the streets and in the shelters of Cleveland, I initiated what has become the Cleveland Homeless Oral History Project (CHOHP). Intrigued with the possibility that oral history could promote dialogue on the streets among the homeless, I bought a thirty-dollar mini-cassette recorder and brought it to our weekly picnics. The initial audio interviews examined the life histories of four homeless men. The project coincided with my entrance into the graduate program in history at Case Western Reserve University and I used the interviews in a seminar paper, a performance piece and pamphlet, 'A Complete Perfect Nothingness.'[2]

As I transcribed these interviews, however, I realized that my goal of promoting dialogue on the streets was only partially fulfilled. While the individuals I interviewed knew they were being recorded, they were clearly talking to me. I was the one who had collected and compiled their profound words, which I now had before me at my desk. My desire to have the interviewees talk to each other resulted in some unconventional theoretical approaches in my first paper. However, the limitations of the printed format, measured in terms of its cool reception by the most important intended audience, the homeless themselves, prompted me to switch over to video. I began to see this project more explicitly as a collaborative one, unlike mainstream academic research on homelessness. [. . .]

Presently there is no accountability in the relationship between the state and the homeless subject or between the academic and the homeless subject. Defining the homeless as a primary audience would be a significant act in and of itself, and an acknowledgement of the inability of the present political process to deal with the phenomenon of homelessness. Such an approach necessitates more than just having the homeless as an audience or as spectators, but also having them as active participants in the formation of a collective analysis. James Jones's research on the Tuskegee syphilis experiment makes it clear that researchers cannot ethically study misery in a detached scientific fashion.[3] It is not enough to critique the closed and ineffectual circle of discussions on present homeless policies or academic debates on homelessness without working towards building a movement of people who can add weight to the critique and leverage social change as a result. Clearly one group of people with the biggest stake in seeing things change for the better are homeless people themselves.

The Cleveland Homeless Oral History Project is based on the supposition that a democratically organized research project built on the framework of what Michael Frisch terms 'shared authority' can play a significant role in movement building. Frisch goes beyond the model of arguing that the goals of oral and public history should be to impart skills and knowledge to the disempowered. He argues for 'a more profound sharing of knowledges, an implicit and sometimes explicit dialogue from very different vantages about the shape, meaning and implications of history.' He argues that this dialogue will 'promote a more democratized and widely shared historical consciousness, consequently encouraging broader participation in debates about history, debates that will be informed by a more deeply representative range of experiences, perspectives and values.'[4] I would add that the dialogue built on this basis needs to go beyond the way we view history, but also influence the way we design public policy and more importantly, the way we reproduce the social organization of the communities we live in.

Will such an approach violate the academic commitment to objectivity? While it is clear from Jones's research that there is an ethical dimension that requires us to eschew a detached position when studying suffering and human misery, does this necessitate that we forego our commitment to 'the truth'? By providing a 'bullhorn' to the oppressed and excluded, do we give up our critical authority and give in to 'bad science'? Helen Longino argues that all science is influenced by background assumptions that shape our questions and influence our interpretations of data. Rather than foregoing empiricism and peer review, Longino argues that a scientific community is closer to objectivity when it is more inclusive and democratic Acknowledging that theories can never attain the status of 'single truth,' Longino contends, 'We can nevertheless rank theories as to their acceptability, in particular their worthiness as basis for collective action to solve common problems. That theory which is the product of the most inclusive scientific community is better, other things being equal, than that which is the product of the most exclusive.'[5] By broadening the scientific community through the process of sharing authority with the homeless, one does not give up objectivity; rather one produces more objective and effective research. Theories and solutions that garner support are effectively implemented, and [those that] successfully address common problems are objectively better than those that do not. [. . .]

In the summer of 1999, I conceived the CHOHP video project with a fairly simple design rooted in the principle of reflexivity – making the actual research accessible to the homeless. While bringing food downtown, I discovered that Cleveland's Public Square was full of electrical outlets. Earlier in the day preachers and church groups made use of these outlets to proselytize when they brought food to the Square. Through experience I learned that homeless folks were not readily willing to speak into a microphone in front of a large crowd.[6] However, the audio interviews demonstrated they would talk extensively in a more relaxed setting. By videotaping interviews and bringing a television and VCR to the Square, it became possible to create a format where people could talk to a homeless audience extensively about their experiences with and analysis of homelessness. Others on the Square expressed interest in watching these tapes the following week, and invited me to show the videos in other settings such as the shelters. The project developed to the point where homeless spectators requested a reshowing of particular interviews from earlier weeks – establishing a grassroots canon of homeless voices. While the interviewees spoke on wide-ranging issues, it became apparent from these requests that certain analyses resonated with homeless audiences.

Early on when I switched from tape to video, I moved away from asking questions that centered on the life histories of the narrators and asked them both what they felt the historical causes of homelessness were and what they thought could be done about the present situation. This move occurred following my initial video interview with Anthony Ball. I asked him what questions he would like to ask homeless folks, and he replied:

> I guess if I was to ask any kind of questions . . . I don't know, it's hard maybe to ask anybody else questions who is living out here and living a certain way in the streets . . . I don't want to get too personal in someone else's business, but the thing I would want to ask them are what are they doing for themselves to try and make things better for themselves and for other people.[7]

Avoiding direct life history questions provided a means for each of the narrators to be more flexible in their presentation of their experiences and avoid being in a position where they felt they had to provide a confessional. One man, Levi Israel, specifically stated that he would like to see a world where we do not have to probe into the lives of the oppressed.[8] Moving away from personalized life history questions and asking what the interviewee believes to be the causes of homelessness explicitly brings the interviewee into the process of analysis. Nearly all participants combined their experiences with a larger political and structural explanation of the causes of homelessness. Talmadge Wright, whose work on homelessness has furthered the field of critical sociological analysis, argues that this nexus between experience and social structure is at the root of agency. His work *Out of Place* stresses that this recognition of the agency of the homeless has been lacking in most research on homelessness. However, as he argues, recognizing the agency of the homeless is absolutely necessary if we are ever going to see any substantive social change.[9]

Beyond bringing me to change my interview format, Anthony Ball also prompted me to reevaluate and ultimately change the interview medium. Ball continually asked me what I was doing with his interview beyond just showing it on the Square. He wanted to hear his voice 'amplified' by broadcasting the videos to a larger audience. While I had made a concerted effort to ensure that the interviews were broadcast to a homeless audience, I could think of no reason why they should not be broadcast to a broader audience as well. The problem, however, was a technical one. The unedited videos began accumulating and did not present themselves in a readily consumable format. Furthermore, I did not have the skills or access to equipment to do the editing. There was no one willing to take the project on voluntarily, and I did not have the resources to pay someone else to do the project.[10] Access to broadcasting a finished product on television presented another significant hurdle. On top of these barriers, I was not readily convinced that it would be worth all the effort, especially when radio could accomplish the same ends. Radio as a medium had added benefits. A sizeable number of people staying in the shelters, under the bridges, and on the sidewalks of downtown Cleveland carry portable radios with them. Live interviews with the homeless broadcast from the studios of WRUW, CWRU's college radio station, would be readily accessible to a homeless audience and could reach households and cars throughout the city and outlying suburbs.[11]

In the summer of 2000, I began conducting weekly one-hour [radio] interviews with different homeless people each week. As the word spread, people began tuning their radios in on Tuesday mornings and playing our broadcast at drop-in centers and homeless shelters. While it is impossible to determine exactly who your listening audience is when broadcasting a radio show, the fact that we began receiving calls from homeless people who had questions and comments demonstrated that broadening the audience turned out not to mean reaching the middle-class college-educated public we had expected. While we received calls from suburban listeners, the majority of non-homeless callers were working-class city residents interested in the topics addressed by the show's homeless experts.

Like academics, the homeless narrators in the video and radio project did not all share the same analysis of the causes of homelessness. However, it became clear through repetition that there were certain themes that were broadly accepted and discussed. How these themes could and would be identified and who would identify them posed certain problems if I was to stick with my desire to keep this a collaborative project. Certainly I could not go off and do it on my own. In developing the concept of reciprocal ethnography, Elaine Lawless stresses the importance of building a research structure that includes spaces for the collective discussion of research and development of analysis with her research subjects.[12] Drawing from her research model, I organized weekly workshop and research sessions in a drop-in center and emergency shelter in the winter and spring of 1999–2000. During these sessions we watched the video interviews, we brainstormed, and we set about identifying core themes of an analysis of homelessness from the bottom up. Beyond identifying the themes, throughout the entire year in 2000 we prioritized them and developed strategies to promote substantive social change.

While no narrators touched on all the themes, the workshops allowed for the creation of a collective analysis that could evaluate the interviews in a critical manner and identify the most compelling theories. This process produced a multi-factored understanding of homelessness that goes beyond traditional academic analysis. Intriguingly enough, the majority of the issues raised are not inherently 'homeless issues,' but are issues that affect a broad number of city residents. The analysis has a built-in capacity for coalition building. While the space here does not allow me to do complete justice to this analysis, the basic contours of it can be discussed. The workshop participants identified six major themes essential to understanding the present state of homelessness. These themes are not listed in order of importance and were not seen as distinct but understood as interrelated. The first strand of the analysis identifies public and economic policies that led to disinvestment and decline in working class neighborhoods following the 1966 Hough Riots – policies that ultimately paved the way for the gentrification of these areas. John Appling, a participant in the Hough riots and the 1968 Glenville riots, argues:

> But to cut a long story short, if you go down into the Hough area now, it is a planned thing . . . Because back in the sixties when the Hough riots were going down, people couldn't get to work. They were scared to come down Chester. They were scared to come down Euclid. They were scared to come down Superior. Because you see, in order to get downtown to the center, the work district, you had to come down through them streets. And they say, never again will it be like this here. And if you look around here today, it is not like that anymore. If you go down to the Hough area, you have $300,000 homes down there now. You have got apartments that cost 700, 750, 800, $900 a month now, which we cannot afford. The whole area in which I was raised up in, until I was a grown man, now is taken over by Cleveland Clinic, Mt. Sinai, and [University Hospitals].[13]

The second theme identifies the destruction of the single room occupancy hotels, better known as the flop houses, and the subsequent development of sports arenas, the Rock and Roll Hall of Fame, and other downtown 'revitalization' projects as central to the rise of homelessness. Ralph Pack, a former employee at one of these hotels, reflects:

> They wanted to make downtown look real photogenic and make it look real clean. So they cleared out all the old hotels and all the places that were frequented by the poor guys so that when the well-to-do tourists . . . came in they wouldn't see all this . . . They wanted to create a complete new image for downtown Cleveland of everyone prosperous, of everyone doing real well, so they really made a sweep on all the poor people there.[14]

The role of the retrenchment of the welfare system in the creation of homelessness is the third theme. Thomas Smith argues:

> I think if welfare did a better job and gave checks for rent you would have less homeless people . . . It took me four years to get disability. I had four operations. Cut from top to bottom. Eventually they will amputate this one leg. It really ain't the main cause of my being homeless – the disease itself. Mainly it's the welfare department.[15]

The fourth theme consists of the expansion of the criminal justice system as a result of the war on drugs and the criminalization of the poor. Hakeem Ali reasons:

> Ohio itself has thirty-one prisons in the state. [There are 1.6 million people incarcerated.] And that rises at 68% each year. So we're either building more prisons for the rich people to get rich or we're building more prisons to make society safer. It is not making society safer. What it is doing is taking poor white men and poor black men and incarcerating them for a limited time. And they come out angry. Now they're angry when they come out here again, instead of working with their addictions. . . . So we're talking about America using their money anyway they want, instead of using it for the people. It should be for the people and by the people.[16]

Jason Maiden notes that increasingly the homeless have been arrested merely for being homeless:

> The topic is the police coming down and telling us we cannot lay on the sidewalks period. . . . Now we must find places where they can't see us. Now they want to come around the holiday season and get homeless people off the streets – show things off for the people in the suburbs. That's all they want to do is see things pleasant. They don't want to see us lying on benches, trying to get money. I think it is uncalled for.[17]

Anthony Ball argues that this expansion of the prison population impacts people well beyond the time they serve for their alleged crimes:

> But being a felon, I can tell you right now that I can't go to the RTA [Regional Transit Authority] and sweep their floor because of my background. I can't go to the Renaissance Building because I can't even talk to a person anymore because you are talking to an automated system. I did that for about almost three or four weeks. The only places I can probably get a job with quickness is the slave labor, which is the temporary agencies. You can't get no housing with them folks, because you don't get paid enough. After Uncle Sam gets your money and the temp agency gets your money, you ain't got nothing left.[18]

Which leads us to our fifth theme – the rise of the temporary industry. Clarence Dailey recalls:

Back in the sixties and seventies you could basically walk off one job or get fired from one job and be back on another job within an hour or two. Now with the temp agencies, they have taken over control. The companies do not really want to hire anyone because they do not want to pay the benefits, the vacations, the sick pay and take on the responsibilities.[19]

Finally, the sixth theme consists of the establishment of an inhumane shelter system that is akin to an open penitentiary. Robert Molchan emphasizes this point, 'Actually you are in a penitentiary more or less. The only thing is you have the freedom to get up and go.'[20] Clarence Dailey highlights the level of disgust he has towards the shelter system – a sentiment that most of the homeless people I have interviewed share:

They have a site down at 2100 Lakeside where 300 men or more come in there every night. They have about 300 beds and you have about 50 to 100 people sleeping on the bare floor with one blanket up under them. Sure it is cold out there. It is better than sleeping on the streets. But they are warehousing people just like Hitler did in the days of old.[21]

These six points are most concisely summed up by the notion that every which way you look, people other than the homeless are profiting off of the institution of homelessness – be it the real estate developers, downtown leisure and retail business interests, the temp agencies, the prison industries, or the shelter providers. It is precisely because of these entrenched interests that homelessness as a phenomenon has not been effectively addressed. It is also because of these entrenched interests that the homeless have concluded in the workshops that they, along with other segments of the working-class, must take the lead in a movement for social change.

The workshops have gone beyond analyzing what Levi Israel terms 'The Downpression Man.'[22] They have sought to identify strategies for social change. While it has been useful to establish an analysis of the matrix of oppression, it has been even more important to identify avenues of resistance. Discussions throughout the year 2000 made it clear that there were two areas where the homeless felt that they should focus their attention. Not surprisingly, these areas consisted of gaining aspects of control in their working lives (the temp agencies) and their home lives (the shelters and the streets). Nearly all the homeless grassroots activism has arisen in these two sectors since the Cleveland Homeless Oral History Project began. However this activism has not been narrowly drawn. Individuals have been clear to draw interconnections to other issues as they have articulated what they are fighting for.

CHOHP has already had an indirect impact on the public debate in Cleveland. Many of the folks I have interviewed were involved in a series of protests in the summer of 1999 that led to the closing of one shelter due to its poor management and unsanitary conditions.[23] Later that same year Jason Maiden's taped interview on arrests of the homeless during the Christmas season actually spurred a flurry of protests and public hearings. In interviews with the mainstream press, where he critiqued the mayor's policies of criminalizing the homeless, Maiden stressed that the homeless chose to sleep outside because the conditions in the shelter were so miserable.[24] [. . .]

What is perhaps more surprising is the degree of success the protests had. The first protest led to a major reorganization of Cleveland's emergency shelters. The second series of protests resulted in an injunction against Mayor Mike White's holiday policy and a subsequent settlement in which the city explicitly agreed not to arrest or threaten to arrest 'any individuals, including homeless individuals, for performing innocent, harmless, inoffensive acts such as sleeping, lying or sitting in or on public property.'[25] The fact that the protests provoked these responses suggests that the relationship between the homeless and the constellation of interests invested in homelessness began to become unsettled.

The following summer a group of homeless individuals, all of whom had been involved in the CHOHP project, refused to leave a building they had squatted for well over a decade. These individuals argued their case to the public on the CHOHP radio show weeks prior to the eviction. On the day of the eviction, this small band of homeless individuals ground the development process of the city to a halt. All the top-level officials in the mayor's administration negotiated over walkie-talkies with the homeless in the building, while the local media broadcast reports throughout the afternoon. In their press conferences, the homeless made it clear that their occupation of the building was directly related to neighborhood development practices and shelter conditions. Although the building was eventually taken, the standoff resulted in the widespread broadcast of an oppositional analysis of homelessness and an embarrassment for the city administration.[26]

The weekly workshops eventually evolved into what has become the Day Laborers' Organizing Committee (DLOC). By the spring of 2001, the DLOC had successfully secured a ban prohibiting recruiters from temp agencies from entering the city's emergency shelter. In the fall of 2001, eighteen homeless day laborers testified before Cleveland City Council regarding the exploitation and abuse they faced at the temp agencies. The DLOC has since networked with local service unions in the city and has set up an advisory council to establish an alternative hiring hall accountable to day laborers. The organization has also worked with attorneys to draft municipal legislation to regulate day labor agencies operating in Cleveland.[27] Meanwhile, many CHOHP members have worked with the Northeast Ohio Coalition for the Homeless to establish a shelter residents' council and address the pervasive problems in the emergency shelter. In May 2002, Raymond Robinson collected 350 signatures from residents at 2100 Lakeside demanding that the Salvation Army be removed from operating the shelter for the city and the county and that the homeless residents be placed in charge of the facility. The petition prompted the convening of a high level meeting at City Hall and has resulted in significant changes at the shelter as the Salvation Army has scrambled to retain its control.[28]

This flourishing of activity clearly demonstrates that the homeless are more than victims but are agents and perhaps the most effective agents for social change. It not so much that CHOHP has produced discussion and analysis where there was none. Rather it has created links between multiple discussions that were already occurring in the smoke rooms of the shelters, under the bridges, in the parks, and on the steam grates of downtown Cleveland. If there is anything that CHOHP has done, it is to connect people who were thinking about similar things so that they could talk to one another and further develop an analysis of homelessness. The process of creating a shared analysis in a formal research setting has emboldened people to act. [. . .]

Notes

1   John Appling interview, 5 September, 1999. All interviews, tapes, and transcriptions in possession of author.
2   Daniel Kerr. 'A Complete Perfect Nothingness', *XCP*: *Streetnotes*, Fall 1999 (http://bfn.org/~xcp/kerr.html).
3   James H. Jones, *Bad Blood*: *The Tuskegee Syphilis Experiment*, New York: The Free Press, 1981.
4   Michael Frisch, *A Shared Authority*: *Essays on the Craft and Meaning of Oral and Public History*, Albany: State University of New York, 1990, pp. xxi–xxii.
5   Helen Longino, *Science as Social Knowledge*: *Values and Objectivity in Scientific Inquiry*, Princeton University Press, 1990, p. 214.
6   In the summer of 1997, we brought down a microphone and amplifier in order to set up an open forum for the homeless.
7   Anthony Ball interview, 30 May, 1999.
8   Levi Israel interview, 30 May, 1999.
9   Talmadge Wright, *Out of Place*: *Homeless Mobilizations, Subcities, and Contested Landscapes*, Albany: State University of New York, 1997, p. 6.
10   CHOHP has received small amounts of funding from individuals, the CWRU History Department, and some material support from WRUW. The expenses have also been limited. From 1996–2002 the project has approximately cost $4000. My personal income has come from stipends as a teaching and research assistant.
11   As a graduate student I had no problems entering the staff training program and obtaining my own show. To secure my position in the station, I gave up my role as student senator and became the WRUW Public Affairs director. The organization of the show also meant that I stopped conducting video interviews as I juggled my time commitments. Over the whole project, from 1996 to the present, I have on average committed two evenings and one morning every week to CHOHP research.
12   Elaine J. Lawless, *Holy Women, Wholly Women: Sharing Ministries of Wholeness through Life Stories and Reciprocal Ethnography*, Philadelphia: University of Pennsylvania Press, 1993.
13   John Appling interview, 5 September, 1999.
14   Ralph Williams Pack interview, 6 June, 2000.
15   Thomas Smith interview, 12 September, 1999.
16   Hakeem Rahman Ali interview, 31 October, 1999.
17   Jason Maiden interview, 28 November, 1999.
18   Anthony Ball interview, 30 May, 1999.
19   Clarence Dailey interview, 20 March, 2000.
20   Robert Molchan interview, 20 March, 2000.
21   Clarence Dailey interview, 20 March, 2000.
22   Levi Israel interview, 30 May, 1999.
23   Olivera Perkins, 'The Homeless Object to Treatment at Shelter', *Plain Dealer*, 7 July, 1999.
24   Andrea Simakis, 'Lawsuit Sends 4 From Street into Spotlight to Fight Policy', *Plain Dealer*, 10 January, 2000.

25   Michael O'Malley, 'New Shelters to Offer Men Beds, Services', *Plain Dealer*, 12 October, 1999; Rena Koontz, 'Leave Homeless Alone, Judge Rules', *Plain Dealer*, 24 December, 1999; Lynn Key, *et al.* v. City of Cleveland (N.D. O.H. 1999) No.93–CV–3143.

26   Michael O'Malley, 'Homeless Men Vow to Remain in Building When Wreckerss Come', *Plain Dealer*, 1 August, 2000; Michael O'Malley, 'Homeless Holdouts Give in to Orders to Vacate Abandoned Building', *Plain Dealer*, 2 August, 2000; Michael O'Malley, 'Camelot Falls; Judge Stands Up for Occupants', *Plain Dealer*, 3 August, 2000.

27   Josh Greene, 'Temporary Insanity: Dangerous Work, Low Pay, No Future', *Free Times*, 7 February, 2001; Michael O'Malley, 'Homeless Temp Workers Fight Long Days, Low Pay', *Plain Dealer*, 26 August, 2001; Michael O'Malley, 'Temporary Workers Gain Political Support: Day Laborers Consider Forming Own Hiring Hall', *Plain Dealer*, 5 September, 2001. For more on the Day Laborers' Organizing Committee, see www.clevelanddloc.com.

28   'Resident Committee Victory at 2100 Lakeside', *The Homeless Grapevine*, Issue 56.

William Westerman

CENTRAL AMERICAN REFUGEE TESTIMONIES AND PERFORMED LIFE HISTORIES IN THE SANCTUARY MOVEMENT

This chapter provides an example of the direct use of oral history in a particular political struggle, that of the Central American refugees who use their own life-story testimonials to educate North Americans about the situation in their countries, and to gain financial and political support. Westerman shows how these testimonials are constructed for maximum political effect and presented through a range of narrative forms: as performance, in writing, and etched into the bodies of victims of torture. William Westerman is Director, Program for Immigrant Traditional Artists, International Institute of New Jersey. Reprinted from *International Yearbook of Oral History and Life Stories*, Vol. III: *Migration and Identity*, pp. 167–181, edited by Rina Benmayor and Andor Skotnes (1994) by permission of Oxford University Press.

To testify is to bear witness, to tell what you have seen or felt. A religious experience, perhaps, or a crime. Then to come forward and speak. To deliver the word.

DECEMBER 1987. WE ARE STANDING in the Cathedral of San Salvador, El Salvador, tape recorders in hand. There are around two hundred people occupying the Cathedral, just dispersed with tear gas and rubber hoses from the National Ministry of Justice. Young men are taking off their shirts to allow witnesses to photograph the red welts on their backs from the beatings. Scattered among the people in the church, at the doors, in the pews, and before us, dressed in black, their heads covered by white scarves, are the women of COMADRES, the

Committee of Mothers and Relatives of Political Prisoners, Disappeared, and Assassinated of El Salvador. They are standing on the front steps of the Cathedral with banners and megaphones, telling all of San Salvador of the injustices they have witnessed. They are blocking the doors, making sure only those who bring no harm can enter. 'Who are you?' they ask us. A North American delegation. Come on in.

One woman stands before us, and our tape recorders and cameras. She tells us why she is there, about the demonstration violently disrupted by the police. She tells us that a 22-year-old baker had been found dead just several days earlier. He had been held for a brief time in one of the political prisons. They found his corpse, the body mutilated, the skin peeled back in strips from his arms and his thighs, burns from a live wire tied around his tongue. She and the other women of COMADRES were protesting at the Justice Department to demand why.

She asks if we would like to hear her personal testimony. Yes, we tell her, shaking, while our eyes check the doors guarded by the other women for security. She gives us her testimony, and tells us about those in her family she has lost to the death squads, the police, and the government. A daughter. A son. A grandchild. She will go on fighting, speaking out, she says, until the end, until she finds justice, because she has nothing else left to live for. Only a hope that one day there will be justice, one day she might not live to see. Still, she speaks.

Most of us North Americans in the Cathedral that day had previously heard these stories, these testimonies, but without having been to Central America. Since 1980 we had been hearing these accounts across the United States, in churches and synagogues, schools and union halls. They had been brought north to us, on foot, by bus, by plane, by hundreds of thousands of refugees from El Salvador and Guatemala. In the words of one Arizona priest, in 1980 for the first time:

> Not only were there people who came here [to the church] daily for food, for handouts, that were stranded, but there were a new breed of people who came and not only were without food and clothing, but had a story to tell. And it was that story of horror, of terror, from not Mexico but from El Salvador, and from Guatemala, that demanded a new pastoral response.[1]

They came by the thousands: as many as 750,000 fleeing death squads and war in El Salvador which left over 75,000 dead; fleeing massacres, assassinations, torture and repression, hunger and disease in Guatemala, which left at least 30,000 dead as well as up to another 70,000–100,000 'disappeared', killed and buried in clandestine cemeteries.

All the refugees came with stories, histories of why they left and how they arrived. But a select few, at least a thousand, came forward in some way, and began to tell their life stories in public, to North Americans, as a way of informing the US (and Canadian) public about the repression in El Salvador and Guatemala, repression largely funded by our own US Government.

Most of those who came forward to speak during the years 1982 to 1987 were affiliated with the well-known Sanctuary movement, a loose conglomeration of over four hundred congregations which sponsored, transported, and provided legal, medical, and other assistance to Central American refugees, many of whom were undocumented.[2] Though protected by the Geneva Conventions ratified by the US Senate and the US Refugee Act of 1980, most were considered unwelcome by the Reagan and Bush administrations, under which fewer than 3 per cent could obtain political asylum.[3] Some refugees only spoke because they had to, to a judge or lawyer during deportation proceedings, if they got that far. But others, some associated with Sanctuary and some not, spoke out and continue to speak out in public, and these have included union leaders, students, human-rights workers, health workers, businesspeople, peasants. Many spoke out, in the hopes that, as one Salvadoran said to me, 'Once these people listen to us, I believe that they are not going to be the same anymore.'[4] In other words, they hoped that the US public would be moved to act and to question their own government, just as they had done in their home countries.

Those refugees who chose to go public were mostly between eighteen and thirty-five years of age, reflecting in part the age of those who had been most involved politically. Rather than deliver a political 'analysis', the refugees usually delivered a life history in public, which they themselves referred to as 'testimony', a direct translation of the Spanish *testimonio*, or 'personal experience'. These testimonies, lasting between twenty and forty-five minutes in length, were delivered in Spanish, through an interpreter, or preferably in English, since translators became notorious for their errors or failure to capture subtle shades of meaning. English also became the language of choice because North American listeners were more inclined to pay attention and be directly affected by hearing a testimony in their own language. When Spanish was used, it was more formal than usual conversational Central American Spanish, with fewer colloquialisms and clearer pronunciation, both because this accommodated the translators, who often spoke Spanish as their second language, and because the testimony took on the nature of a formal oration.

Such testimony could be given in a variety of contexts, usually in religious settings. Most commonly the personal testimony was a formal component of the ceremony in which the refugee was welcomed into sanctuary. On those occasions, it might also have been released in written form. But testimony would also have been given in a variety of other situations: in private house meetings and gatherings, in elementary and secondary schools, at colleges and universities, in churches and synagogues, in union halls, in law offices, at governmental hearings, even at fashion shows, and on regional tours to areas where there were interested people, but no formal sanctuary communities. It could also have been given in the course of a formal interview with a reporter or with an ethnographer, as in my case as part of a long-term, field-based study.

We can now safely say that testimony was effective, because of the rapid growth in the Sanctuary movement and other Central American solidarity movements during the early 1980s. The Sanctuary movement in the southwest US actually grew out of the experience of listening to the stories of refugees just having crossed the border. A number of Sanctuary workers I interviewed remembered distinctly the first time they ever heard a refugee speak and could relate to me the story they heard. Word of mouth, personal visits, and refugee narratives were responsible for the participation of most of the active congregations. The Sanctuary movement might possibly have grown anyway had there not been personal testimony, but the success in converting the sceptical and the 'apolitical' to a politicized stance, as well as the involvement of the religious sector in the larger Central American Solidarity movement, was largely due to the strength of a few individuals who learnt to speak out, to bear witness to the injustice they had known and were committed to end.

What emerged was an overall consistent traditional pattern to these narratives. Testimony was always in the first person, with episodes concerning third parties – children, siblings, parents – mentioned, but usually only in relation to the speaker. Most examples I heard and compared showed the same structure, including six definite sections: (1) introduction and background, (2) life and activity in the home country, (3) persecution, (4) escape, (5) exile, and (6) analysis and call to action.[5] This is the general chronological pattern, too. This structure was found to be the most successful with North American audiences. While the structure seems intuitive, the choice of autobiography was instead cultural and practical, as Central Americans realized North Americans were much more willing to listen to personal experiences than political discussion. Fundamental parts of the story would not be omitted, but short episodes, details, and descriptions could be lengthened, shortened, or dropped altogether, depending on the audience. The important themes and episodes, according to one refugee, are those 'which are marked in your life'.[6]

Certain historical episodes (such as the military take-over of El Salvador's National University, the assassination and funeral of Archbishop Oscar Romero, or fleeing from aerial bombardments, to name a few) were part of the experience of so many people that they recurred as traditional motifs. Other, more personal episodes were of course unique to the teller, such as a story of capture and torture, but similar thematically to those told by others. Thus each testimony was personal, yet commented upon the larger social picture.

Rather than existing in isolation, these testimonies were each part of that larger mural of the recent history of Central America, and they corroborated one another by offering overlapping perspectives of the same historical event. Indeed, considerable interchange and story-sharing did go on among refugees in the United States. The structure of having two or more refugees in one evening's house or church meeting made such public interaction unavoidable, but also refugees worked together in human rights and church offices and socialized together, trading experiences informally and analysing speaking strategies more formally in business meetings. Discussions among refugees yielded pointers and suggestions, with less experienced speakers learning about form, and these same newer arrivals giving updates on recent political developments at home. Though individual experiences were often different, through refugee interactions testimonies become 'traditional' in their structure.

In the case of Central America refugee narratives, each story was the story of an individual, but only moved people to action when placed within the context of an entire nation of similar testimonies. Hearing one testimony was not sufficient. Nor was content alone the significant feature, and eventually it became important for North Americans not only to hear a variety of refugee testimonies but to visit Central America and hear the testimonies of those who had not left and who continued (and continue) to experience repression on a day-to-day basis while struggling for justice. And it became important for Central Americans in the United States to develop a speaking style that would engage listeners, without making an audience feel threatened or become bored. That meant concentrating on human, anecdotal narrative and removing political commentary that could be construed as inflammatory or accusatory.

More recent research, including a brief trip to El Salvador in 1987, made me aware that testimony in North America was merely that *testimonio* in Central America which had been brought north. In other words, the concept of testimony was not devised in and for the United States, though the idea of delivering testimony to North Americans *in their own country and language* was. As a verbal form conveying historical or eyewitness information, thousands of people continue to speak out in El Salvador and Guatemala, painting a canvas so large and complex that together it gives an oral historical portrait of a people at war, seeking justice.[7] What went on in the United States, the testimony from those who had left or escaped, was only a small part of a larger phenomenon. [. . .]

Why did (and do) these people speak out, and why did they speak out in the form that they did, that is, telling their personal history? For one thing, these personal narratives were also religious testimony within the framework of the widely practised theology of liberation. This radical reinterpretation of official, standard religion emphasizes the liberation of the poor and oppressed from the repressive situations and societies in which they live. Developed at the grass-roots level since Pope John XXIII, and becoming widely practised in Latin America since 1972, it became closely linked with the liberation movements in Nicaragua, El Salvador, and Guatemala, and elsewhere in Latin America.[8] Liberation theology focuses on the active role of the community and the individual in ending the sinful state of oppression and violence perpetrated by the state and in building the Kingdom of God on earth. This religious interpretation is not limited to theory alone, but also demands action.

Testimony, then, became one such form of action. The conversion experience of liberation theology is known as 'conscientization': the process of becoming conscious of the often unjust political and social reality and its root causes. In bringing the message of liberation theology to North America, refugees had to first make North Americans aware of the social, economic, and political conditions in Latin America, as well as of the political reality in the United States and the role of the US Government in maintaining conditions as they are throughout Latin America.

Clearly, the personal testimony in this context was indeed religious, and one essential purpose of giving testimony was to bring about the conscientization in North Americans. Most of the refugee speakers were devoutly Roman Catholic, and many had backgrounds in the practice of liberation theology in the Christian base communities, the local study- or worship-groups through which the popular church is organized. Giving testimony and denouncing oppression is therefore one way of being a good Christian. The refugees asked North Americans for a similar conversion, such that US citizens would side not with the oppressors (the governments of the United States, El Salvador, and Guatemala) but with the oppressed. The refugees asked for – and in many cases secured – a commitment to social change and social justice.

Also from liberation theology comes an idea central to testimony and crucial for its success: the creation of solidarity between North and Central Americans, between the middle and upper classes of the North, and the poor and oppressed in

Latin America (as well as, I might add, the poor and oppressed in the North, too). The Central Americans were more than aware of the distance between the two cultures; that distance is in itself responsible for the problem of North American apathy and ignorance concerning the US Government's actions or its heavy involvement in Central American affairs (up to $1.5 million US tax dollars a day were spent in El Salvador alone for some years, for example, not to mention the deployment of US military advisers in combat, US funding of the Nicaraguan *contras*, and the militarization of Honduras). Refugee testimony was personal and included the essential function of conveying a part of the history that was not recorded in the official media of the state and dominant culture.

In order to achieve this awakening, intimacy needed to be created[9] and personal identification with the refugee became essential. The refugee had to present himself or herself as a complete, three-dimensional, feeling human being in order to show, quite simply, that the war and repression had very real victims. By performing their life histories, the refugees presented themselves as fully human; and as they described their pain and their experience they encouraged identification, sympathy, and empathy, leading, they hoped, to action on the part of the listeners. In the words of one Salvadoran in Philadelphia, 'The [North American] people, they can feel us, you know, they can – they can hear us, they can see us, they can *think* [of us] . . . human beings – we have been suffering that, that situation.'[10] Testimony was, in an oft-quoted phrase of Archbishop Oscar Romero, 'the voice of the voiceless', and in North America it had the additional feature of making these statistics human.

Intimacy and personal identification ideally led to more politicized solidarity, going beyond empathy to concrete work on behalf of the poor and oppressed. Paulo Freire, the Brazilian educator and theorist, writes that the:

> oppressor is solidary with the oppressed only when he stops regarding the oppressed as an abstract category and sees them as persons who have been unjustly dealt with, deprived of their voice, cheated in the sale of their labor – when he stops making pious, sentimental, and individualistic gestures and risks an act of love.[11]

Speaking itself became one way to render the oppressed no longer as abstractions, but as representatives of all too real human suffering in Central America. Speaking, and committed listening, became one such risky act of love, a love which in the words of theologian Gustavo Gutiérrez, 'seeks also to liberate the oppressors from their own power, from their ambition, and from their selfishness . . . One loves the oppressors by liberating them from their inhuman condition as oppressors, by liberating them from themselves.'[12] Refugee testimony was a manifestation of this act of love, even when it involved disagreement or conflict.

The functions of testimony, then, were fourfold. First, speaking itself was a political act, an act of denouncing the injustice from which the refugees fled. It was also a religious act, a way of concretizing faith so that it transcended belief to include action as a manifestation of that belief. Thirdly, testimony created solidarity between the refugees and those representatives of a people whose government was held responsible for creating refugees in the first place, and in turn, that solidarity led to further political action by US citizens. And fourthly, there was and continues to be a therapeutic function, in the sense that speaking out is a way of making sense of a destructive, violent past, a past in which one often felt victim, and of triumphing over that experience, turning it into a motivation for living and working in the pursuit of certain social ideals. One Salvadoran told me that when he first entered this country he had hoped to remain anonymous, but his outlook changed after being encouraged to speak out. For him, it was a way of overcoming feelings of help-lessness and depression.[13] I would also say that, significantly, testimony need not have been a spoken narrative. I have heard songs of personal experience, seen narra-tive embroidered tapestries from refugee camps, and have heard refugees mention 'testimony of life', that is, when one gives one's life for the purpose of social justice, as in the case of a martyred priest or nun.

Testimony can be visual too; one refugee asked me in Spanish (the first time I ever met him, in fact), 'You want my testimony? This is my testimony', and he pulled up his sleeve to reveal a deep gouged out scar from a bullet wound in his shoulder, received, as I later found out, when he was taken out to a garbage dump with other prisoners, lined up and shot.

Testimony is about people rising from a condition of being victims, objects of history, and taking charge of their history, becoming subjects, actors in it. History no longer makes them; they make it, write it, speak it. On one level, this concerns the everyday struggle to stay alive. But this also concerns at another level the role of the individual in history, and how all of us depict that experience in our narra-tives. Anthropologist Barbara Myerhoff, in describing a life-history class among elderly Jews in Los Angeles, commented that:

> Conditions sometimes make the members of a generational cohort acutely self-conscious, and then they become active participants in their own history; they provide their own sharp, insistent definitions of them-selves, their own explanations for their past and their destiny. They are then knowing actors in a historical drama which they themselves script, rather than subjects in someone else's study.[14]

Becoming the subject, the 'active participant' in one's own history requires, according to Freire, questioning, speaking out, being critical of one's own life.[15] Freire has written, in his earlier *Pedagogy of the Oppressed* – that:

> There is no true word that is not at the same time a praxis. Therefore to speak a true word is to transform the world . . .
> Human existence cannot be silent, nor can it be nourished by false words, but only by true words, with which men transform the world. To exist, humanly, is to *name* the world, to change it . . . Men are not built in silence, but in word, in work, in action-reflection.
> But while to say the true word – which is work, which is praxis – is to transform the world, saying that word is not the privilege of some few men, but the right of every man.[16]

Testimony was, and in Latin America continues to be, precisely this, the naming of the world by denouncing the oppression, the beginning of dialogue between Central and North Americans, and the liberation of individuals, and eventually a people, through the process of becoming historical narrators, and thus actors. Testimony is a word that transforms, but moreover, a word that emerges from the critical examination of one's own life by those deeply involved in the shaping of history. To give testimony is to bear witness; it is to tell the unofficial story, to construct a history of people, of individual lives, a history not of those in power, but by those confronted by power, and becoming *empowered*.

Finally, at the risk of romanticizing refugee testimony, I would like to make the argument that this utilitarian speech was also a folk art form and that it subscribed to a traditional aesthetic which was both conscious and well defined. The terms 'art' and 'aesthetic' can be misleading, suggesting the creation of pleasure or beauty. But certainly folklorists recognize that not only can the utilitarian be art but functional qualities can also render something aesthetic. With folk art, the judgement of what is 'good' or 'aesthetic' often rests with the community itself, and this was very true of refugee testimony. Good testimony, as defined by the refugees, was that which was most effective in moving the audience to a new level of understanding or action. The good speaker, like a good story-teller, was responsive to the different interests of each audience. He or she would have prepared those topics to be emphasized and would have decided on the level of political analysis to be included, for example, concentrating on repression against workers in a talk to a labour union audience. What would make the content or structure 'good' was the effect the talk had on the audience, to move them, motivate them, make them reflect. The best testimony was that which was easy to understand, got the point across, and reached people on an emotional and moral as well as intellectual level. That required having an important story to tell, and understanding how to turn that personal experience into something that others – people who in this case were linguistically, culturally, politically, often religiously, and economically different – could appreciate. The testimony was more important than the abilities of the speaker, the process of subsequent action ultimately more important.

Unlike many forms of narrative story-telling, the goal was not to come up with, in folklorist Richard Bauman's words, 'artful texts, identified on independent formal grounds',[17] though many testimonies were beautiful in the sense of being emotionally moving. But as this was a group of people speaking from a politically marginal position, most often in broken English or poorly translated Spanish, their materials were determined by necessity and their aesthetic ideals by political as well as cultural and religious factors. Without recognizing that, we might fail to appreciate what is good or beautiful – that is, artistic – in these narratives and might miss their message altogether. Furthermore the performers could 'be both admired and feared – admired for their artistic skill and power and for the enhancement of experience they provide, feared because of the potential they represent for transforming the status quo'.[18] That status quo could be of course political, but also personal, since the refugees implicitly (and sometimes explicitly, later) asked for commitment and action in everyday life that North Americans generally were unprepared – and may otherwise have felt unable – to give. Though in some ways this separated them from the North American population to whom they were talking, such narratives helped to establish them as representatives of the struggles for social justice that were being waged back in their countries of origin. Thus there was a tension between allying themselves with the North Americans with whom they had to, wanted to, work everyday, and remaining distinct, Salvadorans and Guatemalans with their own histories, identities, and experiences that were separate from those of their North American audiences.

In that context, inflammatory speeches which emphasized too much political analysis would have been threatening to a North American audience and were dismissed by refugees as ineffective. Often, it was the most personal, and most understated talks that had the most impact. John A. Robinson has noted that one possible motivation for telling a personal narrative is 'to instigate action . . . in a way that avoids preaching or invoking one or another type of authority'.[19] Such narratives can be one method of accomplishing this because the 'very typicality of an incident . . . recommends it for narration, rather than its remarkableness'. This may be particularly true when the action in the narrative is typical for the speaker, but not for the audience. Hence, 'commonplace activities may excite great interest in listeners who are unfamiliar with the sphere of life to be discussed'.[20] By personalizing the history of Central American, then, the refugees could offer authority without being seen as authoritarian. And, it was the unfortunately commonplace quality of the episodes which made testimony so effective. The atrocities and the poverty described are part of the everyday life of Central Americans. Thus a narrative told in an understated, almost offhand manner could actually be more effective than a fiery speech, since the content had not been presented as something remarkable. The implication was that the miserable situation was almost normal, but still not acceptable. If it were not seen as normal, such acts of violence and oppression would seem isolated and would to some extent not be cause for such alarm or concentrated political activity in response.

We can also therefore begin to understand these refugees as historical actors by looking further at the genre of performed life history. The life histories became powerful tools in the construction of a more just society when wielded by devoted performers skilled in their use. As Myerhoff notes, such actors '"make" themselves . . . an activity which is not inevitable or automatic but reserved for special people and special circumstances'.[21] If, in Dell Hymes's words, the acceptance of responsibility determines a 'breakthrough into performance', then testimony was an example of performance *par excellence*. They accepted – even grabbed – responsibility 'not only for knowledge but also for performance . . . [in order] to shape history'[22] and not only for verbal performance but for historical performance as well. By being witnesses from Central America, they earned the right to be authentic speakers, the right to take on that responsibility. Their tradition demanded of its bearers careful attention to an aesthetic, sensitivity to an audience, the memory of the past, a view to the future, and considerable bravery just to assume the responsibilities of performance.

Notes

1   Interview with Fr Matthews (pseudonym), Nogales, Arizona, 2 August 1986. Because of the legal history of the Sanctuary movement and people involved in it, although some people were willing to allow me to use their names, I have made the choice – preferring to err on the side of safety – to use pseudonyms.

2   By 1988 the structure of personal testimony began to change, at least outside the south-western, border areas of the country. The focus shifted away from 'protecting

the refugee' to defending the right of the civilians, and especially the displaced, back home. As interest in the Sanctuary movement waned (some congregations remained active into the 1990s), the focus on publicly performed life stories faded too.

3   For the best summary of the legality of Salvadoran and Guatemalan refugees, see I. Bau, *This Ground is Holy*, Mahwah, N.J., 1985, pp. 39–56.

4   Interview with Diego (pseudonym), Los Angeles, California, 11 August 1986.

5   Which could really be two sections, depending on the individual. In order to determine exactly, it would be necessary to examine linguistic and paralinguistic markers, such as particles and pauses, to see exactly how each speaker structured the narrative and where the 'sections' were divided. The outline I have provided above refers primarily to a plot structure, rather than a linguistic one.

6   Comment made to me by Gregorio (pseudonym), a Salvadoran in Philadelphia, in 1986.

7   Collections and examples include M. Argueta, *One Day of Life*, (trans by B. Brow), New York, 1983 (orig. published 1980), the testimony of a Salvadoran peasant woman in novel form; A. Hernandez, *León de Piedra*, El Salvador, 1981; M. Lopez Vigil (ed.), *Marxismo y cristianismo en Morazán: Testimonio del Padre Rogelio*, El Salvador, 1987; examples published in R. Golden and M. McConnell, *Sanctuary: The New Underground Railroad*, Maryknoll, N.Y, 1986; R. Menchü, *I . . . Rigoberta Menchú*, (ed. by E. Burgos-Debray, trans. by A. Wright), London, 1984; and V. Montejo, *Testimony: Death of a Guatemalan Village* (trans. by V. Perera) Willimantic, Conn., 1987.

8   Two of the best introductions to liberation theology in Latin-American politics are P. Berryman, *The Religious Roots of Rebellion*, Maryknoll, N.Y, 1984; and P. Lernoux, *Cry of the People*, New York, 1980.

9   Part of this process, then, is what S.K. Dolby-Stahl calls the creation of intimacy. 'The higher the percentage of "private" folklore embedded in a story, the more likely the creation of intimacy is a major motivation for the storytelling' ('A literary-folkloristic methodology for the study of meaning in personal narrative', *Journal of Folklore Research*, 1985, vol. 22, pp. 47–48). The motivations for creating the intimacy in this case are significant. In order to overcome the cultural, linguistic, historical, and political differences, some sense of a 'shared inner life' between Central and North Americans had to be created.

10   Gregorio, 1986.

11   P. Freire, *Pedagogy of the Oppressed* (trans. by M.B. Ramos), New York, 1970 (first published 1968), pp. 33–35.

12   G. Gutiérrez, *A Theology of Liberation* (trans. by Sister C. Inda and J. Eagleson), Maryknoll, N.Y, 1973 (first published 1971), pp. 275–276.

13   Personal interview with Diego, Los Angeles, 11 August 1986. His experience was by no means unique. See also I. Agger and S.B. Jensen, 'Testimony as ritual and evidence in psychotherapy for political refugees', *Journal of Traumatic Stress*, 1990, vol. 3, pp. 115–130; and A.J. Cienfuegos and C. Monelli, 'The testimony of political repression as therapeutic instrument', *American Journal of Orthopsychiatry*, 1983, vol. 53, pp. 43–51.

14   B. Myerhoff, 'Telling one's story', *Center Magazine*, 1980, vol. 13, no. 2. p. 22.

15   P. Freire, *The Politics of Education*, (trans. by D. Macedo and L. Slover), South Hadley, Mass., 1985, p. 199.

16   Freire, *Pedagogy*, pp. 75–76.

17   R. Bauman, 'Verbal art as performance', *American Anthropologist*, 1975, vol. 77, p. 293.

18   Ibid., p. 305.
19   J.A. Robinson, 'Personal narratives reconsidered', *Journal of American Folklore*, 1981, vol. 94, p. 61.
20   Ibid., p. 62.
21   Myerhoff, 'Telling', p. 22.
22   D. Hymes, *'In Vain I Tried to Tell You'*, Philadelphia, 1981, p. 134.

Chapter 39

Rosanne Kennedy

STOLEN GENERATIONS
TESTIMONY
Trauma, historiography, and the question
of 'truth'

This chapter explores the contested memory of Australian Aborigines who were
taken from their families and placed in foster families or state institutions, and
compares how this memory is produced and treated in different contexts: oral history
recordings compared with autobiographical writing; in law courts and 'memory
commissions'; by historians and in self-help advocacy groups. Drawing upon theoretical approaches to Holocaust and abuse survivor testimony, Rosanne Kennedy
argues that personal testimonies should be regarded as sophisticated interpretative
narratives that incorporate sharp social and historical insights, and not simply as
evidence for interpretation (or rejection) by historical 'experts'. Rosanne Kennedy
is Senior Lecturer in the School of Humanities at the Australian National University.
This chapter was first published as a paper in *Aboriginal History*, 2001, vol. 25,
pp. 116–131, as part of a special section '"Genocide?": Australian Aboriginal
history in international perspective', edited by Ann Curthoys and John Docker.

I N RECENT AUSTRALIAN Aboriginal history, testimonies have played
a significant role in bringing into the public domain knowledge about the
practices and effects of the removal of Aboriginal children from their families and
communities. Broadly defined, the category of testimony includes a wide range of
texts, such as autobiographical narratives, oral histories, semi-official testimonies
such as those published in *Bringing Them Home*,[1] legal testimonies, Link-Up testimonies, psychotherapeutic testimonies, filmed testimonies and videotape testimonies.
While testimony has proven an invaluable means of transmitting experiences and
memories of people whose stories often go unrecorded, the category of testimony
is a contentions one – especially for historians, who are often concerned with
establishing what actually happened in the past.

Not surprisingly, controversy concerning the status and value of testimonies erupted during a Stolen Generations panel discussion featuring Bain Attwood, Peter Read and Robert Manne.[2] In essays published since the conference, Manne contends that Aboriginal witness has become the object of a 'collective hysteria'. For instance, conservative critics such as Ron Brunton and Paddy McGuinness have characterised Stolen Generations testimonies as exemplifying 'false memory syndrome', thereby implying that witnesses have fabricated memories of removal in a sympathetic cultural and political climate.[3] In this essay, however, I focus on Attwood's essay, 'A matter for history', which was published in the weekend *Australian Financial Review*.[4]

Unlike conservative critics such as Brunton and McGuinness, Attwood does not vilify Stolen Generations testimony as false memory syndrome. He does, however, treat testimony as a particularly troublesome kind of evidence for historians who are keen to provide a factually authoritative account of practices of separation. On the one hand, in viewing testimony as evidence to be interpreted by the historian, he undermines the witness's position as a valuable interpreter of events. On the other hand, his essay can be read allegorically as a story about the declining status of academic history as the guardian of the 'truth' of the past. It raises a number of significant issues, not only for history as an academic discipline, but for our understanding of the discourse of history in Australian public life. These issues include how we conceive of history, who owns the past, and who can speak as an authority on the significance of past events.

Questions of testimony, memory and historiography have been discussed in great detail in an international context, particularly in relation to the Holocaust. Following a critique of Attwood's argument, I suggest alternative critical methods for reading, analysing and evaluating Stolen Generations testimonies. In particular, I discuss two approaches that may enable us to read testimonies not simply as evidence, which places the historian in the role of expert, nor as literature, which makes them marginal for history's purposes of establishing what happened in the past, but as contributions to historiography in their own right. The first approach, represented here by Dominick LaCapra, uses a psychoanalytic framework to address issues of trauma, memory and affect in the context of the Holocaust. Drawing on LaCapra's work raises questions of how the concept of trauma is currently being used in relation to the Stolen Generations, and of whether a psychoanalytic approach is appropriate or productive. The second approach – a discursive approach – focuses on issues of interpretation, agency and authority in the process of making witness. I draw on discursive approaches that have been developed by James Young, who analyses Holocaust testimony, and by the feminist theorists Linda Alcoff and Laura Gray, who analyse the discourse of sexual abuse survivors. In the final section, I show how these approaches can be used to analyse Stolen Generations testimony.

Stolen Generations historiography: symbolic or forensic?

Attwood argues that our understanding of past practices of separating Aboriginal children from their kin is in danger of being obscured by the dominance of a simplistic and monolithic narrative. The Stolen Generations narrative is the product of 'narrative coalescence' – the accumulation and convergence of stories of separation – that has occurred over the past two decades. He attributes a foundational role in this discursive process to Peter Read's 1980 essay, 'The Stolen Generations', which provided an interpretative framework through which to make both historical and moral sense of policies, practices and experiences of separation.[5] In the wake of Read's essay, and with the formation of Link-Up in the early 1980s, many people who had been removed began to tell their stories. In addition, the 1996 National Inquiry into the Separation of Aboriginal and Torres Strait Islander Children from their Families sought out, listened to, recorded and published many testimonies, bringing them into public circulation. According to Attwood, these minor narratives gradually coalesced into a master narrative of the Stolen Generations, which attributes all removals to the government's allegedly genocidal policy of assimilation. This master narrative collapses differences between separation and removal, and has produced 'simplistic histories of colonialism in Australia'.[6] Attwood apparently shares Peter Novick's scepticism towards 'collective memory' – a memory that is shaped by the concerns of the present, rather than the actualities, of the past.[7] Rather than settle for a 'myth' of the past, Attwood advocates the need for more historical research, and for testimonies to be corroborated by research. While I share Attwood's desire for a historical discourse that does justice to the complexities of the past, I am concerned with the rhetorical, methodological and political implications of his argument.

Attwood contends that narrative accrual has resulted, in part, from changes in the production and significance of narratives of separation. During the 1970s narratives of separation were produced in collaboration between a historian and an informant. By contrast, during the 1980s and 1990s they tended to take the form of autobiography. As autobiography, they were 'more the product of memory and discursive practices other than history' and 'were becoming increasingly symbolic'. During the same period, narratives of separation expanded their historical reach and significance. Although they began 'as local or family histories', by the 1990s, 'the [Stolen Generations] narrative was taking on the cast of a national history'.[8] Drawing on Hayden White's well-known categories of chronicle and narrative, I propose that the shift Attwood traces can be described as a shift from chronicle to interpretive narrative.[9] When testimonies were produced in collaboration with historians, they constituted an oral history chronicle, and as such, a source of evidence. Once the historian is no longer involved as a collaborator, the narrative becomes 'more symbolic', and is consequently more properly regarded as interpretive narrative (with implications of fiction) rather than evidence. It is worth pausing to ask: what does 'symbolic' mean, and what rhetorical work is this label doing?

To say that these narratives became more symbolic is to say that the narrators interpreted their experiences according to a set of over-arching symbols, tropes and literary figures. In Attwood's view, the use of symbols gives a false meaning to the past because it obscures or neglects details and events that do not fit the narrative pattern, and thereby denies historical complexity. Thus, rather than telling what really happened in the past, with all the inconsistencies and particularities of an individual's separation, the narrator instead produces a predictable moral tale of innocence and culpability. Yet it must be noted that in singling out testimonies as 'symbolic', Attwood is denying the metaphorical nature of historical discourse itself. As Hayden White and others have convincingly argued, literary figures and tropes are at work in all discourse, including history.[10] James Young has argued in relation to Holocaust testimonies that all narratives, including those that are presented as simple reports of fact, produce a style, if only the style of 'the rhetoric of fact'. In his view, 'the aim of such a style is not to write unmediated facts, but to convince the reader that such facts . . . have been established'.[11] Likewise, Alcoff and Cray contend that 'when individual narratives are related as if they were not narratives but simple reports' this obscures 'the way in which all experience is itself discursively mediated'.[12]

If all experience is discursively mediated, why is the symbolic or literary nature of testimony a cause of concern for the historian? I propose that the central issue for Attwood is not the symbolic nature of testimonies, but who is producing historical meaning. He claims that autobiographies are not simply recording the effects of practices of separation, but are now 'telling the broader, collective history about the past'.[13] Witnesses are no longer offering their testimony as evidence to be interpreted by the historical expert. Rather, they are themselves active producers of historical meaning, which Attwood apparently finds unsettling.

Judicial historiography?

Although Attwood criticises the courts for ignoring the evidence that historians could provide in Stolen Generations cases, he uses a legal metaphor to describe historical methodology. He argues that telling 'the collective history about the past' is a 'forensic task' that testimonies 'are not traditionally thought capable of doing' mainly because 'memory can be notoriously malleable and so unreliable'.[14] As Derrida and De Man have pointed out in relation to the language of philosophy, concepts are not pure; they always involve metaphors and histories of metaphors.[15] According to the Oxford English Dictionary 'forensic' means 'used in courts of law'. Historically, 'forensic' is associated with 'forum', which in Roman antiquity was a 'place of public discussion'. Forensic thus has connotations of theatre, and entails the rhetorical acts of argument and persuasion. Given that historical writing is always 'literary', that it can never by a pure language of 'fact' and 'truth', why does Attwood use a legal metaphor to describe historical method? As historian Carlo Ginzburg has argued, the analogy of history with law draws attention to the concepts of 'proof' and 'truth', which lends credence to the view that history is primarily a matter of finding 'fact' rather than of telling stories.[16] Attwood's use of a legal metaphor must be regarded as a rhetorical move, the aim of which is to distance history from literature, with its implications of fiction.

The analogy between history and law implies that historians should assess testimonies for their 'truth content', using methods of proof similar to those used in law, such as checking testimony against other evidence for accuracy. Thus, Attwood criticises the Stolen Generations narrative, as it developed in the 1990s, because it drew on 'oral testimonies not supported by the findings of historical research.[17] In *Cubillo v. Commonwealth*, Justice O'Loughlin uses a medical analogy to describe the process of proof in law, further revealing the metaphorical nature of all discourse: 'The task of the Court is to examine the evidence – both oral and documentary – in a clinical manner, devoid of emotion.'[18] The metaphor of the clinic suggests that the court should not be emotionally swayed by testimony; by analogy, neither should the historian. The analogy between history and law casts the historian in the role of the judge, and the narrator in the role of a witness who is doubted until proven reliable. It treats 'literary' aspects of testimony (such as tone, style, structure, affect, symbols) as features which hinder an analysis of its factual content.

In practice, the analogy between history and law is troubling in part because Stolen Generations testimony has not fared well in the courtroom. In *Cubillo v. Commonwealth*, Justice O'Loughlin accepted some parts of Lorna Cubillo's evidence, but rejected other parts. Stating that he did not believe that either Cubillo or Gunner [two aboriginal witnesses] had been 'deliberately untruthful' he expressed concern 'about their ability to recall, accurately, events that occurred so many years ago when they were small children'. It is not surprising that a judge would question a witness's ability to recall events that occurred fifty years earlier. More troubling, however, was his assessment that 'they have unconsciously engaged in exercises of reconstruction, based, not on what they knew at the time, but on what they have convinced themselves must have happened or what others may have told them'.[19] By using the term 'subconscious reconstruction', he implied that the reconstruction that occurred in Cubillo and Gunners' testimonies was motivated by political, ideological or emotional commitments that were in some way suspect. Had he acknowledged that all testimony, grounded as it is in memory, entails a process of reconstruction, then perhaps he might have assessed their testimony differently.

In the light of Justice O'Loughlin's advocacy of a 'clinical' approach to testimony, it is surprising that he allowed negative emotion to colour his assessment of Cubillo's testimony. At one point, he says that she became 'progressively defensive, evasive and argumentative' in her testimony. He later speculates that Cubillo was unloved at the Retta Dixon Home not through any deficiency in the missionaries, but probably because of her difficult personality. The judges subjective judgement that 'she created an unfavourable impression' suggests that he found her testimony unreliable not simply because it was 'reconstructed' but because she was a difficult and challenging witness.[20]

Given that Attwood has argued that the Stolen Generations narrative is endangering historical truths, it is worth considering his view of historical truth in the light of the analogy with law. His essay reveals two conflicting views of how historical truth is produced. One view, associated with the linguistic turn in historiography, imagines historical truth as a product of interpretation. As Hayden White has convincingly argued, facts do not give rise to their own meaning; rather, meaning is a product of the combination of a choice of plot-structure, an explanatory framework, and an ideology.[21] Attwood treats Read's 'Stolen Generations' essay and the Stolen Generations narrative more generally, as exemplifying the dangers of myth and fiction that result from an excessive and uncontrolled use of narrative and reliance on memory. By contrast, he advocates a return to an empiricist practice of history in which 'a precise description of the unfolding of events is meant to carry its own interpretation, its own truth.'[22] The latter view is exemplified in the work of Robert Manne, who produces interpretative narratives with a moral meaning, but defends these narratives as an accurate representation of events, as substantiated by meticulous research and detailed description.[23] As Saul Friedlander points out, for empiricist historians such as Manne, there are no clear categories of 'attestable fact' and 'pure interpretation'; rather there is a continuum.[24] Attwood's use of a judicial metaphor is a rhetorical means of promoting the view that historical 'truth' is a process of fact-finding, rather than of narrative interpretation.[25]

The notion of truth as grounded in historical sources is foundationalist in that it conceives of evidence, metaphorically, as the foundation or bedrock of truth. Attwood subscribes, however uneasily, to this foundationalist conception of truth. He criticises the Stolen Generations narrative, arguing that in its presentation 'some of the important "grounding" in historical "sources" that are held to verify what happened in the past, and which provide the basis for the discipline of history's claims to truth, has been lost'.[26] By placing both 'grounding' and 'sources' in quotes, he signifies that he is aware of the post-modernist debates that surround these terms. Yet, at the same time, he does not qualify the notion of 'truth'. Thus contradiction produces ambivalence; while he advocates a foundationalist view of truth, he simultaneously indicates that he does not enthusiastically embrace it.

Stanley Fish, a theorist of interpretation, suggests that foundationalism is motivated by the desire to ground truth in something other than interpretation, which is believed to be guided by the contingent and fallible beliefs of the day.[27] Attwood's suspicion of testimony as unreliable because it is based in memory, and as requiring checks against other 'historical sources', protects these 'other sources' from scepticism by treating them as if they do not need to be interpreted. If the meaning of all evidence is constructed, however, then there is nothing intrinsically different about testimony. The constructed nature of evidence means that the historian or literary critic should not read any text, including testimony, as a 'window' onto the past, but as a document that must be interpreted. In *Writing and rewriting the Holocaust*, James Young argues that '[o]nce historians recognise their own activity as meaning-makers, they might be more comfortable with the meanings created in the survivors' testimonies.'[28] For once historians accept that all evidence is constructed – that it only becomes meaningful, and indeed, only functions as evidence, through particular discursive frameworks – then they must acknowledge that they, like witnesses, are meaning makers, not detectives or judges who 'find fact'.

The recognition that the meaning of all evidence is discursively produced leads to an unsettling realisation: that only the culturally conferred status and authority of the historian distinguishes his or her interpretation of evidence from the interpretations found in testimonies. What is ultimately at stake for Attwood is the status of the historian. LaCapra argues that 'a neo-positivist understanding of history as a dry and sober matter of fact and analysis and . . . suspicion of memory as inherently uncritical and close to myth . . . positions history in a purely enlightened realm that may divert attention from the continual need . . . to examine one's implication in the problems one studies'. He adds that 'the problem of subject-position and voice is particularly acute' where one is dealing with 'extremely traumatic phenomena in which one's investment is great.[29] Imagining history as a 'forensic task' positions the historian as a judge – as one who is emotionally distanced from and sits in judgement on the past. A judicial approach to historiography, and the retreat to an authority allegedly grounded in factual accuracy, protects the historian from the need to consider his or her own subject-position in relation to the events under consideration. In claiming that the act of determining historical meaning is a 'matter for history', and that historical truth should be determined through forensic methods, Attwood's essay has the effect of restricting debates about the meaning of the Stolen Generations to historical experts. He fails to imagine a significant role for Aboriginal people, intellectuals, and the public in determining the meaning and significance of the Stolen Generations and the broader history of Aboriginal dispossession.

Among researchers who write about testimony, there is consensus that memory poses problems, and recognition that testimony should not simply be accepted as a source of historical fact. In the face of these caveats, many scholars have developed productive approaches to testimony, which accept it as an invaluable contribution to historiography. In considering these approaches, I am mindful of a question suggested by LaCapra's work on the Holocaust: that is, in what ways do traumatic events, and the testimonies that bear witness to them, challenge us to rethink the requirements of historiography?[30] But first, I must ask, can the removal and separation of Aboriginal children, and the destruction of Aboriginal culture, be described as 'traumatic events'? For whom?

The traumatic event: injury and interpretation

Over the past twenty years, and with increasing frequency in the last several years, the removal and separation of part-Aboriginal children, and the destruction of Aboriginal culture, have been described as traumatic events. In some cases, the concept of trauma has been used in passing, to convey the extreme suffering and the extraordinary nature of events that characterised separation and removal. This kind of usage occurs in Read's early 'Stolen Generations' essay. In other cases, the use of trauma appears to be more deliberate. Notably, the authors of the *Bringing Them Home* report frequently use the related concepts of trauma and post-traumatic stress disorder to characterise both the event of separation, and its effects on individuals who had been removed, and their mothers, kin and communities. In addition to including specific case studies, the authors draw on the work of various psychological experts to support their interpretation that:

> Separation and institutionalisation can amount to traumas. Almost invariably they were traumatically carried out with force, lies, regimentation and an absence of comfort and affection. All too often they also involved brutality and abuse. Trauma compounded trauma.[31]

What should we make of the use of the discourse of trauma? Who benefits from it? What are the limitations?

In his recent book, *Post-traumatic culture: injury and interpretation in the nineties*, American literary critic Kirby Farrell provides a cultural analysis of the uses of the concept of trauma in the 1890s and 1990s. He argues that '[p]eople not only suffer trauma; they use it, and the idea of it, for all sorts of ends, good and ill'. For instance, '[t]rauma can be invoked to substantiate claims on the empathy of others, as a plea for special treatment, or as a demand for compensation'.[32] In the context of the Stolen Generations, the discourse of trauma has been used to describe real distress, both emotional and physical, to convey the damage that has been done by misguided policies, to mount a moral campaign for an apology, to invite empathy, and to legitimate claims for reparation. The use of the concept of trauma in *Bringing Them Home*, a report which also applied the concept of genocide to removal policies, can be seen as a rhetorical move to legitimate the – in my view problematic –

analogy between the Stolen Generations and the Holocaust. One of the potential drawbacks of the discourse of trauma, however, is that it may individualise and pathologise the experience of removal, and people that have experienced it. People who were removed or separated may be referred to as suffering from post-traumatic stress disorder, or as having some kind of symptom or displaying the effects of trauma, and may thereby be reduced to victims or examples of 'effects' of trauma. Not surprisingly, one Link-Up witness declares that 'I am much more than "a long-term effect".'[33]

One feature of post-traumatic culture is the confrontation with events that have long been repressed. Although Farrell draws his case studies from the United States and Britain, his claim that '[t]he present cultural mood reflects the contagious effects of clinical and political trauma, with predictable spasms of anxiety and rage, depression and mourning'[34] also applies, I believe, to the responses to the Stolen Generations, and Aboriginal dispossession more generally. In Australia the 'discovery' of policies of removal, assimilation and absorption have produced responses of shock and dismay, and have threatened national pride. In this context, it is worth noting that not only has the idea of trauma been used to characterise the Stolen Generations, it has also been used by historians to characterise cultural and political responses to these events. Manne titles his analysis of the conservative attack on the Stolen Generations *In denial*. Denial is a psychoanalytic term, which implies an unconscious repression of memories of events that are too painful or challenging to confront. Anna Haebich, in a section of *Broken circles* titled 'Remembering and forgetting', draws on psychoanalytic theories to discuss how Australians could claim not to have known about policies of removal.[35] As LaCapra has argued, the application of psychoanalytic concepts (such as transference, denial, repression, acting-out, and working-through) should be 'a matter of informed argument and research';[36] he calls for 'a more critical, vigilant, and reflective elaboration of these concepts'. To date, however, these essentially psychoanalytic concepts have been used loosely in Australia, without a careful theoretical reflection on their appropriateness. A more detailed critical analysis than I can offer here is necessary to adequately explore the uses to which trauma and other psychoanalytic concepts have been put with regard to the Stolen Generations.[37]

Testimony as interpretation: a discursive approach

Some of the approaches that are potentially most fruitful for analysing Stolen Generations testimony have been developed by scholars working on Holocaust testimony. In *Writing and rewriting the Holocaust*, Young maintains that the value of testimonies 'lies not in their supposed neutrality as source material but in their record of "telling history"'. Thus, testimonies should not be evaluated according to the demands of proof or truth. Rather, they should be read and analysed for their insights into how people involved in past events interpreted those events and their implications. For instance, we should consider 'the manner in which survivor-witnesses have understood and expressed their experiences, the kind of understanding they now bring to such disaster, and the ways in which they now understand the world in light of the Holocaust. It is specifically the subjective nature of memory, the fact that the testimony is situated and embodied, that makes it valuable to the historian or critic. Rather than treat testimony as evidence, which inevitably raises questions of proof and truth, Young encourages us to treat it as an interpretation of experience, and as an intervention into the field of historical discourse. Young notes that historians are dependent on 'this kind of reconstructed source material' but they often distrust survivor testimonies because they tend to be 'laden with pathos . . . and so dependent on individual memory alone.'[38]

LaCapra has addressed the question of being affected by events and their pathos at length. While not equating memory with history, he views memory as posing special challenges for history because 'it points to problems that are still alive or invested with emotion and value'. Like Attwood, he argues that, '[i]deally, history critically tests memory', but he insists that the historian must be prepared for 'a more extensive attempt to work through a past that has not passed away.' Testimony is a 'crucial source for history' because it positions the historian or analyst as a 'secondary witness' who 'undergoes a transferential relation, and must work out an acceptable subject-position with respect to the witness and his or her testimony.' By transference, he refers to 'the tendency to become emotionally implicated in the witness and his or her testimony with the inclination to act out an affective response to them'.[39] In other, words, what makes testimony particularly important for the historian or critic is its affective nature – the way that it reveals a past that has not yet been mastered. Historians such as Read, Haebich, Clendinnen and Manne have, in their writings, responded affectively to Stolen Generations testimonies, and have implicitly or explicitly questioned their own implication, and the implication of all Australians, in these events – although they do this without recourse to psycho-analytic notions of transference and working-through.[40] One question, then, is whether the use of psychoanalytic concepts such as transference, working-through and mourning would enrich the analysis of our implication in the events we study, and more broadly, the public response to these events.

The politics of Stolen Generations testimony: rethinking agency and authority

The Holocaust has become a touchstone for scholars working on questions of trauma, witnessing and affect in the United States. The analogy between Holocaust and Stolen Generations testimonies is limited, however, because the contexts in which these testimonies are produced and consumed, read and viewed, debated and discussed, are very different. As Peter Novick has argued, Holocaust memory may be so obsessive in the United States precisely because the United Slates was not positioned as a perpetrator nation. In addition, the Holocaust and its survivors are removed from present-day politics of American national idenity.[41] Consequently, in the United States, remembering the Holocaust does not raise the same political and moral difficulties that confronting Aboriginal dispossession, including policies of child removal, raises in Australia. How Australia responds to the Stolen Generations, and whether it re-evaluates the historical record with regard to Aboriginal dispossession, has significant implications for the reconciliation process.

Given the overly political context in which the Stolen Generations is being debated, a critical methodology for reading testimonies must consider not only issues of trauma and affect, but also questions of power and subjectivity. In this context, I have found the Foucauldian approach elaborated by Linda Alcoff and Laura Gray, who have written about issues of agency and authority in relation to survivors' narratives of sexual abuse, to be useful for analysing Stolen Generations testimonies.[42] Drawing on Foucault's analysis of the discourse of sexuality and the structure of the confessional encounter, they argue that a tension characterises the discourse of sexual abuse by survivors. On the one hand, this speech can be transgressive of dominant social and power structures, by revealing and insisting upon the reality of unthinkable categories such as 'husband rapist' and 'father rapist'. On the other hand, however, survivors' narratives are often 'recuperated'. They are used in a way that reinforces dominant social relations and power structures, which in turn disempowers girls and women.

Alcoff and Gray argue that one of the primary contributing factors in the process of recuperation is the role of the expert mediator.[43] When survivors tell their stories, particularly on television talk shows and in newspaper articles, they are asked to recite the explicit details of the sexual assault, which are used to attract viewers and increase ratings. The woman may be asked provocative questions about how she was dressed and where she was when the attack occurred, and whether she knew her attacker. An expert mediator, usually a psychiatrist or therapist, is called upon to interpret the woman's story. The expert may present her experience, and its continuing effects, as an example of a 'syndrome', 'symptom', or 'effect'. The expert may discuss ways that women can behave to lessen the incidence of attack or abuse, and what the survivor can do to heal herself, and recover her pleasure in sex. In sum, the expert often shifts the focus from the perpetrator to the victim, who is represented as 'the problem'.[44] Typically, the woman has been disempowered in the encounter, by being reduced to an object to be analysed, rather than being treated as a subject of her own discourse. By treating the individual as a victim, the expert neglects the patriarchal structures and cultural factors that contribute to ongoing sexual violence against women and girls.

In Australia, this kind of disempowering strategy has recently been used, to sensational effect, against Lowitja O'Donoghue [a Pitjantjatjara woman and Founding Chair of the Aboriginal and Torres Strait Islander Commission]. Conservative journalist Andrew Bolt used comments she made about the circumstances of her removal from her mother to cast doubt on the notion of a 'stolen generation'.[45] Her comments were pounced on by [Conservative Prime Minister] John Howard, who took them as support for his own policy of refusing to offer a national apology. In the process, her interpretation of her own experience, and of the broader significance of the Stolen Generations, was silenced. In representing O'Donoghue as at best, having unintentionally misled the public, or at worst, an outright 'liar', Bolt constructed her as an unreliable witness. Bolt's (mis)representation of O'Donoghue shifted attention from an analysis of the racist social conditions that allowed her father, an Irish station worker, to remove his five children from their Aboriginal mother without her full consent, to O'Donoghues reliability.

Although without malicious intent, Attwood took up the role of the 'expert' in relation to Sally Morgan's subjectivity in his critique of her book My place. He asked why she constructed herself as 'Aboriginal' in her autobiography, and what psychological need this construction filled for her.[46] As Tim Rowse has rightly pointed out, in taking a biographical approach to Morgan's text, Attwood set himself up as an 'expert' who knew more about her than she knew about herself, and who was especially equipped to judge the historical and psychological correctness of her identity.[47] In positioning himself as an expert, Attwood reduced Morgan to an object of analysis, thereby stripping her discourse of agency and authority.

How can this kind of situation, in which the witness's words are used against her, be prevented? Alcoff and Gray outline the conditions for 'subversive speaking' – speaking which will not disempower the person giving witness. Conditions for subversive speaking include eliminating or reconfiguring the role of the expert mediator, and abolishing the split between experience and interpretation. Like James Young, they argue for the need to create speaking situations in which 'survivors are authorised to be both witnesses and experts, both reporters of experience and theorists of experience.' For personal testimony to be 'politically efficacious' a witness must recognise her role as an interpreter of her own experiences, and not simply a reporter of facts. Citing bell hooks, they argue that if 'women do not merely "name" their experiences but also "place that experience within a theoretical context . . . storytelling becomes a process of historicization. It does not remove women from history but enables us to see ourselves as part of history"'. In such a scenario, survivors might use testimony and memory 'as tools of recuperation' rather than as 'instruments for recuperation'. Such a transformation, in their view, 'will alter existing subjectivities as well as structures of domination and relations of power.'[48] I would like to tie together the threads of my argument by showing how the methodological approaches I have canvassed might be used to read Stolen Generations testimony.

Reading Stolen Generations testimony

The distinction that I mentioned earlier, between oral history narratives and symbolic narratives – which I labelled as a distinction between chronicle and narrative, or evidence and interpretation – can be used to characterise two groups of Stolen Generations testimonies produced in the context of the National Inquiry [into the separation of Aboriginal and Torres Strait Islander Children from their families, 1997]. The testimonies in the [National Inquiry's] *Bringing Them Home* report mostly take the form of chronicle, and function as evidence that is interpreted by the authors of the report. By contrast, the testimonies in the Link-Up (NSW) [an organisation that links separated Aboriginal families] submission to the National Inquiry take the form of interpretive narrative. The narrators not only tell their story, but also frequently interpret the meaning of their experiences, and reflect on the broader significance of separation and of Australian Aboriginal history.

Although these two groups of testimonies were produced during the same period (1996–1997), their styles are very different. The style of the testimonies in *Bringing Them Home* could be described as a 'rhetoric of fact', while the style of the Link-Up testimonies is far more confrontational, and to use Altwood's terminology, 'symbolic'. The differences in the Link-Up and *Bringing Them Home* testimonies suggest that the chronological distinction Attwood posits between pre-1980s and post-1980s testimonies does not hold up. Whereas he sees a chronological break in the styles of testimonies, with pre-1980s testimonies being more of the style of 'oral history', and those produced in the later 1980s and 1990s being more fully interpretive, in fact, in the context of the National Inquiry both styles exist simultaneously. This suggests that testimony should not he treated as a monolithic category.

What would most probably account for the differences in the narrative forms and styles of these testimonies are the differing conditions of production. Conditions of production include the purpose for which the testimonies were produced, the immediate audience for the testimonies, whether the witnesses knew the audience, whether there was a situation of trust, whether the setting was formal or informal, and other such issues.[49] In response to some of the criticisms of the report, Sir Ronald Wilson has pointed out that the National Inquiry was not a legal inquiry; therefore, it was not obligated to prove the truth of the testimonies. Rather than treat the testimonies as evidence, he focuses on the affective dimension of the inquiry – the healing work it did in listening empathetically to people who had been harmed by policies of removal: 'The objective clearly is not retribution, but understanding and healing'. Much of the report was, he notes, 'expressed in the words actually spoken to us by those who suffered personally from the processes of separation . . . The report must he read with an open heart and mind, and with a willingness to listen, and to listen intently.' The Report argues that 'reparation can only begin when there is an understanding that comes through listening, followed by an acknowledgment of the shameful deeds of the past and a genuine expression of regret.'[50]

At the same time, however, the Report did provide interpretive frameworks, such as the concepts of trauma and genocide, to make sense of the testimonies. Although the Report was not a judicial inquiry, it did make a moral and legal case for reparation. It presented witness testimony as documentary 'evidence' – as an authentic and factual report of events – thereby downplaying issues of memory and construction. As Young points out, '[f]or a survivor's witness to be credible, it must seem natural and unconstructed'. He observes that the separation of testimony and interpretation suggests that only the interpreter is making meaning in the test, and that the testimony 'is a pure and normative rendering of events', in which case it appears as if the 'maker of meaning is the event itself'. In the Report, testimony and interpretation were separated, and testimony functioned, rhetorically, to support the case for reparation. To say that the *Bringing Them Home* report used the 'rhetorical trope of the eyewitness'[51] is not to deny either the authenticity or the evidential value of the testimony, or even to say that they should have taken some other approach. Clearly, the use of witness testimony as evidence was effective in producing empathy in readers, and in persuading a good proportion of the public of the need for reparation. Ironically, however, in the process of making its case, it represented Stolen Generation witnesses as victims, and as embodiments of traumatic symptoms and syndromes. It also denied them the agency to interpret their own experiences. It must be noted that some of the witnesses who came forward may not have had the cultural resources available to them that would enable them to interpret their own experiences.

In contrast to the National Inquiry, Link-Up is an Aboriginal organisation that is devoted to helping people who have been separated to trace their families, and work through the effects of separation, including identity issues. Link-Up's aim, in part, is to empower survivors of separation and removal, to provide a supportive environment and a network as people come to terms with their past and future, to enable people to speak authoritatively about their own experiences, and to aid the healing process. Link-Up testimonies are produced in a group forum in which the other participants have either shared experiences of separation, or are involved in the healing process. A key premise of Link-Up's analysis is that the separation of Aboriginal family members, although systemic, took multiple forms and had multiple effects. This approach provides witnesses with the resources to interpret their experience. For instance, learning to analyse the social, political and historical forces at work in producing separation may enable people who have been separated to stop blaming themselves and their families for their circumstances.

The testimony I have selected for analysis is from Link-Up's submission to the National Inquiry. The testimony, entitled 'Sometimes quickly, sometimes slowly', is by a woman who was adopted by and grew up in a non-Aboriginal family in the 1950s and 1960s. The narrator, adopted as a baby, did not learn that she was Aboriginal until she was in her twenties. This testimony is not a simple report of fact. Indeed, it tells us little about the events of the author's childhood. Rather, the author cites concepts such as 'passing', 'denial' and 'racism' to make sense of her experience. For instance, she comments that 'The only uncle I have found, could not tell me – would not tell me – where all the other uncles and aunties are. . . . He's spent his life passing as an Indian. His wife passes as something else.' She speculates that his art of passing is a strategy to avoid 'having their kids taken away', which nonetheless perpetuates the effects of removal: 'This means his kids, and now their kids . . . don't know who they are or where they come from either. Removal just keeps being passed on, today, now.'[52] Later in the testimony she talks about how her birth mother is too ashamed and in denial to tell her non-adopted children about her and another sister who were adopted out. 'Part of the reason they can't be told about me is because it's tied in with her history and that's hidden from them too – because it's Aboriginal history.' Thus, she is separated from her siblings and they from her, and '[t]he removal continues'.

In this testimony, the witness-narrator does not take up the position of victim and thus she denies the reader or critic the possibility of identifying vicariously with her trauma. Rather, she addresses us as White Australians, and therefore, as implicated bystanders or potential collaborators. Not, perhaps, collaborators to the actual processes of removal, but collaborators in the conspiracy of silence and denial that has made removal, and the repetitions of removal to this day, possible. The narrator comments, for instance, on the ways in which White Australians have denied Aboriginal history:

> Aboriginal history is not something you can hide away from everything else . . . I . . . believe that's what the whole of White Australia has done over many generations, without even knowing it . . . Yeah, they've gone into removal from where they really are and who they really are, where they really fit in – no wonder they can deny or condone the removal of other people. I'm not talking about all White people here . . . but I do think that many White Australians have been set up to do so.

This testimony does not ask for our empathy. It asks for us to become critically conscious of our own subject-positions in the ongoing practices of denial, including the denial of Aboriginal history. It asks White Australians, and others who identify with that subject-position, to work out where we fit into this history of separation, and into Aboriginal history more broadly. That question is very different from the question of where Aboriginal history fits into White Australian history, which is the way White Australians are used to thinking about Aboriginal history. In offering her interpretation of the role of both Aboriginal and White Australians in practices of denying Aboriginal history and Aboriginal identity, she challenges White Australians to examine their own role in past and present practices that support racism.

Notes

1   National Inquiry into the Separation of Aboriginal and Torres Strait Islander Children from their Families 1997, *Bringing Them Home: Report of the National Inquiry into the separation of Aboriginal and Torres Strait Islander children from their families* [Commissioner: Ronald Wilson], HREOC, Sydney.

2   The Life Stories Conference at Monash University, 14–17 July, 2000.

3   Robert Manne, 'A crude case of absurd historical denial', *Agora: Victorian Historical Association*, 34(4), 1999, pp. 10–11; Robert Manne, 'Right and wrong', *Spectrum, Sydney Morning Herald*, 31 March 2001, p. 11; Ron Brunton, 'Betraying the victims: the "Stolen Generations" Report', *IPA Backgrounder*, 10(1) February 1998, p. 9.

4   *Australian Financial Review*, Friday 15 December 2000, Review: 1–7.

5   Peter Read, *A rape of the soul so profound: the return of the stolen generations*, St. Leonards, NSW: Allen and Unwin, 1999, pp. 46–70.

6   Bain Attwood, 'A matter for history', *Australian Financial Review*, 15 December, 2000 Review: 1–7.

7   Peter Novick, *The Holocaust and collective memory*, London, 1999, pp. 3–4.

8   Attwood, op. cit., p. 5.

9   Hayden White, 'The value of narrativity in the representation of reality', in *The content of the form: narrative discourse and historical representation*, Baltimore: Johns Hopkins University Press, 1987.

10   Hayden White, 'The historical text as literary artefact', in *Tropics of discourse: essays in cultural criticism*, Baltimore: Johns Hopkins University Press, 1978, pp. 81–96.

11   James Young, *Writing and rewriting the Holocaust: narrative and the consequences of interpretation*, Bloomington: Indiana University Press, 1988, p. 9.

12   Linda Alcoff and Laura Gray, 'Survivor discourse: transgression or recuperation?', *Signs: Journal of Women in Culture and Society*, 18(2), 1993: pp. 260–290, p. 283.

13   Attwood, op. cit., p. 6.

14   Ibid.

15   See for instance: Paul De Man, *Allegories of reading*, New Haven: Yale University Press, 1979; Jacques Derrida, *Of grammatology*, Baltimore: Johns Hopkins University Press, 1976.

16   Carlo Ginzberg, 'Checking the evidence: the judge and the historian', reprinted in *Questions of evidence*, ed. J. Chandler, A. Davidson, and H. Harootunian, Chicago: University of Chicago Press, 1991, pp. 290–303, pp. 294–295.

17   Attwood, op. cit., p. 5.

18   *Cubillo v. Commonwealth of Australia 2000*, Justice Maurice O'Loughlin, Federal Court, 11 August, paragraph 79.

19   Ibid., paragraph 125.

20   Ibid., paragraph 728–9.

21   Hayden White, *Metahistory*, Baltimore: Johns Hopkins University Press, 1973.

22   Saul Friedlander, 'Introduction' in *Probing the limits of representation: Nazism and the 'Final Solution'*, Cambridge: Harvard University Press, 1992, pp. 1–21 and p. 7.

23   Robert Manne, *The culture of forgetting: Helen Demidenko and the Holocaust*, Melbourne: Text Publishing, 1996, pp. 162–163; and Robert Manne, 'Stolen generation', *Quadrant*, 42(1–2), 1998: pp. 53–63.

24   Friedlander, op. cit.

25   As I have argued elsewhere, narrative plays a major role in producing the meaning of evidence in legal trials, See Kennedy, Rosanne 'Legal sensations: sexuality, textuality and evidence in a Victorian murder trial', in *Romancing the tomes: popular culture, law and feminism*, Margaret Thornton (ed.), London: Cavendish, 2000.

26   Attwood, op. cit., p. 6.

27   Stanley Fish, *Doing what comes naturally: change, rhetoric, and the practice of theory in literary and legal studies*, Durham, NC: Duke University Press, 1989.

28   Young, op. cit., p.16.

29   Dominick LaCapra, *History and memory after Auschwitz*, Ithaca, New York: Cornell University Press, 1998, pp. 16–17.

30   Ibid.

31   National Inquiry, op. cit., p. 196.

32   Kirby Farrell, *Post-traumatic culture: injury and interpretation in the nineties*, Baltimore: Johns Hopkins University Press, 1998, p. 21 and p. 24.

33   Link-Up (NSW) Aboriginal Corporation and Tikka Wilson (ed.), *In the best interest of the child? Stolen children: Aboriginal pain/White shame*, Canberra: Aboriginal History Monograph 4, 1997, p. 126.

34   Farrell, op. cit., p. 16.

35   Anna Haebich, *Broken circles: fragmenting Indigenous families 1800–2000*, Fremantle: Fremantle Arts Centre Press, 2000, pp. 563–570.

36   LaCapra, op. cit., p. 43.

37   See Jill Bennett and Rosanne Kennedy, 'Introduction', and Rosanne Kennedy and Tikka Wilson, 'Reading testimonies of the stolen generations', both in *World memory: personal trajectories in global time*, Jill Benett and Rosanne Kennedy (eds), Macmillan: London, 2003.

38   Young, op. cit., pp. 163–165.

39   LaCapra, op. cit., pp. 8–12.

40   [See also…] Christine Watson '"Believe me": acts of witnessing in Aboriginal women's autobiographical narratives', *Journal of Australian Studies* 64 (2000): pp. 142–152.

41   Novick, op. cit.

42   Alcoff and Gray, op. cit.

43   Ibid., p. 282.

44   Ibid., p. 276–278.

45   Andrew Bolt, 'I wasn't stolen', *Herald-Sun*, Melbourne, 23 February 2001.

46   Bain Attwood, 'Portrait of an Aboriginal as an artist: Sally Morgan and the construction of Aboriginality', *Australian Historical Studies*, 99, October 1992: pp. 302–318, p. 1.

47   Tim Rowse, 'Sally Morgan's Kaftan', *Australian Historical Studies*, 99, October, 1992: pp. 465–468. See also John Docker, 2001, *1492: the poetics of diaspora*, London: Continuum, for the chapter on Sally Morgan's *My place*.

48   Alcoff and Gray, op. cit., pp. 282–283.

49   Ken Plummer, *Telling sexual stories: power, change and social worlds*, New York and London, Routledge, 1995, for a discussion on how these issues impact on narrative.

50   Sir Ronald Wilson, 'Preface' in *The stolen children: their stories*, ed. Carmel Bird, Milsons Point, N.S.W., Australia, 1998, pp. xxiii–xv.

51   Young, op. cit., p. 17 and p. 22.

52   Quoted in Link-up and Wilson, op. cit., p. 125.

Chapter 40

Irina Sherbakova

THE GULAG IN MEMORY

In totalitarian regimes power is maintained in part through the control of memory. Using interviews with survivors of the Soviet prison and labour camps, Irina Sherbakova evokes the impact of fear and distortion upon individual remembering, and how remembering is a process of struggle for survivors and in the social and political life of a nation. Irina Sherbakova is Head of Educational Youth Programmes for the Memorial organization in Russia. Reprinted with permission from L. Passerini (ed.), *International Yearbook of Oral History and Life Stories*. Vol. I: *Memory and Totalitarianism*, Oxford, Oxford University Press, 1992, pp. 103 115.

THE UNIQUENESS OF our Soviet situation lies in the decades through which historical truth within our country lived on only through underground memory. Publications which appeared in the West, broadcasts from foreign radio stations, and manuscripts secretly circulated in samizdat form only began to seep through comparatively widely as recently as the 1960s and 1970s. Before that there was only silence, or at the most, rare whispers between intimates, because to tell anyone about the prisons and concentration camps was deadly dangerous.

I began collecting accounts of the Stalinist camps myself in the mid-1970s. At first I only recorded women whom I knew well as close family friends: often I had listened to their stories since my childhood. Gradually the circle of people I was recording widened, as I was sent from one person to another. I started to use a tape recorder in 1978. Altogether, I have now recorded 250 ex-prisoners. Sometimes I have listened to someone for months, but with others I have only talked for a few hours. The interviewees fall into several groups, but the largest number are 'victims of 1937', imprisoned at the height of the terror, followed by those convicted in the renewed repressions of the late 1940s and early 1950s. A much smaller group of my interviewees started their prison lives in the 1920s. The first of them all was imprisoned in 1919, and the last in 1953. Two-thirds of them are women, which may well be a typical proportion of survivors generally. In terms of nationality, the majority are Russian, one-third are Jewish, and the rest are Polish, German, Latvian, Armenian, and so on. As to social background, the majority come from the urban intelligentsia – doctors, teachers, scholars, students, or journalists – while others were party workers or from the armed forces.

For the Soviet regime, memory itself was intrinsically a serious threat. The entire history of the past, and above all of the revolution and the civil war, was rewritten and mythologized. Memory was made to function in a truly Orwellian style: what had been peace was now declared war, and the Soviet version of memory became oblivion.

The time span of many decades, compared with just twelve years of Nazi power in Germany, has shaped the character of memory and recollection. Those who fell before the waves of repression in the 1920s – beginning with members of the so-called 'exploiter classes', former aristocrats and White officers, followed by Social Democrats and social revolutionaries, and later by Trotskyites – were, as a rule, unable to emerge from the Gulag system before the 1950s. My interviews include many of this kind. For example, Daria Samaelova was first arrested while still at school, at the age of seventeen, on the grounds that her older brother had also been arrested as a Trotskyite opposition sympathizer. This was in 1927, in the city of Baku in the Caucasus; she was released after two months. But a year later she was arrested again and deported for three years. In 1933 she tried to re-enter normal life and, hiding her past, enrolled as a student in Moscow University. But after a year she was rearrested and exiled to Tartaria. Then in 1936, she was once again rearrested, this time receiving a prison sentence of ten years for Trotskyist counter-revolutionary activity. In 1946, after her release, she was permanently exiled to Kolyma (in the far north-east of Siberia). Samaelova was only rehabilitated after 1956. And far from being a unique case, hers was a characteristic path which hundreds of thousands of others followed. It is unusual only in that she survived such a past to be still alive today, so that I was able to record her history.

Obviously it is impossible to repress the memory of such a fate: that would mean forgetting one's entire life. The effect is rather different: more of a confusion – especially in the memory of prisons and camps – of the superficial distinctions between imprisonment and freedom. Today they all repeat the observation, which is now a commonplace, that the Soviet Union in the mid-1930s was itself an immense concentration camp: even if millions of its people, particularly of the generation born after the revolution, considered their 'cell' the brightest and most beautiful in the world. Thus, those who had served their term and were released into freedom still felt – either consciously or unconsciously – that the Soviet Union itself was a concentration camp, and therefore chose not to return to the 'big world', but instead settled down in Siberia or the far east of Russia, living near the camps, continuing to work on the camp farms on different tasks as exiles. The most far-sighted of them did understand the system. But where could they go, where else could they settle? Ex-prisoners were forbidden to live in the big cities, and in smaller towns a stranger would always be under suspicion. Their fears were sound, for a new wave of repression followed in the 1940s, and those so-called 'recidivists' who had settled down in new places were rearrested and sent off into exile: an exile which is often remembered as scarcely less terrible than the concentration camps, with no work, nothing to eat, and nothing to provide warmth. Indeed, those who were sentenced to the camps in the post-war period – with the exception, of course, of those sent to hard-labour camps – often told me, 'You were better fed in the concentration camps than in freedom.' The camps formed a network spread over Siberia, the far East, Kazakhstan, and so almost the whole country, which was essential to the immense Soviet industrial and agricultural projects, supplying a labour force which therefore had to be fed. Life was certainly tough in these camps, but their objective, in contrast to many of the camps in the repressions of 1937–39, was never annihilation through mass executions or death through starvation. The prisoners in the post-war camps adapted themselves to these conditions, and prepared to spend their whole lives in the camps, to which they had already been typically sentenced for ten to twenty-five years. When release came, after the death of Stalin, it was neither anticipated nor easy, and this is partly why there often is a lack of clarity and coherent perspective, and in some respects confusion, in their reminiscences. For them freedom did not come in a single, swift joyful act. Release demanded trouble, letters, and petitions. Re-entry into ordinary life was slow. They had long struggles to win rehabilitation, a flat, or a pension. In the Soviet situation it was very difficult to perceive the end of repression in an individual's fate, not merely in memory, but simply in real life. For many of them the repressions have scarcely finished even in the most recent years, when they have at last been able to talk openly about their own pasts.

What and how did they remember and recollect, thirty or fifty years ago – and today?

It may sound paradoxical, but we in Russia today are certainly persuaded of how short the span of human memory can be. In the last three or four years we have so thoroughly examined – as well as watched on the screen and heard on the radio – so many reminiscences of the repression, the prisons and the concentration camps of the pre-Stalinist, Stalinist, and post-Stalinist periods, that very quickly it suddenly seems as if this past was always known and remembered. Yet a mere ten or fifteen years ago, when the events of the 1920s–50s were much closer and their witnesses younger, it seemed that everything of the past had disappeared into oblivion, and that living witnesses were lone individuals: for they were still in deep concealment.

The first wave of recollections of the camps and prisons poured out during the Khrushchev thaw, when the first ex-prisoners began to talk about their experiences. Those who came back can be roughly divided into two groups. There were those who wanted to forget what had happened to them. When I first began my recording in the 1970s, I encountered, among the families of ex-convicts who had married and had children after their release, some members who did not know about their wife's or mother's past. But there was another group who right through their imprisonment, sometimes subconsciously and sometimes explicitly, had wanted to remember. A determination had developed in them that what had happened to them and those with them should be fixed in the memory and perhaps later recounted: and this had helped them to survive. Many others who wrote their reminiscences in 'fresh footsteps' in the late 1950s and early 1960s spoke about this. They often took the attitude that if the chance to recollect was missed it would be irretrievably lost to us. Perhaps we can recall the recording of the stories – the fresh stories – in the late 1950s, of those who were waiting in queues at the military prosecution offices to obtain their certificates of rehabilitation. At that time there were some among those returning who undertook Moscow 'lecture tours', orally recounting camp experiences, because interest about the Gulag was so high among the intelligentsia on the other side of the barbed wire. But, in literary form, the facts about the prisons and camps were as a rule tragi-comic. In particular, this was the time when certain expressions and terms from camp jargon began to pop up constantly in conversational language. Nevertheless, the real picture of the repressions and of prison and camp life remained entirely hidden. For beyond imprisonment glimmered a ghastlier fantasy. The reality of the camps had been terrible and fantastic enough, but the whole horror was submerged in the incredibly depressing and petty everyday struggles for survival. This was why the appearance of Solzhenitsyn's novel, *One Day in the Life of Ivan Denisovich* seemed so important. I well remember how, reading it as a schoolgirl, I was above all puzzled: I could not understand what had produced such a powerful impression on my parents. I had expected something horrific, freezing the blood in my veins, but all that Solzhenitsyn offered was hunger, cold, filth, and unmanageable labour, a mere biological existence, in which every rag and every tiny crumb of bread took on an existential significance. But ex-prisoners at last saw a rendering of part of their lives in the novel, and a stream of recollections poured out with the journal reviews. However, the camp theme was very soon officially prohibited again, while official biographies began to use formulas to symbolize that a person had suffered under the repressions: 'In the 1930s and 1940s he worked in the far North', or 'his life was torn apart in 1937'.

But by now it was already impossible to force all the witnesses to subside again. The books of Solzhenitsyn and the recollections of Evgeny Ginsburg and Varlam Shalamoff were reprinted and broadly circulated in samizdaty. Above all, some ex-convicts were asserting the need to talk about their past and of being together with other survivors. Quietly, those who had been in Kolyma, Vorkuta, or Inta were meeting. Nor was this surprising. Among those repressed under the infamous political Decree 58, especially in the 1930s, were many active city intellectuals. It was well known that in almost every concentration camp a university could have been opened. Links made in the camps were often maintained in liberty. People met together and continued to reminisce or even read aloud their testimonies, which had been introduced as court evidence.

On the other hand, to speak to outsiders brough a fear, a fully justifiable fear, that everything might be repeated. With my informants in the 1970s, I constantly used to find that they became instantly silent on seeing my tape recorder. An additional hindrance was their memory of the false confessions, obtained through physical and psychological tortures by the NKVD – the People's Commissariat of Internal Affairs, the internal security police – which were preserved somewhere in the archives. Only now, after having at last got the opportunity of getting to know some official investigation papers, including the minutes of interrogations, and reading the incredible evidence from their nearest and closest – husband, lover, or friend – have I finally been able to confront what forced victims either to keep their silence or to expunge whole sections of their consciousness. Recently, an archivist told me the story of a woman who applied to him to be shown the papers on her father, who had perished in the late 1930s. When he looked at this evidence he discovered that the unique accusatory material was that of this very daughter, who was then aged sixteen. They had taken her to the interrogation and, already frightened by this, she had used some careless phrase of her father, in an argument with him – just letting off steam – the previous evening. But afterwards, of course, she did everything to put this out of her consciousness and indeed she 'forgot'.

But the perpetually recurring question was how those who were strong and brave people in ordinary life came to denounce themselves and others. The limit of endurance was very plainly explained to me by Ivan Fitterman, an important constructor at the largest automobile factory in the country, who was arrested in the 1950s and sentenced to twenty-five years as a participant in Zionist plotting. He was in the notorious Sukhanovskaya prison, within 40 kilometres of Moscow, which was intended to destroy all who persisted with resistance: 'If they needed to get evidence from you, they got it. Or they killed you. If you did not sign what you were given, you knew that the moment they waved their hand at you, you might be no longer necessary for their evidence.'

'The investigator responsible for our rehabilitation', recalled Irma Kin, the widow of a famous Soviet journalist shot in 1938, herself imprisoned for ten years in the camps, 'showed me documents about my husband. I knew his handwriting; I read how he denounced himself – and I began to be hysterical. But he said to me, "I thought you were a strong woman."'

For many years people found it hard to understand why the punitive administration so persistently sought these confessions. Probably there is one explanation: that in a totalitarian society in the period of total terror, the general guilt needed to be shared by all – by both victims and executioners.

In general, the problem of who were victims and who were executioners in the Soviet context is extraordinarily complex. It is not a myth that those who were shot sometimes died with the name of Stalin on their lips, maintaining to the last minute their belief that their beloved leader knew nothing of the repression. Those arrested in the early and mid-1930s included a high percentage of believing communists. Many even returned from the concentration camps as convinced communists and rejoined the party, by no means merely for the sake of their pension and privileges, or for an easier way of fitting into normal life – although that was one reason – but because they continued to believe in the excellence of communist ideas, explaining their own misfortunes in terms of mistakes and distortions, and also continued to believe in the personal virtues of Stalin. Lenin remained a sacred image, and all that was necessary, as they would then say, was to return 'to Leninist lines'. The ironic consequence of the Gulag system was that both victim and executioner could share a common ideological platform. Neither the investigators, nor the guards or the administrator of the camps could be ideological enemies for arrested communists. Hence, the first thought of those arrested often was that the arrest must be a mistake, a misunderstanding; that the investigator was not an enemy, like the Gestapo, but a Soviet man who simply needed to be convinced that you were not guilty. It happened in some cases that the NKVD investigators turned out to be acquaintances whom they had met in general friendship, and who by no means turned on full moral or psychological pressure. 'There look, but if we had behaved ourselves well, we could be drinking tea together with you at Mr H.'s', recalled Olga Penzo, a ballerina arrested in 1937.

Hence some of those things seem wholly incomprehensible to someone of a different generation: like those pages in the album of an ex-convict, where I noticed among the photographs from the late 1950s a snap of herself with other women at one of the Crimean health spas. One of these women, it was explained, had been the governor of the camp in which my informant had spent some years. Already in the Khrushchev period they had met again in the spa and were photographed together as long-remembered acquaintances. 'She wasn't the worst from there', Katya Gavralova, who had spent eight years in the Kolyma camp, explained to me – 'there were some much worse than her'.

Now, there are former camp administrators who write letters to ex-prisoners asking them if they will confirm, for their personal records, that they were decent and discontented with the party organization. And the ex-prisoners reply: 'Yes, he wasn't so bad, at least he didn't steal from people, or starve them as much as the governor of the next camp.' It is important to note that among survivors a large percentage survived through being in relatively privileged situations, working in the administrative structure close to camp authority.

None of this is surprising: it was similar in the Nazi concentration camps. The difference was that in the Soviet camps the victims were often identifying themselves with the very regime which was inflicting their repression. Thus I have often heard such views expressed as: 'When I was in the prison or camps I was ashamed in front of young women students, or foreigners, about what was happening in my Soviet country.' After the war it was still shameful in front of Latvian women, Estonians, or west Ukrainians. And the source of this shame was in their genuine loyalty to the regime, even in the camp or prison. This is the striking meaning behind the apparently absurd remark in the story of a German woman who came as a political immigrant to the Soviet Union in the 1930s and was arrested there: 'How glad I was that I could participate in the building of socialism at Kolyma, how much more incongruous it would have been for me to have served my sentence in some Nazi prison.'

Sometimes the links between the two sides were superimposed quite fantastically. Tamara Galkina was the wife of an important military man, but she fell in love with a young subordinate and went off with him. He had an active career in the NKVD. In 1937 they came in the night but, to their surprise, they did not arrest him, but took her – to her first husband, who was being held in connection with the Tukachevsky case. Her first husband Mikhael was shot, and she herself was sentenced to ten years in the camps. Meanwhile her second husband went into the Gulag as a high-up administrator and at the moment of her release he arrived in Magadan, the capital of the Kolyma region, as a general, one of the chief administrators of the immense network of camps in the far east. He summoned Tamara to him. She knew that after her arrest he had given evidence against her, refuted her, and then divorced her. He now proposed that she should stay with him. She refused. But years later, after her rehabilitation, when he was already retired, they were reconciled, and right up to his death they regularly called on each other, and drank tea together like old friends.

However, this NKVD general was an exceptional success among those who were arrested and those who were shot. In the 1930s tens of thousands of the NKVD workers themselves perished. They led the repressions from the start; they prepared the process of fabrication of documentation; and then they imprisoned themselves. There were many occasions in later year when the sometime tormentor stumbled on his victim in a camp where both were imprisoned.

In the Soviet situation it was possible for a man to change his life role several times: to shoot White officers in the civil war, to participate in the crushing of the Kronstadt rising, then to struggle actively against the socialist opposition, destroying social revolutionaries and Trotskyists, and later to lead collectivization and the breaking-up of kulak farms with an iron fist, and finally in 1937 or 1938 to become a victim of repression himself. As late as the 1970s, I still often hear ecstatic and uncritical recollections about participation in the civil war, or in collectivization: everything was good and proper, until they were struck by the sudden blow of their own arrest.

There are some questions which I always put to my informants: at the moment of their arrest, how far did they understand what was going on in their country; when were their eyes opened, if they were opened – on arrest, in prison, in the camps, or even later? Very few of them correctly appreciated what was happening because, as a rule, the earliest people who found themselves under threat, either because of their background or because of their political beliefs, were already overrun by the gathering speed of the machine of terror in the 1920s. The least prepared and most blind were the communist victims of 1937. 'It seemed an inexplicable nightmare', I heard again and again, or 'The only thing which came into my head was "It's a Fascist conspiracy."' 'I scarcely understood anything', recalled Dina Yankovskaya; 'as a scientist, a biologist, when at the beginning of 1939 by a happy chance I found myself released from prison, I threw myself into writing letters to the government: to confirm that all those people in prison with me were innocents, and that the NKVD had been infiltrated by Fascists.' The only surprising thing about her story is that rather than immediately rearresting her, they sent her son to the battle-front. She herself survived the Leningrad blockade, before the authorities, after nearly ten years, recollected her letter and arrested her.

'I understood nothing at that stage,' a Comintern worker, Georgei Rubinstein, told me, 'so that after my arrest my first thought in the Lubyanka prison was "They're testing me through a routine task."'

Not surprisingly, nor deliberately do interviewees evoke how far what was happening in the prisons recalled the theatre of the absurd. The wife of a well-known Soviet aviator, who, like him, was arrested, was forced during her interrogation in the Butyrskaya prison to write her husband a letter just as if she was at liberty: everything was in order, she was well and active, the children were studying, and so on. Other arrested women managed – from their cells – to change their clothing, have their hair done at the hairdresser's, and arrange to see their husbands, who also needed to think that they were free. Understandably, they remember the details of such absurd episodes throughout their lives.

In recollections of the Gulag there is always a great significance in the detail, in episodes, in the fine particulars of life: both because of its continuous meanness and equally because it was on this that life itself depended. As a rule, it is the first arrest or the first cell, which is remembered best of all, probably because it came as such a powerful shock to one who, up to that very moment, had been an innocent person. Often, they still hold the whole view of what they saw in their parting glance as they were marched off, their last look at their old life: a handful of sweets scattered on the table, the teapot on the cooking range, the linen on the washtub, the unfinished report on their last work trip which had seemed so important, or the kind neighbours who had managed to return a borrowed coffee grinder just five minutes before the arrest. Each spare little shred of clothing, the stockings given to someone, the mittens stolen from you, they all remained fixed in the memory for decades.

With the millions of Soviet people who had gone through the camps scattered across the whole country, I never cease to be surprised by the part played by unexpected encounters, meetings, intersections, or coincidences: how a man saw someone, how a woman was in prison with someone else. For example, I remembered an episode from Evgeny Ginsburg's beautiful memoir, *Life's Hard Path*, set in the Butyrskaya prison: 'People peered eagerly into their faces – who were they? What about those four, for instance? In such absurd evening dresses with exaggerated *décolletés*, and high-heeled slippers . . . Everything crumpled, pulled at . . . That's the guests of Rudzutak. They were all arrested at his house as his guests.' Jan Rudzutak had been a major political and party activist and a Politburo member at the moment of his arrest. What had happened to these women who flashed past in the pages of Ginsburg's book to be devoured by the vast camp system? And then, fifty years later, one of these same women was sitting in front of me; she had been arrested, with her husband, in May 1937 in Rudzutak's dacha. Her appearance in the prison had certainly been absurd. 'They didn't allow us to take in anything – our summer silk dresses and underwear were torn, stuck over our shoulders, our stockings were ripped. At the last minutes before our prison transfer I received money from someone and we bought whatever there was in the prison chest.' So an orange top-shirt replaced a scarf on the head, a green football outfit, trousers, and on her feet the high-heeled slippers disappeared and towels were wrapped around. 'This was how I started the journey in December. It was a pure miracle I survived.'

Over many decades, life in the Gulag gave birth to endless rumours, legends, and myths, most of all of course about famous people – long previously believed executed by shooting in Moscow – who were said to have been seen by someone in some far distant camp somewhere. There were constantly recurring themes and details in such stories. For example, at least four women described to me exactly the same scene: how, many years later, when they were able to see themselves in a mirror again for the first time, the image they saw was the face of their own mother. Even as early as the 1970s, I myself recognized incidents recounted to me orally which were also scenes described in Solzhenitsyn's *Gulag Archipelago* or other printed recollections. But now story-telling about the camps has become so general that recording oral memory has become much more difficult. The vast amount of information pouring out of people often seems to happen through an immolation of their own memories to the point where it begins to seem as if everything they know happened to them personally. As a result, while earlier it had been especially important for me to learn details of their lives in the camps and prisons, now it became much more interesting to catch the 'alienation effect' of being at the same time both witnesses and questioners, of how they were themselves fifty or forty years ago. Especially recently, the moment has come for many – although certainly not all – to make a clear distinction between their present and past selves. The painful wound of semi-rehabilitation and the continuing necessity of silence over long years has now left them. On the contrary, ex-prisoners frequently perceive themselves as bearers of important information. The pain of the past recedes and they – especially the women – can talk about the torture of the prisons almost as if it had not been their own. An English-language teacher, Dina Slavutskaya, after describing to me how she had been forced to stand continuously for three days and nights during her interrogation – a form of torture in which she was forbidden to sit or even lean, and through which she has become lame for her entire life – at the end of her story asked; 'but have I told you something dreadful enough?' 'When I saw the prisoners in Kolyrna sifting gold,' another woman told me, 'I vowed to myself that if I survived and eventually came out, I would never wear a single gold piece – but now look at me: look at my ear-rings, my chain, my ring.'

So far, I have not referred to the continuing contrasts between the stories told by men and those told by women. As a rule, women describe in much fuller detail the everyday routine of the prisons and concentration camps, the clothing, and the appearance and character of people; they speak more calmly and with more detachment about the tortures and agonies they had to bear; and they are more frank about emotional and sexual life in the camps. Indeed, love in the camps is still one of the most painful and difficult themes to speak about. Women see themselves as generally better able to adapt to imprisonment and they much more often stress the crucial importance of friendships and human relationships in this. They also give more emphasis to family relationships: above all to the tragedy of being parted from their children. Men, by contrast, are more reserved. They more often highlight a moment of personal humiliation. They are more often analytical. Men also usually give more detailed and elaborate descriptions of work, occasionally illustrated by drawings; and they sometimes have a better memory for the names of people they met, and for dates. Hence sometimes, although not always, it can be useful when a man and a woman exchange memories together: a husband and wife, if both are ex-convicts, can add to and correct each other's accounts.

Some of the memories which once were the most painful of all have often now softened. In the 1950s and 1960s, for example, the problem of informers remained very acute. There was of course an immense multitude of people who had helped with the arrests and who had become interrogators in the prisons and camps. Those who returned in the 1950s could very easily meet up with the people who had put them in prison – at work, as guests, or on the street. It was extremely difficult to prove who had informed on them and usually any attempt would only end in public scandal. A strange process is now taking place, one which can be illustrated by an incident which I witnessed myself. At one of the Moscow meetings of the Memorial society, which brought together ex-convicts with those who were studying the history of the repressions, one woman, who had been arrested in about 1939, said to me in a completely calm voice: 'but over there is the man who informed on me'. And she greeted him quite normally. Catching my perplexed expression, she explained: 'Of course we were then just eighteen, his parents were old Bolsheviks who were repressed, and then they tried to recruit me too. And of course he was repressed later on himself.' I felt that what she said was the outcome not of a lack of concern for or forgetting of her past, but of a realization, which now at last had come to people of the shameful things which the system itself had done to them. In such a situation people need to behave in their own different ways but it is very important not to presume that somebody still carries the same moral self-estimation they once bore in the past. It was much more difficult in the past than today. Now survivors, or at least those who have not lost the ability for self-reflection, are often changing their own self-evaluation. 'How could I have agitated for those unlucky women to go to the collective farms?' one of my women informants castigates herself: 'I never asked myself that, when the KGB came for me – I thought they were arresting me again, but instead they informed me of the death of my brother, for whom I had looked for years in the camps – my first thought was not about him, but about myself. I thought, "Thank God, they didn't put me in."'

The question now often arises, especially from younger people, of the possibility of opposition in the concentration camp conditions. It is well known that there were of course major forms of direct resistance in the post-war period, including armed escapes, and eventually after Stalin's death uprisings and strikes in the camps themselves. But it seems to me more important, both from my discussions with the 'last' true witnesses now, and also from talking with them in the 1970s when they were younger, that ultimately the only true form of resistance was a determination to conserve one's humanity. It was sometimes undoubtedly very difficult not to become a camp of wolves, faced with the pitiless law of camp life: 'You die today, I die tomorrow.' And, together with the survivors themselves, we do have now, at last, a final chance of evaluating their past journey, with neither partiality nor anger.

Chapter 41

Patricia Lundy and Mark McGovern

'YOU UNDERSTAND AGAIN'
Testimony and post-conflict transition in the North of Ireland

'In the last three decades truth-telling has come to be seen as a key element of post-conflict transition in societies throughout the world.' This chapter considers 'the contribution of community-based truth-telling to achieving truth and justice' in Northern Ireland, and details the significant practical challenges of participatory oral history and the personal and political benefits of a 'victim-centred approach to truth-telling that can be transferred not only to other communities in the north but to other parts of the world'. Patricia Lundy is a Lecturer in Sociology at the University of Ulster in Northern Ireland; Mark McGovern is a Reader in the Centre for Studies in the Social Sciences at Edge Hill College of Higher Education in England. Reprinted with permission from *Words and Silences*: *Journal of the International Oral History Association*, 2004, new series, vol. 2, no. 2, pp. 30–35.

Oral history, community-based truth-telling and post-conflict transition

> We haven't been the victors so history hasn't been written by us. It's only now when we can see the changes coming and the demand for change being strong that people are confident enough to write the story and give the history that has never been told.[1]

IN THE LAST THREE DECADES truth-telling has come to be seen as a key element of post-conflict transition in societies throughout the world.[2] At least twenty-four countries emerging from conflict have held some sort of official truth-telling process, often called a truth commission. The North of Ireland is not one of them. Indeed, the North is beginning to appear decidedly out-of-step with other post-conflict societies because of that absence.

Thirty years of conflict between the British State and armed groups from the nationalist/republican and unionist/loyalist populations in the North were more or less brought to a conclusion by the signing of the Good Friday Agreement on 10 April 1998. Five years later the possibility of establishing an official truth process to address the legacies of the past still appears a very distant prospect. This is not due to any lack of debate on the issue. Widespread discussion of the pros and cons of various truth-telling mechanisms for the North have been ongoing for several years.[3] However, fears that a truth commission in the North may not help in achieving the desired goals of truth, justice and progressive social change have limited progress in this direction. So too have the political circumstances of post-conflict transition. None of the major parties to the conflict regarded a specifically past-focused mechanism as a priority in the negotiations leading up to the signing of the Agreement. Indeed *not* confronting the causes and competing explanations of the conflict was part of a deliberate State strategy to obtain a *realpolitik* concensus. The consequence of what Christine Bell describes as the 'constructive ambiguity' of the Irish peace process has been a 'piecemeal approach' to dealing with the past.[4]

This article outlines and examines the work of the Ardoyne Commemoration Project (ACP). People from the Ardoyne community of North Belfast carried out the project, beginning in 1998 and spending the next four years engaged in collaborative oral history/participatory action research. Their goal was to record and publish testimonies collected from relatives and friends of the ninety-nine residents of Ardoyne killed during the years of armed conflict. The book *Ardoyne: The Untold Truth* was published in August 2002.[5] The paper first provides a brief description of Ardoyne, the impact of the conflict upon it and the nature of the Commemoration Project. It then assesses the contribution of community-based truth-telling to achieving truth and justice in the process of post-conflict transition in the North of Ireland. In doing so the authors reflect upon their personal experiences as members of the ACP and joint authors/editors of *Ardoyne: The Untold Truth*.

Ardoyne, the ACP and collaborative oral history

> Defending your neighbours was what it was all about in Ardoyne. This is an area with a militia mentality because of its geography. Our location dictated everything. We were surrounded and we had to stand up for ourselves because there was no one else to do it for us. That's Ardoyne.[6]

Ardoyne is a working class area in North Belfast with a population of roughly eleven thousand people who are republican, nationalist and catholic. Similar working class areas surround it on three sides except that people there are loyalist, unionist and protestant. North Belfast had one of the highest levels of deaths directly attributable to the three decades of the North's 'low intensity' war.[7] As a heavily militarised and much demonised nationalist enclave in North Belfast, Ardoyne was particularly vulnerable to attack. Between 1969 and 1998, ninety-nine members of this community were killed, one of the highest death rates of any area in the

North. Most were victims of either British State security forces (28%) or loyalist paramilitary groups (50%).

This has given rise to a number of specific truth and justice issues. For example, the question of impunity enjoyed by State forces and loyalist groups remains to be fully examined. In all the cases of those killed directly by the State forces there were subsequently no arrests, charges or convictions brought, though many of the victims were clearly innocent unarmed civilians. Allegations of long term collusion between loyalist groups and State intelligence agencies have recently been confirmed by a government inquiry. However, as yet no further action has resulted from these (still unpublished in full) findings.[8] In addition, silences have continued to surround the circumstances of those killed by Irish republicans. Roughly 10% of Ardoyne's victims were killed by local republican organisations (principally the Irish Republican Army, IRA) either as alleged informers or unintentionally during attacks on the British army. This also raises important issues for local truth-telling and focuses attention on the divisive legacies of conflict within as well as between particular communities.[9] Taken together, a culture of denial and omission concerning past events may be contributing to the continuation of conflict into the present, even if it is now largely unarmed.

The Ardoyne Commemoration Project started in 1998, against the backdrop of the emerging peace process and the growing highly politically charged debate on which and how victims should be remembered. All those involved (except one of the authors) were from Ardoyne and all worked as volunteers. Around thirty interested individuals – some were relatives of the dead, some were community activists – came together to explore various ways to commemorate the dead of Ardoyne. After much discussion, they decided to do so through a book recording the voices of those who knew them best. A committee of five was set up to organise and begin work on the project. Initially, and naively, the project was envisaged as a yearlong job. Eventually it took four years to produce a final text of over 350,000 words, after conducting, transcripting, editing and re-editing over three hundred in-depth interviews. The original under-estimation of the task was due largely to the lack of experience of those involved. This was very much a bottom-up initiative.

Community participation was a defining feature of the project, guiding and shaping its development. A key goal was to generate a sense of control over the work amongst those taking part. This was due to several factors. Those involved, because they belonged to the community, were well aware of the impact on relatives of prevailing negative, demonising media (and often academic) representations of the area and its population. Similarly, a conflict in which the British intelligence agencies had employed a wide range of invidious counter-insurgency strategies had engendered a deep distrust of any and all outsiders to the community. Generating a level of trust required not only that local people carry out the work, but that interviewees felt sure that what eventually appeared in print was what they wanted to be said. The project also came to be informed by a radical participatory action research approach to 'history-making'. As Anisur Rahman argues, this involves a challenge to domination resulting from control over the 'means of knowledge production [including] the social power to determine what is valid or useful knowledge.'[10] Validating popular knowledge and experience required that people felt a genuine sense of control at key moments of the process.

The project also acted as a conduit for a great deal of interchange and discussion. The desire to share authority between the ACP and the interviewees – an essential aspect of collaboration in oral history – was most explicit in the decision to hand back the transcribed interview to the interviewee after an initial edit.[11] He or she then had complete control to add, take out or change words. This was also done in discussion with ACP volunteers. The text was then re-worked and returned to each interviewee for final approval before publication. Families also had access to the transcripts of other interviewees. While the general rule was that people could only make changes to their own words, questions and observations could be raised with the ACP. The handing back phase undoubtedly added years to the work of the project, but was regarded as a key to achieve genuine collaborative control of the decision-making process. That said, the sheer scale of the work meant that collaboration could only take place within the limits of time and resources.[12]

Clearly this process also impacted on the nature and status of the evidence produced. A wide range of influences, both personal and political, might affect how people want the public remembrance of their loved ones to take place. Similarly, the role of collective memory and the communal construction of the past on individual narratives cannot be ignored.[13] But in the end, the efforts involved in sharing authority often added greatly to the richness, depth, diversity and complexity of the testimonies. For those involved in the project it also gradually became clear that this process was itself as important a contribution to post-conflict transition as any outcome might prove to be.

Oral history, participation and justice in the North of Ireland

> I have only found out recently, in the last few months, when I read the inquest papers the extent of the injuries and what happened to my brother . . . We have launched a campaign and I just want to get to the truth of what really happened that night. We all know we will never get justice . . . [that] they will get away with it, but its important even to have them stand there and admit what they did.[14]

Projects that focus on participation might play a key role in the wider process of truth-telling and post-conflict transition in the North of Ireland. First, a project like ACP places 'on record' the experiences and insights of loved ones whose evidence may, at some future point, be part of an official truth and justice process. This is important because there is little likelihood of any significant judicial redress for past human rights violations in the near future.[15] Second, by highlighting the ongoing legacy of the past within a particular area, such projects create greater awareness of the need for a society-wide truth-telling process. In this respect it is important to understand that the ACP is part of a patchwork of disparate truth and justice and oral history projects taking place in many (mostly nationalist) communities throughout the North. Some of these have recently come together to form Eolas (Irish for information), a network of organisations seeking to widen the debate on post-conflict truth-telling.[16]

The work of a project like the ACP, however, is not only about generating future debate and initiatives in truth-telling. It is a contribution to truth and justice in its own right. As a number of authors have argued, post-conflict truth mechanisms can have a number of different goals. Unfortunately these are not all necessarily mutually conducive. Key amongst them has been the restoration of dignity for victims.[17] This is closely linked to the supposed cathartic effect that such a process is believed to have. But one of the problems in the way that official truth-telling processes have developed is that the goal of restoring dignity has often been sacrificed for what are seen as greater goods. This has occurred for a number of different reasons, including the desire of judicial reform, demands of societal reconciliation and sheer political expediency. For example, Clint van de Walt *et al.* argue that the desire to represent the 'fantasmagoric harmony' of Archbishop Tutu's 'rainbow nation' in the South African Truth and Reconciliation Commission constrained survivors to 'speak' their experiences within the discourse of 'reconciliation'. This meant that what then was 'unspoken' remained 'inexpressible . . . non-symbolised surplus' and that (*à la* Lacan) is precisely what defines trauma.[18]

There may be many good, sound arguments as to why particular social and political ends might be given precedence over the immediate needs of victims. Post-conflict truth-telling is never going to be an ideal process. However, the emphasis on institutionalised truth-telling may need to be addressed. A process that wants to bring to the fore the needs of victims and targeted communities, particularly in affording an opportunity for them to speak out, may need to take a more diverse and multi-sited approach. In such circumstances projects such as the ACP can play a pivotal role in either countering or balancing the work of a Truth Commission. Such a victim-centred agenda should also be seen as a matter of radical social and political practice. It is also an instance where oral history can play a key and direct political role. It would be overly prosaic and optimistic to believe that the setting of the oral history interview, no matter what lengths are taken to make the interviewee feel safe, is a context within which a fully therapeutic experience could (or indeed should) take place. Nor should the oral history practitioner underestimate the ethical dilemmas such an occasion invites.[19] However, devising means of speaking that create genuine co-generative dialogue through participatory control at least reduce the possibility of inducing the sort of second order trauma identified by van der Walt *et al.* in South Africa. In doing so a public space can also be opened up to create dialogue both within and between communities. This is not going to be an easy process. But it represents a valuable opportunity for people to re-evaluate their own individual and collective past, to (as one Ardoyne resident put it) 'understand again'.

Conclusion: the value and limits of community-based truth-telling

> What is justice? I'm very confused about my idea of justice . . . One week you feel that the killers have done their time and there was a war going on. Then there are other weeks when you think 'I wish they would shoot the bastard or hang him.' It's very confusing. But I think something needs to be done now. I think the families and friends that have lost someone need to express what happened to them. We are often too

quiet. In those days you were expected to just go back to your house and that was it. That was people's way of dealing with it, but they didn't deal with it, they buried it and forgot about it but it is still there and they need to bring it out.[20]

The problems facing community-based truth-telling in the North of Ireland should not be underestimated. Researching a violently divided society presents a whole series of ethical and methodological issues.[21] Community oral history projects face immense hurdles and limitations when operating in such a context. Given the sensitivities involved in such work it is always therefore important not to raise the expectations of victims beyond what is achievable. It is also quite likely that there will be no common agreement on what constitutes truth and justice. What is evident, however, is that the 'need to bring out' what is 'still there' for victims is likely to mean that truth processes will continue to be a key feature of post-conflict transition.

The lack of official truth-telling in the North of Ireland has been due largely to the absence of conducive political circumstances. Transition has also seen a high degree of institutional continuity, limiting the possibilities for truth and justice in a number of ways. However, those conditions have allowed alternative approaches to come to the fore. For the ACP that meant adopting a collaborative oral history perspective that produced a focus on building genuine participation into its approach to truth-telling. The benefits of participation for the ACP provide lessons for a victim-centred approach to truth-telling that can be transferred not only to other communities in the north but to other parts of the world.

Notes

1   Gerard McGuigan, Ardoyne resident and former local Sinn Fein councillor, interviewed by Patricia Lundy and Mark McGovern (ACP), Ardoyne, May 2003.

2   See for example, Priscilla Hayner, *Unspeakable Truths: Confronting State Terror and Atrocity*, London: Routledge, 2001.

3   See, for example, Eolas, *Consultation Paper on Truth and Justice: a Discussion Document*, Belfast: Relatives for Justice, 2003; Healing Through Remembering, *The Report of the Healing Through Remembering Project*, Belfast: HRT, 2002; Patricia Lundy and Mark McGovern, 'The politics of memory in post-conflict Northern Ireland', *Peace Review*, 13, 1, 2001, pp. 27–34.

4   Christine Bell, 'Dealing with the Past in Northern Ireland', *Fordham International Law Journal*, 26, 4, 2003, pp. 1095–1147.

5   Ardoyne Commemorative Project (Patricia Lundy and Mark McGovern), *Ardoyne: the Untold Truth*, Belfast: Beyond the Pale Publication, 2002.

6   Sean Colligan, Ardoyne resident and former republican activist, interviewed by Patricia Lundy and Mark McGovern (ACP), Ardoyne, February 2000.

7   Of a total of roughly 3,630 conflict fatalities almost half occurred in Belfast, with just under 550 victims (396 of them civilians) in the North of the city alone. The majority of these were from the nationalist/catholic community. See Marie-Therese *et al.*, *Northern Ireland's Troubles: the Human Costs*, London: Pluto Press, 1999; David McKitterick *et al.*, *Lost Lives: the Stories of the Men, Women and Children who Died as a Result of the Northern Ireland Troubles*, Edinburgh: Mainstream Publishing, 1999.

8   See, John Stevens, *Stevens Enquiry 3*: *Overview and Recommendations*, Belfast, Stevens Inquiry, 2003.

9   It should be noted, too, that the local IRA was also responsible for the deaths of dozens of other victims either killed in the area (including twenty-two members of the British army) or in and from adjoining loyalist communities.

10   Anisur Rahman, *People's Self-development. Perspectives on Participatory Action Research: a Journey Through Experience*, London: Zed Books, 1993, p. 83.

11   Michael Frisch, *A Shared Authority: Essays on the Craft and Meaning of Oral and Public History*, New York, SUNY, 1990; Alicia Rouverol, 'I Was Content and Not Content: Oral History and the Collaborative Process', *Oral History*, 28, 2, 2000, pp. 66–78.

12   Randy Stoecker, 'Are Academics Relevant? Roles for Scholars in Participatory Research', paper presented to the American Sociological Society Annual Meeting, May 1997.

13   Alistair Thomson, Michael Frisch and Paula Hamilton, 'The Memory and History Debates: Some International Perspectives', *Oral History*, 22, 2, 1994, pp. 33–43.

14   Ann Stewart, sister of IRA Volunteer Jackie Mailey (shot dead by the SAS (Special Air Service), 21 June 1978), interviewed by Tom Holland (ACP), Ardoyne, May 1999.

15   In May 2001 the European Court of Human Rights held that the failure of the British state to carry out effective investigations into State killings and allegations of collusion in four cases brought before them contravened the 'Right to Life' of the victims, as defined in Article 2 of the European Convention on Human Rights. However, there were limitations to these rulings and it is unclear how the decision might underpin other, and future, legal proceedings. See, Fionnuala Ni Aoláin, 'Truth-telling, Accountability and the Right to Life in Northern Ireland', *European Human Rights Review*, 5, 2002, pp. 572–559; and 'The Evolving Jurisprudence of the European Convention Concerning the Right to Life', *Netherlands Quarterly of Human Rights*, 19, 1, 2001, pp. 21–42.

16   Amongst those groups involved in Eolas are nationalist/republican victims and relatives groups (Relatives for Justice, Bloody Sunday Trust, Firinne), ex-prisoners organisations (Coiste na n-Iarchimí) and oral history projects (ACP, Duchás). See Eolas, *Consultation*.

17   Paul Seils, 'Reconciliation in Guatemala: the Role of Intelligent Justice', *Race and Class*, 44, 1, 2001, pp. 33–59.

18   Clint van der Walt *et al.*, 'The South African Truth and Reconciliation Commission: "Race", Historical Compromise and Transitional Democracy', *International Journal of Intercultural Relations*, 27, 2003, p. 262.

19   David Becker, 'Dealing with the Consequences of Organised Violence in Trauma Work', in *Berghof Handbook for Conflict Transformation*, Berlin, Berghof Research Centre for Constructive Conflict Management, 2001; Maxine Birch and Tina Millerm 'Inviting intimacy: the Interview as Therapeutic Opportunity', *International Journal of Social Research Methodology*, 13, 3, 2000, pp. 189–202; David Jones, 'Distressing Interviews and Unhappy Interviewing', *Oral History*, 26, 2, 1998, pp. 49–56; Wendy Rickard, 'Oral History: More Dangerous than Therapy? Interviewees Reflections on Recording Traumatic or Taboo Issues', *Oral History*, 26, 2, 1998, pp. 34–48.

20   Paddy Meehan, son of Patrick Meehan (shot dead by loyalist paramilitaries, 17 June 1976), interviewed by Tom Holland (ACP), North Belfast, March 2000.

21   Marie Smyth and Gillian Robinson (eds), *Researching Violently Divided Societies: Ethical and Methodological Issues*, London: Pluto Press, 2001.

Chapter 42

Nigel Cross and Rhiannon Barker

THE SAHEL ORAL
HISTORY PROJECT

The SOS Sahel Oral History Project recorded stories from men and women in sub-Saharan Africa about their changing environment and ways of life. Through oral history young, local aid workers developed a more mutually respectful relationship with their elders, and memories of effective social relations and land use were used as a resource for community and environmental survival. Nigel Cross was Research Director of the Sahel Oral History Project. Rhiannon Barker was Coordinator of the Sahel Oral History Project and is now a freelance consultant in public health research. Reprinted with permission from Nigel Cross and Rhiannon Barker (eds), *At the Desert's Edge*: *Oral Histories from the Sahel*, London: Panos/ SOS Sahel, 1991, pp. 1–16. This book was published as part of the Panos Institute's Oral Testimony Programme, which explores and illustrates the potential of oral testimony in the development process, and gathers, publishes and amplifies the views and experiences of individuals and communities in the South on specific development themes.

O RAL HISTORY IS BOTH a methodology and an academic discipline. It has not yet been widely used in a development context. One aim of the Sahel Oral History Project was to explore how the application of oral history techniques can assist the development process. By talking at length with farmers, pastoralists, refugees and other groups, we hoped to gain a better understanding of traditional land-use practice, land tenure, farming and pastoral systems, the causes of desertification, and many other aspects of Sahelian life. Our aim was not only to record indigenous knowledge and improve rapport with those with whom SOS Sahel and its partner agencies work, but also to develop a practical methodology which could then be incorporated into development planning, project implementation and evaluation.

We do not claim that *At the Desert's Edge* and its supplementary material will become a seminal text for historians of Africa. In most of the places where we worked, there was no written record to support or contradict the oral testimony. In some instances it was possible to record the first tentative outlines of village histories, but this, though fascinating, was peripheral. The principal aim was to record the perceptions of Sahelian men and women – which are neither right nor wrong – about their changing environment and way of life. All history is informed by someone's testimony – his or her story. We did not set out to accumulate facts, but rather to find the stories, to improve the techniques for their collection and, most important of all, to demonstrate their value and utility.

The pace of change

Social change in the Sahel has been rapid. Many children now have access to formal education. While this may increase their own economic prospects, it also leads to a loss of cultural continuity. Traditional knowledge is considered 'out-of-date' by young villagers as well as outsiders. Recording traditional knowledge both rescues it from oblivion and demonstrates its value to a younger generation. Environmental and economic pressures in the Sahel have combined to create a period of unprecedented social dislocation. Academic analysis of economic, social and physical change, while it may be objective, lacks the authenticity of first-hand testimony and fails to capture the important subjective aspects of these upheavals.

Not the least of our concerns has been to offer alternatives to the received image of Sahelians as passive, grateful beneficiaries who have been helped to fish or farm (the aid agency cover photo), by giving some 500 men and women – classic development 'targets' – the chance to talk back and to broadcast their experiences, priorities and perspectives.

We have not edited out the tragedies or the disasters as these are graphically described by those who have lived through them, but the same witnesses demonstrate their ingenuity and tenacity, and reflect on the 'good life'. The interviews reveal the complexity of everyday Sahelian life: people's relationship to and care of the environment; the position of men and women on the land and in the household; and changes in family relationships and social customs. As the interviews make clear, these individuals are neither emaciated victims nor happy peasants. They are themselves.

The process

The preliminary research, identification of sites, liaison with other agencies and development of a questionnaire were carried out between January and May 1989. The interviewing began that June and continued until October 1990. Over 500 interviews were completed, of which just under half were with women. A small proportion were group interviews, bringing the total number of respondents to more than 650. The project worked in eight countries – Senegal, Mauritania, Mali, Burkina Faso, Niger, Chad, Sudan and Ethiopia – at nineteen sites, in seventeen languages.

From the outset, interview sites were linked to ongoing development projects. This strategy provided participating agencies with new, village-authored extension and evaluation materials and the Sahel Oral History Project with a ready-made base. Although it is never easy for development agencies to provide such support, there was a high level of cooperation. As a control, interviews were also conducted in non-project areas. In general, project sites were easier to work in – the relationship that had already been established between the project and the people proved an enormous asset.

A major consideration in the selection of interview sites was that they should cover a range of tribal, economic and social groups. These were divided into five main categories:

- refugees (political and economic): Eritreans and Tigreans in Sudan, ex-pastoralists in Nouakchott, Mauritania
- pastoralists and agro-pastoralists in Mali, Niger, Chad and Ethiopia
- farmers in rainfed areas in Mali, Burkina Faso, Niger, Sudan and Ethiopia
- farmers in irrigated riverine areas in Senegal and Sudan
- fishermen in Mauritania and Chad

We chose interviewers from extension workers, research students and local journalists; inevitably a mixture of luck, judgement and availability circumscribed our choice. The most successful interviewers were good communicators who had a natural curiosity and interest in the respondents. In terms of grasping the complexity of some of the questions and to ensure effective transcription and translation, a relatively high level of education and literacy was essential. Given the nature of the fieldwork – with the inevitable frustrations created by limited transport, inaccessibility of interviewees and difficult living conditions – the energy and enthusiasm of the interviewer was as important as previous interviewing experience. Undoubtedly the most successful interviewers were those who had a thorough knowledge of the area and, in most cases, had been born and brought up within it. They could, in the fullest sense of the phrase, 'speak the same language'.

Finding the right questions

The first task of the project was to prepare a guide for interviewers outlining a standard methodology, together with a draft questionnaire. Initial research for the guidelines involved consultation with development agencies and academics. An interview outline was tested in Sudan. Further consultation, and feedback from interviewers, led to a number of changes. In addition, discussions were held with development workers on each interviewing site prior to the work, in order to establish their own priorities.

To draw up a questionnaire which can be used effectively in many different countries, even though they share common problems and conditions, is a near impossible task. Questions which would strike a European as being neutral and rather mundane, such as 'How many children do you have?', may prove offensive. To divulge such facts to a stranger may tempt fate – an open invitation to God to take a child away.

A cultural bias in the interview outline was inevitable – we saw the project as having a development education role and so were seeking to inform a Northern public as well as an 'expert' audience. We found ourselves seeking answers to questions which members of the community concerned might never have thought to ask. To balance our concerns, interviewers were given scope to exclude anything they felt unsuitable, and encouraged to include questions of their own design. Similarly, questions were added or subtracted depending on the specific country or site and according to the prevailing political, social and environmental conditions.

Working with women

Most of the Sahelian countries in which we were working have strong cultural and religious influences which tend to restrict the movement of women and inhibit easy communication between the sexes. To avoid marginalising women, one male and one female interviewer were sought for each site. But employing women proved much more difficult than men, largely because of cultural constraints restricting their freedom to travel. Women interviewers had less work experience than men and generally needed more training and confidence building.

Despite the extra work involved, the policy of employing women proved critical to the success of the project. On a number of occasions, as an experiment, men were asked to interview women and women to interview men. Their comments on this experience were enlightening. Women generally found the interviews ran smoothly. The men, on the other hand, appeared at a loss to know what to ask women and their questions quickly dried up. Some said that they found talking to women boring and unenlightening, but it is also possible that male respondents found women interviewers less intimidating than the other way around.

As interviewees, women again required a higher investment of both time and energy. In the first place, they were harder to involve since their domestic chores could rarely be postponed – there was always grain to grind, wood to collect or a meal to prepare, and they preferred to be interviewed while continuing their chores. Men were more inclined to lay down the task at hand, benefiting from a male culture which sets aside time and space for communal debate. They generally talked with greater ease for long periods of time without faltering, whereas women usually needed much more encouragement. Women also tended to reflect less critically on their life situation, attributing their hardships to fate rather than external factors, making it more difficult for the interviewer to follow up further lines of questioning.

Problems sometimes arose from men wanting to take over or disrupt interviews with women. Men would decide that they should act as mediators between their wives (or other female relatives) and the interviewer. In some cases it appeared that the woman was reassured by male encouragement; at other times the consequences were disastrous, with the woman feeling unable to talk about certain issues and the man asserting that he knew the woman's mind better than she. It was also noticeable that men often laughed at the questions to women and the women's responses, whereas they took their own contributions much more seriously.

Training

The time allocated to interviewing in each country was about one month. In this period interviewers were recruited by the project coordinator and the actual interview process was completed on two to three different sites. Within this tight schedule, a short three-day training programme was devised which provided an invaluable component of the work.

The first day of training was spent on a thorough review of the questionnaire outline and guidelines, together with some role play where the new interviewer would test interviewing methods and also play the part of respondent. On the second day the coordinator carried out the first one or two interviews, using the interviewer as an interpreter. The flexibility of the interview structure was stressed, with the coordinator demonstrating the value of follow-up questions. On the third day a sample interview was conducted, transcribed and analysed.

Selection

On each site we sought to interview roughly equal numbers of men and women. Initially, interviews were exclusively with the elderly, but as the project progressed it became clear that it would be useful to include younger people in each sample to allow comparisons between the differing perceptions of two generations.

Before interviewing began, those helping to facilitate the work were asked to identify the different economic, social and ethnic groups in the community, to ensure the interviewers covered as wide a spectrum as possible and were not simply choosing to talk to close friends, neighbours or relatives. While the majority of the interviewees were farmers or pastoralists, we also sought specialist occupations such as midwife, hunter, traditional healer, blacksmith and village chief. In most instances people were contacted through the village chief or head of the women's committee. Although this was often time-consuming, once the interviews were endorsed by respected members of the community, the respondents had greater confidence and were more willing to cooperate. We always took care to stress that there was no material advantage to be gained by participating in the interviews, beyond the intrinsic value of sharing knowledge and experience.

Our method of selection was not statistically random since our sample, averaging perhaps twelve men and twelve women in each community, was too small and the logistics too difficult. Some people were selected by the chief, others by village groups, and some were self-selected. On occasion, people were too busy to talk or were simply suspicious of the questions and unwilling to participate.

In refugee camps, and other situations where a well-established social structure was absent, selection methods were more haphazard. Where a community leader could be identified, the channel of communication was relatively easy. More often the camps, lacking ethnic and social homogeneity, had no elected representatives, obliging us to wander from house to house making our own introductions. Interviewees, however, seemed prepared to accept this rather intrusive approach.

The interviews

The majority of interviews were conducted with individuals, although there were also a small number of group interviews of up to fifteen people. While our main interest was specialised material on the environment and work practices linked to personal histories and anecdotes from individuals, group interviews were useful as they provided a consensus account. Individuals in a group situation are often animated by the discussion to follow through certain lines of inquiry in greater detail. Also, in many Sahelian societies the group is the familiar and preferred forum for discussion, especially with strangers.

Most interviews were conducted in private homes or in the shade of a lone but convenient tree. In some instances the village chief would call people to the village square or to his house. We encountered several problems in interviewing in the open: the heat of the sun rapidly wilts the interviewer and respondent; strong winds interfere with the microphone, affecting the quality of the recording; and droves of curious, often disruptive, onlookers are attracted to the site. Wherever possible we sought shelter and quiet.

Interviews lasted between forty minutes and two hours, although initial introductions, rapport-building, tea ceremonies and other hospitalities often extended the time. Two hours is about the maximum sensible period for such intense dialogue. The interviewer has to be constantly alert, planning the next question, encouraging the respondent to talk and looking for interesting areas of knowledge and experience to examine in detail. Since the 'fatigue factor' is high, no more than three thorough interviews were conducted in one day, with an obligatory break after five days of interviewing.

All interviews were recorded on cassette and interviewers were encouraged to take notes to supplement the recordings. A number of people found the note-taking difficult, complaining that it slowed down the dialogue, distracted them from the questions and meant that they lost valuable eye contact with the respondent. Despite this, we stressed the value of brief notes as a useful means of cross-checking, providing back-up for a bad or faulty recording, and for recording non-verbal expressions and descriptions.

Translation

Following the interviews, the interviewer translated and transcribed the tapes into French or English. Transcription is a tedious and time-consuming process and fraught with problems, to which there are no easy answers. An extension worker from Mali poignantly described the type of problem she faced translating the inter-views from Bobo into French. Bobo, she explained, is rich with subtly worded proverbs which cannot easily be translated. She cited the following example: 'If you want to stop the mouse, you must first get rid of the smell from the soumbala spice.'

Apparently the proverb refers to the value of a good upbringing. In the past children were brought up to be polite and obedient and therefore could be relied upon to behave well. Today children fail to receive proper instruction from their parents, and for this reason cannot be blamed for behaving badly, just as the mouse is not to blame for taking the soumbala spice when it smells so enticing. Given the complexity of the proverb, the extension worker finally opted for a gloss which omitted the proverb itself. Indeed, so much of Sahelian expression is laced with proverbs which are often exclusive to a particular group that only members of the group can fully understand the meanings and implications. The outsider is left bemused – for example: 'Les termites sont loin de la lune.'

The response

An analysis of the material collected reveals that the project did not recover as much indigenous knowledge, in its specifics, as originally intended. For instance, recipes for medicines, meals and organic fertilisers, and accurate descriptions of plant uses, changing vegetation, animal numbers and herd composition, are often mentioned only in vague terms. The fact that many rural populations have been made to feel that their traditional techniques for agriculture, veterinary and medical care, are in some way 'backward' and unscientific was undoubtedly a constraint. They are aware that the educated élites, who come on sporadic visits, tend to promote the adoption of new technologies and encourage a more scientific approach to development and conservation. For this reason many are reluctant to divulge methods of animal treatment, land conservation practices, or herbal remedies, which may label them as ignorant or out of touch with the 'modern' world.

Our questions about traditional veterinary practices in a camp for sedentarised pastoralists in eastern Chad met with blank faces, shoulder shrugs, and a denial of the existence of any such systems. It was only after the interviewers began to talk in positive terms about techniques they were acquainted with from other areas that the respondents were persuaded to share their own extensive knowledge.

No time for numbers

Then there is the problem of trying to search for common ground across the different modes of cultural expression. The desire for quantification and specificity that preoccupies research in the North is not an easy notion to convey to a Sahelian farmer. Efforts to find out the number of cattle in his herd will more often than not provoke raised eyebrows, derisive laughter and evasive responses. 'God is generous, I have enough animals to fertilise my fields!' . . . 'We have to make do with whatever God gives us.' The question is comparable to asking Europeans or North Americans for their bank balance or an inventory of their assets. Similarly, the question 'How many hours does it take you to grind your corn?' may be answered, 'I begin when I return from collecting the water and finish when my husband returns from the field.'

Responses which involve reference to figures, dates, weights and times are often spoken in French or English. Because such numerical accuracy is not perceived as relevant, it is not usually contained in the local language. For this reason the accuracy of ages, dates of specific droughts and famines is questionable. Indeed, throughout the interviews phrases such as 'in the past' are always preferred to something more precise such as 'in 1919' or 'in 1940'.

It is difficult to know how such constraints on the collection of indigenous knowledge can be effectively overcome. It may be that the problem lies not so much in the method of collection as in the setting of inappropriate targets. Is there simply too romantic a notion of indigenous knowledge? Such knowledge, after all, is not static but evolves to suit a changing environment. It must be open to the acceptance of new equipment and technologies. Farmers and pastoralists will adapt to whatever method serves them best, be it traditional or modern, old or new; archaic practices are usually retained not from nostalgia but because they still serve some purpose. But, as the interviews make clear, some traditions are retained through inertia or prejudice. There are reactionaries in every culture, but in the Sahel today such conservatism can lead to a cruel lack of development – particularly for women, as evidenced by the widespread resistance to education for girls.

One obvious drawback in employing non-specialist local interviewers is their lack of academic training in the detailed environmental or agricultural field. They could run through the checklist of questions but did not have the specialist knowledge to follow up on detailed points of concern and interest. On one site, in Kordofan, western Sudan, we tried a different approach. The coordinator, herself an agriculturalist working in the region, was briefed by an authority on Sudanese ecology who had worked in the area thirty years earlier, producing the first published botanical and environmental surveys. The questions were more informed, and the ability to cross-check details of change against the written and remembered record led to the interviews being much more specific than at other sites.

However, although a tight interview conducted by a specialist can get closer to accurately recording traditional knowledge, it also moves further away from the respondent's priorities and views. These may sometimes be incoherent or even factually wrong, but they have an integrity of their own. There is, then, a tension between the interview that seeks to focus on indigenous knowledge, and the interviewer who solicits opinion and impressions. For the former the 'facts' are primary and the respondent is secondary – a cipher; for the latter it is the other way round.

Perceptions of change

Despite these reservations, the interviews as a whole, although 'unscientific', describe a wide range of environmental knowledge and traditional farming and pastoral systems. Farmers talk about tried and tested methods of improving soil fertility; pastoralists explain how they control animal reproduction, the pastures preferred by each of their animals and the ideal ratio of males to females. Healing methods and herbal remedies are mentioned in varying degrees of detail. There is a great deal of repetition [. . .] which we have taken as evidence of a consensus about environmental and social change. Some of these 'findings' are new, some confirm hunches and others restate the obvious.

Change is everywhere recorded – no one can be left in any doubt that Sahelians have a thorough understanding of their own predicament, and of the causes of desertification. Whereas thirty years ago farmers were able to grow sufficient crops for subsistence plus a surplus for sale, they are now often cultivating from three to five times as much land in the uncertain hope of a yield that will provide enough for their subsistence. Many of the men are seeking employment in the towns so that their families, left behind in the villages, have enough to eat.

Plant breeders have succeeded in developing new varieties of sorghum and millet requiring a shorter growing season, which are able to take better advantage of the meagre rainfall when it occurs. But the extension services are still woefully inadequate and the costs of introducing new technologies often prohibitive.

Those who had led a nomadic life and lost their livestock through lack of pasture have been forced to settle and attempt to make ends meet by cultivation or by seeking employment in the towns. Many long to return to their nomadic way of life and attempt to rebuild their stocks, preferring sheep and goats (especially the latter), since they reproduce more rapidly and are better able to survive on the scanty pasture than cattle and camels.

The shift from pure pastoralism to agro-pastoralism and herding for wages (from absentee owners) is visible across the Sahel. When – and if – more 'normal' rainfall returns, the pasture will be slow to recover, passing through various stages of rehabilitation before approaching the levels of former years. A prerequisite for any recovery, which is well understood, is for livestock numbers to be kept well below the actual carrying capacity of the existing pasture.

There is clear agreement among those interviewed about the main reason for environmental degradation: inadequate and sporadic rainfall. Man-made factors are also cited: pressure on land due to rising population and the fact that more and more pastoralists, whose herds have been decimated by the droughts, are turning from pastoralism to farming. Bush land is being cleared with increasing rapidity to make land available for cultivation. The increased pressure on land and natural resources has disrupted what was a 'previously amicable relationship between farmers and pastoralists': conflicts between the two are frequently reported.

Although the majority of the interviewees felt that degradation was attributable to climatic change, many were confident that steps can be, and are being, taken to counter the damage. Trees are being planted; the fertility of the soil has been improved by adaptations to traditional farming methods, such as compost holes and bunds to reduce soil erosion and improve infiltration of water.

Patterns of life

It was also our aim to record social and cultural change. In this, the Sahel Oral History Project exceeded its expectations and has established a fuller picture of community history and social evolution than originally anticipated. It has revealed the extent of the breakdown of traditional relationships between groups: adults and children, sedentary farmers, pastoralists and agro-pastoralists, men and women.

Much of the information contradicts received development wisdom and provides ample evidence that many standard generalisations simply do not stand up, or are so general as to be seriously misleading. For instance, the interviews highlight the dangers of generalising about women's position in rural communities. According to Fatchima Beine, president of the women's committee of Abalak village, Niger: 'Before, when natural resources were abundant, women did not have to work so hard. Now, however, women do the same work as the men and during the day they work in the field.' But in Tibiri, another village in the same district, local farmer Sayanna Hatta commented:

> New technologies have helped to lighten a woman's load, she no longer has to spend several hours a day grinding grain due to the presence of diesel-powered mills; there are wells and pumps from which she can collect water. The men plough the fields and if the family don't have enough food then it is the men who have to go in search of supplements.

As always, there are marked differences in circumstances within villages and between communities that are lost in generalisations. 'Years ago all the wood we needed was near. It used to take us only five minutes to collect. Now it's a ten-hour trip, so those who can afford it buy it from the men who sell it in the market' (Rékia, woman farmer, Takiéta, Niger). As far as fuelwood collection is concerned, the gap between women with some money and women without has widened.

In the Nile province of Sudan, married women whose husbands have remained in the area as farmers welcome their improved quality of life: 'Now we don't have to pound the dura, or pull water from the deep well; also our participation in agricultural work has decreased' (Um Gazaz el Awad, Shendi); 'When I was young I used to do some work on my husband's farm. But now women are just sitting at home waiting for the men to bring money to them' (Hajeya Juma Ahmed). But in the same area the widow of a pastoralist has had to work as a paid seasonal labourer and is the sole breadwinner for a family of eight.

The value to projects

Development projects are often caught up in an almost obsessive drive to produce quantifiable results which can be presented to donors as proof of the project's success. In this quest for measureable achievements, other more subjective parameters are either forgotten or ignored. We believe this study, in creating a dialogue between development workers and local communities, has demonstrated the value of improved communication at all levels of project activity.

Each development project associated with the interviews was at a different stage, so it was possible to assess the value of participation throughout the project cycle. In Niger we conducted interviews before the project started; the woman interviewer was subsequently employed by the project to manage the women's programme. In Mali the project was at an early stage, in Sudan about half-way through. It became clear that it is never too late to use oral history as a project evaluation tool, but it is most useful if implemented at the planning stage. In Niger, for example, the interviews were used in the project design and followed through thereafter, and extension workers now set up oral history interviews each time they enter a new village.

Feedback from project sites shows that interviewing work conducted by extension workers has had a number of spin-offs – it is an effective method for creating links with new communities, and also a valuable training tool. The coordinator of the interviewing work in Mali notes in her report that the work provided her with a new training area, from which both she and extension workers have benefited. She concludes:

> The general utility of this research to the project is that it does something to counteract the idea that farmers are ignorant, conservative and fatalistic. Such preconceptions persist amongst our staff, although they are more subliminal than explicit. Little attempt is made to link the techniques we are trying to popularise with the farmers' own experiments. Thus the extensionist appears as a giver of solutions and the farmers' own capacities are undervalued. And, seeing themselves as surpassed, the farmers are less likely to volunteer suggestions, further aggravating the imbalance . . . The more details we have of farmer's knowledge and ingenuity, the more we can hope to counteract these problems of attitude.

In the same vein, a Senegalese non-governmental organisation (NGO), Fédération des Paysans Organisés du Département de Bakel, noted:

> We wanted to participate in this project from the start because we realised that it would be of benefit to our own work . . . We felt that it would be particularly useful to our literacy trainers. In this respect the results have gone beyond our expectations. What might have seemed like a lot of extra work from the outside in fact worked to our advantage. We put our trust in young inexperienced workers and were delighted to discover that they were able to carry out the work well . . . In addition they discovered a rich well of knowledge. We have decided that we cannot leave it here; we will continue the oral history work in our own project.

Thus not the least of the benefits of employing oral history methods in a development context is the impact on project workers, nearly all of whom have acquired valuable new insights, often into their own communities. If oral history techniques are institutionalised in project work, they can increase understanding and sensitivity towards the participating community.

A two-way process

A major obligation of the oral historian is to 'return the compliment'. When 'outsiders' initiate a programme of research, there should be a commitment to seeking new ways of ensuring that the resulting material is of value to the people who provided it. The NGO Fédération des Paysans at Bakel, for instance, published the interviews in Soninke, the local language, for use both as a local resource and as a tool in their literacy programme.

Perhaps the most immediate and practical value of the Sahel Oral History Project has been in identifying the benefits to projects and project workers of taking the time to learn, through interviews, as much as possible from individual life histories and reflections. Secondly, when such work is collected together, important 'under-researched' areas become apparent and can be followed up to ensure that objectives of the developers take into account the many variations in attitudes and priorities of the individuals who make up the community.

To end with a story from Mali: there was once a village so wealthy that the young people decided to make it a youth village of eternal joy, by killing all the old people. On the chosen day there was a single youth who had pity and hid his father so as not to have to kill him. In the new, joyful village of youth, all were strong and worked for themselves, and there were no old people to feed. One day the village was visited by a delegation from the local government, who suspected that something was wrong. They asked the young villagers if they could make a rope out of sand. Impossible. Wild attempts were made to gather up the soil, to no avail. The youth whose father was alive crept off to consult him. The father advised the boy to ask to see the old sand rope first. Thus the delegation realised that this boy's father at least was still alive, and while the others were punished, he was spared.

Chapter 43

Sanjiv Kakar

LEPROSY IN INDIA
The intervention of oral history

In this study of oral history in leprosy projects in India, Sanjiv Kakar describes how memories are used to improve historical understanding *and* contemporary care strategies. Oral history has helped to break down the silence and stigma which surrounds leprosy, and interviewees have become activists in community health and education schemes. Kakar also shows how the oral testimony of leprosy patients can 'enable a more sensitive reading of colonial records' and 'help to fill in the gaps within colonial histories' which denied the experience of leprosy patients in the community. Sanjiv Kakar is a Senior Lecturer in the Department of English at the College of Vocational Studies, University of Delhi. Reprinted with permission from *Oral History*, 1995, vol. 23, no. 2, pp. 37–45.

Introduction

THERE ARE AT THE PRESENT TIME at least two and a half million patients of leprosy in India, who constitute about one-third of the world's leprosy population. Leprosy is prevalent in virtually every state of India, ranging from a mere 1,522 cases in Haryana, to an estimated 272,000 cases in the state of Bihar, while Orissa and Tamil Nadu have the highest prevalence rate in the country.[1] In the early 1980s, with the commencement of the National Leprosy Eradication Programme (NLEP), districts with a prevalence rate of five or more patients per thousand of the population were identified as hyperendemic, and phased introduction of the Multi Drug therapy (MDT) began. Treatment time is substantially reduced with MDT to between six to twenty-four months for most cases, which represents a significant improvement on the earlier dependence on sulfone monotherapy, which entailed continuous drug intake over several years.

Leprosy is a chronic bacterial infection caused by *Mycobacterium leprae*. It attacks mainly the superficial tissues, especially the skin and the peripheral nerves. If untreated it can lead to physical deformity, such as destruction of hands and feet, nose collapse, and muscular atrophy. Injuries caused to anesthetic areas invite ulceration. With timely and adequate treatment, these deformities can be prevented. Early clinical signs include skin patches of heightened colour with anesthesia, accompanied by sensitivity of nerves and muscular weakness. Diagnosis can be confirmed with skin smear tests and other laboratory investigations.

Where seventy per cent of the population live in rural areas, not surprisingly the overwhelming number of patients are rural. From the Leprosy Control Programme of the early fifties, the rural patient came to be recognised as the focus of the Programme. With the launching of the NLEP, and a target of total eradication of leprosy by AD 2000, the endemicity of a *district* became the criteria for priority-based intervention, and the rural patient, virtually non-existent in colonial records, moved to centre-stage. Oral narrative is the only means for such patients, especially those without access to literacy, to enter into the arena and tell their own story. It is a story that has remained largely untold. Voluminous government records, laden with statistics on endemicity and eradication strategies, form the principal archive for information about leprosy in the contemporary period, but these are unhelpful on the matter of the subjective experiences of a patient when confronted with a disease which carries with it a long history of discriminatory practices. Urban, educated patients who might commit their experiences to writing and thus feature as subjects in their own history are anxious to retain anonymity, and are reluctant to recount their experiences; in this manner they perpetuate the myth that leprosy affects only the poor.

Any engagement with leprosy in contemporary India must negotiate the events of the last century, when western medical systems and practices were introduced; these included the separation of leprosy patients from other ill people, the marginalisation of the hospital, and the concurrent patronage of the asylum for the exclusive confinement of leprosy patients. The Lepers Act of 1898, the major legislation on leprosy of the nineteenth century which authorised such forcible confinement (for vagrant patients only!) remained on the statutes well into this century, until the slow process of repeal spreading over the last three decades finally terminated in 1991, with its repeal by the state of Bihar. Some of the perspectives on leprosy formed during the colonial period have lingered into the present, often intermixed with indigenous systems of knowledge; these include an exaggerated fear of infectivity, and the use of both Indian and western medicine for treatment. It is regrettable that recent scholarship on medicine in colonial India, which might have developed these themes further and suggested deeper correspondences, has bypassed entirely the study of leprosy, and its relationship with the entire apparatus of western medicine, in its scientific, cultural and ideological aspects.[2]

In this paper I attempt to redress the historical lacunae by reproducing interviews with leprosy patients in India conducted over the last few years. Following this, I consider how oral history offers a unique archive for the study of leprosy in contemporary India, as well as providing essential data for any interventionist offensive. Next I [. . .] discuss how oral history can also serve as a guide to our reading and rewriting of the colonial history of leprosy. Finally there are some examples illustrating how this oral history project can in truth benefit from an engagement with colonial sources.

Listening to leprosy patients

This exercise in oral history was undertaken during 1991–93, in four leprosy hyperendemic districts (with a prevalence rate of five or more per thousand of the population) in India: Durg and Rajnandgaon (Madhya Pradesh), Salem (Tamil Nadu), and Cuttack (Orissa). The successes of the MDT have encouraged the emergence of cured patients who are now actively engaged in leprosy control and eradication work. This is a relatively new phenomenon and it signifies a break-through in the assault on community prejudice about leprosy; for this reason, of the many patients interviewed, I rely heavily here on the testimony of patient activists. Because written narrative is virtually silent on the woman patient, a special effort was made to interact with women leprosy patients, and with children. As this oral history project relates to a commitment to the eradication of leprosy, it focuses on leprosy endemic districts where the health education offensive has enjoyed some success, so as to consider not only the situation of leprosy patients within a village community, but also its transformative potential. (The NLEP is not equally efficient in all districts, nor are the health education strategies uniform everywhere.) Virtually all the patients who were interviewed had received MDT; some had been declared as Released From Treatment (RFT). Questions related to patient percep-tions on contagion of leprosy, transmission, curability, experiences of discrimination, and patient participation in the detection of new cases. Some patients were detected afresh during the course of surveys of schools and far flung villages; they were motivated to begin treatment immediately. Of the many interviews conducted, two have been selected for presentation here.[3]

Durg

Thanwarin Bai is a resident of Khapparwada village. This interview takes place outside her hut, which is virtually on the borders of the village. The leprosy worker who has been visiting this village for several years, and who continues to visit once every month with the mobile clinic, and the District Leprosy Officer are the only others present. Occasionally they must assist in interpreting the local Chhatisgarh dialect. Both are on intimate terms with the patient, who now functions as a 'janbhagidar', literally a social communicator, an inmate of the village who has volunteered to assist in leprosy detection and with monitoring of patient progress.

> *What were your experiences as a leprosy patient?*
> Then I was living in another jhopri (hut) but not this one, this I got much later from a government scheme to help those who were very poor. When the villagers found out that I had leprosy they forced me to move out. How long could I hide it, the sores on my feet were visible to all, I had trouble walking, and when bathing in the river the other women would see the patches on my body . . . So I had to go, this was the custom in those days. So I built myself another jhopri on the outskirts of the village, near the cremation site, and I lived there alone.
>
> *What about your family, you have a son . . .*
> What could my son do, he is the barber, the village threatened him with a collective boycott if he continued to keep his mother with him. He

has to feed his family. What could he do all alone? He kept me as long as he could, but once the signs become so visible, how long can you hide it?

When did these events take place?
(After some hesitation and consultation with the others) The end of 1987. I lived there alone for some months, my son would bring me food and whatever I needed, I grew food also. Then the leprosy workers came and they brought me the medicine, this was the new medicine, MDT, which had newly come to our village. Then they spoke to the villagers to allow me to return home, but there was no success; they kept coming, and then they formed a swasth samiti (health association) with some sympathetic villagers, and finally I was able to return to the village, and the boycott threat against my son was lifted.

Is your treatment now completed? What was your attitude to the medicine at the beginning? Did you believe that leprosy could be cured?
Now I am RFT. When they first came I said, well, what do I lose by taking the medicine, I have lost everything already, so what will I lose by taking it? I did not really believe that it would cure me, but it was free, so I took it. In fact we did not think at all about cure of leprosy, we thought, why has God cursed me? You think of cure only when you think of illness. But all the same I ate the medicine and then after some months I began to notice the difference.

What is the status of leprosy in this village now (October 1991)?
There are 960 people in the village, including children. There are four cases undergoing treatment. The clinic comes here on the 7th of every month, at 11 a.m., just where you are sitting now. The patients come sometimes on their own, sometimes I have to call them. It is not easy to get them here regularly, and the clinic cannot wait for them, they have to visit so many villages. People should have the sense to look after their own bodies, but they do not.

What is the attitude of the villagers to leprosy at the present time? How do they respond to your detection work?
I have visited every home in the village, I have detected some patients too. I have personally examined the girls and the women, the ones who will let me. Always the leprosy workers are telling me to examine the women, how else will they get examined, the men cannot check women's bodies? Earlier it was the custom to evict patients from the village, now that has changed. People have learned to tolerate patients, but they do not love them. Some of the people abuse me: they say, 'First you get leprosy and you bring shame on this village. Now you detect more cases and you bring more shame.'

You live here alone? Where is your son?
When I returned he wanted me to live with him, but I built my hut here. I will always live here.

You have anesthesia on your feet, why are you not wearing your slippers (microcellular rubber)? Have you not been given a pair?

I have no ulcers, you can see . . . I soak my feet in water . . . not everyday, where is the time? I have my slippers in the hut. Wearing every day will spoil them, and where will I get another pair? I got these after a lot of difficulty.

Cuttack

Nirankar Sarangi is a resident of the Gandhipalli leprosy colony in Cuttack. Two leprosy colonies exist side by side; originally on the outskirts of the city, urban expansion has now integrated the colonies with the city. The leprosy colony is indistinguishable from any other shanty colony in Cuttack. Many leprosy patients consider this their home, and live here by choice, visiting their villages for brief periods. The patient speaks only his mother tongue, Oriya, so another resident translates into Hindi.

How old are you?
(Laughs) I don't know for sure.

Can you tell us roughly . . . 50s, 60s?
Not so old. Not yet sixty.

Tell us about this place.
This is a leprosy colony, there is another one nearby also. All the patients here have completed treatment or are under MDT. This is our meeting hall, today you can see that people are watching the test match. It is not always so crowded. We all live together like one family. During the recent elections the politicians came many times to talk with us about our problems. We always support the same candidate, the whole colony votes as one block, so our votes are important to them. We told them about the high cost of living, and about the shortage of the special rubber chappals (slippers).

Tell us your story, from the time that you contracted leprosy.
As a child I lived in Ganteshwar village. I got leprosy when I was very young. I continued going to school but one day because the patches on my skin were so obvious, the headmaster removed me from the school. I continued to live at home, until the age of about twenty-two years. The progress of the disease was slow. Over the years the problems at home kept on increasing. Some of our relatives would refuse to visit our home because of my presence. They were afraid that they would get leprosy from me. A cousin of mine had been married when he was a child; now he was grown up and ready to receive his bride, but her family refused to send her to live with us because . . . of me. All these years I had tried so many remedies from the local doctors, to no avail. We had spent a lot of money also. Finally, in 1956, that is a date that I remember, I left home for the famous Hathibadi Health Home. We had heard about this,

it was a major centre in Orissa state for the care and treatment of leprosy patients. I had only sixty rupees in my pocket, which my mother had given to me. From here I moved to the Leprosy Home and Hospital, here in Cuttack. In those days the treatment consisted of sulfone tablets, and injections of Chaulmoogra oil on the discoloured skin patches. These injections were very painful. Earlier the oil used to be administered orally, which was nauseating, and many patients could not tolerate it. Often we would say, leprosy is preferable to the treatment. I would return home for holidays, and to collect money. Many many years later I had a course of MDT here itself. Now I am cured, but the deformities on my hands and feet will remain with me for always.

Have people's ideas about leprosy changed over the years. Are patients still harassed? How do people view leprosy now?
That varies. Many people still fear leprosy, but it is less than in earlier years. We used to call it the 'bada rog' (big illness) in my village. Now when I go home and meet people they can see that I am cured.

What is the condition of leprosy patients in your village now? Are they receiving MDT?
I don't know.

I will ask you a very important question. Please do not be offended, and answer truthfully. Now that you, a Brahmin, have experienced untouchability because of leprosy, and you know what it means for another to feel polluted by your touch, does it not transform your attitude to the caste system?
For me everyone is equal.

Are you willing to interdine with people from any caste? Including Harijans?
Everyone is the same.

Do you actually do so here?
How can I, even though I have no personal objections, here I am a priest, I am in charge of the temple, so I can only eat food cooked by certain hands . . .

Eradication strategies and community development

Virtually every account of the rural patient underlines the vital importance of the village community. Where the community is hostile, patients have no choice but to cover up tell-tale patches as best they can, for fear of being persecuted: finally these become too pronounced, or deformities set in, and this is the stage when the patient is banished from the village. All this is inimical to the functioning of any leprosy eradication programme, which depends on early detection, (both with a view to ensuring complete cure without the patient suffering any physical deformity, and to render the patient non-infectious as quickly as possible), and timely and regular medication. It is simply not possible for the handful of leprosy workers, mostly non-medical staff to physically verify every single village. Where the vast majority of people do not recognise the early signs of leprosy, only community participation can generate knowledge about leprosy, persuade fellow villagers to come forward fearlessly for treatment, convince them of the efficacy of the Multi Drug therapy, monitor and motivate patients who tend to default (in the early stages leprosy is characterised by an absence of pain and discomfort, so patients do tend to be casual about discoloured, anesthetic skin patches), and care for those cured patients who have deformities and who require simple physiotherapy like regular soaking of feet in water to prevent ulceration. Those who have completed treatment often require a measure of rehabilitation to enable them to make a living.

Oral history can assist in garnering up to date knowledge about attitudes to leprosy and the condition of patients. Interventionist offensives must be devised according to local need, for there is tremendous regional variation even within villages close to each other. While some villages in Rajnandgaon, such as Dhangaon, and Dhorabhata, have supportive communities and patients are not subjected to harassment, in others like Khaprikala villagers fear even to touch the corpse of a leprosy patient for fear of contagion. Nardah village (Durg district) has a level of tolerance which allowed a patient to remain home, and visit the village temple every day, without any hindrance; both patient and community shared the stoic belief that a scourge which emanates from God may be revoked by Him; that this patient was an educated man, a physical training instructor in a regional undergraduate college, who denied himself the benefit of medical treatment, indicates that the health education effort here must necessarily be different from other nearby villages, where very different conditions prevail.

Attitudes to contagion, transmission, and curability vary enormously, as interviews with patients reveal. In Tamil Nadu in the south, sexual promiscuity is often cited as causing leprosy; or else leprosy is attributed to the lick of a long earthworm, locally known as 'monna pambu' (a theory of correspondence identifies the blunted fingers of a leprosy patient with the blunt ends of the earthworm). In central India prejudice can take very severe forms, drawing from a fear that leprosy spreads from casual physical contact, and from a belief that such a divinely originated curse brings shame upon the entire village; this often leads to prompt eviction of the patient from the village. Oral narrative is the only means to learn of local conditions, of patient perceptions, and to devise programmes, including rehabilitation schemes, that suit local needs. Oral narrative is the only means for poor, underprivileged patients like Thanwarin Bai to have their say, and to record their own histories.

Oral history also enables leprosy workers and other medical personnel in the field, far removed from the corridors of power, to record their perspective on official policy. Such perspectives, which emanate from the site where official policy comes into contact with the patient, can offer significant insights. For instance, the official Government of India definition of a leprosy free area is when the incidence of leprosy is reduced to one case per 10,000 of the population. Leprosy workers, however, call for multiple criteria: for a working definition which will help them to achieve this target, one which is concerned with process rather than merely with the end result; they stress factors such as freedom from ignorance, freedom from ulcers (for the care of patients with deformities by the community is a valuable

index of the level of community awareness and sensitivity), and freedom from deformity (which would indicate whether patients are detected in the early stages). The
unanimity regarding the need for effective treatment of the child patient, and a
shared concern that child deformity must be prevented by timely medication and
physiotherapy, brings the differences between the official perspective and the field
perspective into sharp focus. Child deformity is taken very seriously by officialdom
as a signal failure of the Programme, and this often results in suppression of such
cases by field staff, for fear of incurring official displeasure; whereas the leprosy
workers want definitions that make visible such glaring instances of failure, so as to
prevent recurrence, and to enable the child to receive first priority in surgical
correction. Interviews with leprosy field workers reveal that for strategic reasons
they represent leprosy as being wholly non-infectious, as easily curable, and the
medicine as having no side effects. Privately they admit that children are more
vulnerable than adults and must be protected; but the only means to protect healthy
children is to deny infectivity, so that the child can remain at school and undergo
treatment. Any other means only results in suppression of cases. [. . .]

Oral history/reeived history

The patient in the community, surely a crucial category, is denied in the colonial
discourse on leprosy. Making this visible is perhaps the most significant contribution
of this oral history project to the study of leprosy in colonial India. The dialogue
between leprosy in contemporary India based upon oral narrative, and the history
of leprosy in colonial India, based upon elite, written sources cannot be an easy
one. Even if attitudes toward leprosy have remained largely unchanged over the
decades in some quarters, nonetheless historical periodisation cannot be wished
away. At the same time, any attempt to reconstruct the condition of the leprosy
patient in the colonial period cannot remain within the confines of colonial representation. The narrative of the patient within the community makes visible the very
limited nature of the colonial intervention in the case of leprosy, and its wilful
disregard for the overwhelming number of patients. The Lepers Act of 1898
provided 'for the segregation and medical treatment of pauper lepers', and it
invented its own definition of leprosy by representing it exclusively as 'the process
of ulceration';[4] this legal definition of leprosy was not supported by medical
opinion at the time. Colonial intervention was confined to urban areas, and only to
vagrant patients in advanced stages of the disease; as this exercise in oral history
reveals, there are many worlds beyond.

Oral narrative can also help to fill in gaps within colonial histories, and enable
a more sensitive use of such histories. For instance, the widespread prevalence of
discriminatory practices directed at leprosy patients at the present time serves
to problematise confident assertions of colonial officials that such practices were
wiped out by imperial writ; one official wrote that 'under the British rule, when
law and legal procedure predominate, families or communities have no power in
this way to drive a leper from his house and property against his will . . . and
so his Honour believes that lepers . . . commonly live in their houses with their
families and defy the public opinion of the community'.[5] To take the example of

contagion, the oral testimony of leprosy patients can enable a more sensitive reading of colonial records. Patients' testimony reveals that leprosy may be regarded, simultaneously, as a contagious disease and as a curse, thus it is extremely difficult to isolate a single cause for exile of patients. As virulent community hostility often coincides with the process of ulceration, this might suggest that ulceration is regarded as the more contagious phase, were it not for the fact that leprosy patients regularly exhibit their ulcers when begging for alms at pilgrimage sites, and this does not provoke visible panic from the general public. This kind of understanding of the complex nature of popular responses to leprosy is a useful aid in approaching even highly competent and able investigation, such as the *Report of the Leprosy Commission, 1890–91* where this complexity is not recognised, and is read instead merely as a native difference: 'It has all along struck the Commission that though a native on being questioned will, as a rule, state that leprosy is a contagious disease, yet his own acts do not support his statements.'[6] Colonial sources are unsympathetic to the problematic encounter between the native patient and western medicine; such paradigms which have continued into the present are especially amenable to elucidation by oral history.

The testimony of the female patient is particularly valuable, and challenges considerably her colonial representation. The female leprosy patient achieves visibility in colonial official records only when her sexuality is perceived as constituting a threat to order within the asylum. There are references to separate wards for male and female patients in the asylums, and to homes set up to receive babies of patients at birth. Beyond this, the female patient simply does not exist, except as an appendage to male patients. Missionary publications, reluctant to comment on sexuality, which has no place in their representation of leprosy in terms of sin and redemption, are doubly silenced on female sexuality. Oral narrative reveals, on the other hand, the trauma of the mother who is separated from her children, or the condition of a wife who is discarded by her husband when he learned that she has leprosy. There are also numerous instances of healthy wives who remain with diseased husbands, even following them into exile. This points to new directions and the need to locate other sources to reconstruct the life of the female patient in the last century. What happened to healthy wives of leprosy patients? Did abandoned women patients remain, alone, on the fringe of the village, or did they join mobile bands and wander from temple to temple, from shrine to fair? Did they remarry? Did they bear children? Why was female fecundity such an issue in official and missionary records? Is this related to the fact that male potency declines with advancing leprosy?

Some of these issues may be contextualised with a reconstruction of the situation of one such patient, based upon interviews with villagers. Her name is Basanteen Bai. Residents of Dhangaon village (Rajnandgaon) remember her, and narrate her story. She married and moved to her husband's home in the nearby village of Asra. A young mother with two infant children, her husband evicted her from their home when he discovered that she had leprosy; this action was supported by the Panchayat, the village assembly of Asra. Basanteen Bai was forced to seek refuge at her parents's home. This incident appears to have taken place some three decades ago. Basanteen Bai's family took her for treatment to the Wesleyan Leprosy Home and Hospital at the district centre. It was a fair distance away, so a degree of anonymity was assured. I was unable to retrieve the records of her condition from amid the meticulously maintained records at this institute. Miss R. Bibbee, the Medical Superintendent reveals that it was fairly common for patients to register under an assumed name. Medical staff at this institute describe the attitude towards the leprosy patient in the sixties: the fear of contagion prevailing even amongst doctors, and the unwillingness of para-medical staff to even touch the patient; how the compounder would wrap up the sulfone tablets in some paper and toss them across the counter to the patient; how the few coins that the patient left by way of payment would be soaked in antiseptic for several hours before anyone would dare to touch them. Whenever she needed a fresh supply of medicine, Basanteen Bai would have to trek many miles; as even today patients frequently complain that medicines get damaged by rain and humidity, it is questionable how regularly she consumed her medication. In spite of this, Basanteen Bai continued with the treatment for some months. Doctors advised her to avoid contact with her children, and specifically to desist from breast-feeding her baby. One morning she wandered off, and threw herself across the railway track that borders one flank of Danhgaon. This story, brief though it is, throws into relief the sterility of official testimony. It also provides an entry point for the analysis of hospital and asylum records.

Colonial sources provide a history of leprosy in nineteenth-century India, however fragmentary and ideologically charged this may be, and engagement with this archive can prove fruitful. For instance, the references to patient mobility across the country, and to visits to sites of pilgrimage, point to areas where oral history projects might profitably be conducted, especially as patient mobility is not conducive to uninterrupted medical treatment, and this can locate weak spots in the leprosy eradication programmes that are currently underway. Other documents, such as this letter from the High Priest of the Baidyanath Temple, Bengal, dated 8 May 1889, can serve to explain the rationale behind such congregation at temples:

> Baidyanath means the Lord of the Physicians and it is to Him that persons suffering from incurable diseases resort for their recovery from all parts of India . . . The *Susruta*, a great Hindu medical authority, declares leprosy to be a contagious disease. Another book recommends that bodies of dead lepers should not be burned, but buried in holy places . . . It is therefore clear that it is the duty of the relations of lepers to keep them beyond the reach of their fellows.[7]

Such sources can provide a basis for approaching popular perceptions of leprosy, and in assessing the relations of these to the high Sanskrit tradition.

There are indications that at the present time AIDS is being interpreted in some parts of India through the metaphor of leprosy. The visibility of leprosy in India, coupled with a body of prejudice about AIDS enables this connection to take place. In some villages of Kerela AIDS is being referred to as 'the rich man's leprosy', and patterns of community hostility towards AIDS patients are reminiscent of similar patterns of discrimination and marginalisation meted out to patients of leprosy. Oral history can help to prevent such situations from developing, and enable us to draw upon the experiences of the leprosy eradication effort to ensure that we cope with AIDS whilst remaining human and humane.

Notes

1   Figures for 1991: 'National Leprosy Eradication Programme Guidelines, 1993', New Delhi, Leprosy Division, Ministry of Health and Family Welfare.

2   Studies on health policy in colonial India make very occasional or no mention at all of leprosy. See R. Macleod and M. Lewis (eds), *Disease, Medicine and Empire: Perspectives on Western Medicine and the Experience of European Expansion*, London: Routledge, 1988; R. Jeffery, *The Politics of Health in India*, Berkeley: University of California Press, 1988; T. Dyson (ed.), *India's Historical Demography: Studies in Famine, Disease and Society*, London: Curzon Press, 1989.

3   [A third interview is included in the original article – eds.]

4   Lepers Act, 1898, also known as Act. No. 111 of 1898, V/8162, India Office Collections, [the original article includes an additional section on 'Colonial Representations of Leprosy' – eds].

5   H. Maude, Officiating Junior Secretary Govt. of Punjab, to the Officiating Secretary Govt. of India Home Dept., Lahore, 16 December 1889, Rpt. in P.S. Abraham (ed.), *Journal of the Leprosy Investigation Committee*, February 1891, no. 2, London: Macmillan, p. 44.

6   *Leprosy in India*: *Report of the Leprosy Commission in India*, 1890–91, Calentta: Govt. Printing, 1892.

7   Sailojananda Ojha, High Priest, Baidyanath Temple, Bengal, to the Private Secretary to the Viceroy, dated 8 May 1889, in *Papers Relating to the Treatment of Leprosy in India, 1887 to 1895*, pp. 15–16.

Select bibliography

Handbooks and bibliographies

Hays, P. (1992), *Speak for Yourself*, Namibia: Longman.

Hutching, M. (1993), *Talking History*: *A Short Guide to Oral History*, Wellington, New Zealand: Bridget Williams Books/Historical Branch of the Department of Internal Affairs.

Matters, M. (1995), *Oral History Cataloguing Manual*, Chicago, Ill.: Society of American Archivists.

Perks, R. (1990), *Oral History*: *An Annotated Bibliography*, London: British Library National Sound Archive.

Perks, R. (1995), *Oral History*: *Talking About the Past*, 2nd edition, London: Historical Association.

Ritchie, D.A. (2003), *Doing Oral History*: *A Practical Guide*, 2nd edition, New York: Oxford University Press.

Robertson, B. (2000), *Oral History Handbook*, fourth edition, Adelaide: Oral History Association of Australia (South Australia Branch).

Taylor, P. (1996), *Telling It Like It Was*: *A Guide to Making Aboriginal and Torres Strait Islander History*, Canberra: Australian Institute of Aboriginal and Torres Strait Island Studies.

Thompson, P. (2000), *The Voice of the Past*: *Oral History*, third edition, Oxford: Oxford University Press.

Wilton, J. (1996), *Oral History in Australia*: *A List*, Sydney: Oral History Association of Australia (NSW Branch).

Yow, V.R. (2005), *Recording Oral History*: *A Guide for the Humanities and Social Sciences*, 2nd edition, Walnut Creek, Calif.: AltaMira Press.

Collections and reflections on theory and practice

Armitage, S.H. with Hart, P. and Weatherman, K. (eds) (2002), *Women's Oral History*: *The Frontiers Reader*, Lincoln: University of Nebraska Press.

Attwood, B. and Magowan, F. (eds) (2001), *Telling Stories*: *Indigenous History and Memory in Australia and New Zealand*, Crows Nest, New South Wales: Allen & Unwin.

Bertaux, D. (ed.) (1981), *Biography and Society: The Life History Approach in the Social Sciences*, London: Sage.

Bornat, J. (ed.) (1994), *Reminiscence Reviewed: Perspectives, Evaluations, Achievements*, Buckingham: Open University Press.

Bornat, J., Perks, R., Thompson, P. and Walmsley, J. (eds) (2000), *Oral History, Health and Welfare*, London: Routledge.

Chamberlain, M. and Thompson, P. (eds) (2004), *Narrative and Genre: Contexts and Types of Communication*, New Brunswick, N.J.: Transaction Publishers (previously published by Routledge, 1998).

Darian-Smith, K. and Hamilton, P. (eds) (1994), *Memory and History in Twentieth Century Australia*, Melbourne: Oxford University Press.

Dunaway, D. and Baum, W. (eds) (1996), *Oral History: An Interdisciplinary Anthology*, 2nd edition, London: AltaMira Press.

Evans, G.E. (1987), *Spoken History*, London: Faber.

Ferreira, M.M. and Janaina, A. (eds) (1996), *Usos & Abusos da História Oral*, Rio de Janeiro: Fundação Getulio Vargas.

Frisch, M. (1990), *A Shared Authority: Essays on the Craft and Meaning of Oral and Public History*, Albany: State Univeristy of New York Press.

Gluck, S.B. and Patai, D. (eds) (1991), *Women's Words: The Feminist Practice of Oral History*, London: Routledge.

Green, A. and Hutching M. (eds) (2004), *Remembering: Writing Oral History*, Auckland: Auckland University Press.

Grele, R. (ed.) (1995), *Envelopes of Sound: The Art of Oral History*, 2nd edition, Chicago, Ill.: Precedent.

Huen, P.L.P., Morrison, J.H. and Guan K.C. (eds) (1998), *Oral History in Southeast Asia: Theory and Method*, Singapore: National Archives of Singapore and Institute of Southeast Asian Studies.

Jeffrey, J. and Edwall, G. (eds) (1994), *Memory and History: Essays on Recalling and Interpreting Experience*, Lanham, Md.: University Press of America.

Lummis, T. (1987), *Listening to History: The Authenticity of Oral Evidence*, London: Hutchinson.

McMahan, E. (1989), *Elite Oral History Discourse: A Study of Cooperation and Coherence*, Tuscaloosa: University of Alabama Press.

McMahan, E. and Rogers, K.L. (eds) (1994), *Interactive Oral History Interviewing*, Hillsdale, N.J.: Erlbaum.

Meihy, J.C.S.B. (ed.) (1996), *(Re)introduzindo a história oral no Brasil*, São Paulo: Xamã.

Myers, L.E., Sharpless R. and Charlton, T.L. (2006), *Research Handbook for Oral History*, Lanham, Md.: Rowman & Littlefield.

Passerini, L. (ed.) (1992), *International Yearbook of Oral History and Life Stories, vol. I, Memory and Totalitarianism*, Oxford: Oxford University Press.

Personal Narratives Group (eds) (1989), *Interpreting Women's Lives: Feminist Theory and Personal Narratives*, Bloomington: Indiana University Press.

Plummer, K. (2001), *Documents of Life 2: An Invitation to Critical Humanism*, London: Sage.

Portelli, A. (1991), *The Death of Luigi Trastulli and Other Stories: Form and Meaning in Oral History*, Albany: State University of New York Press.

Portelli, A. (1997), *The Battle of Valle Giulia: Oral History and the Art of Dialogue*, Madison: University of Wisconsin Press.

Rogers, K.L., Leydesdorff, S. and Dawson, G. (eds) (1999), *Trauma and Life Stories: International Perspectives*, London: Routledge.

Samuel, R. and Thompson, P. (eds) (1990), *The Myths We Live By*, London: Routledge.

Schneider, W. (2002), *So They Understand*: *Cultural Issues in Oral History*, Logan: Utah State University Press.

Schwarzstein, D. (ed.) (1991), *La História Oral*, Buenos Aires: Centro Editorial de America Latina.

Seldon, A. and Pappworth, J. (1983), *By Word of Mouth*: *Elite Oral History*, London: Methuen.

Stricklin, D. and Sharpless, R. (eds) (1988), *The Past Meets the Present*: *Essays on Oral History*, Lanham, Md.: University Press of America.

Thompson, P. and Burchardt, N. (eds) (1982), *Our Common History*: *The Transformation of Europe*, London: Pluto.

Tonkin, E. (1992), *Narrating Our Pasts*: *The Social Construction of Oral History*, Cambridge: Cambridge University Press.

Vansina, J. (1965), *Oral Tradition*: *A Study in Historical Methodology*, London: Routledge & Kegan Paul.

White, L., Miescher, S.F. and Cohen, D.W. (eds) (2001), *African Words*, *African Voices*: *Critical Practices in Oral History*, Bloomington: Indiana University Press.

Periodicals

Bios – Zeitschrift für Biographieforschung, Oral History und Lebensverlaufsanalysen [Germany], vol. 1 1988–

História Oral [Brazil], vol.1 June 1998–

História y Fuente Oral [Spain], no. 1 1989–

International Journal of Oral History, vol. 1 1980–1990

International Yearbook of Oral History and Life Stories, vol. 1 1993–vol. 4 1996

Life Stories/Recits de Vie, [UK/France], no. 1 1985–no. 5 1989

Oral History [UK], vol. 1 no. 1 1969–

Oral History Association of Australia Journal, no. 1 1978–

The Oral History Forum (formerly the *Canadian Oral History Association Journal*), vol. 1 1975/6–

Oral History in New Zealand, vol. 1 1988–

Oral History Review [USA], no. 1 1973–

Voces Recobradas [Argentina], no. 1, 1998–

Words and Silences/Palabras y Silencios [International], no. 1 1997–

Key studies using oral history

Amin, S. (1995), *Event, Metaphor, Memory*: *Chauri Chaura, 1922–1992*, Berkeley: University of California Press.

Bozzoli, B., with Nkotsoe, M. (1991), *Women of Phokeng*: *Consciousness, Life Strategy and Migrancy in South Africa, 1900–1983*, London: James Currey.

Broadfoot, B. (1973), *Ten Lost Years 1929–1939*: *Memories of Canadians Who Survived the Depression*, Toronto: Doubleday.

Caplan, P. (1997), *African Voices, African Lives*: *Personal Narratives from a Swahili Village*, London: Routledge.

Cruikshank, J. (1998), *The Social Life of Stories*: *Narrative and Knowledge in the Yukon Territory*, Lincoln: University of Nebraska Press.

Field, S. (2001), *Lost Communities, Living Memories*: *Remembering Forced Removals in Cape Town*, Cape Town: David Philip.

Fraser, R. (1979), *Blood of Spain*: *The Experience of Civil War 1936–9*, London: Allen Lane.

Fyfe, J. (1990), *The Matriarchs: A Generation of New Zealand Women Talk to Judith Fyfe*, Auckland: Penguin.

Genovese, E. (1974), *Roll, Jordan, Roll: The World the Slaves Made*, New York: Pantheon.

Glassie, H. (1982), *Passing the Time in Ballymenone: Folklore and History of an Ulster Community*, Dublin: O'Brien Press.

Gluck, S.B. (1987), *Rosie the Riveter Revisited: Women, the War, and Social Change*, Boston, Mass.: Twayne.

Greenspan, H. (1998), *On Listening to Holocaust Survivors: Recounting and Life History*, Westport, Conn.: Praeger.

Haley, A. (1977), *Roots*, London: Hutchinson.

Hammerton, A.J. and Thomson, A. (2005), *Ten Pound Poms: Australia's Invisible Migrants*, Manchester: Manchester University Press.

Hareven, T. (1982), *Family Time and Industrial Time: The Relationship Between the Family and Work in a New England Industrial Community*, Cambridge: Cambridge University Press.

Hinton, W. (1983), *Shenfan: The Continuing Revolution in a Chinese Village*, London: Secker & Warburg.

Hofmeyer, I. (1993), '*We spend our years as a tale that is told*': *Oral Historical Narrative in a South African Chiefdom*, London: James Currey.

James, D. (2000), *Doña María's Story: Life History, Memory and Political Identity*, Durham, N.C.: Duke University Press.

Kay, B. (ed.) (1981/1982), *Odyssey: Voices from Scotland's Recent Past*, two volumes, Edinburgh: Polygon.

Kennedy, E.L. and Davis, M. (1993), *Boots of Leather, Slippers of Gold: The History of a Lesbian Community*, New York: Routledge.

Langer, L. (1991), *Holocaust Testimonies: The Ruins of Memory*, New Haven, Conn.: Yale University Press.

Lanzmann, C. (1985), *Shoah: An Oral History of the Holocaust*, New York: Pantheon.

Lowenstein, W. (1978), *Weevils in the Flour: An Oral Record of the 1930s Depression in Australia*, Melbourne: Hyland House.

Maloof, J. (1999), *Voices of Resistance: Testimonies of Cuban and Chilean Women*, Lexington: University Press of Kentucky.

Parker, T. (1983), *The People of Providence: A Housing Estate and Some of its Inhabitants*, London: Hutchinson.

Passerini, L. (1987), *Fascism in Popular Memory: The Cultural Experience of the Turin Working Class*, Cambridge: Cambridge University Press.

Portelli, A. (2003), *The Order Has been Carried Out: History, Memory, and Meaning of a Nazi Massacre in Rome*, New York: Palgrave Macmillan.

Roberts, E. (1984), *A Woman's Place: An Oral History of Working Class Women 1890–1940*, Oxford: Blackwell.

Roseman, M. (2000), *The Past in Hiding*, Harmondsworth, London: Penguin.

Rosengarten, T. (1971), *All God's Dangers: The Life of Nate Shaw*, New York: Knopf.

Summerfield, P. (1998), *Reconstructing Women's Wartime Lives*, Manchester: Manchester University Press.

Terkel, S. (1970), *Hard Times: An Oral History of the Great Depression*, New York: Pantheon.

Thomson, A. (1994), *Anzac Memories: Living With the Legend*, Oxford: Oxford University Press.

Van Onselen, C. (1996), *The Seed is Mine: The Life of Kas Maine, a South African Sharecropper, 1894–1985*, New York: Hill & Wang.

Wigginton, E. (1985), *Sometimes a Shining Moment: The Foxfire Experience*, Garden City, N.Y.: Doubleday.

Zhang, X. and Ye, S. (1989), *Chinese Lives*, Harmondsworth, London: Penguin.

Useful contacts

1 International

International Oral History Association
Website: www.ioha.fgv.br/
Email: almut.leh@fernuni-hagen.de
Publications: *Words and Silences*, vol. 1, no. 1 June 1997–; *Newsletter*, no. 1 September 1998–

H-Oralhist
A member of the H-Net, Humanities & Social Sciences On-Line initiative, H-Oralhist is an international network for scholars and professionals active in studies related to oral history. It is affiliated with the Oral History Association [US].
Website: www.h-net.msu.edu/~oralhist/

In the First Person/Oral History Online
An online index of over 2,500 oral history collections in English from all over the world, assembled by Alexander Street Press [US].
Website: www.alexanderstreetpress.com

2 Europe

Oral History Society (UK)
c/o Department of History
University of Essex
Colchester
Essex CO4 3SQ
United Kingdom
Website: www.ohs.org.uk

Email: rob.perks@bl.uk
Publication: *Oral History*, vol. 1, no. 1, 1969–

Institute für Geschichte und Biographie/Institute for History and Biography (Germany)

Haus der FernUniversität
Liebigstraße 11
58511 Lüdenscheid
Germany
Website: www.fernuni-hagen.de/INST_GESCHUBIOG/welcome.shtml
Email: Alexander.vonPlato@fernuni-hagen.de
Publication: BIOS – Zeitschrift für Biographieforschung, Oral History und Lebensverlaufsanalysen, vol. 1, 1988–

Koninklijk Instituut voor Taal-, Land- en Volkenkunde (KITLV)/Royal Netherlands Institute of Southeast Asian and Caribbean Studies (Netherlands)

PO Box 9515
2300 RA Leiden
The Netherlands
Website: www.kitlv.nl
Email: stcijlen@kitlv.nl

Italian Oral History Association/Associazione Italiana di Storia Orale

Comitato Organizzatore
c\o Circolo Gianni Bosio
via Sant'Ambrogio 4
Roma 00186
Email: stefaniaficacci@hotmail.com

Oral History Centre, St Petersburg (Russia)

European University at St Petersburg
Gagarinskaya St., h. 3.
St Petersburg 191187
Russia
Website: www.eu.spb.ru/en/history/oralhist.htm
Email: history@eu.spb.ru

WebCT Oral History Research in the Nordic-Baltic Area (Estonia)

Department of Estonian and Comparative Folklore
University of Tartu
Estonia

Website: http://webct.e-uni.ee/public/TUOHaLHRitNBA/index.html
Email: tiiu.jaago@ut.ee

Malta Oral History Society

15/16 Triq I-Imnajqar
Birkirkara
9 Triq J. Pace
Bormla
Malta
Email: jchir@arts.um.edu.mt

3 North America

Oral History Association (USA)

Executive Secretary
Dickinson College
PO Box 1773
Carlisle, PA 17013–2896
USA
Website: http://omega.dickinson.edu/organizations/oha/
Email: oha@dickinson.edu
Publication: *Oral History Review*, no. 1 1973–

Canadian Oral History Association/Société Canadienne d'Histoire Orale

PO Box 2064 Station 'D'
Ottawa
Ontario K1P 5W3
Website: http://oral-history.ncf.ca/
Emai: skidmore@uwo.ca
Publication: *The Oral History Forum* (formerly the *Canadian Oral History Association Journal*), vol. 1, 1975/6–

4 West Indies/Caribbean

The Cayman Islands Oral History Programme

The Cayman Islands National Archive
Government Administration Building
George Town
Grand Cayman
Cayman Islands
Email: cina@gov.ky

Oral and Pictorial Records Programme (Trinidad and Tobago)

Main Library
The University of the West Indies
St Augustine
Trinidad and Tobago
Email: khelenes@library.uwi.tt
Website: www.mainlib.uwi.tt/

Jamaica Memory Bank

Email: acij@anngel.com.jm
Website: www.instituteofjamaica.org.jm/ACIJ/jmb_main.html

Social History Project (Jamaica)

Department of History & Archaeology
University of the West Indies
Mona Campus
Jamaica
Email: kathleen.monteith@uwimona.edu.jm
Website: www.mona.uwi.edu/history/shp/

Folk Research Centre (St Lucia)

Mount Pleasant
PO Box 514
Castries
St Lucia
Email: frc@candw.lc
Website: www.stluciafolk.org/

Oral History Project (Barbados)

Department of History & Philosophy
University of the West Indies
Cave Hill Campus
Barbados
Email: ohp@uwichill.edu.bb

National Oral History Programme (Barbados)

National Cultural Foundation
West Terrace
St James
Barbados
Website: www.ncf.bb/

5 Latin America

Mexican Oral History Association/Asociación Mexicana de Historia Oral
c/o Direccion de Estudios Historicos
Allende 172
Tlalpan
México D F 14000
Emails: mcamarena.deh@inah.gob.mx *or* ppensado@institutomora.edu.mx

Brazil Oral History Association/Associação Brasileira de História Oral
Fundação Getulio Vargas – CPDOC
Praia de Botafogo 190, 14 Floor
22250–900 Rio de Janeiro RJ
Brazil
Website: ww.cpdoc.fgv.br/abho
Publication: *História Oral*, vol. 1 June 1998–

Instituto Histórico de la Ciudad de Buenos Aires (Argentina)
Avenida Córdoba 1556
Planta Alta (CP 1055)
Ciudad Autónoma de Buenos Aires
Argentina
Email: historiaoral_ihcba@buenosaires.gov.ar

6 Australasia

Oral History Association of Australia
c/o Oral History Program
State Library of New South Wales
Macquarie Street
Sydney, NSW 2000
Australia
Website: www.ohaa.net.au/
Email: rblock@sl.nsw.gov.au
Publication: *Oral History Association of Australia Journal*, no. 1, 1978–
Website for National Library of Australia's Oral History Directory: www.nla.gov.au/ohdir/

National Oral History Association of New Zealand/ Te Kete Körero-a-Waha o Te Motu
PO Box 3819
Wellington
New Zealand

Website: www.oralhistory.org.nz
Email: megan.hutching@mch.govt.nz
Publication: *Oral History in New Zealand*, vol. 1, 1988–

7 Asia

Japan Oral History Association
Inage-ku
Yaoi-cho 1–33
Chiba-shi
Chiba-ken
Japan
Website: www.joha.jp/site/index.php
Email: sakurai@L.chiba-u.ac.jp
Publications: *Newsletter*, 2004–

Oral History Centre (Singapore)
National Archives of Singapore
National Heritage Board
1 Canning Rise
Singapore 179868
Website: www.a2o.com.sg/
Email: Yap-Wong_Hwai_Fey@nhb.gov.sg

Brunei History Centre
Ministry of Culture, Youth & Sports
Bandar Seri Begawan BS 8610
Negara Brunei Darussalam
Website: www.history-centre.gov.bn/eng-s_research.htm
Emails: pusat@brunet.bn *or* sejarah@brunet.bn

8 Africa

Centre for Popular Memory (South Africa)
Historical Studies
University of Cape Town
Private Bag
Rondebosch
Cape Town 7701
South Africa
Website: www.popularmemory.org
Email: rmeyer@humanities.uct.ac.za

Index

Aboriginal history 364–5, 368–9, 449–50, 506–20
accuracy of oral evidence *see* memory: reliability as evidence
adult education 47, 374–5, 447, 451–2, 460
advocacy and empowerment x, 5–6, 11, 75–81, 117, 186–95, 272, 311, 328–30, 369, 447–559; *see also* development projects, oral history: social and political change, reconciliation programmes
Africa ix, xiii, 2, 10, 14–24, 89, 143–54, 155–65, 382–92, 450, 538–48; *see also* individual countries
Agee, J. 97–8
ageing and older people 447–8, 459–70; *see also* life review, reminiscence work
Alcoff, L. 507, 509, 515–16
Allison, F. 211–12, 221–9
Anderson, K. 61, 76, 116, 129–42, 448
anthropology ix, xii, 3, 5, 12, 55, 57, 59, 86–7, 94, 115–16, 129, 143, 193, 279, 283–309, 311, 353, 382–89, 454
archives and oral history xiii, 80–1, 102–10, 262–4, 333–4, 336, 338–9, 343–61, 366, 438, 440–3, 468; *see also* cataloguing and indexing, libraries and oral history
Argentina 6, 83–101, 568
Armitage, S.H. xiii, 4, 6, 73–82, 448
arts and artists ix, xiii, 337, 342, 425–33
Asia xiii, 167; *see also* individual countries
Attwood, B. 506–20

audio editing and production 393–405, 419–22, 429–30
audio tours 396–7, 425–33
Australia xiii, 3, 7, 43–53, 93–4, 178–9, 289, 376–81, 449, 506, 508
autobiographical writing ix, 12, 28, 43–53, 93–4, 178–9, 289, 376–81, 449, 506, 508

Barker, R. 450, 538–48
Bass, R. 435, 438, 441
Baum, W. 350, 363, 366
Benjamin, W. 99–100
Benmayor, R. 337, 434–45, 448
Bennett, O. 143–54
Bertaux, D. 458
biography 5, 12, 57, 60–6, 130, 149, 156, 230–43, 399, 466
black history 2, 14–24, 47, 64, 77, 105, 109, 117, 155–65, 186, 280, 329, 396, 453, 458, 469, 474–84; *see also* Aboriginal history, colonial history and memory, ethnic communities, indigenous people, racism, slavery
Blee, K. 215–16, 322–32, 449
blogs (web-logs) 349
Borland, K. 80, 215, 310–21, 449, 466
Bornat, J. 117, 185, 335, 447, 456–73
Botswana 382–91
Bozzoli, B. 117, 155–65, 448
Brazil 7, 412–13, 568

Brehaut, L. 364, 369
Brewster, K. 336, 350
Briggs, C. 143, 145
Britain xii, 2, 4, 18, 43–53, 177–83,
    232–43, 245, 255–60, 337, 374–81,
    417, 425–33, 456–73, 531–7
broadcasting *see* film, video and television,
    internet, radio oral history
Bruemmer, B. 352, 356
Brunei 569
Bruner, J. 24
Burkina Faso 539
Burton, S. 166–76, 448
Butler, R. 459–60
Butler, T. 337, 425–33, 448, 450

Canada 346, 496, 566; *see also* North
    America
Caribbean 469, 566–7
cataloguing and indexing 8, 104–10, 349,
    352–3, 365–6; *see also* archives and oral
    history
Central America 87, 118, 449, 495–505;
    see also individual countries
Chad 539, 544
Chambers, R. 149, 151
Chesneaux, J. 44, 50
childhood and child-raising 29, 105, 109,
    203, 283–304, 379–81, 417–18, 420,
    458; *see also* family history, youth
China 26, 400, 411–12
civil rights *see* black history
Clifford, J. 59, 89
Cohen, D. 296
Coleman, P. 463
collective memory *see* memory: social and
    collective memory
colonialism and colonial memory
    214–15, 283–309, 448, 451, 453,
    508, 550, 556–8
commemoration 7, 244, 248–50,
    333
communication studies *see* linguistics and
    communication studies
communists and communism 36, 43,
    46, 250–1, 459, 521–30; *see also*
    labour history, socialist history
community activism 47, 430–2, 448,
    485–94; *see also* development
    projects
community history 3–6, 30–1, 43–53,
    148, 185, 213–14, 219, 261–70,
    422–3, 441–4, 450, 452, 469,
    485–94, 531–7; *see also* local history

community publishing 46, 185, 334–5,
    376–81; *see also* autobiographical
    writing, community history
compact discs (CDs) 103, 111, 335, 340,
    369, 371, 395, 419, 428, 435; *see also*
    computer applications
computer applications 8, 102–14, 366,
    421, 434–45; *see also* blogs, compact
    discs, digital versatile discs, digitization,
    email, internet
confidentiality and anonymity 194, 387,
    468–9
'conversational narrative' 86, 93, 163
copyright *see* interview relationship:
    copyright and consent
Coutinho, E. 412–13
crime and criminals 29, 115, 397, 490
Cross, N. 143–54, 450, 538–48
cross-cultural interviewing *see* interview
    relationship: cultural or cross-cultural
    dimensions
cultural studies 4, 43–9

Daspit, T. 448, 474–84
Davis, M. 278
Davies, S. 417
demography 27, 257–8
Depression (inter-war) 256, 266–7, 476
development projects x, 5, 143–54, 264,
    450, 455, 538–48
dialect 35; *see also* memory: language and
    memory, transcription
diaries 45, 116, 131, 135, 146–7, 212,
    233–42, 272, 349, 458
digital versatile discs (DVDs) 103, 111
digitization 1, 8, 102–14, 118, 335–6,
    340, 345, 349–55, 370–1, 393–405,
    421, 428, 434–45; *see also* computer
    applications
disability 117–18, 121, 184–97, 265, 448,
    453, 457, 460, 465; *see also* health and
    welfare
documentary sources 1, 27–8, 33–4,
    37–41, 84–5, 157–8, 186, 272, 349,
    408; *see also* interpreting oral evidence:
    and documentary sources
domestic work and domestic service ix, 80,
    214, 283–309, 417, 420
drama *see* theatre and oral history
dreams 249, 389
Dryden, J. 346–7
Duberman, M. 56, 278
Dublin, T. 266
Dunaway, D. 394

economics 6

economic history 27, 29; *see also* work

editing oral history transcripts 110–14,
128, 334–5, 339–40, 367–71, 374–92,
534; *see also* audio editing and
production, presenting oral history,
writing oral history

education, history of 28; *see also* adult
education, higher education, literacy,
schools and oral history

elite history 2, 40, 323, 327, 452; *see also*
political history

El Salvador 495–6, 498–500

email 6, 8, 81, 337, 349, 435–42

empiricism 49, 51, 57, 271–2, 510;
see also positivism

empowerment *see* advocacy and
empowerment

England 43, 115, 166–76

environmental history 149–53, 422, 450,
538–48; *see also* place: meaning of

Estonia 565

Ethiopia 149, 539

ethnic communities ix, 75, 166–76,
266–7, 323, 434–5, 448, 453; *see also*
black history, migration, racism,
refugees

ethnography 4, 59, 62, 89, 95–6, 287,
311, 385, 497; *see also* anthropology

Europe xiii, 7, 98, 334, 450, 564–5; *see
also* individual countries

Evans, G.E. 2, 31, 190

exhibitions 130–1, 337, 394, 396–8,
416–24, 427–33; *see also* museums and
oral history

Eynon, B. 350, 352

family history ix, 2, 26–9, 112, 117,
131–5, 146, 160, 177–83, 185, 220,
258, 276–7, 283–321, 383–92, 400–4,
407, 413–14, 417–24, 461–4, 479,
506–20, 558; *see also* childhood and
child-raising

family memory 2, 9, 14–24, 117, 177–83,
310–21

fascism 3, 49, 66, 256, 275, 325, 459

femininity 314–15

feminism 43, 205; *see also* feminist theory
and methodology, women's
movement

feminist history 6, 12–13, 26, 45, 50–3,
73–82, 278, 322, 327–30, 468; *see also*
feminist theory and methodology,
women's history

feminist theory and methodology 5, 57,
61–2, 73–82, 120, 190, 215, 279,
311–20, 466; *see also* interview
relationship: and gender

Fillipelli, R. 346, 355

film, video and television xiii, 50, 102–14,
262, 336, 341, 394–5, 406–15, 468,
486–8; *see also* interviewing: video
interviews

Finnegan, R. 117, 177–83

Fogarty, J. 334, 344, 349, 356

folklore research 2, 9, 35, 47, 311, 317,
353, 465, 502

food 299–302

Fortier, N. 347

Foucault, M. 50, 515

Foxfire 55, 474, 477–9, 484

France 26, 50, 208

Fraser, R. 49

Freire, P. 500

Freud, S. 60, 246

Frisch, M. 3, 8, 102–14, 215, 269, 335,
338, 365, 368–9, 371, 411, 417, 448,
457–8, 465–6, 486

Gambia 19–24

gay and lesbian history 186, 214, 271–82,
448, 453

genealogy *see* family history

gender *see* feminist theory and
methodology, memory: and gender

geography 425–33, 538–48; *see also*
environmental history, place: meaning
of, rural life, urban history

Germany 26, 202, 230–43, 256, 325, 327,
565

Glassie, H. 89, 92–3

Gluck, S. B. xiii, 4, 6, 61, 73–82, 105,
213, 215, 448

Good, F. 334, 362–73, 448

Gramsci, A. 46, 183

Gray, L. 507–09, 515–16

Green, A. 337, 416–24, 448

Grele, R. xi, 55–6, 66, 86, 93, 347, 351,
366

griot 2, 20–24, 144

Guatemala 496

Haley, A. 2, 14–24, 38, 448

Harris, A.K. 55–6

health and welfare 5, 75, 135–41, 258,
447, 451, 455, 457, 470, 549–59; *see
also* disability

hermeneutics 57–60

'hidden history' and oral evidence ix, 6,
    45, 78–9, 156, 271–2, 287–8, 322,
    345, 447, 457–8, 555; *see also* oral
    history: aims and achievements
higher education 30–1, 33, 48, 64, 74,
    105, 199, 398, 416, 434–45, 465–6,
    486
history (the discipline and profession) xii,
    1–5, 25–31, 43–53, 57, 93, 115, 345,
    406–8, 414, 457, 480, 506–20
History Workshop movement 48
Holocaust xi, 54, 98, 105, 118, 121,
    198–210, 212, 216, 230–43, 337, 449,
    507, 512–14
homosexuality *see* gay and lesbian history
Hoopes, J. 55
H-OralHist discussion list xiii, 107, 263,
    366, 564
housing and homes 489; *see also* domestic
    work and domestic service,
    homelessness
homelessness 5, 7, 336, 448–9, 485–94
human rights 496–7, 506, 534
Humphries, S. 185
Hymes, D. 503
Hyslop, D. 370

immigration *see* migration
India 149–53, 451, 549–59
indigenous people ix-x, 5, 219, 382–92,
    448–9, 453–4, 468; *see also* Aboriginal
    history, Native Americans
Indonesia 214, 283–309
interdisciplinarity xi-xii, 1, 5–6, 57–64,
    211, 458, 471; *see also* interpreting oral
    evidence
International Oral History Association 7,
    564
internet xi, xiii, 8, 13, 105–6, 112–14,
    118, 121, 262–3, 335–7, 340–1,
    349–55, 395–9, 435, 442–3 ; *see also*
    blogs, computer applications, email
interpreting oral evidence x, xiii, 3–6,
    40–1, 74–72, 92–101, 129–42,
    211–332, 345, 506–19: audio-visual
    analysis 33–5, 134–5, 213–14, 219,
    264–5, 393–405, 410–13; biographical
    interpretative method 466; cohort
    analysis 257; collaborative group analysis
    75–7, 304, 417–22, 438–41, 480–1,
    488–9; cultural meanings and analysis
    129–42, 508–9; and documentary
    sources 211–12, 217, 230–43, 441,
    451; interviewee involvement in

interpretation ix, 6, 31, 40–1, 49,
    75–81, 148, 184, 193–5, 215, 220,
    262, 269, 310–21, 335, 368, 374–81,
    387, 447–9, 464–71, 486–94, 516,
    534–5 (*see also* 'shared authority', oral
    history: participatory projects); linguistic
    and textual analysis 34–5, 129–42, 334,
    380–1; literary analysis 5, 86, 157;
    narrative analysis xiii, 4, 35–6, 86,
    92–3, 139, 180, 214, 219, 273–5, 290,
    294–304, 310–16; psychoanalytic
    interpretation 116, 135–41, 179,
    199–208, 217, 236–41, 245, 507,
    513–14; qualitative data analysis
    software 106; quantitative analysis 213,
    218, 255–60, 544; researcher
    subjectivity 55–72 (*see also* reflexivity);
    secondary analysis of archive interviews
    213, 218–19, 262–7, 334, 339; socio-
    historical thematic interpretation 73–81,
    84–5, 157–8, 186–7, 213, 218,
    255–60, 263–72, 441, 462–3, 466,
    488–91; *see also* audio editing and
    production, editing oral history
    transcripts, feminist theory and
    methodology, memory, interview
    relationship, presenting oral history,
    reflexivity, representativeness and
    sampling, storytelling and performance
interviewing 115–210: bilingual interviews
    117, 121, 168–72, 400–1; equipment 8,
    112, 336, 393–4 (*see also* tape
    recorders); field journal 436–8; group
    interviews 116–17, 145, 147–8, 375–6,
    542; life history interviews 117, 145–6,
    156, 160–1, 184–97, 198–210, 245,
    389, 487; locating and selecting
    interviewers 167, 187, 263, 268, 436,
    479, 540, 542 (*see also*
    representativeness and sampling);
    location and context 91, 144–5,
    148–9, 190, 222–3, 409, 543;
    longitudinal interviews 146–7, 211–12,
    221–9, 443; non-verbal communication
    66, 103, 124–5, 246, 314, 409–10,
    412–13; non-'Western' techniques
    143–55, 166–76, 540–3; payment and
    gifts 144, 168, 386–8; preliminary
    discussions 158, 187–9; questions and
    interview guidelines 117, 121, 125–7,
    131–3, 141, 156, 159–61, 164–5, 268,
    438–9, 482–3, 540–1; summaries and
    interview logs 365–66; techniques 30–1,
    39, 63–7, 76–8, 93, 115–210, 245–7,

267–9, 384, 430, 478, 482–3, 543; use of artefacts 116, 121, 148–9, 190; use of photographs and audio-visual material 116, 120, 148–53, 187–95; video interviews 119, 410–11 (*see also* film, video and television); *see also* feminist theory and methodology, interview relationship, memory, oral history: project preparation, oral history: training, radio oral history, transcription
interview relationship ix-x, 4–6, 39–41, 54–72, 74–81, 86–92, 115–210, 327–30, 385–6, 409–10, 456: and age 64, 159–60; and class or status 55, 64, 95, 159–61, 169–71, 190, 412–13; copyright and consent 118, 121, 188–9, 334–9, 350, 367, 439, 468, 476, 481 (*see also* confidentiality and anonymity); cultural or cross-cultural dimensions 61, 116–17, 120–1, 143–54, 160–1, 166–76, 302–3, 382–91, 400–1, 540–1; and gender 61, 64, 116, 146, 158–61, 384–92, 541; impact of interviewer 54–72; 'insiders' and 'outsiders' 117, 132, 157–63, 167–8, 186, 212, 226, 263, 328, 540, 545; inter-generational 31, 55, 159–61, 386, 448, 450; intermediaries and third parties 116–17, 145, 167–8, 187–90, 541; intersubjectivity 61, 63; interviewee's experience of interview ix, 54–72, 86–100, 162–3, 168, 187–90, 200–8, 246–7, 302–3, 327–30, 459; interviewer's experience of interview 1, 39, 54–72, 116, 141, 198–208, 246, 263–4, 391, 459 (*see also* reflexivity); interviewing friends 121, 171; interviewing members of your family 117, 121, 310–21, 400–4, 412–13; power, equality and ethical issues 8, 30, 52, 61–2, 66–7, 88–90, 96, 118, 121, 188–95, 246, 302–4, 325–32, 374–81, 410, 461; therapeutic nature of 98–9, 118, 121, 135–41, 198–210, 246, 386–7, 403, 459, 501 (*see also* memory: trauma); transference and counter-transference 60, 65, 116, 120; *see also* confidentiality and anonymity, interpreting oral evidence, interviewing, transcript review by interviewee
Ireland xiii, 7, 178, 450, 531–7
Israel 199
Italy 3, 32–42, 49, 277, 458–9, 565

Jack, D. 76, 116,
James, D. 6, 83–101, 448
Jamieson, R. 363–4, 370–1
Japan 117, 166–76, 569
Jewish history 49, 95, 98–9, 186, 432; *see also* Holocaust
journalism 2, 115, 366, 463

Kakar, S. 451, 549–59
Kennedy, E.L. 271–82, 448
Kennedy, R. 506–20
Kerr, D. 7, 117, 336, 448–9, 485–94
Klempner, M 118, 198–210
Koonz, C. 325–6, 328–9
Kuhn, T. 9, 448, 474–84

labour history xi, 6, 27–9, 47, 49–50, 66, 83–101, 250–1, 256, 266–7, 448; *see also* communists and communism, socialist history, work, working class history
La Capra, D. 507, 511–12, 514
Langer, L. 206, 231–2, 237
Langness, L.L. 387
language *see* memory: language and narrative form
Larson, M. 336
Latin America xiii, 6–7, 83–101, 334, 454, 499, 568; *see also* Central America, and individual countries
Laub, D. 199–200, 204–7
Lawrence, J. 375
learning disability *see* disability
legal contexts for memory work x, 5, 116, 449–50, 454, 509–12; *see also* reconciliation programmes
leisure and entertainment 29, 310–21, 420
lesbian history *see* gay and lesbian history
letters 34, 45, 131, 135, 212, 233–42, 272, 458
libraries and oral history xiii, 343–61; *see also* archives and oral history
life review (remembering in later life) 5, 98–9, 217, 252; *see also* ageing and older people, reminiscence work
Linde, C. 94, 212, 226
linguistics and communication studies ix, 4, 12, 63–4, 363, 365
literacy 184, 187, 192, 407; *see also* adult education
local history 26, 30, 108, 265–7, 407, 469; *see also* community history
Lorde, A. 273

Lummis, T. 213, 255–60
Lundy, P. 7, 449–50, 531–7

Mace, J. 334–5, 374–81
McGovern, M. 7, 449–50, 531–7
McLellan, M. 448, 474–84
McMahan, E. 410–11
Malcolm X 14, 38–9
Mali 539, 547–8
Malta 566
Manne, R. 507, 510, 512, 514
masculinity 249–50, 421–2
Mauritania 539
medical history see health and welfare
Meihy, C.S.B.M. 7
memory: and class 273–5, 297; and gender
   117, 120, 129–42, 170, 220, 278–81,
   529; intergenerational transmission of 2,
   14–24, 98–9, 178–9, 217, 422–3,
   474–84; language and narrative form
   xiii, 9–20, 35–6, 94, 117, 126, 132–42,
   143–5, 168–72, 180, 193, 290,
   294–304, 369, 390, 410, 498–9,
   510–11, 516–18; memory studies 7, 13,
   213, 216, 287–8; nature of 32–42,
   98–100, 211, 277–8, 412–14, 456;
   nostalgia 47, 284–6, 441; public-
   individual interaction xii, 3–4, 35,
   43–53, 118, 129–42, 212–3, 218, 228,
   244–54, 256–7, 279–81, 290–7,
   324–5, 429–30, 449, 463, 508–9, 534;
   reliability as evidence (bias, distortion,
   selection, etc.) x, 2–3, 37–40, 85–6,
   93, 157–8, 180–1, 211–12, 230–43,
   323–4, 417, 506–19; retrospectivity
   (past-present relationship) x, 3–4, 37–8,
   223–9, 230–43, 299, 326–7, 510; self-
   interpretation and coherence ix, xiii, 4,
   12, 38, 45, 78, 97, 138–9, 168, 180,
   200, 216, 223–8, 245, 328–30, 449,
   461–2, 511–14; self-representation and
   identity 83–5, 96–99, 135–41, 162–3,
   174, 212, 216–17, 245–53, 275–9,
   288, 421–2, 456; sensory memory 215,
   219, 285–6, 299–302, 429–30, 527–8;
   silences, suppression and forgetting 3, 7,
   38, 88–9, 99, 118, 121, 124, 129–42,
   161, 198, 232, 249, 256–7, 294–7,
   328, 441, 521–30; social or collective
   44–53, 99–100, 213, 217–18, 244–54,
   508, 534 (see also family memory,
   national memory, popular memory);
   subjectivity and meaning ix, 1, 3–4, 6,
   36–7, 49, 56, 86, 116, 129–42,

158–63, 214, 271–2, 458–9, 513–14;
   and totalitarianism 449–50, 454,
   521–30; and trauma 99, 118, 121,
   198–210, 212, 221–9, 230–43,
   246–53, 294–7, 449, 456, 464, 467,
   501, 506–30; see also family memory,
   history, interpreting oral evidence, life
   review, popular memory, storytelling
   and performance
mental health see health and welfare
Mexico 87, 95, 434, 568
middle-class history 274–5, 310–21
migration 26, 29, 117, 155–76, 178–9,
   400–4, 413, 434–5, 448, 453; see also
   ethnic communities, refugees
military history 28, 221–30, 244–54
Miller, G. 337, 425–33, 448, 450
Mink, J. 344, 356
Moon, S. 448, 474–84
Moore, K. 363–5
Moss, W. 344, 346, 356
multimedia history 102–14, 393–405; see
   also computer applications
museums and oral history ix, xiii, 50, 262,
   336–7, 341–2, 396–8, 416–24, 427,
   468; see also exhibitions
music 34, 395, 401, 429, 463
Myerhoff, B. 59, 95, 97–9, 392, 501, 503
myth and legend 30–1, 45, 117, 157,
   178–83, 244–53, 279–81, 418, 422,
   508, 522, 528

narrative see memory: language and
   narrative form, interpreting oral
   evidence: narrative analysis, storytelling
   and performance
national memory 44, 213, 244–54, 290–4,
   506–19, 521–30
Native Americans 95, 132, 148
Negoechea, G. 7
Nesmith, T. 348–9
Netherlands 202, 207, 283–309, 565
Neuenschwander, J. 350
Nevins, A. 2
New Zealand xiii, 337, 416–24, 568
Nicaragua 499
Niger 539, 546–7
Nishimoto, W. 369
Nixon, R. 474–84
Nkotsoe, M. 117, 155–65
Nora, P. 7
North, N. 171
North America xi, xiii, 7; see also Canada,
   United States of America

Northern Ireland 531–7
Novick, P. 57, 62, 508, 514

objectivity 54, 63, 449, 486–7
O'Farrall, P. 3
oral history: and academic researchers 1–8,
    25–32, 43–50, 74, 93, 262, 264, 406,
    465, 468, 486–7; aims and achievements
    1–13, 25–31, 48–53, 73–81, 84–5,
    447, 457–8, 483–4 (see also 'hidden
    history' and oral evidence);
    bibliographies 560; critics of x–xi, 2–4,
    10–11, 33, 49–53, 344 (see also
    memory, representativeness and
    sampling); definition of term ix,
    118–19; and funding 334, 345, 354,
    416, 427, 481; guides and handbooks x,
    54–5, 58–9, 119–20, 130, 267, 363,
    560; and the history profession ix, 23,
    26–31, 43–53 (see also history);
    international movement xi, xiii, 1, 7–9;
    journals xii, 7, 54, 62, 73, 395, 411,
    562; large projects 73–82, 105–6,
    255–60; origins and development xi,
    xiii, 1–115, 334–5, 457; project
    preparation and research 77, 436,
    478–9, 539–40; and social or political
    change 1, 7, 31, 48–9, 75, 82, 143–54,
    184–6, 253, 447–559 (see also advocacy
    and empowerment, legal contexts for
    memory work); and training x, xii,
    74–5, 130, 337, 344, 354, 434–45,
    468, 474–84, 471, 540–1
Oral History Association (USA) 14, 55,
    75, 105, 263, 343–5, 350, 411, 475,
    566
Oral History Society (UK) 564
oral tradition 2, 10, 14–24, 178–83, 389;
    see also family memory, folklore
    research, myth and legend, popular
    memory, storytelling and performance
orality 4, 33–5, 102–4, 113, 362–7, 381,
    393–405, 407, 409, 418

Palestine 76, 80, 431
Passerini, L. 3–4, 10, 49, 56, 86, 118,
    179, 256, 275, 326
Parker, T. 61, 75, 80, 123–8, 327
Patai, D. 61, 75, 80, 327
people's history 1–3, 48, 263, 369
Perks, R. 354
phenomenology 57–8, 60
photographs see interviewing: use of
    photographs

place, meaning of 100, 265–7, 422,
    425–33; see also environmental history
political history 29, 220, 258–9, 322–32,
    412–13, 448–9, 485–94, 495–505
political science 61
popular memory 4, 43–53
Popular Memory Group 4–5, 43–53, 245,
    449
Portelli, A. xii–xiii, 4, 11, 32–42, 86, 211,
    277–8, 324, 458, 461, 466
positivism and post-positivism 1, 3, 5, 62,
    157, 255, 511
post-conflict resolution see reconciliation
    programmes
post-modernism 5, 78–9, 86, 96, 219,
    272, 334, 348, 398, 420
post-structuralism 157
presenting oral history ix, xiii, 8, 77–8,
    110–14, 262, 333–446; 459, 467–70,
    471, 548; see also arts and artists, audio
    editing and production, audio tours,
    community publishing, computer
    applications, editing oral history
    transcripts, film, video and television,
    exhibitions, multimedia history, radio
    oral history, theatre and oral history,
    writing oral history
preservation see archives and oral history
psychoanalysis and counselling 4, 57, 60,
    131, 200–1, 460
psychology ix, 3, 5, 7, 12, 60–2, 118,
    136–40, 199, 387, 447, 460, 463
public history ix, 44–53, 267–9, 333–8,
    369, 406–7, 486
publishing see community publishing,
    writing oral history

questionnaires and question structures see
    interviewing: questions and interview
    guidelines

race and ethnicity see black history, ethnic
    communities, indigenous people,
    interview relationship: cultural or cross-
    cultural dimensions
racism 54, 215, 266–77, 322–32, 518
radio oral history xii, 123, 335–6, 341,
    393–41, 400–4, 411, 468, 488–9
Read, P. 335, 507–8, 510, 512, 514
reflexivity 54–72, 279, 312, 391, 402,
    409, 441, 487; see also interview
    relationship: interviewer's experience of
    interview
refugees 5, 448–9, 468, 495–505, 540

Reimer, D. 346, 348

religion 66, 115, 322–32, 401–2, 417, 465, 496–7, 499

reminiscence work 3, 5, 98–9, 117, 335, 374–81, 447–8, 451, 456–73; *see also* ageing and older people, life review

representativeness and sampling 3, 30, 40, 79, 213–14, 257–60, 385, 420, 467

Ritchie, D. 167, 335, 349

Robinson, J.A. 198–9, 503

Rosengarten, T. 56, 110

Rosenstone, R. 407–8

Rosenthal, G. 327

Rouverol, A. 465–6

Rowbotham, S. 6, 50

rural life 2, 131–5, 143–65, 382–92, 412, 538–48, 549–59

Russia 26, 565; *see also* Soviet Union

Rwanda 450

Salazar, C. 324

Samuel, R. 85, 333

schools and oral history ix, 3–4, 26, 47, 55, 199, 337, 448, 452, 474–84

Scotland 115, 337

Senegal 539, 548

sexuality 160, 458, 557; *see also* gay and lesbian history

sexual abuse 199, 205, 294–7, 449, 467, 507, 515–16

'shared authority' 215, 269, 398, 448, 465, 468, 486, 534

Sherbakova, I. xiii, 449–50, 521–30

Shopes, L. 4, 213–15, 261–70, 469

Shostak, M. 335, 382–92, 448

Singapore 569

Sipe, D. 336, 406–15

slavery 14–24, 74, 394, 477–8, 483

Slim, H. 116, 143–54

social history 27–8, 48–9, 344, 347–8, 376, 417

socialist history 2, 4, 6, 28, 31, 40–1, 43–53; *see also* communists and communism, labour history

sociology ix, xii, 3, 5, 11, 47, 49, 57–8, 61–2, 79, 156–7, 457–8, 464

Sommer, D. 283–4, 296

soundscapes 397–8, 419, 425–33

South Africa 7, 26, 117, 155–65, 337, 450, 535, 569

Soviet Union 118, 449–50, 421–30; *see also* Russia

Spain 49

Spielberg, S. 105, 199

Stanley, L. 61

statistics 27, 255–60; *see also* interpreting oral evidence: quantitative analysis

Stoler, A.L. 214–15, 283–309, 448

storytelling and performance 6, 35–7, 77, 80, 88–92, 116, 143–4, 162, 177–8, 214, 273–5, 296–304, 310–18, 384, 389, 456, 498–503; *see also griot*, interviewing: non-verbal communication, memory: language and narrative form, oral tradition

Strassler, K. 214–15, 283–309, 448

Sudan 144, 539

Swain, E. 333–4, 343–61

Taiwan 403

tape recorders and audiotape 2, 112, 115, 123–4, 349, 386–7, 485; *see also* interviewing: equipment

technological change 26, 102–14, 349, 393–405, 406–7

Tedlock, D. 59

television *see* film, video and television

Terkel, S. xiii, 55–6, 115–16, 123–8, 335, 466

testimonio 87, 95–6, 454, 497–9

theatre and oral history 50–1, 335, 340, 411, 463–4, 467, 469–70

therapy *see* interviewing: therapeutic nature of, memory: and trauma, psychoanalysis and counselling

Thompson, P. 1–2, 25–31, 49, 85, 116, 143–54, 185, 257, 324, 345, 411, 457–8

Thomson, A. 212–13, 215, 244–54, 369

transcript review by interviewee 194, 363–4, 366–70, 376–81, 464, 534

transcription 33–4, 103–8, 130, 172–3, 264, 334, 339, 362–73, 376–8, 437–8, 461, 543; *see also* interviewing: summaries and interview logs

translation 171–3, 335, 340, 369, 386, 388–92, 411–12, 497, 543; *see also* interviewing: bilingual

trauma *see* memory: and trauma

Treleven, D. 351, 367

Tuchman, B. 348–9

Turkey 7

Turner, V. 5, 59, 63

unemployment *see* Depression, homelessness

United States of America 2, 14–24, 54–82,
    102–14, 129–42, 201, 221–9, 261–82,
    310–32, 334–42, 393–415, 434–45,
    465–6, 474–505, 514–15; *see also* North
    America
urban history 29, 83–101, 268, 271–82,
    374–81, 425–33, 485–94, 531–7

Vansina, J. 19
video *see* film, video and television,
    interviewing: video interviews
Vietnam War 199, 211–12, 216, 221–9,
    248, 252

Wales 26
Wallot, J.P. 347–8
Walmsley, J. 117, 184–97
war crimes *see* legal contexts for memory
    work
war memory 45–6, 198–254, 291–4,
    531–7
war veterans 38, 199, 211–13, 221–19,
    244–54, 459
welfare *see* health and welfare
Westerman, W. 449, 495–505
Wigginton, E. 55, 474
witnessing 5, 118, 449, 502, 514–15
women's history xi, 2, 6, 27–9, 61,
    73–82, 116–17, 129–42, 155–76,
    271–332, 382–91, 420, 462–4, 516,
    546–7, 557–8; *see also* feminist
    history
women's movement 4, 50, 74–5, 448; *see
    also* feminism
work 74–5, 84–5, 127, 131–5, 137–41,
    258–9, 266–7, 283–309, 416–18, 423,
    458, 490–1, 538–47; *see also* domestic
    work and domestic service, labour
    history
working-class history ix, 2, 6, 27–8, 40–1,
    45–52, 84–101, 271–82, 416–24, 448,
    489
World War I 10, 212–13, 244–54, 256
World War II 2, 17–18, 45–6, 74–5, 93,
    256, 290–4, 327, 401, 412–13, 426,
    467, 476
World Wide Web *see* internet
writing oral history (books or articles) 49,
    56, 193, 262, 310–21, 334–5, 374–92,
    399, 407, 442, 481, 534; *see also* editing
    oral history transcripts, presenting oral
    history

Young, J. 507–9, 511, 513–14, 517
youth 26, 418; *see also* childhood
Yow, V.R. 5–6, 54–72, 116, 215

Zachert, M.J.K. 343, 346–56